Sacred Pleasure

SACRED PLEASURE

Sex, Myth, and the Politics of the Body

Riane Eisler

HarperSanFrancisco

A Division of HarperCollins*Publishers*

Permissions begin on page 496 and are considered a continuation of this copyright page.

The Partnership Way, a workbook developed by Riane Eisler and David Loye for applying the partnership model to all areas of our lives, is available in bookstores. For information about the International Partnership Network, write to the Center for Partnership Studies, P.O.Box 51936, Pacific Grove, CA 93950.

FIRST EDITION

Library of Congress Cataloging–in–Publication Data
Eisler, Riane Tennenhaus.
    Sacred pleasure : sex, myth, and the politics of the body / Riane
Eisler.
      p. cm.
    Includes bibliographical references (p. 464) and index.
    ISBN 0–06–250293–X (cloth)
    ISBN 0–06–250283—2 (pbk.)
    1. Sex customs—History. 2. Sex—Religious aspects. 3. Body,
Human—Religious aspects. I. Title.
HQ12.E47 1995   95–5861
306.7'09—dc20   CIP

95   96   97   98   99 ❖ RRD(H) 10   9   8   7   6   5   4   3   2   1

This edition is printed on acid-free paper that meets the American National Standards Institute Z39.48 Standard.

To David

Contents

Our Sexual and Social Choices: An Introduction   1

Sex, pleasure, and pain. Dominator and partnership sexuality. Sex, spirituality, and society. The opportunity and the challenge.

Part 1: HOW DID WE GET HERE?

1. **From Ritual to Romance: Sexuality, Spirituality, and Society**   15

   Ancient sexual symbols. New and old sexual realities. The social construction of sex. Woman, sex, and religion. Sex, the Church, and the troubadours.

2. **Animal Rites and Human Choices: The Roots of Dominator and Partnership Sex**   34

   Our human origins. The uncommon chimps. Rites of sex, friendship, and sharing. The partnership and dominator alternatives. Sex, evolution, and choice.

3. **Sex as Sacrament: The Divine Gifts of Life, Love, and Pleasure**   53

   A new view of Ice Age art. Myths of renewal and rites of spring. The mystery of sex and the celebration of life and pleasure. The sacred marriage and the cycles of birth, death, and regeneration. Ancient hymns of love, goddesses, and kings.

4. **Sex and Civilization: The Early Roots of Western Culture**   72

   Modern archaeology and ancient myths. Prehistoric art, life, and sex. Partnership and high civilization. Sex, spirituality, and social structure.

5. **From Eros to Chaos: Sex and Violence**   84

The contradictory proofs. The nomadic onslaughts. The puzzle of dominator origins. Pastoralism and psychological armoring. The "danger" of sexual love. Sexual violence, the institutionalization of trauma, and our legacy of pain.

6. **The Reign of the Phallus: War, Economics, Morality, and Sex**   103

Women, sex, and Athenian democracy. Homosexuality, heterosexuality, and free love. The cult of the phallus, memories of partnership, and the mutilation of the Hermes. Laws, militarism, patriliny, and power. The economics and politics of dominator morality. The domestication of women and the dehumanization of men.

7. **The Sacred Marriage in a Dominator World: The Metamorphosis of Sex, Death, and Birth**   126

Heroes, monsters, and the sacred marriage. Sacrifice, demons, and sex. Changing myths for a changing world. The blending of dominator and partnership myths. Sex, Eros, and Thanatos.

8. **The Last Traces of the Sacred Marriage: Mysticism, Masochism, and the Human Need for Love**   143

The mystical journey and the mysterious power of sex. From the sacred marriage of the Goddess to male brides of God. The divine demand for suffering and the ecstasy of pain. The romance with death and the human need for love.

Part 2: WHERE ARE WE AND WHERE DO WE GO FROM HERE?

9. **From Ancient to Modern Times: Setting the Stage**   161

The politics of the body. Pain, pleasure, and the sacred. The human yearning for connection. The evolution of love, language, and consciousness. The biology and chemistry of love. The push of evolution and the challenge of transformation.

10. **Waking from the Dominator Trance: The Revolution in Consciousness and the Sexual Revolution**   179

Modern history and the history of intimate relations. The family, human rights, and the dominator trance. The forward push and the backward pull. Personal, social, and sexual change. The struggle over sex, consciousness, and our future.

11. **Bondage or Bonding: Sex, Spirituality, and Repression**   201

Sex, religion, and domination. Obsessing on sex and distorting spirituality. Women's sexual slavery. Sexual and political repression. Sadomasochism, rebellion, and submission. From bondage to bonding.

12. Making Love or Making War: Eroticizing Violence　　222

*Sex, brutality, and human nature. The male script for violence.
War and the war of the sexes. Male fantasies and inhuman realities.
The double standard for violence, Pavlov's dogs, and androcratic
men. The normalization of horror and the challenge of change.*

**13. Sex, Gender, and Transformation: From Scoring
to Caring**　　244

*Gender, ideology, and society. Renegotiating sex and gender. From
masculinity to masculinities. Sex, winners, and losers. The many
faces of the men's movement. Women, men, and partnership.*

**14. Getting Out of Prince Charming's Slipper:
Sex, Femininity, and Power**　　265

*The girl, the prince, and the body. What are we teaching our
daughters? The household nun and the sexual vampire. Masochism,
motherhood, and feminism. Reclaiming woman's sexuality.
Resacralizing the erotic.*

**15. Sex, Lies, and Stereotypes: Changing Views of Nature,
the Body, and Truth**　　287

*Eggs, sperm, and myths of gender. Sacred blood or the curse?
Women, men, and nature. Renaming the sacred and the obscene.
Redefining the normal, abnormal, and perverse. Postmodernism,
reality, and relativity.*

**16. Morality, Ethics, and Pleasure: Sex and Love in the Age
of AIDS**　　308

*AIDS and traditional morality. Population, contraception, and
abortion. Morality, domination, and accountability. Sexual
standards, sexual policies, and sex education. Tradition, family,
and values. Love, the body, and pleasure.*

**17. Sex, Power, and Choice: Redefining Politics and
Economics**　　330

*Genes, politics, and economics. The economics of prostitution.
Women, work, and value. Power, productivity, and reality.
Rethinking work, welfare, and economics.*

**18. Toward a Politics of Partnership: Our Choices
for the Future**　　347

*The emerging politics of intimate choice. The old politics of violence.
The new politics against violence. Empathy, gender, and the
"feminization" of politics. The groundswell for transformation.
Spirituality, justice, and the body politic.*

19. The New Eves and the New Adams: The Courage to Question, the Will to Choose, and the Power to Love   372

Our creative adventure. Remything the sacred. Relearning love. The challenge, the creative opportunity, and the real culture wars. Redefining courage and recreating our lives. The future of sex, love, and pleasure.

The Dominator and Partnership Models   403

Use of Notes and Bibliography   407

Notes   409

Bibliography   464

Acknowledgments   484

Index   486

Permissions   495

Our Sexual and Social Choices: An Introduction

Sacred Pleasure is a book that quite unexpectedly demanded to be written. My plan, as I mentioned in the closing pages of *The Chalice and the Blade*, was to write a different book.[1] But fortunately the creative process is guided not only by our conscious plans but by far deeper stirrings. So gradually, though not without a struggle, I began to shift from what I thought I wanted to write to what I now see I needed to write.

As I was putting together the materials and notes for the book I was originally planning, there was one chapter that kept getting bigger and bigger. This was the chapter called "From Chaos to Eros: Dominator or Partnership Sexuality." First the materials started to overflow from one to two, and then three, four, and five file folders. In a very short time, there was a whole box. Then a second, a third, and a fourth.

At that point, I began to see that this was not a chapter. It was the book I was going to write. Moreover, as I got more deeply into it, it turned into a book that not only challenges many of our most basic assumptions about sex; it also puts at issue much of what we have been taught about love, spirituality, politics, and even pain and pleasure.

Sacred Pleasure explores the past, present, and potential future of sex. It looks at both sex and the sacred in the larger context of our cultural and biological evolution. It demystifies much in our sexual history that has been confusing, indeed incomprehensible, shedding new light on matters still generally shoved under the rug of religious dogma or scientific jargon. It shows that the struggle for our future is not just political in the conventional sense of the word, but revolves around fundamental issues of pain and pleasure. Above all, it helps us better understand—and thus break free of—the agonies we chronically suffer in our search for healthier and more satisfying ways of living and loving.

For me, writing this book was an exciting journey of continually amazing discoveries. Sometimes it was a deeply troubling journey, as I had to come to grips with all that in our culture to this day links sexuality with violence and brutality. Other times what I found was so strange and funny it made me laugh out loud. And as I read everything I could lay my hands on about sex, ultimately what I found led to a whole new theory not only about the evolution of sex, but about the evolution of pleasure, politics, consciousness, and love.

Sex, Pleasure, and Pain

I should say from the beginning that although I think much that I deal with is universal, my focus has been on Western society. Even here, though we will also look at homosexual relations, I have focused primarily on heterosexual relations and how these affect, and are in turn affected by, different social forms—already in itself a huge subject.

I should also say that my aim has not been to accumulate knowledge just for its own sake. I was strongly motivated by the increasingly critical need for transformative knowledge: for the new tools for personal and social transformation that our time of mounting ecological, political, and economic crises requires if we are to have a better future, perhaps a future at all. Thus, my research was set up to try to answer questions that for most of us are far from being just matters of intellectual curiosity.

Why, when avoiding pain and seeking pleasure are such primary human motivations, have we for so long been taught that the pleasures of sex are sinful and bad? Why, even when sex is not condemned as evil (as in modern pornography), do we so often find it associated not with erotic love but with the marketing of women's bodies or with sadism and masochism, with dominating or being dominated? Was it always so? Or was there a time before sex, woman, and the human body were vilified, debased, and commodified?

What really lies behind rape, incest, and other forms of sexual violence? How and why did these practices arise? Most important, what personal and social changes can help us move toward a healthier, less dysfunctional, less hurtful way of structuring sexual (and more generally, human) relations?

My search for answers to these questions took me into fields ranging from biology, psychology, sexology, and sociology to economics, archaeology, art history, literature, and mythology. Time and time again I kept coming back to the profound human yearning for connection, for bonds forged by love and trust through both sexuality and spirituality. I became particularly interested in the ecstatic experience, and in the at first seemingly incongruous erotic imagery in so many Eastern and Western religious traditions.

Gradually I began to see that this connection between sex and spirituality was not accidental; that in fact it has very ancient roots. I also began to understand why *love* is the key word not only in romantic but also in mystical literature, and why the poetry of mystics, like that of lovers, is so often erotic.

The more I probed, the deeper the questions went. Eventually I began to look at not only sex and spirituality, but also pain and pleasure in a completely different way—hence the (to some people) heretical book title *Sacred Pleasure*. I began to see that neither human society nor human history can be understood without taking into account the very different ways a society can use pain or pleasure to motivate human behavior. Even beyond this, I began to see the central, though amazingly ignored, role pain and pleasure have had in the evolution of culture, and even of life. I also saw how the evolution of our highly developed human capacities for sexual pleasure and for the intense pleasures of love was a potential turning point in the extraordinary history of this planet.

At that moment, it was as if a hundred light bulbs had just gone on. For I began to see that much that is happening in our time is about what for shorthand I have come to think of as the pain to pleasure shift: the shift to a social system that can support, rather than chronically block, these highly pleasurable human capacities.

This in turn made it possible for me to see that it is not coincidental that so much of our traditional religious imagery sacralizes pain rather than pleasure, or that the capacity to inflict pain, rather than to give pleasure, has been idealized in so many of our epics and classics. It helped me understand how and why our lives came to be poisoned by notions like "pain and pleasure are two sides of the same coin," "spirituality and sexuality are at opposite poles," and "the war of the sexes is inevitable." Most important, I began to understand that to overcome the pain and guilt, the exploitation and alienation, the tragic and often comic obstacles that have so embittered both women's and men's lives will require fundamental changes not only in how we view sex, spirituality, and society, but in how we view the human body, power, pleasure, and the sacred.

Dominator and Partnership Sexuality

No subject arouses more curiosity than sex. It is indeed fascinating, as we will see in the pages that follow, how varied sexual attitudes and behaviors can be. But this book does not just present a pastiche of intriguing sexual tidbits from many cultures over thousands of years. It organizes what otherwise appears to be random information into patterns.

Sex is one of our most basic human drives. Moreover, sexual relations are more physically intense, and often more fully felt, than any other personal relations. This is why the way sexual relations are constructed influences all other relations. But this is not just a one-way process. How sex and sexual relations are defined is in turn also profoundly influenced by a society's economic, religious, and political structure.

Sacred Pleasure contrasts two different ways of constructing human sexuality within the larger framework of two very different ways of organizing human relations: one relying more on pain and the other more on pleasure. In the pages that follow we will see how beneath the great variety of sexual customs and mores are two underlying possibilities for our species: what I have called the dominator and partnership models.[2]

In the dominator model—beginning with the ranking of one half of humanity over the other—rankings backed up by fear or force are primary. Hence, societies orienting primarily to this model rely heavily on pain or the fear of pain to maintain themselves. Moreover, to maintain relations of domination and submission, the natural bonding of the give and take of sexual pleasure and love between the female and male halves of humanity has to be blocked or distorted.

This is why societies orienting primarily to the dominator model—which have historically ranked men over women, kings over subjects, and man over nature—have built into their basic social structure a number of devices that distort and repress sexuality. One, with which most of us are all too painfully familiar, is the vilification of sex and woman. A second, which has only in recent years begun to attract scholarly and popular attention, is the equation in both heterosexual and homosexual relations of sexual arousal with domination or being dominated.

The most familiar example of the first is of course the Western religious dictum that sex is dirty and evil. In this view, sex is for only one purpose: conception. And those who violate this dictum—be it through masturbating, homosexual sex, or heterosexual sex for pleasure—are to be punished, not only through temporal means here on earth but for all eternity by God.

Moreover, as in the biblical story of Eve's causing humanity's Fall and the Christian *Malleus Maleficarum* (a book blessed by the fifteenth-century Church as the manual for witch-hunters), woman is sinful, a "carnal" creature suitable only for propagation, for providing men with sons. Therefore woman, along with human sexuality, must be rigidly, indeed violently, controlled.

But it is important to stress, as I will in this book, that this way of interfering with the sexual relations between the female and male halves of humanity—without which our species could not go on—is not just something we find in our Western religious traditions. Rather, it is a mind-set found in a number of rigidly male-dominant societies. We find it, for example, in fundamentalist Islamic Iran, where, at the orders of "moral" men like the late Ayatollah Khomeini and his mullahs, people have been executed for "sexual crimes"—and the "necessity" of controlling woman "for her own good" has actually been made part of the curriculum at the University of Teheran.[3]

This embedding of mistrust and control into the sexual relations between women and men has been an extremely effective way of ensuring that not only our most intimate relations but all our relations are tense and mistrustful. For if God created a world where man cannot even trust woman—the person with whom through both sex and birth he has the most intimate physical relations—how can he be expected to trust anyone? If women are so inherently untrustworthy, how can they trust each other, or even themselves? Moreover, if God decreed that men must control and dominate women, why—as in the all-too-familiar "holy wars" where to this day killing and pillaging are said to be God's will—should not the same also apply to other men and other nations?

All this leads directly to the second major device for using sex as a way of conditioning both women and men to fit into a social system based on force-and-fear-backed rankings. This is the conditioning of both women and men to equate sexual arousal with the domination of woman by man (and in homosexual sex, of the individual who plays the feminine role). Of course, even in the most rigid dominator societies, there are men and women who manage to avoid these patterns. And, as we will see, in the last few decades both men and women have frontally challenged these and other gender stereotypes, with the growing recognition by many men that they too are losers in the dominator "war of the sexes," that in the end it prevents them from getting what they really need and want. But the fact that so much in our society still eroticizes domination has, to varying degrees, tended to condition men to think of sex in terms of domination and control rather than affiliation and caring, and to even see domination and control as integral to their basic "masculinity" or sense of self. And what better way of unconsciously programming women to accept subservience and domination than through the erotization of female submission?

The modern pornography industry offers the most dramatic contemporary example of this kind of conditioning. For while some of what it markets is erotica—that is, materials depicting the giving and receiving of erotic pleasure—it tends to dehumanize both women and men and to confuse sexual pleasure with the sadomasochistic inflicting or experiencing of pain. However, this way of maintaining and reinforcing dominator relations is hardly new. It most probably goes back to the time in our prehistory when, as we are now learning, there was a major shift in the mainstream of our cultural evolution—from a partnership to a dominator model for all relations.[4]

As we will see, both women and sex were viewed very differently in our earlier prehistory. For there is mounting evidence from archaeological excavations that for thousands of years women and men lived in societies where the norm not only for sexual relations but for all relations—from those between parents and children to those between humans and nature—was not domination and exploitation.

But even though there was in our prehistory a fundamental change, I want to emphasize that what we are talking about here is always a matter of degree. No society conforms completely to a partnership or dominator model.

In fact, no society, no matter how rigid its rankings of domination, can survive without at least some partnership elements. However, as the historian Mary Elizabeth Perry points out, in societies that orient primarily to a dominator model, these elements are co-opted.[5] They are exploited at the same time that they are distorted and suppressed, with caring and nonviolent behaviors relegated to "inferior" groups such as women and "effeminate" men—in other words, to those who are dominated rather than those who dominate.

I also want to emphasize that in a partnership model all is not peace, love, and cooperation, with never any violence, pain, conflict, or fear. But it is a type of social organization where chronic violence, pain, and fear do not have to be built into the basic or institutionalized social structure. Therefore, societies primarily orienting to partnership rather than domination can rely more on pleasure than on punishment (or fear of pain) to maintain social cohesion. For—once again beginning with the fundamental difference in our species between women and men—in a partnership model of social organization difference is *not* automatically equated with inferiority or superiority, with in-groups versus out-groups, with dominating or being dominated.

Hence this type of social organization does not require the misogyny, or hatred of woman, that serves to justify the subordination of one half of humanity by the other. There is here no need to vilify woman as a carnal and dangerous temptress so much less spiritually evolved than man that she is even excluded from the priesthood (or direct access to the divine). Neither is there a cultural need to rank man and spirituality over woman and nature, or to inhibit the sexual bonding between women and men through religious dogmas of "carnal sin." Nor does domination have to be eroticized to perpetuate the "war of the sexes." Quite the contrary, the innate human impulse toward enjoying the giving and receiving of sexual pleasure can be encouraged through partnership sexuality—and so also can bonding through the mutually fulfilling giving and receiving of affection.

Indeed, in partnership-oriented societies, sex can be a form of sacrament, a peak experience, as here the sexual union of two human beings can be a reminder of the oneness of all life, a reaffirmation of the sacred bond between woman and man and between us and all forms of life. Once again, this is not to say that partnership sex is always an act involving love or what we call higher consciousness, or that in the partnership model there are no rankings of any kind.[6] But in societies that orient primarily to partnership rather than domination there is no structural requirement to implant the kinds of attitudes and behaviors needed to maintain a system based on rankings backed by force and the fear of pain. Consequently, here sex can be a means of linking based on the giving and receiving of pleasure and it can also be both spiritual and natural.

Sex, Spirituality, and Society

The view that sex has a spiritual dimension is so alien to everything we have been taught that it takes most people completely aback. But actually this view is rooted in ancient traditions vividly expressed in prehistoric art that earlier scholars often found too embarrassing to deal with, and in some cases to even fully see. These traditions not only provide important information about our past, but have profound implications for our present and future. And they are traditions about which we in fact have long had many clues.

For example, in Western mythology we find many references to the sacred sexual union scholars call the *hieros gamos.* This probably was an ancient partnership rite before it was distorted into a means for kings to legitimize their rule through union with a high priestess as the representative of the ancient Goddess. Another clue is what nineteenth-century scholars termed temple prostitution. This was the practice we read about in Mesopotamian records where priestesses apparently initiated men through erotic rites into mystery cults in which giving and receiving pleasure—rather than enduring pain, as in many dominator religions—was viewed as an important spiritual experience.[7] Thus, in the Sumerian narrative of Gilgamesh, hailed by scholars as the first Western epic, we read that a woman (whom translators alternately call a "love-priestess" of the Goddess, a "temple whore," or a "temple courtesan") transforms the wild Enkidu from a beast to a human being by having sex with him—thereby helping him "become wise, like a god."[8]

There are also strong vestiges of sex as a religious rite in Eastern religious traditions—for instance, in Indian erotic iconography and Tantric yoga. But here—as in the Mesopotamian stories where love-priestesses are reduced to "prostitutes"—the use of erotic pleasure as a means of raising consciousness (or attaining higher spirituality) for both partners has also already been largely co-opted by a male-centered dominator view.

In the pages that follow we will examine many other fascinating examples, such as May Day celebrations, which most probably derived from prehistoric sexual rites and in which lovemaking was still customary well into the twentieth century. And we will also see how throughout recorded history there have been attempts to reconnect us with our prehistoric partnership roots.

For example, there were the troubadours, and their female counterparts, the trobaritzes. Flowering in the twelfth century courts of southern France (the same area where millennia earlier woman's sexual power was venerated in Paleolithic cave art), their poetry celebrated both woman and love. This courtly romantic love they sang about was in some ways a resurgence of partnership sexuality, of sexual love as both sensual and spiritual. It was also during this time that Mariology flourished. This was the veneration of the Virgin Mary, which from this perspective can be seen as a return to the worship of the prehistoric Goddess in her aspect of the merciful and compassionate Mother. Also prominent at this time were unusual Christian sects such as the Cathars, who, in sharp contrast to the Roman Church, accorded women high status in religious affairs.[9]

But the Cathars, like other "heretics" who rejected the notion that woman is of an inferior and nonspiritual order, were mercilessly persecuted by Church authorities. So also were the so-called witches and other women who still clung to vestiges of the prehistoric worship of a Great Goddess and her divine son, the Bull God (who by then had become the horned and hoofed devil of Christian iconography). Most thought provoking to us now, these women who were tortured and burned at the stake were often also healers who still knew ancient methods of birth control and taught them to other women.

The emerging new knowledge about our past also sheds new light on today's search for a new spirituality and a new sexuality. For in terms of the conceptual framework of the partnership and dominator models, the two are *not* unrelated. Rather, they are integral parts of the strong contemporary movement to shift to a society that orients primarily to partnership rather than domination—and with this, to healthier, more satisfying, and more sustainable ways of structuring our relations with one another and with nature.

The Opportunity and the Challenge

According to Freud, who correctly assessed the key importance of sex in all human relations—but who unfortunately tended to confuse dominator sexuality with human sexuality—"man" must at all times be wary and controlling of nature, including his own.[10] But ours is a time when "man's conquest of nature" threatens all life on our planet, when a dominator mind-set and advanced technology are a potentially lethal mix, when all around us institutions designed to maintain domination and exploitation are proving incapable of coping with the massive social, economic, and ecological problems they have created.

It is a time of epochal crises. But for this same reason, it is also a time of epochal opportunities—a time when, as we struggle to create for ourselves and our children new ways of thinking and living, women and men all over the world are challenging many of our most basic assumptions.

In this book we will take a close look at some of these assumptions—and at our sexual, social, and spiritual alternatives. In "How Did We Get Here?" (Part I), we start by contrasting contemporary sexual images (along with the often brutal practices they reflect) with ancient erotic images, as we begin to look at the sometimes amazingly obvious clues to an earlier and very different spirituality, sexuality, and society. After this brief overview we will go back even farther, to what anthropologists call protohistory, to take a fresh look at an extraordinary yet generally neglected and often misunderstood evolutionary development: the first emergence of hominid and human sex. From there we move on to prehistory, to a time when sexual attitudes—along with all aspects of women's and men's lives—were very different from how we have been taught things always were, and by implication always must be. We will see how both sex and spirituality were, during a time of great chaos and dislocation, drastically altered. And in the closing chapters of Part I—as we move from prehistory to early Western history; to ancient Greece, Babylon, Palestine, and Rome, and from there to the Christian Middle Ages—we will see how, in a vivid alternation of horror story and tragicomedy, both sexuality and spirituality became distorted in dominator societies. But we will also see how, even despite this, earlier partnership traditions such as the ancient sacred marriage survived—although often in truly bizarre forms.

In "Where Are We and Where Do We Go From Here?" (Part II), we shift to our own time to examine the modern sexual and spiritual revolutions as part of a larger revolution in consciousness, which in turn is integral to the modern struggle to create a less painful and violent world. We will start by taking a fresh look at some basics: the human body, pain, pleasure, power, love, and the sacred. We will explore what (borrowing the Chilean biologist Humberto Maturana's term) we may call the biology of love—and how a dominator social and sexual organization at every turn distorts and blocks the profound human yearning for connection, for bonds forged through love and trust rather than fear and force. We will also take a fresh look at politics from a perspective that takes into account our intimate relations—between parents and children as well as women and men—and probe in depth how dominator sex is still a major obstacle to both personal and social health. Most important, we will see that the more fulfilling, pleasurable, passionate, and at the same time more spiritually satisfying relations we all want *are* possible, once we leave behind a fundamentally imbalanced system, with all its built-in obstacles to human fulfillment and actualization.

In short, following the general sequence of human cultural evolution, Part I takes us from protohistory to the end of the Middle Ages, and Part II covers the period from the Middle Ages to present times—focusing on the unprecedentedly powerful contemporary partnership movement and the strong resistance to it. Nonetheless, ours will not be a linear course, either in time sequences or in themes. For *Sacred Pleasure* is above all a book about connections, a book that, like our lives, keeps recombining basic elements in different ways in different contexts.

In this sense, it is very different from books that, in line with the compartmentalized and specialized approach of much of contemporary scientific thinking, tend to focus on one thing, or at best, one thing at a time. I have chosen this more holistic approach because only by as much as possible looking at the whole picture can we change the lens through which we evaluate what is or is not "reality." I have also chosen it because it flows from the *cultural transformation theory* I introduced in *The Chalice and the Blade*, which provides the conceptual framework for this book.

To briefly summarize, *cultural transformation theory* proposes that, in the language of nonlinear dynamics, the dominator and partnership models have for the whole span of our cultural evolution been two basic "attractors" for social and ideological organization. Drawing from chaos theory and other contemporary scientific theories that show how living systems can undergo transformative change in a relatively short time during states of extreme disequilibrium, *cultural transformation theory* shows how these same principles apply to social systems. Specifically, it shows that many beliefs and practices we today recognize as dysfunctional and antihuman stem from a period of great disequilibrium in our prehistory when there was a fundamental shift from partnership to dominator model ascendency. And it proposes that in our chaotic time of escalating disequilibrium we have the possibility of another fundamental cultural shift: this time in a partnership rather than dominator direction.[11]

This book expands *cultural transformation theory* by grounding it in the experience—and politics—of the body. It also expands its scope by going farther back in time and probing the evolution of both sex and consciousness, as well as by focusing on the foundational matter of pain and pleasure as levers for human motivation. It shows that the degree to which a society orients to a dominator rather than a partnership model profoundly affects the degree to which it relies on pain rather than pleasure for its maintenance. It examines how through a variety of means, including the sacralization of pain rather than pleasure, dominator systems have idealized the institutionalization of pain. And it shows that much that is happening in our time can be seen as an attempt to shift to a system where pleasure—not in the sense of a short-term escape or distraction, but in the sense of healthy, long-term fulfillment—can instead be institutionalized, and even sacralized.

This book also further expands the templates of the partnership and dominator models by focusing on the interconnections between different approaches to both sex and spirituality and whether a society is more authoritarian and warlike or more peaceful and democratic. Conversely, it shows that successfully challenging and replacing unhealthy assumptions about sex and spirituality requires that we understand how both are interwoven into a larger whole that encompasses economics, politics, family, literature, music, and all other aspects of social and cultural life. For only by trying to simultaneously look at how all these elements interconnect can we see the underlying patterns—and thus move toward more satisfying and equitable alternatives.

It is my hope that through its in-depth exploration of our sexual and social alternatives, *Sacred Pleasure: Sex, Myth, and the Politics of the Body* can be a useful tool for the many women and men today struggling to finally free ourselves from a basically antipleasure and antilove system. I am convinced that we *can* regain the lost sense of wonder about human sexuality, the ecstasy of pleasure, and the miracle of love. I am also convinced that the still-ongoing modern sexual revolution, with all its upheavals of accepted norms, offers us an unprecedented opportunity not only for a much more satisfying sexuality but for fundamental personal and social change.

To the extent that in its earlier stages this sexual revolution made it possible for us to talk openly about sex and to look at sex as a legitimate source of human pleasure, it has already been partly successful in taking us toward healthier and more pleasurable ways of living and loving.[12] But to the extent that it did not unlink sex from violence and domination—and did not offer us any viable alternatives—it has failed to bring us closer to these goals.

Now we have the opportunity to move to a second phase, to a *real* sexual revolution. This is the opportunity to go deeper, to the sexual, spiritual, and social choices before us. It is an opportunity to at long last break free of the fetters that have so long distorted our most basic relations: with one another, with our natural habitat, and even with ourselves, with our own bodies. Above all, it is the opportunity, and the challenge, for both women and men to construct for ourselves and our children a world where pleasure rather than pain can be primary—a world where we can be both more free and more interconnected, integrating spirituality and sexuality in a new, more evolved understanding of and reverence for the miracles of life and love.

1

HOW DID WE GET HERE?

CHAPTER 1

From Ritual to Romance: Sexuality, Spirituality, and Society

Candles, music, flowers, and wine—these we all know are the stuff of romance, of sex and of love. But candles, flowers, music, and wine are also the stuff of religious ritual, of our most sacred rites.

Why is there this striking, though seldom noted, commonality? Is it just accidental that *passion* is the word we use for both sexual and mystical experiences? Or is there here some long-forgotten but still powerful connection? Could it be that the yearning of so many women and men for sex as something beautiful and magical is our long-repressed impulse toward a more spiritual, and at the same time more intensely passionate, way of expressing sex and love?

Because we have been taught to think of sex as sinful, dirty, titillating, or prurient, the possibility that sex could be spiritual, much less sacred, may seem shocking. Even stranger in a world where female genitals are sometimes described as "cunts" (one of the most obscene swear words in the English language) is the idea that women's bodies—and particularly women's vaginas—could be sacred.

Yet the evidence is compelling that for many thousands of years—much longer than the thirty to fifty centuries we call recorded history—this was the case. In traditions that go back to the dawn of civilization, the female vulva was revered as the magical portal of life, possessed of the power of both physical regeneration and spiritual illumination and transformation.

Far from being seen as a "dirty cunt," woman's pubic triangle was the sacred manifestation of creative sexual power. And far from being of a lower, base, or carnal order, it was a primary symbol of the powerful figure known in later Western history as the Great Goddess: the divine source of life, pleasure, and love.[1]

Ancient Sexual Symbols

In the south of France, where some of the earliest European art has been found, there are many images of the sacred vulva. Some of these, in cave sanctuaries near Les Eyzies in the Dordogne region, go back thirty thousand years.[2] As archaeologists point out, the cave was symbolic of the Great Mother's womb. Its entrance was thus a symbol of the sacred portal or vaginal opening.

This association of the divine vulva and womb with birth, death, and regeneration is a major mythical theme in prehistoric art. It probably goes back all the way to the Paleolithic (or early Stone Age), is clearly present in the Neolithic (when agriculture began), and in various forms still survives in the Bronze Age and even later historic times.

Many sculptures of what archaeologists call Venus or Goddess figurines, as well as other ceremonial objects excavated from all over the ancient world, have highly emphasized vulvas. Since prehistoric art is primarily concerned with myths and rituals, there is little question that these vulvas are of religious significance. For example, in the Neolithic community of Lepenski Vir in the Iron Gate region of northern Yugoslavia, fifty-four red sandstone sculptures carved on oval boulders were found placed around vulva- and uterus-shaped altars in shrines that were themselves in the shape of the pubic triangle. Dating back more than eight thousand years, some of these sculptures have engravings of the face of the Goddess with V-shaped decorations pointing to the sacred vagina.[3] Similarly, a group of Goddess figures from Moldavia in northeastern Romania dating to about seven thousand years ago have highly stylized pubic triangles decorated with V-shaped chevrons.[4]

A six-thousand-year-old Goddess figure from Bulgaria, the throned "Lady of Pazardzik," has her arms folded over her prominently etched vulva. Her sacred triangle is ornamented by a double spiral, an ancient symbol of regeneration. Strikingly similar is a Japanese Jomon pottery Goddess from approximately the same time with double spirals on her torso and a highly stylized inverted pubic triangle.[5]

In a Cycladic platter from about forty-five hundred years ago, a highly stylized vulva is flanked by branches under a large number of spirals in what looks like a spiral sea.[6] In other places, the vulva is represented by symbols from nature, such as a flower bud or a cowrie shell. In fact, cowrie shells found among skeletons from more than twenty thousand years ago indicate that the practice of placing these shells in burials as symbols of the female power of regeneration goes back to remote antiquity. The ancient Egyptians often decorated their sarcophagi with cowries. And even as late as the Roman Empire, the cowrie shell was still seen as a powerful symbol of regeneration and illumination.

In ancient Indian religious tradition, the female pubic triangle was viewed as the focus of divine energy. It is to this day in Tantric yoga associated with what is called *kundalini* energy, which, when awakened through the pleasures of sex, rises through the body to bring about a state of ecstatic bliss. This Indian worship of the divine vulva, which in some places persists even now, is graphically illustrated by a relatively recent Indian sculpture: a twelfth-century relief carved on the walls of a Goddess temple in southern India of two holy men seated at the foot of a giant vulva, their hands raised in prayer.[7]

There are also indications that the male phallus was in ancient times an object of veneration. Although the evidence for this is strongest from Bronze Age times, phalluses, and particularly depictions of the union of the phallus and vagina, are found as early as the Paleolithic, in imagery strongly reminiscent of the sacred lingam-yoni figures today still found in India. For example, at Le Placard in France, archaeologists found a carved object they at first called a *baton de commandment* (stick of command), which upon closer examination turned out to be a highly stylized elongated phallus above a vagina. One of the most interesting aspects of this ancient find is that like other Paleolithic artifacts, it has a series of notches that have now been identified as marking phases of the moon—leading Alexander Marshack to conjecture that this carving probably relates to a myth about "menstruation or pregnancy, or to a rite related to one or the other."[8]

In excavations at Savignano and Lake Trasimeno in northern Italy, archaeologists have found carvings that show, as the archaeologist Marija Gimbutas writes, "a fusion of the phallus with the divine body of the Goddess."[9] At another site in Italy, a sculpture in a shape that suggests both a phallus and a highly stylized Goddess figurine was found in the Gaban cave, near Trento. As if to reinforce the sacral connection between female and male sexuality, there is also a carving on this sculpture. A pair of crescent horns symbolize the male principle, and the vulva is represented as a flower.[10]

One of the most beautiful examples of this artistic tradition depicting sex as sacred comes to us from Mesopotamia. It is a terra cotta plaque sometimes identified as "Lovers Embracing on Bed," probably the Goddess Inanna and her divine lover about to consummate their sacred union.[11] It was fashioned about four thousand years ago. And like many earlier Neolithic Goddess figurines, it clearly delineates, indeed accentuates, the sacred pubic triangle.

New and Old Sexual Realities

These ancient sexual images are clearly not anything like what we today call pornography (a term derived from the Greek that literally means "depictions of prostitutes"). In fact, the contrast between these two kinds of sexual images is so striking they almost seem to come from different planets. Although the pornographic images that today fill so many books, magazines, films, and video cassettes also focus on vaginas, phalluses, and sexual intercourse, here, rather than being revered as sacred, women's genitals are considered obscene. And rather than being associated with a female deity, pornographic sex is often linked with male coercion and violence and with female submission and degradation.

Indeed, the way sex is generally portrayed in pornography is not even erotic (in the sense of Eros as the god of sexual love). For in pornography sex is hardly ever associated with love, or even caring.[12] Quite the contrary, pornographic images and stories are often expressive of contempt for women, and sometimes even of murderous hatred.

For example, a cover of the widely circulated pornographic magazine *Hustler* featured a picture of a man shoving a jackhammer into a woman's vagina over the "humorous" caption "Foreplay."[13] An "artistic" spread in *Penthouse* displayed nude women hanging from trees on hooks, like pieces of dead meat. In the same vein, another issue of *Hustler* used for its cover a picture that has now become a "classic": a naked woman, upside down, with only her legs and lower torso remaining intact, the rest coming out as hamburger from a meat grinder.[14]

Of course, pornographic images are only one expression of how our society views female and male bodies and how it conceptualizes sex. As we will explore in Part II, there are many other ways—from religious edicts aimed at controlling sexual behaviors, and even sexual thoughts, to the more general allusions to sex found in films, television programs, books, and articles about how women and men act in relations where sex is involved. But pornography is the most explicit, both in its nudity and its depiction of the elsewhere-taboo act of coitus. And it also most explicitly expresses cultural beliefs and practices in which sex is more like making war than making love. For here, besides the general theme of women (sometimes little girls) as merely male sex objects, we find women in chains, women being humiliated, degraded, beaten, tortured, and even killed.

Moreover—as evidenced by the infamous "snuff" films where we are now learning some women were actually killed—it is not only in pornographic magazines, films, and videos seen by millions of men and boys that sex is in our society linked with the degradation, humiliation, domination, torture, and even killing of women. Although this is something most of us would rather not come face to face with, all this does not just happen on the pages of a magazine, a movie screen, or a video cassette; it all too often happens in real life.

We only have to look at the lurid press accounts of serial sex murderers to verify that sex-related killings of women are not confined to fantasy. A recent newspaper story told of a young woman who had been kept chained inside a wooden box by a man who kidnapped her in a market parking lot and kept her as his "sexual slave" for more than two years. While this is an unusual case, the enslavement of thousands of girls and women in houses of prostitution and military bordellos worldwide is not. It has been widely documented by numerous INTERPOL and UN-ESCO reports, even though (despite the 1949 United Nations Convention for the Suppression of the Traffic in Persons and the Exploitation of the Prostitution of Others) it remains by and large unprosecuted.[15] The beating of women by men they have sex with is also far from uncommon—as tragically evidenced by the many thousands of women in the United States who are afraid to leave men who severely beat them, lest they carry out their threats to kill them—even though this battering too remains by and large unpunished, or punished by far lighter sentences than the beating of strangers.[16]

As for other forms of sexual violence and domination, the FBI estimates that in the United States a woman is raped every six minutes, with a recent U.S. Bureau of Statistics study indicating that in some states more than half the victims are girls under eighteen. An estimated 250,000 U.S. children, most of them girls, are sexually molested in their own homes every year—usually by males in their families.[17]

In other nations that are now beginning to keep such statistical records (and where women are also beginning to more openly report sex-related crimes), the picture that emerges is equally grim. For example, in Malaysia, about 49 percent of rape cases reported in 1985 involved children younger than fifteen years, and in most cases (67.8 percent) the perpetrators were natural fathers, stepfathers, or brothers.[18] In regions where we as yet have almost no statistics about this fundamental aspect of people's lives—such as most parts of Africa, Asia, and Latin America—there are other indicators of widespread sexual violence against girls and women. Indeed, in a number of respects the situation may be even worse in some of these places than in the West.

A horrible practice estimated to affect more than one hundred million women and little girls in parts of Africa, Asia, and the Middle East is genital mutilation.[19] Unlike male circumcision, with which this practice is sometimes erroneously equated, this is not a matter of the ceremonial cutting of skin. It consists of cutting off all or part of the clitoris (to deprive women of sexual pleasure and thus presumably the desire to "stray") and/or cutting off the labia and tightly sewing up the vaginal opening (making sexual intercourse impossible until a larger opening is again cut before marriage).[20] And this terribly painful sexual violence—which causes not only extreme physical trauma (from severe infections to death) but also incalculable psychological damage—is still sometimes in our day and age justified as an ethnic tradition. Or it is extolled as a religious rite said to be morally necessary to control women's sexuality.

In Iran and some other fundamentalist Islamic nations where the "sexual purity" of women is a major religious theme, young women condemned to death are routinely raped before they are killed. And though this practice too is still justified as moral because under Islamic law a virgin cannot be put to death, as we will see, it actually stems from economic concerns: the view that a virgin is valuable male property and thus should not be destroyed.[21]

But here I want to make a fundamental point. To understand, and change, brutal sexual myths and realities—be they in the Middle East, Africa, Asia, or the United States—we have to go beyond geographic, ethnic, and religious differences. The critical issue is *not* whether a culture is Eastern or Western, industrial or preindustrial, secular or religious, Northern or Southern. It is the degree to which a culture or subculture orients primarily to one of the two basic alternatives for social and sexual organization described in the introduction to this book: a dominator or a partnership model.

From this perspective, it is not coincidental that in the rigidly male-dominant, markedly authoritarian, and chronically warlike ancient societies we will look at in chapters 5 and 6 a man's "honor killing" of his wife (and sometimes his daughter, sister, and even mother) for any real or suspected sexual independence was socially condoned—as it still is in some autocratic, chronically violent, and rigidly male-dominant Middle Eastern and Latin American cultures to our day. For these are all cultures that orient closely to the dominator model.

Neither is it coincidental that those parts of the world where today we see the strongest movement toward partnership—where people are frontally challenging male dominance, warfare, and authoritarian controls in both the family and the state—are also the places where sexual violence is beginning to be openly challenged and condemned. Nor is it coincidental that prehistoric images of women's bodies, and even more specifically of women's sexuality, communicate to us a reverence for life and pleasure rather than an obsession with domination and pain. For the fact that sexuality was once associated with the sacred rather than with the sordid, brutal, and—in the true sense of the word—obscene, also did not happen in a vacuum. As we will see, it evolved in societies where women and men had a more equal partnership: more generally equitable and peaceful societies where the highest power in the universe was still seen as the power to give, nurture, and illuminate life, rather than the power to dominate and destroy.

This is not to say these were societies free of all violence, pain, and destruction—any more than it is to say that if we succeed in moving to a more partnership-oriented world there will never be any acts of sexual or other violence. But it is one thing to recognize the destructive side of nature, and ourselves, and the fact that sometimes people are violent and abusive. It is quite another to organize society so that—in order to maintain rigid rankings of domination—violence and abuse become institutionalized and (as with the unprosecuted male violence of both warfare and the war of the sexes) bound up with gender-specific socialization processes.

Which in turn leads me to a very important point I want to underscore in this stage-setting chapter: that what we are here dealing with is *not* a question of innate "masculine" or "feminine" characteristics and behaviors any more than it is a question of men against women or women against men. There were obviously both women and men in the prehistoric societies that created sacred images of women's and men's sexuality. There are today men who reject masculine stereotypes that equate manliness with dominating the "opposite sex," just as there are women struggling to free themselves from feminine stereotypes of a passive or masochistic sexuality. But at the same time, there are still men fixated on sexual "scoring" (or sex as a kind of win/lose Nintendo game) and women for whom the idea of their own bodies as sacred is so counter to everything they have been taught about sexuality that it seems to them sacrilegious.

Clearly, such marked differences in both female and male sexual attitudes and behaviors are totally inconsistent with still-prevailing notions of a fixed and immutable female and male sexuality. But they are consistent with the masculine and feminine roles that go along with two very different ways of constructing social and sexual relations: one emphasizing domination, fear, and pain, and the other mutual trust, partnership, and pleasure.

The Social Construction of Sex

Sex is an innate—indeed, indispensable—human activity. But sexual attitudes and practices are learned. We see this in the evidence all around us today, when millions of women and men have radically changed their sexual attitudes and behaviors in the span of less than a generation. We also see it in the evidence of scientific experiments showing that even monkeys, whose behaviors were once thought to be purely instinctual, have to learn the sexual act—as in the famous experiments by the psychologists Harry and Margaret Harlow on monkeys brought up in isolation, with no experience of being fondled or even touched, who then did not know how to mate.[22]

In short, sex does not, as a once-popular song had it, "just come naturally." Rather, as illustrated by the jarring differences in the prehistoric and contemporary sexual symbols and images we have been comparing, sex is to a very large degree socially constructed.

As Jamake Highwater writes in *Myth and Sexuality,* how a society at a particular time and place constructs sexuality (both heterosexual and homosexual) is inextricably intertwined with its myths. Like other scholars, Highwater does not use the term *myth* in its popular sense, meaning falsehood, but, on the contrary, meaning the expression through images and stories of that which is believed to be an immutable or sacred truth. He repeatedly shows that sexual attitudes and behaviors have been a highly variable expression of the different values carried by the myths that explain the "truth" about the world to us, and that even images of the human body are from society to society and from time to time transformed by the flux of different mythical visions.[23] Or in Michel Foucault's words, they fluctuate in accordance with periodic rewrites of "the politics of truth."[24]

Thus, the notion that the human body as part of nature is somehow inferior to the mind and spirit is already articulated in European history during classical Greek and Roman times, especially by some of the philosophers known as Stoics. But it is only later with Saint Paul, and then conclusively with Saint Augustine, that the Christian idea that the human body, and particularly the body of woman, is corrupt—even demonic—begins to take hold.

The mythic vehicle used by Augustine to support this notion was in its time, as the religious historian Elaine Pagels points out, a radical reinterpretation of the biblical story of Adam, Eve, and the Fall.[25] For according to Augustine, the Fall from Paradise—which was supposedly caused by woman—made both sex and the human body irreversibly corrupt. Moreover, according to Augustine, the normal acts of sex and birth are, for all of humanity and for all time, the instruments of God's eternal punishment of every woman and man for this "original sin."

Augustine believed, and the Church eventually accepted, that to their dying day all human beings born on this earth through sexual intercourse bear the curse of Eve's and Adam's sin of disobedience. As Augustine declared in the Christian classic *The City of God*, every child born of the sexual union of woman and man is born tainted with sin—which is sexually transmitted through the male semen. He wrote:

God, the author of all natures but not of their defects, created man good; but man, corrupt by choice and condemned by justice, has produced a progeny that is both corrupt and condemned. For, we all existed in that one man, since, taken together, we were the one man who fell into sin through the woman who was made out of him before sin existed. Although the specific form by which each of us was to live was not yet created and assigned, our nature was already present in the seed [semen] from which we were to spring. And because this nature has been soiled by sin and doomed to death and justly condemned, no man was to be born of man in any other condition."[26]

Specifically, it is this original sin that condemns women to be ruled by men, and men in turn to be ruled by autocratic kings, emperors, and popes. For according to Augustine, Adam's and Eve's sin not only forever damned sex and denied us immortality, condemning all of us to death. In essence—and in keeping with the dominator system's rigid hierarchies maintained through fear and force—it also forever doomed us to being controlled by kings, emperors, and popes "divinely ordained" to so rule.

As Highwater incisively puts it, after Augustine the human body and human sexuality became "a form of divine retribution"—a carnal burden that could only be partly escaped by truly spiritual men by tormenting their flesh. As for women, they were in this Christian mythos even more sinful than men. As the medieval Church's *Malleus Maleficarum* put it, "all witchcraft comes from carnal lust, which in women is insatiable."[27]

All this, of course, made it a Christian duty to procreate without pleasure—as Highwater remarks, "quite a chore." It also meant, as Augustine and later Christian leaders such as Bishop Ambrose insisted, that having so misused their will in disobedience of God, humans had forever forfeited their right to govern themselves. Hence, authoritarian rule, and with it political tyranny, were "the inescapable necessity of our universal fallen nature."[28]

Again *not* coincidentally when viewed from the perspective of *cultural transformation theory,* this notion of the universal corruption of humans through the sin of Adam and Eve—and thus the eternal necessity of iron-clad social and political control—coincided with the transformation of the Christian movement from a persecuted sect preaching and practicing nonviolence, compassion, and empathy (in accordance with the partnership teachings of Jesus) to the religion of the Roman emperor himself.[29] As Pagels points out, in his own persecution of first the Donites and then the Pelagian Christians (who denounced the "unholy alliance" between Catholic Christians and the Roman state) Augustine unhesitatingly allied himself with imperial officials. Indeed, as she also notes, this man, canonized by the Church as a saint, came to find military force "indispensable."

But I again want to emphasize that while the Augustinian myth of a sexually and politically doomed humanity is unique to Christian tradition, the idea that the realm of nature—including the human body—is inferior to the realm of mind and spirit is not. To varying degrees it is found in both Eastern and Western religious mythologies designed to impose and maintain dominator-dominated political and sexual relations.

For example, according to the Persian philosopher Zoroaster, there is a cosmic polarity between good as light and evil as dark, with nature and matter (the dark or earthly) inherently corrupt. Zoroaster is believed to have lived from 628 to 551 B.C. (before Christ)—or as religious scholars today prefer to call it, B.C.E. (before the Common Era).[30] But although from a different time and place, Zoroaster's philosophy is very much like that of the Christian Augustine. It holds that "man's" soul is imprisoned by matter, and that the female (who is said to be soulless) is the mother of all demons. And, like the medieval Christian notion that woman is a carnal source of evil, according to this much earlier Middle Eastern ideology, cosmic darkness and evil were awakened by a female creature—whose Persian name translates into English as "menstruation."[31]

In many Hindu religious myths, women are also of a lesser order than men. A shocking (though still generally glossed over) example is the well-known story of how the supreme Hindu deity, Vishnu, was saved from death in his crib—when a girl baby was deliberately put in his place so she would be killed instead.

Even in Buddhist mythology, one of the temptations the Buddha had to resist in order to attain enlightenment under the Bo tree was the temptation of lust and sensual pleasure. Accordingly, in some Buddhist sects monks are not only celibate, but forbidden any contact with women—including even the shaking of hands.

Like the view that the human body is somehow corrupting to the spirit, this view of woman, and particularly woman's sexuality, as dangerous to man also did not spring up in a vacuum. It came out of the fundamental social shift from a partnership to a dominator model as the primary social "attractor" that, as we will see, brought with it a fundamental shift in how both pain and pleasure were socially constructed. Wherever this shift occurred—be it in India or Ireland, Persia or Japan, Europe or Asia Minor—it characteristically entailed the elevation of man over woman and of the so-called spiritual or otherworldly over what is of this world, including our own bodies. Most dramatically, it required an almost total reversal and vilification of precisely what was once revered: nature, sex, pleasure, and—above all—the life-creating-and-sustaining sexual power of woman.

Woman, Sex, and Religion

Our Paleolithic and early Neolithic ancestors imaged woman's body as a magical vessel. They must have observed how it bleeds in rhythm with the moon and how it miraculously produces people. They must also have marveled that it provides sustenance by making milk for the young. Add to this woman's seemingly magical power to cause man's sexual organ to rise and the extraordinary capacity of woman's body for sexual pleasure—both to experience it and to give it—and it is not surprising that our ancestors should have been awed by woman's sexual power.

Nor is it surprising that male genitalia, along with the bull and other horned and hoofed animals as symbols of male potency, should have been viewed with reverence and awe. Or that the sexual union between woman and man, the source of life, love, and pleasure, should have been for our Paleolithic and Neolithic ancestors an important mythical-religious motif.

Indeed, what is surprising is that the ancient link between sexuality and spirituality could have been forgotten—or rather, that it is not consciously remembered. Because if we closely reexamine both Eastern and

Western myths, it is evident that its unconscious memory still lingers on in most world religions to our day.

In India, the lingam and the yoni (the male and female genitals) are still associated with the sacred. In Tibet, the famous phrase *om mani padme hum* (the jewel in the lotus) has many layers of mystical meaning. It refers to the primal unity within a larger whole of what we today tend to think of as polarities: light and darkness, creation and destruction, fire and water, and woman and man.

In China a similar image is represented as the diamond body born of the golden flower. In medieval Western mysticism, paralleling the jewel in the lotus, we find the image of the dewdrop in the rose. Even the Christian description of nuns as the brides of Christ and of Jesus as the bridegroom of Mother Church[32] must harken back to an earlier view of sexual union as union with the divine.

In the Kabbala, a collection of medieval Hebrew mystical writings, we find innumerable references to the Shekinah—the feminine source of divine wisdom—along with prescriptions for holy men to seek spiritual union with her. There are also Christian images that harken back to the earlier iconography honoring woman, life giving, and sexuality. For example, the so-called Vierges Ouvrantes that were venerated in the Christian Middle Ages depict the pregnant body of the Virgin Mary in much the same posture as some of the pregnant so-called Venus figurines from the Paleolithic.[33]

The numerous medieval icons and Renaissance sculptures of Mary and the Baby Jesus are likewise direct descendants of earlier representations of the Goddess and her divine child. And one of the most remarkable—and, once we really look at it, obvious—examples of an artistic tradition that goes back to the Paleolithic and Neolithic is a Renaissance painting of the Goddess Aphrodite (reproduced in Joseph Campbell's *The Mythic Image*) where we find rays of light emanating from her vulva onto a group of men.[34]

As we saw earlier, around that same time we find men venerating the sacred vulva in twelfth-century Indian religious sculptures. Also from this same general period are the famous erotic Indian temple friezes that in recent decades have been featured in Western art books (such as *The Sensuous Immortals,* published by the Los Angeles Museum of Art). Like the Neolithic and Bronze Age sculptures described earlier, these Indian sculptures depict the act of sexual union as a religious rite. And even though these Indian temples already date from a time after the Aryan or Indo-European invaders superimposed many of their dominator values over the earlier indigenous Goddess-worshiping cultures, they are still arresting examples of erotic partnership: of the give and take of ecstatic sexual pleasure.

Here, because of current publicity, I should note that what these sculptures depict is nothing like what allegedly goes on in secret demonic sexual cults today. Whether there are such organized cults or not (now being hotly debated) is not the point. The point is that the scenes in Indian erotic friezes are not by any stretch of the imagination sadistic, brutal sexual acts—much less the occult or secret worship of the devil. To begin with, these temple sculptures emphasize the give and take of mutual pleasure, not the inflicting of one-sided pain. They were created as part of the religion of their time and place, for all to see. And, as depictions of sexual union between widely worshiped deities, they were not designed to demonize or corrupt but rather to instruct and inspire both women and men.

These Indian images of sacred erotic rites most probably have the same ancient roots as the Indian Tantric tradition mentioned earlier, where the central rite is *maithuna* or sexual union. The purpose of this rite is to awaken the *kundalini* or divine energy, which is often explicitly identified with *shakti*, the creative power of the Goddess.

Because the Tantric writings that have survived are already shrouded in many overlays of later dominator cultures (both Hindu and Tibetan), their emphasis is on the male. We are told that through *maithuna* a man achieves union with the life-giving or primal power of the Great Mother. But if *maithuna* is the path to union with the divine for the man, this is clearly also so for the woman. For it is through woman's body—through her sexual arousal and her sexual pleasure—that the erotic energy of the Goddess is evoked. In Tantric practice, the man merges with the divine by giving woman sexual pleasure, thus helping to sustain the ecstatic experience for both. But woman's body is the divine vessel—in Western symbology, the Holy Chalice or Grail.

Another fascinating, though still generally ignored, aspect of Tantric yoga relates to birth control. While woman's power to give life was revered—and perhaps precisely *because* it was revered—there are in Tantric practice indications of a partnership between women and men to avoid accidental conception. For Tantric sex is explicitly and exclusively designed *not* for impregnation. Its sole purpose is to enable both women and men to experience, through the most prolonged and exquisite erotic sensations, the spiritual experience of ecstasy.

It is interesting in this connection that originally in Indian iconography the infinity sign (∞) apparently meant sexual union: two becoming one. Composed of two circles next to each other—one clockwise and the other counterclockwise, with neither one above the other—it symbolized equality between female and male, leading to wholeness or infinity. But an important clue to what happened in our prehistory is how later Indian iconography deftly shifts the emphasis to the male: the infinity symbol is now described as referring to two male deities—still, revealingly, the twin sons of the primal Goddess Saranyu.[35]

Again and again in the chapters ahead we will see the results of this reversal and co-option of earlier religious symbols. We will also see that this was part of a massive remything process with profound political implications that stood many of the old sexual and social myths—and realities—on their heads. And we will further see that some of the most striking clues to this remything process come to us not from Eastern religion, but from our own Western heritage.

To give just one example, there is in the Old Testament a section that in any other context would immediately be recognized for what it is: a poem of erotic love. In the Song of Songs (or as it is called in the Authorized or King James translation of the Bible, the Song of Solomon), we read of a beautiful Shulamite, the rose of Sharon, whose "lips are like a thread of scarlet," as her bridegroom sings to her, and whose "two breasts are like two young roes that are twins, which feed among the lilies."[36] Even more explicitly sexual are her own declarations of passion: "Let him kiss me with the kisses of his mouth; for thy love is better than wine," she sings to her lover. "I am my beloved's and my beloved is mine . . . a bundle of myrrh is my well-beloved unto me; he shall lie all night betwixt my breasts."[37]

What, we may well ask, is this erotic poem doing in the Bible, the most sacred of Western religious texts? Religious scholars have often tried to explain the Song of Songs as symbolic of Yahweh (popularly mistranslated as Jehovah) taking Israel as his bride, and thus of God's love for his people. But nowhere in it is there any mention of Yahweh or God. Instead, in passages such as "thy belly is like a heap of wheat set about with lilies" and "thy navel is like a round goblet," it celebrates woman's body. And in one of its most famous passages ("the flowers appear on the earth; the time of the singing of birds is come, and the voice of the turtle is heard in our land")[38] it celebrates the return of spring—as we will see, a key theme in Paleolithic and Neolithic religion.

We know from biblical scholars that the Old Testament was heavily edited over hundreds of years by school after school of priestly writers fashioning a text suitable for their theocratic rule.[39] We also know that although this collection of writings contains many important ethical teachings, it all too often treats women as evil temptresses and/or sexual property to be rigidly controlled by men. So why would the men who

edited and reedited the Old Testament have included in it a hymn celebrating woman's sexuality as sacred and ecstatic?

I do not believe that the inclusion of the Song of Songs in the Old Testament was just an inadvertent slip, as seems to be the case with other
biblical passages that offer clues to earlier forms of worship (for example,
Jeremiah's vehement rantings against the people's "backsliding" to the
worship of "the Queen of Heaven," a direct allusion to Goddess worship).[40] Rather, I think that this erotic poem (or more properly, combination of poems, for that is what it is) was put in the Bible precisely because
long-established sacred hymns celebrating sexuality, love, and the return
of spring (such as the Sumerian hymns of the Goddess Inanna we will
look at later) still retained such a strong hold on popular imagination.[41] In
other words, I believe that either consciously or, more likely, unconsciously, the men who decided to include the Song of Songs in the Bible
were using the time-honored political device of co-option.[42]

By incorporating already watered-down and fragmented passages associated with earlier traditions of Goddess worship and sacral sex into
their writings about a transcendent male divinity who ruled his earthly
flock in the same way a husband now ruled his wife—for example, by al-
luding to a royal bridegroom and a woman in his harem, rather than to
the Goddess and her divine bridegroom—they were effectively co-opting
or taking these passages over. And this process of co-option became ever
more pronounced as generation after generation of first Hebrew and then
Christian religious authorities continued to reinterpret the meaning of the
Song of Songs to better fit the myths, and realities, they sought to impose.

Sex, the Church, and the Troubadours

In later chapters we will explore this process of co-option in more detail, along with many other clues in Western religious writings to a time
when sexuality was sacred. But to close this chapter, and quickly take us
from ritual to romance, I want to briefly focus on still another compelling—yet also generally ignored—piece of evidence for a time when
the pleasures of sex were seen as sacred rather than sinful: the extreme
vilification of sexual pleasure by the Christian Church.

As we saw earlier, Augustine's dogma that sex is inherently, and eternally, sinful became one of the mainstays of the political alliance between
Christianity and the Roman emperors. But why did the Church fathers
feel it necessary to take such an extreme position? Why were they so
adamant about the evils of sex? Why did they condemn this most natural
of acts—and this most natural of pleasures—and proclaim, as did

Clement of Alexandria, that even within marriage, to engage in sex for any other reason than procreation is to "do injury to nature"?[43]

Again, religious scholars have offered a number of explanations. Some say that these men, who compulsively practiced sexual abstinence and often brutally mortified their flesh, were so sexually frustrated that they became emotionally and mentally imbalanced. But even assuming that all of them were sexually abstinent (and there is much evidence that many were not) this is still begging the question of how all this got started in the first place. It certainly fails to explain why the Church fathers should have deemed it necessary to threaten those who disobeyed their commands about sex not only with severe earthly penalties but with the most painful of eternal punishments—with nothing less than eternal torture in the fire and brimstone of hell.

Once again, a better understanding of the Church's hysterical antisexuality and violent repressiveness requires a larger context. And by this I do not just mean the politics of the time, whereby Jesus's teachings of love, tolerance, and peace were co-opted by a rigidly male-dominant, hierarchic, and all-too-often violent institutionalized "orthodox" Church. I mean the still-surviving vestiges of a much earlier Western religion, which Judaism, Christianity, and Islam after many violent persecutions finally eradicated and replaced.

As G. Rattray Taylor has documented in his now-classic *Sex in History*, the Church's persecutions of heretics—including the torture and burning of many thousands, and according to some accounts millions, of women accused of being witches—were not random. Rather, the Church most frequently focused on those "heretic" sects that honored women, gave them positions of leadership, and/or worshiped a female deity. And often the Church claimed that these sects engaged in immoral sexual practices.[44]

What I am here suggesting is that the Church's "moral" condemnation of sexuality was far more than a psychological quirk. It was an integral part of the Church's highly political strategy to impose and maintain its control over a people who still dimly remembered, and clung to, much earlier religious traditions. If the Church was to consolidate its power and establish itself as the one and only faith, the persistence of myths and rituals from an earlier, well-entrenched religious system—in which the Goddess and her divine son or consort were worshiped, women were priestesses, and the sexual union between woman and man had a strong spiritual dimension—could not be condoned. These remnants had to be eradicated at all costs, either through co-option or suppression.

And so the Church took the position it did: that sexuality was tainted with sin unless used by men solely for the obviously necessary act of procreation. Thus, the Bull God, who in the ancient religion was the son or consort of the Goddess, became the horned and hoofed devil of Christian iconography. And sex, once a sacred gift of the Goddess—along with woman—became the source of all carnal evil.

None of this is to suggest that the Christian Church is to blame for all our sexual ills. The association of sex with male domination and control began many thousands of years before Christianity became the official Western religion. In fact, it may well be that in at least some instances the Christian condemnation of sexual "licentiousness" was due to the by-then all-too-common association of sex with violence and domination.

But the Church did *not* then—any more than it does now—condemn the association of sex with violence and domination or with sado-masochistic infliction of pain. Instead, it condemned sexual *pleasure.* And this truly unnatural condemnation of sex, and the horribly bloody ex-tremes to which it led, only make sense if we look at them from this larger perspective. For then we can see that an important factor was the me-dieval Church's suppression of all remnants of an earlier religious tradi-tion that associated sexuality—as well as woman, and not just man—with the spiritual and the divine.

Once we begin to reexamine the course of European social and sexual history from this perspective, we can also begin to unravel another seem-ing mystery: why the Church would deem it necessary to so vilify woman, even to the extent of giving papal blessing to the claim made in the *Malleus Maleficarum* (the manual used by the Church for its witch-hunts) that woman is by nature more sinful because she is more carnal than man.[45] Even beyond this, it helps us better understand why popes would bless the torture and burning of women for imaginary sexual crimes, including "consorting with the Devil."[46] For though there were other factors behind the witch-hunts, including the replacement of tradi-tional female healers by Church-trained male physicians,[47] it was pre-cisely woman's sexual power that was in the older religion venerated and sanctified.

But even despite the Church's fanatic condemnations of sex and its vi-olent persecution of women—which is what the witch-hunts were[48]—the seeds of the old forms of worship were too embedded in the deepest lay-ers of European culture to be completely eradicated. Thus, during the Middle Ages, when under Church auspices the great European cathedrals were built, every one of these magnificent cavernous structures was, like Notre-Dame at Chartres, dedicated to Our Lady, the Holy Mother—mak-ing it possible for the people of Europe to at least in some form openly re-tain the ancient worship of the Goddess.[49] Also during the Middle Ages in the same south of France where woman's sexual power was once venerated in Paleolithic cave sanctuaries, there flourished the poets known as troubadours and trobaritzes, whose songs of courtly love honored woman as man's spiritual inspiration and celebrated erotic love between woman and man.[50]

In their love songs, the troubadours and trobaritzes celebrated a love between woman and man that was out of wedlock—and thus not controlled by the Church, with its by-then rigid rules on marriage and its prohibition of divorce. In some lyrics, particularly the later ones, this romantic love was a chaste love—that is, a love without sexual consummation. But in many of the songs, particularly those written before the Church-launched Crusades against the Albigensians of the south of France (the only Crusades by Christians against Christians), the lyrics of troubadour and trobaritz poetry are clearly sexual, without the obligatory proclamation of chasteness of the later poets.

The songs of the trobaritzes, or women poets, are of particular interest in this connection. As Bonnie Anderson and Judith Zinsser write, their lyrics often called for forthright declarations of love, regretted missed opportunities, and delighted in anticipation of the consummation of passion.[51] And one of the most interesting aspects of the men's lyrics is that they sing of a love where the lady, not the knight, makes the choice—a complete departure from the customs of that time when men, including knights, routinely raped women, and girls were routinely "given away" in marriage by their fathers, with little if any say in the matter.

As was fitting for their time, and for the circumstances of their romances (usually of a knight with another man's wife), troubadour and trobaritz love songs are often full of sorrowful laments and frequently have tragic outcomes. But their main import is the celebration of women and of romance—and the ritualistic courtship between a noble lady and her chosen love.

In terms of the old religion, this was certainly a toned-down version of earlier myths of the sacred union of the Goddess and her divine sexual partner. But in terms of medieval life it was a radical challenge to prevailing norms.

Indeed, the troubadour ideal of a more gentle manhood, from which our term *gentleman* derives, was in itself a violation of prevailing norms.[52] And it is for this ideal of gentleness, even reverence, toward women—and of a romantic and highly ritualized love between woman and man that has both a strong erotic and a strong spiritual element—that the troubadours are today remembered.

It is a powerful legacy, this legacy of romance and ritual that the medieval troubadours and trobaritzes left us despite the condemnation of the pleasures of sex by the Church. And it is a legacy that, as we have seen, stems from much more ancient roots: from a time when sexuality was associated with the sacred rather than the profane and the obscene.

But before embarking on a more in-depth exploration of these prehistoric roots, in the chapter that follows we will journey back even farther in time, to the very beginning of our human adventure here on earth. For if we are to move toward a sexuality and spirituality based primarily on partnership and the give and take of pleasure rather than on guilt, domination, and pain, it is important that we better understand our very earliest history as a species—and equally important, the history of sex itself.

CHAPTER 2

Animal Rites and Human Choices: The Roots of Dominator and Partnership Sex

We may not be conscious of it, but we have all been influenced in how we think of sex by what we have been taught about our sexual origins. Take for example the familiar cartoon of the club-carrying caveman dragging a woman around by her hair. In a few "amusing" strokes it tells us that from time immemorial men have equated sex with violence and women have been passive sex objects. In other words, it teaches us that sex, male dominance, and violence are all of one cloth—and that underneath our veneer of civilization, this is how it is.

This too is the picture of sexuality painted for us by some sociobiologists. In a jargon largely borrowed from capitalist economics, they write that males seek to protect their "parental investment" by fighting their sexual "competitors" and otherwise aggressively promoting their "reproductive success."[1] Here too males are active and females are passive.[2] Indeed, the bulk of the discussion is about males.[3] And, particularly in popularized writings, the emphasis has been on sex, violence, and male dominance.[4]

Most of this kind of literature deals with animals other than humans. But by and large the argument is that we can infer the basics of human mating and sexuality from observations of animals, as presumably our behaviors are similarly determined.[5]

The problems with this approach are many.[6] To begin with, while we humans obviously share many animal traits, we are in significant ways different, indeed unique.[7] To name but a few major differences, there is the much greater role learning plays in human behavior; the unique importance of symbolic communication (ranging from language to art and writing); the infinitely greater capacity of humans to make tools and use technologies to alter our environment and even ourselves; and above all, the enormous importance of culture and social organization in shaping human traits and behaviors, including human sexuality and mating behaviors.

Even beyond this, there have been grave problems of methodological bias, particularly in primate and human sociobiology. For instance, there has been a tendency to focus on competition rather than cooperation and on aggression rather than affiliation, even though both types of patterns are evident in most species. As Frans de Waal writes in *Peacemaking Among Primates*, "Ever since Darwin, the biological spotlight has been on the outcome of competition—who wins, who loses."[8] But, as he points out, "when social animals are involved, this is a dreadful oversimplification," as cooperation is just as important, and sometimes even more important.[9] So one basic problem is what kinds of behaviors are studied and emphasized.

Another basic problem is what kinds of animals are studied and written about. For example, much has been made of so-called orangutan rapes. And very little is made of the saddle-back tamarins, among which there is hardly any aggression between males and females, mating is either monogamous or polyandrous (that is, of one female and more than one male), and adult males do a good part of the child care.[10]

None of this is to say that I think the study of animals is not important or useful. It provides fascinating information about the amazing variability of animal behaviors and social organizations, including their extraordinarily diverse sexual preferences and mating patterns. I also believe that in some ways the observation of animal behaviors and social organizations can help us better understand where we are and where we can go from here. But I say this for reasons very different from those usually given.

I believe that it is *not* helpful, or scientifically appropriate, to take a particular animal behavior and/or pattern of social organization to "explain" (and, in essence, justify) particular human behaviors or ways of organizing human society as natural—and thus, by implication, inevitable.[11] But, as I will develop in this chapter, the study of animals is useful in helping us explore the possible origins of the two forms of social organization we have been discussing: the partnership and dominator models. And it can also help us better understand the important role in both biological and cultural evolution of pain and pleasure—which, as we will see, is in significant ways related to the evolution of sex.

I should here clarify that when I use the term *evolution,* it is not in the sense in which biologists use it in trying to explain how a particular species developed or evolved, but in the much larger sense of the evolution or history of our planet. Accordingly, I apply the term *evolution* to mean change over time at all levels, from the molecular to the cosmic. In other words, when I speak of evolution it is from a systems perspective: one that follows the tradition of systems scientists coming from many disciplines (for example, Vilmos Csanyi and Elisabet Sahtouris from biology, David Loye from social psychology, Eric Chaisson from astrophysics, Fritjof Capra from physics, and Ervin Laszlo from philosophy).[12]

Like many of these scholars, I am interested in the evolutionary movement toward greater variability, complexity of structure, integration of function, and flexibility of behavior. Except that what especially interests me are two key aspects of this evolutionary movement: the development of sex and of consciousness.

If we look at the evolution of life on our planet, we see that the earliest life forms were basically asexual. Reproduction was a matter of simple division and multiplication: first, the division of one cell into two, and then the exponential multiplication of that same rote process. Only later do we find the development of sexual mating between females and males, making possible the recombination of different genes from each parent. What this provided was the opportunity for far more variation among offspring. And this in turn offered many more possibilities for adaptation to the environment—in other words, for evolutionary creativity, variability, and change.[13]

Indeed, if we view evolution as a giant creative experiment—of which we humans are one of the latest, and most amazing, results—we see an extraordinary pageant in which the evolution of both sex and consciousness plays an important part. For between the appearance of simple one-celled organisms three and a half billion years ago and the emergence sixty-five million years ago of the order of primates to which we humans belong,[14] we see the unfolding of life from stationary blobs of matter to ever more complex crawling, flying, walking, and more recently tool-making, talking, and acutely self-aware creatures—life forms capable not only of joining nature in altering our physical environment but also, through our phenomenal human capacity for learning, of fundamentally altering ourselves and our social structures.

Moreover, if we look at this movement toward complexity, integration, and flexibility as one of a number of important themes in the evolution of life on this planet, we see that the customary emphasis on the "survival of the fittest" (with "fittest" in the popular literature generally interpreted as the most aggressively competitive, both sexually and otherwise) says more about the still-prevailing values and social organization than about evolution.[15] And we further see that in the great planetary experiment that the evolution of life on this earth represents, there have been a number of quantum leaps.

The emergence of life and then sex were two such leaps, extraordinary and dramatic changes in the history of our planet. Equally dramatic was the emergence approximately 250,000 years ago[16] of our uniquely complex and flexible human species—which brought with it major changes not only in the evolution of life, but in the evolution of both sex and consciousness.[17]

Our Human Origins

How this evolutionary leap to our species occurred has been the subject of much controversy, as scholars have tried to reconstruct what they call our hominid origins.[18] Since there is no surviving representative of these "missing links" in the evolutionary spiral leading to the emergence of our species, sociobiologists speculating about hominid social organization have primarily looked for models in the social arrangements of our closest animal relatives: monkeys and apes.

Of course, contrary to popular misconceptions, monkeys and apes are *not* our ancestors, so that these models are just that: speculations. Still, because living species of monkeys and apes seem to be descended from the same common ancestor as the primates from which we humans evolved, observations of these animals are more germane than those of less closely related animals farther back in the evolutionary sequence.

We will probably never know for certain how our hominid ancestors structured their social (including sexual) relations. At best, hominid social models give us material for reflecting about a number of possible primate roots for our species. But what these models certainly give us is material for reflecting on ourselves: about prevailing views of human nature and human sexuality—and perhaps most important, about how these views are now beginning to change.

Just as the rhesus macaque, a highly hierarchic, very quarrelsome, and generally aggressive monkey species, has often been used to "explain" such behaviors in humans, a favorite primate prototype for hominid and human evolution has been the savannah baboon.[19] Or I should say, this prototype for hominid evolution was based on the picture of the baboon promulgated before new research by scientists such as Jeanne Altmann, Thelma Rowell, Robert Seyfarth, Barbara Smuts, and Shirley Strum disclosed that baboon society is not as male-dominated and militarily structured as was once believed.[20]

As Linda Marie Fedigan, an anthropologist who has done extensive work in this area, writes, "There are several versions of the model for early humans which make use of the baboon analogy. But they all share in common this basic formula: take one common baboon type society, add hunting and its consequences, and the sum equals early human social life."[21]

The best known of these baboon-derived hominid models is the "man the hunter" theory proposed in earlier decades by such writers as Robert Ardrey, Robin Fox, Lionel Tiger, and Sherwood Washburn.[22] Basically, these men argued that male dominance and a highly hierarchic social organization held together by a great deal of aggressive competition based on fear and force characterized hominid and early human societies. In other words, according to this theory, the development of a dominator society and the development of hominid—and from there, human—society are one and the same.

A salient characteristic of the "man the hunter" theory is that it proposes that the bonding that led to the creation of the first human communities was bonding between males to more successfully hunt. However, as many scientists have now pointed out, hunting is hardly a major activity among nonhuman primates.[23] Nor was it among early hominids; fossil remains indicate that (like apes and monkeys) they too survived primarily on a vegetarian diet. In fact, even for contemporary human foraging societies, the majority of the calories usually come from food that is gathered—so much so that the anthropologist Ashley Montagu argues they should properly be called gathering-hunting rather than hunting-gathering. While meat from big game is valued, the primary diet is composed of vegetables and fruits, as well as very small sources of animal protein, such as snails or frogs. So in its most basic premises, the "man the hunter" theory of hominid and early human social organization rests on very shaky ground.

As an alternative, the paleoanthropologist Adrienne Zihlman and the anthropologist Nancy Tanner have proposed a very different explanation

for the bonding that is the foundation for human society. Their theory—
which orients more to the common chimpanzee as the prehominid prototype—suggests that it was through the sharing of gathered food between
mothers and children, and not through male bonding connected with
hunting, that the social bonds on which human society is based first
evolved.[24]

In contrast to the "man the hunter" theorists—who assume that the
first human tools were sticks and rocks used by men as weapons to kill
other animals as well as humans—they also propose that the first human
tool use was by females to augment, process, and carry gathered food
they shared with their offspring. In support of this, they cite data indicating that chimpanzee females, who like human mothers also share food
with their offspring, are the most adept nonhuman tool users today, often
using sticks to more effectively dig up roots and small forms of animal
protein.[25] And they argue that the hominid mothers who shared their
food with their offspring (and therefore had to gather extra food) also followed this practice, and that they most probably also fashioned the first
containers to carry and store food and initiated the use of stones as mor-
tars to soften vegetable fibers for toothless human babies.

Moreover, they take a far different view of early sexual relationships
from the one proposed in the "man the hunter" model of human origins.
In the former, it was assumed that hominid females were dependent on
males for both food and protection from other males. So it was concluded
that females would choose the most aggressive males to mate with. However, as Tanner and Zihlman point out, among chimpanzees (and in fact
also baboons) females not only gather their own food but often show a
definite preference for having sex with less aggressive males who are
friendly toward them and do not frighten or threaten them.[26] Accordingly, they suggest that among hominid females mating may also have
taken place more frequently with males who were *less* aggressive and
more sociable. In other words, they propose that hominid and early
human sexual relations were based more on bonds of mutual trust than
on fear and force—or put another way, that they conformed more to a
partnership than a dominator model of sexual and social relations.

Setting aside for a moment some of their more technical details, it is
clear that each of these theories of hominid and human origins suggests
that a particular type of social and sexual organization is "natural" for
our species. But there is another way of looking at this matter.

We are a species characterized by immense variability, not only between different individuals but between different groups. As we see all
around us, both women and men are capable of a wide range of behaviors,

from the most self-centered aggression to the most empathic caring. And we humans can have, and in fact do have, relationships structured primarily as fear-and-force-based rankings or as mutually trusting linkings. So one can say that *both* these ways of structuring human relations are natural in the sense that they are part of our human repertoire—and therefore that *both* societies orienting primarily to a dominator or partnership model are human possibilities.

I am therefore proposing as an expansion of *cultural transformation theory* a new theory of hominid and early human cultural evolution: one that is not monolithic but allows for the evolution of various types of social organization. Specifically, I am suggesting that human, and before that hominid, social organization did not follow one single linear path but rather a variety of paths—some orienting primarily to a dominator model and others orienting more to a partnership model.

Such a theory is actually more congruent with the basic tenet of sociobiology and anthropology that (within the limits of the organism's flexibility or lack of flexibility) behavior will be adapted to a given environment, and thus that we can expect to find variability in both animal and human behavior (which is what we in fact do find). A multilinear rather than unilinear theory of hominid and human cultural evolution is also more congruent with the evidence we will be examining about our prehistory. And there is interesting support for such a theory in information that is just coming to light about an only recently studied primate species, the so-called pygmy chimpanzee or bonobo.

The Uncommon Chimps

I say so-called pygmy chimpanzees, because bonobos are actually no smaller in size or weight than common chimpanzees, from whom molecular biologists estimate bonobos diverged only about 1.5 million years ago.[27] And I say only recently studied because bonobos were for a long time mistakenly classified as adolescent common chimps rather than a separate species.[28] So it was not until 1928 that bonobos were "discovered," and not until 1972 that they began to be studied in their natural habitats.[29]

Unlike common chimps, bonobos have a more gracile or slender build, longer legs that stretch while walking, a smaller head, smaller ears, a thinner neck, a more open face with a higher forehead, thinner eyebrow ridges, reddish lips, and long fine hair parted in the middle—in other words, traits that place them much closer in appearance to humans.[30] The genitals of bonobo females are rotated forward like those of human females, making it possible for them to have face-to-face sex like humans rather than with the male mounting like most other primates.[31] Bonobo males are also sexually more similar to human males in the greater length of their penises, which, in contrast to the small organs of other apes, as de Waal writes, "surpass those of the human male."[32]

In the last decade, the scientific observation of bonobos has yielded fascinating new information. Of particular interest—and relevance to what we are here dealing with—is that social interactions among bonobos are far less tense and aggressive than even among common chimps. This is not to say that there is never any violence or aggression. But as Suehisa Kuroda, a Kyoto University primatologist who has been observing bonobos in Zaire, reports, "Their aggressive behavior is mild, and their behavior in general shows high tolerance, especially between different sexes and among females."[33] Thus, Kuroda's colleague Takayoshi Kano (who has studied bonobos since 1974) writes that "unlike common chimpanzees, bonobos have never been observed to kill others of their kind."[34]

But not only are bonobos generally "more pacific and gregarious."[35] Of equal interest is that their social organization is *not* male dominant.[36] In fact, as we will see, theirs is a society in which females, particularly mothers, play key social roles.[37]

These apes also do a good deal of food sharing, which is frequent among humans but rather rare among other primates except between mothers and children. Bonobos, particularly females, not only tend to feed together peacefully; they also frequently approach each other asking that food be shared. Indeed, although there is some question about whether female-male or female-female bonding is most important, Kano, Kuroda, Amy Parish, Frances White, and others who have observed bonobos all stress the importance in their social organization of what Kano terms "strong bonds between males and females" and "high female sociability."[38]

We will return to this matter of affinitive bondings (or friendships) between females and females and between females and males many times. One reason is that in rigidly male-dominated societies females are actively discouraged from forming strong bonds other than as members of male-controlled families and organizations. Another is that while female-male friendship is an integral component of a partnership social organization, it is a major obstacle to the construction of dominator relations—as dramatically evidenced by rigidly male-dominant, hierarchic, and authoritarian fundamentalist Islamic societies, where sexual segregation is a major element in the maintenance not only of male control over women but of the entire system.[39]

The affiliative bonds between bonobo males and females are therefore extremely interesting. Often these bonds are long-term associations between bonobo mothers and their adult sons. But these bonds are also between unrelated males and females, including males and females who have sexual relations. For example, in his observations of bonobos in the San Diego Zoo, de Waal found that when a chain used by an adult male he called Vernon for climbing in and out of a two-meter moat was pulled away by a juvenile trickster, a female (whom de Waal called Loretta) "on several occasions rushed to the scene to 'rescue' her mate by dropping the chain back down"—an affiliative interaction de Waal interprets as stemming from Loretta's empathy for the male with whom she often had sex.[40]

This is not to say bonobos are monogamous. Although sometimes females have been observed mating with only one male, there is evidence indicating this is far from a universal pattern. "Though four instances were recorded in which a female copulated at least twice a day with the same male and no other," Kano writes, "in four cases a female copulated with more than two males in a day. In another case, a female copulated alternately with two males, three times each."[41]

But as Kano, de Waal, and others who have observed bonobos both in the wild and in captivity note, among these primates sexual relations play an important role in promoting social relations based more on mutual benefit—or more specifically, mutual pleasure. As Kano writes, "Most other animals copulate only as an act of reproduction." But for bonobos nonreproductive copulations "diminish hostility and help to establish and maintain intimacy between females and males."[42]

Sex that serves purposes other than producing offspring is of course something else bonobos share with our own species. So also is the fact, as de Waal puts it, that in comparison to "the somewhat boring, functional sex of the common chimpanzee," for bonobos sex is of "every conceivable variation"—from French kissing and fellatio to masturbation and group sex, as if, again in de Waal's words, they were "following the Kama Sutra."[43] Add to this the fact that pygmy chimpanzees sometimes have sex face to face (rather than like most primates, including the common chimp, through male mounting), the fact that females in this species can be sexually active much longer than other animals (including common chimps) and copulate much sooner after giving birth, and what we see among bonobos is suggestive of an important evolutionary development. This is an evolutionary movement toward sex as a means of reinforcing social relations based on the give and take of shared sensual pleasure rather than on coercion and fear.

All of which leads to still another aspect of what de Waal calls the bonobo's "impassioned eroticism"[44]—one that may surprise some readers. This is that a striking aspect of pygmy chimpanzee society is what we would call lesbian sex.

Actually, rather than being unnatural, homosexual relations between primates seem to be far from infrequent—disturbing as this may be to some sexual moralists who condemn homosexuality as unnatural. For example, Barbara Smuts and John Watanabe found that male baboons sometimes use mounting to defuse tension.[45] Bonobos too sometimes use male-male mounting, as well as rump rubbing, as a means of reducing conflict among males. And this also seems to be one of the main functions in bonobo society of sex between females.[46]

Thus Kano writes about a behavior pattern unique to female pygmy chimpanzees that has tentatively been termed genitals rubbing. The setting for this is usually a feeding tree and it usually occurs when the chimpanzees have just arrived in a group at a place where there is a food supply and are getting ready to have their meal. But before so doing, and seemingly as a means of defusing tensions, a highly ritualized sexual interaction between female bonobos often takes place. As Kano describes it:

Female A approaches female B, stands or sits nearby, and stares into B's face. If B shows no response, A may demand attention by touching B's knee or foot with her foot. B may then respond by a slight gesture, such as turning to meet A's gaze. Then either of them may invite the other, by falling on her back, or hanging from a branch. They embrace face to face, and begin to rub each other's genitals together (probably clitoris) rhythmically and rapidly.[47]

Rites of Sex, Friendship, and Sharing

We usually think of rituals in connection with religion. But from an anthropological, rather than a religious, perspective, rituals are formalized behaviors that communicate generally understood symbolic meanings. Because rituals are often associated with situations that are emotionally highly charged,[48] just about every human society has some kind of ritual associated with birth, mating, and death. And because rituals are often designed to reduce tension and promote bonding, we humans have also developed the ritualized movements we call handshakes as a means of communicating friendly (rather than hostile) intent when people meet.

Similarly, species such as wolves and baboons have developed ritualized gestures and sounds that serve to avoid bloodshed when they meet. Dogs, bears, and other mammals use licking to convey what to us looks very much like affection. Embracing is common among many monkeys and apes, since, like humans, these primates seem to have a great need to touch and be touched. And both species of chimpanzee, like humans, have developed the kiss. But what is most interesting is that among primates we also begin to see the use of nonreproductive sex as an adaptive evolutionary development to reduce violent conflict.

This use of sex to reduce tension and promote peaceful coexistence is most dramatic among the bonobos, as here it is frequently used to reduce both intragroup and intergroup tension. As we have seen, it serves to promote food sharing among females when a large group arrives at a feeding site. It is also sometimes linked to the sharing of food between individual females and males, as when Kano observed a bonobo female invite a male to copulate, seemingly with the expectation that he would share his food with her—which in a fascinating analogue of the human custom of sharing a meal before or after sex, he did.[49] And Kano also reports observing how when two different bonobo groups met at the same feeding site, the tension of the encounter was broken first by sex between a female and a male from each group and then when a female engaged in genital rubbing with several females of the other group.[50]

This new knowledge about the bonobos' use of nonreproductive sex as what de Waal calls a "peacemaking ritual"[51] raises interesting questions about primate (including hominid and human) evolution. It certainly contradicts the "man the hunter" idea that social bonding has its origins in the hunt, and with this, the idea that in the social organization of primates (including humans) male bonding has to be primary. And the fact that we see so much food sharing among pygmy chimpanzees (who like other apes and monkeys generally do little hunting)[52] also contradicts another basic premise of the "man the hunter" theory: that food sharing started with our hominid ancestors, and then only when males started to hunt.

As Kuroda notes, "The fact that this pure forest dweller, the pygmy chimp, shows the sharing of vegetable foods suggests the possibility that the early hominids in the forest had already acquired this social behavior, and seems to nullify the hypothesis that food-sharing was originated in the sharing of meat." He proposes that "it should rather be considered that the early hominids in the forest already developed this humanitarian social behavior and that, therefore, it was possible for them to proceed to the open land, where the life requires the every day food sharing."[53]

Some interesting speculations about how this "humanitarian social behavior" developed are also offered by Kano. The first relates to sex—to how, as we have seen, food sharing is greatly facilitated by what he calls the bonobos' "varied sexual repertoire to reconcile and appease." The second relates to family and social organization, to how among bonobos—in striking similarity to the social organization of the more peaceful prehistoric societies we will be examining—mothers play a major social role.

Like Zihlman and Tanner, Kano believes that strong mother-child bonds are what most likely led to food sharing among hominids and humans. He also suggests that the development of a human family composed of parents and children would have been more likely to evolve out of a social organization in which, as among the bonobos, strong and long-lasting mother-son bonds are found. Having experienced such relationships not just as infants but as adults, males could then also form strong affiliative bonds with other females.[54] To this I would add that experiencing these kinds of relations could have served as a basis for a variety of early human family forms—not only families in which mothers and fathers share food and cooperate in caring for their offspring, but also mother-centered families in which all members (including males) participate in this essential task.

Certainly, as Kano writes, among the bonobos the males' greater participation in caring for the young (as well as the generally lower levels of male aggression in bonobo society) are related to what he terms "their prolonged family attachment, in which they become intimate with their small siblings and the siblings' playmates." He notes that "whereas common chimpanzee males become more and more estranged from their mothers during adolescence as they bond with, and become absorbed into the association of adult males, bonobo sons often stay with their mothers even long after they become adults." He further notes that he has never observed "serious aggression by mature males toward young"[55] and has, on the contrary, often seen males "babysitting."

"Many times I have seen males carrying infants on their bellies or backs for short periods," he reports. "Sometimes the mother followed: at other times she was absent, trusting to the babysitter. Once when I was monitoring a group at the feeding grounds, gun fire sounded in the distance. A frightened infant jumped onto a near-by old male, who embraced it firmly, looking in the direction of the shot."[56]

The Partnership and Dominator Alternatives

Gunfire is a threat not only to bonobo infants; tragically, it is endangering the entire species. The pygmy chimpanzees of Zaire are being relentlessly hunted, except by the Mongandu people, whose legends have it that the bonobo and the ancestors of humans "once lived as brothers." Significant populations remain in only a few areas such as the Lomako and Wamba forests.[57]

The extermination of the bonobos would be a terrible loss—not only for their own sake, but because of what their study suggests about a multilinear or pluralistic theory of hominid and human cultural origins. For chimpanzees are not only our closest chromosomal relatives; as Zihlman notes, the existing measurements of early hominid fossils indicate that their body proportions are more like those of the pygmy chimpanzee than those of any other ape.[58] So it does not seem impossible that the social structure of these animals that are so closely related to our species is similar in a number of important respects to that of some of our hominid ancestors.[59]

But once again, I do not believe that the bonobos' social structure should now be *the* model for hominid evolution. As already noted, what I am proposing is that there was most probably more than one type of ancestral hominid and early human social organization, with some groups orienting more to a partnership and others more to a dominator configuration.

I am also proposing that an understanding of these contrasting configurations makes it possible to see different patterns, rather than merely random differences, in the social organization of not only humans but also our closest genetic relatives: the pygmy and common chimpanzees. For if we reexamine pygmy chimpanzee and common chimpanzee social organization from this new perspective, what at first glance may seem to be merely random differences assume specific and recognizable patterns.

Although bonobo social organization is not free of aggression and tension, there is, in comparison with the social organization of common chimps, less institutionalized violence to maintain rankings based on fear and force, and more social fluidity as well as sharing behaviors. Again, this is not to say that among bonobos there are no hierarchies. As already noted, societies that orient to a partnership model are not devoid of all rankings. But as de Waal writes, whereas for many species a major mechanism to avoid constant bloodshed seems to be the maintenance of domination hierarchies through fear and force (that is, through threat of bodily pain), bonobos frequently use bodily pleasure, rather than pain, to avoid tension and violence.

In comparison, while there are certainly also affiliative bonds based on nonviolent and mutually pleasurable interaction among the common chimpanzees, another side of their social organization has increasingly been observed—one that highlights patterns of violence by males toward other males and also toward females and their babies, as well as less sharing and more aggressive behaviors. So while theirs is by no means a rigidly male-dominated, authoritarian, and chronically violent society (the dominator model), it seems to have considerably fewer partnership elements than bonobo chimpanzee social organization.[60]

Most significantly, in these two groups gender relations take on very different patterns. Among common chimpanzees, the primary social bonds are between males and males, with far fewer affiliative bonds between females and males and between females and females. By contrast, among bonobos the primary social bonds are between females and males and between females and females, with strong indications, as Parish, Smuts, and Richard Wrangham note, that female coalitions play an important role in the prevention of male dominance.[61] In fact, in contrast to common chimpanzees, even young females are *not* dominated by males in bonobo society.[62]

Just as significantly, as Wrangham vividly brings out in his comparison of common chimpanzee and bonobo sexuality, in these two groups heterosexual and homosexual relations also follow very different patterns.[63] As Kano commented with some surprise, among bonobos "remarkably, elements of dominance do not enter into sexual activity."[64] And, as we have seen, what we also find here are heterosexual and homosexual relations associated with the sharing of food and with the substitution of sexual pleasure for violent aggression.

Again, this is not to say that bonobos never resort to physical force or the threat of force in their relations. For instance, I have already noted that female bonobo coalitions are an important factor in thwarting male aggression. This also involves the threat (and sometimes use) of force against males by females. But as Smuts notes, "where this all gets really interesting" is that "bonobo social relations are not the mirror-image of those found among chimpanzees, where the balance of power favors males." Of particular interest, as Smuts writes, is that "bonobo females don't use their power to try to keep males subordinate in general, and, in particular, they don't try to control male sexuality. In fact, the potential bonobo females have to dominate males seems to form the basis for the emergence of relatively egalitarian sexual relations."[65]

From the perspective that I am here developing of greater gender equity as a key component of a more generally egalitarian and peaceful social organization, the bonobos' more egalitarian sexual relations are noteworthy. So also is their institutionalization of interactions held together by physical pleasure. It is certainly instructive that both the absence of male dominance and the bonobos' greater sharing of erotic pleasure and food are found in a relatively less tense and more peaceful form of primate social organization—to some degree foreshadowing the more partnership-oriented human societies that, as we will see, developed over many thousands of years in early Western prehistory. Even more fascinating is how, in a rudimentary and nonreligious form, the bonobos' evolutionary experiment with the ritualization of sex as a means of reducing and resolving potential conflicts seems to foreshadow the association of sex and religious ritual that we find in these prehistoric societies.

But having said all this, I want to return to my original premise, which is that while looking at primate behaviors and primate societies is useful in tracing evolutionary themes and identifying recurrent patterns—particularly patterns characteristic of a dominator or a partnership social organization—humans are in many important respects different from other primates. Indeed, we are in critical biological, social, cultural, and sexual respects unique.

Sex, Evolution, and Choice

I have in this chapter suggested a view of evolution as an experimental process in which there are, however, recurring patterns and evolutionary themes. I have also suggested that the evolution of sex was a major factor in the evolution of ever more diverse, complex, and flexible life forms.

What I am now suggesting is that the evolution of human sexuality—particularly of our distinctive human female sexuality, to some extent already foreshadowed in bonobos—was a major factor in the great evolutionary leap to hominids and from there to our own human species. For, as I will develop further, contrary to what we have been taught, human sexuality is not what we have in common with so-called baser or lower animal forms. Quite the contrary, it is what in bits and pieces begins to emerge among primates (particularly bonobos) and then culminates in humans.

Even beyond this, I am proposing that the evolution of our unique capacity for higher consciousness combined with the evolution of our unique capacity for prolonged sexual pleasure unconstrained by seasonality, along with the long caretaking needed for human maturation, provided the potential for a major evolutionary breakthrough toward—in the normative or value-related, rather than descriptive sense—a truly more evolved form of life.

I want to emphasize that when I say "potential" I mean just that, because there is obviously great variability in human behavior and social organization. I certainly do *not* mean, as Teilhard de Chardin proposed, that evolution is the unfolding of some preordained divine plan.[66] In fact, I find it strange that one could suggest that an all-powerful, all-knowing, merciful, just, and loving divinity capable of designing a perfect world would not have avoided the agony and brutality of so much of nature and of life. It makes more sense to me that the evolutionary process is basically self-organizing and open-ended.

But at the same time, if we look at the whole span of our planetary history, there seems to be in it a trial-and-error thrust toward those traits that in the language of spirituality have been called more evolved—traits powerfully expressed in our human striving toward beauty, truth, justice, and love. And I believe that behind this human striving lies the evolution in our species of two unique, and related, sets of biological equipment: our highly developed mental, emotional, and spiritual capacities for thought, feeling, and what we call higher consciousness, and our highly developed sensual capacities for pleasure from male-female (as well as female-female and male-male) and adult-infant bonding, which together can form the basis for a humane social organization. In short, as I will develop in the course of this book, I believe that contrary to what we have been taught (through, for example, the many stories of how spiritually evolved men have to struggle against their sexuality), human sexuality is not a hindrance but rather a help in the human quest for higher consciousness and more culturally and socially evolved and equitable forms of organization. Indeed, I believe that far from being a "baser instinct" or "lower drive," our human sexuality is part of what we might call a higher drive—an indispensable part of what makes our species human.

In this connection, the ideas about sex and society of the Hungarian biologist Vilmos Csanyi are of interest. For while he does not say anything about spirituality or higher consciousness, he does point out that human sexuality provides a biological basis for a social organization structured around the give and take of pleasure and other mutual benefits.[67]

Unlike other primate females, who are sexually active only during a portion of the year (35 percent for common chimps and 75 percent for bonobos), human females can be sexually active year round. Moreover, while other primates also seem to experience orgasms, for humans sexual pleasure seems to be of much longer duration and of much greater intensity,[68] with the human female capable of repeated orgasms. As Csanyi points out, all this is of great importance in promoting longer-lasting pleasurable associations that would encourage cooperation between the sexes[69]—associations that, as the biologists Humberto Maturana and

Francisco Varela note, would have been further facilitated by our complex system of language as a uniquely human tool for communication.[70]

In fact, as we will later examine in more detail, for humans sexual relationships are often accompanied by a bond that extends beyond sex to the whole relationship—with feelings such as the desire to be near one another and affiliative behaviors such as mutual caring and caring for offspring. In light of this, Csanyi believes that the evolution of human sexuality not only made possible what Masters and Johnson call a pleasure bond between females and males, thus enhancing their chances for survival; it also greatly enhanced their offsprings' chances for survival, since the human infant is dependent on adult caretaking for such a very prolonged period of time. So Csanyi argues that, other things being equal, a social organization that encourages, rather than inhibits, more partnership-oriented sexual and social relations between females and males would have been highly adaptive in early human evolution.[71]

While I basically agree with Csanyi's analysis, I am concerned that it may give the impression that what necessarily follows from this sexual pleasure-bonding is a social organization composed of two-parent families where only biological parents are responsible for the care and protection of the young. Actually it can lead to a variety of family forms. A case in point are the Musuo tribespeople who live in the fertile valleys of the Shiaoliang mountain region of Northern China. Here the sexual relations between women and men are based solely on pleasure-bonding between lovers (or as they are called, "ashias"), the family organization is matrifocal (mother-centered) and matrilocal (with both daughters and sons living in their mothers' households), and the responsibility for an equitable distribution of resources is in the hands of the elder women. The most interesting thing is that among these remote mountain tribespeople, whose family organization and sexual mores are said to go back thousands of years, the pleasure bonds between lovers also promote mutual aid between families because, when needed, lovers work in their sexual partners' families' fields and otherwise lend a hand—thereby, in accordance with Csanyi's argument, helping to promote the survival of their own offspring, as well as of their larger community.[72] In short, the sexual pleasure-bonding made possible by the evolution of our human sexuality can lead to a multiplicity of family forms, including mother-centered families such as those today found among the Musuo and, until a few hundred years ago, the Basque, another remote mountain people who, as we will see, lived in a mother-centered family organization that seems to go back many thousands of years—one where mothers and fathers did live together and were jointly responsible for their offspring, but where, although sons could also inherit property, the family's land (as among the Musuo) was vested in the female.

To most of us today, conditioned to think of only male-headed families as normal, such arrangements seem highly improbable. So also, in a world where for thousands of years a dominator model has been primary, does the idea that the year-round sexual activity unique to human females and the pleasure bonds that can flow from human sexuality could help promote partnership rather than dominator sexual and social relations. But it would help explain the data from archaeology and myth we will examine indicating that, for thousands of years in the mainstream of Western cultural evolution, the prehistoric societies that in the more fertile regions of our globe developed our earliest civilizations appear to have oriented primarily to a partnership rather than dominator model. And it would also help explain why sexual images play such a prominent part in the sacral art of these societies, and why they so often celebrate the sexuality of woman.

Again, this is by no means to imply that all early human societies oriented primarily to a partnership rather than dominator model, and hence that this is the only "natural" type of social organization for our species. While some contemporary gathering-hunting societies that originally lived in relatively hospitable environments, such as the BaMbuti and the !Kung, have more partnership than dominator elements,[73] pre-agricultural societies in harsh habitats, such as some Australian aborigines and Eskimos, who rely much more heavily on hunting than gathering, have more dominator than partnership elements.[74] Moreover, the archaeological findings we will examine indicate that incursions from the more arid regions of our planet by highly warlike and male-dominant pastoralist tribes in our prehistory interrupted the cultural evolution of more partnership-oriented civilizations.[75]

Clearly, a dominator model of sexual and social relations is an alternative for our species. But the imposition of this model requires very severe internal and external controls. And its maintenance requires a great deal of fear, force, and pain.

This all takes us back full circle to the fact that ours is a species of enormous flexibility and variability. We are capable of a wide range of sexual and social behaviors. Which of these behaviors we exhibit is to a large degree a function of our cultural and social organization, which is, in turn, largely a function of a number of interrelated factors, such as our physical environment and our technology, as well as of the constant interaction between biological, social, and environmental factors.

But—and this is particularly relevant in our time—it is also a function of still another critical, and increasingly recognized, factor: conscious choice. Because perhaps the most important attribute that distinguishes our species from other life forms on this planet is that—to a degree that is so vastly greater quantitatively that it becomes a major qualitative difference—ours is a species endowed with an enormous capacity for conscious choice.

I am convinced that it is this great human capacity for conscious choice that in our time of mounting economic, ecological, and social crises offers us the greatest hope, not only for more satisfying personal and sexual lives, but for species and planetary survival—and that this is why we today hear so much about a revolution in consciousness.[76] For with consciousness and choice comes the possibility of change.

However, to make choices, we have to believe that we have alternatives. And under the old unilinear theory of cultural evolution as the story of "man the hunter/warrior," we were told that there is for our species only one choice: the dominator model.

In this chapter we have examined evidence for a multilinear or pluralistic view of evolution in which for both humans and other primates a social organization orienting more to a partnership than dominator model is also a viable alternative. In the chapters that follow, we will continue our exploration of human possibilities by examining Western cultural evolution—and sexuality—from this multilinear perspective. For only as we more clearly identify and understand our alternatives can we make more conscious—and adaptive—personal, social, and sexual choices for our future.

CHAPTER 3

Sex as Sacrament: The Divine Gifts of Life, Love, and Pleasure

In Western culture, religious art focusing on sexual imagery goes back more than twenty thousand years to the Paleolithic or Old Stone Age. Here, along with the mass production of sophisticated stone and bone implements, we find an equally sophisticated and extensive production of paintings and sculptures. And one of the recurring themes in this rich and abundant art is the sacredness of woman's body—even more specifically, as we already glimpsed, the sacredness of woman's vagina, breasts, and womb.

Now, we might ask, if female sexual imagery is so prominent in Paleolithic art, why haven't we been told? One reason is the puritanical bent of many of the nineteenth-century scholars who first studied these materials. Another is that, as with protohistory, until recently scholars have tended to focus almost exclusively on one half of humanity—men—with anything pertaining to women considered at best a secondary matter unworthy of extensive or serious study.[1] So when images of female genitalia were even recognized as such, they were dismissed as mere pornography, expressions of what one writer quaintly called "unregenerate male imagination." And they were certainly not considered of any great cultural significance.

Only gradually, against enormous resistance, are these biases starting to change. And as they do, a whole new view of early Western art is beginning to emerge, putting at issue many earlier interpretations of what our ancestors considered important, and even sacred.

A New View of Ice Age Art

In European cave sanctuaries famous for their colorful wall paintings of animals (often in pairs of females and males), archaeologists have unearthed nude female sculptures. Still commonly described as Venuses, these highly stylized, ample-bodied figurines are today generally understood to be ancient images of the powers that give and nurture life, as symbolized by woman's vulva, womb, and breasts.[2]

On the walls, entrances, and other surfaces of these prehistoric caves, which were probably sanctuaries where religious rites took place, are also drawings etched or carved in stone that have until recently been ignored by most archaeologists—or dismissed as meaningless, incomprehensible doodles. But the meaning of these images is comprehensible—indeed unmistakable—once we free ourselves from the still-popular notion that Paleolithic cave art was made by men for men to use in some kind of "hunting magic." For then we recognize these "doodles" for what they are: engravings and carvings of women's vaginas.

Some of these vaginas are naturalistic, such as the engravings of vulvas found in the caves at La Ferrassie, Pergouset, and Lalinde.[3] Some are more abstract or V-shaped, like the vulvas on the carved outlines of two reclining female nudes at La Magdelaine.[4] Sometimes the vulvas are open in sexual arousal or in birth, like the bud of a flower. Sometimes they are highly stylized, in the form of an inverted triangle. And sometimes they are part of a larger tableau in conjunction with other images, human or animal (including the phallus), and with what we now know are notches denoting time sequences (earlier dismissed as "indeterminate markings").

Of these Paleolithic images, the elongated forms originally identified by archaeologists as "barbed weapons" in accordance with the "man the hunter" model of our cultural origins are of particular interest, as they dramatically illustrate the distortions that resulted from this view. For example, when the so-called Montgaudier baton (a 14½-inch engraved reindeer antler) was found in the 1880s by the famous French prehistorian Abbé Breuil, this is what he saw: a common mackerel, two seals, two serpentine forms, a series of "barbed harpoons," and some "indeterminate marks"—all presumably images relating to some form of hunting magic. But more than half a century later another scholar, Alexander Marshack, looked at these carvings again, this time through a magnifying lens that made it possible to more clearly make out worn areas. And what he saw was something very different, something that, in his words, gave "a sudden new meaning to the composition, and to Ice Age art."[5]

Under magnification, the common mackerel turned out to be an adult male salmon with the characteristic jaws of the time of mating or spawning, a time in the spring when seals follow salmon, on which they feed. The fish and the seals, Marshack realized, also represented "time sequenced signs" of "the returning Spring." So did the serpentine forms, which turned out to be nonpoisonous amphibious grass snakes, which emerge from hibernation in the spring. As for the "indeterminate marks"—these turned out to be a schematized head of an ibex with crescent horns (which also reappear in the spring), "an exquisitely rendered sprout" (including roots and first leaves or branches), and a budding flower (which in prehistoric art is sometimes also a symbol of the vulva).

Even more fascinating are Marshack's findings about the so-called barbed harpoons. These linear carvings were originally seen by archaeologists as weapons. Or rather "wrong-way weapons," because the "harpoon barbs" not only pointed the wrong way but were "constantly missing their mark." So eventually the French archaeologist André Leroi-Gourhan reclassified them as "masculine signs" because of their elongated "thrusting" lines. But in fact, under closer scrutiny they turned out to be something very different: line drawings of plants—yet another sign of spring. As Marshack writes: "Under the microscope, it was evident that these were impossible harpoons; the barbs were turned the wrong way and the points of the long shafts were at the wrong end. However, they were *perfect* plants or branches, growing at the proper angle and in the proper way at the top of a long stem."[6]

Thus Marshack was able to clear up not only the mystery of these "wrong-way weapons" but still another "mystery" that earlier scholars had puzzled over: why in the art of a people who lived less by hunting than by gathering there seemed to be so few images of plants. And in the process, he deciphered the meaning of the Montgaudier baton (also a misnomer, since it was so named on the assumption that some "headsman" had used it to command his men)—and of much of Paleolithic art.

As Marshack writes, the images on this ancient object had very little, if anything, to do with hunting magic. Rather, they were "time factored and storied images of creatures whose comings and goings and seasonal habits were known" to our Paleolithic ancestors. And they reflected their interest in, and celebration of, the coming of spring, or, as Marshack put it, "the birth of the 'new year.'"[7]

Myths of Renewal and Rites of Spring

This concern of our ancestors with the birth—or more accurately, the rebirth—of life helps explain the frequent representations of vaginas in prehistoric cave sanctuaries. And it also helps explain why we find images of the phallus or erect penis in these caves.

These images were obviously not connected with hunting. A far more credible explanation is that they figured in stories based on our ancestors' extremely careful observations of the rhythms of nature—observations that, as Marshack notes, are astonishingly scientific in their attention to detail and mathematical precision. And, as illustrated by the Montgaudier baton, these images most probably also figured in scenes of mythical significance associated with rites celebrating the cyclical return of spring —and thus the periodic renewal of life in all its plant, animal, and human forms.

We probably will never know the exact nature of these ancient rites of spring. But it is evident from the many pairs of female and male animals in Paleolithic art that our ancestors were impressed with the existence of two sexes in many species. As Leroi-Gourhan put it, they "undoubtedly knew of the division of the animal and human world into confronted halves and conceived that the union of these two halves ruled the economy of living beings."[8] Except that, unlike us, these people may not have seen male and female as much in confrontation as in sacred union.

Indeed, I think it is highly possible that there were in our prehistory sacred erotic rites on important religious occasions such as the yearly return of spring in early May in which the union of female and male, or man and woman, was celebrated as an epiphany or sacred manifestation of the mysterious powers that give and sustain life. I base this conclusion on a number of factors. One is that sexuality and the rebirth of nature in the spring are prominently featured in Paleolithic religious imagery, and we know that religious symbols and myths are frequently expressed through religious rites. A second is that the erotic rite scholars call the sacred marriage is a theme in the later religious art of both the Neolithic and Bronze Age, and even survives in a variety of forms in much later mystical traditions. A third is that there are clues to such traditions in the many well-known European folk festivals where (in some places well into the nineteenth and even the twentieth centuries) young women and men would go together into the fields to make love on May Day to celebrate the annual return of spring.[9]

Since many Paleolithic and Neolithic sites where sacral sexual images have been found are in Europe, it is not implausible that these customs, although undoubtedly in already greatly altered forms, went back to very ancient times. Certainly they go back to a time before Christianity was introduced into Europe, before the Church took its anti-sexual pleasure stand. For we know that these persistent "pagan" customs were "abominations" to the "men of God" who believed salvation comes through bodily pain rather than bodily pleasure and who sometimes slept on beds of nails, wore hair shirts, and flagellated themselves in efforts to come closer to their flagellated and crucified God.

However, to our prehistoric ancestors, for whom sex was integral to the cosmic order—and for whom the body of woman was *not*, as the medieval Church proclaimed, a source of carnal evil but an attribute of the Great Goddess herself—erotic rites would have had a very different meaning. For them, erotic rites would have been rituals of alignment with the life-giving female and male powers of the cosmos often represented in Paleolithic art. So for them, partaking in the pleasures of sex would not have been sinful but, on the contrary, a way of coming closer to their Goddess.

I want to here emphasize that when I use the term *Goddess* I do not mean anything like a female version of that which we have been taught to think of as God. The prehistoric sacred female imagery we have been examining clearly does not fit into the still-prevailing view of deity as a King, Lord, or Ruler of the World who must be obeyed on pain of terrible punishments. Nor does it represent a disembodied entity residing in some remote celestial realm.

In contrast to how we have been taught to regard the divine, what we have been examining bespeaks a view of the world in which everything is spiritual (inhabited by spirits) and the whole world is imbued with the sacred—plants, animals, the sun, the moon, our own human bodies. It is in this sense that prehistoric religion has sometimes been described as animism or naturalism (where all of the world is imbued with the spiritual or sacred). But prehistoric religion was certainly also anthropomorphic, since human images, particularly female images, were important, often central, religious symbols.

I also want to say that since we have no writings from the Paleolithic and Neolithic there is no way of knowing if they actually used the term *Goddess*, although we do find this term in written records from later Bronze Age civilizations. It seems highly probable that the word *Mother* very early presented itself as an all-encompassing term to describe the creative female powers that so impressed our ancestors as permeating and animating the whole universe. But while the anthropomorphic prehistoric imagery often focuses on woman's maternal aspects, female representations are also sometimes in the form of a young woman and an old woman or crone (perhaps the ancient ancestress or primordial Creatrix).[10] Not only that, sometimes the female images also encompass the male's phallus, as in some Cycladic Goddess figurines. In a number of hermaphroditic or androgynous sculptures, we find still further symbolism of the sexual union of female and male, in this case in the same body.

And sometimes the female imagery is blended with animal imagery, as in the many so-called Bird and Snake Goddess figures of the Neolithic—further reinforcing the conclusion that the way our ancestors imaged what we think of as the divine and the way we have been taught'to do this are very different indeed.

In the same way, the meaning for our ancestors of the sacred sexual rites with which they seem to have celebrated the return of life each year at the beginning of spring and the way we have been taught to think of such matters is clearly not the same. By no stretch of the imagination can ancient images and rites of sexual union be compared to the "satanic" sexual rituals we hear about today. The essence of these "demonic sexual cults" is the torture, sometimes killing, of helpless women and children. By contrast, in Paleolithic art there are no scenes of sexual torture. Nor are there any scenes of the killing of women and children, in association with sex or otherwise. Similarly, to allude to these rites as just obscene prehistoric fertility cults, as some scholars have done, is to place a later, and very limited, interpretation on them. And so also is to equate them with modern sexual orgies. For rather than being forbidden, dissolute, and immoral, these rites would have been socially sanctioned. And instead of being private indulgences, they would have been for the public good—and even beyond that, for an important religious purpose, including what we today would call the attainment of higher consciousness through a sense of oneness with the divine.

The Mystery of Sex and the Celebration of Life and Pleasure

I have here suggested that it is highly probable that the people who inhabited Europe many thousands of years ago celebrated the cyclical return of life each year at the beginning of spring through religious rites in which the sexual union of the female and male principles was a form of sacrament. I have also suggested that these ritual celebrations of the rebirth of nature in the spring, as well as the sexual imagery we see in Paleolithic art, reflected a view of life and religion in which—in contrast to much of our own religious imagery—the celebration of pleasure, rather than the idealization of pain, is primary.

Specifically, what I am suggesting is that our ancestors celebrated sex not only in relation to birth and procreation, but as the mysterious—and in that sense, magical—source of *both* pleasure and life. In other words, I am proposing that prehistoric erotic myths and rites were not only expressions of our ancestors' joy and gratitude for the Goddess's gift of life, but also expressions of joy and gratitude for the Goddess's gifts of love and pleasure—particularly for that most intense of physical pleasures, the pleasure of sex.

To be sure, this has not been the conventional interpretation. Even now some of the scholars whose groundbreaking work is leading to a reinterpretation of prehistoric art tend to emphasize only the life-giving-and-generating symbolism of Paleolithic sexual images. For instance, in some passages in *The Roots of Civilization,* Marshack states that Paleolithic Goddess figures are "not 'sexual' in a modern usage of the term." He states that they are not primarily erotic or even associated with insemination and impregnation. He even assures us that the vulva was somehow "non-sexual," only a symbol of the periodic regeneration of life.[11]

Nonetheless, Marshack writes that the Paleolithic images of vulvas, as well as the Venus or Goddess sculptures, most probably figured in stories and rituals related to copulation. In other words, he acknowledges that what we are dealing with is sex. So in the end he, of course, concedes that these images have an erotic meaning, though not in the debased sense of the word as synonymous with either sinful or pornographic.

I certainly agree with Marshack that the way we have been taught to view sex—and women—is very different from our prehistoric ancestors' views. But what I am getting at is that there is no logical reason for disassociating sexuality—and sexual pleasure—from the process of life giving or regeneration. In fact, I find the suggestion that Paleolithic sexual images had nothing to do with sex astonishing. Certainly the images of female and male sexual organs we have been discussing are sexual. And to assume that these people made the separation that Christian dogma taught—and that men like the Abbé Breuil (who was a cleric) made when they looked at Paleolithic art—between sex for pleasure and sex for procreation is clearly the projection of later beliefs onto earlier times.

As I write this, it again seems to me amazing that there has been so little attention given in discussions of ancient sexual images to this matter of sexual pleasure. But perhaps it is not so amazing if we consider how truly antipleasure our religious cultural heritage has been, and how it has particularly reviled, and even tried to deny, the intense, sometimes ecstatic, pleasures of sex.

So what I am making a case for is the position that for our ancestors *both* life and pleasure were within the realm of the sacred. In short, I believe that—in sharp contrast to much of later religious imagery and dogma, which often sacralizes suffering and pain—our ancestors sacralized pleasure, particularly that most intense physical pleasure we are given to feel: the pleasure of sexual ecstasy.

I also believe that the Paleolithic association of sex with the bounty of nature—particularly with the communal sharing and benefiting from that bounty made possible by the rebirth of nature every year in spring—may have even more ancient roots. It may in some form go all the way back into protohistory, to some of the earliest human groups, who may already have linked the pleasure of sex with the sharing of food through ritualized behavior that (as we saw among the pygmy chimpanzees) also served to reduce tension and aggression, and to instead promote affiliative social bonds.

What I am also getting at here is something that in other connections archaeologists, art historians, and mythologists agree on: that in prehistoric societies there was not the distinction we have been taught to make between nature and spirituality, between the religious (or sacred) and our day-to-day lives (including our sex lives). And what I am further getting at is that if we look at Paleolithic art as an attempt, through mythical images and religious rites, to probe the great mysteries of human existence, we can see that it had more than one dimension.

We can then see that Paleolithic art, like most religious art today, was an attempt to deal with universal human questions: Where do we come from when we are born? Where do we go after we die? Why do we so yearn for beauty and love? What is the meaning of the pain we have to endure? And perhaps most important, and immediate, what is the source of the pleasure that is given us to feel and enjoy—and what can we do to increase our pleasure and decrease our pain?

But the way Paleolithic art answered these questions reflected a world view that is significantly different from that of the Judeo-Christian religion. Paleolithic peoples saw the original source of life on this earth not as a divine Father but as a divine Mother, as the life-force so dramatically manifested in woman's body. And they did not, as the Judeo-Christian Bible does, try to pretend that in the creation of human life woman was a mere afterthought.

Quite the contrary, the creative sexual power incarnated in the body of woman was for them one of the great miracles of nature. A dramatic illustration is the extraordinary carving archaeologists call the Venus of Laussel, carved about twenty-five thousand years ago at the entrance (or vaginal portal) of a French cave sanctuary. For what this millennia-old Goddess figure tells us is not only that woman's creative sexual power was revered; it also indicates that women's menstrual cycles (like the cycles of the moon, sun, and seasons) were seen as wondrous manifestations of the life-giving and nurturing powers of the universe. In other words, rather than being a "curse," here (as among more partnership-oriented contemporary tribal societies such as the BaMbuti)[12] menstrual blood seems to have been seen as a blessing—still one more miraculous gift of the Goddess.[13]

Like other Paleolithic Goddess figures emphasizing woman's sexual power, the Venus of Laussel is wide-hipped and large-bellied, possibly even pregnant. And like the later Mistress of Animals or Lady of the Beasts, as well as the Greek Goddess Artemis and the Roman Goddess Diana, she is associated with the moon. In her right hand she holds a crescent moon notched with thirteen markings: the number of lunar cycles in a year. Her other hand, as if to instruct us of the relationship between the cycles of the moon and women's menstrual cycles, points to her vagina.

Once again, we will probably never know the exact nature of the rites that took place in the ancient cave sanctuary at Laussel. But as Elinor Gadon and other scholars have noted, these prehistoric ceremonies undoubtedly had something to do with both women's menstrual cycles and the cycles of the moon. Like the Neolithic Mistress of Animals and the later Greek Artemis and Roman Diana, the Venus of Laussel was probably also the patroness of young women and of women in childbirth. And like them, she was undoubtedly the protagonist of important myths that were reenacted in this ancient sanctuary in ritual form.

Perhaps these stories were told at puberty rites for young girls or during rites for women who would soon give birth. Perhaps they were part of rituals that included the whole community. In any event, they were clearly associated with the rhythms of nature and the cyclical rebirth of life. And they recognized that both women's and men's sexuality plays an important part in the great cyclic drama of birth, sex, death, and, in terms of their mythical imagery, rebirth.

I say both women's and men's sexuality not just because, as already noted, we find so many representations of female and male animals in pairs in Paleolithic scenes relating to the birth of new life in the spring. I also say it because there are Paleolithic images in which male and female sexual organs are shown together. There is, for example, a stone engraving from Isturitz in the French Pyrenees, dating back to approximately 20,000 B.C.E.,[14] where we find the image of a phallus inside a vagina.[15] As with all cave art, which is in our terms sacral art, this would indicate not only a religious association with the act of coitus but also an understanding of the role of sexual intercourse in the birth (or in their terms, rebirth) of life.

There are also etchings and engravings in Paleolithic art of male hoofed and horned animals standing over pregnant females and of phalluses and vaginas in various combinations. Moreover, the conclusion that the people of the Paleolithic understood a great deal more than we might think about the biological processes involved in procreation is further supported by their extraordinary system of time-sequenced calculations (which archaeologists used to ignore or dismiss as incomprehensible markings).[16] Most significantly, these include a highly sophisticated lunar calendar with extensive notations on the many phases of the moon, which, as we saw in connection with the Venus of Laussel, also seem to have been related to women's menstrual cycles.

The Sacred Marriage and the Cycles of Birth, Death, and Regeneration

This recognition of sex, and particularly of woman's creative sexual power, as central to the cycles of birth, death, and regeneration is also a major theme in the next phase of cultural evolution, which in Western prehistory begins approximately ten thousand years ago. This is the Neolithic era, when our ancestors first began to systematically use what is perhaps the most important human-invented technology: agriculture. In fact, as the British archaeologist James Mellaart points out, there is a re-markable continuity of religious imagery from the Paleolithic to the Neo-lithic. Here too we find female figures representing the life-giving and sustaining powers of the universe. And here too we find the coupling of the female and male principles.

This coupling sometimes takes what at first glance seems to us pecu-liar forms, since the male principle is in the Neolithic, as in the Paleolithic, still frequently symbolized by a horned animal. For example, in Çatal Hüyük (the largest Neolithic or early agricultural site discovered to date) we see scene after scene of the Goddess in combination with bull horns (bucrania) or paintings of bulls. As Mellaart writes, these bucrania proba-bly represent the Great Goddess's son or consort as the representative of male sexual potency.[17] And as he also notes, what we find here is an artis-tic convention that foreshadows later images of a Bull God—who, as we will see at the end of this chapter, was still venerated in historic times.

One of the most fascinating works of art excavated at Çatal Hüyük is a carved relief of a woman and a man embracing and, next to them, the woman with a child in her arms. As Mellaart writes, "This may be one of the earliest representations of the *hieros gamos*, the 'sacred marriage'"[18]— a rite of sacred sexual union that, as already noted, survived as an impor-tant mythical theme well into historic times.

Even more interesting is that the second part of this Neolithic plaque may also be an ancient precursor of a major theme in later historic times:

the thousands of Virgin and Child figures in European Christian art. However, it would here have had a very different meaning. For in this eight-thousand-year-old plaque, the child is obviously the result of the sexual union between the woman and man next to the mother and child—and not of some ostensibly nonsexual divine insemination.

This frieze also represents something akin to what we might today call a lesson in sex education, demonstrating that our Neolithic ancestors understood the connection between sexual intercourse and birth.[19] Beyond that, it is still another piece in the chain of evidence indicating that in the Neolithic, like the Paleolithic, sex was an important religious motif.

An even more explicitly sexual Neolithic sculpture was discovered near Cascioarele in the East Balkans, within the area the archaeologist Marija Gimbutas describes as the civilization of Old Europe. Like the embracing lovers from Çatal Hüyük, the so-called Gumelnita lovers tell us of what seem to have been commonly held beliefs (and myths and rituals) in many of the lands around the Mediterranean. This sculpture, like the frieze from Çatal Hüyük, depicts a woman and a man in embrace. The female figure (probably representing the Goddess or a priestess) has a large stylized pubic triangle. The male is what archaeologists call ithyphallic (a code word scholars use to describe a male with an erect penis). And they are both masked, indicating that they are protagonists in a ritual drama or rite.

As Gimbutas writes:

Possibly the central idea of ritual drama, the "Sacred Marriage", the ritual coition of the male god and a female goddess, is reflected in the little sculpture from Cascioarele. . . . The presence of the masked ithyphallic god also implies a festival at which a wedding ceremony is enacted, the male god marrying the Great Goddess. From the Cascioarele figurine it is seen that she is not a pregnant goddess, but a youthful virgin. She is portrayed in the nude and has a large pubic triangle.[20]

Like the art of the gathering-hunting peoples of the Paleolithic, the art of the agricultural peoples of the Neolithic is full of images from nature: birds, boars, snakes, plants. Its beautiful pottery is often decorated with stylized representations of waves (water), serpentine bands (snakes), and, as in the Paleolithic, V's, chevrons, and cosmic eggs. There are also images of the bull, sometimes as in a late Cucuteni carving, in combination with other symbols of the life-giving powers of nature, such as the bee.[21] And, as in the Paleolithic, a central motif in the Neolithic art of both Çatal Hüyük and Old Europe is the life-generating sexual power of woman.

In fact, one of the most interesting finds from Çatal Hüyük is a figure of the Goddess seated on a throne, flanked by felines, in the act of giving birth. We also find in Çatal Hüyük rooms that appear to have been birthing shrines, sacred places where mortal women sought the Goddess's protection as they too brought forth life.

Other shrines in Çatal Hüyük deal with the opposite side of the natural cycle that so engrossed our ancestors: death. In these shrines, where rites expressing our ancestors' hope for (and faith in) rebirth probably took place, we find the Goddess in association with vultures—still in historic times linked with the return of life to the Goddess's womb after death. These images seem to have related to the ritual practice in Çatal Hüyük of "exposing the dead" to be eaten by vultures before their bones were buried under the sleeping platforms of their survivors—possibly in the hope that their spirits would be returned in one of their children.

In other words, as it still is for us, death was for our Neolithic ancestors an important religious theme, and like most peoples today, they too performed religious rites for the dead. But here again we encounter the problems of interpretation we have been examining. For the failure of most scholars to consider women significant has served to obscure the importance not only of women but also of sex in prehistoric burial customs and rites.

This is dramatically exposed in the British archaeologist Lucy Goodison's comprehensive study of Neolithic and early Bronze Age Aegean burial customs, *Death, Women, and the Sun*.[22] It has been extensively documented that in many Cycladic, Minoan, and other early Aegean burials the dead were interred in round tombs with a small opening facing east to the rising sun. But most of the archaeological literature offers no coherent explanation for the "puzzle" of why these tombs were round, or for the additional "puzzle" of why the opening into them was so "inconveniently" small. But as Goodison points out, if the tomb was viewed as a womb for future rebirth, it would make good sense that it was often round. And if the tomb's opening was intended not for the physical convenience of the living but for the spiritual or actual rebirth of the dead, it would further make good sense that it was small, since it was symbolically a vaginal opening.

As Goodison writes, this interpretation would also help explain evidence suggesting that prehistoric funerary rites and ceremonies were sometimes of a sexual nature. For along with evidence suggesting that dancing by priestesses (even more specifically, ecstatic dancing) was part of prehistoric funerary rites, evidence pointing to sexual rites for the dead would be congruent with the religious thinking of the period—which, as Goodison writes, was "concerned with the issue of human sexual intercourse," and with the then-prevailing belief that there is a connection not only between sex and birth but also between sex and rebirth.[23] Thus, the burials in round tombs would have symbolized the dead's return to the Great Mother's womb—from whence it was hoped they would, after funerary rites designed to facilitate this purpose, once again be reborn.

Goodison's analysis puts at issue still another aspect of earlier interpretations. This is that in many Western archaeological and mythical writings we find female deities almost invariably associated with the earth and moon, with only male deities associated with the more powerful sun. By contrast, based on an extensive analysis of early Bronze Age art (including hundreds of excavated seals from the Minoan civilization of Crete), Goodison demonstrates that the sun was in this earlier period also associated with the female. And of course (even though this too has been generally ignored), this association of female symbolism with the sun—and specifically of female deities with the sun—is evident even in later historic times. Examples are the sun goddess Arina of Anatolia, the sun goddess Amaterazu of Japan, and the Egyptian deities Nut and Hathor (the latter described as both the mother and the daughter of the Egyptian sun god Re). As Gimbutas points out, the female sun Goddess is also well known in Germanic, Baltic, and Celtic mythology, with the sun again associated with death and regeneration.[24]

So the additional puzzle that the small opening of many round Aegean tombs faced east to the rising sun is also solved if, as Goodison proposes, the vitalizing sun was in prehistoric belief systems associated with woman's life-giving powers. Moreover, the association of sex, woman, and the sun would further explain why, as Goodison documents, solar and feminine symbols are so often found in prehistoric Aegean tombs—for they would both be symbolic of regeneration or rebirth.

Given this view of sexuality as the vitalizing principle of the universe, it should not surprise us that there are so many pregnant figures in prehistoric art. Indeed, viewed from the perspective of a system of worship that focused more on the power to give life than to punish and kill, the virtual absence of the pregnant female body from the art of recorded history (except for an occasional discretely robed Virgin who supposedly got pregnant without sexual intercourse) seems strange—in fact, bizarre. It also makes one think anew of the remarkable absence of the act of birth-giving from historic art—in which, by contrast, the act of death-giving (which is virtually absent from Neolithic art) is such a major theme. And it certainly makes it possible to better understand why, as part of the strong contemporary partnership resurgence, women and men are beginning to resacralize the act of birth. For, as we will see, the creation of birthing ceremonies (necessary since most religions fail to provide any, instead, as in the Old Testament, labeling a woman who has given birth "unclean")[25] is part of the contemporary movement to reclaim a view of both our bodies and sex as not only natural but spiritual.

It is hard for us to imagine an art where scenes of men killing are virtually absent, where the act of giving birth is depicted as sacral in sculptures and paintings of the Goddess herself, and where, as suggested by the "sacred marriage" sculptures from Çatal Hüyük and Gumelnita, the act of coitus is a religious rite. It is also not easy for us to imagine menstrual blood as a divine gift, as we are not used to thinking of the human body, much less sex, as spiritual. And it is particularly hard for us to see woman's sexuality—her vagina, her pregnancy, her birth giving—as associated with a deity rather than as something shameful, unfit for polite discussion, much less religious art.

But once we even partially free ourselves from the prevailing views about women and sex, much of what we see in prehistoric art begins to make enormous sense. What we then see is that the central themes of both Paleolithic and Neolithic religious art are the mysteries of sex, birth, death, and regeneration. Only rather than being portrayed as separate and distinct—with sex and birth as carnal acts, and death and reincarnation divine acts of atonement for our sins—here these fundaments of life on this earth can be seen as all of one piece, *both* natural and spiritual. Furthermore, once we begin to recognize the sexual content of prehistoric art, we also begin to more clearly understand the significance (and ancient roots) of some of our earliest known Western writings: the famous hymns of Inanna, the Sumerian Goddess of Love and Procreation.

Ancient Hymns of Love, Goddesses, and Kings

The line between prehistory and history is the written word. It is, however, a blurred line. For often some of the most important information about ancient societies from which we already have written records comes to us from archaeological excavations.

For example, if we read the Old Testament—the most important written record from ancient Palestine—we get a very different impression about the religion of that time than we do from archaeological finds. Despite the Old Testament's exclusive focus on Yahweh as the one and only Hebrew God, archaeological records show that other male deities, such as El, Baal, and Tammuz, were also worshiped. And while the Old Testament rarely mentions the Goddess—and then only in diatribes against "backsliding" to the worship of the Queen of Heaven—the Palestinian goddess Ishtar or Astarte was probably still the most popular and widely worshiped deity of them all (as the religious historian Raphael Patai repeatedly brings out in his book *The Hebrew Goddess*).[26] Moreover, her sacred marriage with Tammuz or Baal (and in some places her sacred marriage with Yahweh himself) continued to be celebrated in sexual rites—as the Old Testament's diatribes against the "whoring" daughters of Zion obliquely confirm.

So written records by no means tell the whole story. But they are helpful, if we look at them in conjunction with both contemporaneous and earlier archaeological finds.

The oldest Western civilization from which we have extensive deciphered written records is Sumer, an area within the Mesopotamian Fertile Crescent (today's southern Iraq), where beginning approximately 3200 B.C.E. a number of powerful city-states emerged. Because the Sumerians inscribed their writing (known as cuneiform) on stone tablets, much has survived the ravages of time.

Most of the thousands of excavated Sumerian tablets deal with economic, legal, and administrative matters. But over the past fifty years, as Sumerologists have collated and combined many fragments of tablets scattered over several American and European museums, a literature consisting of more than thirty thousand lines of text has been reconstructed.[27]

Of this Sumerian literature, perhaps most revealing are the hymns about (and to) the Goddess Inanna, the Sumerian Queen of Heaven and Earth—particularly those poetic and often highly erotic passages dealing with her sacred marriage.[28] In 1983, the noted Sumerologist Samuel Noah Kramer and folklorist Diane Wolkstein reconstructed a cycle of narratives about Inanna, including seven of these hymns. The cycle begins with Inanna's bringing of the gifts of civilization to Sumer. Its climax is her sacred union with the pastoral king-god Dumuzi. And it ends with Inanna's (as well as Dumuzi's and his sister Geshtinanna's) descent into and return from the underworld (death and rebirth).

As Kramer writes, Inanna was Sumer's most beloved and revered deity, the Goddess of Love and Procreation.[29] Every year, during a prolonged New Year celebration, Inanna's sacred marriage to the reigning monarch of Sumer was enacted by a high priestess representing the Goddess.

The Inanna hymns were committed to writing about 2000 B.C.E. However, as Kramer notes, they go back to much earlier oral traditions. Viewed from the perspective of the archaeological materials we have been examining, key elements of these traditions undoubtedly go back to the Neolithic civilizations that flourished approximately 7500–3500 B.C.E., and perhaps even to the Paleolithic (approximately 20,000–12,000 B.C.E.).

So in the Inanna hymns we find a curious mix. There are here elements from an earlier mythology about the sexual union of female and male as partners in a life-sustaining and ecstatic rite. But there are also strands of a later mythology that deals primarily with male kings and gods, their "divine right" to rule, and their battles for conquest and domination.

In Sumer, like in most prehistoric societies, as Kramer explains, "originally, political power lay in the hands of the free citizens." But "as the pressures from the barbaric peoples to the east and west intensified, military leadership became an urgent need, and the king—or as he is known in Sumerian, the lugal, 'big man'—came to the fore."[30] Moreover, as Sumer shifted toward a dominator social order, this rule by "strong-man" kings became legitimized through religious myths in which their power was said to derive from none other than the Goddess herself—through the ancient institution of the sacred marriage.

Thus, like the biblical Song of Songs, the Inanna hymns contain important clues to an earlier time when, far from being a male "sex object," woman was seen as the conduit for what in Indian sacred writings is called the *kundalini*: the powerful divine energy from whence comes both life and bliss. But they also show how this ancient rite was beginning to be co-opted to fit the requirements of the male-dominated, highly hierarchic, and violent social order that, as we shall see, gradually replaced the more partnership-oriented Goddess-worshiping prehistoric cultures through the ascension of "strong-man" pastoral chieftains and later kings.

It is Inanna's marriage to such a king, the pastoralist king-god Dumuzi, that we read about in Sumerian tablets, from which we also learn that at first Inanna does not want to accept him as her husband. She wants to marry a farmer instead:

> The shepherd! I will not marry the shepherd!
> His clothes are coarse; his wool is rough.
> I will marry the farmer.
> The farmer grows flax for my clothes.
> The farmer grows barley for my table.[31]

That Inanna wants to marry a farmer rather than a shepherd is a telling piece of information. It not only speaks of the resistance, particularly by women, to the pastoralists and their harsh and alien way of life; it also tells us that the sacred marriage this hymn graphically describes predates the pastoral invasions. But the fact that, according to the hymns, Dumuzi has been selected as her bridegroom by Inanna's brother bespeaks of the historical realities of the time.

According to the hymns, even though at first Inanna resists marrying Dumuzi, after she meets him they fall in love. But rather than playing the familiar part of the shy and sexually innocent bride we have been taught to value as the "virtuous female," Inanna joyously, indeed boisterously, anticipates their union in language that could not be more overtly sexual.

"My vulva, the horn, the Boat of Heaven, is full of eagerness like the young moon," she announces, before she asks Dumuzi a blunt sexual question still laden with agricultural symbolism: "Who will plow my vulva? Who will plow my high field? Who will plow my wet ground?"[32] "Great Lady," Dumuzi answers, "the king will plow your vulva. I Dumuzi the King, will plow your vulva."

That this shepherd is the king, of course, reflects the new historical reality. But even so, like the Song of Songs, this hymn of Inanna is still in line with earlier Paleolithic and Neolithic traditions when the sacred marriage was associated with the rising of plants from the womb of the Goddess every spring.

When Inanna accepts Dumuzi, she tells him: "Then plow my vulva, man of my heart! Plow my vulva!" And as the hymn continues we learn that "at the king's lap stood the rising cedar. Plants grew high by their side. Grains grew high by their side. Gardens flourished luxuriantly."[33]

Once again in language that (as in the art of Paleolithic and Neolithic times) combines sexual imagery with images of the earth's fecund beauty, Inanna continues her hymn:

> He has sprouted; he has burgeoned;
> He is lettuce planted by the water.
> He is the one my womb loves best.
> My eager impetuous caresser of the navel,
> My caresser of the soft thighs,
> He is the one my womb loves best,
> He is lettuce planted by the water.[34]

Dumuzi answers her in words that again leave no doubt that this sexual rite goes back to agrarian cultures:

> Oh Lady, your breast is your field.
> Inanna, your breast is your field.
> Your broad field pours out plants.
> Your broad field pours out grain.
> Water flows from on high for your servant.[35]

The preparation for this rite by other members of the community—in other words, its symbolic and public significance—is also reflected in

Inanna's call for "the bed of kingship" and "the bed of queenship" to be prepared:

> Let the bed that rejoices the heart be prepared!
> Let the bed that sweetens the loins be prepared!
> Let the bed of kingship be prepared!
> Let the bed of queenship be prepared!
> Let the royal bed be prepared![36]

And even though in this passage we again see the co-option of the sacred marriage to institutionalize the reign of a pastoral king, the erotic language of this ancient epic of sacred sexual union is still sometimes extremely tender. It does not describe casual or impersonal, much less violent, sex. Rather, it deals with the joy of being "hand-to-hand" and "heart-to-heart"—in other words, with the pleasures of sexual love between woman and man.

> He put his hand in her hand.
> He put his hand to her heart.
> Sweet is the sleep of hand-to-hand.
> Sweeter still the sleep of heart-to-heart.[37]

Like her ancient Neolithic and Paleolithic predecessors, Inanna is still the Goddess of old: she who gives us the grains we eat and the water we drink, even the gift of life itself. Dumuzi too is still the Bull God—the principle of male potency. Inanna calls him "wild bull" and "high priest" as she observes that he "is ready for the holy loins."[38]

Moreover, like the art of the Paleolithic and Neolithic, the Inanna cycle deals not only with sex but also with death and rebirth. Specifically, it deals with the periodic death of nature during the barren time of year when plants wither and cease to grow. This aspect of the natural cycle is in the Inanna narratives symbolized by the descent of Inanna and Dumuzi (as well as his sister Geshtinanna) into the underworld, from there once again every year to return and thus be reborn.

So we see that in these Mesopotamian narratives, as in the images we saw earlier from the Paleolithic and Neolithic, the sacred sexual union between woman and man and between the divine female and male sexual energies were not isolated. They were part of a larger cosmic cycle to which erotic pleasure is integral—a cycle that begins with sex and birth and ends with death and regeneration.

In this cosmic cycle, sex still symbolizes the divine energy that makes the world go round: the erotic power of the Goddess, in the words of the hymn, as both the "Lady of Vegetation" and the "Queen of Heaven and

Earth, Queen of all the universe." And in it, the Goddess herself sacralizes love, life, and pleasure, joyfully, again in the words of the Inanna hymn, flowing from "the sweetness" of her holy loins.[39]

It is these "holy loins" that we find depicted in the Mesopotamian terra cotta plaque called "Lovers Embracing on Bed" I mentioned in Chapter 1, dating back approximately four thousand years. The carving shows a woman and man, probably Inanna and Dumuzi, in erotic embrace. His hand is on her hip, above her vulva. She encircles his waist with one arm. And with the other, she lifts her breast—as if, being the Goddess or her representative, she is offering him the bounty of nature, love, life, and pleasure that her body represents.[40]

Because of its erotic nature, many people today would classify such a carving as obscene. But as we can see from the art of the Paleolithic and Neolithic and from the hymn cycle of Inanna, it was a work of sacred art. To many of us, this seems strange, even sacrilegious. But it is sobering to reflect that our sacred images, focusing so much on pain, suffering, and death, might have seemed strange, even sacrilegious, to our Paleolithic and Neolithic ancestors.

It is even more sobering to reflect on what these people would have thought of our pornography. For to people who saw sex as a sacramental act of communion with nature and one another, our sexual images of men humiliating, degrading, mutilating, enslaving, and even killing women in the name of sexual pleasure would have been totally incomprehensible— and patently insane. And they would have wondered, as so many of us do today, how such perverse notions could have taken hold—a question we will pursue as we proceed on our journey of rediscovery to still more deeply probe the sexual-cultural history of Western civilization.

CHAPTER 4

Sex and Civilization: The Early Roots of Western Culture

What kinds of societies produced images of women's bodies, the act of giving birth, and sexual intercourse as sacred? What can we learn from these societies that lasted thousands of years to help us today, as we struggle to break free from a basically antipleasure and antiwoman world view? What led to views about both sex and spirituality so different from what we have been taught?

Until recently, the general assumption has been that human society never was, and by implication never can be, anything except male dominant and warlike—or that if there was anything different in our prehistory, it was so primitive as to be unworthy of much attention. It should therefore not surprise us that many archaeologists still have difficulty with data indicating that Neolithic societies were far more advanced than was previously thought. Or that they often dismiss as "mere interpretation" anything that contradicts *their* interpretation of prehistoric finds.

As the historian of science Thomas Kuhn points out in *The Structure of Scientific Revolutions*, changes in scientific "truths" are often changes in world view or paradigm. As scholars begin to see the world in different ways, they begin to interpret what they see differently. And as new observations are made that do not fit the older paradigm or world view, what frequently ensues is a fierce struggle over the nature of reality—with those in positions of power suppressing, at least for a time, new interpretations at variance with their own.

How fierce this struggle can be is shown by Galileo's narrow escape from being burned alive by Christian inquisitors who clung to views congruent with their religious paradigm. Those who today hold the power to define reality no longer have such lethal means at their disposal. Nonetheless, this kind of struggle still continues in our time. And perhaps nowhere is it as dramatic as in the contemporary conflict between those who still cling to the old views of prehistory and the growing number of archaeologists, linguists, geographers, evolutionary scholars, sociologists, systems scientists, and historians of religion, art, and myth who are today trying to reconstruct a very different picture of Western cultural evolution.

Modern Archaeology and Ancient Myths

The Chalice and the Blade explores this new picture of our past—and its implications for our present and future—in detail. Here I will only sketch it in broad strokes, focusing on three key findings and their implications for sex and spirituality.

The first is that new archaeological discoveries, coupled with reinterpretations of older excavations, support the view that there were in our prehistory more peaceful societies. In extensive excavations of early European Neolithic settlements that had regular trade and other contact with one another, there are few signs of destruction through warfare or of fortifications.[1] Moreover, there is in the rich art of the Neolithic a (to us) remarkable lack of scenes of men killing each other in "heroic" battles and of men raping women.

A second finding is that there were not in these societies the massive inequities we have been taught are characteristic of all ancient civilizations. The comparative size of houses, the nature of their contents, and the funerary gifts in graves point to a more egalitarian social structure. As Mellaart writes, although there were some differences in status and wealth (such as somewhat richer and more elaborate burial gifts accompanying some of the dead), these differences were not extreme.

A third basic aspect of these first cradles of Western civilization is that there is no evidence that women were subordinate to men. There are indications that women specialized in some of the most important crafts of their time: pottery, weaving, and the creation of ritual artifacts and art. Furthermore, from art, burial gifts, and temple models, there is evidence that women were priestesses holding important religious positions.

Indeed, as Gimbutas writes, some of the burials in Old Europe indicate that women played more important religious roles than men. But as she also points out, the fact that women played such important roles in the life of Old Europe does not mean that men rather than women were oppressed.

Nonetheless, until recently, when scholars acknowledged the existence of these kinds of societies at all, they called them matriarchies rather than patriarchies. This perpetuated the assumption that if there is a society where men do not dominate women, it must be a society where women dominate men.

This is why for my work I had to find new words to describe the basic configuration of these earlier societies. I chose the term *partnership* because it is a well-known word that connotes mutuality. I also introduced the word *gylany* to meet the need for a gender-specific alternative to *both* patriarchy and matriarchy.[2]

That I had to coin these new words says a lot about the difficulties of breaking free of the old dominator paradigm. It shows how even our languages (most of which were brought in by the nomadic invaders we will meet in the chapter that follows) have served to maintain the view that there is no alternative to a dominator model of social organization—that it is simply "the way things are."

The curious thing, which only became evident to me as I began to change my own world view, is that we have actually long had clues from some of our most familiar Western myths about a very different kind of social organization. For instance, in the Bible we read of a garden where woman and man lived in harmony with each other and nature—before a male deity decreed that woman should henceforth be subservient to man. In the very next story, the equally famous tale of Cain and Abel, we are informed that brother did not always kill brother.[3] This too is the message of the ancient Greek poet Hesiod's tale of a "golden race" who lived in "peaceful ease," until a "lesser race" brought in their god of war.[4]

In light of what we are now learning from archaeology, there seems little question that these kinds of stories are based on folk memories of a more peaceful partnership-oriented epoch. However, there also seems little question that such stories must have become ever more embellished and idealized as they were passed down from generation to generation. So if the biblical story speaks of a lost paradise and if the earlier people were described as a golden race, it is not because they were pure and unflawed (as gold was believed to be in ancient times). Rather it is because what came later was so much more base and brutal.

It is not realistic to think that there was in these earlier times no violence or oppression, no cruelty or insensitivity. Nor is it realistic to think that there were no hierarchies or rankings of any kind.[5] But the point— and it is a critical point—is that violence, cruelty, domination, and oppression did not have to be idealized or institutionalized in these societies in order to maintain rigid rankings of domination and exploitation.

Consequently, sexuality would not have to be repressed or equated with domination or submission. The natural pleasure bond between men and women would not have to be artificially severed. Nor would men have to be systematically conditioned to equate masculine identity with domination and conquest.

Prehistoric Art, Life, and Sex

As we have seen, the art of the more partnership-oriented societies of our prehistory did not celebrate the power to dominate and destroy (symbolized by the blade). In fact, its focus was on the power to give, nurture, and illuminate life (symbolized since early antiquity by the Holy Chalice or Grail). Even more specifically, it was an art that did not idealize sexual violence.

Like most Western art until modern times, prehistoric art deals primarily with mythical or religious figures and important rituals and rites. However, what figures were chosen, how they were depicted, and their relations to each other tell us a great deal about our ancestors' values and beliefs—including their attitudes toward the human body, women, men, and sex. These figures also provide information about people's day-to-day lives: from what hairstyles and clothing were then in fashion and what musical instruments they played to whether their deities carried weapons and were female and/or male.

Of course, we have to look at art together with other pieces of the prehistoric puzzle such as the remains of settlements, including buildings and their contents, as well as graves and their contents. But when viewed in the context of other archaeological finds, as well as of myths about an earlier more peaceful and egalitarian time, the lack of scenes of rape and killing in the art of these earlier societies is an important clue to their governing ethos.

Although there are certainly gaps in the archaeological record (we only have data from those sites that have been found and excavated), between the art and the excavations of buildings as well as graveyards and funerary gifts, we can at least get some idea of life during Neolithic and Early Bronze Age times.

For example, miniature shrines from Old Europe tell us of Neolithic attitudes about activities that are in contemporary preindustrial societies usually classified as women's work, such as spinning, weaving, making flour, and baking bread. As we see from the many female figures, hearths, ovens, and looms in these temple models, these were some of the activities of the women who served as priestesses in Neolithic societies. And the fact that ovens, pottery wheels, and looms were chosen for depiction tells us that these were highly valued activities—just as the many later depictions of weapons and warriors indicate a high valuing of the activities involved in warfare.

Neolithic art also tells us a great deal about what these people considered important—not only sex, birth, and death, but all natural cycles, from the rhythms of the sun and moon to the rhythm of the seasons. It certainly is an art that honors the creative powers of nature, be it through sexual or birthing imagery, through images of animal and plant forms, or through mythical anthropomorphic figures that were in all probability protagonists of familiar rites.

An interesting feature of these mythical figures is that they are rarely monstrous or demonic in the way that we see after the shift to a dominator model of society. There is a conspicuous lack of images depicting violent heroes obsessed with slaying monsters, so frequent in later times. There are also no indications of a belief system based on the notion that evil, darkness, the body, woman, and nature must be conquered and dominated.[6] Instead of showing men mastering dangerous untamed natural forces, the art of the period speaks more of myths about the interconnection of all life (as in some of the fantastic hybrid human and animal figures) and of rites of alignment with the cyclic rhythms of nature.

This is very important, since scholars have routinely written of prehistoric rites in terms of control. Thus, when faced with indications that our Neolithic and Early Bronze Age ancestors celebrated sex in religious rites, scholars have generally described such rites as attempts to control nature by primitive and superstitious peoples who had no understanding of scientific realities. But sexual rites focusing on the life-generating (in prehistoric iconography, often explicitly sexual) forces of the universe can just as reasonably be seen as attempts to invoke the beneficial powers or energies of these forces than as attempts to control them. Or in terms of the contemporary ideas of the biologist Rupert Sheldrake and the evolutionary theorist Ervin Laszlo about what they call morphogenetic or psi fields, they could be seen as attempts to link up with hidden, beneficial energies (in animistic language, with beneficial spirits), or to avoid negative and destructive energies (or spirits) through alignment with positive and creative ones.[7]

This is not to say that our prehistoric ancestors did not wish to influence the powers that govern the universe to protect and favor them—as many of us still hope to do today through prayers and religious ceremonies. But even though archaeologists tend to write of prehistoric sexual rites solely as attempts to control through magic the fertility of crops and/or the multiplication or fecundity of animals for hunters to kill, control and influence are not the same. As for such contemptuous labels as "primitive" and "superstitious," the fact is that sex *is* magical, not just in a superstitious sense, but in what we in our time might call a scientific sense. As these people observed, sex is necessary if life is to go on. So it was not so irrational of our prehistoric ancestors to view sex and birth as sacred manifestations of the mysterious life-and-pleasure-giving powers of the cosmos.

But again, here we face the problem of projecting later attitudes and belief systems onto earlier meanings. For one thing, I do not think we can assume these people defined the sacred the same way we have been taught. Moreover, even though sex played an important part in prehistoric myths and rites, I do not think that what we are here dealing with is a question of being serious about sex the way most of us have been taught to be serious about religion—as something connected with fear of divine punishment for our "sins," and not as something pleasurable. It is rather a wholly different way of looking at both sexuality and spirituality: one that does not negate the spiritual dimension of pleasure—particularly of ecstatic pleasure—as an experience of wholeness with ourselves, one another, and the universe.

I also again want to stress, as Gimbutas does, that the emphasis in this art on the female regenerative power is not to be confused with "a hierarchical structure with women ruling by force in the place of men."[8] While women seem to have played the leading role in religious rites and myths, there are no indications that men were oppressed. Rather, to again borrow Gimbutas's words, these seem to have been societies with "the sexes more or less, on equal footing"—societies Gimbutas sometimes describes by using my term *gylanic.*[9]

More often Gimbutas uses *matristic* and *matrifocal* (mother-centered) to describe both the religious and family organization of these more peaceful and egalitarian societies. And indeed, as I noted earlier, there is evidence that only a few centuries ago among the Basque (the last known non-Indo-European-language-speaking people in Europe, whose culture is believed to be indigenous to Europe and to go back more than ten thousand years), mothers still played major religious, economic, and political roles, and children bore the names of their mothers.[10] However, if, as Gimbutas believes, in prehistoric Goddess-worshiping societies the bonds between mothers and children were of primary importance and descent was traced through the mother rather than the father, this should not lead us to conclude that children would have been seen as the property of individual women (as children were later to be seen as the property of individual men).[11]

Thus Gimbutas writes of what she calls a "matristic clan with collectivistic principles,"[12] suggesting that here children would have been considered children of the entire clan or tribe. Hence their care and welfare would also have been a communal, rather than merely private, responsibility—an attitude gradually reemerging in our time, particularly in the more partnership-oriented Scandinavian so-called welfare states, where child care is also viewed as a social, rather than solely individual, concern.

Similarly, and again in sharp contrast to what we are accustomed to, women's capacity to give birth would not in these prehistoric societies have been seen as male property but as a sacred gift of the Goddess, herself the mother of all life. As already noted, this view of birth-giving as sacred is vividly reflected in Neolithic friezes and paintings of the Goddess giving birth. But I want to stress that prehistoric images of pregnancy cannot be equated with the contemporary fundamentalist obsession with the fetus or unborn child. The emphasis in this prehistoric art is *not* on woman as merely a baby container. Rather, it is on woman's sexual power—a power that to our prehistoric ancestors was both natural *and* spiritual.

Partnership and High Civilization

It may never be possible, after so many millennia of a very different conditioning, for us to fully understand how sex and spirituality could once have been blended, much less how an erotic spirituality could manifest itself in both religious rites and daily life. But it is possible for us to look at the data with an open mind.

For me, some of the most vivid pictures of how sex could have been at the same time pleasurable and playful as well as sacramental and spiritual have come from studying the remarkable civilization that was first unearthed at the turn of the twentieth century on the Mediterranean island of Crete. Following the lead of the British archaeologist Sir Arthur Evans, it is customary to call this civilization Minoan—even though King Minos (from whom *Minoan* derives) was apparently already from the Mycenaean culture that developed after 1450 B.C.E. when the Indo-European Achaeans took over and absorbed many features of the island's earlier civilization. But since Minoan is the name still used to identify this important Goddess-worshiping culture, to avoid confusion, until a new term gains currency I will use it too.[13]

Because Minoan society was so socially complex and technologically advanced, cultural historians call it a high civilization. But it was in key respects very different from the other high civilizations of that time.

For one thing, there seems to have been a generally peaceful coexistence between the various city-states on the island. As the British cultural historian R. F. Willetts notes, this "contrasts strongly with the internecine rivalries of later Greek states in any comparable area." He writes that "though arms and armor were early developed, and Cretan swords were the best in the Aegean, there is little evidence from Crete itself for their use in human combat (in contrast with, for example, the Mycenaean Shaft Graves)." And he observes that "the cooperative settlement at Early Minoan Myrtos, the long-continued practice of communal burial, and the apparently even development of the several palace regions combine with a general, though not total, absence of fortifications to indicate at least a high degree of mutual tolerance; and the scattered country houses and undefended towns of the later palace period speak clearly of internal peace and external confidence."[14]

Some scholars still try to deny, or ignore, evidence that Minoan society was not only more peaceful but also more egalitarian than other far more publicized ancient high civilizations. Nonetheless, there is a good deal of data indicating that life in Minoan towns was very different from that in most other civilizations of the time. There are here neither pyramids nor ziggurats towering over the much poorer dwellings of the "common people." Most tellingly, Minoan towns display what scholars describe as a remarkably high general standard of living, with none of the sharp differences between haves and have-nots we have learned to associate with "advanced" civilizations.[15]

This is not to say that Minoan society was without hierarchy. However, here an important distinction needs to be made. This is the distinction about which I have written elsewhere in my development of *cultural transformation theory*, between two different kinds of hierarchies. One kind is a hierarchy based on fear of pain through force or other means, which I have called a domination hierarchy. The other is the more flexible and far less authoritarian hierarchy I have called an actualization hierarchy, which goes along with greater complexity of functions and higher levels of performance.[16] It is this second kind, the actualization hierarchy, that probably best describes the administrative and religious structure at ancient Minoan sites such as the Palace of Knossos, which apparently also served as a center for resource redistribution.

I should here add that scholarly consensus is growing that the term *palace* to describe the beautiful, often labyrinthine, structures at Knossos, Zakros, Phaistos, and other excavated sites on Crete is a misnomer.[17] These rambling edifices, with gardens, courtyards, theaters, and a network of roads leading to them both from the towns and the sea, seem to have been combinations of religious, administrative, legal, craft, and trade centers. Here important religious ceremonies took place—for example, the Minoan bull dances where (as we can still see in the famous bull fresco from the Palace of Knossos) young women and men entrusted their lives to each other, working as partners to leap over the horns of what were probably tame (but still potentially lethal) bulls.[18] Here—as evidenced by the exquisite "Snake Goddess" figurines also found in the Palace of Knossos—priestesses communed with snakes in ecstatic trances. And it was also here that artists created the beautiful Minoan sculptured figurines; that craftspeople made pottery, seals, and other fine objects and utensils for both domestic and export use; that grains, oils, and other produce were stored in row after row of huge pithoi or jars; and that councils most probably met to make decisions on important matters such as public works (including the amazingly modern Minoan sanitation system, paved roads, and viaducts).

In this connection, there is also growing recognition by scholars (for example, Emmett L. Bennett, Helga Reusch, Henri Van Effenterre, Helen Waterhouse, R. F. Willetts) that the earlier notion of a king or priest-king ruling in Crete from Knossos is not supported by the evidence.[19] In fact, the only artwork that can reasonably be interpreted as depicting a ruler-divinity is the so-called procession fresco. One important aspect of this fresco is that the central figure (with arms raised in benediction) is *not* (as later "divine kings" characteristically are shown) on an elevated pedestal or of a larger size than the approaching figures bringing it offerings of fruit and wine. Even more important, and revealing, is that the central figure in this fresco is female rather than male.

Accordingly, a number of scholars (Reusch, Waterhouse, Willetts, as well as Jacquetta Hawkes and Ruby Rohrlich-Leavitt) have written about a queen or queen-priestess as the representative of the Goddess officiating in the famous "throne room" of the Palace of Knossos. Certainly, as Reusch points out, the griffins on each side of the "throne" are almost universally associated with the Goddess.[20] The lilies and spirals on the walls are also typical Goddess symbols[21] and the smallness of the "throne" (actually a gracefully carved stone chair that also is not elevated) lends further support to the conclusion that a woman, rather than a man, was its occupant. To this I would add that this may not have been a throne room at all but a room (and it is a relatively small room) in which a high priestess presided over important ceremonies and/or hearings about legal and other matters.

However, as Willetts further points out, it is also highly probable that "male hierarchies had co-existed with the palace priestesses, some in charge perhaps of trade and maritime affairs, others serving as priests."[22]

In short, the social structure of Minoan Crete seems to have conformed more to a partnership than dominator model. And an important aspect of this partnership seems to have been a free and equal sexual relationship between women and men.

Sex, Spirituality, and Social Structure

Like their Neolithic predecessors, the Bronze Age Minoans venerated the creative female principle. They seem to have worshiped a Goddess who presided over birth, sex, death, and regeneration. As the cultural historian Jacquetta Hawkes notes, "This dedication to a Goddess involved also a glorification of the meaning of sex." She writes: "Fertility and abundance were the purpose and the desire, sex was the instrument, and for this reason its symbols were everywhere."[23]

Thus, as Hawkes writes, the dove was an important Minoan symbol "because it was always supposed to be the most amorous of birds." The famous Minoan double axe (or labrys, from whence the term *labyrinth* is derived) also seems to have been a sexual symbol. As Hawkes writes: "Its shape, the double triangle, was widely used as a sign for woman, and the shaft thrust through the central perforation afforded an effective piece of sexual imagery."[24]

This butterfly-shaped double axe was in Crete an important symbol of the Goddess. But it is significant that it is often found placed between the equally important Minoan horns of consecration, the giant bull horns that, as in the Neolithic, were symbols of male potency.

Indeed, as Hawkes writes, there are in Minoan art and later legend indications that the sacred marriage between the Goddess and the Bull God was celebrated every spring as part of a festival that, as she puts it, "may have been the occasion for human rites of copulation."[25] Along similar lines, a Norwegian scholar, Kjell Aartun, recently announced that he has deciphered the hieroglyphic markings on the famous Disc from Phaistos. What Aartun reports is that he found on the Phaistos Disc "an erotic song, a poetically expressed ritual in 30 verses." According to Aartun, the lyrics of this ancient hymn parallel similar ancient literary works, such as the Song of Songs and the hymns of Inanna.[26]

But whether or not erotic rites were part of Minoan ritual, if we closely look at the Minoan portraits of both women and men, it seems clear that sex was a major part of women's and men's lives. Hawkes writes that "in the dress of the men, all emphasis was placed on the narrow waist (enhanced by a massive metal belt) and on the codpiece or penis sheath—a combination at least as provocative as the revelations and concealments of the women." On some occasions, and especially for sports, she continues, "the men wore the codpiece with a much shorter, apron-like garment which exposed the side of the thighs right up to the waist belt." They also "set off their bare torsos and limbs by intricate gold necklaces, armlets, bracelets and anklets."[27] But it is the bare-breasted images of women that tell us the most about Minoan attitudes toward sex.

As Hawkes notes, "The way in which Cretan men and women dressed themselves is particularly significant because it suggests a frank encouragement of sexuality such as would be appropriate to the high status of women in Minoan society, to their uninhibited liveliness in public and the freedom with which they mingled with men."[28] In dresses that look as if they could have been designed by French couturiers (indeed, Evans called one of the frescos of a woman "La Parisienne"), in elaborately and stylishly coiffured hairdos, and above all, in their self-confident, dignified, and at the same time sensuously alive bearing, the women in these pictures are (like the images of the lithe young men in their softly draped short tunics) testimonies to a free and joyful attitude toward sex and a free and high status for women. And since some of these women were priestesses, these images also tell us a great deal about Minoan attitudes toward spirituality.

Hawkes also notes that "although the general fashion was for a strong contrast in the dress of the two sexes, there appears to have been a tendency for ritual transvestism." Thus, when taking part in the sacred bull games, "the women donned the short loin cloth and codpiece." Similarly, "in funerary rites men and women might both wear identical skirts of sheepskin." And, as she further reports, "in celebrating a form of communion, in which both sexes took part, the men put on long, flounced robes."[29]

It is fascinating, but I do not think coincidental, how in many ways some of the Minoan fashions (as well as some of their art) foreshadow much that in bits and pieces has been emerging in modern Western culture. The sensuality of Minoan clothing, the long hair of the men, and the tendency on some occasions toward unisex garments[30] certainly foreshadow some of the fashions of the 1960s in the Western world—when women and men frontally challenged restrictive gender stereotypes of male dominance and female subservience.

Even more fascinating—and revealing in terms of the differences in both sexuality and spirituality characteristic of societies orienting more to partnership than domination—is that the social arrangements of the Minoans also in significant respects foreshadow other elements of the contemporary partnership movement. Minoan civilization flatly contradicts the long-established myth that high civilizations—that is, societies that are technologically and artistically advanced, centralized, affluent, and have developed writing—inevitably orient to the dominator model. As noted earlier, the Minoans' general standard of living was high and there is no evidence of an oppressive ruling class. Although they did use arms to defend their fleets, particularly from attacks by pirates on the open seas, trade rather than wars of conquest played the major economic role.[31] In contrast to its more dominator-oriented ancient counterparts, in Minoan society women maintained their important roles. And the emphasis on public works and government responsibility for people's welfare is also more in line with a partnership rather than dominator orientation. Moreover, here an art flourished that is so vivid and alive in its celebration of the beauties of nature that nothing remotely like it reappears in the West (again, I do not think coincidentally) until the second part of the nineteenth century.

I say that this is not coincidental because the nineteenth century was a time when many long-taken-for-granted assumptions were forcefully challenged in the West. As we will discuss in more detail later, that century saw the emergence of some of the most important progressive ideologies: the antislavery movement, the feminist movement, socialism, and pacifism. It also saw great social and legal reforms. And many of these reforms, such as the more humane treatment of the mentally ill, family planning, and social work as a profession geared to ending patterns of poverty and abuse, were due to the influence of women, who were increasingly breaking down barriers to their participation in public life. In short, while it also retained dominator elements, the greater freedom and joy we find in the Impressionist art of Renoir, Monet, Van Gogh, Cassatt, and Matisse, as well as its focus on the beauties of nature, were not unrelated to nineteenth-century social trends toward a partnership rather than dominator society.

In the same way, rather than being just an anomaly (a unique civilization that, as some scholars have intimated, defies explanation) Minoan society appears to have been the last in a long cultural tradition that, while not ideal or completely violence-free, was characterized by a more gylanic or partnership-oriented organization. So it is again not coincidental that in Minoan art we have a vivid picture of a highly sensual, erotic, pleasure-oriented way of living, inextricably intertwined with the sacred.

In fact, much that is happening in our time seems to have prehistoric partnership roots—a subject we will return to in Part II. But for now, we will stay a little longer in our past, as in the next chapter we probe how earlier sexual and social traditions were in our prehistory interrupted during a time of massive dislocation and chaos—a time when, in the contemporary language of nonlinear dynamics, a critical systems bifurcation took place.[32]

CHAPTER 5

From Eros to Chaos:
Sex and Violence

Eros is in Western mythology the divine embodiment of erotic love and, according to Hesiod, one of the oldest deities.[1] Homer does not write of Eros since, as the classicist Jane Ellen Harrison notes, with him "love is of Aphrodite."[2] Harrison also alludes to a bisexual or androgynous antecedent of Eros,[3] much like the blend of female and male sexual images we see in Paleolithic and Neolithic art. But by classical Greek times (approximately twenty-five hundred years ago), Eros had definitely become male.[4]

He was still, as *The New Columbia Encyclopedia* tells us, "the personification of love in all its manifestations, including physical passion at its strongest." He was still the son of Aphrodite, the Greek goddess of love, one of the most ancient deities in the Olympian pantheon. Only now he was also the son of Ares, the Greek god of war. Accordingly, sexual love was now seen by the Greeks as a winged young man armed with bow and arrow, "carelessly dispensing the frenzies and agonies of love."[5]

By Roman times, as Cupid or Amor, Eros had changed still further, into a naked, winged little boy. He was still the son and companion of Venus (the Roman goddess of love) and as a deity he still retained what we today would call a spiritual dimension, manifesting love and sex as attributes of the divine. But he was now not just capricious—he was at times downright malicious. And now he also had a brother, Anteros, who accompanied him as "the avenger of unrequited love or the opposer of love."[6]

How did all this come to pass? What happened to the Goddess as the divine source of life and pleasure? What became of all the images of female sexual creativity? When did we begin to think it natural that erotic love should come from a weapon? And how, from a sacred marriage between the Great Goddess and her male partner, did we move to an institution of marriage in which—among both the ancient Hebrews and Greeks, the two major influences in historical Western times—woman's sexuality became male property, under the control of male deities and of men?

These questions take us once again to one of the main themes of this book: that neither sex nor spirituality can be understood in isolation from their social and cultural context. To try to understand sacred images of women and sexuality in prehistoric art, we looked in the last chapter at what kinds of societies produced these images. To understand why by classical Greek times sex and love were embodied in an armed male deity, we will in this chapter briefly look at the evidence from both archaeology and myth showing that there was during prehistory a major shift in the mainstream of Western cultural evolution.

Since much of this evidence is examined in *The Chalice and the Blade*, I will here focus primarily on new information. I will also focus specifically on sexuality and spirituality, and how a series of cataclysmic events fundamentally altered both.

The Contradictory Proofs

I have sometimes wondered, as I read ancient Greek myths, whether the mythmakers of that time had a sense of tragicomic irony or whether, like some artists today, they were just "telling it like it is"—without stopping to reflect on what the story or image they had created really says. For example, the Greek story of Zeus's rape of Europa (an ancient name for both the Goddess and the continent) is, like modern cartoons exposing the men who still today equate power with violent domination, something of a political commentary.

Perhaps by classical Greek times, it was relatively safe to engage in political satire (as we see in some of the plays of Aristophanes, who in *Lysistrata* dared to make fun of the by-then habitual practice of warfare). But judging from the archaeological evidence, it would have been totally fruitless, and probably instantly fatal, to poke fun at the men who in our prehistory radically altered the course of Western civilization. For to them, violent domination—be it by man over woman, man over man, tribe over tribe, or nation over nation—was not a regrettable human failing but a highly institutionalized, glorified, and even deified way for men to live and die.

In trying to reconstruct how this dominator lifestyle became entrenched in both Western myths and realities, a number of theories have been proposed. While they differ in important respects, they are all attempts to explain (and often also justify) a shift from what until recently have been called prepatriarchal, matriarchal, or simply earlier "primitive" cultures to a way of structuring human society where—beginning with the ranking of the male half of humanity over the female half—the primary principle of social organization is ranking backed up by fear and/or force.

A once-popular explanation is that when men found out that they too played a role in the procreation of life—in other words, when they found out that sexual intercourse, pregnancy, and birth are connected, and that they too are parents—they violently subjugated women. Not only that, upon their discovery of paternity, men took over both temporal and spiritual power, which thereafter (to use the images from my earlier book) they no longer associated with the life-giving power of the chalice, but with the death-wielding power of the blade.

Behind this theory lie a number of assumptions. One is that men are inevitably aggressive, brutish, and out to conquer and enslave all who are physically weaker unless held back by force or fear—in this case, presumably men's fear of women's magical procreative power. Another is that rather than leading to a feeling of greater partnership and love between women and men, the discovery of paternity would inevitably lead to the sexual subjugation of women by men, presumably, as sociobiologists like to put it, to protect men's "parental investment."

For this theory to work, we have to accept the notion of an inevitably flawed and brutish humanity (or at least, male half of humanity). We also have to ignore the many instances in prehistoric art clearly linking female and male sexual imagery. Even beyond that, we have to ignore the massive evidence of Goddess-worshiping agricultural societies that—long before the shift to a male-dominant order—bred pigs, goats, sheep, and cattle to supplement their food supply, and thus obviously knew that males as well as females play an important role in procreation.

Today the "discovery of paternity" explanation of male dominance is almost universally discounted by scholars. However, some scholars continue to argue that male dominance, warfare, authoritarianism, and even slavery are the inevitable accompaniments of greater cultural and technological complexity—in other words, that this is the price we must pay for progress. This view, explaining the shift to the social configuration characteristic of a dominator—and even more specifically, an androcratic or male-dominated—society as simply a "higher stage" of social and cultural evolution, actually came from a rather unlikely source. It goes back to the so-called matriarchal school of social and cultural origins that in the nineteenth and early twentieth centuries provoked such heated scholarly debate.

If they are today cited at all, works such as J. J. Bachofen's *Myth, Religion, and Motherright* and Louis H. Morgan's *League of the Ho-De-No-Saw-Nee or Iroquois* are generally remembered for already in the nineteenth century pointing out that myths combined with archaeological finds indicated there was a time when women's sexuality was not under the control of men, when descent was traced through the mother, and a female, not a male, deity was credited with the creation of our world—a view that then, as now, outraged many in established scientific circles. But at the same time, many of these works also asserted that even if patriarchy was *not* always the natural and/or divinely ordained human norm, the development of higher civilization required the shift to a male-dominated form of society. And ironically, although not really surprisingly, it is this argument—and not the data on an earlier more mother-centered culture—that was eventually incorporated into what is taught to us as knowledge by an intellectual establishment that to this day vacillates between a number of contradictory "proofs" that a dominator social organization is somehow inevitable.

This, in essence, is the view propounded by the structuralist sociological theories still taught in many Western universities, which propose that progressively more complex and advanced social systems structurally require hierarchies of domination. It is also the generally accepted socialist view that was for generations taught as correct communist doctrine.

For example, the socialist writer Friedrich Engels, cofounder with Karl Marx of scientific socialism, writes in his *Origin of the Family, Private Property, and the State* (published shortly after Marx's death) that "the first class opposition that appears in history coincides with the development of the antagonism between man and woman in monogamous marriage, and the first class oppression coincides with that of the female sex by the male." But, at the same time, even Engels, who along with Marx courageously challenged many forms of oppression, still hails what he himself describes as a brutally unjust, one-sided, male-imposed "monogamous" marriage (actually only so for women) as "a great historical step forward." For in his "evolutionary stages" view of history, it is associated with the move from "barbarism" to "civilization."[7]

Even feminist scholars have been caught in the traps of such contradictory "explanations." One of the most notable examples is the French philosopher Simone de Beauvoir. In *The Second Sex*, a work that has rightly been recognized as a milestone in bringing to light the injustice of woman's position, de Beauvoir constantly vacillates from one camp to the other. In some passages, she asserts that woman has always been subservient to man. In other passages she states that the great ideological and social shift from what she terms matriarchy to patriarchy was indeed a historical fact—however, one necessary if civilization were to progress.[8] Beyond that, in conformity with the scholarly prejudices of that time (the 1940s), she is convinced of the superiority of patriliny and contemptuous of matriliny and of so-called feminine behaviors and values, going so far as to assert that "the devaluation of woman represents a necessary stage in the history of humanity."[9]

I have dwelt on some of the massive internal contradictions in Simone de Beauvoir's classic (and in other respects revolutionary) work to stress that it is not only men who have internalized such biases. Clearly, female as well as male scholars have learned to accept the notion that a dominator society (the configuration of male dominance, warfare, and strongman rule in both the family and the state) is somehow of a higher order—indeed, the "mark of civilization." Not surprisingly, this same notion has also colored the interpretation of the archaeological evidence that what actually seems to have brought about the prehistoric shift to a dominator social organization was *not* some inevitable progression, but rather wave after wave of pastoralist hordes from the arid fringes of our globe.

The Nomadic Onslaughts

Already in the 1940s, the European prehistorian V. Gordon Childe remarked on the archaeological evidence of a dramatic prehistoric shift. Childe reported signs of a change from a matrilineal to a patrilineal organization, the gradual disappearance of once-ubiquitous female figurines, and increasing evidence of warfare.[10] He connected this shift—which he termed "the Late Neolithic Crisis"[11]—with the collapse of village settlements and the adoption of increasingly more pastoral, or roving, animal-based modes of production.

Specifically, Childe connected this late Neolithic crisis with the appearance on the European archaeological scene of a new element: the people prehistorians and linguists call the Indo-Europeans. But Childe, like Hitler, idealized these proto- (or original) Indo-Europeans as the founders of European culture, asserting that they were "fitted with exceptional mental endowments" and were "promoters of true progress."[12]

Few Indo-Europeanists would today so openly idealize the Indo-Europeans or Aryans, as they are also called. This is not only because of the Nazis' all-too-effective use of this mythology to try to justify the extermination of Jews and other "inferior" races. The primary reason, as the

Indo-Europeanist J. P. Mallory notes, is that in fact there are few, if any, cultural achievements that can be credited to the proto-Indo-Europeans since, in his words, one finds them primarily "in the position of destroyers of earlier cultures."[13]

Mallory, Gimbutas, and other scholars also point out that the fact that Indo-European languages almost completely replaced earlier known pre-Indo-European languages in Europe and other regions of the ancient world shows that the fundamental shift in Western culture we have been examining did *not* occur as a natural progression in social evolution. For this new language type is clearly linked to the appearance of a new population group who either destroyed the earlier societies or gradually took them over, so that in the end only a handful of the earlier non-Indo-European languages—such as Etruscan (which was spoken in parts of Italy until Roman times) and Basque (which to this day is spoken in and around the Pyrenees Mountains between Spain and France)—survived.[14]

Summarizing the current consensus of most Indo-Europeanists, Mallory writes that "during the 4th millennium archaeologists perceive a structural reorganization of society across much of southeastern Europe." He observes that "evidence for this comes from the abandonment of the tell sites which had flourished for several millennia; the displacement of previous cultures in almost every direction except eastward; movement to marginal locations, such as islands and caves or easily fortified hilltop sites such as Cernavoda I; and a general reduction in the major Neolithic technologies of both fine ceramic manufacture and copper metallurgy." And he stresses that "this abandonment and movement, often propelling neighboring cultures into one another, operated against a background not only of somewhat elusive traces of hybridization with the steppe cultures such as the Usatovo and Cernavoda I, but also with continuous incursions of mobile pastoralists."[15]

By far the most detailed documentation of this process is provided by Gimbutas, drawing from her own extensive excavations and the work of many other Indo-European specialists and archaeologists. Gimbutas calls the proto-Indo-European intruders Kurgans because they brought with them the Kurgan burial mounds found in the arid area near the Caspian Sea called the Kirghiz Steppes in what is now the Soviet Union, which she believes to have been their homeland. She also charts three waves of Kurgan incursions into Europe: the first wave at approximately 4300–4200 B.C.E., the second at approximately 3400–3200 B.C.E., and the third (and most devastating) at around 3000–2800 B.C.E.

A central theme in the art of the Kurgans (as of later Indo-Europeans) was, as Gimbutas notes, the deification of the power to dominate and destroy, which is in the earliest period sometimes depicted in semi-anthropomorphic figures of gods whose arms are represented as halberds or axes with long shafts, and later by male gods who ride horses and brandish weapons. As she wrote in her last book, *The Civilization of the Goddess*, these armed male deities were well suited to a social organization "with prominent sovereign and warrior classes which had mastered the horse and weapons of war."[16]

In contrast to the Old European symbology of a female Creatrix, in Indo-European symbology male deities created life. In fact, they sometimes did this with their weapons, as, in Gimbutas's words, "the touch of the axe blade was thought to awaken the powers of nature and transmit the fecundity of the Thunder God." And rather than a Goddess taking life back into her womb, here, as Gimbutas writes, "the frightening black God of Death and the Underworld marked the warrior for death with the touch of his spear tip, glorifying him as a fallen hero."[17]

Not surprisingly, this idealization of weapons and glorification of heroic warriors went along with an obsessive preoccupation with death. Since the Indo-Europeans did not believe in the cyclic regeneration of life, provision had to be made, particularly for fallen heroes, in the dank and dark underground world of the dead.[18] Accordingly, as Gimbutas writes, "mortuary houses were built in which the dead took their belongings—tools, weapons, and ornaments which represented their rank—to the afterworld."[19] Also in accordance with this belief system, "chieftain graves" often contained among the funerary gifts bones of animals sacrificed to accompany, and serve, their masters.

Of particular importance were the bones of horses. Indeed, the importance of the horse to these people is stressed by all Indo-Europeanists—for example, in Mallory's book, which by a curious inadvertence has no index entry for women but has seven lines of page citations for horses.

These chieftains were also often buried with their households (wives, servants, and/or children).[20] In other words, in these burials, for the first time in European prehistory, we find graves of high-ranking males that also contain the skeletons of sacrificed women.[21]

The Kurgans also introduced the institution of slavery into Europe. Archaeological findings indicate that in some Kurgan camps the bulk of the female population was not Kurgan but rather of the Neolithic Old European population. What this suggests, as Gimbutas notes, is that the Kurgans massacred most of the local men and children but spared some of the girls and women, whom they took for themselves as concubines, wives, and/or slaves—a practice of warlike pastoralists also documented in biblical accounts of how, during the invasions of Canaan by his pastoralist worshipers, Yahweh ordered that all the inhabitants of conquered cities be slaughtered except for virgin girls.[22]

So there seems little doubt that rather than bringing civilization to Europe (as is still the message of European history classes that begin with the Indo-European Greeks), the appearance of the Indo-European Kurgans in prehistoric Europe marks the beginning of the end of a more partnership-oriented civilization. For what we now see in the archaeological record is the disappearance of millennia-long traditions of painted and incised pottery, temple models, and female figurines, as gradually cultures where women (and "feminine" values) had not been subordinated and despised were either destroyed, conquered, or themselves began to become societies where "heroic" warfare and the rule by force and fear of a small male elite (along with gods of war and thunder) became the norm.[23]

The Puzzle of Dominator Origins

But why should hordes of mounted warriors, sometimes followed by older men as well as women and children in wheeled carts, have ridden west in the first place? Where did these invaders come from? Most important, why did they develop in a dominator direction?

Gimbutas, who does not speculate on why the Kurgans developed as they did, believes that their homeland was north of the Black and Caspian seas, in what are today the Russian steppes. Most Indo-Europeanists also place the proto-Indo-European homeland somewhere in what Mallory calls the Pontic/Caspian region—a territory encompassing more than three hundred thousand square miles across the European and Asiatic steppe—although there are arguments about exact locations as well as other proposed points of origin, some farther east into Asia and others farther west instead.[24]

There is, however, consensus among most Indo-Europeanists that it was during the period from approximately 4500 to 2500 B.C.E. that these proto-Indo-Europeans left Eurasia in wave after wave of migration, to bring both their alien language and their alien ways of structuring social and sexual relations into Europe. And, as other scholars have noted, it is also during this same time that massive cultural upheavals took place in the Middle East.

For instance, Mellaart writes that by about 4500 B.C.E. we begin to see "clear signs of stress" in the archaeological landscape of the Middle East. Old artistic traditions begin to disappear, and in many areas there is evidence of invasions, natural catastrophes, and sometimes both.

The question this raises is what happened, beginning around 4500–4000 B.C.E. and continuing for several more millennia, to trigger such large movements of population. As Gimbutas notes, the domestication of the horse around 5000 B.C.E. gave the pastoralists who overran Old Europe their vehicle of transportation. And, as she also notes, this eventually led to a formidable instrument for armed conquest: the mounted warrior, whose sudden and rapid advance made possible what we today would call the panzer blitzkrieg of that time.[25]

But this still leaves unanswered the question of why so many of these nomadic pastoralists left their homeland. And it also leaves us with the unsolved puzzle of why they developed a social organization that was so warlike and male-dominant.

These questions may never be definitively answered. But another scholar, James DeMeo, who is not an archaeologist but a geographer, has offered some provocative, and in many ways plausible, answers.

DeMeo believes there were actually two homelands from whence came the first known dominator or androcratic societies, which he calls *patrist,* using the terminology first introduced by G. Rattray Taylor.[26] The first, in what is today the Arabian desert, DeMeo believes to be the original patrist or androcratic place of origin. The second is very close to where Gimbutas places the Kurgan homeland in Eurasia. But according to DeMeo, it covered a much larger territory, all the way from the eastern banks of the Caspian Sea into southeast Asia. He calls these areas the central Asian patrist core.[27]

DeMeo ascribes the mass population movements out of these areas— as well as the original emergence of a patrist or dominator social and sexual organization—to dramatic changes in climate. These changes, DeMeo believes, led to the pastoralist invasions that so radically altered the ancient world. In other words, according to DeMeo, these harsh environmental changes were the switch that set off a complex sequence of events—famine, social chaos, land abandonment, and mass migration— that eventually led to a fundamental shift in the prevailing social and sexual organization in the mainstream of human cultural evolution.

DeMeo based his conclusions on a large computerized data base correlating information on climate change over thousands of years with field studies of hundreds of different cultures around the world as well as with archaeological data. From this he constructed a global geographical review of human behavior and social institutions, which, as he writes, revealed a previously unobserved but clear-cut pattern. There was, he found, a correlation in preindustrial tribal societies between a harsh environment, the rigid social and sexual subordination of women, the equation of masculinity with toughness and warlikeness, and the repression and/or distortion of sexual pleasure[28] (all subjects we will return to).

Moreover, of direct relevance to the question at hand is that this kind of social organization itself seems to have originated in times of harsh climatic changes. DeMeo describes these as times when droughts reduced areas that were once green semiforested savannahs to arid steppes and/or deserts. And he asserts that it was from these areas, which now could support only nomadic grazing rather than farming (and during acute droughts, not even that), that wave after wave of nomadic pastoral migrations and invasions ensued.

Specifically, DeMeo reports evidence from archaeological and paleoclimatic studies indicating that the great desert belt he calls Saharasia (extending roughly from northern Africa through the Middle East into central Asia) did not dry out until around 4000 B.C.E. He also presents data indicating that some of the severest environmental changes in the areas adjoining these deserts took place between 3500 and 3000 B.C.E.—a time when incursions by nomadic pastoralists into the adjoining areas of Europe and the Middle East greatly intensified.

DeMeo believes (and we will get back to this) that there is a direct connection between patrist or dominator patterns of social and sexual organization and physical and/or psychological trauma. He proposes that rather than being merely random or accidental, the making of patrist or dominator social institutions was the outcome of traumatic experiences and practices that evolved during severe climatic and environmental changes.

Also, and this is very important, he proposes that once established, these patterns of social and sexual organization were exported into more fertile regions, where this type of social and sexual organization was now perpetuated through the institutionalization of trauma (for example, through traumatic child-rearing practices that effectively inhibit respiration, emotional expression, and pleasure-directed impulses). He argues that these repressive social institutions, which, as he writes, result in "a chronic characterological and muscular armor," to varying degrees still today block not only full physiological and emotional expression but sexual pleasure and full sexual satisfaction.[29] And he repeatedly brings out how the institutionalized distortion of human sexuality—particularly severe and cruel controls over female sexuality—have been primary mechanisms for the maintenance of dominator (or, in his term, patrist) societies.

Pastoralism and Psychological Armoring

I have focused on DeMeo's theories because I believe there is much in them that rings true about the social and psychosexual roots of the dominator model. I do not agree, as DeMeo writes, that there were no dominator or patrist societies before 5000 B.C.E., as I think it is more likely that in some of the more arid areas of our globe this type of social organization developed much earlier—probably as far back as our hominid days. And I also have some qualifications to make about his generalized formulation of sexual repression as the key to what, drawing from the work of the psychoanalyst Wilhelm Reich,[30] DeMeo calls psychological armoring, since I do not think he places enough emphasis on how central the subordination of women is to the distortion of both female and male sexuality.[31] But there seems little question that the repression, or more properly, distortion, of sexuality—specifically, the equation of masculinity with both sexual and social domination and of femininity with sexual and social submission—is critical to the maintenance of a dominator social organization, and particularly to the male socialization for domination and violence (subjects we will return to).

There also seems little question that pastoralist nomads such as the Kurgans originally came from places in which farming was never (or no longer) possible—hence their pastoralist way of life. And there seems little question that, as Reich proposed, "psychological armoring" (the deadening of positive emotions and eventually even the addiction to pain) is the consequence of severe traumas; that traumas can be caused by droughts and other extreme environmental hardships; and that over time physical and psychological trauma can become institutionalized through a variety of customs (all subjects we will also return to). In fact, there are other studies supportive of DeMeo's conclusion that extreme environmental stress can lead to a dominator social organization. For example, the anthropologist Peggy Reeves Sanday's survey of more than a hundred tribal societies indicates that at least in some cultures, in her words, "men react to stress caused by food shortage or by the circumstances of migration by banding together, excluding women from male-oriented power ceremonies, and by turning aggression against women."[32]

I also agree with DeMeo that it is not coincidental that the association of pain with sexuality is characteristic of dominator societies. For there is ample data indicating that practices such as the genital mutilation of males (of which circumcision as we know it today is a far less severe remnant) and the genital mutilation of females (which is still practiced in many of the more extreme patrist or dominator societies in the Middle East and Africa today) have historically been characteristic of those cultures where male dominance, warfare, and authoritarianism (the core dominator configuration) are most extreme.[33]

But I believe that we also need to look at technological and economic factors. I think that it is highly significant that the people who originally spread a dominator or androcratic type of social organization into the more hospitable regions of our globe (where agricultural societies orienting to partnership had originally developed) were nomadic pastoralists. In other words, I think that nomadic pastoralism as a technology is more likely to lead to a dominator organization than is agriculture.

To begin with, nomadic pastoralism as the primary technology for survival develops in areas that either never were fertile or, due to climate and other environmental changes, at some point become unsuitable for agriculture. But nomadic pastoralism (or breeding herds of animals as the primary and sometimes only source of food) is not only the result of inhospitable environments; it is itself a causal factor in making environments inhospitable.

The reason is that nomadic pastoralism (more even than today's cattle ranching) is ecologically unsound. It is a way of using up natural resources through animal grazing without returning even seeds to an increasingly depleted earth. Thus, as the desertification of pastoral lands in prehistory and history demonstrates, nomadic pastoralism is a technology that even in the absence of externally caused climate changes will after a certain time lead to a progressive loss of vegetation—and therefore to a more arid and inhospitable environment.[34]

This environmental depletion would have the most severe consequences in areas that were already so marginal that instead of cattle only camels, goats, and/or sheep can survive—as is still the case today in large parts of the Saharasian steppes. This is because—as we know all too well in our time, when the dominator system threatens to destroy our rain forests—loss of vegetation leads to lower rainfall, and thus to droughts.

So I would add to DeMeo's environmental theories a strong technological and economic factor. Certainly some kinds of agriculture can—and do—also severely deplete the soil, and thus result in reduced vegetation and less rain. But nomadic pastoralism as a technology in itself tends to lead to aridity. And it is this progressive destruction (or domination) of nature without provision for regeneration that must have in our prehistory also greatly intensified another problem that tends to go with nomadic pastoralism: the competition for water and land between neighboring groups of herdsmen.

In short, what nomadic pastoralism tends to produce is a vicious cycle of environmental depletion and increasing economic competition for ever more scarce grazing grounds—and with this, a tendency for violent contests over territorial boundaries. And it is precisely these dynamics—and the increasing warlikeness of prehistoric pastoral peoples—that would in periods of the most severe climate change have led to periodic incursions by pastoralist warriors (from the Kurgans to Ghengis Khan) into more fertile areas to take over by force the lands and property of more fortunate neighbors.

Finally, in trying to piece together the puzzle of dominator origins, there is still another factor relating to pastoralism as a technology that I think is worth looking at. This is that pastoralism relies on what is basically the enslavement of living beings, beings that will be exploited for the products they produce (for example, milk and, when processed, cheese) and that will eventually be killed. In other words, while in agrarian societies the breeding and eventual slaughtering of animals is supplemental to the growing of vegetable and fruit crops, the primary focus for subsistence in most pastoralist economies is on domesticating animals from babyhood to adulthood in order to eventually kill them for food.

This would also help explain the psychological armoring (or deadening of "soft" emotions) that DeMeo believes characterized the origins of patrist or dominator societies. For it is difficult to permit oneself to feel empathy (much less real love) for little creatures that, no matter how endearing, must be killed. It is instructive in this connection that the training of the Nazi SS officers who manned the mass extermination death camps is said to have included the raising of puppies, which they were ordered to feed, play with, and care for in every way—and then kill with no signs of emotion.[35]

Moreover, once one is habituated to living off enslaved animals (for meat, cheese, milk, hides, and so forth) as practically the sole source of survival, one can also more easily become habituated to view the enslavement of other human beings as acceptable. Because once empathy and love are in any context habitually suppressed, this tends to result in what psychologists call blunted affect—a reduced and highly compartmentalized capacity to respond to feelings (affect) other than anger, contempt, and similar "hard" emotions.

What I am getting at is *not* that pastoralism inevitably leads to slavery. Clearly, agricultural people have also had slaves—be they "primitive" tribes in Africa or "civilized" states like ancient Athens and the eighteenth- and nineteenth-century American South. But what we are here probing are the origins of that institution—and of the view of half of humanity as chattel or pieces of property to be controlled and dominated by men. And the almost exclusive reliance on the breeding, enslavement, and finally slaughtering of animals as the primary source of subsistence could also serve to lay some of the psychological foundations for viewing females (first animals, but later women) as merely breeders or sexual technologies for reproduction—as male property whose sexuality has no other function than to be controlled by, and be of service to, their male "owners."

The "Danger" of Sexual Love

Viewed from this larger perspective, it is revealing that women are to this day often said to belong exclusively to the "domestic" sphere. It is also revealing that to this day among some nomadic pastoralists in the Saharasian area only men may slaughter animals (even chickens), with women explicitly forbidden to do so.[36] And it is even more revealing that among these tribespeople sexual love between women and men is explicitly (and I would add, accurately) considered a danger to the preservation of tribal hierarchies of male power.

In her book *Veiled Sentiments,* a fascinating report of her life for nearly two years observing a Bedouin tribe in the western desert of Egypt, the anthropologist Lila Abu-Lughod notes that sexual love between women and men in this rigidly male-dominated pastoralist tribal society is systematically discouraged. She reports how "love matches are actively discouraged, and thwarted when discovered" and how every attempt is made to "minimize the significance of the marital relationship and to mask its nature as a sexual bond between man and woman."[37] She also reports how men are looked down upon (by men and women) for "succumbing to sexual desire, or merely romantic love," because this is equated with dependency, which for men is "inimical to the highest honor-linked value, independence."[38] She further reports how women are effectively conditioned to do something they call *tahashsham* (being modest)—which includes denying any sexual interest in men, and avoiding men who are not kin—and how, even beyond this, women are expected not only to suppress but to effectively deny their own sexuality.[39]

"Good women," writes Abu-Lughod, "deny interest in sexual matters and deny their own sexuality."[40] Indeed, "the woman who does not is called a 'slut' (*qhaba*) or a 'whore' (*sharmuta*)."[41] Moreover, "even married women must deny any interest in their husbands, much less other men."

In fact, so thoroughly are women socialized to view their own sexuality as wrong and dangerous that, as Abu-Lughod reports, "an angry woman will insult another by referring to the size of her genitals (the presumption being that the larger the genitals the more voracious the desire)."[42]

Just as sexual shame and modesty are considered essential for women, "men's honor also rests on their mastery of 'natural' passions and functions, including sexuality."[43] As Abu-Lughod stresses, the significance of sexual expression is very different for women and for men. For men, any witnessed affection for or attachment to a woman (even in front of a man's family) is "interpreted as dependency, which compromises a man's right to control and receive the respect of his dependents." But a woman's free expression of sexuality is seen as a threat to the whole hierarchic male system, as it is, in Abu-Lughod's words, viewed as an "act of insubordination and insolence."[44] For, as is characteristic of rigid dominator societies, a woman's obedience to male control is required as confirmation of absolute male authority—the essential foundation for a social system based on rigid rankings.[45]

As Abu-Lughod writes: "In the eyes of others, a dependent's rebellion dishonors the superior by throwing into question his moral worth, the very basis of his authority. Thus a woman's refusal to *tahashsham* (deny her sexuality) destabilizes the position of the man responsible for her. To reclaim it, he must reassert his moral superiority by declaring her actions immoral and must show his capacity to control her, best expressed in the ultimate form of violence."[46]

In other words, under the man-made rules of this rigidly male-dominant society, terms like *honor* and *dishonor, moral superiority* and *inferiority,* and *responsibility* and *dependence* are used to mask the brutal reality of absolute life-and-death male control over women, and with this, over women's sexuality and reproductive powers. So the still-ongoing "honor killings" of women by some men in parts of the Arab world today are in fact the discharge of a man's "responsibility" to use exemplary violence to maintain male control over women, and particularly women's sexuality—and to express a view of masculinity that equates honor with domination over "inferiors" such as women.

As Abu-Lughod notes, this same basic social function is also served by the still-ongoing fundamentalist Muslim custom requiring the veiling of women. For veiling is not only a way of making women invisible as inferior dependents; the black veil, as she writes, also symbolizes women's sexual shame and natural moral inferiority.[47] Indeed, as she points out, the veil is black precisely because it symbolizes women's shame—as in Bedouin society someone who has been shamed is said to have had his or her face blackened.[48] So the veil is still another symbol of the shameful-ness of being a woman, and particularly of the shamefulness of women's sexuality—and one could argue an example of the interlocking of sexist and racist attitudes.

Yet despite all these massive social inhibitions, women—and some-times also men—in the Bedouin society Abu-Lughod studied still some-times managed to find expression for their yearning for sexual love in both their lives and their poetry. Indeed, many of their *ghinnawa* or poems deal with sentiments of love. But not surprisingly, they usually dwell on the painful aspects of the experience. In fact, many poems, particularly the women's songs, revolve around the theme of what Abu-Lughod calls the wounds of love. [49]

Sexual Violence, the Institutionalization of Trauma, and Our Legacy of Pain

The phrase "wounds of love" takes us back full circle to the andro-cratic metaphor of erotic love as a male deity armed with a bow and arrow. For be it in Saharasia or ancient Greece and Rome—or in our own time—a dominator world view requires that in matters of sexual love the male "call the shots" in a chronic "war of the sexes" in which men are the declared winners.

So the at first glance peculiar image of erotic love as an armed young man bequeathed to us by a rigidly male-dominated ancient Greek society is quite appropriate for such a social organization. And since in this type of social organization men are not supposed to feel pain but rather to in-flict it—as reflected in the Bedouin women's love songs (or for that matter in a whole genre of popular women's songs today)—romantic relations are in fact, not just in poetry, in these societies particularly painful for women.

Of course, these relations are also painful for men because neither women nor men can find fulfillment in a social system that at every turn hinders loving sexual bonding between them. Nonetheless, as the work of Abu-Lughod dramatically shows, this is precisely what is required if the equation of masculinity with domination and control is to be main-tained.

Once again, I want to stress that such habits of thinking and acting are hardly unique to the people of Saharasia. But keeping in mind what we are now learning about the Saharasian desert as one of the likely home-lands of the prehistoric people who—like the Kurgans farther to the north—brought a dominator or androcratic way of life to the more fertile areas they overran, it does not seem accidental that—despite the courageous efforts of progressive Arab women and men—chronic warfare, despotic regimes, and the "honor killings" of women perceived as being sexually free are still so persistent in parts of this desert region. For what all this points to is the legacy of a very rigid dominator social organization in these arid areas of our globe.

We may never be able to completely put together the puzzle of dominator origins. But at least we are beginning to gather some of the pieces of that puzzle—and with this, coming a little closer to understanding the circumstances that originally led to a male socialization that actually prescribes emotional armoring (that is, the suppression by men of feelings other than anger, contempt, and similar "hard" or "masculine" emotions) and a social structure in which women, along with "soft" or "feminine" emotions (such as compassion and caring) are excluded from social governance. For the indications we now have are that the complex of conditions that in our prehistory—and in some places perhaps as early as protohistory—led to a dominator form of social and sexual organization were a combination of technological, social, and psychological factors in which environmental conditions played a major part.

I say perhaps as early as protohistory because, as we explored in Chapter 2, social organizations orienting primarily to a partnership or dominator model are already prefigured in what we are today learning about some of our contemporary primate cousins. And I say complex of conditions because what we are dealing with here is not a simple question of biological, psychological, technological—or even environmental—determinism. Rather it is the interaction of all these factors in a dynamic process of cultural evolution in which (as in biological evolution) both considerations of adaptation or survival and an element of randomness or chance, as well as some degree of choice, are operant.

Thus, we may never know just how some of the Kurgans' cruel customs (such as the killing of wives, concubines, and children to accompany a "strong-man" in death) originated. But by the time they arrived in Old Europe, violence and domination had for them apparently become normal, as it gradually also became in Europe and other parts of the ancient world in the wake of wave after wave of pastoralist incursions.

To briefly sum up the general pattern of what seems to have happened, the prehistoric societies that developed in the more fertile areas of our globe (where nature could be seen as a life-giving and sustaining mother and agriculture could gradually replace gathering-hunting) probably originally oriented primarily to the partnership model. In these areas, the veneration of the feminine creative principle eventually flourished, and myths and rites of alignment with the life-generating creative powers of nature such as the *hieros gamos,* or sacred sexual union, first developed. Of course, the destructive side of nature—such as periodic storms, earthquakes, droughts, and floods, as well as sickness, accidents, and death—would also have preoccupied the people in these regions. But here these destructive forces could be explained more as part of a mysteriously cyclical (and thus interconnected) whole than as adversarial forces in an essentially hostile universe.

By contrast, in the less hospitable, more marginal areas of our globe, the powers that govern the universe would have been seen as far more harsh. Indeed, because of the hardship and suffering one had to chronically endure, they would often have been seen as punitive. Thus, rituals would have tended to be less rites to attempt alignment with the beneficial forces of nature than attempts to somehow placate and otherwise control the unreliable, seemingly angry, destructive forces of nature. And here, especially during times of acute scarcity, hierarchies based on fear and force would have been far more likely to evolve.

As DeMeo points out, in these inhospitable environments—particularly during periods of severe drought, and with this, also severe malnutrition-induced traumas—dog-eat-dog competition and rule by brute force would have been far more likely to develop. And once developed, at least in some groups, these behavior patterns apparently became institutionalized into cultural patterns. For example, there developed religious teachings sanctioning violence against women and children, as well as child-rearing traditions such as the swaddling of babies in rigid halters (which probably began to prevent babies from falling off horses or camels during forced nomadic migrations but still continued to be practiced thousands of years later by settled peoples, surviving in parts of Europe as late as the Middle Ages and even afterward).[50]

In sum, what apparently came to pass over thousands of chaotic years beginning during our prehistory was what DeMeo aptly calls the institutionalization of trauma, not only through systematic cruelty to children and women but also through warfare and despotic strong-man rule. Once again, this is not to say that this had to happen. But it is what we see in the archaeological record left us by pastoralist hordes like the Kurgans. And it is also what we still, to varying degrees, see in societies that are today characterized by chronic warfare, rigid male dominance, and strong-man rule in both the family and the state or tribe.

For to our day, as DeMeo writes, tribal cultures "with behavior patterns and social institutions which tend to subordinate the female, inflict pain and trauma upon infants and young children, punish young people for sexual expression ... and otherwise greatly restrict the freedoms of young people and older females to the iron will of males" also have "high levels of adult violence" as well as "institutions designed for expression of destructive aggression," such as "divine kingship, ritual widow murder (suttee), human sacrifice and sadistic torturing."[51] Beyond this, in these chronically warlike cultures, a sexuality that tends to confuse pain with pleasure is often considered normal—even idealized.[52]

It is this institutionalization of trauma or pain and suffering—and of violence and domination in relations between parents and children, masters and slaves, rulers and subjects, nations and nations, and men and women—that has to varying degrees been our cultural legacy. Institutionally, it is reflected in what are today increasingly recognized as dysfunctional families based on control, in deeply entrenched patterns of violence against women and children, and in chronic warfare. Politically, it is reflected in despotic tribal and state controls, which, as we will see in Part II, characteristically vary in proportion to the degree of male dominance and the rigidity of gender stereotypes. Culturally, it is reflected in surviving myths idealizing male violence and domination and equating true masculinity with the suppression of not only "inferior" peoples but "inferior" feelings—that is, stereotypically feminine feelings such as caring, compassion, and empathy. And sexually, as we will also probe in depth in Part II, it is reflected in the still all-too-prevalent equation of sexual "pleasure" with acts of domination and cruelty.

The heartening and hopeful thing, as we will also see in Part II, is that today millions of women and men all over the world are trying to break free from this painful legacy. But in the next chapter we will still continue our exploration of Western psychosexual history, as we take a fresh look at both sexuality and spirituality in the societies still generally presented to us as the earliest Western civilizations: Sumer, Babylon, Palestine, Greece, and Rome.

CHAPTER 6

The Reign of the Phallus: War, Economics, Morality, and Sex

Homer's *Iliad*, we are taught, is the first great epic in European literature, the treasured repository of much that is noble and valuable in our Western heritage. The action takes place several thousand years after the first Indo-European invasions of Europe, during the Achaean invasion of the city of Troy in Asia Minor. But the *Iliad* too is about the exploits, and spoils, of war. And here, as among the Kurgans, these spoils include women and female children.

In fact, the *Iliad* opens with a famous quarrel between the Greek hero Achilles and King Agamemnon over one of these spoils: a young girl called Briseis, whom Achilles angrily claims as his booty of war.

"And now," he shouts at Agamemnon, "you threaten to take my girl, a prize I sweated for, and soldiers gave me!" But even after the elder Nestor pleads with Agamemnon, "Do not deprive him of the girl, renounce her, the army had allotted her to him," Achilles has to give in to Agamemnon the king in conformity to dominator rankings.[1]

As Homer tells this famous story of heroic male warfare, the only important, indeed the only, issue is whether a king or a hero should rightfully own this "prize of war." Nowhere in the *Iliad* (or for that matter, in most courses on Greek literature) is any question raised about the rightfulness of a young girl being no more than a piece of property, of female sexual slavery.

Even the various female deities who figure in the *Iliad*, such as Hera and Athena, do not concern themselves with such matters. For, like the

mighty Zeus himself, they too are in the *Iliad* wholly absorbed with dis-
putes between men.

Zeus, the most feared of the Olympian deities, is of course himself a
famous rapist and abductor of women. His wife, the goddess Hera (in
some legends still known as the mother of the gods, to whom she gave
the ambrosia of eternal life), has been reduced to the lower rank of wife.
She still has some say but, as we read in the *Iliad,* she is afraid to disobey
her husband, lest he beat her.[2]

As for Athena, while she is still associated with attributes and symbols
of the Goddess of old (such as wisdom and the serpent as a symbol of
oracular prophecy), her main preoccupation too is now the outcome of
the war. For like Ishtar in the Fertile Crescent and the sun goddess Arina
in Anatolia, she herself has now become a patroness of war—a feature
that, as the religious historian E. O. James writes, was entirely absent in
earlier times.[3]

Indeed, so unconcerned is Athena about the fate of women, that it is
she who in one of the most famous Greek plays, the *Oresteia,* casts the deciding vote absolving a son of the murder of his own mother. This she
does on the preposterous ground that only fathers are related to their children—just as she is in Greek myth said to have sprung full-grown from
the head of her father Zeus.[4]

Women, Sex, and Athenian Democracy

As the British cultural historian Joan Rockwell writes, "If matricide is
not a blasphemous crime because no matrilineal relationship exists, what
better argument for sole patrilineal descent?"[5] And of course, if even a
powerful female deity like Athena would not punish the cold-blooded
premeditated killing of a woman by her son, neither women nor men
should see anything wrong with other acts of male violence against
women. Nor should women expect legal protection from "deserved"
beatings, rapes, and even murders.

So, not surprisingly, if we examine the laws of ancient Athens, we see
that women could actually expect little protection from its laws. It is even
questionable whether the often cited "prowoman" law instituted by
Solon (the famous "father" of Athenian democracy), which provided that
brotherless daughters should have a right to inherit their fathers' property, actually offered much protection to women. For heiresses, like all
Athenian women, were forced to be under the legal guardianship of men,
who had effective control over their persons and property—so much so
that women (including heiresses) could not under Athenian law dispose

of any property above the minimal value of one medimnos or bushel of barley.[6] Moreover, it was also Solon who instituted the notorious statute that a father could sell his daughter into slavery if she lost her virginity before marriage.[7]

In fact, as the classical historian Eva Keuls points out, the legal position of women and slaves in Athenian society during its celebrated classical period was not all that different. This is reflected in the legal term for wife, *damar,* a word deriving from the root meaning "to subdue" or "to tame." As Keuls reports, "Like a slave, a woman had virtually no protection under the law except in so far as she was the property of a man. She was, in fact, not a person under the law. The dominance of male over female was as complete during the period in question as that of master over slave."[8]

Keuls's ground-breaking book, *The Reign of the Phallus: Sexual Politics in Ancient Athens,* frontally challenges the idealization of ancient Athens by many other classicists, who tend to either gloss over or ignore the situation of both women and slaves in this "cradle of Western democracy."[9] Keuls draws heavily from the thousands of pictures on Greek vases scattered in museums all over Europe and the United States, which show scenes of Athenian daily life, as well as from laws, speeches, and other records of the life of the period. Consequently, she is able to give us not just another eulogy on classical Athens but a far more realistic picture: one that also tells us a great deal about how the Athenians saw, and practiced, sex.

Specifically, Keuls documents the link between the harsh regulation of women's sexuality and what she calls phallicism—in her words, "a combination of male supremacy and the cult of power and violence."[10] And she repeatedly shows the relationship between ancient Athens' suppression of women, its military expansionism, and the harshness and brutality of Athenian life for most of its population.

At the same time, she also acknowledges the rich artistic and philosophical legacy left us by this remarkable culture, even arguing that "undercurrents of protest were always present," culminating in the year 415 B.C.E. with what she calls "an overt anti-phallic movement" combining both antimilitarism and feminism. In short, Keuls gives us a much fuller picture of ancient Athens: one that includes *both* its dominator and partnership aspects.

The point-counterpoint between these two sides of Athenian society is examined in some detail in *The Chalice and the Blade* in relation to our scientific, artistic, and political legacy from ancient Greece. Here our focus will remain on sexuality—particularly on how, as Keuls vividly documents, the social construction of sex in Athenian society relates to the imposition and maintenance of its dominator aspects.

Like other classicists, Keuls notes that in Athenian households women were segregated in special women's quarters. But unlike many other scholars, she brings out that this was designed to severely restrict women's freedom of movement, and thus to facilitate the strict supervision of their activities, particularly their sexual activities. Keuls even presents evidence that there was in Athens an official women's police, the *gynaikonomoi*, which as Aristotle wrote, served to restrict the movements of women in order to "protect their chastity." She includes the report of a contemporary writer, Aeschines, who "in praise of enforced chastity" reports how an Athenian father, upon finding that his daughter had been "corrupted," walled her up alive in a deserted house.[11] And she also presents ample documentation that as miserable as the situation of "respectable" women was in Athenian society, the situation of other women (prostitutes and slaves) was infinitely worse.

Many writers do not dwell on the unpleasant fact that Athens was a slave society. And even when they do bring this out, they sometimes try to mitigate this fact with implications that the Athenians treated their slaves uncommonly well.[12] Keuls's book belies such assertions. She includes the report of Demosthenes verifying that the Athenians maintained a public torture chamber for the routine torture of slaves in legal proceedings, since a slave's testimony was admissible in court only if given under torture. She provides other evidence that, as she puts it, "slavery was more unmitigated in Athens than in many other ancient societies." One example is "the use of an object called a 'gulp preventer,' a wooden collar closing the jaws, which was placed on slaves who handled food to keep them from eating it."[13] And time and time again, Keuls brings out how the Athenians' seemingly routine brutality (which included public crucifixions and other means of traumatically impressing on the population the importance of obeying authority) was probably felt most cruelly by women.

The most powerless Athenians were women who were also slaves. Apparently many female children were sold into slavery. Or they became slaves by being rescued from the "dung heap," where they had been abandoned by their parents soon after birth to die of hunger or cold in what appears to have been a widespread practice of "exposing" female children. Often these slave girls were used as prostitutes, and were, as Keuls writes, "automatically subject to the unfathomable horrors of that institution, which included abuse by their owners, torture, random execution, and sale at any time to the highest bidder."[14] And all female slaves, whether used by their owners to generate income for them through prostitution or not, were of course sexually, as well as in all other ways, at the mercy of their owners.[15]

Even those prostitutes who were not slaves were strictly controlled. As Aristotle writes, price control of prostitution was an important Athenian institution. Laws even ensured that "girl flute, harp, and cithara players do not charge more than two drachmas for their services."[16] In other words, the income that women could independently generate through one of the very few—indeed, in some situations only—professions open to them was to be severely limited.

To ensure that women's sexuality was in all circumstances under the control of men, there were also elaborate laws against adultery involving severe reprisals. Ex-wives who committed adultery seem to have been fair game for any abuse short of death. For example, if they were seen attending public rituals, anyone could strip off their clothes and kick them. Moreover, husbands of adulterous wives were not only entitled to a divorce (in which women would be left in very poor economic circumstances, as one writer puts it, thrown out naked from the house); it was actually unlawful for men to stay married to a woman who had committed adultery.[17]

To further deprive women of any autonomous power, it was also the practice in Athens to bar women not only from public office and the vote but even from secular education. This obviously served to prevent women from changing their subordinate and isolated situation. But it also had another side effect. As many writers about the period note, it made them "unfit" companions for the educated men. Add to this the belief (reiterated by Aristotle) that by their nature women are inferior and thus (like slaves) naturally meant to be ruled by men—not to speak of the laws and customs that enforced this subordination—and it is not surprising that men in classical Athens were notoriously contemptuous of women.

Hence, also not surprisingly, the most celebrated love relationships in ancient Athens were not between women and men, but between men and men. Or, more accurately, they were between men and boys.

Homosexuality, Heterosexuality, and Free Love

Today we often hear of the Athenians' open practice of homosexuality. But what is still amazingly ignored or glossed over is the well-documented fact that sex between males of equal maturity and power was not socially sanctioned. In this way Athenian society tried to make sure that all sexual relations involving males, be they homosexual or heterosexual, conformed to the dominator model; in other words, that they met the requirement that sex be *not* an act of giving and receiving pleasure between equals, but one of domination and submission.

This is a very important point. For if the only acceptable homosexual relations were between older men and young boys, Athenian homosexuality was not really such a deviation from the dominator norm. In fact, it actually was still another way of reinforcing this model of social and sexual relations, as the boys basically played the subservient roles normally assigned to women.

As the classicist K. J. Dover writes, "No Greek who said that he was 'in love' would have taken it amiss if his hearers assumed without further inquiry that he was in love with a boy and that he desired more than anything to ejaculate in or on the boy's body." Moreover, "if it was known that he had attained his goal," he could expect envy and admiration. By contrast, the boy "could expect strong disapproval if he was thought in any way to have taken the initiative in attracting a lover," as he was expected to play the stereotypically passive and submissive "feminine" role.[18] Most tellingly, if a grown man was thought to play that role, he could not only expect censure and possibly prosecution; he could expect that he would, like women, be regarded with the utmost contempt.

Clearly then the much-discussed "liberality" of ancient Athens towards homosexuality was not so liberal after all. For it too served to maintain the association of sex with domination. Even beyond this, in permitting (indeed idealizing) pederasty it sanctioned the sexual abuse of boys by men—just as Athenian law and custom sanctioned the sexual abuse of girls through child marriage, child prostitution, and the sexual use and abuse of girl slaves by their masters, often in the most cruel ways.

But perhaps nowhere is the equation of sexuality with male brutality and domination as evident as in the ancient Athenians' numerous mythical and artistic accounts and depictions of rape. As Keuls writes, "Rape is the ultimate translation of phallicism into action. Rape is committed not for pleasure or procreation, but in order to enact the principle of domination by means of sex." It is therefore "no wonder," as she concludes, "that the Athenian Greeks were obsessed with it."[19]

Yet this obsession is sometimes handled in very curious ways. For instance, in a book called *The Love of the Gods in Attic Art of the Fifth Century B.C.*—which lists no less than 395 rapes, including rapes by all the major male divinities on Olympus—the author's only explanation for "this explosion of sexual violence on Mt. Olympus," Keuls notes, is to inform the reader that all these tales of rape are "a subtle expression of the Athenians' yearning for the divine."[20]

Of course, it was not only on Mt. Olympus that sexual violence was a favorite Greek sport. On decorated Athenian (or Attic) vases, we see scenes of mythical satyrs chasing and molesting maenads. And we also find scenes showing men beating hetaerae (prostitutes/entertainers), thrusting penises into their mouths, and penetrating them anally, which, as Keuls points out, was in ancient Athens "conceived as humiliating to the recipient."[21]

Many of these scenes were painted on a particular type of drinking cup known as the *kylix*, which was part of the standard equipment for the famous Athenian *symposia*. Today *symposium* is used to describe scholarly meetings, but literally translated it means "drinking party." These social events were held in the men's quarters or *andrones* of private houses, which contained the largest and most luxurious rooms. And, as Keuls writes, they were a "blend of eating, drinking, games of all sorts, philosophical discourse, and public sex with prostitutes, concubines, and other men, but never with wives."[22]

Once again, a great deal has been made of "free love" in Athens, of the frequency of premarital and extramarital affairs in this "pagan" society. But in fact, this free love was only free for men (and then probably primarily for free men, men who were not slaves). For as we have seen, women's sexuality was rigidly repressed and controlled.

While prostitutes (often slaves) were forced to be available to many men, respectable Athenian women were restricted to one man. They were often married off when they were mere children and, as Keuls points out, there are strong indications that the first nuptial night of sexual intercourse with their husbands (who were characteristically much older) was often feared by Athenian brides. There are also indications that for many men intercourse with wives was primarily designed for impregnation (the production of legitimate male heirs) rather than for sexual pleasure or erotic love.[23]

Although this was not always the case, there are further indications that when Athenian men had sexual relations with women (rather than boys) for sexual pleasure, they primarily chose to do so with slaves and prostitutes rather than with wives (who were excluded not only from political but also from social life).[24] The prostitutes men brought into their symposia were probably often what the Greeks called hetaerae, women who played multiple roles as musicians, entertainers, and sexual objects for men. Sometimes these hetaerae were remarkably bright and articulate women who participated in the intellectual discussions from which men's wives and daughters were barred. Occasionally men fell in love with these women, lived with them in common-law marriages, and judging from some of the vase decorations and a number of literary and anecdotal Greek writings, had affectionate relations with them.

But as Keuls notes, "By cruel irony, this relation, the most likely to be based on something resembling harmony and mutual affection, was also the one in which the powerhold of man over woman was the most absolute." With the exception of a few especially fortunate women (the basis for stories about privileged and even wealthy courtesans), most hetaerae were little more than servants, and in fact many were slaves. Like all Athenian women, they did not have any legal status without a male guardian. But unlike respectable matrons, who could claim at least some measure of security once they bore their husbands a male child, they were, in Keuls's words, "almost certain to end their lives in misery."[25]

As one ancient Greek bluntly put it, "We [Athenian men] keep hetaerae for pleasure, concubines for the daily care of our body and wives for the bearing of legitimate children and to keep watch over our house."[26] And this view of women as put on earth solely for the use, and abuse, of males was, as Keuls notes, symbolized by the Athenians' obsession with the male penis as a symbol of male power and authority.

The Cult of the Phallus, Memories of Partnership, and the Mutilation of the Hermes

In front of most Athenians' houses stood a statue of the god Hermes with his penis erect. Scenes of satyrs and men with prominent genitalia are also commonplace on decorated vases and drinking cups. Even in the Athenians' portrayals of babies is this penile obsession evident. For in Attic art, the baby's penis is usually clearly visible—which is how we know that the babies considered worthy of artistic rendering were in classical Athens almost uniformly male. So deeply ingrained was what Keuls calls the cult of the phallus in Athenian thought that, anticipating Freud's theories of penis envy by more than two thousand years, Aristotle held that women were merely incomplete or maimed males—beings of a naturally inferior or not fully human order to be, again naturally, controlled by men.

The extent of this male control—and its often brutal consequences for girls and women—is perhaps best illustrated by the practice of permitting fathers to decide whether a newborn child should be "exposed" (that is, abandoned to die from cold or hunger or to be killed by a wild animal, as outright killing was apparently illegal), and by the fact that most of the exposed babies were female. As a mitigating factor, classicists who mention this sometimes note that not all these babies were eaten by animals or died of slow starvation, as some of them were "rescued." But what they generally fail to mention are the laws that gave abandoned children recovered by another party slave status—or the fact that there were therefore in ancient Athens, as Keuls writes, "armies of enslaved girl prostitutes."[27] Nor do they generally dwell on what it must have been like for the mothers of these babies to have no power or authority to affect the actions—or the laws—that condemned to death children they had carried in their bodies simply for the "crime" of being born female.

But as Keuls writes: "The governing principle in a phallocracy is that the human race is essentially male, the female being a mere adjunct, unfortunately required for the purpose of reproduction. The natural consequence of this notion is the elimination of the female from all social processes."

In classical Greece this took many different forms. One of these was the effective silencing of women. This was in classical Athens achieved by confining women to the women's quarters, forbidding them to speak or even appear in public except on special occasions, denying them any status to go to court, and indoctrinating them with the belief, not unfamiliar to us today, that any woman who does speak up to a man is a "castrating bitch." The complete exclusion of women from public life was, as Keuls notes, also symbolized by the Athenians' veiling of the female form, which, as she writes, "contrasts sharply with the phallic display practiced by men."[28]

Indeed, there are indications that the ancient Athenians may have taken the process of making women both mute and invisible to its logical conclusion: so intent were they on stripping women of any sense of importance, or even identity, that not only in birth records but, in some situations also in daily life, they may even have deprived women of names. As Keuls writes, "We assume that all girls who were kept by their parents to be raised [that is, not exposed to die] were given a name, but we cannot be sure of even that. Their names were not recorded in the records of their phratry or tribe, as were those of boy children." And judging from the existent fragments of Greek Middle and New Comedy, which give a fairly realistic picture of home life in fourth-century B.C.E. Athens, husbands frequently addressed their wives simply as "woman" (which in Greek literally translates as "child bearer").[29]

The practice of marrying girls off at a young age also served to maintain male control, as Socrates makes clear when he asks Ischomachus, "Didn't you marry her as young as possible so that she would have been seen and heard as little as possible?"[30] Barring women from education, and thus keeping them ignorant, also served this purpose. And so did indoctrinating women with an ideology in which male domination and female submission (including female self-sacrifice) was celebrated.

In *The Reign of the Phallus,* Keuls notes how very different the treatment of girls and women in classical Athens was from that of a number of other Mediterranean cultures where women's and men's relations were more egalitarian. She does not, however, in that book trace this difference to earlier times, as she does in one of her later papers, where she points out that the Athenians' devastation of the islands of Melos and Samos, as well as their "hysterical, not to say, pathological misogyny," becomes more understandable as a reaction to cultures still characterized by "female-worship and gender-egalitarian practices"—which the Athenians saw as a threat to their rule of the Mediterranean.[31]

Nor does Keuls particularly dwell on the remarkable culture of the Etruscans, a non-Indo-European-language-speaking people who lived across the Adriatic Sea from Greece and who, as the classicist Larissa Bonfante-Warren writes, "brought art and letters to Italy and to Rome."[32] Among the highly cultured and prosperous Etruscans, whose art bears a striking likeness to that of Minoan Crete, descent was probably still reckoned through the female line. Here, in a culture that still preserved much of its pre-Indo-European heritage, women raised all their children, even if they did not know who their fathers were—as Theopompus (a fourth-century B.C.E. Greek historian) disapprovingly reported. Just as shocking to Theopompus, here wives dined, reclined, and toasted publicly with their husbands on banquet couches—as we can still see in some of the beautiful surviving Etruscan art. And to the great disgust of androcratic observers such as Theopompus, there was here for women a "far too permissive" sexuality—along with a general love of pleasure.[33] As evidenced by the many inscribed bronze mirrors buried with Etruscan women in their rock-cut tombs (sometimes even more luxurious than the men's), here the women were literate. And in contrast to Greek and later Roman women, they bore names of their own.

In short, here (much to the moral indignation of some Greek travelers), thousands of years after the first Indo-European incursions into Europe, women were still in many key ways on an equal footing with men. But, as in Crete with the shift to Mycenaean Indo-European rule, after the Roman conquest of Etruria here too both art and life began to gradually change.

As Bonfante-Warren writes, "At this point in their history, the cruelties so often popularly attributed to the Etruscans first appeared." At Tarquinia and Orvieto, "the world of the dead replaces the world of the living in the Tomba dell'Orco and the Tomba Golini, where the Etruscan

Hades and Persephone reign. The style changes as well. A brooding quality and a melancholy never there before appear." And just as definitely, as
Bonfante-Warren also stresses, the woman's place has also changed. She
writes how, "no longer does she lie next to her husband, but sits by him
primly in Roman style as he reclines"—a clear indication that, as she puts
it, "Rome's patriarchal society had won out."[34]

It is instructive in this connection that the Romans borrowed much of
their culture, and a good part of their mythology, from the classical
Greeks, whom they greatly admired. And it is particularly instructive that
this included the Athenians' open contempt for women, as well as such
other dominator features as militarism and slavery.

But I want to here again underscore that it was not only in Etruria and
some of the Mediterranean islands that remnants of the earlier partnership cultures survived. As I noted earlier, there was even in classical
Athens another side—a side that we can now also see has ancient prehistoric roots. Even in the Indo-Europeanized Olympian pantheon, there
were still powerful female deities (although they were now subservient to
Zeus). In household shrines and even temples, the life-giving aspects of
the ancient Goddess continued to be worshiped. The sacred marriage was
still reenacted in the popular Greek Mysteries cults. And occasionally a
woman could play an important role in political life, as in the case of
Pericles' famous companion Aspasia—although even this brilliant
philosopher from Miletus (who taught both Pericles and Socrates) had to
play this role indirectly, as an advisor to men.[35]

Moreover, in counterpoint to the many Attic vase decorations showing satyrs and other males chasing, molesting, and trying to rape women,
there are also on Attic vases scenes of domestic companionship and affection between women and men. Similarly, in Attic as in later Roman art,
there are images portraying women with sympathy and respect. Some
images of women project a strong sense of personal dignity. And some
even have an air of authority, once again a sign that despite the powerless
roles to which they were assigned, Athenian women somehow found
ways of both accessing some measure of power and inspiring respect and
love.

Also, in sharp contrast to the virulent misogyny of many Greek writings, there are surviving fragments of poems idealizing rather than vilifying women and celebrating love between women and men. In fact, there
is even in one late-fourth-century B.C.E. play a young man who expresses
his remorse at having adopted a "dual standard" in his sexual relations
with his wife.[36] So from both art and literature we have evidence that
even in a society where laws and myths placed such formidable obstacles

in the way of anything other than male dominance and female sub-servience, both women and men hungered for relations based on mutual respect and caring.

Even more interesting, and revealing, are the indications that there may have been in classical Athens an "underground" of partnership re-sistance. For we find clues to periodic protests in plays like Aristophanes' *Lysistrata,* where we read of something rather akin to our own contempo-rary feminist and women's peace movements.[37] Most fascinating, if Keuls is right, one of the most remarkable events in Athenian history—the breaking off in the year 415 B.C.E. the phalluses of the Hermes (the statues guarding free men's houses and public places all over Athens)—may have been such a protest.

This "unsolved crime," which has puzzled many classicists, happened just before Athens was to embark on still another military adventure in its long, and ultimately disastrous, Peloponesian War against Sparta. Keuls makes an interesting case for the likelihood that this "mutilation of the Hermes" was an act of passive resistance to unrelenting "heroic" warfare through "street theatre." Specifically, she presents evidence that the per-petrators of this symbolic act against the omnipresent Athenian statues with erect penises or phalluses representing what she aptly calls the reign of the phallus—the equation of masculine sexuality with domination and violence—were most probably the long-suffering women of Athens.[38]

Laws, Militarism, Patriliny, and Power

If we look back on what we know of ancient Western history from a perspective that accords equal importance to women and men, it seems highly probable there were many other women's rebellions (both collec-tively and individually), not only in ancient Greece but even earlier, in Sumer, Babylon, Palestine, and all the other places where rigid male dom-inance, authoritarian hierarchies, and the institutionalization of violence had by now become the general norm. Indeed, if we look closely at some of the laws in these places, they offer compelling evidence that women must for a long time have resisted their domination.

For what we find are laws where any insubordination by women is punished in the most terrible and brutal ways. For example, the Sumerol-ogist Samuel Noah Kramer reports that under Sumerian law, if a wife was childless because she refused her husband conjugal relations, she could be thrown into the water and drowned. Kramer also writes of a Sumerian text from which we learn that "if a woman said to a man . . . (the text is unintelligible at this point) her teeth were crushed with burnt bricks," and that, inscribed with her offense, these bricks were then hung up in the great gate to the city for all to see.[39] Now, it stands to reason that if women had not continued to rebel, men would not have enacted such brutal laws. For such laws were obviously designed to suppress any individual or collective rebellion by women—and even beyond this, to effectively silence any challenge, even complaint, against men's domestic and social domination.

Oppressive hierarchies of control, be they of men over women or men over men, have throughout recorded history been backed up by force and fear—in other words, by the infliction or threatened infliction of pain. So it is not surprising that we find such brutal laws in a society where women may still have remembered an earlier, freer time—as evidenced by how the Sumerian term *ama-gi* makes a connection between "freedom" and "return to the mother."[40] But what is surprising is that even in the face of such incredibly brutal laws, Sumer (which emerged around 3200 B.C.E.) was, until the recent archaeological discoveries pointing to the Neolithic as the real cradle of civilization, uniformly exalted by historians as the first truly civilized settlement in the ancient world. And what is equally surprising is that the famous Babylonian code of Hamurabi is also still generally hailed by scholars as a major advance in civilization—even though it reveals a legally sanctioned treatment of half of humanity that by no standards can properly be called advanced. For what we find here are laws prescribing that "a flagrantly careless and uneconomical wife" was to be drowned and that "a worthless wife" could be made "a slave in her own house if her husband took another wife."[41]

Laws are extremely useful indicators of the behaviors that are at a particular time and place considered acceptable or unacceptable. Of course, they do not tell us how people actually behave. But far more clearly than literary and historical accounts, laws do tell us what kinds of attitudes and behaviors the people who make the laws (and who have the power to enforce them) want to encourage or discourage.

Since their primary function is to enforce conformity, laws have traditionally been backed up by force or the threat of force (as, in our time, by police power). And laws also articulate standards for what kinds of social, sexual, and economic relations people regard (or are expected to regard) as normal.

So if we look at Sumerian and Babylonian laws regulating the social, sexual, and economic relations between women and men, we see that, like Athenian laws, they were by and large designed to give men nearly absolute power over women in all three of these spheres. And we also again see that they were part of a larger system of social, sexual, and economic relations held together by a high level of institutionalized violence ranging from violence against women and children in the private sphere to warfare and public torture and executions in the public sphere.[42]

These laws—and the "morality" they enforced—played a major role in the process that brought about the fundamental shift in social and sexual relations we have been examining. The shift from descent through the mother (or matriliny) to descent through the father (or patriliny) was a very important part of this process. It led to the invention of one-sided monogamy, along with prostitution, adultery, and illegitimacy, as well as the harsh punishment of women for any sexual (or even personal) independence. Moreover, it was a process that, beginning with the first nomadic incursions into Old Europe and the Fertile Crescent, went along with the institutionalization and glorification of warfare. Most important in terms of what we are here exploring, it was a process in which sexuality, not only women's but also men's, was radically redefined.

I want to pause here to again emphasize that the radical sexual, social, and ideological transformation that accompanied women's gradual loss of personal power and cultural status did not, as is sometimes argued, naturally accompany the move to more complex and centralized forms of social organization. This becomes dramatically evident if we briefly compare the high civilizations of Sumer and Minoan Crete. As the cultural anthropologist Ruby Rohrlich-Leavitt notes, in Minoan Crete, "trade was not superseded by military conquest as the primary means of gaining access to important resources, the kin-based clan structures were not radically transformed to serve the state," and women still enjoyed high status in a complex, already centralized society.[43] By contrast, in Sumer, "the kinship structures were radically changed to fit a rigidly hierarchic system increasingly based on private property and the centralization of political power in the hands of military leaders," and "women were pushed out of political decision making."[44]

This is not to say that even in Sumer women were completely stripped of all their former status and power. For example, women continued in their priestly roles. But gradually even these roles changed. Thus, by the time of the Third Dynasty of Ur (2278–2170 B.C.E.), reflecting radical changes in how sexual relations were viewed, priestesses were described as concubines of the male gods and prostitutes in the temple. As Rohrlich-Leavitt notes, this mirrored the harems of the men who now ruled Ur. "The organization of the temple priestesses, the Sal-Me," she writes, "was headed by the priestess who was the god's 'true wife,' and who might be the eldest daughter of the reigning king. At the bottom of the hierarchy were very many common temple prostitutes." And in between were the women who were now called "the gods' concubines," as Rohrlich-Leavitt reports, often women of royal descent who were still permitted to "bear the children of unknown fathers" and who still "owned property and carried on business in their own names."[45]

In ancient Palestine (which enters Western history about two thousand years after Sumer), there is also evidence that women lost status and power only gradually.[46] The fact that even in the heavily edited Old Testament women such as Deborah, Miriam, and Huldah still occupy positions of leadership as judges, and, in the case of Huldah, as prophetesses, may indicate that here too the old norms were slow to change.[47]

However, by and large, here, as by now almost everywhere in the ancient world, positions of leadership—that is, positions of both temporal and spiritual power—were institutionally reserved for men. There would continue to be some women who managed to violate these norms. But these were now only the exceptions, usurping male roles from which women (along with "soft" or so-called feminine qualities such as nonviolence, caring, and compassion) were generally barred.

And while men's sexuality was now everywhere exalted—be it through Old Testament litanies of the many children they begat or Greek and Roman male effigies with erect penises—women's sexuality was increasingly condemned. Not only that, but men's brutal control over women—and particularly over women's sexuality—was now increasingly being justified as necessary to protect women's chastity, honor, and above all, their and the larger community's morality.

The Economics and Politics of Dominator Morality

To our day, from many pulpits of churches, mosques, and other places of worship all over the world, men preach of a God-given sexual morality. For example, the Old Testament laws that rigidly regulated women's sexuality are still presented to us as moral precepts. But if we stop to think about these laws, we have to ask ourselves what a "morality" that required such brutality—for example, that young girls be stoned to death if they were found not to be virgins—was designed to accomplish.[48]

For only when we ask this question do we begin to see that such laws were designed to maintain—once again, through the infliction or threat of bodily pain—dominator-dominated relationships between men and women. Even beyond that, we see that they were designed to regulate economic transactions between men in which women's bodies were essentially sexual commodities to be disposed of, or even destroyed, at will by men.

As we know from biblical laws and stories (such as the well-known tale of how Jacob purchased his wives from Laban by working for him seven years per wife), men routinely sold their daughters in marriage. In other words, marriage was essentially a commercial transaction between men. But to be marketable, a man's daughter had to be a virgin. So in essence an unmarried woman (or rather little girl, since here too child marriage was the custom, as it still is today in some parts of the Middle East) who was not a virgin was "damaged goods." Consequently the stoning to death of "dishonored" girls was not only a way of controlling women through terror by providing an exemplary warning of what to expect if they stepped out of line; it was also a practical measure for the destruction of a now economically worthless asset (thus saving the father any further expense in maintaining her alive).[49]

Similarly, biblical adultery laws requiring that both the adulterer and adulteress be killed also served as economic regulations. They provided for the punishment of a thief (the man who has "stolen" another man's property) and the destruction of damaged property (the wife who has brought "dishonor" to her husband).[50]

Perhaps most telling—and if we really think about it, horrifying—is the *absence* in the Bible of a morality (much less laws) holding men accountable for cold-bloodedly and deliberately causing the "dishonoring" of the women and girl children over whom they had such absolute control. Thus there is no hint that Lot was ever punished, or even censured, for offering his young daughters to a mob threatening two male guests in his house. Quite the contrary, when his two guests turn out to have been angels sent by God, he is actually rewarded. When Sodom and Gomorrah are destroyed, ostensibly for sexual perversions displeasing to God, ironically only Lot and his family (with the exception of his wife) are spared.

Neither is there any hint of punishment or censure in a similar story in Judges 19, where we read of how a father offers a mob of rowdies threatening a man who is a guest in his house his young daughter (a virgin) and his guest's concubine. As we read further in Judges 19, we learn that the guest (a Levite, or member of the priestly clan) actually handed his concubine over to the mob (members of the Benjamite tribe) and that they so brutally gang raped her that when "her master" came out the next morning to command her to get going he found her dead.

There is not the slightest hint in this biblical story that the Levite's handing over his concubine to a mob to be raped violated any legal or moral edict.[51] Moreover, if we read on, starting with Judges 19:29 into Judges 20 and 21, an even more grisly story unfolds—one that makes it crystal clear that under biblical codes of morality, honor, and law, even the men who raped and killed this unfortunate woman were not considered to have committed any crime against the victim—only against her male owner and his tribe. Outraged that men of another tribe (the Benjamites) should have deprived him of his sexual property—even though he himself handed his concubine to them—the Levite now plots his revenge.

In Judges 19:29, we read how upon returning home "he took a knife, and laid hold of his concubine, and divided her, together with her bones, into twelve pieces, and sent her into all the coasts of Israel"; that upon receipt of this "message," after some praying, negotiating, and scheming, the man's brethren and their brethren tribes decided to march forth in war against the Benjamites; and how—after a number of bloody battles that claimed the lives of more than fifty thousand men and destroyed all the Benjamite cities, and after killing every single Benjamite woman and child and all but a small number of men—the victors made an even more bizarre (although equally barbaric) decision. Now, to remedy the fact that the surviving Benjamite men found themselves without wives, the Levites decided to slaughter all the inhabitants of Jabesh-Gilead—except for 400 young virgins, whom (according to Judges 21:14) they gave to the surviving Benjamite men as an offering of peace and reconciliation.

It is difficult to believe that with such contents, there are still people today who try to tell us that everything in the Bible is the word of an Almighty God, of a just and merciful Father whose every command is divine law. But perhaps not, if we remember that not so long ago Christian holy men directed the European Inquisition, the Crusades, and the torture and burning of many thousands, perhaps even millions, of women; that chronic intertribal warfare continues in the Near East to our time; and that in some places "honorable" Muslim men, like their ancient androcratic ancestors, still can kill (even sometimes stone to death) women (their own daughters, sisters, and mothers) for bringing "dishonor" to them and their fellow men.[52]

Once again, I want to emphasize that this brutality is *not* an inherent characteristic of any ethnic or religious group, be it ancient Hebrews, medieval Christians, or modern Arabs. Rather, what we are dealing with are dominator or androcratic customs.

I also want to emphasize that recognizing the barbarity of the dominator elements in our Judeo-Christian heritage should not blind us to the fact that it also contains important partnership teachings.[53] Nor should we conclude from such Old Testament passages that among the ancient Hebrews there was not also love and mutual respect between women and men.

But if we find this, it is not because of, but *despite,* "moral" edicts and laws backing up rigid male control over women and women's sexuality. For obviously such controls cannot serve as the basis for love and mutual respect.

Rather, such controls—and the family values they inculcate—are a major obstacle not only to mutual respect and love between women and men, but also to the construction of a more enlightened society in which human dignity and human rights are truly valued. For as we have seen in the warlike and authoritarian character of the ancient societies we have been examining (and as we will explore in contemporary settings in Part II), the effective reduction of half of humanity to little more than domestic animals to be used and abused by men has throughout recorded history been the cornerstone for a generally uncaring, inhuman, and extremely painful way of organizing interpersonal, intertribal, and international relations.

The Domestication of Women and the Dehumanization of Men

The history of the domestication of women—and particularly the domestication of women's sexuality—still in our time remains largely untold. The brutal enslavement of men in the "great" slave societies of antiquity, such as Greece and Rome, is beginning to receive serious scholarly attention. But the far more brutal and widespread enslavement of women is still, except in feminist writings, generally ignored. If it is addressed at all, it is presented merely in passing, as curious bits of sexual lore rather than the stuff of which important or serious history is made.

But clearly for women this situation was—and continues to be—very serious. And it is (and was) in fact also very serious for the men who for thousands of years have imposed and maintained women's sexual and social domestication. For as we have also seen, the suppression and denial of earlier norms was a process that required the greatest legal and mythical ingenuity. Even more seriously, discouraging any deviation from the new norms required the chronic use of exemplary brutality and force.

The domestication of women—that is, the use of women to serve men and breed for them like domestic animals such as cows or asses (with which, not coincidentally, they are lumped together in the Tenth Commandment)—was also serious for men in still another fundamental way. For integral to this process of trying to convert women into male property was also the need to try to convert men from fully sentient and aware human beings into psychosexual automatons: androcratized men who could perpetuate, condone, and even enjoy personal and sexual relations based *not* on mutuality of benefits and caring but on one-sided exploitation and oppression.

Not that all men then, any more than now, conformed to this ideal of masculinity. Indeed, many men have throughout history rejected these types of roles. But dominator societies are not now, nor were they then, run by such nonconformist men, who are all too often still ridiculed today as "effeminate."

Thus, in ancient Rome, as in Assyria and Greece, public crucifixions were a common method of execution (of which the killing of Jesus by Roman soldiers is the most publicized example). The men who ordered these crucifixions—like the men who in Jesus' name later ordered the public torture, drawing and quartering, and/or burning of "witches" and "heretics"—obviously were used to suppressing, even deadening, any feelings of compassion or empathy. And for men to learn to command— and for women and men to learn to accept—this kind of sadistic cruelty required that both women and men grow up in households governed by precisely the kinds of laws, values, and customs we have been examining.

Thus, under the laws of ancient Rome, the male head of the household, or *pater familias*, was given dictatorial personal and sexual powers.[54] Although twenty-five was a woman's age of majority, for their entire lives Roman women remained under either their fathers' control (*potestas*) or their husbands' control (*manus*). In fact, a common Roman marriage ceremony known as the *coemptio* was a mock sale in which the wife was placed under the husband's hand (*manus*) as his chattel.[55] And unbelievable as this seems to us now, there are writings indicating that women may even have been killed by their husbands for drinking wine in ancient Rome (or at the very least, that such brutality was commended in a "moral" parable on proper family values). Valerius Maximus writes in a text called *Memorable Deeds and Sayings* that a certain man by the name of Egnatius Metellus "took a cudgel and beat his wife to death because she had drunk some wine." And he adds, "Not only did no one charge him with a crime, but no one even blamed him. Everyone considered this an excellent example of one who had justly paid the penalty for violating the laws of sobriety. Indeed, any woman who immoderately seeks the use of wine closes the door on all virtues and opens it to vices."[56]

Yet there is once again evidence that despite such laws, customs, and values, in ancient Rome as in the other ancient societies we have been examining, at least in some cases women and men managed to love and cherish one another. For example, in a letter to his wife, Calpurna, the Roman author Pliny the Younger writes: "You cannot believe how much I miss you. I love you so much, and we are not used to separation. So I stay awake most of the night thinking of you, and by day I find my feet carrying me (a true word, carrying) to your room at the times I usually visited you; then finding it empty I depart, as sick and sorrowful as a lover locked out."[57]

Not only that, but the famous Latin love elegies written by men such as Ovid, Catullus, and Propertius sometimes actually celebrate what we today would call free love (or love out of wedlock) and female sexual independence. In some of these poems, the heroines are sexually autonomous, disdainful of social conventions such as the double standard, and even demand, and obtain, fidelity from their lovers. As Judith P. Hallett writes in her analysis of these poems (which were apparently quite popular in their time), they are remarkable documents in which reversals of male and female roles, a rejection of the double standard, and romantic love as a partnership or "bond of shared trust" between equals are important themes.[58]

As Hallett notes, these poems sometimes employ metaphors of political alliance to talk about woman-man relations. The authors also sometimes depict their love life as "a respectable replacement for rank and wealth"—a stereotypically feminine valuation of the importance of loving relationships. Even more remarkably, they "reveal discontent with both the traditional Roman view of women as demure, submissive chattels and the current [newer] Roman practices which allowed women an ostensible increase in freedom so as to exploit them more fully."[59]

It may thus not be an exaggeration to say, as Hallett argues, that these poems "constitute what present-day social historians would call a 'counter-culture'"—even though it must be added that they also contain some of the sexism and misogynism characteristic of their time. But at least they indicate some attempts to find more partnership-oriented alternatives for men and women to relate to one another.[60]

Indeed, the first century B.C.E. (when the love elegies were written) was a time when many dominator assumptions were being challenged—at least by some. And this was happening both in Rome and in outlying parts of the Roman Empire such as Palestine, where a young Jew named Jesus was preaching a partnership morality: the elevation of compassion, empathy, and nonviolence to social and personal governance.[61]

In Rome it was a time when women had somewhat more personal freedom, when we find indications that at least the women of the ruling classes sometimes exercised a great deal of power. But, once again, by and large they managed to exercise this power *despite* a still firmly entrenched

legal and social infrastructure designed to concentrate personal and economic power exclusively in the hands of men—for example, laws forbidding women to hold office or vote. And even the notorious "immorality"
of upper-class women in that period of Roman history paled in comparison to the sexual excesses of the men of the time.

Ancient Rome, like ancient Sumer, Babylon, Greece, and the Palestine
of the Old Testament, was of course a far more civilized society than that
of the prehistoric Indo-European invaders of Europe that Gimbutas calls
Kurgans. It was far more technologically and culturally advanced. Furthermore, by the first century B.C.E. it was also a far more sophisticated
and cosmopolitan society than either ancient Palestine or Athens.

Still, Rome was throughout much of its history a barbarically cruel society, a slave-based society that brutally conquered a huge empire—a society where the dominator model of male control over women and the
control of "superior" men over "inferior" men governed personal, national, and international relations. As John Peradotto and J. P. Sullivan
write in their book *Women in the Ancient World*, "The Romans gave all
power to the head of the family, as they gave all power initially to the
Kings of Rome, and they would give later all power to the Caesars under
the Empire." As they also note, it was a warrior society,[62] a society in
which "hard" or so-called masculine values were honored and anything
associated with women and the "feminine" was despised—including that
"womanly" emotion we call love.

Moreover, it was a society where, as in ancient Athens, everyday
sexuality was very often both casual and brutal (as we can still read in
novels such as *The Golden Ass of Apuleius*).[63] As in ancient Athens, here
masters regularly abused and sexually exploited their slaves, and sexual
violence was viewed as a prerogative of those in power (as documented
in Suetonius's *The Lives of the Twelve Caesars*).[64] In short, here, as in ancient
Athens, the phallus was supreme (as we can still see today in the phallic
monuments called obelisks that in Rome and other cities commemorate
victorious wars and in the volcanically preserved ruins of Pompeii, where
we also find sculptured erect penises guarding men's houses).

But for all their idealization of the power of the phallus, if we look at
the compulsive sexual excesses of the Romans, we see that what they reflect is actually a sexual powerlessness: the powerlessness to feel real sexual and emotional fulfillment. For what we are today learning about
sexually obsessive and compulsive behaviors is that they generally stem
from an inability to fully experience bodily sensations and a full range of
emotions. In other words, behind the seemingly insatiable appetite for

sex and cruelty of many Romans—their famous sexual orgies and the sadistic sexual practices of some of their emperors[65]—lies a dominator psychosexual armoring that effectively blocks the full experiencing of bodily and emotional sensations.

It is this same psychosexual armoring that in our time continues to drive men to ever more sexual conquests, to the "excitement" of warfare, and to all the other frantic compulsions that fuel both war and the war of the sexes. It is this armoring—and the seething frustrations inherent in a dominator/dominated way of structuring human relations—that in our time still finds expression in mass media that in their celluloid violence and cruelty rival the sadism of the imperially funded Roman "circuses" where cheering crowds watched gladiators in "heroic" mortal combat and Christians and other "criminals" being torn apart and devoured by wild animals. And it is also this psychosexual armoring that is both expressed and fostered by a modern pornographic industry where men's violent domination and humiliation of women (and in hideous image after image, men's cruelty and barbarity to women) is presented to us as exciting and sexually arousing entertainment.

So it is not only women whose sexuality has been suppressed and distorted in dominator societies, to the degree that many women still today are incapable of expressing themselves sexually, much less reaching orgasm. As we will explore in Part II, it is also men's sexuality that has been distorted and stunted, so that for all their obsession with the power of the phallus, many men are still today essentially cut off from the very essence of sexual power: the capacity to freely give and fully experience sexual pleasure.

In the end then the cult of the phallus is not a sexual cult at all. Rather, it is a cult of male sexuality as a symbol of male violence, conquest, and domination. Just as the fight between Achilles and Agamemnon was not really over sex in the sense of sexual love by either one of them for Briseis, but over power, the phallic obelisks that to this day stand even in the Vatican (and for that matter, as the Washington Monument in the capital of the United States) commemorate not men's capacity to give and take sexual pleasure, but men's killings and conquests in war.

This is the sexual iconography we have inherited from the ancient societies we have been examining. It is a very different sexual iconography from that of a time when woman's vulva was the focus of religious art. For now, woman's vulva is obscene—even the "pagan" Greeks and Romans displayed it only in their pornography, as we still do today. Most amazingly, and tragically, it is a sexual iconography in which sexuality is no longer a primal life-force, the source of human creativity and connection, but an instrument for men to subjugate and conquer others, be they women or less aggressive men.

As for spirituality, as we will see in the remaining chapters of our exploration of Western prehistory and history, it too was radically altered. Severed from nature and from the erotic and pleasurable, its focus likewise shifted—as sex, birth, and rebirth were gradually replaced by suffering, punishment, and death as the central motifs of both myth and life.

The Sacred Marriage in a Dominator World: The Metamorphosis of Sex, Death, and Birth

Our most important Western myths come to us from the societies we have just examined, from ancient Greece, Palestine, Sumer, Babylon, and Rome. They are myths that evolved out of an uneasy blend of earlier and later elements: metamorphosized myths for a metamorphosized world.

These myths teach us that to be brave means to risk one's life to kill (as men have been taught to do) rather than to risk one's life to give birth (as women do). They teach us that to be free is for men the noblest goal but that for women it is an ignoble insult—an epithet hurled at sexually "free" or "promiscuous" women. They tell us that morality, sexuality, and spirituality are legitimately defined by men; that women, and particularly women's sexuality, are dangerous; and that true spirituality (like true wisdom, power, and justice) requires detachment from all that (like sex, love, and woman) is connected to flesh and feeling, to real human beings, and to real life here on Earth.

Because such myths have led to so much misery, injustice, bloodshed, and brutality, for some people the solution is to simply get rid of our myths—of everything that is not logical and rational—and focus on changing our realities. But to change our realities, we also have to change our myths. As history amply demonstrates, myths and realities go hand in hand.[1] And this is where the new knowledge from archaeology is so useful. It helps us understand that the most elemental matters—how we view our bodies, sex, birth, and death—can be, and in fact have been, profoundly altered. Not only that, it makes it possible for us to look at familiar myths—including myths about sexual relations and what happens after we die—through new eyes, and to see how different stories and images communicate very different ways of looking at and living in this world.

Our early mythical imagery reflected a world view in which death was neither an isolated event nor a final destination in heaven or hell. Rather, it was part of the same cycle: a cycle of sex, birth, death, and rebirth, in which the Goddess reclaimed what was hers to give, and in which sex played a mysterious but central part. As our ancestors realized that women only give birth after sexual intercourse, they apparently concluded that the rebirth of vegetable and animal life every spring (and even the rebirth of the sun on the winter solstice each year) is also generated through some kind of sexual union. So our ancestors fashioned rites through which we humans too could find union with the mysterious forces that govern the universe, which they associated with the female creative power.

For if plants could be born again and again from the earth (the womb of vegetation) one could believe, even though it was not given to humans to witness that process, that the Goddess—who recycled days and nights, barley and wheat, and spring and fall—would also recycle human life. And one could also believe that through erotic rites of alignment with the mysterious power of sex through which the Goddess performed her miraculous work of birth and rebirth, we humans could not only find protection and solace in our inevitable pain, sorrow, and death but also augment our chances, generation after generation, for a joyful and bountiful life.

But if in a more partnership-oriented era the sacred marriage of the Goddess symbolized both the union of female and male and our oneness with the life-and-pleasure-giving powers of the universe, what kind of sacred union could be celebrated in a world where the worship of the Goddess and her divine son or lover would become ever more subordinate to the worship of violent and warlike gods? And what would happen when during the Christianization of Europe sex itself would be condemned as sinful and women who clung to vestiges of earlier sexual rites would be labeled witches?

In such a world, both the worship of the Goddess and the sacred marriage as an ecstatic religious rite would have to acquire very different forms and meanings. As we will see in the pages that follow, this is precisely what happened—with sometimes the most amazing, indeed bizarre, results.

Heroes, Monsters, and the Sacred Marriage

A fascinating case in point is the famous story of Theseus, Ariadne, and the Minotaur. According to this popular Greek myth, which tellingly takes place on the island of Crete, there was once a wicked king by the name of Minos, who every year required a tribute from the Athenians of seven young women and seven young men to be sacrificed to a monstrous creature, half bull and half man, called the Minotaur. When the action opens, the young Athenians (including Theseus, son of the king of Athens) have just arrived in Crete. Through promises of love, Theseus quickly tricks Minos's daughter, the priestess Ariadne, into giving him a secret only she knows: how to safely enter and leave the underground labyrinth where the bloodthirsty Minotaur dwells. Armed with Ariadne's magic thread and his trusty sword, Theseus descends into the labyrinth, catches the Minotaur by surprise, and speedily dispatches him to Hades (the Greek realm of the dead).

One interesting feature of this story is its vilification of the Mycenaean King Minos. In earlier accounts, Minos is far from evil. Homer, who writes glowingly of Mycenaean times, identifies him as the son of Olympian Zeus himself. Hesiod describes him as the most inspired and just lawgiver of the ancient world. So undoubtedly what the vilification of Minos reflects is the end of Mycenaean control of the Mediterranean and the gradual ascendancy of Athenian power.[2]

Even more interesting, if we look at this story in light of what we know about the important roles played by Cretan women as late as Mycenaean times, is how this myth deals with Ariadne—who, like Queen Arete in the Mycenaean Phaecia of Homer's *Odyssey*, was probably still worshiped by her people as the earthly representative of the Goddess. Even in this Athenian legend, Ariadne is still a woman possessed of great power. It is she who, like Inanna in the Sumerian hymns, holds the secret to the labyrinth, to an initiation-like journey such as Inanna and Dumuzi took to the underworld of death. It is also she who has the knowledge of how to return.

Only now that knowledge and that journey are no longer part of a mythical cycle involving sex, death, and rebirth. Nor is it any longer a journey in which a female deity plays the major role. Instead, it is a journey taken alone by a male hero. And it is not a journey to the realm of a chthonic or underworld Goddess, as in the hymns of Inanna, where her older sister Ereshkigal is queen.[3] Rather, it is to a place under the earth where a hoofed and horned male monster (much like the later devil of Christian iconography) devours human flesh.

Most tellingly, in sharp contrast to the story of Inanna and Dumuzi, in which Inanna returns from the underworld to continue to govern her people, the story of Theseus and Ariadne has a very different ending. For him, it ends with a triumphant hero's journey home to rule as a king. For her, it ends with her people's defeat, the betrayal of her love by Theseus, and her abandonment far away from home on the isle of Naxos.

Just as Greek gods such as Zeus, Apollo, and Ares were Indo-European imports, mythical Greek heroes such as Theseus, Hercules, and Perseus were idealized representations of the men who were now everywhere taking over the ancient world. The qualities these archetypal heroes embodied were not so different from those of the epic he-men of our time, of a Rambo or James Bond. They were consummate killers, noted for their power not to give but to take life. They did not hesitate to use lies and thievery to advance their ends. And, in a world where (eventually, even in Crete) women were gradually becoming male properties, they were frequently not only rapists and seducers but also abductors or thieves of women.

Moreover, as in James Bond and other contemporary macho adventure films, sex with women was for these ancient Greek heroes merely incidental. For rather than a sacred act associated with the worship of the Goddess, sex was now associated with kingly ambition to conquer and to rule—and above all, with violence.[4]

Probably because of the tenacious hold that the institution of the sacred marriage as a legitimization of royal rule still had even by his time, Theseus eventually marries Ariadne's little sister, Phaedra. But like Ariadne, she too is no longer described as the representative of the Goddess. Instead, we are simply told she is also a daughter of King Minos. In other words, the powerful ancient archetype of the Goddess and of the priestess who was her earthly representative has by now been radically altered. And so also has the institution of the sacred marriage, which now no longer takes place—as all ancient sacred marriages did, in the land of the priestess or queen—as tracing descent through the mother and a husband coming to live with his wife would require. Rather it takes place in Theseus's homeland, to which he has taken the little girl Phaedra, who is then brought up as a member of his household: a clear reflection of the shift from matrilineal to patrilineal descent and of the Athenian custom of child marriage for girls.

But these radically altered sexual relations, first between Theseus and Ariadne and then between him and Phaedra, are not the only way in which the ancient sacred marriage is co-opted and debased in this myth revolving around the exploits of a Greek prince/king. Even more dramatic—as I suddenly realized when I reread the part of this story focusing on the Minotaur—is how the sacred marriage is debased, distorted, and in essence parodied in the account of the Minotaur's birth.

What we are told is that the Minotaur is the child of King Minos's wife, Queen Pasiphae. However, he is not the child of Minos but of a beautiful white bull with whom, in punishment of Minos for not sacrificing the bull to him, the Greek sea god Poseidon made Pasiphae fall in love.

The bull as a symbol of male potency goes back all the way to the Paleolithic—as most probably does the myth of a sacred sexual union of the female creative principle with a bull, since in a Paleolithic cave we find an otherwise inexplicable image of a horned animal standing over a pregnant woman.[5] This association of the male principle with the bull is still very clear in the hymns of Inanna (where she refers to Dumuzi as her wild bull) and even much later in Minoan and Mycenaean Crete (where the horns of consecration or bull horns were prominent religious symbols everywhere associated with the worship of the Goddess). So there seems little question that the sexual union of Pasiphae and the white bull is still the sacred marriage of the female principle represented by the Goddess and the male principle represented by the ancient Bull God.

But now, rather than being a rite of central religious significance, it is presented to us as the illicit and unnatural affair of a king's wife. Moreover, rather than bringing forth new life in the spring—or a divine child symbolizing the Goddess's power over birth, death, and regeneration—what this sexual union produces is a monster with an unquenchable appetite for human blood.

In short, just as in medieval Christian dogma sex is linked with sin, in the Theseus legend the sacred marriage between Pasiphae (as the representative of the Goddess) and the white bull (the ancient Bull God) becomes an adulterous act by an unfaithful wife. To top it all off—and in complete reversal of earlier myths and archetypes—the product of this once-sacred union is now an evil and bloodthirsty demon, curiously prefiguring the familiar horned and hoofed devil that in later Christian myth endlessly torments humans in his underground hell.

Sacrifice, Demons, and Sex

The Greeks' demonization of the ancient Bull God as a horrible monster demanding constant human sacrifice is particularly interesting since in Neolithic art the Goddess herself is often represented in half-human and half-animal form, as a bird or snake Goddess symbolizing the unity of all of nature. Minoan and later Mycenaean art is also still full of fantastic hybrid creatures—for example, the griffin, who, like the Egyptian sphinx, is part feline and part bird. But far from being a monster, the Minoan griffin is a beautifully elegant creature. And far from being shown devouring maidens and youths, the picture of the Minotaur we still have from a Mycenaean seal shows him in a rather mundane position, casually sitting on a chair with one leg crossed over the other.

This demonization of earlier deities and religious symbols is a well-documented and recurrent mythical motif in recorded history. As John Maier (coauthor with Samuel Noah Kramer of *The Myths of Enki* and co-translator with John Gardner of *Gilgamesh*) writes, "In Mesopotamia the most striking example is the Imdugud-bird, which becomes demonized as the Zu (or Anzu), the one who brings chaos by stealing the divine *me* and has to be killed for the crime against the universe." Another example are "the protective *lahama*-creatures who, in art at least, lead to the demonic Humbaba, slain by the heroes Gilgamesh and Enkidu (though he was guardian of the cedar forest and connected with the god Enlil)."[6]

Very often this demonization of earlier mythical figures is linked with accusations of human sacrifice. For instance, just as the Greeks transformed the ancient snake Goddess into the terrible Medusa and the bird Goddess into the frightful Harpies, they also claimed that the Titans (the older gods of Greek cosmology) ate their own children. In the Middle East, the demonic Lillith is another case in point. In some Hebrew legends she is said to have been punished by Yahweh for not submitting to Adam—specifically, for refusing to have sex with him in the "missionary" (male above, woman below) position—by every day having to kill thousands of her own children.

But while in historic times both women (for example, the medieval "witches") and female deities (for example, Ishtar and Astarte) are sometimes associated with human sacrifice, there is little evidence from prehistoric art or other finds to support the view that human sacrifice was a prominent part of our heritage from earlier Goddess-worshiping societies. To begin with, there is no artistic imagery of human sacrifice in Paleolithic, Neolithic, or Minoan art. In fact, rather than youths and maidens being fed to a monstrous Minotaur, what we find in Minoan art are scenes of youths and maidens dancing with bulls in what appears to have been an important ritual of both athletic skill and religious devotion.

From our perspective, this bull dancing is a very strange ritual, particularly as we are used to the idea of bull fights where matadors (the Spanish word for killers) enrage a bull with flesh wounds and then butcher it with a sword in a ritual act of domination and conquest. But in terms of an ideology *not* of conquest of nature but of alignment with both its life-giving and death-threatening powers, the unarmed Minoan maidens and youths dancing with this powerful animal, fabled for both its sexual potency and its destructive potential, would have been quite another matter. Perhaps, in keeping with what the archaeologist Nicolas Platon calls the Minoans' "ardent faith in the Goddess nature," its meaning is what it literally was: a balancing act where these people's legendary love for life was symbolically poised against the ever-present possibility of death. For, particularly in a land of earthquakes, we would expect to find rituals dealing with the recurrent nature of life and death.

Nonetheless, the myth of human sacrifice in Cretan prehistory lingers on, even though there is no solid archaeological evidence indicating that there was ritual sacrifice either in Minoan times or in the Neolithic.[7] Mellaart notes the absence of altars for blood sacrifices in Çatal Hüyük.[8] And Gimbutas points out that most earlier interpretations of archaeological finds as human sacrifice are based on misinterpretations of secondary burials of the deceaseds' bones that we now know were common in prehistoric Goddess-worshiping societies—and that in fact persist in some parts of the Mediterranean even to our day, as documented in a ceremony recorded in Thessaly (northern Greece) in which, revealingly, the female relatives of the deceased still played a central role.[9] For example, Gimbutas writes that the archaeological find in a prehistoric cave in southeastern Italy of the bones of more than a hundred people, where some skulls had been removed before the rest of the bodies were deposited and some had cut marks, "can now be understood within the context of ancient and widespread burial practices in which the heads of the dead were removed to receive special ritual attention before being buried separately" and that "this does not indicate human sacrifice."[10]

Some researchers, such as Vicki Noble and Barbara Walker, even believe that the practice of animal sacrifice may be a dominator (or in their terms patriarchal) practice. They argue that the earliest sacrifice of blood was the "freely given menstrual blood of woman" (like the red ocher in Paleolithic and Neolithic burials, a symbol of regeneration or rebirth) and that the obtaining of sacred blood by killing would only have become "necessary" when woman's sexual power was no longer an important element of both mythology and religious rite. They also argue that stories such as those in the Mesopotamian hymns of Inanna—where both the Goddess Inanna and the bull god/king Dumuzi go back into the underworld for part of the year (the fallow autumn and winter)—were later literalized. In other words, they suggest that what in patriarchal societies became ritual killings were once merely symbolic myths (like the arche-type of a dying and resurrecting goddess or god) or symbolic rites (like the Christian Eucharist, where a priest gives the worshipers a wafer sym-bolizing the body of Christ and wine symbolizing his blood), rather than actual human sacrifices.

While I also am skeptical of claims that human sacrifice was a com-mon practice in Goddess-worshiping societies before the shift to a domi-nator social organization, I do believe that animals were in some early Neolithic (and perhaps also Paleolithic) societies ritually killed. But hav-ing said this, I want to add that there are also indications that at least in some parts of the ancient world, blood sacrifice may have been a charac-teristic pastoralist, rather than agrarian, custom. For example, in com-menting about the allegation that human sacrifice was common in Minoan Crete, Goodison points out that it is actually only with the shift from the Minoans to the more warlike Indo-European Mycenaeans that we begin to find in the art of Crete frequent images of animals in the process of being sacrificed. As she writes, "There is not one seal celebrat-ing the actual act of animal sacrifice from the early period." This is in sharp contrast to the later period, when armed male deities "in positions of command (often standing on an elevated platform) begin to gain pre-eminence" and when instead of "association, accompaniment, respect for, and identification with, the creatures shown," we begin to find expres-sions of domination, as well as the frequent "depiction of tamed, dead and carried animals."[11]

Another interesting piece of support for the view that blood sacrifice (be it animal or human) was a common pastoralist, rather than agrarian, custom is actually contained in one of the first chapters of the Judeo-Christian Bible. For here we learn that the blood sacrifice of the pastoral-ist Abel (the slaughtered sheep) is preferred by Jehovah to Cain's offering of fruits from the earth. And in a total reversal of the historic reality of pastoralists destroying and/or taking over earlier agrarian societies, here Cain, as the representative of the earlier agrarian people, is accused of the monstrous crime of fratricide.[12]

This does not mean that animal, and even human, sacrifice may not have been practiced in the Goddess-worshiping societies of our early pre-history. However, if it had been an important and widespread ritual, we would expect to find depictions of it in the extensive art of these societies, which we do not. In fact, it is only from later dominator-oriented soci-eties—such as the dynastic Egyptians (whose pharaohs sometimes had their wives and slaves buried with them) and the Aztecs (whose ruling

priests tore out the hearts of captured warriors and sacrificed virgins as offerings to their warlike and angry gods)—that we have extensive artistic
records of human sacrifice. It is also from societies that came long after the
cultural shift we are here examining—such as the warlike Carthaginians—
that we find the most persuasive archaeological evidence pointing to ritual
human sacrifice.[13]

Moreover, it is only from later societies that orient to the dominator
model that we find legends of the yearly sacrifice of a divine king, the
son-consort of the Goddess. Thus, in Inanna's hymns, the sacred marriage
is still of central importance and sex is associated with pleasure and the
rebirth of nature. The journey into the underworld (death), though realistically cruel and frightening, is likewise associated with rebirth (the periodic return, first by Inanna and then also by Dumuzi and his sister). And
even though it has been said that in the later Babylonian New Year's
festival (when the sacred marriage of the Goddess and the ruling king
was still celebrated) a king (or his surrogate) may have been ritually
killed, there is nothing to indicate this in the Inanna hymns or any
Mesopotamian text.[14]

By contrast, in the story about a ritual combat between priests outside
a temple to the Roman goddess Diana in a grove in Italy (on which James
Frazer's *The Golden Bough* in large part based its case for prehistoric ritual
human sacrifice), the sacred marriage becomes associated with—and
subordinate to—an act of ritual killing.[15] Similarly, in the Greek myth of
Theseus and the Minotaur, the sacred marriage is incidental, associated
not with pleasure but with divine retribution, with the punishment of
both King Minos and his wife because Minos did not kill a bull as a sacrifice to the Greek god Poseidon.

In other words, where in the older art and myths the central theme is
the cyclic regeneration of life, focusing on sex, love, and regeneration, the
central emphasis of later art and myth is on punishment, sacrifice, and
death—with even the Goddess sometimes, as in the case of Ishtar, now
demanding human sacrifice, be it in war or religious myth. And this emphasis on death and sacrifice is not all that surprising if we consider that
these myths reflect a world in which the greatest power is no longer the
power to give and nurture life, but the power to cruelly and painfully
take it instead. Or put another way, as the theologian Walter Wink observes, if in the myths of this world there was so much attention to monsters and demons as embodiments of evil, it was because there was so
much evil about. And if these myth's protagonists were so violent, it
was, as he writes, because "the story of the gods perfectly mirrors actual
political developments in the state."[16]

Changing Myths for a Changing World

Again, this is by no means to say there was no evil or demonic energy in earlier societies that oriented more to partnership than domination. Human beings have the capacity for violence and cruelty (evil) as well as kindness and caring (good). Indeed, nature is both creative and destructive, and these processes affect all our lives. But the polarization into absolute good and absolute evil we find in dominator-oriented societies (be they primitive or socially and technologically advanced) is not a theme in the iconography of earlier, more gylanic societies, where we do not see the constant opposition between good deities or heroes and a profusion of evil monsters or devils.

By contrast, in the *Enuma Elish,* a Babylonian myth dating back to only around 1100 b.c.e.,[17] creation itself is portrayed as an act of violence: the goddess Tiamat is murdered by the god Marduk and it is from her dismembered cadaver that the world—and a new world order—is formed. According to this story, not only the origin of the world, but our human origins are from violence. For after killing the Mother Goddess to create the world, Marduk kills her spouse, Kingu, and from his blood creates human beings to be the servants of the gods.

The point I am getting at is that there is a reason these myths depict so much violence and justify it through the device of demonizing other peoples and their deities. In order to maintain themselves, rigid dominator societies require the idealization and institutionalization of cruelty, violence, and insensitivity—in other words, of evil. For how else are social and sexual relations based on rigid rankings of domination to be enforced? And since the dominator system also ensures that responsibility for all the evil perpetrated to maintain this way of structuring human relations does not rest where it belongs, it is projected elsewhere—not only in myths but in reality.

One such projection, as we still see all around us today, is scapegoating, or the blaming (and all too often killing) of socially disempowered groups for one's own problems and ills. Thus, when Christians were persecuted by the Romans, they were accused of ritually sacrificing and eating human flesh, perhaps because the Eucharist is a rite of symbolically drinking Jesus' blood and eating his flesh. Accusations of ritual human sacrifice were also leveled against the women tortured and burned at the stake for being witches by Christian inquisitors. And the same charge was made as late as the twentieth century to justify Czarist pogroms against Russian Jews, who were accused of killing and eating Christian children.

Another typical projection is the invention of demons or devils, who in many myths turn out to be distorted versions of the deities of conquered or persecuted peoples. And still another is the projection of evil onto the gods themselves—and with this, the attempt through ritual sacrifice, and in all of these ancient societies through blood sacrifice, to placate angry and vengeful gods and their representatives here on earth.

Once again, I want to emphasize that the more partnership-oriented people of the early Neolithic and Minoan Crete were also concerned with (and afraid of) evil, violence, and death. Death was in the Neolithic often associated with the bird Goddess, possibly because in Çatal Hüyük and other settlements excarnation (or the stripping of flesh from the dead before burial of their bones) seems to have been achieved by vultures, symbolizing the Goddess taking the dead back into her womb. And in both Minoan and earlier cultures, the snake Goddess also symbolized the chthonic or underground realm, which the ancients also apparently associated with a return to the Goddess's womb.

However, to recognize, as these people did, the cyclic nature of life and death and to see the Goddess as she who gives life and takes it back so that it may again be reborn is one thing. To characterize the bird Goddess, the snake Goddess, and other female deities as evil and bloodthirsty demons demanding human sacrifices (which we do not find in Neolithic or Minoan iconography) is a very different matter.

As we have seen, the sacred marriage was in the Paleolithic and Neolithic perceived as the catalyst that activates new life every spring. It does not seem to have had anything to do with placating monsters or demons, with violence, or with legitimizing the rule of kings. Even in the later Sumerian sacred marriage we read about in the hymns of Inanna, the sacredness of female sexuality is still honored, as is its creative power. Lovemaking is still a passionate encounter between a man and a woman, with women overtly initiating and enjoying sexual intercourse. And even though here the sacred marriage is already an instrument whereby men legitimize their rule as kings, there are indications that the king's power is not yet absolute. Although Inanna transfers her powers to Dumuzi to rule in her place, when he forgets that his power came from her, he is deposed to spend half the year in the underworld (from whence he also returns every year, again symbolizing the old theme of the cyclical regeneration of life).

But in another Mesopotamian myth, involving the legendary hero Gilgamesh, already a very different story unfolds. When the Goddess Ishtar (the Babylonian successor to the Sumerian Inanna) proposes marriage to him, he rudely rejects her, accusing her of being unfaithful to earlier lovers and of causing them harm. Then, with the help of his friend Enkidu, a wild man from the hills, he kills Ishtar's Heavenly Bull and throws his thigh (in some translations his genitals) in her face.[18] So besides its shift from the celebration of the power of sex and pleasure to the idealization of the power to cause death and pain, what this myth tells us is that at a certain point at least some kings no longer felt the sacred marriage with the Goddess was needed to legitimize their rule. However, as Maier writes, "The rejection of Ishtar is not the only episode to consider in *Gilgamesh.*"[19] For example, at the end of the story Ishtar is again presented in a favorable light, and a big point is made of the fact that Gilgamesh returns to her worship. But the most important trace of earlier myths and belief systems in the Gilgamesh epic is the episode noted in the introduction to this book, where the wild man Enkidu is humanized by having sexual intercourse with a priestess of Ishtar. In other words, even here we still find traces of a belief system in which sex and pleasure are a humanizing force.[20]

The Blending of Dominator and Partnership Myths

This blending of earlier and later elements in ancient myths is also evident in the so-called Greek Mysteries, which, as I will later elaborate, probably stemmed from earlier religious rites that went underground. As the classicist Jane Harrison writes in *Prolegomena to the Study of Greek Religion*, although its importance decreases with the passage of time, the sacred marriage was probably in some form still part of all three of the most famous classical Mysteries: the Eleusinian, Dionysian, and Orphic.[21]

The Eleusinian Mysteries (known to have been celebrated by thousands of pilgrims from the archaic period of about 800 B.C.E. to as late as the year 150 when the temple at Eleusis was enlarged by the Romans)[22] dealt with the same themes as prehistoric myths: birth, sex, death, and regeneration. As the philosopher Mara Keller writes, they "focused on three interrelated dimensions of life: (one) fertility and birth, (two) sexuality and marriage, and (three) death and rebirth."[23] But as Keller's research traces, the changing versions of the Eleusinian myth also reflect the conflict of cultures between the earlier Goddess-worshiping agrarian peoples and their warlike invaders, with each new version incorporating more dominator elements.

The central myth of the Eleusinian Mysteries revolves around Demeter (the Greek Earth Goddess and Grain Goddess) and her divine daughter, Persephone or Kore, who is, according to Greek myth, abducted into the underworld to be the unwilling bride of its ruler, Hades.[24] In her grief at

Persephone's loss, Demeter (the giver of the gifts of the Earth) no longer makes the plants grow, so that the fertile fields wither and die. To avert catastrophe, Zeus orders Persephone's release. But before Persephone can depart, Hades gives her a sweet red pomegranate seed to eat. And eating this fruit, symbolic of sexuality and fertility, makes it necessary for Persephone to return to the underworld for a third of every year—thus accounting for the annual death and rebirth of vegetation.

This Greek myth of Demeter and Persephone contains some of the same elements as the hymns of Inanna: the marriage between a female and male deity and the journey and return from the underworld realm of the dead. But here sexual union is a subplot to death and resurrection. And even then, the sexual union on which the plot hinges is violent, with a male god raping Persephone and tricking her into returning every year—a clear reflection of a fundamental shift in the relations between women and men.

Further reflecting fundamental cultural changes is what happens in still later versions of the Eleusinian myth. For now the emphasis shifts from the theme of mother and daughter to the theme of mother and son. In these later stories there is another sacred child, variously known as Plutus, Iakchos, Triptolemos, Brimo, or Dionysus. And it is this male deity who eventually replaces Demeter's daughter as the central figure—and who in the Dionysian and later Orphic Mysteries must now go to the land of the dead before his (and the initiate's) spiritual rebirth.

As Keuls writes, "During the period of Attic control over the sanctuary, a deliberate attempt was made to reduce the Earth Mother symbolism of the cult, in accordance with the pattern of 'defeminization' of myths. A new male object of worship was introduced, the boy Iakchos, later called Triptolemos. In the new version of the Eleusinian myth, Demeter gives the secret of agriculture to Iakchos/Triptolemos, who, Prometheus-like, passes it on to men and thus becomes a male fertility figure." Or as Keller writes, "Dionysus, young male god of the grapevine, wine, intoxication, revelry, frenzy and destruction, as well as resurrection, was added rather late to the rites of Demeter, probably not before the 4th century B.C.E."[25]

As we will see, the cult of Dionysus focused heavily on orgiastic violence. Even the Eleusinian Mysteries involved the ritual killing of a pig—in other words, a blood sacrifice—although some scholars believe this was a later addition to the rites.[26] And pigs were also sacrificed in another Athenian festival,[27] the Thesmophoria, when the respectable matrons of Athens (for slaves were not permitted at these festivals) were—very temporarily—permitted to break free from the rigid constraints of their lives, and as Keuls writes, "played at being free."[28] But in contrast to the Eleusinian Mysteries, where women are still associated with the Goddess's creative sexual powers, in the Dionysian myth even the act of birth giving or creation is transmuted into an act of violent destruction.

In one version of the birth of Dionysus (or Zagreus, as he was also known), we are told that when Zeus proposes to make him ruler of the universe, the older gods or Titans are so enraged that they dismember the boy and devour him. The goddess Athena saves Zagreus's heart and gives it to Zeus, who thereupon swallows it and from it somehow produces a second Dionysus/Zagreus. Zeus then destroys the Titans with lightning—and it is from their ashes that the human race springs, part divine (Dionysus) and part evil (Titan).

This dualistic aspect of "man's nature" (the Dionysian and the Titanic) is also central to the Orphic Mysteries (which began as reformed or less debauched versions of the Dionysian rites). The Orphics affirmed that because of the divine (Dionysian) origin of the soul, it could be liberated from its evil Titanic inheritance through initiation into the Orphic Mysteries—dramatically prefiguring later Christian dualism, as well as a male god's violent death and resurrection as the central mythical themes.

In the Dionysian myth, it is the violence of lightning rather than the ecstasy of sex that symbolically gives birth to human life. Similarly, in the Orphic myth, it is the violently severed head of the dead god that symbolizes the creative principle, as it floats on (still singing) even after his body has been dismembered and thrown into the sea.

So once again, as in the Mesopotamian *Enuma Elish*, where life ensues from the dismembered body of the goddess Tiamat, in these Greek myths men and violence have usurped what in fact belongs to women and love: the giving of life itself. But it is not only that neither the Dionysian nor Orphic Mysteries any longer celebrate the Goddess's creative female sexual power; it is that, on the contrary, the key female role in these Mysteries is now that of destroyer rather than creator. According to Orphic legend, it is women who tear Orpheus's body to pieces.[29] And, as we can still see in paintings on Greek vases, it is also the maenads (in other pictures shown sexually "sporting" with satyrs) who tear the body of Dionysus apart.

In ritual practice, this dismemberment was not of a man but of a goat—and judging from vase illustrations, Keuls speculates that this was sometimes done with stage props rather than live animals.[30] But in any event, it is the maenads (which in Greek literally means "raving women") who dismember the dying and resurrecting god—thus reinforcing the

Greek view of women as naturally destructive and dangerous creatures who must be strictly controlled or "tamed" by men, lest they do to them what in these myths they do to the god.

Sex, Eros, and Thanatos

These myths are, of course, products of a radically altered psyche, a psyche appropriate for a radically altered world. It is a world in which the act of life giving has been appropriated by male gods and male priests; in which actual physical birth (being of the flesh and of the female) is devalued and even denied; in which neither life nor woman are any longer affirmed (much less considered sacred and holy). It is a world in which gods must die, kings must die, and sons must eternally kill fathers (as in the Greek myth of Oedipus, which Freud made the basis for his theory of the Oedipus complex) to attain possession of both women and power (which is also now equated with violence). In short, it is a world in which the destructive principle (what Freud called Thanatos, after the ancient Greek personification of death, especially as expressed in violent aggression) is primary.

For now fathers have the right and the power to ritually sacrifice their children (as in the Greek story of Agamemnon's sacrifice of Iphigenia and the biblical story of Abraham and Isaac). Now women are of an inferior order (as in the myth where Pandora, the Greek primal woman, is, like Eve, blamed for all of men's ills). And now the erotic (itself tainted with violence) must—along with women—be controlled by men (as in the later Freudian theories about the need to control the "dangerous" id and libido).

But even in this dominator world, the old yearning for connection, for a harmonious union between woman and man, for a sense of the universe as cyclic and orderly rather than chaotic and violent—in short, for Eros rather than Thanatos—continues to struggle for reassertion in both myth and reality. Thus, in the "reformed" Dionysian myth—the myth of Orpheus—we also find remnants of the older world view in a conception of both masculinity and female-male relations that reaffirms Eros rather than Thanatos.

In some Greek myths, Orpheus is said to be one of the Argonauts (the Greek demigods who, like Theseus and Hercules, fight the Titans, the demonic representatives of the old order, whom the new Olympian gods eventually replace). However, Orpheus is not a warrior/killer/seducer/rapist. Rather, he is a poet and musician, whose lyrical music was said to be so beautiful that when he played wild beasts were soothed, trees danced, and rivers stood still. And, as we can still read in the later Roman stories by Ovid and Virgil, in sharp contrast to the standard strong-man hero, he is a sensitive man who truly loves a woman. Indeed, so strong is his love for his wife Euridice that when she dies fleeing a rapist, Orpheus follows her to the realm of the dead.

The story of Orpheus and Euridice was not part of the Dionysian or Orphic rites, where the union of the feminine and masculine principles no longer played a central part (although, according to some legends, Dionysus "rescues" Ariadne from her lonely grief after Theseus abandoned her on Naxos, and marries her).[31] But it is this story that was to most powerfully capture the European artistic imagination, even inspiring the first operas in the seventeenth century.[32] And, as the social psychologist David Loye remarks, it is precisely the strong partnership themes in the Euridice and Orpheus myth that probably help account for its long-lasting popularity.

Loye points out that Orpheus's yearning for reconnection with Euridice is symbolic of man's yearning for reconnection with woman in a society in which the loving sexual bonding between woman and man is considered a threat to the domination of man over woman. He also notes that as an artist, a man in touch with the more creative or "feminine" part of himself, Orpheus represents the yearning of men for access to their own more humanistic or "effeminate" and creative selves. In short, he points out that what this Orphic archetype represents is men's yearning for escape from a culture that imprisons them in a stereotype of masculinity equated with domination and violence.[33]

This yearning by both men and women for a masculinity not identified with conquest and domination probably also in part accounts for the tremendous popularity, to our day, of another religious myth about a sensitive and caring male: the Christian story of the death and resurrection of Jesus Christ. A fascinating aspect of this myth is that even though the emphasis is also already on the sacrificial death and resurrection of a dying young god, Jesus' birth and conception are again also important themes. Only now, in a strange burlesque of the ancient sacred marriage in which the Goddess played such an active and creative part, his mother is no more than a totally passive baby container. In accordance with the male usurpation of the traditional (and clearly observable) connection of birth with sex and woman, here the holy child is generated entirely by his Father, without anything like sexual intercourse, much less sexual pleasure. And although his mother is still commonly referred to as the Holy Mother or the Mother of God, unlike Jesus and his powerful Father, she is no longer divine.

Actually, this Christian myth is also the result of a number of permutations. It began with tales about a gentle young Jew who could perform miracles. Then it became linked with the ancient Hebrew prophecy of the coming of a Messiah. And only with Paul (the Greek Jew who popularized Christianity in its early stages) did the notion that God sent his only son to die for man's sins enter the picture. In accordance with the biases of his time, Paul also did not make much of Jesus' mother. In fact, the reentry of that part of the ancient myth (about the birth of a holy child from a holy mother) into this religious story did not occur until decades after Paul. But it was undoubtedly an important factor in the story's continuing popularity (as is clearly evident in Catholic countries, where the Virgin Mary is primarily prayed to).

But despite the tenacious hold of such traces of Goddess worship, in Western myth after myth the emphasis continued to shift from Eros to Thanatos.[34] Where once the central theme of myth, and life, was the cyclic unity of birth, sex, death, and regeneration, the first parts of this cycle—sex and birth—increasingly receded into insignificance. And as dominator and partnership elements were constantly recombined in an ever more uneasy blend, dying and resurrecting male deities also moved ever more surely to center stage.

Memories of the sacred marriage of the Goddess (and of myths and rites of sex and birth giving) still remained. But with time—as these memories became more and more dim in male-centered stories—the sacred marriage was even more radically transformed. Until finally, as we will see in the chapter that follows, we begin to find myths of a sacred union, not between woman and man, but between man and God: a sacred marriage in which the female part has completely, and astonishingly, disappeared.

The Last Traces of the Sacred Marriage: Mysticism, Masochism, and the Human Need for Love

For many years, despite my pragmatic bent and empirical training—and for reasons I did not then see, perhaps precisely because of this—I was fascinated by mystical writings. Like many people, I sensed in them an ancient lost wisdom that somehow got buried under all the arcane language, abstract pronouncements, and obscure symbols. But it is only now, after years of studying archaeological data and ancient myths from many lands—and with a clear grasp of the cultural shift from a partnership to a dominator direction in our prehistory—that I am beginning to understand how true this is.

How the symbolism of the sacred marriage survived in both Eastern and Western mystical traditions—and how over many millennia its form and meaning was dramatically altered—is a story we will probably never completely reconstruct. But I think one way this symbolism survived is through the deliberate efforts of women and men who secretly clung to their old religious myths and rites.

Indeed, I have become increasingly convinced that a major reason mystical writings are so full of seemingly incomprehensible symbols is not just, as is sometimes said, that they speak to the intuitive rather than rational part of our minds. I believe that many mystical traditions were probably made deliberately mysterious by their founders so as to conceal, and thus preserve, the myths and rituals once associated with prehistoric religions.

As we have seen, the dominator takeover entailed both extensive re-mything and great physical violence. Undoubtedly the Hebrew and Christian persecutions of heathens and infidels were nothing new, merely the continuation of traditions of religious persecution already well established in prehistoric and early historic times. So the only way to preserve ancient religious traditions in a world of chronic violence and religious persecution would have been through the same method later "heretics" used: by going underground and continuing ancient practices in "mystery cults" with secret codes only divulged to initiates, who (as was the case in the Eleusinian Mysteries) took an oath never to reveal the meaning of the symbols and rites they were taught.

But as the centuries and then millennia went by, the old meanings gradually changed or were forgotten—both through the natural process of change inherent in oral traditions and because the women and men who originally had the keys to the secret codes were long dead. Add to this the continual overlay of dominator elements, and thus continuing reinterpretations, and what evolved truly became ever more mysterious—hence the term *mysticism.*

Yet even to our day, the earlier melding of the sexual and the spiritual is evident in both Eastern and Western mystical traditions. This is one reason many people in the so-called New Age spiritual movement look to mysticism for clues to a more satisfying spirituality and sexuality. Many of these people are particularly drawn to Eastern mystical traditions, as they often preserve more of the prehistoric view that a balanced union of female and male is the essential foundation for balance and harmony in all aspects of our world.

But both Eastern and Western mystical writings are a mix of partnership and dominator elements. So precisely because there is today so much interest in alternatives to religions where our bodies (and particularly our sexuality) are supposed to be base and evil, it is important that we try to untangle the various strands of these two completely contradictory points of view. This, as we continue our journey from Western prehistory to the European Middle Ages—and thus to the threshold of our own modern age—is the subject of this final chapter of Part I.

The Mystical Journey and the Mysterious Power of Sex

The mystical quest—the search for that which mystics sometimes call the Absolute—seems to be a uniquely human experience. And so also does the mystical or ecstatic state, which is said to provide those experiencing it a sense of indescribable inner peace, bliss, and even access to healing powers, along with a sense of unity or oneness with what mystics through the ages have called Divine Love.

There are many roads to an ecstatic or mystic state. The art of the Paleolithic, the Neolithic, and Minoan Crete suggests that probably very early in Western culture, dance was used to attain mystical (or what we sometimes today call shamanic) trances. Since ancient times people have also used meditation, breathing exercises, hallucinogens,[1] fasting, and deprivation of sleep to induce heightened or altered states of consciousness. And, as we have seen, there is strong evidence that sexual ecstasy was once also an important avenue to mystical or ecstatic states.

This ancient perception that sex involves what we today call an altered state of consciousness, and even beyond this, that the sexual union of female and male can be an avenue to spiritual bliss and illumination, is still evident in many Eastern religious traditions. For example, the yin and the yang are in Chinese mystical traditions symbols for the feminine and the masculine. And even though much of Chinese philosophy and religion elevates the male over the female, attributing the negative and passive to the feminine and the active and positive to the masculine, the emphasis in Chinese mystical writings, particularly in the Taoist tradition, is often still on the harmonious balance between the two. Thus, according to some Oriental sages, the heavenly rainbow represented the union between the female and male principles, a bridge uniting heaven and earth. The Chinese also speak of the *tai ch'i* or Great Ultimate, uniting yin and yang.[2] And some Chinese sages specifically teach that the *tai ch'i* is a sexual force associated with the feminine, which (as in the worship of the prehistoric Goddess) energizes and illuminates all life.[3]

The most evident (though curiously ignored) contemporary remnant of the sacred marriage in Eastern tradition is a Japanese rite that made world headlines in 1990, when Japan's new emperor was crowned. At that time the press reported that there raged in Japan a heated controversy about a secret ceremony said by scholars to have its origins in prehistoric times. It was not clear from the press reports whether the new emperor actually had sexual intercourse as part of his coronation ceremonies with a young woman who, according to these reports, was brought into a shrine where this ceremony was held, or whether, as the Imperial Household Agency claimed, the bed in the shrine was used as "a resting place for the Sun Goddess, but the emperor never touches it." What was clear was that a matted bed and coverlet were provided in the inner sanctum where this ancient rite was performed so that the new emperor could commune "in a symbolically sexual way, with the spirit of the Sun Goddess." And what was also clear was that as late as 1990 in modern Japan the sacred marriage to the Goddess was still, as in the hymns of Inanna, considered necessary to legitimize a new male ruler's power. Because in Shinto tradition, it was this union that "rendered the emperor into a deity." Moreover, according to Japanese scholars, this was a ceremony that had its origins in ancient harvest festivals where (as in the European Paleolithic and Neolithic) the union of the female and male principles was linked with the continuing fruitfulness of the Earth.[4]

The many Hindu mystical teachings about the energizing nature of union between the female and male principles also appear to be survivals from very ancient myths and rites. Of particular interest are Tantric Hindu teachings in which, far from being passive, female sexuality is still revered as the energizing principle of the universe. It is especially revealing that Tantric yoga is said to have emerged in India around the middle of the eleventh century as a grass-roots movement that, as Georg Feuerstein writes in *Yoga: The Technology of Ecstasy*, "hailed from the castes at the bottom of the social pyramid in India"—the same castes to which the Indo-European conquerors confined the earlier Goddess-worshiping Indian population.[5]

If we look at Tantric yoga in this larger historical context, we see that it is hardly coincidental that Tantrism came from these castes. To begin with, Tantrism sharply departs from the Aryan aspects of Vedic teachings that the ultimate aim of human existence is transcendence of this earthly realm (a most convenient teaching for keeping oppressed people from trying to change their earthly situation). Most significantly, as Feuerstein writes, Tantric yoga "introduced a battery of means [myths and rites] that hitherto had been excluded from the spiritual repertoire of mainstream Hinduism, notably Goddess-worship and sexuality."[6]

So most likely Tantric yoga was a resurgence of much earlier practices and beliefs (though already with a heavy dominator overlay). As Feuerstein writes, "The great Tantric formula, which is fundamental also to Mahayana Buddhism, is 'samsara equals nirvana.' That is to say, the conditional or phenomenal world is coessential with the transcendental." Accordingly, "the Tantric adepts reclaimed for the spiritual process all those aspects of existence that the mainline traditions excluded by way of renunciation—sexuality, the body, and the physical universe at large." And they did this, to borrow Feuerstein's Jungian language, by "reinstating the anima, the feminine principle," which is called *shakti* power in Hinduism and "depicted in iconography by such goddesses as Kali,

Durga, Parvati, Sita, Radha, and hundreds of other deities . . . or simply as devi ('shining one')—the Goddess."[7]

In other words, Tantric mystical teachings and practices reinstated sexuality, the human body, and even the ancient Goddess to their central place in both myth and ritual. Their symbol for uniting transcendental spiritual bliss with immanent or bodily pleasure was the ecstatic embrace of the female and the male, as exemplified by the sacred sexual union between the Goddess (Shakti) and the God (Shiva).[8]

But although Tantrism taught that "Shiva without Shakti is dead" (that is, devoid of the life-giving creative energy), in Tantric yoga we already find a male-centered practice. And in Tantric writings (until recently almost all by men), the female sexual energy is described from the male perspective, with the woman playing an instrumental—and in that sense secondary, indeed peripheral—role to the male's spiritual enlightenment through sex.

In contrast to some other Hindu teachings, Tantrism idealizes rather than vilifies female sexuality. But at the same time it still elevates the male spiritual experience over both the "inferior" woman and the "inferior" bodily or carnal realm. And most of its textual directives are to the man, who under no circumstances is to discharge his semen but rather conserve it for himself. For women, such sex has the advantage of a built-in birth control device. But the reason given by Tantric writings for this practice is not only male-centered; it is also that even though the male practitioner would seem to indulge in sensual pleasure (bhoga), in Feuerstein's words, "in reality he cultivates transcendental bliss (ananda)."[9]

Still, in Tantric yoga the sexual union between woman and man is a sacred rite: a path to heightened consciousness, and with this, to a sense of oneness or connection with the divine. And here, as in the prehistoric traditions we have been examining, it is the female or Goddess energy (the *kundalini-shakti* force) that is said to illuminate the hearts, minds, and souls of both women and men.[10]

Such glaring contradictions become understandable in terms of the superimposition of dominator elements on earlier partnership traditions. On the one hand, Tantric writings preserve the ancient link between the sensual and the spiritual expressive of a view that the sexual union of female and male is the animating principle of life on this Earth and that when the essential balance between female and male is lost, so also is balance in all aspects of our personal, social, and spiritual lives. On the other hand, these writings are themselves imbalanced. They teach that the bodily or erotic (a mainstay of the ancient sacred marriage) is of a lower order than that which is detached and otherworldly. And they imply that even though (like the ancient Goddess) the woman or yogini is for the male initiate or yogi still the divine source of spiritual bliss, she is also inferior to man.

From the Sacred Marriage of the Goddess to Male Brides of God

In conformity with dominator systems' requirements, this tenet that woman is inferior to man pervades many mystical writings, both Eastern and Western. For example, although many Sufi mystics also use erotic imagery and equate the feminine with spiritual bliss, they do this within a larger Muslim religious framework in which women are viewed as inferior and female sexuality is often depicted as dangerous to men.

The same types of inner contradictions also characterize most Judeo-Christian mystical writings. In fact, as in Muslim tradition, here the rationale for male supremacy is even more extreme than in polytheistic dominator religions. For in these monotheistic religions the female is deprived of all divine power, which is presented exclusively in male form.

Yet even despite such radical remything, as we saw earlier, there are still in the Bible many traces of both the Goddess and her sacred marriage, confirming the archaeological evidence that Goddess worship (and with this, sacral sex) continued to flourish in Canaan during the very years the Old Testament[11] was being established as the only officially sanctioned religious text. For example, Hebrew prophets are constantly exhorting their people against backsliding to the worship of the Queen of Heaven, railing against "the whore of Babylon" and the sinful "daughters of Zion"—obliquely confirming that the sacred marriage was still a popular rite. Moreover, the Christian veneration of the Virgin Mary is directly traceable to the ancient worship of the Goddess. And so also are a number of well-known Catholic saints, as it is to the Church's co-option of earlier pagan deities that many Christian saints owe their origins.

A well-documented example is the famous Irish Saint Brigit, who owed her great popularity to the fact that she was once the powerful Irish Goddess Brigit. An even more dramatic—and radical—example of how this process of co-option served to gradually superimpose dominator elements on earlier partnership traditions is what happened to the Greek Goddess Demeter.

As a first step, the Byzantine emperor Theodosius I in the year 389 issued an edict forbidding the worship of any deities but the Christian Father and Son. But the people of Greece still continued to pray to the Goddess Demeter (the widely revered Giver of Agriculture and Grains) as Saint Demetra, patron saint of agriculture. After some time, though, Saint

Demetra underwent an even more jolting metamorphosis. Now, instead of Saint Demetra, she became Saint Demetrius.[12] In other words, to fit the requirements of the new social (and with it, religious) order, this important female deity was first demoted from divine to saintly status under an all-powerful male God. But ultimately even this was not enough. So she was once again transformed—this time from a female to a male.

That this transformation of a powerful female into a powerful male was a common remything device is also evident from Hebrew mystical writings. For example, the *ain* that in Kabbalistic Jewish mysticism represents the "creative void," as Israel Regardie points out, was in Egypt the goddess Nuit, the "Queen of Absolute Space and the naked brilliance of the night sky blue," jetting forth "the milk of the stars (cosmic dust) from her paps."[13] But in the Kabbala the *ain* is male.

This sex change—and with it, the male appropriation of powers formerly associated with a female deity—was obviously a very effective means of buttressing male power. Indeed, what better way of justifying male dominance than the biblical dogma that man derives his control over woman from a heavenly Father, God, or Lord in whose image he was made? And what better rationale for excluding women from the priesthood (and thus from positions of moral and, what was often the same, legal authority) than the Judeo-Christian and Muslim equation of divine power exclusively with maleness?

But this total masculinization of the divine had still another result. This was a very strange new version of the sacred (or as it was now increasingly called, mystical) marriage—one that, were we not so conditioned to accept anything religious authorities tell us, would immediately strike us as manifestly absurd. For what we begin to find is not only that the female partner in the sacred marriage is secondary or peripheral. What we find is that she—like the Goddess—has been completely written out.

Like much of Eastern mystical lore, Jewish, Christian, and Muslim mystical writings still contain erotic language and female imagery (although, even more than in their Eastern counterparts, these allusions are often tangled up in esoteric symbols, mathematical formulae, and indecipherable metaphysical codes). Like many of their Eastern counterparts, Jewish, Christian, and Muslim mystical writings also tend to relegate the physical to an inferior place—so much so that in Christian mysticism the body is often viewed as intrinsically base. And while the feminine is still sometimes idealized in the abstract (like the Shekinah of Hebrew Kabbalistic mysticism or the Christian Virgin Mary), woman, and particularly woman's sexuality, is frequently presented as a danger to man. But even beyond all this, in these writings we find male-centeredness taken one huge step farther. For now, instead of a sacred marriage between a female and a male, what we begin to find is a "mystical marriage" between a man and his God.

Thus, rather than being the union of the female and male principles, in Kabbalistic and other Hebrew mystical writings (and even in some passages of the Old Testament), the sacred marriage is between a male deity and his worshipers. Moreover, it is now a very unequal union (like marriages in fact became). For now it symbolizes the bond between an all-powerful male deity (God) and a bride or virgin (as God's "chosen people" are frequently called not only in Kabbalistic writings but in the Old Testament itself, for example in Isaiah 37:22, Jeremiah 31:4 and 21, and Amos 5:2).[14] And as we saw earlier, this has even been the interpretation placed by many religious scholars on the highly erotic Song of Songs—even though its protagonists are clearly female and male.

Similarly, using the image of the sacred marriage to legitimize the absolute rule of the "princes" of the Church over all Christians, in Catholic writings the Church becomes the bride of Jesus. And even after the Reformation, the language of the sacred marriage finds its way into the writings of Martin Luther, who likewise uses it to bolster religious institutions and their all-male hierarchies. In his key work *Of the Freedom of a Christian Man* (1520) Luther writes that belief "unites the soul with Christ as a bride to her groom."[15] Or as he put it in a later sermon (1537), "Among all the picturesque allegories which God has given us to portray the Kingdom of Christ, one delightful, affectionate image is the comparison of Christendom or the Christian faith with a wedding, a holy matrimony in which God chooses a Church for His Son to take for his own as a bride."[16]

This notion of a divine entity choosing the Church's hierarchy as a marriage partner is of course a bureaucratic version of the dominator practice we already glimpse in the Sumerian hymns of Inanna: the use of the ancient sacred marriage as a device to legitimize the power of the men who rule in the deity's name. Except that now it is not only that a whole Church hierarchy is legitimized; it is also that we find a union in which both bride and bridegroom are male.

Ambitious men like Luther and other heads of religious institutions also used the metaphor of the mystical marriage to symbolize the union of their deity and his flock. Or more properly I should say *their* flock. For people who did not, like sheep, unquestioningly obey these men, did so at their greatest peril.

By contrast, in most Christian mystical writings, the sacred marriage seems to have a different function. It is usually the ecstatic union between an individual mystic and the deity. But since most mystical writings that have come down to us are by men, it is still usually the union between a male subordinate and a male ruler—with the male mystic (like the male-controlled religious institution) taking the subordinate role of the bride and an all-powerful male God taking the dominant role of the bridegroom.

In other words, what we find here is a homosexual union—made even more strange because most Christian mystical teachings are adjuncts to religions that denounce homosexuality as an unnatural abomination. And while the language describing this mystical marriage is often highly erotic, its intent is clearly not to elevate the sexual or bodily from its despised and subordinate position. Quite the contrary, as Bernard de Clairvaux (sometimes credited as "the real father of the Christian bride mystery") wrote in the eleventh century, "this union takes place in the spirit only, for God is but spirit not body."[17] In sum, what we find in many Christian mystical writings is an all-male union that now takes place only in men's minds.

The Divine Demand for Suffering and the Ecstasy of Pain

De Clairvaux wrote at a time when in the south of France and other parts of Europe troubadours and other "heretics" were again reinstating the worship of the Goddess in the form religious historians call Mariology. During the next two centuries, the great cathedrals of Europe (every one dedicated to Our Lady or Queen of Heaven, as she is explicitly described in the splendid cathedral at Chartres) were still being built on sites where the Goddess had formerly been revered (not coincidentally in vaulted shapes reminiscent of the ancient cave as a womb sanctuary). And images of a Black Virgin or Madonna (black because she represents the fertile black earth or because she traces her roots to the Great Mother Goddess Isis of Egypt) still attracted pilgrims from all over the Christian world,[18] sometimes in shrines dedicated to Mary Magdalene (who according to some legends fled Palestine with a holy child, her son by Jesus, to the south of France).

But at the same time that such vestiges of the worship of the Goddess continued to persist—and undoubtedly because they did—the Church also mercilessly persecuted "heretic" sects still clinging to the sacred marriage as the union of the female principle (the Great Goddess) and the male principle (the Bull God). As late as the eighteenth century, women were still being killed as witches for sexually "consorting with the devil"—that is, with a now-demonized hoofed and horned deity.

Yet even with all this, the ancient sacred marriage as the union of the feminine and masculine erotic and spiritual energies could not be completely stamped out. All through the Middle Ages, and even later, people (including monks and nuns in medieval monasteries) continued to cling to this ancient tradition, albeit in the most strangely altered forms.

For in the context of medieval Christianity, the sacred marriage was now undergoing still another radical transformation. Now—instead of a celebration of life and love—it was increasingly becoming a celebration of pain and death.

This morbid fusion of the mystical marriage with death and suffering is a recurrent theme in the writing of a number of medieval female mystics. Like Catholic nuns do to this day, these women took their vows in a mystical marriage through which they became the brides of Christ. But for them this sacred marriage did not bring the pleasures of sexual ecstasy but rather what they described as the ecstasies of pain.

Thus, Christina Ebner (a nun from the convent of Engelthal near Nuremburg who reported her life and visions in a short work called *Overloaded With Grace*) wrote that her heavenly bridegroom came to her "as one who has died of love."[19] Another nun, Sister Margaret Mary, was, as Sara Maitland writes, "so determined to make a complete gift of herself to the Sacred Heart that she carved 'Jesus' on her breast with a knife. Still not satisfied she burned the letters in with a lighted candle."[20]

The suffering that some of these women inflicted on themselves for the sake of divine love is vividly described by Maitland in an essay she wrote for a book called *Sex and God*. "Women flagellate themselves, starve themselves, lacerate themselves, kiss lepers' sores, deform their faces with glass, with acid, with their own fingers," she writes. "They bind their limbs, carve up their bodies, pierce, bruise, cut, torture themselves." They even speak of their sacred marriage with the divine as Christ's rape of them. And almost uniformly they say that what brought them closer to their divine bridegroom was their suffering—and that it was in return for this suffering that he gave them the love they so craved.[21]

But it was not only women who, as Maitland puts it, abused themselves and abased themselves in the name of mystical love. Now men also equated the mystical marriage not only with total submission (already found in the Old Testament) but also with "ecstatic" suffering—once again for the love of God.

Certainly for women a sadomasochistic relationship with God such as the one described by myriads of women saints who mutilated themselves as a love offering to "their Lord" mirrors the submission that the Church demanded of women in both temporal and spiritual marriage to the male lord (be it as head of family or head of the Church). But this kind of relationship also represents the dominator-dominated relations now demanded not only of women but also of men. For men too were in the Christian Middle Ages required to submit to male "noblemen" and "princes" of the Church who—often in the name of Christian love—oppressed and repressed their "subjects."

This helps explain why the Church was so interested in pain instead of pleasure—a subject we will return to in Part II when we look more closely at sex in Western religion and life. And it also helps explain why, as Maitland writes, "Hagiography [the study of saints] is littered with individuals of both sexes who seem to have organized their whole lives around the greed for violence and death as the way of proving their commitment."[22] For rather than helping them heal this pathological masochism of self-abasement and torture, the Church encouraged it.

By minimizing the importance of what happens on Earth and counseling acceptance of suffering (and even its embrace) as a ticket to spiritual development and divine rewards after death, the Church not only distracted people's minds and energies from seeking less oppressive social alternatives; it actively reinforced the hold of dominator institutions, beginning with the institutionalization of male dominance. So when women equated love and bliss with submission and suffering, and when they saw martyrdom as their highest vocation, it was in part due to their indoctrination to view abject obedience and acceptance of suffering as their greatest womanly accomplishment. But it also stemmed from the Church's general praise of saintly (and divine) suffering, along with its equation of men with spirituality and women with the bodily or carnal.[23]

As Maitland writes, "Once dualistic thought gained ascendancy within Christianity, women were increasingly associated with nature and with the body, while men identified themselves happily with mind and spirit." Thus, "if Christianity was to flagellate and dominate its bodiliness, then women were the obvious and 'natural' matter for the Church to go to work on—and what's more they needed more punishment, since being more bodily they are also more sinful."[24]

However, it is important to again emphasize that contrary to popular belief, this kind of dualism is not a Western idiosyncracy. Nor did it originate with Christianity. It goes back to much earlier non-Christian Eastern cults, such as that of Zoroaster in Persia, as well as to Western philosophers such as the Greek and Roman Stoics, who also argued that man and spirit are superior to woman and nature. As for sex, although many free Greek men indulged in heterosexual sex with wives, concubines, and slaves and often also had homosexual relations with young boys, the

Greek medical writer Epicurus contended, long before Christianity, that sex is hostile to good health. And Soranus of Ephesus, like some of the leaders of the Christian Church, even extolled the virtues of continued virginity within marriage.[25]

Nonetheless, it is in medieval Christianity that the split between body and spirit and between woman and man reaches its apex. And it is also here that we begin to find a totally aberrated, and nonsensical, view of sexuality, as in St. Augustine's dogma about a humanity that is eternally damned, literally condemned to painfully die, due to the very sexual act through which in fact our species survives. Moreover, this view of sex went along with a truly aberrated view of spirituality. For not only did the medieval Church applaud women and men who tried to outdo the suffering of their Lord with the most extravagantly painful and perverse self-inflicted suffering; it often canonized them.[26]

The Romance With Death and the Human Need for Love

Given all the contemporary idealization of an "Age of Faith" before Cartesian rationalism and mechanistic science supposedly severed "man's" connection with the divine,[27] it is hard for us to come to grips with the historical realities of the medieval Christian world. The cultural historian G. Rattray Taylor once described it as "a cross between a charnel house and an insane asylum."[28] It is in some ways an apt description.

For what we find if we look at these realities is a chronically violent world: a world of ceaseless battles between "noble knights" and of Church-blessed "holy crusades" in which men loot, rape, and pillage not only infidel cities and Jewish ghettos but even Christian settlements—as in the infamous Albigenses Crusade launched by Pope Innocent III in 1209 to wipe out the Cathars, a Christian sect where women often assumed leadership and both women and men were committed to nonviolence, charity, and chastity.[29] It is a world in which "men of God" declare that the half of humanity from whose bodies life ensues is carnal and sinful, and "witches" are burnt alive at the stake for the crime of healing through "sorcery" (that is, through folk medicine such as herbs rather than through bleeding and other "heroic" remedies prescribed by the new Church-trained and licensed male physicians). It is a world in which "heretics" and "traitors" who dare to question absolutist dogmas or despotic authority are drawn and quartered, and even stealing a loaf of bread can be a capital offense; where the mass of people live in poverty and filth while the ruling classes hoard gold, silver, and other riches; and where "spiritual" men preach this must all be patiently accepted, holding out instead the promise of a better afterlife.[30] Moreover, this afterlife, they insist, is the reward only for those Christians who unquestioningly obey God's commands, and not for infidels and sinners—which unfortunately includes almost everyone (male or female) trying to have any pleasure, as even dance (long forbidden by the Church as a religious ritual, in contrast to "pagan" times when it played a central part) will soon be forbidden by fundamentalist reformers like Calvin from any part in daily life.

In short, it is a nightmare world where pain is not only ubiquitous but exalted, a world in which man is constantly exhorted to turn against man, against woman, and even against himself—against his own body, which (along with woman) must be dominated and controlled. For both are now seen as lowly and disgusting, as is everything that is not of a higher "spiritual" realm in this earthly "vale of tears."

Not surprisingly then, what we also find is a world where accepting pain and suffering from one's beloved—be it a heavenly deity or an earthly knight or lady—has become the ultimate eroticism. For now, besides all the suffering brides and bridegrooms of God, we find story after story in which suffering and death are inextricably intertwined with love and sex. These are the stories we to this day read as the great romances of our Western heritage—the romances of archetypal figures such as Tristan and Isolde, and Eloise and Abelard, for whom drinking from the "cup of love" is a sure ticket to betrayal, violence, and/or death.

Just as Abelard's and Eloise's sin of carnal love presumably doomed them to the fire and brimstone of hell (as well as leading to Abelard's castration), the sexual union of Tristan and Isolde is what dooms them to die—in still another ironic twist of the ancient sacred marriage from which the Tristan and Isolde legend seems to have derived. For we are told in Gottfried of Strasbourg's thirteenth-century version that the love potion (or symbol of the intoxication of love on which the story turns) was an expression of the will of the Germanic goddess Minne, and that the altar in the Minnegrotte was a bed consecrated to her worship.[31]

Since the favorite subject of poets is now the superiority of "spiritual" suffering to "carnal" pleasure, what is celebrated in medieval romance after romance is not the joy of living and loving. Rather, as Denis de Rougemont's work illustrates, what most of these romances eulogize are the "joys" of anticipation, renunciation, and ultimately death.[32]

Yet even in this dominator world—where suffering is saintly, pleasure is sinful, woman is of the devil, and canonized saints (both women and men) seek salvation by actively mortifying their flesh—women and men still find ways of loving each other, of singing, of laughing, of making love, and even in the midst of so much brutality and morbidity, of giving and receiving from one another some measure of pleasure.

It is still a world where women and men use candles, flowers, incense, and music in sacred rituals and rites. And it is also a world where through a variety of mystical pursuits women and men desperately seek a lost sense of connection with the loving—and even more specifically, the erotic—energies of the universe through permutation after permutation of the ancient sacred marriage.

Alchemists search for mystical union in the laboratory. They write of a "chemical marriage" that would not only transmute base metals into gold[33] but also reunite the feminine and the masculine, as well as the spiritual and the natural.[34] Kabbalists write of woman and man as one body, and even of the Shekinah (a feminine manifestation of divine wisdom) as the creative principle.[35] Christian mystics like Jakob Böhme write of spiritual ecstasy in the language of love and sexual symbolism, asserting that the rift between woman and man and between the human and the divine happened when Adam and Eve were expelled from Paradise.[36]

Like the alchemists, who intuited that the sacred marriage was not merely metaphysical, and the Kabbalists, who in their esoterically coded manuscripts preserved the memory of a feminine creative force, in his intuition of an earlier time before the essential unity of woman and man and the spiritual and physical was fragmented and distorted, Böhme too somehow sensed what we have been examining: the prehistoric shift from a partnership or gylanic to a dominator or androcratic world.[37] It is a fascinating insight. For what Böhme sensed is not only a mystical but, as archaeology now tells us, an actual truth.

Certainly the earlier, more partnership-oriented societies of our prehistory were not ideal. But they were societies where our most intimate connections—the physical connection of women and children through birth and of women and men through sex—were still understood as sacred rather than profane. And they were societies where even at the dawn of human civilization, women and men already seem to have sensed the wisdom that lies at the core of our most exalted mystical and religious traditions: that it is only through connection, through love (be it of a divinity or another human) that we can attain our highest potentials.

The search for this lost wisdom by mystics—and by women and men throughout the ages—is the search for reconnection with our partnership roots. It is the search for a way of relating that is the antithesis of the dominator mode, where in both reality and myth polarization and strife, conflict and separation, winning and losing, dominating and subduing, dismembering and disembodying, conquering and controlling—in short, force, fear, and violent disconnection—are the central themes. And the very essence of this search, as mystical writings have so often brought out, is the search for a means of healing what was so brutally rent asunder with the shift to a dominator world: the fundamental erotic, and with this also spiritual, connection between women and men.

But no mystical initiations, no alchemical magic, and certainly no amount of holy suffering and self-abasement can heal this rift. Indeed, in some ways these practices only widen it. For they either avoid the underlying problem, and thus do nothing. Or they actively reinforce a dominator model of spirituality where at best sexual or erotic love (along with women) is seen as of an inferior order, and hierarchies of violent domination are sanctified through the notion that even the powers that rule the universe (and not just the men who rule the earth) are pleased with human suffering, servility, and self-abasement.

This is by no means to say that the mystic journey, expressive of our yearning for oneness and for love, has not brought comfort to many women and men throughout recorded history. But the point is that the problem is not just spiritual, or even sexual, but rather social.

As we have seen, with the shift to a dominator model of social and ideological organization, woman and man and spirituality and nature were in fact split asunder—and in the process, we were also severed from our own life-and-pleasure-seeking creative erotic energy. So it is only as we again shift toward a more gylanic or partnership-oriented way of living, thinking, and loving that we can heal this rift.

This, from the perspective of a better understanding of where we are and where we are going, is the subject of the rest of this book.

2

WHERE ARE WE AND WHERE DO WE GO FROM HERE?

CHAPTER 9

From Ancient to Modern Times: Setting the Stage

The wonder is not that there are so many problems, so many personal and social tragedies, that we so often form dysfunctional relationships and cause ourselves and others so much pain. Given the load of distortion, misinformation, negative conditioning, and just plain nonsense we have lived with for so long, the wonder is that we have functioned at all.

That even staggering under this load we have still managed to love one another is a tribute to the human capacity, and tenacity, for seeking pleasure rather than pain, caring rather than conquest, and above all, connection—with one another and with all that is creative and loving in ourselves and our world. This human capacity and tenacity also offer us realistic hope that we can at this critical point in human history create a social system that is more balanced and less insane—one where violence and domination, along with sexual and spiritual dysfunction, will no longer be considered "just the way things are." And this hope is today further supported by the fact that much of modern history has been the struggle to break free from our dominator bondage—from millennia-long traditions of violent coercion, inhuman repression, and endless bloodshed.[1]

In the chapters that follow, we will look at this struggle. We will see how almost in the twinkling of an eye—which is what a few centuries are in the history of our species—there have been dramatic changes in how people perceive almost everything, from sexuality to spirituality. These changes have gone along with equally dramatic changes in the structure of the family, government, and other social institutions. For during the last three hundred years, despite massive resistance and intermittent regressions, the dominator "givens" of violence and repression have been challenged with increasing success. And now, as we move out of the twentieth into the twenty-first century and a new millennium, this epochal struggle over our future is coming to a head.

In Part I, we saw that both the partnership and dominator models are possibilities for our species and that even among our closest primate relatives, the so-called common and pygmy chimpanzees, there are significant differences in social organization. We saw that the original direction in the mainstream of our cultural evolution seems to have been more toward partnership, and that this profoundly affected the social construction of both sexuality and spirituality. But then we saw how during a time of great chaos and dislocation there was in our prehistory a major cultural shift.

From here on, we will look at the powerful movement in our time to reverse that shift—and at the strong resistance to it. We will continue to look at the different ways a society can utilize the two most basic levers for human motivation: pain and pleasure. We will continue to look at cross-cultural materials as well as homosexual relations, although we will still primarily focus on heterosexual relations in mainstream Western culture.[2] We will also still focus on the central role traditional stereotypes of sex and gender play in interlocking systems of political, economic, religious, and military domination that rank nation over nation and race over race. But in many ways our course will be very different in this second, and final, part of our journey.

Up to now, we have moved quickly through a very long span of time. It has been like traveling on a river, flowing first in one direction and then, after a very sharp turn, in another. Now, to continue this analogy, our task is to prepare a new riverbed—one that can take us in a partnership rather than dominator direction. But in the process, we still have to navigate extremely turbulent rapids full of sharp rocks and dangerous shoals, with strong currents and crosscurrents going in many directions.

As we look at these currents and crosscurrents, we will take a close look at all our intimate relations: not only our sexual relations, but the relations between children and those responsible for their care. For it is through these foundational relations involving touch to the body that we acquire many of the building blocks for later patterns of either partnership or dominator relations in both our sexual and nonsexual lives. We will also take a fresh look at contemporary developments, not only in sexuality and spirituality, but also in politics, economics, technology, education, communication, and other important aspects of our lives. And we will further expand *cultural transformation theory* by looking at how, on the most basic bodily level, pain and the threat of pain are inherent in a dominator model of social and ideological organization.

But before we go on, I want to first set the stage for what follows. I want to say a few words about the title of this book, how it evolved out of my own changing consciousness, and how it relates to the fact that both pleasure and the sacred are defined very differently in societies orienting primarily to a partnership rather than dominator model. I want to briefly discuss some of what we are today learning about the biology and chemistry of love and the nature of consciousness. And I want to place what is happening in our time in its larger evolutionary context. For more and more I have come to see that underlying the massive ferment of our time is an impasse in our cultural evolution: an impasse that can only be resolved through fundamental changes in how we construct human relations, including our most intimate personal relations.

I also want to speak of something still generally ignored in discussions about personal and social change: the human body. Because stripped to its essentials, social and personal transformation revolves around matters that directly involve the human body. It revolves around how we image our bodies, both our own and those of others. It revolves around who should have the power to define these images. It revolves around how we are touched and in turn touch the bodies of others. And ultimately it revolves around fundamental changes in consciousness about how two very different kinds of power—the power to inflict pain on the body and the power to give it pleasure—can be socially constructed, and thus what kind of power is most highly valued and rewarded or devalued and not rewarded.

The Politics of the Body

One of the most dramatic changes that occurred in my own consciousness in the course of writing this book is that I have become acutely aware that how we image the human body plays a central role in how we image the world—and that this in turn directly impacts how we view ourselves in relation to both. I had long been aware of important feminist writings that directly or indirectly address these issues, from Kate Millett's *Sexual Politics* and Adrienne Rich's *Of Woman Born* to more recent works such as Carter Heyward's *Touching Our Strength* and Paula Cooey's, Sharon Farmer's, and Mary Ellen Ross's *Embodied Love.*[3] But now, more vividly than ever before, and from a new perspective, I began to see that how sex, power, and love are conceptualized at a particular time and place cannot be understood, much less changed, without also understanding, and changing, how we image our bodies as women and men. I also began to understand, on a far deeper level than before, that the way we view our bodies, what we do with our bodies, and who has the power to decide both, are intensely political.

In fact, in terms of the contemporary struggle to leave behind entrenched patterns of domination and violence, they are key political issues. How we image the relations between bodies—and most critically, how we experience these relations in our own bodies—is not only a metaphor for politics in its most basic sense of the way power is defined and exercised. It is how we first unconsciously learn, and continually reenact, the way our human bodies are supposed to relate in all relations, in both what has traditionally been defined as the public and the private spheres.

If early on, in our intimate parent-child relations, and then in our intimate sexual relations, we become conditioned to accept domination and submission as normal, these patterns will unconsciously affect all our relations. Conversely, if early on, in our parent-child relations, and then in our sexual relations, we learn and continually practice mutual respect and caring, it will be very difficult for us to fit into a social system of force-and-fear-backed rankings of domination.

This is why the reconceptualization of the female body from a symbol of sexual and spiritual power to an object under the control of men was integral to the prehistoric shift to a dominator social organization.[4] This reconceptualization of the female body as an object to be controlled by someone outside that body had a number of important results. It certainly justified men's domination and exploitation of women's bodies— be it as instruments for procreation and/or recreation, or to render men services and work in their households. It also gradually led women themselves to image their bodies from a male perspective shaped by the dictates of a dominator system. For while the particular image varied from culture to culture—it could be a heavy or a thin image, an image of a distended neck, a mutilated foot, or mutilated genitals—it was an image that conformed primarily, not to women's own desires and needs, but to what the men in control defined as desirable in women. Even beyond this, in this new social order women themselves gradually learned to control their bodies and those of their daughters to conform to male requirements and tastes—a legacy we still struggle with today, as evidenced by anorexia, bulimia, and other eating disorders resulting from women's

compulsive attempts to reshape their bodies according to outside dictates, no matter how much pain is involved.

However, it was not only women but also men who were profoundly
affected by this externally determined, instrumental view of the human
body. For what now occurred was that the bodies of all women, and most
men, came to be viewed in terms of the needs and desires of those with
the greatest power to hurt, and thus exercise control over, the bodies of
others.

As we have seen, this was the prevailing view in the slave societies of
Western antiquity, where the bodies of all women and most men (the
slaves) were seen as possessions over which a small group of men had absolute life-and-death power. Moreover, in these highly warlike ancient societies, the mass of men were seen as instruments for this elite of men to
engage in power struggles, struggles in which he who could inflict the
most pain to the bodies of others won—yet another aspect of our dominator heritage we are still struggling with today. Which is why the highly
muscular, armored, tough male body of the warrior celebrated in Greek
heroic epics, along with an equally armored male psyche, became the
ideal norm for men,[5] who, in return for offering their own bodies for sacrifice, were then given the bodies of captured women—as we can still
read in the epics of Homer and in the Bible.

The view of the female body as merely male property also profoundly
affected the social construction of both female and male sexuality. Because if one body was there only to serve the other—to give it care, pleasure, and offspring—this not only provided a basic template for all
superior-inferior rankings; it also imposed a particular view of how the
bodies of women and men should relate in their most intimate sexual relations. And this view, which once again we are still struggling with
today, was that both women and sex are "naturally" to be controlled by
men.

This in turn required a number of mechanisms designed to maintain
the ranking of male over female. One, which we have already glimpsed,
is the vilification of both sex and woman. Another, which we will look at
in some depth, is the erotization of domination and violence—a mechanism that is central to the contemporary barrage of pornographic images
of men chaining, whipping, cutting, and in other ways causing pain to the
bodies of women.

Much of the debate about these images has focused on whether they
directly incite crimes of violence against women or whether they just desensitize those who perpetuate those crimes from perceiving that they are

causing pain, while at the same time creating an atmosphere of tolerance for this kind of behavior. But viewed in terms of the contemporary tension between a mounting movement toward partnership and the strong dominator systems resistance, the proliferation of these images can be seen as a response to the partnership thrust by a system that, at its most basic level, maintains itself by inflicting or threatening to inflict pain on the bodies of others.

These images of the human body, and of how two human bodies "pleasurably" relate to one another in ways that are physically and/or psychologically painful to one of the two, vividly communicate a social organization in which the highest power is the power symbolized by the blade: the power to cause pain and to destroy. Even beyond this, they condition us to unconsciously image human relations in terms of someone dominating and someone being dominated.

This is not to say that a dominator-dominated model of sexuality is the only way women and men are socialized to accept, and even welcome, repressive controls. As we will see, there are many other ways of socially conditioning us, in the words of the former Jesuit priest Don Hanlon Johnson, to "become *sensually*, not just attitudinally, obedient" to our "superiors."[6] There are the bodily habit patterns inculcated in us through the painful authoritarian child-rearing practices we will look at in the next chapter. Much of religious asceticism (which Johnson links to sexual sadomasochism) is also an effective way of accustoming the body to dominance and submission.[7] Then there is the threat of eternal bodily pain found in some dominator religions. As Johnson writes, a "profound source of Catholic authoritarianism" has been that "one may burn forever in one's personal flesh." For, as he notes, "with suffering of that order at stake, democracy is out of the question,"[8] since it is far too risky to rely on one's own (presumably flawed, tainted by "original sin") choices and perceptions, rather than on higher (presumably divinely ordained) authority.

Pain, Pleasure, and the Sacred

Before going any farther, I want to reiterate a point I made earlier: that underneath the overlay of dominator teachings and myths there is in Christianity and most other world religions an important partnership core. In fact, it is this core that accounts for the continuing appeal to many women and men of these faiths. However—and this is a matter we will later explore in some depth—the dominator elements in these religions have served, and continue to serve, as powerful means of conditioning women and men to accept, and even sanctify, unjust authority. Moreover, as Johnson notes, they have done this in ways that directly impact such basic matters as our bodies, pain, and pleasure.

Indeed, one of the most dramatic differences between the sacred imagery of the earlier, more partnership-oriented societies and many of our own images of the sacred relates to these basic matters of the body, pain, and pleasure. Because if we stop and look at the sacred images from our dominator heritage, we see that they focus far less on the giving of pleasure than on the infliction of pain—be it in battles between Olympian deities, bloody feuds between Hindu goddesses and gods, or Christ's crucifixion and the martyrdom of Christian saints.

This sacralizing of pain rather than pleasure makes eminent sense from a political perspective, since these images came out of societies in which the power to dominate and destroy represents the highest power. And it also makes sense that in these kinds of societies people have often been conditioned to associate pleasure with selfishness and insensitivity, and even, as we will explore in detail, with dominating or being dominated—and particularly in the case of sexual pleasure, with sadism and masochism, with hurting or being hurt.

All of which takes me directly to the title of this book, *Sacred Pleasure.* At first glance such a title may seem startling, even sacrilegious. But this is precisely why I chose it. Or more accurately, it is why as my own consciousness about both pleasure and the sacred was profoundly altered in the course of writing this book, the phrase "sacred pleasure" kept presenting itself as a way of conceptualizing both pleasure and the sacred that is very different from what we have been taught. For just as the social construction of the body and of power are different in dominator and partnership societies—with the most important symbol of power in the latter being the life-giving and illuminating chalice rather than the life-threatening and destroying blade—so also is the social construction of both pleasure and the sacred.

So when I use the term "sacred pleasure," it is by no means the kind of "holy" pleasure Christian women and men were during the Middle Ages encouraged to derive from self-inflicted tortures and abuses of their bodies. It is certainly not the kind of "pleasure" men were said by Freud to derive from humiliating and debasing women through sexual intercourse, as when he asserted that "as soon as the sexual object fulfills the condition of being degraded, sensual feeling can have free play and considerable sexual capacity and a high degree of pleasure can be developed."[9] Neither is it the kind of "pleasure" people have been taught to derive from the ridicule of others falling down, having pies thrown in their faces, or otherwise being humiliated or hurt. It is also not the kind of "pleasure" we are supposed to derive from winning wars, as when Christians (or Muslims) celebrated the slaughter of infidels in their holy Crusades or, in our time, after the Gulf War, when the United States was full of celebratory joy—with hardly a mention of the thousands of Iraqi men, women, and children maimed and killed. Nor by any stretch of the imagination is it the same view of the sacred conveyed by thousands of religious representations of cruelty and sacrifice—of the human body pierced, crucified, incinerated, impaled, and otherwise hideously tormented—that to our day fill both our museums and our churches.

But I also want to say that my awareness that we have been taught to think of both pleasure and the sacred in very strange ways did not come just as I wrote this book. It came out of a very slow awakening, something akin to what mystics have described as the lifting away one after another of many veils concealing that which we call spiritual or divine. Only what I found in the course of my own spiritual journey—a sometimes tortuous and sometimes joyous quest that took me not to some isolated mountain but to a new way of looking at my day-to-day life—was very different from what I had been led to expect.

I began to recognize that my most important and most deeply felt spiritual moments—the moments when I most intensely felt that inexpressible awe and wonder at the mystery of life—had been possible not because of my social conditioning to associate the sacred with some all-powerful ever-judging entity, but despite it. I also began to see that spiritual development is not something different and apart from such earthly pleasures as sexual ecstasy and loving touch—be it of a child or a lover. On the contrary, I gradually began to understand that these experiences were at the core of my own spiritual development. And I also began to understand, not just on a theoretical but on an experiential level, the urgency of my need to untangle what I had been taught about both pleasure and the sacred.

Still, it was only as I wrote this book that I started to sort some of this out, and most important, that I began to put the many pieces I discovered along the way together in terms of a very different kind of sacredness: one appropriate for a partnership rather than dominator view of what is holy. This is a sacredness that is of this world, rather than of some disembodied, otherworldly realm—a sacredness that derives from a reverence for life, not for what comes after death or before birth. It is a sacredness that does not make a sharp divide between us and what we call the divine. Above all, it is a sacredness that does not view the bodily or carnal as lesser, and therefore unimportant, but rather as an essential part of what, in its basic or integral sense, is holy.

So when I speak of a partnership rather than dominator spirituality, it is in this holistic sense of the word, where what happens on this earth and in our own and others' bodies is *not* divorced from our so-called higher selves. This is why the works of theologians such as Carol Christ, Matthew Fox, Elizabeth Dodson Gray, and Carter Heyward focusing on an immanent spirituality are so important.[10] For I believe that spirituality is *both* immanent and transcendent—and that the integration of the two lies at the core of the spirituality that is today in bits and pieces emerging as part of the contemporary struggle to shift from a dominator to a partnership world.

This partnership spirituality will express *both* our human need for connection in the bodily sense—as in physical union with the loved one— *and* our yearning for oneness with what we call the divine. And rather than presenting great suffering as the road to higher consciousness, and even as the essential attribute of a divine savior, it will focus on showing how we can attain higher consciousness, and thus union with what we call divine, through the great joy that has uniquely and miraculously been given us as human beings to experience from loving and being loved. But once again, this will *not* be love in the abstract. Since this will be a spirituality that derives from a sense of connection rather than detachment, it will also be a spirituality in which love is not otherworldly but very much of this world.

The Human Yearning for Connection

I think one of the great tragedies of Western religion as most of us have known it has been its compartmentalized view of human experience, and particularly its elevation of disembodied or "spiritual" love over embodied or "carnal" love. As we have seen, this compartmentalized view of human experience is not unique to the West. And it is certainly not unique to religion. For instance, the common wisdom (part of our legacy from both ancient Greek philosophers and medieval Christian savants) is that sexual sensations are of a "lower order," that love resides in the heart, and that what we today call higher consciousness is connected only with mental rather than physical states.

In fact, contemporary scientific research indicates that the locus of the sex drive is not in our genitals but in our brains. Even experiments on rats show that electrical stimulation of certain regions of the brain directly results in erections and/or ejaculations, without any genital stimulation whatsoever.[11] And it is not only scientific studies but our everyday experiences and observations that verify this. We know that sexual arousal can come from sexual pictures, or even sexual thoughts. Who a woman or man is sexually attracted to, in all its idiosyncratic variations, is largely a function of something that happens in our minds. And how we interpret states of both sexual and emotional arousal, and what actions we take or do not take as a consequence, are largely determined by what we have learned to think and feel rather than by any innate or mechanical physical drives or "instincts."

The emotion of love likewise involves our brains. In fact, all feelings and sensations—be they associated with sex, spirituality, or love—are in humans mediated by what psychologists call cognition or thought, which is processed in our brains. But since our brains are part of our bodies, it is in our bodies that we physically experience all feelings and sensations, regardless of whether they are conventionally labeled higher or lower.

Thus, it is actually what happens in our bodies that brings on spiritual or trancelike states. People experiencing "higher" states of consciousness, such as yoga masters, often engage in rigorous bodily exercises and are able to sit for hours in positions that most of us could sustain for only a few minutes. This physical dimension of spiritual states is now also being documented in a growing scientific literature on what researchers call altered states of consciousness (in scientific shorthand, ASCs). Experiments show that meditative or trancelike states involve measurable changes in the electrical activity of the brain (or brain waves) as measured by electroencephalographs.

Most interesting, and relevant to what we are exploring, is that sexual orgasm is also increasingly recognized as an altered state of consciousness—as indeed it is.[12] As Julian Davidson writes in *The Psychobiology of Consciousness*, although there are immense individual differences (as there also are in the experiences of individuals in other ASCs), "all orgasms share some of the criteria found in full-blown ASCs." These include changes in "the senses of space, time, identity, as well as strong emotions and great changes in motor output." And as Davidson also notes, "orgasms have been used extensively to induce mystical states."[13]

So it is not surprising that, as we saw in Part I, mystics have often described their experiences in the language of sex. Or that the common—and central—word in the language of both sexual passion and spiritual illumination is love.

This common theme of love in the literature (and experience) of both sexuality and spirituality is not coincidental. It reflects an underlying link that prehistoric civilizations seem to have intuited and modern science is beginning to rediscover. For while we have been taught that human sexuality (which is a striving for connection or oneness), the emotion of love (which is again a striving for connection or oneness), and the spiritual striving for union or oneness with what we call the divine are completely different from one another, at opposite poles, in reality they all stem from the same deeply rooted human need: our powerful human yearning for connection.

Because this yearning is in our species so powerful and so persistent, I believe it is biologically based. This is not to say that only humans have a strong striving for connection. Actually this striving is a recurrent evolutionary theme. Its earliest roots go back billions of years, to the symbiotic union of single cells into the first multicelled organisms that the biologist Lynn Margulis aptly called the first partnership between life forms on our planet.[14] Among colonies of insects, swarms of birds, schools of fish, and herds of mammals, this need for connection is expressed in what we call the grouping or herding instinct, which enhances survival through the greater safety of being close together in large numbers. In life forms as diverse as ladybugs, kittens, monkeys, and humans, we see evidence of a need for physical connection through touch. This physical connection through touch is integral to the survival of species that reproduce by sexual mating. And particularly in mammals, touching is essential for the survival of offspring, who would die without adult protection and care.

But although the striving for connection is by no means unique to our species, it is most highly developed in humans. This is due to a number of peculiarly human traits. Notable among these are the much longer period of helpless dependency of human infants, the human female's capacity for nonseasonal sex and multiple orgasms, and humanity's much greater mental capacities, which play such an important part in the phenomenon we call consciousness.

Looked at from this larger perspective, it becomes apparent that, contrary to prevailing views, humanity's highly developed mental capacities are not of such a different evolutionary order from our highly developed capacities (and needs) for female-male and adult-infant connection. Rather, these are all related evolutionary developments: developments that came together in the emergence of our species. Specifically, they are the evolutionary developments that together give our species the potential for two uniquely human—and related—characteristics. One is the phenomenon we call higher consciousness. The second is the complex of feelings and behaviors that in the realm of both spirituality and sexuality we call love.

The Evolution of Love, Language, and Consciousness

Obviously unloving, cruel, and violent sexual and nonsexual relations are also possibilities for our species. But the evolution in humans of our highly developed potential for the conscious and caring connectivity we call love offers us the basis for a more balanced and fulfilling way of relating to one another and our planet—a way that recognizes our essential interconnection with one another and the rest of nature.

The main evolutionary development emphasized in the emergence of our species is the human brain. And it is our brain (combined with our vocal cords) that directly accounts for the fact that ours is the only species that can communicate through the complex symbols we call words.[15] But as the biologists Humberto Maturana and Francisco Varela note, it is our frontal and nonseasonal human sexuality (combined with the long period of physical dependency of the products of that sexuality) that seems to have provided a major impetus for what they call "a biology of cooperation and a linguistic coordination of action."[16]

Other scholars, for example Adrienne Zihlman and Nancy Tanner, also attribute both the first human social bonds and the origin of language to the need, in a species where there is such a long maturation period, for mothers and infants to communicate. They point out that those infants whose mothers could interact with them through language, instructing, cautioning, and supporting their development, would have a greater chance of survival. And they note that this in turn would have tended to further promote physiological changes (such as larger brain capacity, smaller mandibles, and a large space for a larynx) that also mark the shift to our human species, and with it, the development of language.[17]

Maturana and Varela, however, specifically relate the emergence of language as a human tool to facilitate sharing and cooperation to sex, arguing that the development of language as a means of communicating in intimate relations was facilitated by the human female's year-round sexuality. They note that this would have tended to promote more sustained and cooperative contacts between females and males, and thus more need and opportunity to communicate. And they stress that although many species of birds and fish as well as a number of mammals and primates also have strong male participation in the care of the young, the possibility in humans for year-round sexual bonding between females and males would encourage males to take a more active caretaking role—an important development for a species with an extremely long period of early helplessness.[18]

So, in contrast to what we still find in much of the sociobiological literature, Maturana and Varela emphasize the differences between human and animal sexuality. They also recognize that we are fundamentally different from other animals in still another major respect: our highly developed capacity for awareness of self as distinct from (and at the same time interconnected with) others—in other words, for consciousness. And once again they believe that this too is a development inextricably connected with the emergence of human sexuality.

As they put it, it is "in the intimacy of recurrent individual interactions, which personalize the other individual with a linguistic distinction such as a name," that "the conditions may have been present for the appearance of a self as a distinction in a linguistic domain."[19] And while a few other life forms, such as our primate cousins the gorillas and the chimpanzees, seem to have some capacity to reflect upon themselves, the capacity for conceptual thinking and imaging is clearly most highly developed in our species.[20]

It should therefore also not surprise us that it is in humans that we see the highest development of consciousness. Nor should it surprise us—given our much more developed capacity for communication as well as our capacity for year-round sexual bonding and our need for intimate childhood connections—that we find in humans the highest development of what Maturana calls the "biology of love."[21]

The Biology and Chemistry of Love

Maturana's use of the term *love* may seem to border on the poetic—after all, poetry is the characteristic literature of love. But although the phrase "biology of love" initially takes one aback, there is little question that the human need for love stems from a biological fact: that without love, without at least some measure of caring connections or bonds, we humans do not survive.

We clearly cannot survive as infants without the physical caring of being fed and sheltered. And we also cannot survive without the physical caring of touch—as studies of babies who die for no apparent physical reason in institutions without any loving touching tragically confirm.[22] As the anthropologist Ashley Montagu writes in his pioneering work on this subject, *Touching*,[23] it is from loving touch that we derive our most intense physical and emotional feelings. It is from loving touch that we obtain not only pleasure but also comfort when we are in pain, hope when we despair, and even beyond this, that indispensable sense that we are, after all, not alone in this world but connected with others of our kind.

So, as Maturana writes, it is no exaggeration to say that we humans literally "depend on love and we get sick when it is denied to us at any point in our lives."[24] This is why Maturana asserts that the biology of love is not only the basis for human society but a dynamic deeply imbedded in the history of evolution. It begins with what he describes as the "toleration of another creature in one's own space" found among so many insects, birds, mammals, and other animals. And it culminates in our species with the powerful conscious emotion celebrated in both our secular and religious literature as the most important—and in the spiritual sense of the word, noblest—human experience.

How this emotion became so powerful is also today being reexamined by scientists. And what they are discovering offers an arresting new perspective on still another extraordinary, though still generally ignored, evolutionary development: the evolution of pleasure.

New studies indicate that in the course of evolution, nature began to experiment with chemical rewards that provide our bodies with enormous pleasure both when we are loved and when we are loving to others. What seems to have happened is this. Chemicals such as endorphins (short for endogenous morphines) may originally have come into play primarily as opiates, to mask the pain from a wound and/or provide additional energy for flight from a predator.[25] But at a certain point in evolution, these chemicals acquired a new and very different function. Now, instead of just helping an organism deal with pain in a fight-or-flight situation, these pleasure-inducing chemicals served to promote the bonding involved in the caretaking—and even beyond this, the caring touch—required for the survival of more complex species.[26]

As the psychiatrist Michael Liebowitz writes in *The Chemistry of Love*, it is this reward by chemicals that in our species probably explains the euphoria of "falling in love." For this state, as well as the intense pleasures of sexual love, seems to be associated with rising levels of certain chemicals, probably phenylethylamine, an amphetamine-like substance. Such chemical rewards are most probably also a factor in the pleasure mothers, fathers, and other adults (as well as children) can derive from caring for babies and why people in loving relationships speak of a great sense of contentment—in other words, pleasure. For here again chemicals, probably endorphins, come into play.[27]

Although these studies have only begun, and conclusions are still speculative, they may eventually also help explain the states of euphoric bliss that mystics through the ages have associated with love for the divine. And they may even help us better understand what lies behind the intense pleasure we feel in moments of creation, discovery, aesthetic contemplation, and helpfulness to others.

Most important, what we are now learning about the evolution of both love and pleasure points to the need for some reevaluations of evolutionary theories. For these studies support the conclusion that, like the evolution of sex and consciousness, the evolution of love was a major turning point in the movement toward more complex or highly developed life forms on our planet. They show that when we speak of adaptation we can no longer gloss over our capacity for love—and that in fact the most adaptive development in the evolution of our own species seems to have been the development of our great human capacity for love, and not, as some earlier theorists claimed, our capacity for great violence and aggression.

Moreover, what this new line of inquiry indicates is that the evolution of human love and the evolution of human sexuality are part of a much larger movement. This is the evolutionary movement from the primacy of the punishment of pain to the primacy of the reward of pleasure—and very specifically, pleasure from love—as a major motivator for adaptive behaviors.

The Push of Evolution and the Challenge of Transformation

Viewed from this larger perspective, the powerful contemporary movement to complete the shift from a dominator to a partnership society would seem to be animated by nothing less than the push of evolution. And this is not just because, in our high technology age of hydrogen bombs and holes in the ozone layer, the requirements for maintaining human life and the requirements for maintaining a dominator form of social organization are on a direct collision course. It is because, in any age, the partnership model, which promotes rather than impedes both love and pleasure, appears to be more congruent with the movement of evolution toward what in the normative or valuative sense of the word we call more highly evolved.[28]

This evolutionary movement has been of interest to a number of scholars, including Darwin himself. Despite the fact that today neo-Darwinians consider it a heresy to speak of any kind of movement toward "higher" levels of functioning in evolution, as Robert J. Richards (a leading authority on Darwin) writes, Darwin postulated four stages in the evolution of what he called the moral sense, which he considered "the most important distinguishing feature of human nature."[29] The first was when animals developed social instincts that would bind together closely related individuals. The second was the evolution of greater intellect. The third came with the acquisition of language. And the fourth, Darwin believed, was reached when certain habits could come to mold the conduct of individuals.[30]

Similarly, the biologist Julian Huxley in *Evolution in Action* wrote of "new possibilities" and "the emergence of new qualities of experience."[31] More recently, the psychologist Abraham Maslow wrote of a progression from deficiency or defense needs (which all forms of life share) to higher needs he calls "self-actualization" drives—which he sees as a potentiality of "human nature."[32] And building on Darwin's observations about the origins and development of a moral sense along with the findings of modern brain research, the social psychologist David Loye has constructed a new theory of the gradual evolution of our species' potential for what he calls moral sensitivity.[33]

I should here add that the perspective of these scholars is very different from that of Herbert Spencer and other social Darwinists, who tended to see our species' capacity for manipulating our physical and social environment as some kind of evolutionary apex, and used this conclusion to glorify the "evolutionary success" of predatory nineteenth-century industrialists. It is also very different from that of a priori theorists such as Teilhard de Chardin,[34] who argued that behind evolution lies the unfolding of a preordained divine plan. For example, the astrophysicist Eric Chaisson writes that "rather than claim that cosmic evolution has been teleologically guided by an intelligent or mindful Universe," in his view "the phenomenon of intelligence has, is, and will continue to develop naturally via the principles of cosmic evolution."[35] But (and this is also a subtext for *cultural transformation theory*) these scholars do not ignore the fact that if we look at the whole span of the history of life on our planet, there *are* observable changes from earlier to later levels—as dramatically exemplified by our species' unique potentials for sensitivity to others, creativity, aesthetic sensibility, and love.

However, as we saw in Part I, it is precisely these potentials that must be distorted and blocked in societies orienting primarily to domination rather than partnership if the system—which is one of rankings backed by force and fear of pain—is to be maintained. So it is not only that in terms of simple survival the dominator model is not adaptive in our high technology age. Regardless of a society's technological development, there is a conflict between the requirements for maintaining dominator systems and the requirements for our full development as a species.

If, as appears to be the case, the evolution of human sexuality and our very long period of childhood dependency led to our uniquely powerful human yearning for connection—and with this, to the great pleasure we humans derive from loving and being loved—then a social organization oriented more to partnership than domination is more congruent with our biological evolution. And if, as also appears to be the case, this was the earlier direction of Western cultural evolution—as reflected in a sacred imagery in which the taking of life is virtually absent and the giving and nurturing of life is venerated—then it should be possible for us to meet the great contemporary challenge of fundamental personal, cultural, and social transformation.

But it is one thing to say this, and quite another to say we will inevitably succeed. Blocking transformation are deeply entrenched cultural patterns and institutions. Moreover, a basic tenet of modern evolutionary theory is that what happens in the history of our planet is not predetermined. Just as there is nothing inevitable in the appearance of a species, or in whether a species dies out or survives, there is nothing inevitable about the direction of human cultural evolution.

Today, all around us, once firmly established beliefs and institutions are being challenged, as the old dominator system is disintegrating, moving us ever closer to chaos. But this does not mean that a new partnership culture will inevitably emerge. As *cultural transformation theory* states, during periods of social disintegration or extreme systems disequilibrium there is an opportunity for transformative social and ideological change. However, there is another possible outcome. This is for the dominator system to reconstitute itself in seemingly new institutional and ideological forms that merely co-opt some partnership elements while still preserving the same basic configuration that provides social and economic rewards for domination and conquest and idealizes, and even sacralizes, pain. Hence, as during any other systems bifurcation, more than disequilibrium is required for a different social organization to emerge. What is needed are enough nodules of transformative change to, in the language of nonlinear dynamics, form a new "attractor" that can—while the system is in flux—reconstitute it in a new basic configuration.[36]

The awareness, today mounting all over our world, that we urgently need to alter our institutions and values is a hopeful sign in this direction. But if we are to successfully use this period of both crisis and opportunity to complete the shift from a dominator to a partnership model as the primary cultural attractor, we need to go much deeper. We need to address not only how a society constructs its economic, political, religious, and educational institutions, but also how it constructs such basics as sexuality, gender, and spirituality—and even beyond this, how it uses pain and pleasure to maintain itself.

I should here say that because fundamental change entails the dismantling of many existing beliefs and institutions, the contemporary struggle to complete the shift from a dominator to a partnership social and ideological organization inevitably entails pain—a subject I will return to. I also want to say that even if we succeed in our efforts to leave behind a system that so heavily relies on pain for its maintenance, we will still have pain.

Pain, as well as pleasure, is part of evolution and of life. In fact, in some ways pain can be very useful, not only as a warning that we must heed but as an avenue to both personal and spiritual growth. However, in dominator systems, we cannot even make full use of pain for this purpose, since one of the effects of chronic pain is a blunting of both perception and emotion.

This is one reason there is so much talk today of coming out of denial, of becoming conscious of our pain. Indeed, some of what follows will be painful. But much of it will also be heartening, and even funny.

Certainly the challenge of fundamentally transforming ourselves and our world—even to the extent of changing how we think about our bodies, sex, power, pleasure, and the sacred—is a daunting one. But if there is one constant in evolution it is change. Change is quite literally the essence of what we call evolution, be it biological or cultural. Except that what we will deal with in the pages that follow is a brand new chapter in this creative adventure: the amazing, sometimes amusing, story of how, for the first time in the history of our planet, women and men are *consciously* trying to recreate nothing less than how we live and love.

Waking from the Dominator Trance: The Revolution in Consciousness and the Sexual Revolution

During the second half of the twentieth century, people began to talk of a revolution in consciousness: of radical changes in how we view our world. According to some, the triggering event was the explosion in 1945 of the first atom bomb, alerting us to the possibility of nuclear extinction. According to others, it was the first photos from outer space of our beautiful, ever more threatened planet. According to still others, it was the breakneck speed of the technological, social, and economic changes pushing us toward a "postindustrial" world.

This same period brought important changes in sexual attitudes and behaviors—what the media hailed as a sexual revolution. There were also fundamental changes in the structure of the family. And there was a resurgence of feminism, as women all over the world challenged stereotypical gender roles and relations, and with this, the five-thousand-year entrenchment of male dominance.

These were all major changes. However, they are part of a much larger drama that can only be understood within the broader context of modern history and, even beyond this, the history of consciousness. For, as we will see, they represent only the latest phase in our gradual awakening— as if from a long, painful trance—from the mind-and-body-numbing effects of millennia of recorded, or dominator, history.

Actually these changes in consciousness—in how people see themselves, their relationships, and the world—began in the West as far back as the Renaissance and the end of the Middle Ages. But they were vastly accelerated during the later stages of the Industrial Revolution, which brought massive technological and economic changes that in turn forced major changes not only in work habits but in habits of thinking and living. Such fundamental changes in their turn required much social restructuring, as well as a reevaluation of many long-established "truths." In the process, thanks in large part to the today much maligned Enlightenment, many things that had until then been thought inevitable—slavery, the divine right of kings to rule, the idea that woman's sexuality poses a threat to man's moral and spiritual well-being—began to be reexamined and rejected.[1]

In short, the major technological, economic, and social upheavals that marked the onset of the modern era about three hundred years ago opened the door for a ground swell of partnership resurgence, more powerful than any before. For if from the new perspective of *cultural transformation theory* we take a fresh look at modern Western history, we see that underneath its complex currents and crosscurrents lies the struggle between a mounting partnership thrust and an equally fierce dominator resistance.[2] And we also see that this struggle is not just over political and economic relations; it is, and all along has been, over sexual, gender, and family relations—with the common thread being the challenge to a system based on rankings ultimately backed by force and the fear of pain.

If it has been difficult to see this, it is because most of what we are taught about modern history still focuses on relations between men in the so-called public sphere. But if we reexamine modern history from a perspective in which intimate relations are not viewed as merely incidental, what emerges is a larger, more realistic picture. We then see that the growing awareness that we can make fundamental changes in how men relate to women and in how parents (and other adults) relate to children is integrally related to the modern consciousness that fundamental changes in economic and political relations are possible. And we also see that changes in these intimate relations are not only basic, but in many ways even more important.

For even if it were possible to create a more just and equitable political and economic system without attention to our personal relations—which of course it is *not*—we would still be lacking what human beings so passionately want and need: the fulfillment of truly loving and equitable intimate relations based on mutual respect, caring, and trust.

Modern History and the History of Intimate Relations

For thousands of years, our human need for connection—for bonds forged by love and trust rather than by force and the fear of pain—has been distorted and suppressed. Only by turning woman-man relations into a "war of the sexes" in which women are deemed inferior and dangerous to men, and by conditioning both women and men to accept and condone domination through abuse and violence in parent-child relations, could a system of rigid rankings be maintained.

Still, the yearning for connection persisted. Sometimes, despite all the obstacles, it miraculously found fulfillment. More often, it manifested itself in quiet and not-so-quiet desperation and in the all-too-common obsessive and even violent torment that is the stuff of so many romantic poems and songs. Also, sometimes obsessively and even violently, it sought expression through what we call the spiritual quest, the search for union or oneness with the divine that is the central theme of both Eastern and Western mysticism.

But not until modern times did our powerful human yearning for connection begin to again find collective expression. Gradually, as new technologies destabilized entrenched habits, beliefs, and institutions, there emerged the wide range of social, political, and economic movements that during recent centuries have frontally challenged violence and domination as inevitable in human relations.

In the eighteenth century, the leading philosopher of political democracy, John Locke, proposed that freely chosen representative governments based on responsibility and trust replace autocratic monarchs who for millennia had ruled through force and fear.[3] During that same century, the leading philosopher of capitalism, Adam Smith, offered the "invisible hand" of the free marketplace as a way to end top-down economic control. In the following century, the framers of scientific socialism, Karl Marx and Friedrich Engels, wrote of a time when the state itself might wither away and all power would be in the hands of the people. During that century, Frederick Douglass, Sojourner Truth, and other leaders in the struggle against racism challenged the idea that "superior" races should dominate, exploit, and even enslave "inferior" races. Also in the nineteenth century, Elizabeth Cady Stanton, Hedwig Dohm, Matilda Joslyn Gage, Emmeline Pankhurst, and other leading philosophers of modern feminism wrote of a society where the female and male halves of humanity would no longer be forced into dominator-dominated rankings.[4]

The nineteenth-century abolitionist and pacifist movements and the twentieth-century anticolonial, civil rights, peace, and women's movements shared this cumulating goal of building systems of relations free of painful domination and exploitation. And so also have the far less publicized eighteenth-, nineteenth-, and twentieth-century movements toward a more egalitarian and companionate form of marriage, as well as the movement during this same time—often against vehement secular and religious opposition—to leave behind long-standing traditions of painful punishment of children. In other words, although this is almost never brought out in our history books, at the same time that people began to awake to the brutality and injustice of political, economic, and racial rankings backed by force and fear, there was also, albeit more slowly, a gradual awakening to the brutality and injustice of rankings backed by fear and force in parent-child and man-woman relations.[5]

As we have seen, for much of recorded history the absolute—often life-and-death—authority of the male head of household over women and children was taken for granted. Male violence against women who disobeyed their husbands' orders, or who were suspected of sexual transgressions, was considered only natural and right. Corporeal punishment of children—often in extremely cruel forms—was likewise accepted as not only necessary but, according to some religious writings, decreed by God.[6]

This is not to say that after the fundamental restructuring of the Western family we examined in Part I there was not, even in the most rigid dominator households, some caring and affection. As we saw in Part I, even in the brutally androcratic societies of antiquity there were women and men who really loved each other. There were also undoubtedly loving mothers and fathers who found pleasure in caring for their children. Indeed, since ours is a species that cannot survive infancy without at least some degree of caring and caretaking, there had to be.

But there is little question that in most of these households caring and caretaking were contingent on obedience to authority, and thus consciously or unconsciously tinged with fear of some kind of pain. There is also little question that, as Frances and Joseph Gies write in *Marriage and the Family in the Middle Ages*, "the egalitarian family in which husband and wife share authority and in which democracy extends in some degree to the children, is a modern invention"—or more properly reinvention, since this statement is only true of recorded or dominator history and also ignores partnership-oriented families in some contemporary tribal societies.[7]

Moreover, there is little question that until modern times (and in far too many places still today) violence—usually in the name of sound pedagogy—has been central to what is still sometimes referred to as "traditional" child rearing.[8] There is disagreement as to how extreme and uniform this was. But we know that inflicting bodily pain on children for any kind of disobedience, and even as a corrective for what adults considered a faulty performance, was common in both homes and schools.

Even the cruel custom of swaddling, originally a nomadic-pastoralist "adaptation" to long forced journeys through arid lands, was still common practice in Germany as late as 1864. As Henry Mayhew writes in his book *German Life and Manners as Seen in Saxony at the Present Day* (c. 1864), babies were still in some places as late as the nineteenth century "wound up, in Heaven knows how many ells of bandages, from the feet right, and tight, up to the neck," as if they were mummies, with the bandages only removed once, at most twice a day.[9] Moreover, this cruel pinioning (and the terrible discomfort of being immobilized in their own excrement) was only one way of traumatically habituating children to violent restraint. As Lloyd deMause harrowingly details, "other restraint devices were common"—such as the "hideous engine of torture" (as one woman described it) that in her childhood "held her fast against a steel rod up her spine to a steel collar around her neck."[10]

That this kind of cruelty was not just an exceptional perversion is verified by the fact, as James Thomas Flexner reports, that even Martha Washington felt steel collars should be worn by girls at Mt. Vernon to force them to hold their heads up.[11] It is further verified by studies such as that of Raffael Scheck, who pored through the autobiographies of seventy people born in Germany between 1740 and 1840 (already a time when such methods were beginning to be questioned). He found they uniformly reported severe bodily violence as routine in both their homes and schools (with several reports of brothers and sisters actually killed by violence at the hands of parents or teachers).[12]

In other words, there are ample data showing that this violence was not just symptomatic of an occasional individual pathology but of a social pathology—or more specifically, of the dominator systems-maintenance requirement that people be taught from childhood on to conform to authority through fear of bodily pain. In fact, so deeply ingrained was the view that teaching obedience and subservience is a parental duty that Karen Taylor's study of child-rearing practices in nineteenth-century Boston and Melbourne found that even those who by then doubted that routine physical violence against children is pedagogically sound still advocated it by way of exemplary punishment—to "teach the child that the parents' will is supreme." There were even some who proposed, as a "better alternative" to beatings, that parents establish the "habit of obedience" by tying their children to a chair or lightly burning a child's fingers with hot tea.[13]

Because there is so much documentation of the prevalence of violent and abusive child-rearing practices, some historians—for example, Philippe Ariès, Lloyd deMause, and Edward Shorter[14]—paint a picture of almost unrelieved darkness, giving the impression of almost total parental indifference to children's suffering. They point to research indicating that among both the nobility and the "common people," children were routinely sent away by their parents to wet nurses; that among aristocrats, children were generally raised by hired tutors or governesses; that the poor often sent their children away to work as apprentices or servants when they were still very small; and that from the Middle Ages to the nineteenth century, European children were frequently abandoned along roads and in marketplaces or left in foundling homes, where only a small proportion survived.[15] But others, such as Frances and Joseph Gies, see a less monochromatic picture, arguing that the idea advanced by some of these scholars that until modern times parents had few tender feelings for their children makes no sense. But they too observe that abusive and unfeeling child-rearing methods were commonplace, adding that during much of recorded history the harsh circumstances of most women's and men's lives combined with the extremely high infant mortality rate tended to blunt people's tender feelings, even for their own children.[16]

Most scholars further recognize that for much of recorded history child sexual abuse seems to have been commonplace. Although this is hard for us to accept, there are indications that it was often considered normal. Because if we really think about it, what else is the custom we find in both Judeo-Christian and classical Greek records (and in some societies still today) of little girls sold or given away in marriage when they are still mere children? What else is the practice (also still found in some places today) of parents selling their little daughters into concubinage or prostitution? And what else, for that matter, was the socially accepted ancient Greek pederasty, the homosexual coupling of young boys and grown men?

Moreover, lest we think that childhood sexual abuse was confined to ancient dominator societies, there is strong evidence that in the nineteenth century the sexual abuse of children was still (as it is today) widespread. For example, Karen Taylor found in a survey of nineteenth-century medical literature that doctors often reported finding venereal disease on the genitals, anuses, and mouths of little girls and boys when their parents had the disease—a clear indication that these children were being sexually abused.[17]

The Family, Human Rights, and the Dominator Trance

Taylor, Flexner, Shorter, Ariès, deMause, Scheck, and the Gieses represent a new breed of historians focusing on the history of the family and sex. Poring through court documents, marriage and birth registries, diaries, letters, and other public and private records (often materials hidden in attics and other obscure places left behind by "ordinary people" rather than kings, nobles, and other "important" personages), these scholars are, for the first time, beginning to reconstruct a history of intimate relations—one I hope will one day be fully integrated into what we are taught about our past.

I say this for a number of reasons. One is that this information is important in its own right, as it gives us a far more accurate, and richer, picture than what we find in our history texts of how people actually lived their lives. But the main reason is that it is integral to an understanding of how a repressive and antihuman system has maintained itself—and most important, how it can be changed.

The prehistoric shift from a partnership to a dominator direction entailed a fundamental restructuring of the family. If we are to succeed in our efforts to reverse that shift, we need a much clearer understanding of how the social construction of family and other intimate relations is a major factor in how *all* social relations are constructed. For while it is by no means the whole story, how we are taught to view, and act in, our most intimate relations is a major factor in the social construction of all our relations.

Indeed, as psychologists have now amply documented, the way we see ourselves and our relations with others is not something primarily shaped in the so-called public sphere of politics and economics. Politics and economics certainly channel this shaping. Moreover, there is a constant interaction of the private with the public sphere, both of which are socially constructed to meet the demands of a particular social system. But ultimately, how we see ourselves in relation to others and to the world is largely shaped in the so-called private sphere of our family and other intimate relations. It is here that the patterns of thinking, feeling, and relating that become habitual to us are first acquired. It is through our intimate relations—relations that involve direct bodily contact or touch—

that these habits become entrenched not only in our minds but in our bodies, in our neural and muscular patterns. It is also through these relations that these habits are daily reinforced.[18]

Simply put, it is through our intimate relations, particularly during childhood when we are totally dependent on adults for survival, that we first learn to either respect the human rights of others or to accept human rights violations as "just the way things are." Although there have always been those who rebel, who consciously reject cruelty and injustice in all its forms, most people conditioned from childhood on to accept chronic human rights violations as normal are not likely to create a society where human rights are not also chronically violated. And a major reason for this relates to the psychological mechanism of denial—the suppression out of fear into the unconscious of authentic human needs, perceptions, and experiences—which makes possible the acceptance, and even idealization, of abusive and violent relations by both the dominated and the dominators.

As the psychohistorian Joe Berghold points out, what happens to the psyche of an abused child is similar to what happens in a hypnotic trance.[19] People in hypnotic trances are so influenced by another's suggestions—or more properly, commands—of what they should think, feel, and do that they suppress their own perceptions, feelings, and even will. But in the case of a chronically abusive childhood, this substitution of another's view of reality for one's own becomes habitual. Even one's own abuse, one's own pain, and one's own outrage at such injustice gradually become unreal, repressed into the deepest recesses of one's unconscious mind, or—as required to maintain a dominator system—legitimized as the way things are supposed to be.

Because of this, Berghold argues that real progress can only come as people begin to awaken from the "social trance" that is in vital part produced by what we are today beginning to recognize as traditions of child abuse.[20] This concept of a social trance has been used by other scholars, for example Willis Harman, who points out in *Global Mind Change* that acculturation in many ways works like hypnosis, and that what he terms the cultural trance of conformity has for a long time conditioned people to accept, rationalize, and in his words "legitimize" unjust institutions, oppressive leadership, and distorted images and role models.[21] But in his psychohistorical analysis, Berghold takes this concept from theory to the operations of everyday life.

Like Harman, Berghold believes that once we become truly conscious of how we have been acculturated, we can learn to transcend our conditioning. But his main point is that a history marked by submission to domination, manipulation, and exploitation can be explained in psychohistorical terms as the extension of that susceptibility from the personal to the larger political realm. He points to evidence that people who grow up in families where harsh punishments are the norm are much more susceptible to hypnosis. And he argues that people who in their childhoods are forced to suppress their own reality and accept instead the reality imposed upon them by those in authority, become as adults extremely susceptible to domination, manipulation, and exploitation.

There is certainly ample evidence that people who grow up in families where rigid hierarchies and painful punishments are the norm learn to suppress anger toward their parents. There is also ample evidence that this anger is then often deflected against traditionally disempowered groups (such as minorities, children, and women). Moreover, as the psychologist Else Frenkel-Brunswick documents in the classic work on this subject, *The Authoritarian Personality,* having been conditioned through childhood abuse to surrender their will to the requirements of feared authoritarian parents, such people also tend to be extremely susceptible as adults to surrender their will and minds to authoritarian leaders.[22] In other words, at the same time that they learn to deflect their repressed rage against those they perceive as weak, they also learn to submit to autocratic or "strong-man" rule. Moreover, having been severely punished for any hint of rebellion (even "talking back" about being treated unfairly), they gradually also learn to deny to themselves that there was anything wrong with what was done to them as children—and to in turn do it to their own children.

This psychological mechanism of denial helps explain why—as the Swiss psychoanalyst Alice Miller documents in *For Your Own Good: Hidden Cruelty in Child-Rearing and the Roots of Violence*[23]—generation after generation of parents and children have all too often unconsciously reenacted what was done to them. It helps explain why so many people have unquestioningly followed their "superiors'" orders, no matter how brutal they may be. It also helps explain why throughout history and even in our own time autocratic rulers have enjoyed the loyalty of so many people, even obtaining—as was demanded of these people in their families—their love.

Again I want to emphasize that these kinds of families do not spring up in a vacuum. Quite the contrary, what happens in authoritarian families—including the use of violence to impose authority—is a training to prepare people to fit into an authoritarian social system in which, to maintain rankings of domination, abuse and violence are built into the entire social structure. In other words, what we are here dealing with are interactive psychosocial dynamics that have traditionally involved not just the family but every other social institution in a lifelong process of socialization designed to teach us to view dominator "reality" as inevitable.

Furthermore—and this too is critical—this socialization operates not only on the mental and emotional level; it operates on the physical level, on the level of the body. In fact, it is on this bodily level that childhood conditioning is most effective and enduring, as it is here that authoritarian control is most traumatically experienced and the psychosomatic patterns required for the maintenance of dominator systems first become entrenched.

A dramatic example of how this works is provided by the anthropologist C. Fred Blake's analysis of how the deforming binding of girls' feet practiced for many centuries in prerevolutionary China functioned to teach women to accept, as the very essence of their sense of self, the most painful bending of not only their minds but their bodies to the will of others.[24] From the age of approximately five to thirteen or fourteen, the feet of little girls, not just in the ruling classes but in large sections of the population, were effectively crippled through an ordeal that impeded their bodies' natural development and growth. From the perspective of gender politics, foot binding was of central symbolic importance, molding Chinese social discourse (and hence thought processes) by programming both women and men to view the essence of femininity as conformity to male desires. But on the most fundamental level of cells and neural pathways, it did far more. It trained women from early childhood on to mold both their minds and bodies—and with this, what they imaged as their core identity or self—to the requirements of those in authority, regardless of the misery this entailed.

Moreover—and this too is crucial—the principal agent in this process, on both the symbolic level of describing what her place in the social system should be and on the physical level of becoming the kind of body the social system demanded, was the girl's own mother; in other words, one who herself had molded her body (and her sense of self) to conform to externally defined requirements. Thus, as Blake writes, mothers themselves not only modeled conformity to this equation of femininity and sacrifice of one's own desires, but constantly told their daughters that the sacrifice of their natural capacity to run, dance, and even walk without difficulty—as well as the excruciating pain, including "months, even years, of oozing sores, bandages stiff with dried puss and blood, and sloughed-off gobs of flesh"—were necessary if they were to find the right husband.[25]

Most important, it was also from their mothers that girls learned what Blake calls "the conflation of 'care' with 'pain'"[26]—and with this to themselves one day do the same to their own daughters in the name of love. It taught them to accept that the same touch they associated with love and pleasure should also be the coercive touch that caused them such excruciating pain. Beyond this, through both the foot binding and the punishments inflicted on them for removing their painful bandages, girls learned to suppress not only their own needs and desires but their feelings of rage against both their mothers and the men they had been told required this if they were to take them for wives.

In sum, the foot binding of Chinese girls served to condition women to accept a role in which, for all their lives, they would automatically defer to men and male desires as well as to all those in positions of authority. In that sense, it quite literally produced what, to expand Berghold's term, we may call a dominator trance, legitimizing as the only true, real, and cosmically grounded reality a dominator way of thinking and living. It also served as a vehicle for women to unconsciously deflect some of their rage and pain, *not* against those whose cruel wishes they were implementing, but against other women—specifically their own daughters—in a stunning example of how denial can work to maintain one's own subordination. And it perpetuated the replication, from generation to generation, of this mind-and-body-numbing confluence of care and hurt—and a system in which the human need for love is associated with submission to pain.

The Forward Push and the Backward Pull

As we have seen, to varying degrees this confluence of caring and hurting has been characteristic of dominator child rearing, as it is a very effective way of conditioning people to fit into a system of rankings ultimately backed up by the fear of pain. Sometimes, as in prerevolutionary China, we find more overt violence against little girls. Sometimes, as in some parts of the West today, there may be even more violence against little boys. In some cases, the confluence of caring and hurting is primarily psychological. But even then, because of how our bodies react to psychological abuse in the development of muscular and neural patternings, it is also physical. And it is these same patternings that in dominator societies serve as the basis for a social construction of sexuality that further reinforces the view that human relations are inevitably based on rankings of domination backed up by force or the fear of pain.

Therefore, if we are to shift to a social organization in which the human need for loving connection is no longer distorted and perverted through its association with coercion and the infliction or acceptance of pain, we need to interrupt the replication of these kinds of psychosomatic dynamics. We need to block the mass reproduction of the kind of culturally conditioned mind-set (or to borrow Marx's term, false consciousness) that makes abuse and violence seem inevitable at the same time that, through psychological dynamics such as shame and denial, abuse and violence are rendered invisible. In short, we need to find ways to help us wake from what, not just figuratively but in a very real sense, has been a social trance induced by the institutionalization of trauma that we examined in Part I. And the hopeful thing is that this is precisely what in starts and stops has been happening during the last three centuries, as changes in the relations between women and men and parents and children have gone hand in hand with the political and economic changes that, at least in some world regions, have gradually led to the replacement of despotic governments with more democratic ones.

I will later deal in some detail with the major part that changes in gender relations—and with this, also sexual relations—have played, and continue to play, in changing consciousness and culture. But here I want to stay with how during the last three centuries, particularly in the West, there have been major changes in the family—keeping in mind that these changes cannot be isolated from their larger social context, including changes not only in politics and economics but in gender relations and the social construction of sexuality.

Again, these changes in the family had already begun in the West toward the end of the Middle Ages. But it was not until the end of the eighteenth century, as the family historian Carl Degler notes, that the "modern" family began to emerge. It was still a family in which the male was ranked over the female in both custom and law. But it was also a family in which bonds of mutual affection between husband and wife and between parents and children were increasingly seen as more important than bonds of authority.

As a consequence, the domination of women by men, not only in the family but in society at large, began to be questioned by growing numbers of people—which in turn led to changes in gender roles and relations that, in their turn, profoundly affected parent-child relations. For example, Degler notes that as women gained more respect, the role of the mother—and along with this, a more gentle and loving ideal of parenting—gained more prominence.[27] Similarly, as young women were no longer under such strict parental control and were able to have more contact with young men, romantic love rather than parental orders was also increasingly accepted as the proper basis for marriage. Abusive and violent child-rearing was increasingly challenged. Even the double standard for sex, along with the notion that woman's sexuality must be rigidly controlled by men, was openly challenged—a subject we will also return to in some depth.

As we still see all around us today, these attempts to shift intimate relations from domination to partnership were only partly successful. In fact, by the end of the nineteenth century a massive dominator counteroffensive was also under way. Even so, there were important gains in the continuing democratization of both Western society and the Western family. And although there was enormous resistance all along the way and gains were lost through periodic setbacks, by the second half of the twentieth century, at the same time that the civil rights, anticolonial, women's liberation, and antiwar movements gained momentum, the challenge to relations based on domination in both the private and public spheres again accelerated.

There were obviously many other factors that led to these challenges—notably the economic and social upheavals brought by the gradual replacement in the West of an agrarian and rural economic base by one that was industrial and urban, as well as the accompanying growth in literacy and affordable reading materials. Moreover, with the incipient shift from a primarily manufacturing-based economy to what economists call a service and information economy, the pace of technological, social, and economic change escalated still further, opening the door for even further changes in consciousness—which could now be spread even more quickly through electronic technologies of communication.

But a major factor in these vast changes has been the continuing awakening of masses of people from their dominator trance—an awakening further accelerated by the emergence of the social sciences, particularly by the gradual acceptance of modern psychology as both a new scientific discipline and a new therapy. For what this particular change brought is an insight we today take for granted: that we need to understand painful events in our childhoods, particularly within the psychodynamics of our families, if we are to understand, and successfully change, the way we think, feel, and act.

Clearly, personal, familial, and social change involves far more than an awareness of what happened to us as children. But as we have seen, this growing awareness of the buried side to childhood has been a very important part of the modern revolution in consciousness. As more people have begun to more accurately perceive what was done to them as children, they in turn have tried to leave behind their "instructions" to be abusive and violent to their own children. This in turn has contributed to a further awareness (or lessening of denial) about domination and brutality in both the private and public spheres. Most important, with this awakening from the trancelike acceptance of a chronically painful way of structuring human relations has come the consciousness that there are alternatives to the chronic suffering caused by rankings of domination.

Most recently, as this revolution in consciousness begins to shift into its second stage, changes in beliefs, behaviors, and institutions have been further accelerated by the efforts of grassroots organizations working for women's rights and children's rights (a subject I will return to), as well as by the new attention in both the mass media and the law to widespread patterns of sexual violence against women and children. Once again these changes are also being accelerated by the spread of family therapy and by self-help movements that expose the devastation of the "dysfunctional family based on control" (in other words, the dominator family). Also, even in the face of massive resistance and counter-reaction, they are being further accelerated by the increasing rejection by men as well as women of stereotypical gender roles and relations.

But at the same time that technological and economic changes are continuing to destabilize once firmly established institutions, beliefs, and behaviors, and the challenge to all forms of violence and abuse—be they social or sexual—continues to mount, rapid technological and economic change is also causing enormous stress. Not only is technological change causing great economic and social dislocation, but as dominator elites seek to maintain and even strengthen their hold, disparities between haves and have-nots are widening globally, causing even greater insecurity and privation. And particularly among people who have seen their parents deflect frustration and anger against those who are powerless to defend themselves, this has all too often led to even more violence and scapegoating in both the private and public spheres.

Thus, at the same time that more and more people are rejecting the violence and abuse inherent in authoritarianism, racism, sexism, anti-Semitism, and other forms of political and economic domination, we also find the rekindling of old hates and fears in both the so-called developed and developing world—for example, the angry scapegoating of minorities and poor people (particularly poor women) in the United States, the brutal in-group versus out-group violence that brought Bosnians, Croats, and Serbs into world headlines, the intertribal carnage of Somalia and Rwanda, and the murderous terrorism of religious fundamentalists in both East and West. Similarly, at the same time that the mass media are at last bringing into the open the horrors of such practices as wife battering, child beating, and childhood sexual abuse, we also find the tragic stories of teenage mothers who unconsciously, and at times violently, act out their own bewilderment and distress against their babies, and abandoned and neglected children who band together into "families" of gangs, where they violently act out their pain by deflecting it against their peers and society at large.

So on the one side, as we today shift into an ever more accelerated phase of the contemporary revolution in consciousness, masses of people are refusing any longer to accept violent and abusive relations as simply "the way things are." And increasingly they are focusing on the rejection of abusive and violent intimate relations—as evidenced by popular books such as those of John Bradshaw and Anne Wilson Schaef,[28] and talk shows like those of Oprah Winfrey where people bring out into the open what was once considered too shameful to even admit to oneself. But on the other side, the more technological, social, and economic change accelerates, and the more dominator elites seek to maintain and even extend their power, the more conflict, deprivation, insecurity, and stress there is. And the more scapegoating and incitement to deflect anger and fear onto members of traditionally disempowered groups there is in both the public and private spheres—particularly by those who, due to their cultural conditioning, find it extremely difficult to envision anything except dominator-dominated relations.

In sum, as the partnership thrust has accelerated, so also has the dominator resistance. And one of the most devastating manifestations of an inherently violent and abusive system seeking to reimpose its hold has been an escalation of extreme violence in intimate relations—as grimly shown by the recent spate of killings by men not only of their wives but also their children and often eventually themselves, when women refuse to any longer stay in abusive relations.[29]

Still another manifestation of the strong resistance to the mounting partnership thrust has been an intensive campaign for a return to "traditional family values"—the new code name for an authoritarian, male-dominated, patriarchal family designed to teach both boys and girls to obey orders from above, no matter how unjust or unloving they may be. This campaign has mainly come from fundamentalist and other religious groups who are still told by their leaders that the ranking of man over woman is divinely ordained. So these people are told, and in turn tell all of us, that a return to "traditional" gender roles and relations in a male-headed family is the cure for all social ills—even though studies show that whether two parents are present is less important to a child's development (including his or her potential for criminality) than factors such as

economic stress, parent education level, peer pressures, and the larger environment in which children grow up, and that, contrary to stereotypes,
working mothers are *not* less involved in their children's lives.[30]

However, the religious right's campaign to reinstate families based on
domination is truly just the tip of the iceberg. As we will see, there are
many other equally insidious but far less visible manifestations of the resistance to change by a millennia-old system of social and ideological organization that requires for its maintenance that both sex and women be
rigorously controlled—some of them, like subliminal hypnotic suggestions, exerting a powerful pull on all of us, not only psychologically but
sexually.

Personal, Social, and Sexual Change

All this takes us back to the complex interweaving of sexuality and all
our institutions and values, as well as to the main subject of the second
part of this book: the struggle against dominator sexuality—and how this
is integral to the second phase of the contemporary revolution in consciousness. For just as parent-child relations based on parental control of
children's bodies through force and fear condition people to fit into a
dominator society, a social construction of sexuality based on the control
of women by men also conditions people to regard the control of one individual or group by another as only natural. And this it once again does
on the most basic bodily level, through still further variants of the confluence of pain and pleasure—and with this, care and hurt—that is the
essence of dominator rather than partnership sexuality.

In fact, parenting styles and sexual styles are not unrelated. As we will
see, people who through their families, peer groups, and other childhood
experiences are socialized to view force-and-fear-based rankings as natural also tend to eroticize domination and submission. However—and
this is a crucial point that is also a critical factor in *cultural transformation
theory*—this does not mean that people cannot change their attitudes, behaviors, and relationships as adults.

Indeed, the entire premise of modern psychiatry is that once people
become conscious of unhealthy attitudes, behaviors, and relationships
they can consciously and deliberately change them at any point in their
lives. But while this has been widely discussed, much less attention has
been given to how, as we make changes in our personal attitudes, behaviors, and relationships, we are also empowered to consciously work for
social change—which then in turn supports further personal change.
Moreover, while the importance of sexuality in human behavior and per-

sonality structure was early on addressed by Freud and other psychoanalysts, only Wilhelm Reich, Herbert Marcuse, and a handful of others addressed the interconnection between sexuality and social structure.[31] And even they failed to focus on something that is generally only brought out in feminist analyses: that the social construction of sexuality and the social construction of gender roles and relations are inextricably intertwined and both affect and are affected by all social institutions.[32] Furthermore, despite their recognition of the foundational importance of how sexuality is distorted and repressed in authoritarian societies, these earlier scholars did not understand as well as we can today that—because, like our early childhood experiences, our sexual experiences impact us on the most basic bodily level—changes in sexual attitudes and behaviors play a crucial role in both personal and social healing.

These are all matters we will examine in some detail in the chapters that follow, as we explore the promise a *real* sexual revolution holds for our future, both individually and socially. But before we go farther, I want to clear up a number of misconceptions about what during the 1960s and 1970s was dubbed the modern sexual revolution.

In the first place, contrary to what we are often told, there have been other periods in Western history when sexual attitudes and behaviors were relatively, and in some circles very, unconstrained. In the second place, in significant respects the modern rebellion against traditional sexual mores started in the West long before the 1960s and 1970s.

For example, as far back as the 1870s there were women such as Tennessee Clafflin and Virginia Woodhull who defied massive social censure by challenging the sexual double standard for women and men. In the early 1900s, women such as Alexandra Kolontai and Emma Goldman even wrote of a new sexuality as the basis for a new social order. During the same time, Margaret Sanger defied government harassment and imprisonment to bring contraceptives into the United States. In the 1920s, particularly among artists and intellectuals, there was a strong push for what would later be called sexual liberation. And even though the 1950s were a time of relative sexual (and social) conservatism, they brought the pioneering sex research of Alfred Kinsey.

In the third place, what happened during the 1960s and 1970s was far more than a loosening of sexual constraints. It is true that this was when speaking about sex in public suddenly became acceptable; when many men and "nice" women began to openly live together out of "wedlock"; and when there suddenly emerged in the West a sexual counterculture that carried what had earlier been called a bohemian lifestyle to the children of many middle-class families and to quite a few of their elders. But it was also during the 1960s and 1970s that the ground-breaking research of William Masters and Virginia Johnson revealed that women are just as interested in, and capable of enjoying, sex as men; that it began to seem that the sexual double standard would really soon be a thing of the past; that gradually gay men and women "came out of the closet"; that contraceptives, including the Pill, were not only legalized but mass marketed; and that abortion was decriminalized. It was also during these decades that feminist critiques of dominator sexuality—particularly of the dehumanization and objectification of the female body as merely a male "sex object"—began to sow the seeds for a new kind of consciousness about sex through the works of women such as Susan Brownmiller, Susan Griffin, bell hooks, Laura Lederer, Robin Morgan, Adrienne Rich, and Gloria Steinem, and men such as Harry Brod, Don Sabo, and John Stoltenberg.[33]

Since sex was now beginning to get intensive popular and scholarly attention, it became possible to discern a number of trends. One was the gradual rejection by a large number of women and men of the belief that rather than being healthy and wholesome, sex—and particularly sex for pleasure—is dirty and sinful. A second trend was the attempt by a growing number of women to gain sexual independence: the power to freely choose how and with whom to mate and whether or not to have children. A third was the attempt by more and more women to reclaim the right to sexual pleasure and finally leave behind the notion (supported by both religious and secular dogmas) that women who are sexually active are "bad women" or "sluts." A fourth trend was the spreading recognition that heterosexual sex is not the only "normal" sexuality, that in fact a certain proportion of men and women have historically been, and still are, homosexual. A fifth trend was the gradual demystification of sexuality—which brought with it the explosion of many still widely believed myths, such as beliefs that masturbation is harmful, that women are more carnal than men, that women enjoy rape, and (since dominator myths are often totally contradictory) that only men want, and really enjoy, sex.

As the seventies gave way to the eighties and nineties, there were still other important changes. As female virginity was no longer so widely seen as a man's matrimonial prize, both women and men increasingly recognized that they can be friends and lovers—and that even after they are no longer lovers, they can still be friends. At the same time, more and more women were beginning to question the traditional male model of "sowing wild oats" or "scoring" through numerous impersonal one-night stands—and gradually so also did a growing number of men. Although it was fiercely resisted every inch of the way, sex education began to enter the school curriculum. In part due to the increase in teenage pregnancies as well as fear of AIDS, education about contraception also began to spread, although this too was against great opposition. Books and articles on how both women and men can have more sexual and emotional satisfaction in their relationships proliferated. And, particularly in so-called New Age circles, people even began to explore the link between sexuality and spirituality, attempting to reintegrate the two.

But there were other trends that pointed in a very different direction. One was the vast upsurge of pornographic materials depicting sex as a basically mechanical, impersonal activity devoid of caring or even recognition of another's humanity. Another was that this kind of portrayal of sex, though in less sexually explicit imagery, was also spreading into television and mass market films. Still another was that sex was now incessantly linked with domination and violence—with women or men taking the stereotypically feminine part portrayed as enjoying this treatment—a linking that, as we will see, was not (as is often claimed) a product of modern sexual "laxness," but embedded in ancient dominator traditions, both religious and secular. Moreover, sexual violence was also increasing in real life—even though some of the huge jumps in rape statistics also reflected a far higher incidence of reporting of rape, as people began to view it as a crime of violence rather than an act of sexual passion invited by the victim's improper attire or demeanor.

There was also, as Michel Foucault pointed out, the substitution of sexual rebellion for any real efforts to change power imbalances. For example, the now permissible (and as Foucault noted, often obsessive) social discourse about sex was largely molded by "experts" from medicine, psychiatry, and more recently sexology, whose teachings—if we examine them closely—tend to present dominator-dominated relations as normal.[34] Moreover, this obsessive discourse about sex often became deflected into the puerile rebellion of a smutty language that kept it at the level of preadolescent boys' "dirty talk" and thus led only to a further demeaning of sex. Not only that, but all too often, as in rock lyrics listened to by thousands of young people, the new open forum on sex was deflected into the kinds of words and images that not only debase both women and sex, but extol the most brutal sexual violence as good, manly fun. In the same way, the recognition that sex unlinked from procreation is normal and healthy often became an excuse for pressuring others, in the name of sexual freedom, to have sex whether they want to or not.

The Struggle Over Sex, Consciousness, and Our Future

All of this takes us to a critical point that provides a way to cut through much of the sexual confusion and upheaval all around us. This is that some of what has until now been lumped under the catch-all phrase "the sexual revolution" is in fact part of the dominator sexual *counter*-revolution.

I cannot emphasize this enough. It is easy under the guise of sexual (or any other) freedom for those who hold power to more effectively dominate those who have been socially disempowered. We see this in nonsexual relations, where all too often "free enterprise" has served as a smokescreen for the domination and exploitation of economically disempowered groups such as minorities and women. And we certainly see it in sexual relations, where "sexual freedom" has all too often led to even more exploitive sexual predation, as women are pressured to be sexually available to men simply because they have been taken out to dinner or a show—and (as in the "date rapes" we hear so much about these days) sometimes forced to have intercourse if they refuse. In other words, what we see here is something we already touched on in Part I: the dominator mechanism of co-option—the appropriation and distortion of partnership social trends to maintain or reimpose dominator-dominated relations.

This problem of co-option has been a constant all through the first phase of not only the modern sexual revolution but the modern revolution in consciousness. For example, many of the important intellectual breakthroughs of the Enlightenment were co-opted into the construction of a science that all too often served merely to make oppression and destruction more efficient—a subject we will return to. Important modern economic and political theories, such as those of Adam Smith and Karl Marx, were co-opted in the service of dominator political and economic regressions. And even the all-important deconstruction of dominator beliefs, myths, and stereotypes has itself now begun to be co-opted into a nihilistic attack on all standards and values—which ironically opens the door even wider for those who would reimpose on us the dominator standards and values from a time before the decisive break from our authoritarian past that began to take shape during the eighteenth-century Enlightenment.

This regressive pull is today most visible from the fundamentalist right, often from people who seem to be literally hypnotized by religious leaders who alternately threaten them with the most hideous divine punishments or promise that—in exchange for total obedience—God will choose only them to be saved, while all others are destroyed when Armageddon brings on the end of the world.[35] But their fierce opposition to any change in "traditional" dominator-dominated family and sexual relations is only one aspect of the struggle between dominator regression and partnership resurgence that will determine our future.

Certainly if the fundamentalist right succeeds in seizing power, we will see extreme social and sexual controls. For what they would impose on us is a religious form of fascism in which the ultimate strong-man is a wrathful divine father who countenances neither freedom nor equality, whose power—like that of the men who rule in his name—is imposed and maintained through threats (and intermittent acts) of the most painful violence.[36] And what they would also reimpose on us is strict and, if "necessary," violent control over women and women's sexuality, since this control is both a symbol and a linchpin for all other forms of domination and control. But as we will see, this struggle in our time over such fundamental matters as how we view sex, gender, and our bodies is taking place in far more subtle and ubiquitous ways that transcend such conventional classifications as right versus left and secular versus religious. And while there is a tremendous regressive pull, there is also a very strong and—despite periodic setbacks—cumulatively mounting forward movement.

Whether this movement succeeds or fails today still hangs in the balance. As more and more of us break free of our millennia-long dominator trance, we are becoming aware that much that was once viewed as just reality was socially constructed—and hence, that it can be deconstructed and reconstructed. So a decisive factor in whether we move backward or forward will be whether we not only go much deeper in our deconstruction but also shift the emphasis much more to reconstruction—particularly to the reconstruction of our most foundational beliefs about gender, sex, and our bodies as a central component of what Anthony Giddens has aptly called the democratization of daily life.[37] For only then will we have the solid foundations for sustainable change in both the private and public spheres.

It is too early to project in detail what form this reconstruction will take. But if we succeed in completing the cultural shift from a dominator to a partnership social and ideological organization, we will see a real sexual revolution—one in which sex will no longer be associated with domination and submission but with the full expression of our powerful human yearning for connection and for erotic pleasure. It will be a sexuality that will make it possible for us to more fully express and experience sexual passion as an altered state of consciousness. It will also bring the recognition that erotic pleasure can be imbued with a spirituality that is both immanent and transcendent. And it will combine greater sexual freedom with greater empathy, respect, responsibility, and caring.

I should clarify that by sexual empathy, caring, responsibility, and respect I do not mean inflexible lifelong sexual bonds. While it may embody these qualities, sex in lifelong marriages has all too often been marked by lack of respect, empathy, responsibility, and caring. And what we today call serial monogamy (that is, a series of committed relationships rather than a single exclusive relationship till death), along with a healthy amount of spontaneity and sexual experimentation, are not inconsistent with caring, empathic, and mutually responsible and respectful sexual relations.

Neither, by recognizing the possibility that sex can be spiritual, do I mean that if we succeed in shifting to a partnership society, all sexual relations would have this dimension. But in a society animated by a partnership rather than dominator ethos, all sexual relations—from the most playful to the most fiercely passionate—would no longer be associated with impersonal, mechanical, and/or coercive touch. Nor would the human body, be it female or male, in such a society be imaged as merely an instrument for use, much less abuse, by another.

Is it really possible for us to construct a society in which our yearning for caring connection, for the unfolding of our higher selves through physical and spiritual union with another being—in short, for love—can be socially supported rather than distorted and repressed? I believe it is. But I am also convinced that if we are to construct a society where sex will be linked not with violence and domination but with the truly erotic—with the life-and-pleasure-giving powers within us and around us in the world—we need to fully extricate ourselves from all that has for so long unconsciously bound us to painful and unhealthy myths and realities. We need an understanding of what I have here called the politics of the body, and of how this relates to what has conventionally been defined as political. We need to better understand how and why domination and violence have been eroticized and even, under the guise of spirituality, sanctified. Most important, we need to begin reconstructing not only sexuality and spirituality but all aspects of our lives—since, as we saw in Part I, how sexuality is constructed differs greatly in the context of a partnership or dominator society.

In short, as we will explore in the chapters that follow, we need to move from the first phase to the second phase of both the modern revolution in consciousness and the sexual revolution if we are to create the conditions that will facilitate, rather than impede, the emergence of our species' highest potentials—including our highly developed potentials for the intense love and pleasure that make us unique in the amazing pageant of life on this planet.

CHAPTER 11

Bondage or Bonding:
Sex, Spirituality,
and Repression

Changes in consciousness are a very strange thing. Suddenly we see what was there all the time. And we wonder how it could for so long have been invisible to us.

For much of my own life I had practically no consciousness of any connection between sexual and political repression, much less of how stereotypical gender roles that distort both sex and spirituality can habituate us to domination. When I was a little girl growing up in Cuba, a Catholic country, it never occurred to me to wonder why woman and sex were considered sinful. Nor did it register on me that in the eighteenth- and nineteenth-century writings I read in school about the right of man to life, liberty, and property, the authors meant just that—men, and actually only propertied white men.

Now, like many other people, I am fully, indeed painfully, conscious of such things. I am aware that when Abigail Adams (wife of a future president of the United States) suggested the framers of the American Constitution not forget "the ladies," her husband dismissed this as a laughable idea.[1] Thomas Jefferson, one of the most prominent spokesmen for the new "rights of man" ideals, was himself a slaveholder who owned his slave mistress.[2] Even John Locke—who attacked the notion of the patriarchal family as the "natural" foundation for absolute monarchy, arguing that male and female parents have an "equal title" to power over their children—asserted that there is "a Foundation in Nature" for the legal and customary subjection of women to their husbands.[3] And the French philosopher Jean-Jacques Rousseau, famous for his advocacy of freedom for men, actually advocated the opposite for women, asserting that girls "should be restricted from a young age." For, according to Rousseau, "docility" is something women will "need all their lives, since they will always be in subjection to a man or to men's judgements, and will never be allowed to set themselves above these judgements."[4]

Rousseau's view that women will, and should, always be subjected to men was, as the political historian Linda Kerber writes in *Women of the Republic,* not just a philosophical point. Kerber notes that Rousseau's "sadomasochistic sexual tastes gave him a substantial personal stake" in this position.[5]

This is not to imply that all the men who took such a very different view of freedom and equality for women and for men were sexual sadomasochists. But clearly this double standard for freedom and equality has served to maintain male dominance. Even beyond this, it has blinded us to an absurdity. For how can we speak of a free and democratic society with equality and justice for all at the same time that the domination of one half of humanity over the other half is accepted as only proper and right?

This gender double standard has also made it hard for us to see something else of fundamental importance: that the erotization[6] of domination has been a major obstacle in the modern struggle to create a free and equal society. Because contrary to what we have been taught, freedom and equality are not just a matter of political organization, but of the structure of personal and social life as a whole. To put it even more specifically, as Kerber writes, "sexual style is the adjunct of political style."[7]

To this, on the basis of my research, I would add that sexual style is also the adjunct of religious or spiritual style. This is still another reason the contemporary search for a new politics and a new economics is inextricably related to the contemporary search for both a new sexuality and a new spirituality. And it is also why we will start this chapter with something that will come as a shock to some people: how, in the name of spirituality, religious authorities have used sex to maintain rankings of domination.

Sex, Religion, and Domination

I want to start by reiterating something I said earlier: that there are in our Judeo-Christian religious heritage many important partnership teachings and that the distortion of human sexuality that we are here dealing with is not a function of our religious heritage but of our dominator heritage. Nonetheless, as we saw in Part I, institutionalized religion—be it pagan, Hebrew, or Christian—has in Western history often helped to maintain hierarchies of domination, while at the same time also helping to alleviate some of the suffering caused by these hierarchies. Moreover, as we also glimpsed in Part I, the medieval Christian Church played a major part in actively causing both women and men much sexual guilt, fear, and suffering.

It is common knowledge that even though many clerics were not celibate, and some are even said to have owned houses of prostitution,[8] the medieval Christian Church expended enormous time and energy devising rules and punishments for men's and women's sexual behaviors, even for their sexual fantasies.[9] But if we are to free ourselves from the bondage of millennia-long traditions of sexual, personal, and political repression, we need to more fully understand how and why this was.

According to some Christian authorities, such as Siricius (who became pope in 384), the Church's hostility toward sex—and particularly toward women's sexuality—simply followed the teachings of Jesus. However, as the religious historian Uta Ranke-Heinemann points out, there is no basis for such a claim. What Jesus preached against was a society where men stoned women to death for adultery (as when Jesus stopped such a stoning), where polygamy (or marriage to more than one woman) was considered a God-given male privilege, and where divorce for women was almost impossible whereas a man could cast out a no-longer-wanted wife by simply saying "I divorce you" three times (as is still the practice in some Muslim fundamentalist societies today). So although he did not put it this way, what Jesus actually condemned is what we today would call the sexual oppression of women—and not, as the Church was to later claim, women's sexuality, and even sex itself.[10]

Nonetheless, even though again there is no basis for such a claim, according to Pope Siricius, Jesus would not have chosen to be born from Mary's womb "had he been forced to look upon her as so unrestrained as to let that womb, from which the body of the Lord was fashioned, that hall of the eternal King, be stained by the presence of male seed."[11] Siricius even excommunicated a man called Jovian for questioning the Church doctrine of the so-called "virginity in birth"—that is, that Mary was not only a virgin (which even Jovian believed) but that Mary's hymen remained intact during childbirth (which Jovian, rather sensibly, questioned).[12]

Not that Christianity introduced this hostility toward sex. Even though we are told that Christians taught pagans sexual asceticism—that is, rigid control of, and contempt for, sex—the Church's negative view of both sex and women was already shared by many pagans. For example, the second-century Roman emperor Marcus Aurelius (who violently persecuted Christians) wrote of sex in his celebrated memoirs as "internal attrition and an expulsion of mucus with a sort of spasm"—a comment marked by the same disdain and disgust for the human body as the writings of later Christians who were to denounce pagans as immoral and licentious.[13]

Marcus Aurelius had in turn been influenced in his views by the pagan Stoic philosophers, who also tended to despise women, the human body, and sexual pleasure. In fact, the Stoics also influenced some early Christian sects—for example, some of the more ascetic Gnostics who preached renunciation of all that is worldly and, like some modern Armageddonists, saw no possibility for redemption, except *after* all that is bodily or worldly has been overcome, abandoned, or destroyed.

But it was the Christian Church's hierarchy that declared, as Ranke-Heinemann writes, that "the locus par excellence of sin is sex," that proclaimed woman a constant danger to man, and that enacted edict after edict to "protect" men from women's sexuality through the most incredibly repressive and brutal means. It was the Church that invalidated the marriages of priests, casting out wives without any provision for economic survival. It was the Church's male hierarchy that wrote and tried to enforce synods proclaiming that for clerics any association with women was dangerous (as in the seventh-century Synods of Nantes and Mainz, even forbidding priests to live in the same house with their mothers or sisters and, as in the Synod of Paris of 846 A.D., forbidding any woman to enter where a priest was staying).[14] And it was the Church that, as its ultimate "protection" of men from the "danger" of women, launched the Christian witch-hunts—which left some towns almost without any female population, killed many thousands (according to some estimates millions) of women so accused, and deprived Western medicine of invaluable herbal and other healing knowledge that had until then been passed on by pagan priestesses and healers from generation to generation.

As I reflect back, it is strange, indeed truly incomprehensible, that it is only recently that the Church's arrest, torture, and murder of so many women has begun to be recognized as nothing less than a full-scale religious war against women. And it is just as strange that Christian historians to this day fail to note that the Church's teaching that both woman and sex must at all costs be controlled by man served to maintain male dominance—and that, even beyond this, it served to condition both women and men for all forms of repression and domination.[15]

Clearly the Church's obsessive vilification of sex and woman was a means of preventing sexual bonding between women and men. If men have to be protected from being "polluted" by woman's sexuality, sexual love is dangerous. And so also is any relaxation of male control over women.

But the Church's constant association of sex not with pleasure but with eternal punishment and pain was not only a way of alienating men from women, and thus justifying and maintaining male dominance; it also served to alienate men from their own bodies, their own emotions, and above all, from their human need for loving connection. And in so doing it effectively served not only to distort men's and women's sexuality; it also effectively conditioned men and women to distort their most basic human need for connection (the need for sex and love) into an acceptance of domination, coercion, and repression.

For if one could accept, for one's own good, the Church's coercive control over one's own sexuality—over how one touched and was in turn touched by others, and even over how one thought about one's body and the bodies of others—surely one could, and would, also for one's own good, accept all other coercive controls. If sexual or bodily pleasure was sinful, perhaps it was not so sinful instead to cause others bodily pain, also for their own good (as the Church itself did). And if the conception of life itself was considered sinful by God, it was perhaps also not so sinful to take the life of others in the name of God (as the Church also did).

So at the same time that the Church continued to mouth Jesus' message of peace and love, it could command the institution of the brutal Inquisition and Crusades. It could continue to preach that we are all "brothers" through Jesus Christ, and at the same time condone the virtual enslavement of women to their husbands, along with the enslavement of men by men and nation by nation.[16] And at the same time that the princes of the Church spoke of men's liberation from the "tyranny" of the flesh through abstention from any sexual pleasure, they could also enact the most complex, cruel, and manifestly absurd rules to tyrannically control the most intimate sexual behaviors and even sexual thoughts of the women and men in their "earthly flock." And it is this control over peoples' bodies that is the ultimate mainstay of dominator social organization.

Obsessing on Sex and Distorting Spirituality

But there is still another, more insidious, way in which the Church's self-appointed role as the controller of sex served to maintain a system of fear-and-force-backed rankings. And ironically, it served—and continues to serve—basically the same purpose as much of the pornography the Church vehemently condemns to our day.

On the face of it, the Church's dogma that unless it is strictly for procreation and *not* for pleasure, sex is sinful even in marriage, signals a disgust and contempt for sex—which is certainly there. However, if we probe deeper, what we see is *not* what one usually expects from contempt and disgust: the avoidance of anything to do with its object. Quite the contrary, what we find is the Church's minute attention to every conceivable and inconceivable aspect of sex. In short, what we find under the guise of spirituality is actually an obsession with sex.

In one way, this is not surprising, since by its emphasis on lifelong celibacy the Church undoubtedly succeeded in producing many chronically frustrated, and thus sexually fixated, men. But the way these men fixated on sex is the key.

For it is not only that under the guise of spirituality the Church hierarchy demanded acceptance of rigid sexual controls by both its priests and its flock. Nor is it only that, under the guise that men are more spiritual than women, the Church insisted that men must control women, particularly women's sexuality. What the Church did through its constant association of sex with the most horribly violent divine punishments is that, once again under the guise of spirituality, it effectively eroticized domination and violence.

Indeed, what we find if we look closely at the endless Church pronouncements, edicts, and laws about sex is the very same thing that in the next chapter we will see in the pornographic erotization of domination and violence. For the Church's warnings that sexual pleasure is sinful were hardly abstract. Rather, as we will also see in the next chapter, they were both verbally and pictorially delivered through the most vivid images of bodily torture and excruciating suffering in hell. So even though it was in the name of forbidding sexual pleasure rather than, as in pornography, attaining it, the Church too constantly associated sex with violence and domination.

Moreover, when the Church asserted that even in marriage intercourse is sinful unless it is solely for procreation, it felt compelled to prescribe that even then it must never be performed except in the male-above, female-below position—once again effectively linking sex and domination. Thus, the Dominican Roland de Cremona enjoined corpulent persons to slim down so they could assume what is still today described as the missionary position. And the Church official who wrote the *Codex latinus Monacensis 22233* actually asserted that the wife's agreeing to depart from the "normal" position was as serious a sin as murder.[17]

Similarly, when these men refused to grant Communion to anyone who confessed (as people were told they had to) the "sin" of having had sex to enjoy pleasure, they effectively again taught their flock to associate sex with domination and punishment[18]—as well as making it possible for priests to constantly pry into people's sex lives, and thus themselves constantly fantasize about sex in all kinds of possible variations. The same purposes were achieved when popes, bishops, and priests worked for years on penitentials and punishment tables for every kind of sexual "sin."[19] In all these cases these men could legitimately obsess on sex while still claiming both bodily and mental purity—at the same time that they exercised control over the most intimate bodily details in people's lives.

Thus, from the eighth century on, confessors were directed to ask about birth control, particularly of women. They were also given precise instructions from their superiors as to penances for oral intercourse, nonmissionary positions, abortion, anal intercourse, bestiality, and just about everything else one can think of in relation to sex.[20] For example, we learn in the Decree of Burchard of Worms that priests were instructed to deal with male confessors by asking and telling them the following:

Have you coupled with your wife or another woman from behind like dogs? If so, then ten days of penance on bread and water. Have you coupled with your wife during menstruation, then ten days of penance on bread and water. If your wife went to church after having a baby, but before being purified, then she is to do penance for as long a time as she should have stayed away from church. And if you have coupled with her during this time, then you will do twenty days of penance on bread and water."[21]

In their dealings with women, the Church hierarchies were often more severe. Thus, Bishop Caesarius decreed that "no woman may drink a potion that makes her incapable of conceiving"—and that every time she did she would "be held accountable for that many murders."[22]

Since male control over women was a mainstay of Church doctrine, it should not surprise us that (even though, once again, Jesus said nothing to justify this) the medieval Church forbade women contraception. In fact, this prohibition also tied in with the Church's persecution of the women who still retained some of their earlier spiritual power as priestesses and healers, since before the witch burnings herbal and other contraceptive information had apparently been passed on from generation to generation by these women.

Nor should it surprise us—if we keep in mind that woman's sexual power was in the Old Religion associated with her capacity to give life, and thus with both menstruation and birth giving—that the Church prohibited sex with a woman who was menstruating or had recently given birth. Given the Church's sanctification of pain (instead of, as in the earlier religion, pleasure), we should also not be surprised when we read that the bishop of Paris, William of Auverge, wrote in the thirteenth century that because pleasure hinders the soul's development, it was "happy news" that "some young men remain cold with their wives, even when they are beautiful."[23]

Yet one cannot help being taken aback on reading how at about the same time another archbishop, Stephen Langton, wrote that a woman must always be sexually available to her husband, lest he seek sex elsewhere, even at the risk of her own life—that "the wife must rather let herself be killed than her husband sin."[24] Trying to explain this religious blessing for sex on demand in the context of the Church's virulently anti-sexual-pleasure stance, Ranke-Heinemann notes how it fits with the Catholic notion of sex as a sickness and marital sex as its "medicine."[25] And it is true that this view was still held by the father of Protestantism, Martin Luther, who also spoke of sex in marriage as "medicine."[26]

But practically speaking, as Ranke-Heinemann writes, this notion that "married men were like mortally ill patients headed for eternal damnation unless their nurse-wives sacrificed themselves for them, even risked their lives to fulfill their conjugal duty, to supply the medicine against incontinence at all times" meant "the sexual enslavement of women."[27] And it also again highlights how the Church's obsession with controlling sexuality has very little to do with spirituality in the sense of a more evolved consciousness or sensitivity, much less with Jesus' teaching that we do unto others as we would want them to do unto us.

In truth, it is monstrous that under the guise of saving men from sin a cleric should command women to willingly give up their lives just because their husbands feel like having sex. And of course such a command is also fundamentally inconsistent with the Church's position that unless it is solely for procreation, sex is intrinsically sinful.

But what we are here dealing with has as little to do with logic as it does with spirituality. What it has to do with is the dominator double standard for women and men—not only for sex, but for spirituality, morality, and even life and death.

This double standard has for millennia been justified by teachings that in the eyes of God men are of a higher spiritual order than women. It manifests itself in the fact that although men are in Christian dogma deemed to be more spiritual than women, women are in actual practice expected to be far more spiritual than men—more noble, giving, and self-sacrificing. Under this double standard, no matter how kind and caring a woman is, unless she completely sacrifices her own welfare (even her life) for that of others (particularly her husband and children), she can never hope to be considered the spiritual equal of man. And even then, she will only be looked on as the exception to the rule that woman is less spiritually and morally evolved than man.

Similarly, while men's sexual urges (and their sexual lapses) were considered natural by the Church (and thus more readily forgiven and even condoned), when women gave in to their sexual urges even once, they were branded for life as harlots. And this was so even though the Church also preached that carnality is the essence of womanhood—and thus should logically have been more, rather than less, forgiving of any female sexual lapses.

It is this same double standard for women and men that organized religion has helped maintain through stories such as the Fall from Paradise, blaming woman for all men's ills—despite the obvious fact that it is actually men, and not women, who through recorded history have been primarily responsible for such barbarities as chronic warfare and despotic strong-man rule. And of course it is this double standard that, lest the story of Adam and Eve in the Garden repeat itself, has served to justify male control over women—a control that were it by men over men would immediately be called slavery.

Women's Sexual Slavery

It is particularly revealing, and shocking, that even though the Church had something to say about almost everything regarding sex, when it came to women's sexual slavery, it was conspicuously silent—as most religious institutions still are even today. Indeed, it did not prohibit, or even comment about, its most blatant forms.

For instance, it was the custom of some European men to protect their "honor" by forcing their wives to put on metal or wooden "chastity belts."[28] But the misery of these women—the painful infections caused by devices preventing them from properly cleansing their bodies, their inability to do anything about their chronic irritation and unrelievable sexual arousal, as well as their humiliation and degradation—were apparently of no concern to their husbands (or the historians who usually write of such things in passing, as titillating bits of sexual lore). Nor was it of any concern to the Church.

Of course, female sexual slavery was hardly introduced in Christian times. In fact, the exploitation by men of women's productive and reproductive (including sexual) services that we find in such "advanced" European civilizations as ancient Greece and Rome may in some ways have been ameliorated when the Church condemned polygyny. And by making divorce difficult for both women and men instead of as before only for women, the Church also challenged the custom of many of the barbarian tribespeople during the early Middle Ages of a man just throwing out a no-longer-wanted wife.[29]

However, the Church never took a vigorous position against the also customary Germanic practice of men killing adulterous wives.[30] Nor, as already noted, did it take a position against wife beating or the domination of women by men that it serves to maintain.[31] In fact, the English common law governing marriage, which in large part derived from earlier Church law, permitted a man to beat his wife if she did not perform her services to his satisfaction, just as slave owners were permitted to beat their slaves if they were not satisfied with them.

Under this same common law (which served as the model for the family laws of England's American colonies), husbands not only had coercive power over their wives' bodies; they also had complete control over their wives' property. This even included property wives inherited in their own right, or earned by their own labor, which (as is also customary in slavery) legally belonged to their husbands.[32] In fact, under the English common law, like slaves, wives were nonpersons, even to the extent that they could neither sue nor be sued. Thus, if a wife was injured by a third party, damages went to her husband to compensate him for the loss of sexual and other services, just as a slave owner would be compensated if a slave's body was injured.[33]

Again, because this view of women as male property still lingers in our world today, it is hard for us to deal with the fact that the legal status of women until recent times was, and in some cases still is, at best that of partially emancipated slaves. Blinded by the double standard for male and female repression, we tend to deny this unpleasant reality—despite the many clues pointing directly to it.

A familiar example is the widespread custom of fathers giving away their daughters in marriage, leading them to the altar where their husbands take them over. A less well-known example is that when American colonists imported Blacks from Africa and looked for models of laws to govern their status as slaves, they chose the English common law governing the status of married women.[34] Still another example is that a common rationale for strict control over Black male slaves in the American South was their "dangerous, untamed" sexuality—just as taming women's "dangerous" sexuality has through much of Western history been a rationale for men's strict control over women.

Just as slaves who rebelled against their masters, or subjects who killed their rulers, have throughout recorded history been subject to the most terrible punishments, if a woman killed her husband it was under the English common law considered treason in the same way as when a subject killed the king. Therefore the penalty was not only death, but a slow and horrible death through public torture.[35] In other words, in all these cases excruciatingly painful exemplary public punishment was inflicted to discourage others who might contemplate rebellion.

But it was not only that women who sought freedom by rebelling against male control were cruelly punished (a custom that, as we saw in Part I, goes back to early Western codes of law); women's marital subjection and sexual servitude to men was often also guaranteed by economic constraints, by the fact that for many women marriage was the only respectable job opportunity. There were in the Middle Ages trade guilds of women. And women from the peasantry worked as servants in men's households (where they were often at their masters' sexual mercy). There was prostitution, a profession where "fallen women" traded their sexual services to many men rather than just one in order to survive economically. And, despite all the obstacles, there were always a few women who managed to make their way into the professions and the arts. But for most women of the nobility and later the middle classes, the expected profession, and often the only option for livelihood, was to get married and to stay married, no matter how miserable or even brutal their situation might be.

And what being married meant is that—whether she loved her husband or loathed him, whether he was kind or cruel, attractive or repulsive, gave her pleasure or pain—she was by law required to have sex with him as part of her marriage contract (which also required her to bear as many children in her body as her husband desired). Specifically, since marital rape only began to be recognized as a crime of violence in the late twentieth century, it meant that wives were legally required to be sexually available to their husbands, even if it was by force against their will.

That some women and men still managed to have relatively egalitarian relations, and that there was, despite all this, real affection between many wives and husbands is, once again, testimony to the great power of the human yearning for caring connection—as well as to women's ability, against incredible odds, to assert their humanity and have some say in their lives. But this does not change the fact that those women who were not able to transcend the dominator stereotypes of docile femininity, or who were not lucky enough to marry kind men, were legally at the mercy of their husbands, just as slaves are at the mercy of their masters ("master" not coincidentally being the traditional appellation of the male head of household well into modern times). In short, it does not change the fact that for much of recorded history marriage was a legally sanctioned form of female sexual slavery.

So here again we come back to the gender double standard, and with it, the double standard for slavery. If one says slavery, most people today recoil in horror. But if one says the sexual slavery of women, many people still today are merely titillated. What it evokes is not outrage at cruelty and injustice, but sadomasochistic pornographic fantasies or, at best, the kinds of women's romances sold in supermarkets where masterful males sweep women off their feet and torrid love scenes, initially against the heroine's will, precede their riding off together into the sunset.

In these romances, the heroine is powerless to resist either the romantic hero or her own forbidden sexual feelings. And, as in the famous Rudolf Valentino film *The Sheik*, where an Arab prince abducts the heroine and forces himself upon her, these stories usually have "happy endings."

But in real life it is quite another matter. For centuries, and still today, women have been abducted to be imprisoned in the harems of Arab sheiks. As Kathleen Barry writes in her powerful book *Female Sexual Slavery*, there are eyewitness accounts of modern slave auctions in parts of Africa and Asia where heavily drugged women, sometimes still dressed in the clothes they had on when abducted, are sold to the highest bidder.[36] These sales often involve children; for example, a well-documented 1990 public auction in the slums of Karachi of girls from Bangladesh aged eight to ten described at a 1991 conference on slavery.[37]

These women's and children's suffering, and all too often untimely deaths, tragically belie the notion that sexual slavery is a happy fate. Indeed, for the thousands of ever younger girls who are today sold and bought in India, Nepal, Thailand, and other nations to staff Asian red-light districts as their predecessors become infected with AIDS, it all too often means certain death.

Some of these little girls are sold by their own parents, either into prostitution or forced marriage. And even when a case receives wide public attention, like that of the little girl shown in a 1993 *60 Minutes* television program whose sale under a phony marriage certificate to an old man from Saudi Arabia was foiled by a courageous airline stewardess, nothing much changes. What happened was that the child was first put in a detention camp for juvenile offenders. And when feminist groups protested, rather than being permitted to go with the woman who saved her (and who pleaded that the Indian court allow this), she was handed by the authorities to the very parents who had sold her—at the same time that rather than being jailed or even fined, her purchaser went scot-free.

That such things can happen to a child even when the sale of children into marriage is supposedly illegal in India—and that even despite this, the child's parents were in no way penalized—is horrifying. But this lack of official action against sexual slavery is unfortunately not the exception but the rule. For example, there are many accounts of how girls and women are brutally terrorized to discourage them from even trying to escape from the brothels (including military bordellos and camps of migrant workers) to which, in some cases, their own parents have sold them, and of how even when they do try to escape, there is no one they can go to for recourse, as often the local authorities either directly or indirectly profit from the prostitution industry.

Even INTERPOL and other international organizations aware of this trade in women and children have done hardly anything to interfere. This is despite the fact that in Asia alone an estimated million or more women and children are every year "traded like commodities on a stock exchange"[38] without government interference (and often with tacit government approval)—and even though there are numerous United Nations conventions prohibiting slavery, and sexual enslavement has specifically been declared a violation of international law.[39]

Sexual and Political Repression

Clearly involuntary servitude is slavery, whether the services are sexual or not. But the erotization of domination has conditioned us to accept the sexual enslavement of women by men as not only normal but exciting. And it has also obscured the fact that the sexual enslavement of women has historically and cross-culturally gone hand in hand with the political and economic enslavement of *both* women and men.

To illustrate, in some fundamentalist Muslim theocracies, where the most repressive provisions of the Shari'a (Muslim "divine law") are still (or again) in force, to this day women are effectively imprisoned by men who are legally allowed to severely restrict women's freedom of movement. This was vividly brought out during the Gulf War when a handful of courageous Saudi Arabian women defied the prohibition against their even driving cars—for which they and their families were later to pay dearly.[40] And not coincidentally, such rigidly male-dominated societies are also places where absolute monarchs and/or coercive priestly hierarchies rule both men and women with an iron hand.

Similarly, the brutal genital mutilations designed to make sure women do not sexually "stray" are characteristically found in parts of Africa, Asia, and the Near East where dictatorial governments rule their people through fear and force. In the same way, the enforcement of women's sexual slavery through "honor killings" (found in parts of Latin America as well as Asia and the Middle East) is also characteristic of places where repressive regimes see nothing wrong with using physical violence to deprive both women and men of political freedom.

This too is not coincidental. Men who think it honorable to kill their own wives, daughters, sisters, or even mothers for being too sexually free have learned that freedom is at best a selective matter, one that "inferior," "weak," or "dangerous" people (in their eyes, people like women) are not entitled to enjoy. In fact, how male contempt for women transfers into contempt for "effeminate" enemies was dramatically illustrated during the Gulf War, when after the Iraqis were defeated, Kuwaiti men expressed contempt for Saddam Hussein by putting lipstick on (and thus feminizing) an Iraqi poster of him.[41]

The denial to women of free access to contraception and abortion—still another form of sexual slavery—has also historically and cross-culturally characterized politically repressive regimes. This too is not coincidental. For men conditioned to see nothing wrong with depriving their "loved ones"—their own wives, daughters, sisters, or mothers—of freedom of choice even to the extent of forcing them against their will to get pregnant, or once pregnant against their will to give birth to an unwanted child, can far more easily be conditioned to accept the curtailment of other freedoms, such as freedom of speech and assembly. Thus, both Hitler's and Stalin's renewed emphasis on criminalizing abortion when they gained power was not only a matter of wanting larger populations (and thus more men for gun fodder) but of dominator systems dynamics.[42] We see the same dynamics even today in the United States, in the fact that those who would return us to the "good old days" of authoritarian control by religious hierarchies (as well as to "holy wars") have been waging a no-holds-barred campaign to once again deprive women of abortion and reproductive freedom of choice.

In short, be they secular or religious, Christian or Muslim, ancient or modern, Eastern or Western, the times and places where we find the greatest sexual repression of women are generally also the times and places where political repression is most severe. Yet even today the systems connection between freedom or repression for women and political freedom or repression is still generally ignored.

Part of the problem is that political oppression—or as political scientists like to put it, "man's oppression"—is considered a major issue fit for serious study, while under the gender double standard what happens to women, and particularly what happens to women sexually, is considered trivial. Another part of the problem is that the connection we are here dealing with between social and ideological structure and how different human bodies are imaged—and specifically how relations between the male body and the female body are imaged—is still almost nowhere addressed. Still another part of the problem is the rigidity of academic compartmentalization and specialization, which helps ensure that, except for feminist scholars, even those who today seriously study gender and sexual relations usually still focus solely on the psychological and not the political implications.

A notable exception to this fragmented approach was the German psychoanalyst Wilhelm Reich, who introduced what he called sex-economic sociology to explain both the rise of Hitler in Germany and why in Russia "the replacement of private capitalism by state capitalism has not in the least altered the typical helpless and authoritarian character structure of the masses of people."[43] A refugee from Nazi Germany and a Marxist profoundly disillusioned with Soviet-style communism, Reich in 1933 published his masterpiece, *The Mass Psychology of Fascism.* In it he noted that one of the most effective means through which repressive systems have historically maintained themselves is through the authoritarian family, which is "the factory of its structure and ideology," and particularly through "sexual suppression." He also noted that fascism was "not a modern phenomenon but one with deep historical psychosexual roots."[44]

When I first discovered Reich's *The Mass Psychology of Fascism* in the early 1970s (it was banned in the United States, but I was able to get a copy from an underground press), I was tremendously excited. But after a while I was also saddened. Not only because this important work had been banned, but because despite Reich's important insights into how both male and female sexuality have been distorted to maintain hierarchies of domination—and despite his assertion that sexual repression and political repression are inextricably intertwined—in the end Reich again drifted off into the all-too-familiar male-centered scholarship. And he thus lost sight of the centrality of something he himself noted: that at the heart of the sexual and political repression he so deplored lies the sexual and political domination of women by men.[45]

What Reich failed to note is that even though the social construction of male sexuality in dominator societies tends to deprive men of their full capacity for sexual pleasure, the issue is not one of sexual freedom alone. In fact, sexual freedom for men is *not* inconsistent with a repressive, authoritarian, and highly violent society in which men are conditioned to express the kind of sexuality that equates masculinity with domination.

For example, in Nazi Germany, underneath a lot of puritan rhetoric, Nazi men were hardly forbidden sex. On the contrary, shortly before the Nazis' defeat, as a spur to his troops' flagging morale, Hitler promised that decorated war heroes would be legally allowed to marry more than one woman as a reward for their heroic manliness.[46]

Similarly, the highly violent and repressive Samurai culture of Japan hardly restricted male sexual freedom. As among the ancient Athenians, among Samurai warriors both heterosexual and homosexual relations were openly sanctioned. But (as among the Greek warrior aristocracy) sexual relations between men were only considered proper if they were between *un*equals—with the older warrior taking the "masculine" role and a young boy taking the role that would otherwise be taken by a woman. And not surprisingly, as among the ancient Athenians, in Samurai society sexual relations between males were also favored precisely because women were held in such contempt.[47]

Even in fundamentalist Iran, despite severe "moral" restrictions and even executions of men and women for sexual "immorality," within religiously sanctioned limits men have a great deal of sexual freedom. One example is how, after the mullahs took control, they institutionalized what they call temporary marriage—in essence, a religiously administered sexual trade in women to take the place of the prostitutes these men executed when they closed down the Iranian brothels.[48] So not even in theocratic dominator societies is male sexuality always repressed. Moreover, in many dominator societies, free sexual access to women by men is actually facilitated rather than prohibited by both law and custom.

In sum, the critical factor when it comes to political repression is not whether male sexual freedom is repressed (as by the medieval Christian Church) or whether it is deemed men's inalienable right (as by many men today). The critical factors in politically repressive societies are, first, the repression of female sexual freedom and, second, the distortion of both male and female sexuality through the erotization of domination and violence. And these two factors are inextricably interrelated, not only to each other, but to the maintenance of the habits of thinking and feeling that stand in the way of fundamental social, economic, and ideological change.

Sadomasochism, Rebellion, and Submission

It is therefore all the more ironic that still today men and women actively committed to creating a more truly democratic society—one where there is no longer a double standard for those who have traditionally held power and those who have not—sometimes take the same stance as their most reactionary opponents when it comes to domination in sexual relations. Most people who consider themselves liberals denounce any justification for political and economic domination on the grounds that the dominated groups have tacitly, or even expressly, consented to it. They point out that oppressed groups are socially conditioned to consent to their oppression, and that such consent is never freely given in relations of power imbalance. Yet some of these same people still try to justify the sexual domination of women by men by asserting that this is what women want—in other words, what they consent to. In fact, they sometimes take the stance that feminists who object to pornographic images of the sexual domination and exploitation of women are unfeminine and antisexual—rather than recognizing that what these feminists object to is hardly sexual pleasure but the use of sex to model, and inculcate, unconscious patterns of domination and subjection.

Even more ironic is that in recent years a number of men and women have proclaimed that acts of sadomasochism—of sexual cruelty and sexual bondage—are somehow politically liberating. For example, at an event advertised as a "Torture Circus" held in California at the Santa Cruz Art Center Theater on May 17, 1991 (featuring chainings, whippings, and mutilations in the name of avant-garde art and politics), one of the show's organizers (a woman) claimed that the show was "a form of politics we desperately need to do in the '90s."[49] This woman prided herself on being in the forefront of a modern revolution for sexual and political freedom. But by organizing a public event featuring chainings, whippings, body piercing, and other forms of violence, she had unwittingly become coopted by the same dominator sexual counter-revolution that is today being mass marketed by a billion-dollar pornography industry.

Objectively, to equate sexual freedom with sexual excitement from the chaining, torturing, humiliation, and degradation of others seems totally insane. And in the sense of insanity as a failure to perceive reality, it is. But in the context of a socialization to equate sex and violence, to mistake pain for pleasure, and to experience "loving" as hurting or being hurt, it is understandable. And the fact that this socialization remains largely unconscious makes it even more powerful. Because as long as it remains beyond our conscious understanding, it also remains beyond our ability to consciously bring about change.

Of course, the word *bondage* says it all. For bondage is not only a metaphor for sexual sadomasochism, for tying up or chaining the woman or man playing the traditional feminine part in a sexual scenario; it has for millennia been the description for slavery, for that ultimate act of repression short of taking away life: the taking away of freedom.

Certainly the chains, the whips, and the other paraphernalia of torture associated with sadomasochistic sexuality are hardly new. Nor are they by any stretch of the imagination instruments of freedom. They were always, as they still are, instruments of repression. As we have seen, they go way back into history, to times when the torture of one human being by another was a staple of daily life.

But while public torture (and even the torture behind closed doors of political prisoners) is today properly condemned by almost everyone in the "civilized" world, some people still indignantly defend private (and now even public, as in the so-called torture circuses) sadomasochism as long as it has a sexual component. In other words, as long as it is contextualized in the relationship of men and women, or of homosexuals taking the traditional dominator-dominated roles of men and women, it is not condemned as torture—but defended as freedom.[50]

To be sure, in a society where until recently the only acceptable sexual activity was heterosexual intercourse in the missionary position, it is understandable that any sexual "transgression" should be seen as an act of personal, and even political, rebellion. And since experimenting with sadomasochistic sex brings into the open the power imbalances that have for millennia characterized sexual relations, sadomasochism (or S/M, as it is sometimes called) may, at least for some people, serve as a stage in the process of bringing to consciousness what is otherwise concealed in the unconscious. Moreover, as the sociologist Gini Graham Scott notes in her study of the S/M subculture (which she aptly calls the sexual subculture of domination and submission), if sexual experimentation also involves the flexibility of switching roles, for people habituated to masculine and feminine stereotypes it may bring some expansion of consciousness, making it possible for them to see that, at least in this instance, they do not automatically have to be locked into a dominant (or conversely submissive) role because of their gender.

Nonetheless—and this is the crux of the matter—even if, as Scott documents, a certain percentage of men find the notion of being dominated by women who cruelly punish them sexually arousing, and a certain percentage of women also find this kind of sexual role reversal exciting, in either case sexual relations (and thus male-female relations) are still equated with domination and submission; that is, with relations of inequality.[51]

All of which takes me to a number of basic points. The first is that because the erotization of violence and domination has been central to the social construction of sex for millennia of dominator history, most of us— and not just women and men actively involved in the S/M subculture— are to varying degrees sexually aroused by sadomasochistic fantasies. In other words, what we are dealing with unconsciously affects us all. The second point is that we humans have a need for variety, and therefore for exploration and experimentation—including exploration of the outer limits of intense pleasure. Which in turn leads to a third point: that since both pain and pleasure are intense sensations, sometimes the border between the two is not sharply delineated. We all know that too strong a pleasure can be painful, just as there is sometimes no clear line between intense bliss and a sudden watering of the eyes for joy.

But this is not the same as the falsification that pain *is* pleasure, that to become sexually aroused requires inflicting pain either on oneself or on another. And it is certainly not the same as pretending that the erotization of violent domination and submission is politically and personally liberating, rather than further conditioning us to accept domination and submission in other spheres of life.

It is interesting in this connection that the argument is sometimes made that engaging in sadomasochistic sex represents an expression of trust by the masochist that the sadist will not really hurt her or him. While this may be true, the problem is that this way of expressing trust is itself a reinforcement of the notion that the powerless should trust the powerful, and thus willingly submit to their bondage.

Not only that, but the equation of sexual arousal with either the infliction or suffering of pain reinforces the same kinds of psychosomatic dynamics we looked at earlier in examining the confluence of caring and hurting in child rearing. It links coercive touch with our human need for physical connection, programming us on the most basic level of nerves and muscles to associate pleasurable bodily sensations with domination and submission.

From Bondage to Bonding

In his book *Touching,* the anthropologist Ashley Montagu points out that even this most elementary act of human connection has all too often in traditional child rearing been distorted into an act that teaches us to link pain with pleasure. Thus, through the punitive touching on the buttocks we call spanking, children are often effectively conditioned to associate control through the infliction of pain with sexual arousal. Rousseau, for example, wrote in his memoirs that the spankings by his governess elicited both pain and sexual arousal and were a major factor in his sadomasochistic sexual tastes when he grew up.[52]

But Rousseau did not see how his view of sex as an acting out of domination and submission affected not only his behaviors but his thinking— so much so that he could write of repression as natural for half our species, at the same time that he argued that freedom is an inalienable human right. Neither, as evidenced by these massive contradictions and denials in his thinking, did Rousseau see—when he despotically made the unilateral decision to put all five children borne him by his mistress Thérèse in foundling homes (even though some of his friends offered to raise them, as he writes in the amazingly hypocritical passage I have included in the notes)[53]—that without an end to the institutionalization of domination and submission in personal relations, political institutions based on democratic ideals have no solid foundations. Most critically— and understandably, since he lived in a time when the religious denigration of all that is bodily was still so strong—Rousseau did not deal with the conflict between freedom and repression where it ultimately plays itself out: the place where we all live, within our own bodies.[54]

Because ultimately the way repressive controls are imposed and maintained is through control of the human body, through the fear of pain and the fear of death. Therefore ultimately the human body is also the site of resistance to repression—which is why sadomasochistic sex is far from being an act of political rebellion. Quite the contrary, it is a way rebellion is co-opted and deflected. It is a way of ensuring that we continue to carry, deeply embedded in the actual physicality of our bodies as well as in our unconscious minds, precisely the model of human relations that Freud, Hegel, Sartre, and other important figures who confused the dominator psyche with the human psyche have presented to us as inevitable: one where the only alternatives are for the slave to become a master or the master to become a slave.[55] In short, it turns what on the surface seems like a deviation from the norm (and thus rebellion) into what is actually an acting out of the norm through a sexual ritual of domination and submission.

Certainly the erotization of domination and submission is not the only way dominator systems maintain themselves. There are many other ways, individually, socially, in economics, politics, religion, and the family. But because it unconsciously conditions us to accept, participate in, and even seek relations of domination and submission, the erotization of domination and submission cannot be ignored.

I here want to add that if we find sadomasochism not only in heterosexual sex but among homosexuals, it is because homosexual sex has also often been distorted into dominator-dominated relations. In fact, the French playwright Jean Genet powerfully revealed almost half a century ago how homosexual relations can be exaggerations of the traditional heterosexual scripts—with the woman playing the masculine "butch" role in lesbian relations dominating the woman playing the role of the "femme," and the "manly" male homosexual contemptuously dominating the man taking the despised feminine role of the "queen."

But having said this, I also want to say that there is today a very strong and conscious movement away from these kinds of sexual stereotypes among many lesbians and gay men. And it is with this movement among both homosexuals and heterosexuals—and the changes in consciousness it reflects—that I want to close this chapter.

Clearly it does not help if we berate ourselves, or others, for having become conditioned to eroticize domination and submission. Becoming so habituated creates a pattern akin to addiction—one that involves bodily rewards (sexual excitement, and thus probably, as in other addictions, the release of endorphins) for personally and socially destructive behaviors. Furthermore, habits that developed over so many centuries—even millennia—do not go away overnight. So even once we recognize how the social construction of sexuality into a no-exit ritual dance of domination and submission affects us all, we cannot just by some magic act of will drive it away.

However, as we know from the contemporary study of addiction, coming out of denial is an important first step. It makes it possible for us to envision healthier, more satisfying alternatives. And the hopeful fact is that despite all the resistance from both inside and outside us, people all over the world are today beginning to do just that.

All over the world, women and men are today questioning their most basic assumptions regarding just about everything, from power and sex to love and spirituality. These are signs that we may at long last find ways to leave behind our attachment to habits of thinking, feeling, and acting that have habituated us to confuse pain with pleasure and bondage with bonding. But before we go on to all this, we will first in the next chapter look more closely at a psychosocial dynamic that goes along with the erotization of domination: the erotization of violence.

CHAPTER 12

Making Love or Making War: Eroticizing Violence

During Western prehistory there was, as we have seen, a fundamental shift in how sex was conceptualized. From an act associated with the sacred, with religious rites, with the Goddess herself, sex became associated with male power over women. Then religious authorities taught men that the bodily or carnal is, like woman, of a lower order. So it became man's duty to control and subdue not only woman (who was viewed by some medieval Christian theologians as so base that they even debated whether she had a soul) but all that is bodily or carnal. All this put men at war with their own bodies. And it also put them at war with women—hence the term "war of the sexes."

Even in the most rigid dominator societies, not all men became active combatants in this war. On the contrary, sometimes men have joined women in rejecting both war and the war of the sexes. For example, during the 1960s, as U.S. sentiment against the Vietnam War mounted and the women's liberation movement was born, a new slogan was coined: Make love not war. But like most slogans, it did not go deep enough—to the fact that in the dominator mind making love *is* making war.

We vividly see this in our language, where many of the words we are taught to express hatred and contempt have sexual meanings: for instance *bitch, bastard,* and *fuck* (as in "fuck you" or "mother-fucker"). These words are accurately called by men "fighting words," since they have often been followed by acts designed to cause injury and death. In the same way, the crude insult "cunt" (a slang word for women's genitals) is hurled at women to express hatred and contempt, often in conjunction with acts of physical violence.

This association of sex with brute force is jarringly apparent in military jargon: the language that describes acts explicitly designed to cause injury and death. In fact, this language and the language of sex are often interchangeable. Just as the aim of soldiers is to take enemy territory, a man sexually "takes" a woman. A man who makes many sexual "conquests" used to be called a lady-killer. In military language a man's sexual organ is jokingly referred to as his gun. (I have actually heard military wives teach their little sons to so refer to their penises as a "polite" term.) Combat analysts write of new weaponry as "penetration aids"—just as sexual intercourse is customarily described as male "penetration" of the female (with only the most occasional mention of how the male organ is in this act also engulfed by the female genitalia).[1] And generals and politicians speak of nuclear weapons as providing more "bang for your buck" (*banging* being a common male slang word for sexual intercourse).

But unlike military warfare, which is even in dominator societies sporadic, the war of the sexes is integral to daily life and thought. And while military warfare is freely acknowledged and fought in the open, the violence of the war of the sexes has until recent times simply been ignored, as if it did not exist. Even beyond this, the most brutal and explicit images of sexual violence, which constitute the most blatant propaganda for this war, are still widely viewed as only smut or pornography—to some people an exciting and to others a prurient or dirty aspect of human sexuality.

But the erotization of brutality and violence not only serves to maintain the domination of one half of humanity by the other, which, as illustrated by classics like Shakespeare's *Taming of the Shrew,* is the goal of the war of the sexes. Nor does it only condition men to enjoy warfare, which likewise has the express goal of conquering and dominating others. It is an effective means of maintaining a way of living, and dying, in which both women and men learn to accept violent and coercive touch as not only normal but exciting.

Again, I want to stress that not all women and men are successfully socialized in this regard. In fact, many men as well as women react with horror to violence and cruelty. Nonetheless, when added to the childhood dynamics we examined earlier, the systematic erotization of domination and violence helps explain how—having been conditioned to associate with sexual arousal every conceivable and inconceivable brutality and violence—men all over the world have beaten, tortured, and even killed other human beings (be they political prisoners, religious heretics, or women), and seemingly enjoyed it.

Sex, Brutality, and Human Nature

As I was writing this chapter—and it was a painful chapter to write—I realized how for much of my life I too had not been conscious of how pervasive violence against women is, or how the association of sex with domination and violence fuels, and at the same time conceals, this violence. I also became even more acutely aware of how the psychological mechanism of denial has throughout dominator history made it possible for us to cope with brutal realities, particularly if they were believed to be inevitable. For denial not only makes it possible for us to pretend brutality and violence do not exist, shoving our perceptions and experiences into our unconscious minds. It also makes it possible for us to accept two contradictory versions of reality—both of which reinforce the dominator status quo.

On the one hand, the association of sex and violent domination is said not to exist except in the case of just a few perverts. On the other hand, this same association is said to be not only normal but inevitable—just part of human, or more specifically, male nature.

Thus, only a few years ago the well-known British writer Colin Wilson could state that sex killings are of interest to the "sexually normal" because "the sexual act has a close affinity to murder" since, according to Wilson, "murderer and victim are in the same sort of relation as the male penetrating the female."[2] This was also the view of Robert Stoller, who went so far as to contend in *Sexual Excitement: The Dynamics of Erotic Life* that "putting aside the obvious effects that result from direct stimulation of erotic bodily parts, it is hostility—the desire, overt or hidden, to harm another person—that generates and enhances sexual excitement." In other words, it was Stoller's contention that "harm and suffering" are central to sexual excitement, and that the debasement and fetishization (dehumanization and objectification) of the "sexual object," and even the use of sex in a "search for revenge," are normal.[3]

For Stoller the sexual object was a woman, or a man playing the part of a woman in a homosexual relation. And the protagonists of his hostile sexual scripts were regularly male, even though he actually maintained that a woman chooses sexual masochism "because through it she triumphs over men, whom ultimately she controls because she is the provocation to which they respond."[4]

I should add here that it is not only men but also women who have made these kinds of bizarre pronouncements. An example is Freud's disciple Helene Deutsch. Freud had contended that "sadism can be readily demonstrable in the normal individual" (in Freud's male-centered world, read "man") because "the sexuality of most men shows an admixture of aggression, of the propensity to subdue."[5] To this Deutsch added that this all works out because female masochism is also "normal."

Indeed, women who take the position that dominator-dominated sexual relations are only natural gain far more academic and media attention than those who question this.[6] And there is always a new authority to tell us that it is "man's nature" to be violent and cruel, both sexually and otherwise.

The fact, however, is that images of cruelty and brutality are not, as in later times, an important theme in the art of the prehistoric societies we looked at earlier. Nor do we there find any hint of the erotization of brutality and violence. Quite the contrary, as we have seen, it is an art that shows a reverence and awe for woman's sexual power.

Moreover, if male violence were a genetic given we would not find so much cultural variation in male violence, not only from period to period but from society to society. Nor would we find, as we do, a correlation between rigid dominator-dominated gender stereotypes and a high level of social violence.[7]

Not only that, if male cruelty and violence were, as we are often told, simply a matter of male hormones, most, if not all, men would be cruel and violent while women would never, or hardly ever, be—which is clearly not the case. There are studies correlating the hormone testosterone (which is present in much larger quantities in men) and violent behaviors, although other studies dispute this. But even if testosterone plays a role in male violence, and men as a group are therefore more predisposed to learn violent behaviors, the social context (including whether men are systematically taught violent behaviors) is still critical. For testosterone levels rise and fall depending on the social situation, going up where aggressive behaviors have a social "payoff."[8]

Indeed, recent studies indicate that how any kind of physical and emotional arousal is labeled—and therefore what actions are taken as a response—varies greatly depending on the social cues. For example, in what was billed as a health experiment, male subjects were told they were getting a vitamin injection but were actually given an adrenaline shot, which causes significant hormonal arousal. The men were then divided up into different groups and asked to wait until the "vitamin" took effect in separate rooms where confederates of the experimenters, who had been instructed to comport themselves in two very different ways, were waiting. For some of the subjects, the confederates created what the experimenters called the "anger condition" environment by asking intrusive and insulting personal questions and otherwise acting in annoying and offensive ways. For others, a "euphoria condition" environment was created by the confederates, who were the essence of niceness and friendliness, acting in playful and giddy ways, inviting the subjects to join in the fun. What the researchers found is that these two very different kinds of social cues profoundly affected how the men in their experiment responded—with reactions ranging all the way from angry feelings and hostile behaviors in one group to feelings of happiness and giddy behaviors in the other.[9]

So clearly, cruel and sadistic acts do not just follow from hormonal arousal alone. We always have to take into account the social context—including how people have been socially conditioned to interpret what happens in their bodies and how they should react to it.

But perhaps most tellingly, if it were true that because of hormonal or genetic factors men are innately violent, there would be no need to at every turn teach boys and men violence. In other words, even if it is true that men as a group are more predisposed to learn violence than women (which is all one could reasonably say in light of the enormous variability of human behavior and the tremendous role learning plays in it), this would be all the more reason *not* to systematically reinforce such a tendency through every conceivable social cue—including the systematic linking of sexual arousal with violence and cruelty.

The Male Script for Violence

The erotization of violence is not the only way men have throughout recorded history been taught, and still continue to be taught, to associate enjoyment with violence. The systematic association of enjoyable activities, such as games and toys, with violence starts in early childhood, when parents hand little boys toy swords, guns, and more recently missile launchers and video games where the object is to win by killing. It continues throughout adolescent and adult life—for example, through books, songs, films, comic strips, and TV programs idealizing the hero as the warrior/conqueror. And women have actively collaborated in this teaching—for example, when mothers call their sons "sissies" (that is, weak sisters) when they cry, and when girls deride sensitive boys as "wimps" or "wuzzes," saying they prefer tough "he-men"—in some cases even men who slap women around as a way of expressing their "love."[10]

So the erotization of violence is part of a larger male socialization that to varying degrees follows what the psychologist Silvan Tomkins calls the macho script for what is today often called hypermasculine socialization.[11] Tomkins, who is well known in psychology for his development of "script theory" (which proposes that personality is formed through a combination of innate and cultural scripts), shows how this script is taught to men to prepare them for their culturally prescribed roles.[12] He begins his analysis by noting something we examined earlier: that nomadic pastoralists living in environments of extreme scarcity seem to have been the first to develop societies ruled, in Tomkins's words, by warriors and "masculine adversarial deities celebrating prowess and death over life and community."[13] And he shows how the scripts for masculinity first developed in these societies are still with us today in very different environments—and how they have been passed on and lived out from generation to generation "at once self-validating and self-fulfilling."[14]

"Scripting the Macho Man," an article Tomkins wrote in 1988 with the psychologist Donald Mosher for the *Journal of Sex Research*, analyzes how "macho" scripts are part of an ideology in which males are viewed as superior to females and emotions associated with masculinity are considered superior to those associated with femininity. As Mosher and Tomkins document, these scripts teach men that only certain kinds of feelings are "masculine," feelings such as disgust, anger, and contempt—in other words, feelings appropriate for those who are to dominate. They also teach men to have contempt for "inferior feminine" feelings, such as distress, compassion, and empathy—just as stereotypical female socialization teaches women that "masculine" feelings, which they too are taught to see as superior (along with men), are off limits for them.

To so split our species into a "superior" male in-group and an "inferior" female out-group is not an easy task. Neither is the accompanying splitting of humanity's emotional repertoire into "masculine" and "feminine" feelings. This is why it has to begin in early childhood and continue all our lives. It is also why, as Tomkins and Mosher note, the socialization of boys and girls for androcratic "masculinity" and "femininity" is most clearly evident in the types of families that most effectively condition children to fit into dominator-dominated rankings: families where parents (having experienced similar treatment) frequently fail to respond to a child's cries of distress by comforting it (modeling empathy) and instead ignore or even punish the child for crying (modeling callousness or lack of empathy).

It is in these families that we also most vividly see how boys are systematically taught that for males to express (or even feel) "soft" emotions is shameful, that such feelings are appropriate only for "inferior" girls and women (or for equally inferior "sissies" or "effeminate" men).[15] For in accordance with the macho script, it is made clear to boys that they are being punished not just because they are expressing such feelings, but because by so doing they are being "feminine" rather than "masculine."

Add to this the fact that boys soon learn that there is a payoff to "masculine" emotions—that while anger is forbidden to girls and women, for boys it is, as Mosher and Tomkins put it, "instrumental in securing desired goals" (in other words, is rewarded)—and it is not hard to see how, again in Tomkins's and Mosher's words, the unrelieved and intensified neural stimulation of painful distress is in boys transformed into the "manly" emotion of anger. So after a while boys learn either consciously or unconsciously that the cultural script for men is: "'Don't cry, be tough, have contempt for those who cry' and 'Don't cry, get mad, and make them cry instead'."[16]

To further ensure they learn to be properly "masculine," boys are also taught contempt and disgust for the "feminine" emotions of fear and shame—and thus never to admit that they are afraid or wrong. But in the process, as Mosher and Tomkins stress, boys are taught to feel disgust even for themselves when they have "feminine" emotions. On top of this, since "real men" must always be in control of their own despised "feminine" side, as well as strive for control over others, they are also taught to be suspicious of "relaxed enjoyment," which, as Mosher and Tomkins note, is likewise associated with women and "effeminate men."[17]

So in the end, what the properly socialized macho man is left with is only the "enjoyment" of victory over an opponent—be the opponent another man or a woman. As Mosher and Tomkins note, "in his dangerous world of perceived scarcity," there is for the macho man only the "intense excitement" that for him becomes associated with "the joy of victory or the agony of defeat."[18] And it is this same kind of "intense excitement" that for macho men becomes associated with "enjoyable" relations with women.

Thus it is that in initiations to macho manhood a boy must not only show he is not afraid of other males; he must also show that he can sexually master females. And in so doing, he learns still another major component of the macho script: the association of sex not with mutual pleasure, much less caring, but with violent domination. This is why fraternities (as well as gangs) often initiate boys into "manhood" not only through acts of reckless daring and endurance of pain, but through exhibitions of their sexual "power" over women in front of their peers—as in the fraternity gang rapes that have only recently begun to be recognized as crimes of violence rather than "boyish pranks."[19]

Indeed, it is in these male peer groups—from armies and urban gangs to sports teams and fraternities—that men (and boys) are taught to bond around power over out-groups (be they women or "inferior" and/or "dangerous" men).[20] And it is also in these all-male peer groups that, as we will see, "scoring" (or sexually conquering women) becomes integral to proving a man's masculinity.

So it is not only, to again borrow Mosher's and Tomkins's words, that the "Four F Philosophy"—"Find them, fool them, fuck them, and forget them"—"encapsulates the macho's sexual ideology." It is also that to participate in "gang bangs" and otherwise sexually conquer, harass, or intimidate women in the presence of male friends, or to recount these scenes in their presence, "bonds the male group together in a camaraderie of shared hypermasculinity"—with the final result that "the social stratification into the strong or the weak has subsumed a sexual differentiation as strong *and* masculine or weak *and* feminine."[21] For though the macho man or boy must defer to the dominant leader and thus may accept a submissive role within the in-group, he may never do so with "inferior" out-group men or women.

War and the War of the Sexes

Since this script for masculinity is our inheritance from ancient warrior societies, it should not surprise us that the place where we most clearly see how the erotization of male violence serves to fuel both war and the war of the sexes is in the institution specifically designed to train men to kill: the military. Throughout dominator history, the military (not so long ago considered the only honorable career for noblemen) has prepared men not only to kill people of "dangerous" or "inferior" tribes and nations; it has also trained them to kill their own people if the authorities perceive them as a threat to their rule. So it was, and still is, necessary to teach these men not to give in to "soft" emotions such as empathy, compassion, and caring. And what better way to teach men to suppress such feelings than by using the worst insult conceivable to "real" men—that if they do, they are acting like women?[22] Even beyond this, what better way to train men to actually enjoy their macabre tasks than to systematically associate cruelty and violence with sex and women?

Once again, this is not to say that military or political strategists then, or now, sat down to consciously and deliberately figure all this out. But the fact is that even now, as the social scientists William Arken and Lynne Dobrofsky observed in their study of American military training, "the relationships of masculinity and violence and masculinity and sex dominate formal as well as informal military socialization patterns."[23]

They report that in boot camp training, "military discipline simultaneously embarrasses and reminds the recruit of his penis-as-power link by requiring him to hold his rifle in one hand, while his other hand grasps his crotch," and to shout:

> Sir:
> This is my rifle
> This is my gun
> This is for fighting
> This is for fun![24]

Similarly, just as "joystick" (slang for penis) is a name pilots give to the control lever of female-named combat aircraft such as Betty Boob, in boot camp jargon sex and violence are also linked. Indeed, so intertwined are the two that land mines designed to explode at groin height are frequently given female names such as Bouncing Betty, exploiting the familiar male fear of castration—and rationalizing the violent domination of women by men.

Arken and Dobrofsky report that in basic training men are systematically encouraged to see sexual conquest as manly—in their words, to see women as "objects for men's sexual exploitation." So, not surprisingly, men often talk about sexual violence in the same terms as military violence—as exciting and fun. And also not surprisingly, wife beating and other forms of violence against women were, as they still are, a major problem in military families.[25]

Again, this is by no means to say that all men in the military physically abuse their wives or that all men who go through military training are successfully socialized to be active combatants in the war of the sexes, or even in war. But there is little question that the military script linking "real" masculinity with violence and conquest (including sexual conquest) functions to maintain dominator rankings through both war and the war of the sexes. And there is also no question that some men do internalize this script, that they learn to despise and suppress in themselves anything associated with what they are taught is soft or feminine—that is, feelings of love and empathy, even empathy for themselves—and to equate sex with brutal conquest, even killing.

This becomes only too evident if we look at some recently published excerpts from the writings of men from two nations that during World War II fought each other: Germany and the United States. For, like a gangrenous wound split open, they burst upon us the full horror of a male socialization that systematically links violence and cruelty with sex and women.

It is very difficult to read these writings because what they reveal about the men who wrote them is so monstrous. And in a very real sense these men are monstrous, having lost the human capacity to see others as living, sentient beings and to identify with their pain. Certainly the German men whose writings are examined in Klaus Theweleit's *Male Fantasies* were monstrous killers and torturers. They were members of the elite Nazi Freikorps, who between 1923 and 1933 became the core of Hitler's infamous SA—the elite troops who not only terrorized Germany during the short-lived Weimar Republic but also were to play a central role in the horrors of World War II, including Hitler's extermination of millions of Jews, Poles, Russians, and/or individuals perceived as dissidents.[26]

These men wrote of women's bodies (or more accurately, women's sexual body parts, which is how they described women) with undisguised disgust and contempt. As Theweleit writes, woman's sensuality seemed to them "castrating," "animal-like," "dangerous"—a threat to their masculinity, and often, as in the many stories where they kill women, to their lives. In fact, the Freikorps stories typically link sexual intercourse with death (or, more accurately, with women's death). And even in a rare story, such as the one about Lieutenant Bewerkron and Red Marie, where the flicker of a human relationship enters the picture, the outcome is the same. We are told that "poor Bewerkron would have to get a firm grip on his heart if he were going to carry out his errand of mercy." But then it turns out that his "errand of mercy" is to betray his lover's trust by telling her, so she will not be afraid all night, that he will save her—and in the morning, with her trusting eyes hopefully fixed upon him, ordering his men to shoot her.[27]

The Freikorps writings repeatedly bring us back to how sexual relations are in these men's minds equivalent to the relations of combatants in war. Indeed, by and large the only relationship between the women and the men in these stories *is* through the men's acts of cruelty and violence. It is through the clubbing, whipping, burning, trampling, shooting, and ripping apart of women's flesh, particularly of women's genitals, buttocks, and breasts—or as Theweleit puts it, through the reduction of women's bodies to "a bloody mass."[28] And it is precisely this process— "the pleasurable perception of women in the condition of bloody masses"—that, as Theweleit notes, "seems to deliver the real satisfaction" these men seek.

"It's as if two male compulsions were tearing at the women with equal strength," Theweleit writes. "One is trying to push them away, to keep them at arm's length (defense); the other wants to penetrate them, to have them very near. Both compulsions seem to find satisfaction in the act of killing, where the man pushes the woman far away (takes her life), and gets very close to her (penetrates her with a bullet, stab wound, club, etc.)." He concludes:

It is only after she has been reduced to this state that her sensuousness meets with an almost appreciative tolerance. The "red roses" of her sex only blossom from the wounds on her dead, deformed, opened-up body. Whatever it is about the sensuous woman that excites these men lies beneath the surface, under her skin. It looks very much as if the killings are conceived as corrective measures, which alter the false appearances of the women so that their "true natures" can become visible.[29]

And what is this "true nature"? It is, of course, the "bloody mass." For in these dominator fantasies, and all too often realities, women's bodies and women's sexuality are associated not with life and pleasure but with the "bloody mass" of destruction, with the "satisfaction" of cruelty and domination, and ultimately with the putrefaction of the body and with death.

These too are central themes in the writings of a very different group of men: the young American pilots of the U.S. Air Force 77th Tactical Fighter Squadron who half a century later published a pamphlet called the *Gambler's Songbook* that, in their words, "is a collection of over seventy-five years of tradition, our thoughts, our songs and our games."[30] One of the songs included in this collection of three-quarters of a century of military tradition is "I Fucked a Dead Whore." It begins as follows:

> I fucked a dead whore by the roadside,
> I knew right away she was dead.
> The skin was all gone from her tummy,
> The hair was all gone from her head. . . [31]

Then there is a song its authors call "These Foolish Things (Remind Me of You)." Here are some of its lyrics:

> A sloppy blow job in a taxi cab,
> A cunt that's covered with syphilitic scabs,
> These foolish things remind me of you.[32]

In these songs too, the bodies of women both excite and disgust the men. But above all, as in the Nazis' fantasies, in them women are nothing but pieces of meat—and even beyond that, disgusting pieces of meat, rotten and as in the first song, dead. In short, as Joan Smith notes in her remarkable book *Misogynies*, these too are songs in which woman, and particularly woman's sexuality, is a symbol of death and pain rather than of life and pleasure.[33] Moreover, as we read in still another song called "Ghost Fuckers in the Sky" (describing the rape of a "slant-eyed bitch"), they are songs in which sex is repeatedly associated with violence—or more specifically, with the violent domination of "the enemy" (woman) by men for whom only a dead woman's pussy is sweet.

Male Fantasies and Inhuman Realities

To deal with all this horror, it is tempting to think that these kinds of fantasies can be explained as psychological aberrations, the products of minds hardening themselves for the horrors of war. But these fantasies are neither unique to brutal fascists nor American fighter pilots. We find these very same fantasies in pornographic books, films, and videotapes of women being bound, chained, pierced, and sexually tortured that today are mass marketed to boys and men all over this country, indeed world-wide. And now we do not even have to go to porno shops and adult the-aters (like the military, traditionally male preserves) for such images, as they can be found in the porno magazines at many newsstands.

Again, it is tempting to think that this is just pornography, the product of dirty minds. But the truth is that our entire culture is permeated by the erotization of cruelty and brutality to women, so much so that we have learned to take it for granted.

We see it in our movies, in theaters all over the United States, and from there, the world, where men's rapes, whippings, chainings, tortures, and killings of women are mass marketed as entertainment. Films shown not in porno houses but in Main Street theaters—Alfred Hitchcock's criti-cally acclaimed woman-murder film *Psycho* (the prototype for a whole genre of "slasher" films); Sam Peckinpah's lovingly detailed depictions of women being beaten, whipped, and raped; box office hits like *The Chain Saw Massacre* and *Henry: Portrait of a Serial Killer* (a stomach-turning guide on how to get away with sexual murders)—endlessly link male violence and sexuality. So also do film classics such as Rudolph Valentino's *The Sheik*. More subtly, but just as effectively, "macho" movie stars such as Humphrey Bogart, Marlon Brando, Clint Eastwood, Jack Nicholson, and Arnold Schwarzenegger (all noted for roles in which they slap, beat, kill, or otherwise brutalize women) further convey the message that sex and violence go together.

Music videos that link sex with violence and domination are common television fare. In addition, both children and adults yearly see thousands upon thousands of murders, beatings, and other acts of brutality that link masculinity with violence and domination right on their home television screens. Then there are novels read by thousands of people, such as Bret Easton Ellis's *American Psycho* (1990), in which the hero gets his sexual thrills by cutting off a woman's fingers, pouring acid into her vagina, stabbing her in the throat, and finally, in front of another woman, sawing her head off and putting his "cock, purple with stiffness, into the corpse's bloodied mouth."[34] No less grisly are records listened to by millions of young people, many of them children—records by groups such as 2 Live Crew (whose 1989 "Nasty as They Wanna Be" was held "not obscene" even though it is a call to sexual brutality, with lyrics such as "bust your cunt," "break your backbone," and "I wanna see you bleed"); NWA (who "rap" about tying a woman to a bed, raping her, and then killing her with a .44 Magnum in their song "One Less Bitch");[35] and Cannibal Corpse (whose lyrics for the song "Entrails Ripped From a Virgin's Cunt," about disemboweling a young girl "tied to my mattress/devirginized with my knife," end with "internally bleeding/vagina secreting/her blood-wet pussy I am eating").[36]

Even in our advertising, sometimes subtly and sometimes not so subtly, male violence and domination are presented as sexy. This is the message of the 1989 Revlon ad where a smiling Frank Sinatra pulls a woman with an equally frozen smile to him by the pearls around her neck. It is the message of countless album covers glamorizing sexual sadism and of ads for albums like that displayed on a billboard on the Hollywood Sunset Strip in 1976 showing a bound and bruised woman with legs spread-eagled over the caption "I'm black and blue from the Rolling Stones and I love it!" It is even the message sometimes found in fashion ads—for example, in a number of issues of *Vogue*, where sexual sadism against women was elegantly marketed not only as sexy but as chic.[37]

Again, it is tempting to think that all this is a recent aberration, the by-product of "too much sexual freedom." But in reality it is only the latest, and most explicit, elaboration of long-established themes. Indeed, if we stop to think about it, we see that the equation of male sexuality and violent domination is a favorite subject of some of our most revered writers.

Thus, from Leo Tolstoy, a man described by some of his biographers as the greatest modern writer and even as a modern saint, we have *The Kreutzer Sonata*, a thinly veiled autobiographical account of his sadistic relationship with his wife, Sophie, symbolically expressed in the story of a man who, to overcome his revulsion for women and sex, murders his wife. The legendary D. H. Lawrence would have us believe in "The Woman Who Rode Away" that his invented heroine becomes sexually aroused by the realization that she is about to be ritually slaughtered by half-naked savages. The famous poet Robinson Jeffers fantasizes in his "Roan Stallion" that a woman would actually want to have intercourse with a huge horse, even though it would rip her apart. And the central message of such "important" contemporary writers as Henry Miller (who rhapsodizes about the sexual degradation of women) and Norman Mailer (whose hero in *An*

American Dream finds honor and renewal in brutally killing his wife) is once again that what is sexually arousing to men (and presumably also to women) is *not* the giving of pleasure but the inflicting of pain—and even more specifically the debasement, torture, humiliation, domination, and even killing of women.[38] Indeed, the parallel between some of the passages in Mailer's book and those of the Freikorps men and the sadistic lyrics in death metal songs such as "Entrails Ripped" are striking, and sickening.

Still, there are those today who claim that all these images of women's brutalized bodies and all this linking of sex, cruelty, and violence have no real effect, that they are just fantasies, not realities. However, if this were so, why would the military deliberately use the erotization of violence to teach men to kill? And why, if linking sex with violence has no effect on sexual and social behavior, would savvy media professionals link sex with whatever they are trying to sell—from cars to Coca-Cola—to influence peoples' buying behavior?

If war propaganda is effective in dehumanizing members of "enemy" nations, making it possible for men to hurt, kill, and degrade other human beings—as it clearly is—why would images of women as merely body parts for male sexual use and abuse not have similar effects? Why, like propaganda for other wars, would stories and images that dehumanize women not blind people to the reality of women's suffering?

The answer is that it is precisely because this propaganda has been so effective that many men and women still today cannot see these seemingly obvious connections. Indeed, were this propaganda not so successful, we would all be aware of something we already glimpsed in Chapter 1: that the term "war of the sexes" is a metaphor for what has been an incredibly violent war against women—a war in which the casualties are far higher than in many well-publicized armed conflicts.

The true magnitude of worldwide violence against women is staggering, almost impossible to comprehend. And so is the fact that only now is it beginning to be officially documented, and thus more generally recognized and reported.[39]

For example, according to the U.S. Senate Judiciary Committee, in the United States more women were victims of rape in 1989—one year alone—than Marines wounded in all of World War II.[40] In 1990, the U.S. Surgeon General reported that domestic violence was the single largest cause of injury to American women—way ahead of auto accidents. And after it too finally started to look at violent crimes from a gender perspective, the FBI announced that three out of four American women (75 percent) can expect to be the target of at least one crime of violence in their lifetimes.[41]

In other parts of our globe, the incidence of violence against women may be even higher. Wife beating is still socially accepted in many regions and even the deliberate murder of girls and women for any suspected sexual independence is in some countries not viewed as a criminal act but rather as a matter of male "honor."[42] According to a 1991 United Nations report, due to selective malnutrition, bride burning, and other forms of violence, 25 percent of Indian girls die before the age of fifteen.[43] And the press has in recent years begun to report something that, as we have seen, is actually a very ancient form of gender-specific violence: selective female infanticide. But revealingly, this violence only became "important" front page news when it was reported from China because of the U.S. government's anticommunism and anti–population control crusade—and *not* because its targets were female babies.

The tragic truth is that if violence against girls and women were considered newsworthy, it would make headlines every day—and would have done so for most of recorded history.[44] So it is indeed a major step in the modern revolution in consciousness that at long last newspeople, social scientists, and women and men all over the world are beginning to perceive the true nature, and horror, of the war of the sexes—and how its violence serves to maintain the domination of half of humanity by the other.

Still, even today it is mainly in the feminist press that we find article after article about the worldwide failure of courts and other authorities to punish the perpetrators of this brutality, that we learn that in parts of Africa, Asia, and Latin America it is still today often openly sanctioned in the name of tradition.[45] As we saw earlier, this failure of laws and courts to protect women from violence is also deeply embedded in Western tradition. This helps account for the fact that until recently, women did not generally report this violence. And it also in large part accounts for the fact that as this gradually changed we have seen a huge jump in violent crime statistics. For as I noted in chapter 1, if a man beat up someone he did not know he was customarily arrested and taken to jail—whereas if he beat up a woman with whom he had a sexual relationship, it was police practice to either ignore it as a "domestic squabble" or at best to just walk the man around the block until he "cooled off."

So perhaps it should not surprise us that even today, in tragic case after case, when American women report to the police that men threaten to beat or kill them they are told that there is no way of protecting them until the man actually "does something"—and of course by then it is too late. All the same, it is shocking to discover the extent to which our laws and courts still protect men from police and legal prosecution—rather than protecting women from male violence—and that even when it comes to police protection from violence there is a double standard.

A horrifying case in point is what happened a few years ago with a California man who cut off his victim's arms after he brutally raped her and left her to die on a deserted road (which she miraculously survived). When he was released for "good behavior" and neighbors (who understandably did not want this monster around) threatened him, *he* was protected by a police guard assigned to be with him around the clock—at taxpayers' expense.[46]

The Double Standard for Violence, Pavlov's Dogs, and Androcratic Men

There is today a heated controversy about whether there is a relationship between increases in brutal acts of violence (particularly rapes and sex murders) and the contemporary barrage of explicitly violent imagery in the media, music, art, and literature.[47] As with other human behaviors, it is impossible to attribute acts of violence to a single cause. For instance, a recent study of 4,269 men in Denmark found that when taken together, rejection in childhood and birth complications strongly pointed to violence-prone men—even though there was no significant correlation when only one of these factors was considered.[48] So the question is not whether there is a direct causative relationship between violent imagery and acts of violence, as has been found in a number of "copy-cat" sexual murders and rapes. The question is whether images of violence produce a cultural climate that, particularly for those individuals already predisposed to violence due to psychological or physical factors, increases the likelihood that they will act out this predisposition. And still another question is how this cultural climate affects the general perception of violence, particularly when it is violence against women.

Clinical experiments show that men who watch violent pornography are less likely to see rape as hurtful to women and more likely to say they would rape if they thought they could get away with it.[49] In fact, men exposed to only five X-rated movies linking sex and violence, as the researchers Daniel Linz, Edward Donnerstein, and Steven Penrod write, "came to have fewer negative emotional reactions to the films, to perceive them as significantly less violent, and to consider them significantly less degrading to women."[50] So even where violent pornography does not directly incite violence against women, those who see it are desensitized to women's suffering, leading them to more readily tolerate violence against women by disassociating it from real pain and instead associating it with sexual arousal.

This in turn contributes to a social climate in which the acts of those men who in fact, not just fantasy, are violent against women are also more easily condoned. And just as in authoritarian regimes relatively few men have to violently terrorize people to maintain their subordination, the maintenance of male dominance only requires that a certain number of men be violent against women. For in both cases it is enough to have in- termittent violence to terrorize the subordinate groups, and thus effec- tively control attempts to change the status quo.

Not only that, but the conditioning of both women and men to view sexual violence against women as arousing and exciting—and thus as not only acceptable but desirable—makes it possible for both women and men to treat cruelty and violence that is specifically against women as of a different order than cruelty and violence that is also against men. Put another way—and in sharp contrast to the contemporary denunciation of violence against groups that include males (such as racist and anti- Semitic violence)—it makes it possible for many people to view violence against women as merely a "women's issue."

But the erotization of violence not only serves to maintain male domi- nance. The resulting acceptance of bodily violence against women as triv- ial and/or sexy forcefully reinforces a male socialization for all kinds of violence—which is why the erotization of violence has been such an inte- gral part of military training. For if men can successfully be taught to equate violence, and even killing, with sexual arousal—like the Nazis of the Freikorps or the American pilots who wrote the *Gambler's Songbook*— they will also be sexually aroused by hurting and killing, be it hurting or killing women or other men.

How this works through a mechanism that has long been studied by psychologists trying to understand how emotional, and even physiologi- cal, responses are acquired began to become clear to me in the course of my research for this book. Generally known as conditioning, this mecha- nism was first experimentally documented by the pioneering Russian sci- entist Ivan Pavlov. What Pavlov did was to ring a bell every time he fed the dogs in his famous experiments. But after a while, he stopped putting out any food when he rang the bell. And what he found is that the dogs had become so conditioned to associate food with the ringing of a bell that they salivated every time it rang—even when there was no food any- where around. In other words, Pavlov obtained the same emotional, and even physiological, response from what he called the conditional or sec- ondary stimulus as from the primary or unconditional one.[51]

Along the same lines, the sexual arousal of men by a woman's body (the primary stimulus) is in dominator cultures regularly associated with domination, cruelty, and violence (the secondary stimulus). So after a while—even when there is no sexy woman or other sexual image to produce sexual arousal—cruelty, domination, and violence themselves can produce the same emotional and physiological response. As Linz, Donnerstein, and Penrod write, what probably ensues is "a misattribution process," where subjects begin to misattribute their arousal to violence.[52]

Again, this is not to say that everyone exposed to this conditioning will respond in this way. But particularly for those men already predisposed to violence, the repeated association of sexual pleasure with violence and cruelty will make it more difficult to overcome such predispositions. This is what Leonard Berkowitz has suggested in his "stimulus-response association model."[53] And it is also congruent with Albert Bandura's research on modeling, which suggests an interactive, mutually reinforcing process whereby conditioning men to link sex with violence is in itself a factor predisposing them to violence.[54]

This kind of conditioning of men and boys—who are the target market for all the modern pornography associating cruelty and violence against women with sex—is particularly important in societies where people are also taught that cruelty and violence are inhuman and immoral. For unlike in more barbaric or "pure" dominator societies, there is here a need to selectively reinforce only the cruelty and violence that maintains the society's most basic rankings of domination: those of men over women and of "superior" over "inferior" groups (groups that, like the Jews in Nazi Germany and the defeated Iraqis in Kuwait, are often derisively labeled "effeminate").

So it makes sense that during our time of powerful partnership resurgence we should find an exponential escalation of images linking sex and violence, not only in pornography but throughout the mass media, including music, advertising, and even cartoons and comics. For this not only warns women of what they can expect if they do not return to their "traditional" roles; it also provides a constant barrage of social cues that link sexual arousal with violence and domination. And as we have seen, how physiological arousal (in other words, the surge of chemicals that accompanies physiological excitability) is interpreted by humans varies greatly depending on the social cues.

However, I again want to emphasize that this association of sex and violence is not new. As I noted earlier, it has to varying degrees helped to shape the construction of both male and female sexuality throughout most of our "civilized" history, teaching us, generation after generation, to link the pleasurable sensations of sexual arousal with the inflicting and suffering of pain. Indeed, it is remarkable that anyone who knows anything about ancient history could accept what we are sometimes told: that sexual sadism is a modern invention that began with the Marquis de Sade (from whom the term *sadism* derives).

For example, predating de Sade (who both wrote about and practiced sexual sadism) by almost two thousand years, in Suetonius's accounts of the lives of Roman emperors we learn that men like Caligula had a seemingly insatiable taste for sexual cruelty and violence.[55] We also know from Roman records that women who were to be sadistically tortured and killed were often stripped of their clothing before crowds in the Roman Colosseum. Moreover, if we read some of the Christian writings of the time, we learn that not only the Romans who came to "enjoy" their torturing expected these women to be naked. The Christians who wrote and read of these women's martyrdom also shared this expectation. As Margaret Miles notes in *Carnal Knowing: Female Nakedness and Religious Meaning in the Christian West,* "The regularity with which the female body and female nakedness were featured in *Acta* and popular novels indicates that their readers expected such details, though they seldom note male martyrs' nakedness."[56]

Not only that, but despite the fundamentalist Christian charge that pornography is a symptom of the modern drift away from religion, we find in Christian religious art almost the identical images of sexual sadism we do in modern pornography: of nude women being tortured, dismembered, and killed. For example, in Christian paintings detailing the martyrdom of female saints, we find the same association of woman's nude body with fully clothed men holding whips and knives that we find in modern pornography. Thus, in a fifteenth-century painting by Master Francke that hangs in the National Museum of Finland, we see a naked Saint Barbara tied to a post (much like many women in pornographic images today). On her right stands a man holding a whip. And on her left is another man holding one of her bare breasts in one hand and a knife in another about to cut it off. In another painting, Saint Agnes is portrayed suffering a similar fate. As Miles writes, "Her breasts were cut off, and she was often depicted carrying her large, firm breasts on a platter."[57]

Miles further notes that, in the name of moral warnings against carnal sin, Christian art often shows "sinners" being punished in a prescribed sequence of tortures. "The damned," she writes, "were tortured particularly in the organs involved in their sins; for example, 'the breasts and abdomen of the lustful woman are sucked out by toads and repulsive serpents.'"[58] As in modern pornography, here too women are depicted bound or chained, with particular emphasis given to sexual torture. For instance, in *Inferno,* a work done in 1396 that can still be viewed in San Gimigniano, Italy, a masked devil is shoving a sharp pole into a bound woman's vagina.[59] Similarly, in medieval etchings and engravings show-ing the interrogation of women accused of being witches, we see some of the very same images we see today in pornography, of bound and chained naked or partly disrobed women being tortured by men.

Except what we here see are not man-made fantasies but man-made realities. For these are by and large scenes from Church-commissioned re-ligious art, the art made by men for the very same men who were in real life sadistically tormenting women.

The Normalization of Horror and the Challenge of Change

Again, there will be those who argue that because the erotization of cruelty and violence has been so prevalent, it is natural. However, the tremendous flexibility of human behaviors makes almost every kind of behavior natural in the sense of being part of the range of our biologically available possibilities. This is very different from the normal as defined by psychologists and sociologists in terms of norms. These are behaviors that fall within the scope of what at a particular time and place is ac-cepted as natural—even if it is considered undesirable. For example, the fact that there are constant wars has for five thousand years been consid-ered normal by most people, even though most people do not consider this desirable. Similarly, there was a time in U.S. history when slavery was considered normal, just as there was a time in Chinese history when it was considered normal for men to find sexually arousing the deformed feet of girls forced by their parents to be stunted in their natural growth, and with it, their natural capacity to move about.

In other words, what is considered normal varies greatly among human societies and is to a very large extent a matter of learning. Even more specifically, it can be changed, as dramatically illustrated by the fact that all over the world both women and men are today beginning to reject the erotization of violence and domination, and with this, a way of living and "loving" that can never be emotionally fulfilling—and that, even be-yond this, has effectively sexualized the horror of cruelty and violence, rendering it attractive instead of repellent.

I should say here that even once we free ourselves from our condition-ing to view sexual violence and cruelty as normal, there will still be peo-ple who will be sexually aroused by violence and cruelty, and some who will act this out. Moreover, regardless of our social norms, a certain de-gree of fascination with horror will undoubtedly remain.

We humans are by nature curious and the unfamiliar is fascinating, even if it is also frightening or grotesque. Moreover, fear itself is a state of physical and emotional arousal, which up to a point can be exciting. And

of course the grotesque and horrible also reflect certain realities of a natural world where some species eat other species alive and natural disasters such as earthquakes, storms, and epidemics can, and often do, have
horrible consequences.

But it is one thing to recognize this horror, and even to be fascinated
by it. It is quite another to deliberately institutionalize, and even sexual-
ize, horror as a means of conditioning people to view it as normal.

Thus, public torture was considered normal in some of the rigidly
male-dominant and authoritarian Western societies of antiquity, as were
the most sadistic executions of criminals, traitors, heretics, or anyone
whom the authorities saw fit to so torment (for example, the Romans' crucifixion of Jesus). Public stonings (which sometimes take many hours) of
women accused of adultery, and even in some cases of just remarrying
after divorce, are still in our time found in rigidly male-dominant and authoritarian areas of Bangladesh and other parts of the Muslim world
where religious courts hold sway.[60] It has been reported that in Kuwait
(where after the 1991 Gulf War, the severed heads of people who collaborated with the Iraqis were displayed on posts) people's hands are still
chopped off for theft. And only a few hundred years ago, Christian kings
and clerics still ordered public drawings and quarterings, disembowel-
ings, and the burning alive of women accused of being witches—which,
like the Roman circuses, were presented as spectacles for public entertainment.

Naturally, people exposed to all this horror become desensitized to
suffering—be it that of others or their own. And if on top of this, horror
can be sexualized, people not only become desensitized to the pain of others, but their neural arousal becomes associated with sexual arousal—
thus further contributing to the maintenance of a system that replicates
itself through pain or the fear of pain.

But this kind of system is not the only possibility for our species. Indeed, despite all the insensitivity and pain considered normal in much of
recorded history (during which to varying degrees a dominator social organization has prevailed), women and men have still somehow managed
to relate to one another in sensitive and pleasurable ways. Even in the
midst of hate, cruelty, and violence, we have again and again managed to
instead give and receive love and to find joy not only in sexual passion
but in the simplest of human gestures, in the touch of someone's hand, a
kiss, a friendly smile. In fact, so strong is our human need for pleasure
that even in the most horrible times we have still managed to find it in the
most ordinary of natural events: a sunset, the blossoming of a flower, a
moonlit sky.

Only now, as we begin to become more conscious of both how we got here and where we are, there is the realistic possiblity that an end to much of the horror we have learned to accept as normal may finally be in sight. For what is different in our time, as we will see in the chapters that follow, is that for the first time in recorded history, women and men are consciously and concertedly joining together to challenge cruelty and violence—not from the top down but from the roots up—beginning with such basics as how we define sex, love, and even what it means to be a woman or a man.

CHAPTER 13

Sex, Gender, and Transformation: From Scoring to Caring

It is sometimes said that when women say yes to sex, it is because they want love, and when men say they love a woman, it is because they want sex. But like most gender stereotypes, these are vast overgeneralizations.

Women are sexually aroused by men, just as men are by women. And although convention forbids "good" women sex just for pleasure, women can, and do, enjoy sex out of sheer lust.[1] Moreover, men, like women, also yearn for love. In fact, despite the notion that romantic love was invented in the West, and then only a few hundred years ago, a 1991 study of 166 cultures by William Jankoviak and Edward Fisher found clear evidence of romantic love in 147 of these cultures.[2] And surveys have shown that both women and men consider caring, trust, respect, and honesty central to satisfying relationships.[3]

Nonetheless, in dominator societies men are supposed to prove their masculinity by not becoming too emotionally involved with women, which is viewed as a loss of control, and instead having sex with as many women as possible. As illustrated by archetypal male heroes such as Odysseus and Don Juan—and flatly contradicting the notion that impersonal, uncaring sex is a modern invention—this sexual "scoring" script for real men is hardly new. What *is* new is that not only women, but also men in larger numbers than ever before are taking a close look at their stereotypical gender scripts and rejecting those aspects that limit and distort not only sexual relations but all our relations.

It is true that many men still brag of their sexual conquests, men like the American basketball star Wilt Chamberlain, who proudly claimed he had sex with twenty-five thousand women, and even "spiritual" gurus such as Sri Rajneesh, who boasted he had sex with more women than any other man in the world. It is also true that many women are still drawn to such men. But both women and men are beginning to recognize that teaching men to see intimacy as effeminate and to keep score of sexual "wins"—at the same time that women are taught to believe their whole lives should revolve around intimate relations with men—is a truly no-win prescription for *both* women and men.

More and more men are also beginning to recognize that teaching men they must always be in control is a prescription for not only emotional dysfunction but also for sexual dysfunction. Because as sexologists tell us, it is the ability to give up control—to let go—that is basic to a full orgasmic sexual experience, as it is to a peak spiritual experience.

Even beyond this, there is a growing consciousness that the traditional male socialization to be contemptuous of "soft" emotions does not turn men into real men but into lesser men. It blunts men's capacity for feeling, be it of pleasure or pain, and suppresses in them those very feelings of empathy and caring that make us uniquely human. And because it produces men who will consider it manly to use violence—be it in intimate or in international relations—at this point in our technological and cultural evolution this kind of socialization poses a threat to human survival.

Gender, Ideology, and Society

Women and men are the two halves of humanity. So it is no exaggeration to say that the contemporary questioning of stereotypical gender roles is nothing less than the questioning of what it means to be human—or that if it succeeds it will bring fundamental changes in all aspects of our lives, from sexuality and spirituality to economics and politics.

To fully grasp this, we need to return to something I touched on earlier: *cultural transformation theory* and some of the other new scientific theories that take us beyond the old linear cause-and-effect approaches that still pervade much of our thinking. This is why I want to start this chapter by quickly sketching the emerging new understanding of how complex living systems—which is what social systems are—form, maintain themselves, and change.

I have already mentioned nonlinear dynamics and the chaos theory associated with the Nobel Prize winner Ilya Prigogine and others.[4] Emerging primarily from physics, chemistry, biology, and systems science, these new theoretical approaches are part of a larger framework sometimes called the new scientific paradigm. Unlike the conventional Aristotelian scientific paradigm, this new scientific paradigm no longer mistakes what *is* for what *must* or *should be,* as it no longer deals with living systems, be they biological or social, as static or fixed. On the contrary, one of its main contributions is that it shows how during periods of great system disequilibrium—periods such as ours—seemingly small changes can come together to form the nuclei of a fundamentally transformed system.[5]

Accordingly, the *cultural transformation theory* I have developed over the past two decades views social systems as self-organizing, self-maintaining, and capable at certain bifurcation points of fundamental transformation. But as the social psychologist David Loye points out, when we move from nonhuman to human systems, a whole new set of factors have to be considered—including human consciousness, and with it, the question of human agency in both social maintenance and change.[6] Therefore, taking as a departure point Marx's remark that humans make history but not under circumstances of their own choosing,[7] the aim of *cultural transformation theory* has been to construct a conceptual framework that can help us better understand how these circumstances can be changed in ways that promote human development and actualization.

As I noted in the Introduction, *cultural transformation theory* is based on the perception that our cultural evolution has been shaped by the interacting impact of the dominator and partnership models as two basic possibilities for social organization, and that just as there was in prehistory a shift from partnership to domination as the primary social "attractor," we are now trying to shift in the other direction: from domination to partnership.[8] In the construction of this theory, I have taken into account environmental, biological, social, economic, technological, and psychological factors, focusing on their interaction and on how they affect, and are in turn affected by, socialization processes. I have particularly focused on gender socialization, since it so profoundly affects human consciousness about all aspects of our lives, from how we view our bodies to the degree to which we feel we have both personal and social choices.

Applying the interactive approach provided by *cultural transformation theory* to the study of social systems makes it possible to cut through many confusing controversies, such as the futile "which-came-first-the-chicken-or-the-egg" debate as to whether a particular set of beliefs or ideology is the cause or the result of a particular social and economic structure. It makes it possible to see there is a constant interaction between ideology and social structure, just as physicists are now discovering that matter and energy are in a constantly interactive flux. It also helps explain why the upheavals of shifting from a primarily agrarian to an industrial economy, and now in the West from manufacturing as the economic base to a more information-and-service-oriented economy, have been accompanied by major changes in consciousness—including the mounting questioning of stereotypical gender roles and sexual relations. And it makes it possible to better understand how these changes in consciousness have in turn led to further changes in economics, politics, the family, and religion—in other words, to changes in material conditions, social institutions, and individual (including sexual) behaviors.

However—and this is a point I again want to underscore—whether all this will in the end lead to fundamental changes still hangs in the balance. Just as biological organisms are maintained by their organs, the institutions that form the organs of a social system are also designed to ensure the larger whole of which they are a part survives. So, like the organs in a biological body, the institutions that form the social body of a dominator society (from the male-dominated family to the military) work together to maintain themselves as part of a larger, interconnected whole. And just as our bodies continuously reproduce or replicate their cells, in social systems this also involves the basic evolutionary process of reproduction or replication.

Except that in social systems, as the work of Vilmos Csanyi highlights, this replicating or copying process involves more than the replication of structures (institutions and organizations, such as governments, schools, and churches). It heavily relies on the replication of ideas, symbols, and images.[9] And it particularly relies on gender socialization to implant these ideas, symbols, and images in the minds of the individuals whose active involvement or agency is needed to maintain these structures.

This is why, through both words and images, dominator institutions replicate the idea that war and the war of the sexes are inevitable, and that men must be victors in both. It is also why there is an urgent need to replicate partnership ideas and images—particularly to replace dominator gender stereotypes—if we are to construct a social system that is not chronically violent. Of course, partnership ideas and images alone, without structural or institutional changes, cannot bring about this shift. But the spread of these ideas and images is an essential part of this process, not only because it raises our consciousness to the possibility of more satisfying and sustainable alternatives, but because it is essential to counter the powerful backward pull of dominator ideas and images that are constantly regenerated by religious and scientific authorities, politicians, educators, and in our time, the mass media.

To illustrate—and bring us directly to this critical matter of how the social construction of sex and gender is inextricably intertwined with all aspects of social and ideological organization—on the surface it would seem to make no sense that stories eroticizing conquest and domination should become particularly frequent in times before or during wars. Nonetheless, as the social psychologist David Winter has documented in his extensive probe of the rise and fall in the number of stories where males prove their manliness through their repetitive sexual conquests of women, this is exactly what happens.[10] And looked at from the perspective I have just sketched, it makes a lot of sense that this happens. Because, as we have seen, the male socialization for sexual conquests plays a major part in the socialization of men for military conquests.

But—and again this can best be understood if from the perspective of *cultural transformation theory* we look at social systems as self-organizing and self-maintaining—this intensified production and dissemination of what Winter calls Don Juan stories[11] happens not because political and military leaders deliberately conspire with writers, playwrights, and composers to pump out such tales. It happens because of the dynamic interaction between the ideas and images that provide the material for dominator consciousness, the institutions that maintain this type of society, and the gender roles or scripts required for both women and men to fit into the kinds of institutions that maintain it.

Certainly people who hold power in dominator structures both consciously and unconsciously strive to hold on to that power. But the dynamics of social systems maintenance are far more complex. They involve human agency within the demands of institutional structures, and thus, to paraphrase Anthony Giddens, the continuous reproduction of certain forms of social conduct across time and space.[12] Hence they are inextricably intertwined with the socialization of both women and men for the kinds of roles—and with this, the kinds of habits or routines—that must be constantly recreated, and when faltering, reinforced, if despite outward changes in form, social institutions are to maintain their basic or underlying character.

These then are some of the reasons the modern women's and men's movements—still often trivialized and ridiculed in both academia and the mass media—are of such profound social and political significance. They are not the only movements that in our time challenge an institutional infrastructure based on rankings of domination backed up by force and fear of pain. As we have seen, this has been the aim of all modern progressive political movements. But other movements have not specifically addressed the invisible thread of gender that connects the political and the personal, much less such "peripheral" issues as sex and spirituality. Hence the socialization of men to equate their very identity or masculinity with domination and conquest and the relegation to women of stereotypically feminine characteristics such as compassion and caring has not generally been seen as important. Nor has it been addressed by most historians and political scientists—even though the challenge to stereotypical gender scripts has actually been a major theme in Western history during the last three hundred years.

Renegotiating Sex and Gender

Many people still view any attempt to change gender and sexual scripts as not only unnatural but unprecedented. However, there have throughout recorded history been such attempts.[13] And particularly during modern Western history (that is, during the three hundred years since the Enlightenment), these attempts have been especially vigorous.

For instance, based on his study of modern English and American history from a gender-sensitive perspective, the sociologist Michael Kimmel documents how during the late seventeenth and early eighteenth centuries in England "a virtual pamphlet war erupted as both men and women attempted to renegotiate the structure of gender relations and develop new definitions of masculinity and femininity."[14] Like both earlier and later attempts, this too was during a time of technological, economic, and social ferment, when many traditional roles—and with this habits and routines—were challenged. It thus brought some weakening of androcratic rule. But at the same time, it also saw the regrouping of dominator elites.

For example, threatened by industrialization, the landed gentry sought to maintain their control through what historians call the enclosure of their lands, depriving the peasants who had been their tenant laborers of all means of livelihood, forcing them to move in droves to cities, thus ironically contributing to even more rapid urbanization, industrialization, and rebellion against the upper classes. In the same way, as men too sought to maintain control (sometimes, as in our time, with the active help of collaborating women), in Kimmel's words, "women were chipping away at the edges of traditional expectations."[15]

Some women, such as the playwright Aphra Behn, openly rejected marriage as a form of sexual slavery. Others, as we read in the 1706 Pamphlet "The Duty of a Husband" (written in response to Samuel Johnson's earlier "The Duty of a Wife"), wanted to change marriage into a bond of "mutual love," one where a man "not like a Tyrant rule his Wife, as if she was his Slave for Life." There was also (as in the 1960s and still today) a heated debate about premarital and extramarital sex. Women often accused men of seduction and abandonment. Men wrote eloquent defenses of premarital sex—and so also did some women. However, as Kimmel notes, no sooner did women "attempt to claim sexual agency, to seek sexual gratification actively," than they were restrained "either by traditional morality" or by accusations of "sexual insatiability."[16]

Also during this period, homosexuality became more prevalent (or just more open), and many men adopted more colorful and frillier dress. But when men challenged traditional stereotypes of masculinity, they were accused (sometimes by women) of "pettiness, vanity, and femininity," and of "being French"—thereby, as Kimmel writes, "linking feminization to treason, and traditional masculinity to patriotism."[17]

In the end, although somewhat modified, traditional gender stereotypes—along with the traditional sexual double standard—prevailed. In fact, less than a century later in Victorian England, women were to be rigidly divided into "good" (or asexual women, who endured sex as their duty but did not enjoy it) and "bad" or "fallen" women (with whom men could do as they wished).

Still, the modern struggle over gender roles and sexual relations was far from over. Particularly in the United States, women were during the nineteenth century vigorously challenging the notion that femininity means social and sexual subordination. As they pushed to gain entry into the "men's world" or public sphere of politics and economics, these pioneering feminists profoundly humanized the lives of women. Moreover—vividly illustrating how the social construction of gender roles affects all aspects of society and ideology—as they gained greater entry into areas from which they had traditionally been banned, these women also profoundly humanized the lives of children and men.

They lobbied for the repeal of oppressive family laws and access for women to higher education, but they also worked for more humane treatment of the mentally ill and for public education. They developed whole new service professions, such as social work and nursing, which profoundly impacted health care. Since drunkenness was then (as now) often used as an excuse for violence against women, some feminists also crusaded for temperance—as the cultural historian Theodore Roszak points out, *not* out of prudishness but for the sake of simple self-defense.[18] They actively worked together with men in the antislavery movement. They also worked with men in the development of the modern labor movement, particularly to outlaw child labor and the virtual imprisonment of women workers in unsanitary and unsafe sweatshops—a common practice tragically illustrated by the Triangle shirtwaist factory fire where 146 women were burned to death.[19] They brought attention to the exploitation of women and children in the sex trade. And for more than seventy-five years they defied ridicule and even threats of violence to argue that half the population should no longer be denied the most basic of political rights: the right to vote.

Many men, and also women, ridiculed this demand as unnatural and unfeminine. But there were also those who strongly supported it, including men such as the famous liberal philosopher John Stuart Mill and the black abolitionist leader Frederick Douglass, who joined in the struggle to have the Thirteenth Amendment to the U.S. Constitution giving freed male slaves the vote also include black *and* white women.[20]

Finally, half a century after the Thirteenth Amendment was adopted, American women pushed through the Twenty-first Amendment to the U.S. Constitution to make the phrase "universal suffrage" a reality. But then, in part because school and university textbooks and curricula as well as religion and the media—in other words, what was replicated and disseminated as knowledge and truth—were still overwhelmingly controlled by male elites, the movement to renegotiate gender roles and sexual relations again dwindled. There were of course still attempts by individual women to broaden their life options. However, organized feminism as a mass movement was a thing of the past—or so women were told, as they are again sometimes told today.

In reality feminism only lay dormant. And when it once again resurged as the women's liberation movement during the 1960s, it was with a force never before seen in recorded history. Never before had so many women all over the globe demanded a renegotiation of gender scripts in both the private and public spheres. Never before had so many men been drawn, sometimes willingly and even eagerly, other times reluctantly and recalcitrantly, into this renegotiation. Most important, never before, not even during the height of the nineteenth-century feminist movement, had these renegotiations about sex and gender been at such a deep and all-pervasive level.

In family relations, the contemporary renegotiation of gender scripts lies at the heart of the movement to shift from a dysfunctional family based on control—that is, a family structured around male domination and abusive child rearing—to a partnership family based on mutual trust and respect. In business, organizational development experts cite findings that more "feminine" or nurturing leadership styles make for greater worker productivity and creativity, and that sexual harrassment has detrimental effects on productivity and morale. At the same time, women are beginning to break through the gendered "glass ceiling" barring them from top management. In politics, women are also challenging the stereotypical definition of leadership as male, with the result that unprecedented numbers of women have been elected to office in many countries—from the United States, India, and Japan (where they still have approximately only one-twentieth representation in national legislatures) to the Scandinavian nations (where approximately one-third of national legislators are female).[21] Even in religion, gender roles and relations are being renegotiated. Women are challenging their exclusion from spiritual leadership and being ordained in mainstream congregations. Some of these congregations are even changing the Judeo-Christian script requiring that the divine be only a Father, Lord, or King by again including Mother in the appellation of deity. Outside mainstream congregations, women and men are beginning to explore a new Goddess spirituality as a more nature-and-pleasure-affirming faith. Even the view that spirituality precludes women and men from fully enjoying our unique human capacity for erotic pleasure is being challenged, along with the notion that women are less (or alternately, more) lustful than men.

Just as critically, men are today in larger numbers than ever before questioning their stereotypical scripts for masculinity. This too is on a much deeper level than ever before. For individual men, this questioning holds the promise of far greater freedom to explore and express their full humanity. For both women and men it holds the promise of far more satisfying intimate relations. And for society at large—in a world where what has been considered normal for men has been the standard by which all our institutions (from the work place and the family to religion and politics) have been constructed[22]—it holds the promise of fundamental changes in all aspects of human relations, from international relations to our most intimate sexual relations.

From Masculinity to Masculinities

Just as many women are today challenging the notion of an immutable, unalterable femininity, men during the 1970s began to question the notion of a single "normal" masculinity. Much of this questioning stemmed from the growing recognition by many men that both women and men are capable of both what are stereotypically described as masculine and feminine feelings and behaviors. But much of it has also stemmed from the growing awareness of some men of the enormous costs to them of constructing social institutions so that men are expected to live, and all too often die, in accordance with roles that constantly place them in situations where they have to experience fear and pain—at the same time that they are taught that the most shameful thing for a man is, like a woman, to express fear and pain. Or, to borrow the words of the sociologist Rob Koegel, much of it is directed at "healing the wounds of masculinity"—wounds that, as he brings out, stem from a social construction of masculinity appropriate for a dominator rather than partnership social and ideological organization.[23]

Thus, as Mathew Callahan writes in *Sex, Death, and the Angry Young Man*,[24] men are becoming aware that even when they reach the top of a particular dominator pyramid, they must still be wary (that is, afraid) of other men trying to dislodge them from their positions of control. And all too often they must even be afraid for their lives—as grimly attested to by the endless wars of recorded history, where men have been wounded, crippled, maimed, killed, and sometimes left behind to slowly die (as during the Napoleonic Wars, when in one battle alone fifty thousand dead and wounded men were abandoned on the blood-soaked field of Wagram).[25] Then there is the violence and pain of boys' fistfights and of their often deadly gang fights—as in the drive-by shootings in American inner city ghettos today, where the leading cause of death among young Black men is murder by another young man. Not only that, but the "real" masculinity today in some circles termed the "deep masculine" is, as Tim Beneke writes, ideally approached through "aggressive initiation where boys endure physical pain and injury in the presence of older men" in preparation for a manhood "one proves through taking distress like a man"—that is, without any verbal or other expression of one's feelings.[26]

Of course, there are many factors behind male violence, such as poverty, drugs, and, particularly in the United States, lack of adequate gun-control laws. But the fact is that in the United States, as in most other parts of the world, it is women—not men—who are the bulk of the poor and the poorest of the poor,[27] and they too have access to drugs and guns. So when we look at the statistic that almost 90 percent of violent crimes in the United States are crimes by men, often against other men,[28] we again come back to the stereotypical male socialization for domination and violence—a socialization today magnified a thousandfold by an entertainment industry that presents violence not only as manly and heroic but as great fun.

The heartening thing is that, despite all this socialization pressure, so many men have failed to conform to this ideal of a tough, violent, and unfeeling "macho" masculinity, or do so only in part.[29] But even for these men, the costs of this type of socialization are high. To begin with, if their failure to conform is too apparent, they suffer great humiliation. Moreover, whether they fully or only partly conform, since this male socialization is part and parcel of the dominator war of the sexes in which someone has to dominate and someone has to be dominated, they too have to pay some of the emotional costs of this war—as attested to by all the songs and romantic literature written by men that focus less on the joys than on the agonies of love.

But here again, ironically, men's stereotypical socialization for conquest and control itself creates part of their pain. According to the "macho" script, only men are supposed to have power. So any show of power by women (which of course includes the power to reject men or otherwise hurt them) is not only painful in itself; it is also painful in the sense of being perceived as a loss of manhood. And on top of all this, because distress is something men are not supposed to feel, these feelings themselves (natural when one is hurt) become the source of even more pain from not living up to internalized cultural expectations.

Small wonder then—as more men become conscious of all this—that some men are today undertaking nothing less than what in his book *The Making of Masculinities* Harry Brod calls the "deconstruction and reconstruction of masculinity."[30] For instance, the psychologist Joseph Pleck in an essay in Brod's book challenges the long-accepted assumption that psychological maturity requires that men and women acquire male or female "sex-role identity"—in other words, that, as psychology students are still taught, learning the traditional gender scripts is the road to human maturity and full development.[31] Similarly, in a recent issue of *Masculinities* (the official publication of the Men's Studies Association) Ken Clatterbaugh points to the current revivals of "essentialist" gender roles through fundamentalism, neoconservatism, sociobiology, and some neo-Jungian mythopoetic writings as attempts to make something that is socially constructed appear as instinctual or biological.[32] Another scholar, Michael Messner, calls for a whole new definition of success for men: one that through a more equal involvement of men in parenting will not only give more satisfaction to men's lives, but have far-reaching humanizing effects on society.[33] Along the same lines, the sociologist Scott Coltrane reports that his research on couples where men actively participate in parenting shows that this improved and enriched their relationship with their children as well as with their wives. Moreover, based on his cross-cultural study of ninety nonindustrial societies, Coltrane reports that societies in which there is high paternal involvement in child rearing are "characterized by egalitarian beliefs and generally similar gender roles" as well as by relative nonviolence in all areas of life.[34]

But it is not only in the new academic field of men's studies that dominator stereotypes of masculinity are today being challenged. As Coltrane's work documents, men are beginning to reject these stereotypes in real life. Younger men in particular are beginning to discard stereotypical definitions of fatherhood as a distant disciplinarian-provider role, instead becoming more involved in the intimate caretaking still generally classified as "mothering."[35] For example, shortly before he was assassinated John Lennon publicly announced, "I like it to be known that, yes, I looked after the baby and I made bread and I was a househusband and I am proud of it."[36]

More and more men are also asking themselves the questions John Lennon asked: "Isn't it time we destroyed the macho ethic? . . . Where has it gotten us all these thousands of years?"[37] For instance, in *The Male Predicament*, James Dittes writes about how both women and men have been crippled by stereotypical gender roles and relations.[38] And Michael McGill's *Male Intimacy*, reporting research on men's problems with intimacy (and findings that men have far fewer close relationships than women), probes the many reasons why "men aren't more loving and why they need to be," concluding that rather than having "more power and control by withholding themselves from relationships," men are limited by their fear of intimacy in their ability to act powerfully in relations—and that men need to learn that masculinity and intimacy are not inimical.[39]

Another subject men write about is how traditional stereotypes of masculinity have inhibited their capacity for sexual pleasure. For example, in *Delivering the Male* Clayton Barbeau concludes that "the male mystique" is a major obstacle to healthy sex. "Healthy sexuality," he writes, "finds expression as a free gift, not as a compulsion, and arises out of the desire to give and receive pleasure in union with the beloved." Speaking more personally, he continues: "I cannot express tenderness in my love relationship if I am—because of my miseducation in the male mystique— afraid of showing tenderness. My sexual love-making cannot be a total communication of myself, if I am unwilling to give myself away in intimate sharing."[40]

Nonetheless, as we have seen, this intimate sharing is precisely what men are forbidden in their stereotypical "scoring" script for sexuality. For here, as in the legend of Don Juan and Casanova's *Memoirs*[41] (a work sometimes touted as a minor classic), control and power over women, not giving and receiving pleasure—much less union with the beloved—is the prime motivation.

Sex, Winners, and Losers

Actually, Casanova's autobiographical writings (which also tell of his fraudulent lotteries, petty thefts, and observations of the prominent figures of his time) are not all that well written. In fact, in their repetitive boasts of his "victories" over women, they are boring. But they do provide an early record of the sexual malfunction psychologists today call sexual compulsivity.

Sexual compulsivity can take many forms, and not only men but also women can be afflicted by it. But while most women and a certain number of men are primarily driven by the "feminine" need for pleasing others (that is, giving pleasure as a way of gaining acceptance and love), for men conditioned to equate masculinity with conquest (as for Casanova and Don Juan), the issue is not love—or even sex. Rather, it is the domination of the female "adversary" and/or the frequency of "performance."

Indeed, as we saw earlier, for some of the men with this compulsion, the aim is to give pain instead of pleasure—which the sex torture killer takes to its logical brutal extreme. But for most men with this compulsion the "pleasure" of humiliating the conquered woman (or in homosexual relations, the man who takes the woman's place) suffices. Thus, in re-counting his maneuvers to get the women he compulsively pursues to "surrender," Casanova makes it clear that what excites him is not sex but overcoming women's resistance and imposing on them his will. Hence, once he has psychologically or physically overpowered a woman, and once this victory has been duly recorded in his memoirs, he sets out to find another body to add to his tally of sexual conquests.

Of course, this "sexual conquest" mentality is not exclusive to men. Women too are sometimes infected by it, though they may not count their conquests by how many men they have sex with but by how many men's hearts they have broken. But whereas women have traditionally been censured for this, men's conquests of women have generally been ad-mired—even prescribed by the dominator script for real masculinity.

One effect of this script has been that for many men sexual love has tended to become extreme possessiveness. Again, this is not unique to men. But it is in men that it has most often assumed its most violent ex-pression, as in the all-too-familiar fictional—and real-life—stories where a man shows his "love" for a woman by beating or even killing her when he suspects her body is not his exclusive possession.

Another effect has been a drastically reduced possibility for men to ex-perience emotional (rather than only physical) intimacy with a woman. And still another effect has been an impairment in male sexual function-ing. As Tompkins and Mosher write, the hypermasculine script's equa-tion of "relaxed enjoyment" with the "inferior" feminine role would tend to make sex (no matter how often a man "scores" or even how often he comes) a limited sexual, not to speak of emotional, experience. Moreover, as Wilhelm Reich observed, male ejaculation is not the same as a full or-gasmic experience.[42]

I want to here emphasize that all this is a matter not of absolutes but of the degree to which men have internalized rigid masculine and feminine role definitions. For instance, the psychologist Else Frenkel-Brunswick found that men who defined human relations in terms of rigid masculine-superior and feminine-inferior roles often described sex as merely a "hygienic release of tension." And it is significant, as she also reported in the classic work on this subject, *The Authoritarian Personality*,[43] that these were the same men who scored high on the F (for fascist) psychological measurements: men characterized by extreme prejudice and intolerance toward Jews, blacks, and other "inferior" and/or "dangerous" out-groups.

Similarly, a 1971 study of German political extremists from both the right and left (including members of the leftist terrorist Baader-Meinhof gang) found that these men generally suffered from problems of sexual dysfunction, including the inability to achieve orgasm.[44] Again, these were characteristically men who defined their masculine identity in terms of control, violence, and the suppression of empathy. Many of these men had sadistic or masochistic fantasies in which they felt pleasure in torturing or wounding someone or in being punished by others. They frequently reported unpleasant sensations during any kind of sexual activity. However—and not surprisingly, since what is sexually exciting to such men is not giving and receiving pleasure but rather a sense of power over another human being—members of the Baader-Meinhof gang frequently reported erotic excitation during political discussions and demonstrations.[45]

So not only is the hypermasculine script for sex generally devoid of caring. Ultimately it is also devoid of pleasure—except, as Tomkins and Mosher keenly observed, the "pleasure" of imposing one's will upon another through fear and force.

Of course, not all men buy into this script. But that it has impaired the way many men perceive, and experience, sex is dramatically brought out by Don Sabo's remarkable article "The Myth of the Sexual Athlete," published a few years ago in the men's journal *Changing Men*.

Sabo, who played organized sports for fifteen years, begins by describing his inner conflict as a boy between a socialization for "masculine control" and his need for "feminine intimacy." "Inside," he writes, "most of the boys, like myself, needed to love and be loved." Yet "the message that got imparted was to 'catch feels,' be cool." He then relates how when he went to college and became part of the "jock" subculture, at Sunday breakfasts the topic was often the "sexual exploits of the night before," including "laughing reports of 'gang bangs.'" So after a while, for him and for most of his buddies, dating became a "sport" where sex was basically a game in which "winners" and "losers" vied for domination and women were viewed as "opponents."[46]

Not surprisingly, as Sabo points out, this "man-as-hunter/woman-as-prey" sexual script made it hard for men to form loving relationships.

And in the end it became an obstacle to sexual functioning since, again in Sabo's words, it led young men to "organize their energies and perceptions around a performance ethic" which turned them into sexual "achievement machines." The more obsessively these "sexual athletes" fixated on "masculine" frequency of performance rather than "feminine feelings," the more driven they were to "score" and to have and maintain erections. However, the more preoccupied they became with "erectile potency and performance," the less able they were to enjoy sex—and to avoid the "unmanly" sexual dysfunction of impotence they so feared.[47]

As Sabo also notes, not only "jocks" but many other men have internalized this "eroticism without intimacy" script—men in fraternities, motorcycle gangs, the armed forces, and urban gangs.[48] In fact, what Tomkins and Mosher call "the callous sex scene" is often in such groups part of the initiation into manhood.[49] And of course this impersonal, scoring-type sex is today mass marketed through both hard- and softcore pornography, as well as through much of corporate advertising.

But even with all this, more and more men like Sabo—men who only a short time ago bought into dominator sexuality—are becoming conscious that even when men are "winners" in this adversarial kind of sex, they too are losers. Just as important, more and more men are also becoming conscious, in Sabo's words, that "until equality between the sexes becomes more of a social reality, no new model of a more humane sexuality will take hold."[50]

The Many Faces of the Men's Movement

Clearly not all the men who are today taking a new look at masculinity and sexuality share such views. As Susan Faludi notes in *Backlash*, among the thousands of books and articles out on the "masculinity question" are also quite a few fiercely woman-hating, hypermasculine tracts.[51] And still more contain a mix of dominator and partnership ideas.

Just as there are many different factions in the women's movement, there are also different—sometimes totally opposed—factions in what the media generally lump together as "the men's movement."[52] Those men who are working for gender equity, to reduce male violence, and to change their own thinking and behavior so they can have more satisfying love relations, are clearly on the partnership side of the line. Clearly on the other side of the line are those men openly working against equality for women, either denying there is inequality or claiming women should be, and want to be, dominated by men. Where it gets less simple is in groups such as Robert Bly's "Wild Man" workshops and other groups that still urge men to identify with dominator archetypes such as the warrior and the king, while at the same time often talking about equal partnership between women and men and a more generally just and equitable society.

Certainly the impulse behind many of the men's groups that have been given so much press, where men meet in sweat lodges, drum in the woods, and tell stories about warriors and kings, is toward a less limited masculinity. This is particularly true for the white-collar and professional men (who can afford these workshops) looking for a new masculine script in which men are not so constrained by stiff codes of basically adversarial interaction with other men, and in which, as leaders of these groups put it, men can "bond."

But although it is touted as new, the script for men offered by some of these groups is actually not all that different from the old macho script—except that it is dressed up in New Age clothes. As in the old macho all-male peer groups, once again male identity is defined in negative terms, as *not* being like a woman. As in the old macho script of contempt for the "feminine," Bly berates his followers for being "too soft" or "feminine"—and thus "unmanly"[53]—expressing horror of being "controlled" by women, from whom, according to him, men must at all costs be independent. To this end, men must even distance themselves from their own mothers, lest they be contaminated, in Bly's words, by "too much feminine energy."[54]

One of the most ironic things about Bly is that he originally preached that men should embrace their "feminine principle," that as he said in a Great Mother conference he conducted in the 1970s, this is essential for world peace. But of course the contemporary struggle between the dominator and partnership models is not only between different groups; it also takes place within the same organization—and within the same individual.

Still, I cannot help but think that men like Bly would think and act very differently if all of us were taught a history that tells us about gender relations. For example, we would then all be familiar with the hypermasculinity revival of the nineteenth century, when also in reaction to feminism, men wrote of their "horror" of a nation losing "its manhood"; defined manhood in ways that, as Theodore Roszak writes, "cheapen compassion and tenderness" and "ennoble violence and suffering";[55] and in the end created the "macho" cultural climate that set the stage for the bloodbath of World War I. In short, we would know, and be warned, that all this talk of a New Age masculinity of "real" manhood is not merely empty rhetoric; that no matter how it is packaged, exhorting men to again emulate the old dominator archetypes of king and warrior is dangerous—not only to women, for whom it presages a return to the "good old days" of open, unashamed male dominance, but to men and children of both genders.[56]

Moreover, if we were taught psychology from a gender perspective, we would all also be aware that one of the ways this destructive type of masculinity is maintained in dominator societies is precisely through the long-accepted and totally arbitrary notion (as Pleck writes in critiquing it) that for a man to develop normally he must learn *not* to identify with his mother—that the mark of masculinity is a man's separation from, and rejection of, any "feminine" identity.[57] For we would then be aware, as another psychologist, Knoll Evans, points out, that the prohibition against identifying and thus empathizing with his mother is a way of teaching a man not to feel "soft" or "feminine" emotions and thus not to empathize with any woman[58]—not even, in Roszak's words, the "woman most desperately in need of liberation," the "'woman' every man has locked up in the dungeons of his own psyche."[59] And we would further know that it is precisely in those societies and families where women are most rigidly dominated by men that mothers are the most controlling of their sons— the male on whom they can most effectively vent their pent-up anger and frustration.[60]

In sum, we would know that to the extent that men's groups today buy into the old macho scripts, they are reinforcing precisely the kind of society and family where men and women (and this obviously includes mothers and sons) both consciously and unconsciously hurt one another in all the ways that men (and women) complain they have been hurt. We would know that myths such as Freud's Oedipus complex—which sets up the angry sons to take over from the equally angry fathers and in the process "possess" as many women as possible (including in fantasy even their own mothers)—and Jungian-type archetypes that still idealize "heroic" male violence do *not* reflect the human psyche, but rather the dominator psyche: the same psyche that today threatens all life on this planet.

And we would immediately see the difference between, on the one hand, encouraging men to feel self-pity and continuing to blame women for their problems and, on the other, helping men to feel empathy for both women and men—including themselves. Finally, we would recognize something that is actually quite obvious: that men, like women, need close loving bonds with *both* women and men, including *both* mothers and fathers.

Having said this, I want to also say that I think the contention of Bly and other New Age writers that men (and I must add, women) need new initiation rites into adulthood is valid. In fact, I hope this recognition will eventually lead to truly new rites of passage for men—rites, however, very different from those in *Iron John*, from macho-script "callous sex" scenes, and from all the other ways of inculcating in men contempt for women and the "feminine."[61]

I also want to say that I think the recognition that men need new role models is very important—and that a key issue, implicit in some of men's fears of becoming too "feminine," is the need for men to find new role models for assertiveness. Because the point is not for men to now take the submissive stance traditionally associated with femininity, but for both women and men to learn to express their needs and desires in a strong and assertive manner without intimidation or violence.

Finally, I want to say that the recognition by Jungian and New Age men's groups that there has to be a spiritual dimension to the "new masculinity" is very important. But it is my hope that what this will eventually lead this segment of the men's movement to deal with are the core spiritual questions raised by sages throughout history: questions about the need for men to adopt in their behavior values such as empathy and nonviolence, and questions dealing with fundamental issues of equality and justice.

Women, Men, and Partnership

To me, the most encouraging aspect of the contemporary men's movement is how many men are in fact probing precisely these core spiritual and social issues. It has been my good fortune to live with one of these men, my partner and husband, the social psychologist David Loye, and to see how his research and writing has increasingly focused on gender, first in *The Partnership Way* [62] (which we wrote together) and then in the books he is now completing on the relationship between social structure, gender, and what he calls moral sensitivity. I am particularly excited about this new work, and will return to it later, as it not only provides the first unified scientific perspective on morality but traces moral development through biological and cultural evolution.

Another man who has passionately written about these core spiritual and moral issues from a gender perspective is John Stoltenberg, whose book *Refusing to Be a Man* is unprecedented in its outright rejection of dominator masculinity—as is the fact that a book with such a title got published at all. A collection of thirteen essays that, as Stoltenberg writes in his introduction, "might provoke some people to outrage," it expresses Stoltenberg's outrage at the profound injustice of traditional gender and sexual relations, and particularly at the erotization of male supremacy, which as Stoltenberg notes "makes inequality feel like sex."[63]

In an essay on "Pornography and Male Supremacy," Stoltenberg writes: "Once you have sexualized inequality, once it is a learned and internalized prerequisite for sexual arousal and sexual gratification," sexual freedom becomes a license for men to more effectively hunt and subdue women. "Pornography," he continues, "institutionalizes male supremacy the way segregation institutionalizes white supremacy." Stoltenberg has even had the courage to criticize some of the pornography of gay men, an act vociferously condemned by some political liberals. Only, as Stoltenberg points out, the problem is hardly one of gay men or of erotic images; it is that all too often "the values in the sex depicted in gay made sex films" are "very much the values that male supremacists tend to have: taking, using, estranging, dominating—essentially power mongering."[64]

But unfortunately, rather than publicizing the work of men such as Stoltenberg, who have the courage to join hands with other men and with women to heal a distorted male sexuality that has helped maintain a dominator society, the media still tend to give greatest publicity to those men's groups that see women, and particularly feminism, as a threat to their masculinity—just as they tend to focus on the more separatist (or as they inflammatorily put it, "man-hating") factions of feminism, thus again presenting feminists as men's enemies. And, tragically, in so doing, they are pointing the very men searching for new ways of relating to themselves and to women in precisely the direction that *cannot* help them develop the new models of masculinity they say they want and need—instead of giving them information about the ideas and groups that can.

For example, there are today men's groups such as Men Against Rape, Men Against Domestic Violence, and Men to Stop Battering. There are organizations such as the National Organization of Men Against Sexism, national conferences with themes such as "Building Bridges for a Multicultural Men's Community,"[65] and publications such as *Changing Men* and *Masculinities.* Recognizing that women and men share essentially the same human goals, such organizations, conferences, and publications are important, and unprecedented, signposts on the road to partnership. Together with national women's organizations such as the National Organization for Women (NOW), the National Women's Political Caucus (NWPC), and the Older Women's League (OWL), international conferences such as the WEDO (Women's Environment and Development Organization) 1994 conference "Women and Power," national conferences such as "Empowering Women: Achieving Human Rights in the 21st Century,"[66] and publications such as *Ms., Woman of Power,* and *Women's International News,* they provide the nuclei for the gradual consolidation of the women's and men's movements into an overarching partnership movement: an integrated movement for progressive change that places both sexual and gender relations at the center rather than the periphery of the political agenda.

I say gradual because, particularly for women who have for so long been conditioned to defer to and please men, separate women's and men's groups are essential. Although, as I will develop later, the partnership movement is the logical melding of the women's and men's movements with the environmental, human rights, and other progressive movements, this is not to say that the women's and men's movements will soon be unnecessary. Quite the contrary, both will be essential for a long time, as some of the strongest threads in the cultural warp and woof that hold repressive institutions together are dominator stereotypes of sex and gender.

Moreover, to recognize that there are aspects of "traditional" masculinity that idealize the very behaviors that today endanger human survival is not to say that everything stereotypically taught men as masculine needs to be left behind. In the same way that there are traits stereotypically labeled feminine, such as empathy and caring, that men can (and if permitted, do) share—traits that do *not* make a human being less of a man, but rather more so—there are traits stereotypically labeled masculine that are excellent human traits for both men and women. These too are traits that both women and men can (and if permitted, do) share—for example, stating what one wants rather than feeling one has to manipulate or placate, as socially disempowereed people are taught they must do.

In short, the point of all this is not that everything now taught men as masculine is dysfunctional or that everything taught women as feminine is superior—much less that women are superior to men. Nor is the deconstruction and reconstruction of gender stereotypes and sexual relations about moving to a "unisex" society where women and men become the same. On the contrary, what the women's, men's, and partnership movements are about is the creation of a far more interesting and exciting society, one where diversity—be it based on gender, race, religion, or ethnic origin—can be truly valued.

Certainly these movements are not about constructing a bland, passionless sexuality. On the contrary, they are about constructing a far more intense and passionate sexuality. Nor are they about moving to a world in which there will no longer be any fighting or conflict. Rather they are about constructing a world where both men's and women's life scripts contain many different types of behaviors—including the today urgently needed creative conflict resolution skills that in both interpersonal and international relations can successfully be applied to the inevitable clashes of

human needs and desires that are all too often still dealt with through violence. And it is to construct this far safer, more satisfying, and more interesting world that, after millennia of the dominator war of the sexes, women
and men all over the world are today coming together—not as adver-
saries—but as partners in a jointly beneficial enterprise.

In later chapters we will look at some of the key elements in this unprecedented endeavor, as well as some of the obstacles in its way. But first
we will in the next chapter shift from masculine to feminine stereotypes
for sex and gender—and to how, unlike Sleeping Beauty, millions of
women are today beginning to wake from their long dominator trance.

CHAPTER 14

Getting Out of Prince Charming's Slipper: Sex, Femininity, and Power

When I was growing up, first in Cuba and then in the United States, I often felt I was an outsider. I thought it was because I was a refugee child uprooted by the Nazi takeover of Austria from the country of my birth. Certainly this was an important factor. But now I realize that there was another factor—one I think also lies behind some of the loss of self-esteem by teenage girls we today read about.[1] Because on some deep unconscious level it must have registered on me as I was growing up that I was indeed an outsider in a world where in practically everything taught me in all the schools and universities I attended there was hardly anything written or thought by those who, like I, had been born female.

It was not until many years later that I began to consciously understand how male authorities—beginning with a male deity—had defined everything about me: from how my body should look to find favor in their eyes to what I was permitted to do, or even imagine. I never had the slightest hint that for thousands of years, woman—as the earthly representative of the Goddess, from whom all life is born and to whom all life returns at death—was a powerful temporal and spiritual figure, the archetype of all that is erotic, pleasurable, and alive. Nor did I have any way of knowing that the limiting archetypes of femininity I had been exposed to were the result of a fundamental social and ideological shift.

I was never taught that in ancient Greece once-powerful female divinities such as Hera (still known as the mother of the gods) were during this shift made subservient to a far more powerful, often violent, Zeus.

Nor was I taught that in Hebrew scriptures the Goddess was completely written out—with even the creation of life attributed entirely to a male deity. Indeed, there was nothing in my education about how a Goddess Creatrix was worshiped for thousands of years, much less that her sexuality was one of the attributes that made her divine.

On the contrary, I was presented with the two primary Western religious archetypes that I now realize allocate the ancient Goddess's sexual and mothering powers to two mortal, and clearly subordinate, women. One, fashioned by the Christian men who needed a mother for God's divine Son, is the "unsullied" Virgin Mary who gives birth to a holy child *not* through the sexual union of a female and a male deity, but through the asexual insemination of a mortal woman by an all-powerful male Creator.[2] The other, embodying the Goddess's sexual powers, is also not a female deity but a mortal woman: Eve, who, like Delilah, is a temptress blamed for leading man to ruin.[3]

These have been our most important feminine archetypes for most of recorded Western history. Even in our time when we sometimes speak of a "sex goddess," we mean something very different from the Goddess of old who in her body incarnated the mysterious powers of sex and birth. For even though their sexual power was acknowledged, film icons like Marilyn Monroe, Rita Hayworth, and Brigitte Bardot were little more than sex objects for men. Moreover, rather than being a sacred marriage, sexual union with such women was for men (both on and off screen) basically an emblem of superior male power—a far cry from Dumuzi's marriage to Inanna.

Just as archetypes equating manliness with conquest and domination are inappropriate for a healthy masculinity, these archetypes are inappropriate for a healthy femininity. But they *are* appropriate for a society of inbuilt power imbalances in the relations between women and men. Female archetypes splitting woman into an idealized mother-wife or a despised temptress-whore effectively teach both women and men that good (asexual) women like Mary passively accept the male's superior power, whereas bad (sexual) women like Delilah and Eve wield power over men with disastrous results. Not only that, most of our archetypes of femininity basically deny women any independent existence, defining them only in terms of how they further (or hinder) male-defined goals. Above all, they strip women of legitimate power, be it temporal or divine.

Today women all over the world are beginning to recognize how sexist imagery, like racist imagery, has served to maintain relations based on domination rather than partnership. They are becoming aware that these images are inculcated into our unconscious minds when we are still very small, and that they are constantly replicated in a myriad of different forms to counter any fundamental change. Even more important, women are again beginning to tap into the powerful archetype of the prehistoric Goddess—for example, as the novelist Alice Walker did, transforming Aunt Jemima from a symbol of servile nurturance into a modern Black Madonna.[4]

In short, women are today trying to imbue disempowering images from religion, folklore, and fairy tales with power—or if that is not possible, at least expose them for what they are. And in the process they are radically transforming long-entrenched assumptions about the body, sexuality, and spirituality.

The Girl, the Prince, and the Body

Like some of our religious myths, many fairy tales still contain traces of earlier times. In fact, unlike most of our religious myths and literature (which, except for romantic novels and other "women's market" specialties, generally have male protagonists), the central characters in some of our best known fairy-tales are female. Not only that, some of these female figures, like the good fairy in "Cinderella" and the wicked sorceresses in "Snow White" and "Sleeping Beauty," can even perform magic—that is, feats associated with supernatural power. But despite these traces of prehistoric traditions, the primary message of the fairy tales we tell our daughters and sons is not one of female power, but of female powerlessness.

In some cases, we can actually trace the transformation of these stories over time. For example, the folkloric anthropologist Alan Dundes tells us that it was not until three hundred years ago that the story we know as "Little Red Riding Hood" was made by the French writer Charles Perrault into a moral fable warning girls against listening to strangers lest they be gobbled up by a wolf (an image with some possible sexual symbolism, since sexually predatory males were as late as the 1950s known as wolves).[5] According to Dundes, in earlier folklore the story's protagonist had been an inventive girl who triumphed over the villain.[6] But by the time the story was again refashioned by Jacob and Wilhelm Grimm in 1812 to become the version we have today, she is swallowed up whole (red hood and all) on top of her equally helpless grandmother by the wicked wolf. And even when she gets out, it is not through anything she does, but because a brave woodsman cuts open the wolf's stomach.

This rescue of passive females by active males is also the theme of "Cinderella" and "Sleeping Beauty." Only in these stories the relationship between the hero and the heroine is sexual, since in both the heroine eventually marries the prince. But once again, it is a marriage very different from the ancient sacred marriage in which the female was imbued with divine power and the sexual union of female and male was central.

To begin with, in these stories there is hardly any touching, except for a dance or a kiss. Moreover, the emphasis is on the girl's physical attractiveness, and not on anything even remotely associating female sexuality with spiritual or temporal power. On the contrary, the central message of these fairy tales is once again that the male has all the power—either because he has some kind of magical potency (as when the prince awakens Sleeping Beauty with his kiss) or because he is the temporal ruler of the realm (as in "Cinderella"). So that all a girl can do is wait for Prince Charming to find her, and hope that he will find her attractive enough to be chosen.

Thus, despite her misery, Cinderella has no other plans, or even ideas, except that a prince will marry and save her. But there is in this fairy tale classic still another, even more disempowering, message. This is that for a girl to be saved from a life of misery, her body must fit certain specifications. In fact, if she cannot fit these specifications she must deliberately maim her body—as in the case of Cinderella's stepsisters, who cut off parts of their feet in vain attempts to fit into the story's famous slipper.

It is tempting to dismiss this as merely something in a fairy tale, a fanciful notion of no real consequence in life. But as illustrated by the crippling foot binding practiced in prerevolutionary China because men found it sexually arousing and the genital mutilations still practiced in many African and Middle Eastern cultures because men will not marry unmutilated women, for millennia women have done just that—often (like the stepmother in "Cinderella") counseling, or even forcing, their own daughters to be mutilated in order to fit male sexual desires and expectations. In fact, it is what many women in modern Western societies continue to do to our day—be it by cramming their feet into "fashionable" pointed-toe stiletto-heeled shoes that cripple not only their toes but their backs, or through the potentially fatal self-starvation of anorexia and the life-threatening binging and purging of bulimia.[7]

There are obviously other reasons for the epidemic proportions of bulimia and anorexia in our time.[8] But a major factor is that during the last few decades the message of the old dominator fairy tales has been amplified a thousandfold. Now it is blared at us incessantly by billion-dollar cosmetics, diet, and fashion industries telling women that to attract a Prince Charming they must fit their bodies to the specifications dictated by these industries—specifications that idealize a debilitating and unhealthy thinness of body along with the kind of face that only a tiny minority of women will ever have, no matter how hard they diet or how many beauty aids they buy.

The desire to look good and to adorn one's body is universal and healthy. But what these ads and stories keep telling girls and women, using the best writers and artists money can buy in a hypnotic cacophony of arresting images and words, is that unless they constantly make themselves over—unless they devote their lives (and massive amounts of money) to forever "improving" their bodies and their faces—they will never be acceptable to, much less loved by, the only people whose tastes and wishes matter: men. Moreover, this mass marketing of low self-esteem, escapism, and the notion that the only way a woman can prove her worth is by pleasing men is not only through ads. Unlike other publications, be they newspapers like the *New York Times* or men's magazines like *Esquire,* women's magazines are subjected to a practice that in any other context would be denounced as interference with a free press. This is that women's magazines are expected by their advertisers—as a condition for placing their ads—to print "informative" stories about products such as cosmetics and clothes. Even beyond this, as one editor put it, they are expected to "present a happy face"[9]—and thus (as the publishers of *Ms.* magazine found when they violated this rule and ads were canceled or not placed)[10] only lightly touch on women's real needs and problems, such as domestic violence, job and racial discrimination, poverty, and reproductive choice.

So not surprisingly, it is primarily in feminist magazines free from such severe curtailments of editorial freedom that we find in-depth discussions of such issues—as well as of the enormous damage to girls and women (and society) from brainwashing half the population for passivity and low self-esteem. And it is only here that we find the recognition that socializing women to focus only on pleasing men and on an exaggerated emphasis on physical beauty—or more specifically, male-defined standards of feminine beauty—actually hinder the very goal they supposedly serve: to help women land, and keep, a man.

For the final irony for women—and tragedy for both women and men—is that the cultural messages from the ads and stories that fill women's magazines are precisely the formula for unsatisfying male-female relations. Men can never meet the exaggerated expectation that they will provide all meaning, content, and purpose in women's lives. Women can never meet the exaggerated expectation (their own and those of men) that they will be eternally beautiful, young, pliable, and pleasing. And so, as we read in volume after volume of popular psychology and self-help books, both women and men are chronically disappointed, frustrated, and confused—as neither women's nor men's most basic emotional and sexual needs are adequately met.

Yet as lunatic as it is to keep bombarding women with the message that we are not good enough—that we must constantly remake ourselves to gain male approval and love—it is perfectly understandable from the perspective of a dominator model for gender relations. For to maintain dominator-dominated relationships, it is essential that women (like members of other subordinate groups, such as African Americans and Native Americans) learn to devalue themselves. And it is further essential that women have no other aspirations than to please men—and, most important, that they have no other options.

What Are We Teaching Our Daughters?

This leads directly to another message of the seemingly harmless fairy tales that fathers and mothers continue to tell their daughters: a message about sex and the female body that is in the true sense of the word obscene. For not only do all the stories about passive, helpless girls who have to be rescued by a man on whom their very survival depends (like the proverbial young woman tied to the railroad tracks) teach little girls to have rescue fantasies rather than developing their own abilities and talents. What these stories also implant in the minds of little girls is a feminine script in which they are taught to view their bodies as commodities to trade for security, happiness, and—if they somehow manage to land not just an ordinary guy but a prince—status and wealth. On top of this, they imply that this is basically what men are for; that the astute girl will strive not to form a loving relationship, but to ensnare the most economically and/or politically powerful male. So ultimately the message of "innocent" fairy tales like "Cinderella" is that not only prostitutes but all women do—and should—trade their bodies to men, preferably to men (like the princes in fairy tales) of ample means.

Of course, most parents would be horrified if they realized that these are the kinds of ideas they are putting into the suggestible minds of their children. I certainly did not realize what such stories were teaching my own daughters. And even now, I still find myself suddenly aware of perfectly obvious things I never noticed before.

For instance, it was not until recently that I saw how truly disgusting it is that Cinderella has been presented to untold millions of little girls as praiseworthy for never speaking out, much less rebelling, against injustice: for crying in silence and working from dawn to dusk in miserable exploitation as the perfect drudge. As often as I had read that story, I had never realized how that too was part of training her to fit into the prince's slipper—in other words, to meet the specifications for the kind of woman that makes a submissive wife.

It also took me a long time to fully understand another message to girls and women in the Cinderella story: that women should not and cannot trust other women, much less look to them for protection against men. For the only grown woman in the story was not only vile to Cinderella; she also gave terrible counsel to her own daughters, whom she ordered to cut off pieces of their own bodies to fit into the story's fabled little slipper.[11] And it is only now that I fully understand still another aspect of this still-popular story. This is that by portraying all these women so frantically anxious to do their utmost to please the prince and his representatives, "Cinderella" not only teaches girls to "happily" fit into the prince's slipper (in other words, to be what *he* wants in the ways *he* specifies); it also teaches women to cooperate in maintaining their own powerlessness.

Perhaps one of these days someone will do a new version of "Cinderella": one in which, like many girls and women are beginning to do today, she reclaims her power. But of course "Cinderella" is not the only story that idealizes as feminine virtues passive acquiescence to exploitive drudgery, chronic suffering, and outrageous injustice. Nor is it the only story that romanticizes the emotional (and physical) mutilation of women—along with the exchange of their bodies (and thus their sexuality) for the privilege of both sexually and nonsexually serving a man.[12]

There is, for example, Sheherezade, the exotic Oriental slave (in some versions, princess) who in that story's "happy" ending manages to save her life by telling a thousand and one tales—and thus gets to spend the rest of her days imprisoned in the harem of a man who (until she came along) entertained himself every night by having sex with, and then killing, still another woman.[13] Then we have all the medieval tales of knights who rescue helpless damsels in distress. And for those who want more modern fare, there are the thousands of adventure films, cartoons, and TV shows in which the heroine (usually wearing as few clothes as possible) is yanked from the jaws of monsters (or other dangers) *not* through anything she does but merely by being sexy—thus, once again, using her body as currency to pay for her deliverance by a powerful male.

And there is hardly anything to counter this, as heroines modeling spunk and independent action—such as Portia in Shakespeare's *Merchant of Venice,* Jo in Louisa May Alcott's *Little Women,* and Daniel Defoe's *Roxana* (who is actually rewarded rather than punished for being sexually independent)[14]—have been as rare as the proverbial bird in an arctic clime.

Fortunately, more publishers and producers are bringing out stories about self-directed, vital, and spirited women: heroines like Ántonia in Willa Cather's *My Ántonia,* Sybylla Melvyn in Miles Franklin's *My Brilliant Career* and *The End of My Career,* and more often than not, real women in autobiographical writings such as Sojourner Truth's *The Narrative of Sojourner Truth,* Beryl Markham's *West With the Night,* Emma Goldman's *Living My Life,* and Judy Chicago's *Through the Flower.* But at the same time, and not for the first time in modern history, these kinds of stories are also being countered by the ever-escalating replication of dominator stories and images designed to get women back "in their place," not only by depicting women who are "too independent" as frustrated, lonely, and unwomanly, but all too often through graphic images of sexually active (or just "sexually provocative") women meeting a violent end.

The Household Nun and the Sexual Vampire

I say not for the first time in modern history because (although this is still ignored in most history, literature, and art courses) during the nineteenth century, in the wake of the first modern wave of organized feminism, there was in the West a veritable ideological war against women—a war that, fittingly, often portrayed the only good woman as sexually (and sometimes literally) dead. The men who fought this war were primarily writers, artists, and intellectuals. Along with like-minded religious and scientific authorities, politicians, lawyers, and philosophers, these men saw themselves as the vanguard of a new era of evolutionary progress. As the cultural historian Bram Dijkstra writes in his book *Idols of Perversity,* "Science had proved to them that inequality between men and women, like that among races, was a simple, inexorable law of nature." So "when women became increasingly resistant to men's efforts to teach them, in the name of progress and evolution, how to behave within their appointed station in civilization, men's cultural campaign to educate their mates, frustrated by women's 'inherently perverse' unwillingness to conform, escalated into . . . a war largely fought on the battlefield of words and images."[15]

To teach women what was expected of them (and in keeping with the emphasis on commerce and industry that accompanied the rise of the middle classes and the replacement of a still primarily agrarian with a mercantile-industrial society), the "virtuous" women portrayed by these men carefully guarded their virginity and refused to trade it for anything short of marriage. Dijkstra fittingly calls this type of heroine, so popular in the nineteenth century, "the household angel." For even in marriage she often retained her "purity"—which in the art of the period somehow became synonymous with looking deathly pale and listless (in other words, too weak to resist anyone).[16]

On the one hand, this nineteenth-century archetype of proper femininity was an ethereal figure hoisted up by men to an imaginary pedestal of otherworldly virtue. In compliance with the fashion of that day, she had to be so tightly laced that she was indeed often deathly pale and listless, as would be only fitting for an ideal femininity that, in Dijkstra's words, was a "paragon of renunciation." In accordance with nineteenth-century ideas about Woman as the Civilizer of Man, this bloodless creature was also supposed to provide a refuge and (although never too obtrusively or insistently) a "gentler" conscience for her husband when he returned every day from his forays of predatory capital accumulation. At the same time, she was to provide him her body for childbearing, regardless of the costs of incessant pregnancies to her health. And on proper occasions she was also to serve as a kind of display rack, conspicuously showing off emblems of his worldly success by wearing resplendent jewels and fancy dresses.

As a counterpart to this model of the ideal wife and mother (the now secularized archetype of the Holy Virgin or Madonna), there was in nineteenth-century literature and art still another, and as time went on more pervasive, image of woman. Instead of representing vestal purity, noble docility, and proper "feminine" dependence, this woman was the wild and degenerate embodiment of all that is dangerous and subhuman. Consumed by animal lust and atavistic cruelty, relentlessly seeking to drag man down from his lofty spiritual heights, this woman was the demonic archetype of the evil temptress, like Eve and Pandora before her, the carnal source of all evil.[17]

Like Pandora's famous "box" (still a slang word for vagina), woman's sexuality was once again blamed for all men's ills. And like the religious men who a few centuries earlier wrote the *Malleus Maleficarum* as a manual for hunting and burning "witches," the poets, novelists, and artists who waged the nineteenth-century war against women also focused on woman's sexuality—and even more specifically, woman's sexual power—as the ultimate danger to man. In images replicating the anti-woman propaganda of classical Greek and Roman mythology, woman became the bloodthirsty Cybele to whom in classical antiquity the genitals of bulls had to be given to assuage her insatiable hunger for seed. She became Diana, "the many-breasted idol of promiscuous, wasteful, earthbound fertility."[18] She became the "Cruel Whore of Babylon," sacrificing men to her cruel goddess, or a maenad tearing man apart limb by limb.

And, particularly as the nineteenth century drew to a close, she became the Sexual Vampire, sucking man dry not only of his precious semen but of his lifeblood.

As Dijkstra writes, "Female vampires were now everywhere." And they were not just the lurid monsters of men's poetic imagination but nasty, stupid, everyday creatures like the "gold digger" that Kipling wrote was as hungry for coin as for blood. Indeed, the female vampire came to represent woman as the personification of everything that was despicable, violent, and abhorrent in a modern dominator world.[19] And lest there should be any doubt as to who she *really* was, this vampirous woman was now sometimes explicitly associated with the "modern woman": the "man-hating" feminist who (like Lucy in the popular Victorian novel *Dracula*) was sexually independent.

As they did with Lucy, men had to make this woman pay for her insurgency. And this she often had to do with her life. So now, as Dijkstra writes, in story after story the sexually independent woman (or "Polyandrous Virago") was turned by men into "that ideal creature of feminine virtue of the mid-nineteenth century: the dead woman."[20] In fact, as in the poetry of Edgar Allen Poe, the dead woman and the ideal woman became almost the same.[21]

In reality, neither the household nun nor the sexual vampire had much to do with women and their lives. As the historian Barbara Kanner writes, "the Victorian ideal of the completely leisured, completely ornamental, completely helpless and dependent middle-class wife or daughter with no function besides inspiring admiration and bearing children" is contradicted by studies showing that women, particularly in the professional classes, sometimes had strong personal partnerships with their husbands and played important roles in their business and political lives, and that some women even chose to remain spinsters and thus retain more independence.[22] And of course the majority of women—the poor— had no choice but to work both inside and outside their homes, doing heavy and menial labor. But this ideal of proper femininity was a good way of making women who could not, or would not, conform to it feel uneasy, even abnormal.

Similarly, paintings such as Elihu Vedder's *Sphynx of the Sea-Shore* (suggesting cannibalism, or more accurately "man-eating") and other images of dangerous female sexuality were also effective tools for making women feel ashamed of their sexual desires, and for making men understand it was their duty to subdue women's "bestial wiles.[23] In sum, when added to other antiwoman propaganda—such as the message of nineteenth-century religious authorities that woman's subordination was decreed by God, and of nineteenth-century scientific authorities that woman's intellect is genetically inferior to man's and even that biologically, paternity is more important than maternity—they were effective tools for convincing both women and men of the wisdom, and inevitability, of male dominance.

Masochism, Motherhood, and Feminism

It is truly a testimony to women's innate strength of heart, mind, and soul that throughout recorded history so many women have transcended this massive socialization for low self-esteem, passivity, and powerlessness, somehow finding the will and the way to express at least some part of what they are and can be. On the other hand, it is also not surprising that women, like members of other socially disempowered groups, have also often learned to identify with those who dominate them.

Like some of the house slaves who during the American Civil War fought on the side of their masters to protect their right to enslave them, many women still think any challenge to male dominance is unfeminine. Indeed, like the Chinese mother-in-law who was expected to terrorize her son's new wife as was once done to her, women have often themselves acted as agents for the maintenance of male supremacy. Women have also all too often helped maintain, or at least taken advantage of, the economic exploitation of other women, particularly women of other races, castes, and classes, as in the case of white women in the United States with primarily African-American and Latin-American servants, upper-caste Indian women with lower-caste Indian servants, and Saudi Arabian women with servant women imported from other regions of the Middle East.[24] Women have also all too often countenanced and actively participated in anti-Semitism, racism, and other forms of dominator scapegoating.[25] And, as already noted, women themselves often perpetuate dominator stereotypes of masculinity, at the same time that they condemn as "unfeminine" women perceived as too assertive and active rather than (as befits stereotypical femininity) being discreetly manipulative.

For example, women have all too often bought into the view that men are weak if they are sensitive, or if they find it difficult to accept the notion that "real" men must prove their masculinity by being aggressive and even violent. And women have all too often been even harsher than men in their judgment of other women as immoral and/or unladylike.

Indeed, even though many women have internalized the view that women should not dominate others, they have often also internalized a value system in which the power to dominate others is most highly valued.

So often women have themselves been controlling and abusive when their social roles permitted it—for instance, as mothers in cultures where physical and emotional abuse is considered good parenting, or in some cases when they have been given the opportunity to take on a ruling role, like the regent mother of a young prince.

This recognition that for much of recorded history women have not just been passive victims is very important. It not only takes us away from the polarization of women and men into victims and oppressors to an understanding that what we are dealing with here is a generally oppressive system; it also makes it possible for us to recognize that women, like men, are profoundly influenced by what they are taught. Moreover, it makes it possible for us to recognize that women are *not* innately more passive, submissive, or manipulative than men.

To recognize that throughout much of recorded history women, like men, have often actively collaborated in their own and others' domination and oppression is also to recognize that once we become aware of our true situation we do have the power for change. And in truth, it is only then that we have this power. As the nineteenth-century feminist philosopher Charlotte Perkins Gilman wrote, "Until we see what we are, we cannot take steps to become what we should be."[26]

This is not the place to go into the feminist deconstruction and reconstruction of femininity in depth. There are many excellent books that do this, some of which I have already cited. Nor is it the place to go into the growing recognition by feminists of the urgent need, in both theory and practice, to address interlocking systems of domination based on sexism, classism, racism, and other forms of institutionalized oppression.[27] Neither is it the place to look at the relationship between the feminist challenge to dominator politics and economics and the transformation of both sexuality and spirituality, as I will do this in a later chapter. Here I want to briefly focus on just a few aspects of the contemporary changes in consciousness about what it has meant, and can mean, to be a woman.

The first is the growing consciousness of the incredible human costs stemming from the male preference characteristic of male-dominant societies, where (particularly in more rigidly male-dominated regions) even mothers and fathers consider it a misfortune when a little girl rather than a little boy is born.[28] In places such as China, India, and Bangladesh (where mothers sometimes kill baby girls when they are one or two days old by pouring scalding chicken soup down their throats as a sacrifice so they will be given a son, because their own status, and even survival, heavily depends on this), the cost has all too often been a girl-child's life.[29] But even in less brutal circumstances, when the birth of a baby girl is greeted with the traditional quip "Hope next time it's a boy," the human costs are enormous. For how can girls and women in such a cultural climate be expected to develop any solid basis for self-esteem? How can they be expected to develop their full human potentials? How can they be expected not to feel envious (as in Freud's famous diagnosis of penis envy) of men's privileges, and hence to unconsciously resent them? And how can they help internalizing these negative messages and thus come to believe that if they suffer, it somehow must be their fault?

This internalization of misogynist or woman-hating messages takes me to a second area where we are today seeing important changes in consciousness: the belief that women enjoy, and even seek out, pain. Certainly, when human beings are devalued, they develop psychological problems. But as more and more women are beginning to realize, this is a far cry from the false myth of female masochism. And while it is true that women sometimes make choices that may seem like choosing subservience and suffering, in reality this often boils down to women just doing their best to survive.

For example, women sometimes endure abusive relations because they have been effectively conditioned to blame themselves for their suffering and to hope that if they somehow manage to change so as not to anger their abusers, everything will turn out all right.[30] In extreme cases—like concentration camp inmates, with whom these women's psychological states have recently been compared—they sometimes stay in brutally abusive relations because constant messages that they are no good coupled with systematic patterns of violence and abuse have destroyed in them the last vestiges of independent will. But the main reason women stay in physically and/or emotionally abusive relations is not so much psychological as practical. They often do so because they are afraid that if they leave, men will carry out their threat to kill them (as they all too often do) and/or because they all too accurately perceive that they do not have any good alternatives. For the alternative to an abusive relationship for many women and their children is at best a marginal existence on welfare or, as we increasingly see around us, sleeping out on the streets.

Of course, men also often choose to do things that are sure to cause them pain. For instance, in male peer group initiations in both tribal and industrial societies a man's willingness to expose himself to pain is required as proof of his manhood. But the difference is that in men the choice to endure pain is considered valor, whereas in women it is considered masochism.[31]

This leads to another area where women are today questioning what we have been told about women's roles and lives: motherhood. As

Adrienne Rich writes in *Of Woman Born*, there is a big difference between women's experience of motherhood and the still-prevailing social construction of motherhood.

Rich notes that despite the idealization of motherhood, and in part because of it, there is a tendency in our society to automatically blame mothers for every conceivable ill that afflicts their children, even for any crimes they commit. Indeed, as psychologists such as Phyllis Chesler and Paula Caplan have pointed out, modern psychiatric theory has all too often been an exercise in mother bashing.[32] This is not to say that mothers, and particularly mothers socialized to transmit dominator norms to their children, do not unconsciously, and sometimes consciously, engage in abusive and violent behaviors that damage both their daughters and sons. Just as women in rigid dominator societies often express their self-hate as "inferior" women in ambivalence and hostility toward their daughters, they also unconsciously, and sometimes consciously, express some of their resentment and ambivalence toward men in their relations with the only males over whom they can, at least for a time, legitimately wield power: their sons.[33]

But the recognition of these problems is hardly what we find in mainstream psychiatric theory. What we instead find are psychiatric constructs such as the Freudian Oedipus and Electra complexes—which supposedly describe the normal relations between parents and children but actually describe the tangled masculine and feminine psychology of a society where young men periodically replace old men as dominators and women are only supposed to exercise power indirectly, by manipulating men. Thus, Freud claimed that every son wants to kill his father so he can take over his power and have sex with his mother. And he also asserted that every daughter wants to kill her mother so she can replace her in having sex with her powerful father—dismissing what women who came to see him for help told him about the trauma of having been sexually abused by their fathers.

This in turn leads to still another important area where we are today seeing major changes in consciousness. At the same time that women are beginning to recognize that their real experiences have often been discounted by the male authorities who have defined reality for us, they are also beginning to realize that what many women are expressing today is not new—that in fact, as Dale Spender writes, "for centuries there has been a long and honorable tradition of women who have resisted and protested against men and their power.[34] For me, reading books such as Spender's *Feminist Theorists: Three Centuries of Key Women Thinkers* was a turning point. For the first time, in page after page recording the lives and ideas of women such as Aphra Behn, Margaret Fuller, Lucy Stone, Matilda Joslyn Gage, Emma Goldman, and Hedwig Dohm, I found myself: my own feelings, thoughts, and aspirations. I began to realize, with shock and rage, how truly bereft I had been of this essential experience. Above all, reading these works made me realize how essential it is for us to ensure that the voices of the women who century after century managed to trust *not* what they were told but their own observations, experiences, and feelings are not lost again.

Until now, each generation of women has had to start anew, since as Spender points out, "this tradition of feminine resistance" was correctly perceived as dangerous to the dominance of "those who have the power to suppress and remove evidence"—in other words, the religious, philosophical, scientific, political, and economic establishments.[35] So it should not surprise us that precisely because so many women are today rejecting dominator stereotypes of femininity, the replication of misogynist images is in our time even more blatant than in the nineteenth century—ranging from unrepresentative media images of feminists as unattractive man-hating outcasts (who, because they are too ugly to fit the prince's slipper, try to turn more properly feminine women into "bra-burning," "castrating bitches")[36] to films such as *Fatal Attraction* (where female sexuality is a mortal threat not only to man but to his whole family) and *Boxing Helena* (where a man chops off a woman's arms and legs and keeps her in a box—thereby, according to this truly sick and sickening romanticization of absolute male power over women, obtaining her love).[37] And unfortunately, rather than vigorously countering this propaganda, both the liberal establishment and the mainstream press still all too often trivialize women's needs, problems, and aspirations.

As a result, women (and men) are today again, as in the nineteenth century, being conditioned to see feminism as negative and dangerous. And even though it is to the courageous struggle of feminists that women in the Western world owe every one of their rights and freedoms—from the right to vote and hold political office and the right to contraception and abortion to access to higher education, the freedom to take a job without their husband's permission, and the right to keep the earnings from such a job—a whole generation of young women are again being taught to disassociate themselves from that "unfeminine" label.[38]

Yet even despite all this, the contemporary deconstruction and reconstruction of femininity is moving ahead as never before in recorded history. And in the process, it is making important inroads in that most fundamental matter of how our bodies are imaged, who has the power to do this imaging, and how the relations between female and male bodies are depicted.

Reclaiming Woman's Sexuality

Along with feminist gains in the struggle for equal employment op-portunities—such as laws ending sex segregation of want ads in which all the high-pay and high-status jobs had been under "Help Wanted Men"—during the 1970s the view of women's bodies as merely bargaining chips for obtaining a few privileges from men was gradually put at issue. During this same period (when women were fighting for rights, rather than privileges that could be withdrawn at will), another long-accepted Western stereotype was put at issue. As for the first time in American history girls gained the right to enter athletics en masse, they began to question, and reject, the notion that for women physical development means only larger breasts—in other words, that sexually attractive women cannot have strong bodies.

Indeed, as in the United States and other Western nations women in feminist consciousness-raising groups began to openly speak about their own sexual experiences, women began to realize that much that they had been told about their own sexuality was based on false information. For example, as women began to share their sexual feelings and experiences, they realized that for women long and sustained sexual pleasure is not nymphomania, but a normal and healthy aspect of their capacity for mul-tiple orgasms. Women also began to more readily accept both bisexuality and homosexuality. And women began to break their silence about such once shameful subjects as rape and incest.

At the same time that feminists pressured judges and law enforcement officials to treat rape as a crime of violence against women rather than something women provoked, the reporting of rape increased exponen-tially. As feminist scholars began to seriously study incest, the astonishing prevalence of child sexual abuse—of children of both genders, but pri-marily of girls—was also discovered. Thus, in *The Secret Trauma: Incest in the Lives of Girls and Women,* Dianna Russell reported that 38 percent of the 930 women she interviewed in San Francisco had memories of having been sexually abused.

This information verified women's much earlier reports, which Freud later discounted as hysterical fantasies—a psychiatric label still widely used to effectively deny the reality of women's experiences. And it also brought to light how this sexual abuse works as still another mechanism for maintaining male sexual control over women. For what better way to accustom girls and women to associate sex with absolute submission to male sexual control as a condition of their very survival than through the violation of their bodies, and their trust, by the very men who are supposed to care for and protect them?

Even women's sexual fantasies, particularly women's so-called rape fantasies, now came under scrutiny. In accordance with gender stereotypes of femininity as powerlessness, women had been told that they naturally had such fantasies because women naturally wish to be dominated. But as Molly Haskall wrote in her 1976 article, "Rape Fantasy: The 2,000-Year-Old Misunderstanding," what began to become clear as women shared their own experiences and observations (rather than accepting what they were told they were feeling or ought to feel) is that in some ways these fantasies were actually about sexual power, not powerlessness. What women fantasized about was not the terrible pain of having one's vagina ripped open or being beaten, maimed, or killed by a rapist. Quite the contrary, what they usually fantasized about was, in Haskall's words, being able to make men "go mad with desire"—in other words, about their own sexual power.[39]

Like men, women have obviously also been influenced in their fantasies by the constant association of sex with violence and domination we examined earlier. Moreover, in a society where men are supposed to hold all the power, there is either implicitly or explicitly an element of coercion in the sexual relations between women and men. But what women now began to understand is that sexual fantasies in which women are powerless to resist sex, as Dr. Carol Cassell writes in her book *Swept Away: Why Women Fear Their Own Sexuality*, made it possible for them to justify, and act on, their natural sexual feelings.[40]

Most important, they began to see that such fantasies are not innate. For instance, many of the more independent women Nancy Friday interviewed a generation later for her book *Women on Top* had fantasies in which men took the masochistic role—not a surprising role reversal in a society where domination and submission have for so long been equated with sex. In the main, however, women's fantasies were now increasingly about sexual experimentation and venturesomeness, rather than merely role reversal.[41]

In sharp contrast to earlier times when all the books on sex (including sex manuals) were by men, women now also began to write reams of books and articles explicitly dealing with sex—books such as Shere Hite's *The Hite Report* and Barbara Ehrenreich's, Elizabeth Hess's, and Gloria Jacobs's *Re-making Love: The Feminization of Sex*. Even women from the religious right began to write openly about sex, advising women to be sexually active and to enjoy it—of course, always remembering that they are doing so to please the "king of the house."[42]

But as part of their reclamation of female sexuality, women during the last three decades have not only been talking and writing more openly about sex; as women have begun to gain more personal, economic, and political power, they have also more openly, and far more actively, been engaging in sex. Indeed, in significant ways the sexual revolution of the last three decades has been a revolution, not in the sexual behaviors of men, but in the sexual behaviors of women.

In the mainstream media this has at best been mentioned in passing. For example, in a 1984 *Time* article on the sexual revolution, the historian Vern Bullough is quoted as stating that "there hasn't been a change in male sexual patterns in the 20th century." This quote I believe is too extreme. But as that article points out, "studies tend to agree that changes in male premarital sexual behavior since the '30s have been rather modest," whereas "premarital sex rates for women more than doubled between the 1930s and 1971, and sharply rose again to a new peak in 1976."[43]

These findings make sense if we keep in mind that for men sexual freedom has for much of dominator history been a given—that even during times of the most virulent Christian denunciations of sex (and women), most men, including some popes, were freely having sex. So it is important that when we talk of the sexual revolution of the 1960s and 1970s we be appropriately specific.

What was most significant about the first phase of the modern sexual revolution was not only that it brought a weakening of the old dogma that except for procreation in marriage, sex is bad. As Ehrenreich, Hess, and Jacobs repeatedly note, what radically changed—and thus both directly and indirectly impacted the sexual relations between women and men—was that women at first tentatively, and then more determinedly, began to reclaim their own sexuality.[44] And central to this was the reclamation of women's right to sexual pleasure—a reclamation that came hand in hand with women's reclamation of at least some measure of economic and political power.

Perhaps the most dramatic manifestation of this was the demolition of the Freudian myth of the vaginal orgasm. In retrospect, it seems odd that this notion that women can somehow achieve orgasm without clitoral involvement could have been so widely believed. But it was not until the research partnership of William Masters and Virginia Johnson clinically established that the clitoris (and not the vaginal walls, which actually have relatively few nerve endings) is the primary source of female sexual arousal—and until this was verified through surveys such as Shere Hite's drawing from women's own experiences and observations—that the myth of the vaginal orgasm was finally discarded.

The dogma that if women did not experience orgasm during intercourse they were somehow immature, if not downright abnormal, was perfectly congruent with the old male-centered view of sex. As we still read in most sex manuals, even though the clitoris is the primary seat of female sexual sensitivity, its stimulation has at best been considered foreplay, a prelude to what Hite wryly calls "the main event" through which men usually achieve their orgasm. So from that perspective, it is not all that surprising that it was not until women began to reclaim their own sexuality that this manifestly false belief—which as Stephen Jay Gould writes in his trenchant article "Freudian Slip," "shaped the expectations (and therefore the frustration and often misery) of millions of educated and 'enlightened' women" made to feel abnormal by a brigade of psychoanalysts and hundreds of articles in magazines and marriage manuals— was abandoned.[45]

To be freed from such false assumptions was a great boon to women. And because it facilitated a much longer, less restricted, more intense, and thus far more passionate exchange of sexual pleasure, it was also a great boon to men.

But it is only now, as we begin to enter the second phase of the modern sexual revolution, that still another fundamental aspect of the belated scientific recognition of what Gould calls "the sham of the vaginal orgasm" can be seen. This is that by failing to fully recognize the importance of the clitoris, scientific authorities also failed to fully recognize that in the human female there is an anatomical separation of the central locus for sexual pleasure (the clitoris) from the vaginal opening through which coitus (or the act required for reproduction) takes place. And by so doing they helped maintain the sham to our day promulgated by some religious authorities that sex purely for pleasure is of a base or animal nature— when in fact it is precisely this decoupling in the human female of the capacity for sex purely for pleasure from reproductive sex that *distinguishes* our species from most animals. In other words, what they failed to note is that it is actually only reproductive sex that can properly be classified as of a purely animal nature.

Not only that, but what has consequently often been ignored by those who have defined reality for us is that while reproductive sex is something we share with other species that reproduce through sexual intercourse, there are aspects of human sexuality—including the human female's capacity for year-round sexual activity and both the female's and male's capacity for prolonged sexual passion, sexual love, and erotic spirituality—that are uniquely human. And this in turn has made it difficult for scholars to recognize some important implications of our unique human sexuality—including the connection between sex and spirituality that for thousands of years played such a key role in societies oriented more to partnership than domination.

Resacralizing the Erotic

As we saw in Part I, there are still mystical traditions in which our human capacity for year-round and prolonged sexual pleasure is recognized as an avenue to spiritual illumination. But it is only today—as more and more women and men struggle to shift their intimate relations from domination to partnership—that the connection between sex and spirituality is once again being more generally rediscovered.

Some of the books exploring this connection are by men—for example, Georg Feuerstein's *Sacred Sexuality,* Peter Redgrove's *The Black Goddess and the Unseen Real,* William Irwin Thompson's *The Time Falling Bodies Take to Light,* and Robert Anton Wilson's satirical *Coincidence.* But most are by women, as a new genre of women's writings about sex is gradually beginning to emerge: writings that link sex with a full-bodied spirituality imbued with erotic pleasure.

In critical ways these writings are even more radical departures from convention than the more explicit books on sex now being written by women. For what they deal with is the reclamation of nothing less than woman's ancient sexual power—and with this, the powerful archetype of the prehistoric Goddess.

Some of these writings are by theologians (or as some prefer to be called, the*a*logians) such as Carol Christ, Elizabeth Dodson Gray, and Judith Plaskow. Others are by poets like Audre Lorde and Barbara Mor; artists such as Judy Chicago and Monica Sjöö; and art historians such as Elinor Gadon and Gloria Orenstein. Some are by lesbians and others by heterosexuals. Some are by women such as Vicki Noble, Starhawk, Luisah Teish, and Donna Wilshire, reclaiming for themselves powerful ancient roles as healers, shamans, and ritualists or priestesses.[46] Most invoke the ancient Goddess as the source of erotic power, although a few, like Carter Heyward, still write of her as God.[47] But whatever term they use, their focus is on resacralizing both woman and the erotic—which they define as inclusive of, but not exclusive to, sexuality—and on the erotic as empowering.

The power these women speak of is not the power to dominate and control others through fear and force. Rather, it is the power to give and nurture life and the power to give and receive love. Above all, it is not the power to inflict pain but the power to give and receive pleasure, and through the pleasure bond to enhance all of life.

As Lorde writes in a work where she describes the erotic as "a resource within each of us that lies in a deeply female and spiritual plane":

The sharing of joy, whether physical, emotional, psychic, or intellectual, forms a bridge between the sharers that can be the basis for understanding much of what is not shared between them, and lessens the threat of their difference. . . . When we live outside ourselves, and by that I mean on external directives only rather than from our internal knowledge and needs, when we live away from those erotic guides from within ourselves, then our lives are limited by external and alien forms, and we conform to the needs of a structure that is not based on human need, let alone an individual's. But when we begin to live from within outward, in touch with the power of the erotic within ourselves, and allowing that power to inform and illuminate our actions upon the world around us, then we begin to be responsible to ourselves in the deepest sense. For as we begin to recognize our deepest feelings, we begin to give up, of necessity, being satisfied with suffering and self-negation, and with the numbness which so often seems like the only alternative in our society. Our acts against oppression become integral with self, motivated and empowered from within.[48]

Or as Noble writes in a passage where she speaks of the ancient link between woman's sexual power and shamanic or healing traditions:

The garden within is the sacred sanctuary where we reconnect with the Goddess, the deep Feminine, the underground source of female empowerment and expression. We were once deeply rooted in that place, expressing power and sexuality from there without any splitting. That's the unambiguous wholeness we see in the ancient female figurines. We were snake and bird, earth and sky, body and spirit. We could invite the male into that place for an encounter, and he came.[49]

Similarly, Gadon speaks of "reclaiming the mystery of our erotic natures." And Heyward writes of the erotic as "life-force," "creative energy," even "nurse-maid of wisdom," and of "probing the Sacred—exploring divine terrain—through sexual experience."[50]

Like the artists of the prehistoric Goddess-worshiping societies, these writers see woman's body as both the immanent and transcendent symbol of the power to give life, love, and pleasure—a symbol that must be reclaimed if both women and men are to achieve spiritual healing. In fact, for many of them, it is specifically the reclamation of woman's sexual power that is the key to both spiritual and social healing: to the creation of a world where the beauty and mystery of woman's creative sexual power will be honored, instead of being linked with sin and degradation or viewed as a commodity for male consumption.

In short, these women are not only deconstructing, but also reconstructing, sexuality. And they are not alone in this process, as we will see in the chapters that follow, as we continue our exploration of how the modern sexual revolution and the modern revolution in consciousness are all of one cloth—and how both are in our time entering a new stage in which our most foundational assumptions, and relationships, are being reexamined and refashioned.

CHAPTER 15

Sex, Lies, and Stereotypes: Changing Views of Nature, the Body, and Truth

In his hit 1989 movie *Sex, Lies, and Videotape,* Steven Soderbergh tells the story of two women and two men. Each is a familiar sexual stereotype: a wife who is frigid, her nymphomaniac sister, a husband with a Don Juan type of sexual addiction, and his impotent friend. But the way Soderbergh handles the story is far from stereotypical.

Instead of presenting him as a glamorous man who, in the Casanova and later Hollywood swashbuckler traditions, wins the hearts and bodies of all the women he encounters, Soderbergh makes the Don Juan of this story a ridiculous figure who ends up losing his wife, his mistress, his job, and even the respect of his male associates. By contrast, the frigid wife and the husband's impotent friend (standard foils for comic ridicule) are treated with compassion and gentle humor as they try together to find mental and sexual health. Instead of stigmatizing the mistress as a slut for her voracious sexual appetite and for sleeping with her sister's husband, Soderbergh has her gradually emerge as a sympathetic character, struggling against the same repressive family background as her sister through sexual rebellion rather than shutdown. Moreover, it is the women and not the men who in this film most openly and graphically talk about sex, even going so far as to let themselves be videotaped on the subject—in the case of the wife's sister, masturbating at the same time.

In short, what this film does is to stand a lot of conventional sexual stereotypes on their heads. Still, the old stereotypes about the nature of men, women, sexuality, and spirituality linger on, despite the fact that they pose major obstacles to fulfilling sexual relations—and even despite the fact that today in all fields, from biology, physiology, and psychology to theology, law, and philosophy, once firmly entrenched beliefs are being demolished, with the most unexpected, and sometimes extremely funny, results.

Eggs, Sperm, and Myths of Gender

When most of us read about human reproduction in biology texts, we assume we will find factual descriptions of natural phenomena. But as the anthropologist Emily Martin documents in "The Egg and the Sperm: How Science Has Constructed a Romance Based on Stereotypical Male-Female Roles,"[1] what is taught about sexual reproduction in our biology classes is still in important respects less about the natural world than about "cultural beliefs and practices as if they were part of nature." Martin shows how "the picture of egg and sperm drawn in popular as well as scientific accounts of reproductive biology relies on stereotypes central to our cultural definitions of male and female." Not only that, it conveys the impression "not only that female biological processes are less worthy than their male counterparts but also that women are less worthy than men."[2]

For example, a best-selling text called *Molecular Biology of the Cell* informs the student that oogenesis (the making of eggs by the female) is "wasteful" since of the seven million egg germ cells found in the female embryo only three hundred thousand remain at puberty. To bring this home, the authors comment that "it is still a mystery why so many eggs are formed only to die in the ovaries."[3] But, as Martin notes, the real mystery is why the male's vast production of sperm is not described by textbook writers as wasteful—in view of the fact that a man produces one hundred million sperm per day during an average reproductive life of sixty years (well over two trillion sperm in a lifetime) and that for every baby he produces he wastes more than *one trillion* sperm.[4] Nonetheless, rather than remarking on the fact that an astronomical number of sperm die in a man's body during his lifetime, the typical textbook employs what Martin aptly calls a breathlessly admiring prose in dealing with the sperm. For example, in the classic text *Medical Physiology* edited by Vernon Mountcastle, we read that "whereas the female sheds only a single gamete each month, the seminiferous tubules produce hundreds of millions of sperm each day"—skillfully juxtaposing the term *sheds* for the female to the term *produce* for the male, even though of course these hundreds of millions of sperm (which as one writer enthuses, would span almost one-third of a mile were they placed end to end) are in fact a far more extreme example of "wastefulness" than anything connected with the production of ova by the female.[5]

But the problem is not only that the standard descriptions of male biological processes are typically couched in positive terms whereas female biological processes tend to be described in negative terms; the way that the egg and the sperm supposedly behave is practically a carbon copy of the way women and men are expected to behave in dominator cultures. As Martin writes:

It is remarkable how femininely the egg behaves and how masculinely the sperm. The egg is seen as large and passive. It does not move or journey, but passively "is transported," "is swept," or even "drifts" along the fallopian tube. In utter contrast, sperm are small, "streamlined," and invariably active. They "deliver" their genes to the egg, "activate the developmental program of the egg," and have a "velocity" that is often remarked upon. Their tails are "strong" and efficiently powered. Together with the forces of ejaculation, they can "propel the semen into the deepest recesses of the vagina."[6]

In fact, as Martin notes, the real story of what happens between the egg and the sperm is radically different. Researchers at Johns Hopkins University have found that the forward thrust of the sperm is extremely weak, which certainly contradicts the assumption that sperm are "forceful penetrators." And actually the strongest tendency seems to be for the sperm to pry itself off the egg rather than to penetrate it.[7]

But so strong are prevailing cultural expectations that for some time the researchers who made these discoveries continued to write papers and abstracts as if the sperm were the active party that attacks, binds, penetrates, and enters the egg. The only difference was that the sperm were now seen as performing these actions weakly. As Martin writes, "Not until August 1987, more than three years after the findings described above, did these researchers reconceptualize the process to give the egg a more active role." Only what they then did was yet another rehash of gender stereotypes.

For now they began to describe the ova as an aggressive sperm catcher, "covered with adhesive molecules that can capture a sperm with a single bond and clasp it to the zona's surface." In the words of their published account:

The innermost vestment, the *zona pellucida*, is a glycoprotein shell, which captures and tethers the sperm before they penetrate it. . . . The sperm is captured at the initial contact between the sperm tip and the *zona*. . . . Since the thrust [of the sperm] is much smaller than the force needed to break a single affinity bond, the first bond made upon the tip-first meeting of the sperm and *zona* can result in the capture of the sperm.[8]

In other words, still using the same military sexual language, they simply reversed the two roles, with the ova now, as Martin writes, cast as the "dangerous" sexual vampire, capturing and entrapping hapless male sperm[9]—when in fact what the new research suggests is an interactive process between egg and sperm. Yet so strong are the old gender stereotypes that even researchers such as Gerald and Helen Schatten, who admit that "recent research suggests the almost heretical view that sperm and egg are mutually active partners"[10] still find themselves presenting this partnership in terms of domination and submission. Thus, the Schattens write that "the sperm and egg first touch when, from the tip of the sperm's triangular head, a long, thin filament shoots out and harpoons the egg."

But what we actually find out is that "remarkably, the harpoon is not so much fired as assembled at great speed, molecule by molecule, from a pool of protein stored in a specialized region called the acrosome" and that it "may grow as much as twenty times longer than the sperm head itself before its tip reaches the egg and sticks."[11] As Martin writes, "Why not call this 'making a bridge' or 'throwing a line' rather than firing a harpoon?"[12] Indeed, why use the analogy of a harpoon, which pierces and injures, for something that is actually a sticking together or bonding of two surfaces?

Along similar lines, why should a textbook describe an electron micrograph of an enormous egg and a tiny sperm with the caption "A Portrait of the Sperm" when, as Martin wryly points out, this is like showing a photo of a dog and calling it a picture of the fleas?[13] Or why should another researcher, Paul Wassarman, in an article for *Scientific American* focusing on the specific molecules in the egg coat involved in egg-sperm interaction, report findings that male and female gametes "recognize one another" and form "interactions," and still write of this interactive process as if the sperm were the protagonist—the one that penetrates and fertilizes the egg and produces the embryo?[14]

The answer is of course that biologists, like all of us, are affected by the prevailing sexual stereotypes. But the problem is that the images, models, and metaphors they then employ to interpret their data in turn profoundly influence society. And what is particularly damaging about the scientific literature on sexual reproduction is that, by attributing these stereotypes to biological cells, dominator-dominated sexual relations are made to seem beyond alteration.[15]

This is why critiques such as Martin's are so important. They not only help us deconstruct earlier falsifications of nature and reality, they point us toward different alternatives. Thus, Martin suggests that biology itself provides another model that could be applied to the egg and the sperm:

the cybernetic model, with its feedback loops, flexible adaptations to change, coordination of the parts within the whole, evolution over time, and changing response to the environment. In so doing, like many other feminist scholars, Martin helps us move from deconstructing to reconstructing the way we imagine our world and ourselves—and with this, the way we think, feel, and act.

Sacred Blood or the Curse?

Perhaps nowhere is the denial of positive images to female sexual processes as jarring—and harmful—as when it comes to the uniquely female process of menstruation. In the medical textbooks, menstruation is generally described in negative terms as the "debris" of the uterine lining or as a result of "failed production."[16] In lay terms it is to our day often called "the curse"—as if this natural process were some supernaturally ordained calamity to punish women for failing to be born male.

This view that woman's monthly bleeding is a biological defect or even a malediction is very appropriate for a social system in which women are dominated by men. Thus, the view that menstrual blood is not only a curse for women but dangerous to men is characteristic of rigidly male-dominated tribal societies. Here a girl's first menses—signaling that she is now sexually a woman—is characteristically believed to render her unclean, indeed polluting, to her family and her tribe. As Mary Douglas has noted, this belief justifies male superiority and the creation of separate and unequal male and female social spheres.[17] Above all, it serves to justify strict control over women, particularly women's sexuality.

Accordingly, a girl's first menses is often followed by practices that initiate her into a restricted and inferior status. Usually this takes the form of enforced isolation.[18] Sometimes this is almost an immurement, confining a girl in a tiny lightless space, in some tribes for months and even years—a brutality that would in any other context immediately be recognized, and condemned, as cruel and unusual punishment rather than just a peculiar ethnic custom.

As the anthropologist Colin M. Turnbull writes, in some African villages a girl's first menstrual bleeding is considered "a calamity—an evil omen." Therefore, the girl who is "defiled" by it is promptly secluded. "The period of seclusion varies from tribe to tribe, and even from village to village," Turnbull continues. "Sometimes it is just for a week or two; sometimes it lasts a month or more. And sometimes it lasts until the girl is betrothed and can be led from her room of shame to be taken away by her husband."[19]

In sharp contrast, Turnbull reports what happens on the occasion of a girl's first period among the more partnership-oriented BaMbuti Pygmies of the Congo forest, where in Turnbull's words "woman is not discriminated against." "When a young Pygmy girl begins to flower into maturity and blood comes to her for the first time," he writes, "it comes to her as a gift received with gratitude and rejoicing." Instead of being condemned to solitary confinement, she and all her young friends go to a special house where "together they are taught the arts and crafts of motherhood by an old and respected relative." Here "they learn not only how to live like adults, but how to sing the songs of adult women."[20]

So rather than using menstruation as the occasion for a rite of passage that impresses on a girl—and her tribe—that as a woman she is of an inferior nature, for the BaMbuti a girl's first menstrual blood means she has been blessed—as they put it, "blessed by the moon." They celebrate this occasion through a festival they call the *elima,* and "day after day, night after night, the elima house resounds with the throaty contralto of the older women and the high, piping voices of the youngest."[21] Most significantly, as Turnbull also observes, a girl's first moon (as the BaMbuti call menstruation) "is a time of gladness and happiness, not for the women alone but for the whole people." And after its first celebration, a girl's menstruation is simply accepted as a natural part of life rather than, as in more androcratic tribes, a continuing occasion to isolate women and impress on them (and the tribe) their inferior, dangerous, and thus truly cursed nature.

This view that menstruation is not a curse is also characteristic of other more gylanic or partnership-oriented societies such as the Pueblos of North America. As the anthropologist Ruth Benedict writes in *Patterns of Culture,* the Pueblos' "handling of menstruation is especially striking because all about them are tribes who have at every encampment small houses for the menstruating woman. Usually [in these other tribes] she must cook for herself, use her own set of dishes, isolate herself completely. Even in domestic life her contact is defiling, and if she should touch the implements of the hunter their usefulness would be destroyed. The Pueblos not only have no menstrual huts, but they do not surround women with precautions at this time. The catamenial periods make no difference in a woman's life."[22]

An interesting footnote to the BaMbuti's association of the moon with women's menstruation—already found more than twenty thousand years ago in the Paleolithic cave sanctuary at Laussel—are scientific studies indicating that patterns of light affect menstrual cycles and that in the absence of other forms of nocturnal light, ovulation tends to coincide with the full moon.[23] Today, when artificial light is a commonplace, women's cycles are generally longer and not in rhythm with the moon. But even today women living together—for example, in dormitories, sororities, and jails—still often bleed together. And of course, woman's menstrual bleeding is completely unlike other forms of bleeding, since it is associated not with injury, illness, and death but with woman's sexuality and her capacity to bring forth life. So it is not surprising that woman's menstrual blood would once have been considered magical.

Nor is it surprising that in societies where women were not dominated by men—and women thus did not have to be rendered powerless in both reality and myth—woman's "blood magic" could have been seen as a sacred gift rather than a defiling curse. Perhaps there was even a time, as some scholars propose, when there were special rites in which women's menstrual flow was a "magical" fertilizer for the soil.[24] And perhaps, as some of these scholars also suggest, it was before and during menstruation that women once accessed their strongest shamanic healing and oracular powers—and thus that women's high sensitivity just before and during menstruation was then seen not as irrationality, but as an altered state of consciousness made possible by women's special biology.[25]

At a time when in industrial societies reports of premenstrual and menstrual disorders are increasing, it is certainly important that we no longer ignore women's hormonal cycles (as do our male-centered work and leisure arrangements).[26] And it is just as essential, if women are to regain a healthy sense of self-worth, that we teach little girls that women's monthly bleeding cycles are a natural aspect of womanhood that was once, and again can be, honored.

But there is still another aspect of this shift in attitudes toward women's natural cycles—one that has equally profound implications for women as well as men. This is that recognizing the value and integrity of women's natural cycles goes along with a much-needed shift in attitudes toward nature and the human body—a shift through which the dominator obsession with male superiority and control over both women and nature could finally be left behind.

Women, Men, and Nature

As we have seen, in dominator ideology male control over women is justified by dogmas placing man and spirituality above woman and nature. But these dogmas also require that men view their own bodies (which, like women's bodies, are obviously part of nature) as objects to be controlled. These attitudes were in the West exacerbated by Christian teachings of the inferiority of both women and the bodily or carnal, including the Church's condemnation of sexual pleasure. However, as we have also seen, this dualistic (or more accurately, dominator) view of men and spirituality as superior to women and nature is characteristic of many Eastern religions, philosophies, and even mystical traditions.

So the view of nature as something to be controlled, which is so decried today by environmentalists and others trying to find healthier and more sustainable lifestyles, can hardly be blamed, as some writers have, on Newtonian science or Cartesian rationalism.[27] Newtonian science and Cartesian rationalism certainly represent a detached, male-centered approach. But they are merely mechanistic updates of much earlier views. Indeed, the supposedly modern view that nature (and thus also the human body) is to be conquered and controlled by men can in Western tradition easily be traced back to the Babylonian *Enuma Elish*, where, as we saw, Marduk creates the world by dismembering the body of Tiamat. Moreover, although it is in a less violent form, the notion that males can, and should, control nature is central to the biblical creation story that is a cornerstone of Jewish, Christian, and Muslim religion. What we are told here is that all of nature was created simply because a male deity ordered that it be so—and even beyond this, that when God created humans in his image, he gave man dominion "over every living thing that moveth upon the earth."[28]

This notion that man can, and should, have absolute dominion over the "chaotic" powers of nature and woman (both of which are in Babylonian legend symbolized by the goddess Tiamat) is what ultimately lies behind man's famous "conquest of nature"—a conquest that is today puncturing holes in the earth's ozone layer, destroying our forests, polluting our air and water, and increasingly threatening the welfare, and even survival, of thousands of living species, including our own. This is also what lies behind a medical approach to the human body that all too often relies on unnecessary and/or harmful chemical and surgical intrusions— an approach that in Western medicine goes back to the "heroic" remedies developed by the Church-trained doctors who during the late Middle Ages gradually replaced traditional healers (many of them women burned as witches) and their more natural herbal and other treatments. For here too the guiding philosophy is one of omniscient doctors giving orders and of detached external control; in short, of domination over rather than partnership with nature.

None of this is to say that modern science and medicine have not made major contributions to human welfare—which they clearly have. But it is just as unsound to insist that modern science and technology alone can solve our mounting ecological problems as it is to blame all these problems on modern science and technology.

Indeed, the stereotypes of modern science and technology as either villain or savior obscure the real issue. It is not *whether* we should, or should not, develop science and technology. It is rather *how* science and technology should be developed and applied.[29]

There are in nature both creative and destructive forces, and a major achievement of human culture has been the development of technologies to better deal with, or at least minimize, the damage from destructive natural phenomena such as periodic floods, earthquakes, and other natural disasters. Medicine has also made great strides toward curing and preventing destructive viral, bacterial, and hereditary diseases. We obviously want to continue developing these kinds of technologies. But we also need to learn to work more in partnership with nature, including partnership with the human body as part of nature.

For instance, rather than merely seeking to control nature's periodic floods using modern technology to dam rivers, we need to understand how dams can under certain circumstances also have adverse economic and environmental effects, as in the case of the famous Aswan Dam in Egypt—which wreaked havoc with the natural cycles of soil enrichment through the Nile's periodic flooding, leading to massive use of chemical fertilizers, and with this, not only to great ecological damage but, in the long run, to drops rather than increases in crop productivity.[30] Another example is that rather than seeking to deal with bodily malfunctions through massive chemical therapies, which often create more health problems, we need to move toward what is today accurately called a more holistic approach to the human body—one that recognizes the interaction between mind and body and the great untapped power we humans have to heal ourselves.

This takes us to something else that is still also rarely brought out: that largely because women have not been socialized to believe they should "conquer" nature, women today play a major role in articulating and disseminating this more holistic or partnership-oriented view of natural processes. There are many books by women dealing with this issue. For example, Rachel Carson's *Silent Spring* was the first clarion call for the modern ecology movement. *Our Bodies, Ourselves* was a landmark book in holistic medicine, a powerful tool in women's struggle to reclaim our bodies, and with this, the authority to heal that was (after the Church's extermination of Europe's women healers during the witch-hunts) monopolized by male physicians. And ecofeminist books such as Carol Adams's *Ecofeminism and the Sacred*, Lorraine Anderson's *Sisters of the*

Earth, Irene Diamond's and Gloria Orenstein's *Reweaving the World,* Susan Griffin's *Woman and Nature,* Carolyn Merchant's *The Death of Nature,* and Vandana Shiva's *Staying Alive: Women, Ecology and Development* vividly show that the devaluation (and conquest) of woman and the devaluation (and conquest) of nature are all of one cloth.[31]

Taking this more partnership-oriented view of both women and nature an important step farther is Elizabeth Dodson Gray's *Sacred Dimensions of Women's Experience.* For this work not only stresses the need to understand and change gender stereotypes if we are to make real progress; it puts at issue nothing less than what is and is not sacred.

Renaming the Sacred and the Obscene

As we have seen, how we define what is sacred is integral to how we define reality. Thus, Gray writes: "It is not accidental that in the Genesis 2 account of creation Adam 'named' all the animals. Naming is power, the power to shape reality into a form that serves the interest and goals of the one doing the naming."[32]

It is all too evident that a dominator way of naming reality is not serving the best interests of either women or men. It has led to chronic violence and injustice and is ecologically unsound. Even beyond this, the view of the world as a pyramid ruled from above by a remote, otherworldly deity robs both women's and men's day-to-day experiences of wonder and meaning, investing only that which distances us from life with holiness.

Perhaps the most glaring example is that while we have no lack of religious ceremonies to deal with death, we as yet have hardly any rites to imbue the act of giving birth with sacred meaning. Quite the contrary, in the Bible we are told a woman is tainted and unclean from giving birth[33]—a complete reversal of the ancient view of giving birth as a sacred act in image after image of pregnant and birthing Paleolithic and Neolithic female figures. So the fact that women and men are today beginning to consciously resacralize giving birth through rituals of celebration is a very important partnership sign.[34]

These rites, like the rites some mothers and fathers are fashioning together with their daughters for their first menstruation, are much needed ways of investing important occasions in our lives with both meaning and joy. For why should we only imbue the passage to death with spiritual significance? Why should we ritually ignore the transition—and miracle—of our passage into life? Surely rituals of birthing, as well as the

honoring of both girls' and boys' biological coming of age, can greatly en-
rich our lives, investing these inevitable and natural human experiences
with positive rather than negative meanings, honoring the importance,
and sanctity, of the human body.

Certainly calling a girl's first menses a blessing rather than a curse and
honoring this experience with a religious celebration gives it a very different meaning. Similarly, religious rites celebrating the act of birth giving
reflect very different ways of thinking and feeling about this uniquely female experience than those conveyed by still-prevailing stereotypes of
birth as a dreaded experience that only an obstetrician (usually a male)
can help ameliorate.

Obviously there is pain in childbirth. But giving birth is also a moment of awe and wonder, a moment when the true miracle of aliveness,
and of woman's amazing part in that miracle, is suddenly experienced
in every cell of one's body. It is in that sense truly an altered state of
consciousness, a moment of such inexpressible exultation that, having experienced it, it seems to me unconscionable to deprive women who give
birth of its conscious memory by the still-customary oversedation.

I want to be clear here that this is not meant to overidealize pregnancy
and birth giving, particularly in a society that gives little actual support to
pregnant women (especially if they are poor) and still considers the pregnant female form unsightly. Much less do I want to imply that every woman
should give birth. Just as the choice of some women, and men, to abstain
from sex can be a satisfying one (indeed, for some of the women who in periods of very rigid male dominance became nuns, an eminently reasonable
one), the choice of women and men not to have children can also be very
satisfying—and in our time of population explosion, quite reasonable.

Neither do I mean to imply that those women who choose to have
children should not use the best scientific advances to reduce the pain,
and danger, of childbirth. But precisely because women are now beginning to reassess and reclaim birthing, because midwives are struggling to
regain their ancient roles, and because women are learning natural
birthing techniques including deep breathing, we are also learning how
harmful many accepted medical practices are—from forceps deliveries
and thousands of unnecessary Caesarian operations[35] to the once manda-
tory exclusion of fathers from the birthing room and the "hygienic"
separation of mother and child shortly after birth, when bonding with
parents is so important.

As women today return to more natural childbirth techniques, they
increasingly report positive experiences of childbirth—often describing it

as a labor of love, one in which, as Sydney Amara Morris writes, "we confront that which ultimately connects us with every sentient being and with the essential nature of the universe."[36] Not surprisingly, many men who have been included in the birthing process also report truly memorable experiences, as well as a much stronger sense of connection with their children. Also not surprisingly, as women become less loath to acknowledge to themselves and others that natural processes such as birthing and breast-feeding can actually give rise to sensations of erotic pleasure and that women's times of menstrual bleeding are often those when they are most sexually receptive and aroused, women also report much more positive and pleasurable feelings about their bodies—and about being women.

I will return to this matter of reclaiming the erotic as a natural, pleasurable, and even sacred part of life rather than something sinful and obscene, as it is so central to everything we have been examining. But here I want to go on to another important change in how we perceive and name matters relating to the human body: one that relates not to the sacred, but to how we define what is and is not obscene.

We have long been told that images of the nude human body, and particularly of the human body experiencing sexual pleasure, are obscene. This type of thinking—which curiously even considers depictions of women in the act of giving life unfit for "innocent" eyes, at the same time that images of men in the act of taking life are considered perfectly acceptable and normal—led to laws prohibiting the publication and distribution of all sexually explicit materials. Then, during the first stages of the sexual revolution, these laws were increasingly ignored, as pornographic books, magazines, videos, and films became widely available and, far more slowly, sex education was gradually introduced into schools.

However, the debate over obscenity is far from over. The most publicized aspect of this debate has been the argument between those in the traditionally conservative establishment who would still prohibit all sexually explicit materials as obscene, and those in the traditionally liberal establishment who would protect all sexually explicit materials, regardless of their content or consequences. But there is another view, one that again highlights how renaming gives us the power to redefine reality.

This view is based on a fundamental distinction between, on the one hand, erotica and sex education and, on the other, pornography. Probably the best-known application of this new view—which cuts through many myths and stereotypes about obscenity—is the "civil rights" antipornography legislation first introduced during the late 1970s by the law profes-

sor Catharine MacKinnon and the writer Andrea Dworkin.[37] This legislation does not deal with *erotica*—in other words, with materials that celebrate sexual love and the sharing of sensual pleasure and treat the human
body with dignity and respect. It only applies the term *pornography* to
those sexually explicit materials that dehumanize women and glamorize
domination and violence. And it therefore only provides legal remedies
against the makers and distributors of materials that fall under this definition of pornography, as distinguished from sex education or erotica, on
the grounds that such materials are central to creating and maintaining
the inequality of women and men and that, in many cases, they are dangerous to women's safety.

This legislation challenges the absolutist position of both the politically conservative male establishment and the politically liberal male establishment. And in the process, it shifts the argument over pornography
from a coercive or punitive morality of censoring obscenity (under this
definition, any sexually explicit materials) to a morality of caring and responsibility—one where protecting the right to freedom of speech and
press of powerful commercial interests that control the production and
distribution of pornographic materials is balanced with the protection of
the right of women to legal recourse for injuries to them individually and
as a group from these materials.

This must be a careful balancing, as freedom of speech and press are
central to a free and equitable society. But in fact there has always been
such a balancing. For example, there are libel and slander laws restricting
the right of one person to destroy the good name and reputation of another. Similarly, there is the prohibition against falsely shouting "Fire!" in
a crowded theater, on the grounds that it impairs people's right to be protected from the danger of being trampled in a stampede.

Indeed, this balancing of different rights has been central to the entire
history of human rights, which has from the very beginning been the
struggle between those who hold power trying to maintain their absolute
rights and privileges, and traditionally disempowered groups trying to
narrow those rights and privileges through laws that protect their rights
instead. So what we are here dealing with is essentially a continuation of
this struggle.

But once again, it requires that we make a fundamental distinction
between the protection of two very different kinds of rights. One is the
right of those who do not hold power to speak out against violence and
injustice without fear of governmental suppression—which is the basis
of the First Amendment to the U.S. Constitution. The other is the right of

institutionally disempowered groups (such as women and Blacks) to protection from members of institutionally powerful groups (such as Whites and men) when they advocate violence and injustice against these groups—which is also in line with constitutional intent, in this case, the protection of people's life, liberty, and property.

This is not always an easy distinction to enforce. Personally, I strongly favor class actions and other suits for damages but still have some qualms about prior restraints, as I am concerned about censorship. Nonetheless, I believe that those who directly or indirectly instigate acts of violence and oppression must be held accountable—a principle that was recently incorporated into the U.S. legal system through "hate crime" laws holding those who propagate hatred against Blacks or Jews accountable when this incites acts of violence. And I also believe that when the right to freedom of expression clashes with the right of women and children to be protected against sexual violence, the rights of women and children come first, and that only when sexual images debase, brutalize, and objectify another human being should terms like *obscene* and *pornographic* apply.

Redefining the Normal, Abnormal, and Perverse

I further believe that a fundamental renaming is long overdue in still another area: the question of what is and is not sexually perverse. For example, today we know from study after study that masturbation—or as I would like to see it renamed, self-pleasuring—is healthy. For example, Dr. Helen Singer Kaplan reports that "both little boys and girls stimulate their penis and clitoris as soon as they acquire the necessary motor coordination."[38] There is also evidence that women who have a history of masturbation are more likely to have satisfactory sexual relations with a partner.[39] There is even scientific evidence that postmenopausal women who either masturbate or have regular sexual intercourse have much healthier vaginal tissue and urinary tracts than women without any sexual outlet.[40]

Nonetheless, masturbation has been—and by some people still is—called unnatural, sinful, and very dangerous. For instance, in the eighteenth-century work *Onania* (so named because in the Bible Onan was slain by God for "spilling his seed on the ground"), we read that this "self-abuse" causes insanity.[41] In the nineteenth-century *Dictionary of Practical Medicine,* Dr. James Copland attributed the decreased life expectancy and greater morbidity of men who remain unmarried to what he termed the "pollutions" of masturbation.[42] Preachers decried its immorality and parents were told to tie their children's hands to bedposts at night, lest they cut short their life spans, go blind, go insane, or at the very least permanently injure their genitals. This of course was still another way of conditioning people to associate sex with control and violence. And in some cases, such as the unfortunate young man in a British insane asylum whose fingers were crippled from being restrained from this "perversion," there was indeed permanent physical damage—from the treatment, rather than the "perversion."[43]

Another supposed sexual perversion for which nineteenth-century doctors sometimes prescribed even more sadistic treatments was "nymphomania," which became a medical obsession during a period of feminist rebellion that sometimes included demands for greater sexual freedom. In fact, as Carol Groneman points out, doctors (all men, who therefore had no direct experience with what is and is not normal female sexuality) sometimes diagnosed nymphomania for just about anything that to them seemed out of line with the nineteenth-century idea that normal women have far less sex drive than men—from women feeling more passion than their husbands to adultery and even flirting.[44] And to ensure women conformed to this view of female sexuality (actually one that, as Thomas Laqueur notes, represented an abrupt shift from an earlier male construction of female sexuality as lustful),[45] some of these men offered a new cure: surgery.[46]

One type of surgery was the removal of nondiseased ovaries.[47] A second and even more popular surgical procedure was clitoridectomy. In fact, as in the ritual sexual mutilation of girls in some parts of the world still today, the clitorises of little girls were sometimes cut off.[48] For instance, Groneman reports that a certain Dr. Block in 1894 did a vaginal examination of a nine-year-old girl, according to his own account, "to determine the degree of her perversion (diagnosed as masturbation tending toward nymphomania)." He reported that "as soon as I reached the clitoris the legs were thrown widely open, the face became pale, the breathing short and rapid, the body twitched from excitement."[49] This led him to conclude that the clitoris alone was responsible for her "disease" and he performed a clitoridectomy.

Since the clitoris is the seat of female sexual excitement, today we would say that the child's response was perfectly normal, and that the perversion was Dr. Block's sexual sadism. But it is sobering that even now we sometimes read in the medical literature that women with strong sex drives are nymphomaniacs who are "excessively" interested in sex because they are actually frigid, hence their "insatiability"[50]—this, even though sex researchers long ago determined that many women have the capacity for multiple orgasms. Not only that, even though we now know that all orgasms directly or indirectly involve arousal of the clitoris, the myth that the only mature orgasm for women is the vaginal orgasm lingers on. For instance, in the 1990 *Kinsey Institute New Report on Sex* we still find many letters from women haunted by the fear that they are abnormal if (like more than half of all women) they do not reach orgasm when the only form of stimulation is intercourse.[51]

Similarly, oral sex or anything other than the "missionary position" is still considered perverse by some people (a view earlier codified in many American states through laws making these practices a crime). And many people still view homosexuality as a perversion—even though homosexuality has often been socially accepted.

For example, the Jesuit missionary Joseph Francois Lafitau in the early eighteenth century wrote of Native American and Meso American "berdaches"—men who dressed like women and married other men. Similarly, among the Kaska of the sub-Arctic, women could marry other women and often had influential social roles.[52] And we have all heard of the Island of Lesbos, from which the term *lesbian* derives, and of the famous bisexual poet Sappha (usually translated as Sappho) who wrote love poetry to both men and women.

To me, one of the most interesting findings from the recent spate of research on homosexuality is that in some ancient societies there were homosexual priesthoods—for example, the men who served as priests in temples of the goddess Isis until the Christian Roman emperor Constantine murdered most of them as part of his campaign against paganism.[53] What this finding highlights is that while a certain percentage of people in every society seem to have a homosexual predisposition, how this is expressed is to a large extent socially constructed. In some societies, homosexuality has been associated with warriors—for instance, in the days of classical Athens or in the case of the Egyptian Mamelukes, who acquired "sons" by either buying slaves or taking boys as prisoners of war. But homosexuality can also be associated with very different roles, including those of shamans and healers still found in some Native American tribal societies today.

Similarly, in dominator societies a factor in some women's choice of a lesbian lifestyle has been painful experiences in their relations with men,[54] just as a factor in the preference of some men (like the Samurai and ancient Greek warriors) for sex with males has been their culturally induced contempt for women.[55] Of course, there is even here not only a negative but also a positive element: the validation of love between woman and woman and man and man. But in a partnership society, these sexual choices could be primarily motivated by positive rather than negative factors.

Certainly in societies orienting primarily to partnership homosexuality would not be treated as some terrible perversion, but simply as another form of difference. What would be considered a perversion is the hate, opprobrium, and all-too-often violent persecution of people simply because their sexuality is different from the socially imposed norm.

However—and this is a critical point we will return to in the next chapter—this does not mean that every kind of sexual activity would be approved in a partnership society. Except that here the question would not be what kinds of sexual relations one engages in, but whether sexual relations do or do not violate other people's human rights. Thus pederasty would not be condoned, much less valued. Neither would sexual harassment, coercion, or any other type of sexual behavior that effectively denies another person's freedom of sexual choice. And rape and other forms of intimate violence would be just as unacceptable in homosexual relations as in heterosexual ones.

In other words, to reject some of the traditional notions about what is and is not a sexual perversion is not the same as rejecting all standards. All of this takes me to a final matter I want to address in this chapter: the position, sometimes today advanced under the guise of "postmodern" thinking, that because much that was once seen as truth is no more than a cultural construct, the only truth is that there is no truth—and hence no basis for formulating any standards.

Postmodernism, Reality, and Relativity

I want to start by saying that postmodernist (or as they are sometimes called, poststructuralist or postpositivist) forms of analysis often contain important insights about the social construction of what at different times and places has been seen as knowledge and truth.[56] Many of the diverse, and often conflicting, writings in the postmodern debate—from the works of scholars such as Hans-Georg Gadamer, Jürgen Habermas, and Thomas Kuhn, to those of Jacques Derrida, Michel Foucault, Julia Kristeva, Thomas Laqueur, Jean Francois Lyotard, Richard Rorty, and Joan W. Scott[57]—have made very important contributions. Moreover, through a variety of new approaches (from deconstructionism and social constructionism to semiotics and new forms of feminist analysis) many of these works have dismantled the myth of scientific objectivity, showing that language is integral to meaning and often promoting more pluralistic and multicultural perspectives. Indeed, following the earlier deconstructive scholarship of feminists and Marxists, these kinds of analyses are providing what Kenneth Gergen calls a "coup de grace"[58] to many religious and scientific dogmas that maintain hierarchies of privilege and power.

I also want to say that at a time when so much that was once considered knowledge and truth has been discredited—when all around us myths and stereotypes are collapsing like so many houses of cards—it is understandable that there should be a tendency to take this deconstructive process to extremes. Also understandable, when viewed in terms of the strong resistance to fundamental change, is that at a time when more and more people are rejecting the notion that sexual, racial, and religious differences are a proper basis for ranking "superiors" over "inferiors," the very important principle of valuing diversity should sometimes be co-opted into a cultural relativity that in fact serves to maintain the status quo.

But to shove all ethical questions under the rug of a cultural relativity that insists that one must look at human societies and human history only in terms of the values of the studied group, no matter how barbarous the ethnic custom or historic period, lulls one into an almost somnambulistic state of ironic detachment, one in which, posing as a defender of ethnic diversity, one can justify every kind of behavior. Moreover, merely substituting detached irony (the battle cry of postmodern discourse) for detached objectivity (the battle cry of modern science) is hardly a new approach to scientific inquiry. Actually, in many ways it comes to the same. For what is lacking in both is feeling, or more specifically, empathy—a lack that has all too often made modern science a tool for maintaining the massive inequities and imbalances inherent in a dominator status quo.

Of course, the claim of some postmodernists that truth, values, and meaning are dead is hardly new. It goes back a hundred years to the dadaists and nihilists of the turn of the twentieth century, and long before then, to the ancient Greek and Roman skeptic philosophers. Cynicism has long been a refuge of disillusioned idealists, an escape from the painful realities of a world where, in actuality and not just in "narrative structures," our human relations have all too often been chronically painful.

Certainly the observation that meaning is the product of "signifiers" (human-made words and other symbols that vary from place to place and time to time)[59] helps us understand that how we interpret reality is profoundly influenced by our cultural conditioning. So does Gadamer's observation that we make sense of the world through prejudices and pre-understandings that are built into the language we inherit and use.[60] But to imply that therefore everything is no more than a matter of interpretation obscures the most basic of facts: that if we cut someone they bleed, that if we care for someone they flourish, that when cruel behaviors are socially sanctioned there is enormous suffering—and that we each bear some responsibility not just to observe and interpret, but to act.

Put another way, it is instructive to realize that how pain and pleasure are experienced—and even how they are defined—is to a certain degree culturally constructed. But this does not change the reality that there are acts that cause great physical, as well as psychological, pain and that whether or not these kinds of acts are socially condoned and institutionalized has very real consequences.

This bedrock recognition that there is such a thing as a sentient human body and real human experiences lies at the core of what the historian Kathleen Canning calls the "uneasy encounter between feminism and poststructuralist theory."[61] At the nexus of this encounter lies the "postfeminist" proposal that as part of the deconstructionist attack on categories, the term *woman* be abandoned as a category for analysis.[62] Obviously, like all categories—from nations and universities to houses, flowers, and stones—the category *woman* includes many differences as well as commonalities. But the human brain cannot function without categories. Indeed, as brain research and cognitive science demonstrate, it is our capacity for categorizing that makes it possible for us to sort out what would otherwise be an overwhelming barrage of senseless sensory input. Moreover, as many feminists point out, to suggest that we abandon the category *woman* as a descriptive term in academic writings at a time when the omission of women's experiences, contributions, and even presence in historical, literary, and philosophical discourse is just beginning to be challenged in the academy is indeed postfeminist in the most regressive sense of the word.[63]

Equally regressive is the claim of some postmodernists that all communication is characterized by "irrepresentability" and "irreference," and hence that every account of an event or experience is equally legitimate or illegitimate. For this sidetracks the insight that how we construct social relations is not fixed or predetermined into a view of life as merely a game in which, to borrow Jean Baudrillard's term, various "simulations" vie with one another in a world of such total irreference that "even illusion is no longer possible because the real is no longer possible."[64] As Richard Kearney points out, "It is a short step indeed from Baudrillard's kind of thinking here to the claims of pseudo-historians like Faurrison or Irving that the gas chambers never existed."[65]

The representation of events and experiences as just a series of simulations or "hyperrealities" is, as the art historian Suzi Gablik points out, also characteristic of much that is today labeled deconstructionist art.[66] Thus, Andy Warhol's famous painting of Marilyn Monroe with repetitive frames of her as merely a series of blips or frames on a TV screen does make the legitimate point that much in today's consumerized mass culture is no more than a media construct. But by dealing only with this surface image, it creates the same stupefying mythology television does in both its advertising and its programming: trivializing and homogenizing rather than, as great art has done, helping us see below the surface. So in Warhol's work the reality, and the meaning, of Monroe's existence—her childhood sexual abuse, her struggle for identity as a human being rather than as just an expression of male sexual fantasies, her untimely death— are again covered up by her pop culture image, like her famous nude calendar and her photo with skirts flying up, a reflection of someone else's culturally conditioned imagination. Moreover, as in the television screens that such art mimics, by assigning to anything and everything equal meaning (or lack of meaning) as merely a repetitive series of images, the message of this art is also that since everything is devoid of intrinsic meaning, there are no meaningful alternatives.

If we really think about it, it is absurd to argue that just as we turn television channels to tune in and out of different programs, all life is about is flipping from one "value-neutral" experience to the next.[67] There clearly *is* a reality to violence, cruelty, and indifference to suffering (be it that of other people or our own)—a reality that profoundly affects the possibilities for our very survival. And while all reality is in human society filtered through what postmodernists call the text or discourse of language and other culturally constructed symbols—symbols that in dominator societies have often served to sacralize, glamorize, eroticize, or even invisibilize violence, cruelty, and suffering—this is all the more reason that it makes no sense to argue that we must now question the "authority of experience" and instead look only at text or discourse.

The real irony of all this is that while this type of "ironically detached" thinking is often described as radical, the notion that in our "postmodern information age" every bit of information—and with it, every belief and action—is as good, or bad, as any other just as effectively ridicules those working for a more humane society as do those from the political right who use labels like "do-gooders" and "bleeding hearts" to mock anyone working for positive social change. For if everything is just relative, just a matter of someone's interpretation, why bother to try to change anything? Why even bother to react to injustice and brutality, much less work for a more humane and just society? Why not just do whatever one wants, no matter how someone else may "interpret" it? In short, why have any standards, conscience, or even consciousness at all?

In reality, of course, no society can function without standards. This is why those postmodern thinkers who derisively dismiss any attempt to find a basis for standards as "essentialism" and even "fundamentalism," subscribing instead to a veritable cult of "irrepresentability" and "irreference," are in effect opening the door for a massive dominator regression. Because the old dominator standards are familiar (as expressed by the term *traditional*), and because they are effectively mass marketed not only through the media but through much of our secular and religious education, they will inevitably fill the vacuum created by rapid change—unless partnership standards are developed and disseminated instead.

History makes this amply clear. For example, after the rebellious 1960s, during the 1970s and 1980s we saw the resurgence of "traditional" values, such as heroic warfare, racism, and sexism, along with fundamentalist religious dogmas. At the same time, we also saw the revival of the old "trickle down" economics that in the 1930s led to the Great Depression, with politicians once again telling the majority of Americans and other people in the world to be content with scraps from their masters' tables—as in the good old days when those below understood, and stayed in, their place.

What is urgently needed is therefore not only deconstruction, but reconstruction. It makes just as little sense, like rebellious adolescents, to blindly reject all existing rules, be they about sex or other human relations, as it does to blindly accept them. What makes sense instead is to reexamine existing rules and to distinguish between those designed to promote mutually responsible and caring relations and those designed to maintain fundamental imbalances of power where cruelty, violence, and indifference to suffering are justified as moral. For instance, there are rules about sex, such as the prohibition of incest and child molestation, that are obviously appropriate standards for partnership relations, as they serve to prevent abuses of power. But there are other rules, such as the sexual double standard for women and men, the justification of cruelty and violence in the name of sexual morality, the intolerance of sexual diversity, and the notion that men must control women's sexuality for women's own good, that are obviously only appropriate for dominator sexual and social relations.

In short, rather than, so to speak, throwing out the baby with the bath water, we urgently need to develop a coherent system of ethical standards appropriate for a partnership rather than dominator world. This is what we will explore in the chapter that follows, as we look at our intimate (including sexual) relations *not* in terms of what we have been taught is moral or immoral, but in terms of what is fair, caring, and ethical—or unfair, uncaring, and unethical.

CHAPTER 16

Morality, Ethics, and Pleasure: Sex and Love in the Age of AIDS

There is a saying that "all's fair in love and war." It reflects the belief that fairness is irrelevant in intimate relations. It also highlights that by even speaking of sex and ethics in the same breath we are today breaking new ground.

For example, in the Bible we read how King David not only committed adultery with Bathsheba, but got rid of her husband Uriah by having him sent to the battlefield and making sure he was put in the thick of the fighting so he would be killed—which he was. Yet David continued to reign as king, at the same time that biblical laws mandated the stoning to death of women for extramarital sex.[1]

These are both extreme cases. But part of our dominator heritage is an unfair, and unfeeling, morality of coercion in which those who hold power and those who do not are subject to very different rules.[2]

When it comes to sex, this double standard for morality is sometimes justified on the grounds that it is natural—that since women can get pregnant from sex while men cannot, it makes sense to punish women but not men for having sex outside marriage. But if the object is to prevent childbirth outside marriage, strict punishment of those who impregnate women to whom they are not married would achieve the same goal. Moreover, also under the guise of morality, women are in dominator societies often prevented from deciding not to have children—in other words, forced to give birth, whether they want to or not. All of which is a reminder of something we saw in Part I: that the rules designed to strictly control women's sexuality were not devised to protect morality, but to protect men's ownership of women's sexual and nonsexual services, as well as of any children they bore.

Because these are the real underpinnings of much of our so-called traditional sexual morality, I am here deliberately using the term *sexual ethic* instead. This is not to say I think we should just abandon the term *morality*. We need to redefine morality—just as we need to redefine other basic concepts, including love. But the term *sexual morality* is so laden with dominator baggage that it will take some time to achieve these ends. And in the meantime, there is an urgent need for new sexual standards, not only for individual women and men but for the makers of social policy— particularly since we today face a deadly sexually transmitted disease that has reached epidemic proportions.

AIDS and Traditional Morality

There are some who believe the dangers of AIDS are exaggerated by rightist religious zealots to scare people into returning to traditional morality. But while there may be this motive, the dangers of AIDS have not been exaggerated. If anything, they have sometimes been downplayed.

According to predictions from the World Health Organization (WHO), 1 million cases of AIDS were expected in 1991, in addition to another 249 million cases of other sexually transmitted diseases, including 25 million cases of gonorrhea, 3.5 million cases of syphilis, 20 million cases of genital herpes, and 120 million cases of trichomoniasis—diseases which, according to Dr. Hiroshi Nakajima, director of WHO, can greatly increase (even triple) a person's risk of contracting AIDS.[3] But by 1992 it was clear that even the WHO estimates were too conservative. As a group of researchers headed by Dr. Jonathan Mann of the Harvard School of Public Health found, the AIDS virus was spreading with "astounding rapidity."

The Harvard study was based not on official information from governments (which, as Mann noted, often suppress reports about AIDS and other diseases) but on analyses of hundreds of programs around the world. What it showed was that by early 1992 at least 12.9 million people had been infected with HIV (the virus that transmits AIDS), including 7.1 million men, 4.7 million women (the fastest growing infected group, up in two years from 25 percent to 40 percent), and 1.1 million children (some of whom acquired it through infected blood transfusions, but most of whom were born of mothers infected with the virus). One in five of those infected had developed AIDS, and nearly 2.5 million had died. And the predictions were that within three years the number of people who developed AIDS would exceed the total who developed the disease during the entire history of the epidemic.[4]

But while pretending there is no AIDS epidemic just avoids the issue, a return to traditional morality is certainly *not* going to prevent the sexual spread of AIDS—any more than it prevented syphilis from reaching epidemic proportions in the nineteenth century. To begin with, it is precisely because of the lingering power of traditional morality that all over the world government and religious leaders have failed to do even the simplest things that could have prevented AIDS from reaching epidemic proportions—as to do so would have meant not only talking openly about sex but advising people to use preventive contraception. For example, the Harvard AIDS study found from a survey of thirty-eight countries that one-third of the leaders had never spoken about AIDS at all, while another third had spoken occasionally, and only since 1989. In other words, violating the most rudimentary ethical dictates, these men had deprived their people of even the most basic information about the dangers they face and how to prevent them.[5]

Even now, although it is widely known that the only effective protection from the sexual transmission of AIDS for both women and men is a latex condom together with the generous use of spermicides,[6] religious leaders, including the pope, still place enormous pressure on national governments and international agencies to deny people sex education as well as access to contraceptive techniques. Perhaps most shocking is that when the pope visited Africa in 1993—a time when it was already well known that millions of women and men on that continent were HIV infected, when whole villages were beginning to be decimated by the AIDS plague—he still preached wherever he went that the use of contraception is a sin. For example, in Uganda (a country where, even though one out of eight people is infected with HIV, both Catholic and Anglican bishops have fought efforts by the government and other groups to promote condom use), Pope John Paul II told thousands of young people that "the sexual restraint of chastity is the only safe and certain way to put an end to the tragic plague of AIDS."[7]

It is impossible to estimate the terrible toll in human suffering and human lives exacted by this religious opposition to the only realistic way to halt the AIDS epidemic. For instance, in Africa—where already by 1990 20 to 30 percent of pregnant women were infected in major cities such as Blantyre in Malawi and Kigali in Rwanda,[8] and where heterosexual transmission is the major cause of the spread of the virus—countless women (including married women infected by their husbands) have given birth to infected babies. Had the pope and other religious leaders instead pressured government officials to educate their people about contraception and make condoms generally available, many of these babies (and women and men) now doomed to painfully die could have been saved.

Moreover, if so many religious leaders worldwide would stop talking about AIDS as some kind of divine retribution for sexual immorality, we would not see the horrible treatment of AIDS victims that is reported by the international press. For example, a February 1992 Nepal newspaper tells the story of a young woman named Geeta Danuwar. After working three years in a Bombay brothel—to which she was sold by her own brother—she sought refuge in her home town, only to die an "isolated," "untouched," and "humiliated" death, with villagers "pointing their fingers, saying she is bearing the punishment of her deeds."[9] Similarly, in places such as San Francisco, where the disease first spread among homosexuals, gay men have often been vilified as they slowly and painfully died.[10] And grisly stories out of Africa even report men cutting out the vaginas of prostitutes infected with HIV in revenge, without considering that, like the thousands (according to some estimates almost one million) prostitutes infected in Asia, these women obviously did not get the virus in a vacuum, and in many cases were in fact infected through sexual intercourse with infected men.

Needless to say, the point of all this is *not* to now blame heterosexual men, rather than prostitutes or gay men, for AIDS. The point is that it is not a problem that can be dealt with either through traditional morality or through the scapegoating to which it leads.

Scapegoating is one of the ways dominator systems maintain themselves. It diverts people's fears and frustrations from those who have the power to do something about the problems that give rise to these painful feelings to those who have little or no power. So instead of venting their anger at the civil and religious authorities who, in the name of traditional morality, have done little or nothing to effectively deal with AIDS, and holding them accountable, people have turned on the "sinful" prostitutes and homosexuals. And instead of recognizing that the AIDS epidemic is in important respects the result of dominator social and economic structures and religious attitudes, people continue to waste their time and energy vilifying and persecuting those very individuals who are suffering the most from a disease that most of them were either ignorant about or, like the majority of infected prostitutes, in no position to defend themselves against.[11]

In fact, since in many countries the sex tourist industry is basically sanctioned by the government, with huge profits flowing to its owners and the local and national officials with whom they work, the parties responsible for the rapid spread of AIDS in places such as Thailand and India are primarily the men in power. But aside from general condemnations of the evils of prostitution, religious leaders worldwide have done little about this industry, neither vigorously preaching against its exploitation of sex workers (often mere children) nor pressuring governments and international agencies to hold those who most profit from it accountable.

Similarly, in Africa, where the rapid spread of AIDS is to a large extent due to the poor health of the population—a condition in turn due largely to extreme poverty and lack of adequate health care—it is those who hold power who actually bear a good share of responsibility for the devastation of AIDS on that continent. For, tragically, it is a continent of callous exploitation and domination by a truly immoral alliance of foreign industrial interests from the North with indigenous Southern elites who, like the foreign interests they work with, seem to have little empathy for their own people's suffering. But, once again, most of the world's religious leaders speak of economic injustice only in general terms, rather than pointing to the political and economic infrastructure that supports it, or vigorously lobbying national and international agencies (as they do on other matters) to hold those who callously profit from it accountable.[12]

And it is precisely this lack of empathy that in still further respects underlies the AIDS epidemic. For although there are other factors (such as contaminated blood transfusions and the injection of drugs with contaminated needles) behind the spread of HIV,[13] a strong case can be made that at its root lie not only dominator politics, economics, and morality, but also dominator sexuality—that is, sex without an ethic of empathy and accountability.

To start with, if we look at the fact that AIDS is sexually transmitted only when the virus enters into the body through its fluids—usually through a cut, wound, sore, or other break in tissue—we come upon a striking, though largely unremarked, factor in the AIDS epidemic. This is that although the sexual transmission of HIV often occurs because women and men have sores (in the case of the venereal disease chancroid, festering ulcers) on their genitals,[14] this is not the only way AIDS reached epidemic proportions, either among male homosexuals in the United States or women and men in parts of Africa and Asia. Among homosexuals, it spread in large part through casual (sometimes totally anonymous)[15] and uncaring anal sex, which (in contrast to more caring and bonded homosexual relations) entails a much higher probability of tearing tissue. Its rapid spread through the sex tourist industry in Asia has also by and large been through uncaring sex—all too often sex where there is no concern for tearing tissue, as dramatically illustrated by filmed performances of Asian prostitutes "entertaining" their customers by picking up two-edged razor blades with their vaginas.[16] And, as medical researchers have noted about the epidemic spread of AIDS in parts of Africa, besides the poverty and lack of health care behind the rampant spread of other sexually transmitted diseases that cause genital sores and ulcers, another factor has been what the *New York Times* termed "little-known sexual practices that might also raise transmission rates."[17]

For example, the *New York Times* reported that in parts of central Africa, including Zambia, Zaire, Zimbabwe, and Malawi (all places where AIDS cases have been soaring), "some women engage in 'dry sex'"—a practice "designed to increase friction during intercourse" and otherwise narrow the vaginal opening through swelling.[18] As Dr. Subhash K. Hira found in Zambia, women who used herbs, chemicals, stones, and cloths to reduce lubrication and cause vaginal swelling (a practice apparently designed to please men by narrowing the vaginal opening) seem to have a greater chance of infection because of the increased chance of abrasion.[19]

Even beyond this, clitoridectomies, infibulation, and other cuttings of vaginal tissue required by religious or ethnic customs (since men will not marry women who have not been so mutilated) increase women's chances of sexual lacerations in many parts of Africa. And so also do other traditional practices, such as the marriage of little girls to older men, once again often resulting in the tearing of their genitalia.

These kinds of practices have long been known to create a host of physical and psychological problems for girls and women. But perhaps, as Fran Hosken (editor of *Women's International Network News*) notes, in view of the AIDS epidemic, they may now be looked at in a different light.[20] For as Hosken wrote as far back as 1986 in an editorial letter to the *New York Times*, the spread of AIDS through heterosexual intercourse in large parts of Africa has been accelerated by traditional sexual practices, "including the requirement by Muslims (as well as some other cultures) that blood must flow on the wedding night to confirm the bride's virginity, clitoridectomy and genital mutilation, child marriage, widespread sexual violence and rape."[21]

Obviously, uncaring and violent sex is not exclusive to African or Asian heterosexual relations—as is all too vividly demonstrated by the enormously high incidence of rape in the United States. Indeed, the point I am making is that neither sexual preference nor geography, much less racial characteristics, are what we are here dealing with. Rather, it is the dominator character of sexual intercourse. Or, put another way, it is dom-inator sex, not sex per se, that is the problem.

But, once again, the men who head the world's powerful religious hi-erarchies remain conspicuously silent about uncaring and violent sex—even when it is as extreme as genital mutilation and rape. Instead of pressuring world leaders to hold men fully accountable for rape, they ex-pend their considerable resources on trying to stop women and men from the "sins" of contraception and abortion. Thus, Pope John Paul II's re-sponse to the mass rapes of women in Bosnia was not to back those who are today working to have mass rapes finally recognized as war crimes. Rather, it was to pray that the violated women not have abortions.

Population, Contraception, and Abortion

It is tragic—and because of their enormous influence, unconscion-able—that the men who in the name of various divinities claim absolute moral authority (and in the pope's case, infallibility) are so out of touch with the realities of people's lives. Not that these men intentionally inten-sify people's pain and suffering. Quite the contrary, an important goal of all the world's major religions is to ameliorate people's pain and suffer-ing. This is one of the reasons sensitive men and women have often been attracted to the religious life, particularly to religious orders that provide people with food and run schools, orphanages, and hospitals. Certainly these enterprises have done much good, often making horribly deprived lives at least a little more bearable. But unfortunately even then, due to the alliances between heads of religious and political hierarchies, these efforts have all too often themselves become enmeshed with barbarous inhumanities—as happened in the Americas when Church-backed mis-sions were instrumental in the enslavement, and even annihilation, of the "heathen" Indians. Moreover, in instance after instance, the "traditional sexual morality" preached by these religions has prevented, rather than promoted, ethical national and international policies.

Perhaps nowhere is this as obvious as in relation to the shocking fact that due to lack of adequate family planning, *every year* 90 million more people swell our numbers, with predictions that if present growth rates continue, in just the fifteen years between 1985 and the year 2000, world population will have increased by 1.5 billion people (approximately the total world population just one hundred years ago), climbing to an astro-nomical 10 to 14 billion before the end of the twenty-first century—more than *double* the 5.6 billion that already so overburden our planet today.[22] Already this exponential growth in population has been a major factor in the destruction of forests and croplands, the wiping out of many species, and the pollution of the earth's air and water. Overpopulation is also a major factor in both civil wars and wars of conquest.[23] Moreover, in the more affluent industrialized regions, even moderate population growth, coupled with high rates of consumption, threatens finite world resources. Not only that, but in the most overpopulated regions of our globe, every day thousands of little children (as well as women and men) slowly die of starvation, with the places where hunger, poverty, and disease are highest (such as sub-Saharan Africa) those where women have only minimal access to family planning.[24]

So by any humane, and rational, standards, doing everything possible to dramatically reduce birthrates should be a top moral priority for all the world's secular and religious leaders—particularly since both maternal and infant mortality rates are highest precisely in those areas where women are forced by lack of contraception and abortion to bear children that cannot adequately be cared for. However, instead of vigorously promoting safe and effective birth control technologies and sex education, most of the men who head the world's powerful religious hierarchies more often either actively oppose, or at best passively condone, them. For example, even though polls show that in the United States 87 percent of Catholics believe couples should follow their consciences on whether to use contraception and 83 percent believe the Church should approve the use of condoms to prevent the spread of AIDS, Bishop Raymond Boland of the National Conference of Catholic Bishops recently insisted that the Church's anticontraception position stems from the Gospels[25]—despite the fact that there is absolutely nothing in the Gospels about this.[26]

Sometimes these men still make the old argument that "it's all in God's hands," as Fareed Nu-man from the American Muslim Council put it, because "if the population gets too big for the world to bear, the natural order will take care of it through famine, disease, etc."[27] Or, as the pope has done in recent years, they claim unbridled population growth should not even be an environmental issue, that the only focus should be on "consumption and better distribution of wealth." And this rhetoric continues, when in fact *both* factors are operant—and despite the fact that even though there are important official Catholic statements on the need for a more just redistribution of wealth, the Vatican has yet to redistribute its enormous wealth or, as attested by former priests who did join such grass-roots struggles, to actively support those who in many Catholic countries are fighting for just that.[28]

Neither—although population experts point out that the only real way to reduce population growth (as well as abortion) is to emancipate women, educate women, and allow women options beyond mother-hood[29]—have powerful religious leaders like the pope done anything to support equality for women. Quite the contrary, the Vatican continues to view contraception and feminism as intertwined evils.[30] Consequently, in conjunction with highly organized fundamentalist Protestant groups in the United States, the Catholic Church has vigorously worked to block not only funding for family planning but—as in the pope's 1994 declaration that women entering the priesthood is not even open to discussion—efforts to advance the status of women.[31]

So successful has this antifeminist and pronatalist religious pressure been that in 1985 the American government stopped contributing to the United Nations Population Fund, an agency that provides health care to women and infants and population information and assistance to needy families in the developing world.[32] Similarly, both the Reagan and Bush administrations systematically undermined women's constitutionally protected right to abortion in the United States, at the same time that they prohibited U.S. funding for international organizations that provide family planning and health services.[33]

All this was promoted by people who have been told by religious authorities that to do so is prolife. But in line with the dominator religious emphasis not on life on this Earth, but in some remote hereafter, the only life many of the leaders of the anti–family planning movement seem to care about—indeed obsess about—is life *before* birth and *after* death. For instance, studies show that those U.S. politicians who consistently voted on the antiabortion side generally also voted against gun control and for military aid to the Contras, while at the same time voting to cut funding for health, education, and welfare (including even school lunches for disadvantaged children)—thus demonstrating the most callous indifference to human life after a child is born.[34] And once again, they have ignored the realities: that for the vast majority of women abortion is the choice of last resort—and that rather than stopping abortions, making abortion illegal only criminalizes it.[35]

This is not to say that abortion is a simple issue, even when one believes, as I do, that the fetus, like the ovum and the sperm, is only potentially a human life. But as the feminist theologian Rosemary Radford Ruether writes, the only real way to substantially reduce abortions is by "ameliorating the circumstances that put women in this situation of involuntary and unbearable pregnancy."[36]

Thus, abortions have continuously declined in Scandinavian countries since the 1970s, when restrictions on abortions were lifted, because this was accompanied not only by widespread availability of contraception and sex education but by government child-support policies and policies to raise the status of women.[37] By contrast, in countries where abortion is illegal, including the Catholic countries of Latin America, abortion has not been stopped—and is instead a major contributor to very high rates of maternal mortality. For example, in Colombia one fourth of all pregnancies are terminated by illegal abortions, which are responsible for 60 percent of that nation's high rate of maternal deaths.[38]

In short, both to reduce abortions and to effectively deal with overpopulation what is urgently needed are policies that support not only reproductive freedom of choice for women but freedom for women from the traditional constraints that have served to maintain male control. But these are precisely the kinds of policies that go against a traditional sexual "morality" that was from its very inception designed to maintain male control over women.

This is dramatically highlighted by what happened at the 1992 Earth Summit in Rio de Janeiro. At this gathering of world leaders to discuss how to prevent the irreversible degradation of the environment and continued poverty for much of the world, the Vatican successfully derailed a recommendation for the development of safe contraceptives and considerably watered down all references to the need for family planning. There were several reasons for the Vatican's success in tipping the scales against any serious consideration of overpopulation as a major factor in environmental devastation. These included fears by some Southern leaders that the population issue would divert attention from their campaign to expose the major role of the North in creating environmental problems through overconsumption and economic injustice. But there was a common thread in the coalition the Vatican successfully put together to push its anti–family planning agenda: it contained not only many Catholic countries but also many Muslim nations that share with the Vatican strong opposition to any real change in the "traditional" roles of women.[39] And this same thread again made it possible during the 1994 UN Conference on Population and Development in Cairo for the Vatican to form alliances that, once again under the guise of "morality," diverted media attention from the worldwide suffering of women and children due to inadequate reproductive health care and family planning[40]—as well as from the fact that, as Population Communication International points out, there is a direct connection between every one of our social, economic, and ecological problems and our world's astronomical population growth.[41]

Morality, Domination, and Accountability

I here want to pause to say that if I have often focused on the Catholic Church, it is because it has been so powerful throughout Western history and because, having spent many years in a Latin American Catholic country, I am more familiar with it—and *not* because this kind of moral irresponsibility is exclusive to it. Certainly Pope John Paul II is not the only man in a position of power who uses lofty terms like *morality* or *patriotism* to justify pronatalist policies.[42]

There are many factors behind the persistence of such policies in our world today even in the face of all the evidence that they are a prescription for global disaster. In the pope's case, a factor is said to be fear that admitting a religious teaching was wrong undermines authority—which is apparently why it took the Church hundreds of years to admit what everyone long knew, that it had been wrong in rejecting Galileo's findings.[43] Still another reason for the persistence of pronatalism, even in face of the global population crisis, is that the more people a particular leader (secular or religious) controls, the more power that leader has—especially if that leader is in a position to dictate what people should or should not think and do without being held accountable for the consequences. And, to this day, this continues to be the situation for many of the world's religious leaders, who still rely on the same divine right to moral authority that has long been rejected in democratic societies as the basis for political authority.

This issue of accountability—or rather lack of accountability—is one of the central problems we are here dealing with. For how can there be a just morality in a system where the only accountability is in a one-way upward line, moving vertically from inferior to superior? Yet this is the only kind of morality appropriate for a dominator social organization, where "superiors" are never accountable to "inferiors"—be they a man's wife, children (and in earlier times, slaves), or the "subjects" or "flock" of a man's temporal or spiritual realm.

In *Moral Transformation* and other books under way, in his formulation of a new moral transformation theory, David Loye explores the basic immorality of what is involved here in terms of a dominator morality as contrasted to a partnership morality.[44] He also shows how this dominator morality—with its double standard for those who hold power and those who do not—is still very much with us and how one of its main functions is to inculcate in those who do not hold power that it is only moral for them to comply, and even cooperate, with their own domination.

In political relations, this "morality" has all too often served to justify violence against those who rebel against brutal and unjust authority—so successfully that the soldiers and policemen charged with meting out this violence have often been recruited from the very groups calling for greater political accountability. In economic relations, it has often served a similar function, as when both church and state justified violence by the economically powerful and their agents (again often people from economically exploited groups) against those struggling for greater economic equality, as well as any attempts to change the economic status quo by holding those in power more accountable.[45] In sexual relations, this "traditional morality" has also effectively served to justify the denial of freedom and equality to women, and even to justify violence against them. Moreover, here again "morality" has been used to enlist members of the dominated group to enforce their own domination—as in the case of "moral" women who condemn, vilify, and even collaborate in punishing women deemed too sexually free, at the same time that they make excuses for, and even admire, men's sexual exploits.

How effective this kind of sexual "morality" still is was exposed in a sex scandal that made U.S. headlines in 1993. The site was Lakewood, California, a small, conservative, middle-class, church-going community, where a group of high school boys, many of them popular football players, organized a competitive game where a boy scored one point for every girl he had sex with. As one boy later made clear, in this game the girls (including a ten-year-old they were accused of molesting) represented little more than numbers. But, as *People* magazine reported in a story called "The Body Counters," when some of these girls finally came forward to complain, many of the boys' parents took the view that their sons should not be held accountable as they were "only doing what comes naturally"—that "the real villains are girls of loose morals who are now crying rape." In fact, one of the boys' fathers actually bragged to reporters about what "virile specimens" his sons were. As a result, the boys, who were totally unrepentant, were welcomed back by many people at their school as heroes, while the girls who had accused them of rape and sexual molestation were branded "sluts," or as one woman put it, "trash."[46]

Still more jarring for what it tells about traditional sexual morality are the sex scandals involving the Catholic Church that have begun to surface in recent years. The cumulating pattern has been of people coming forward to accuse not only priests and nuns but even high Church officials of sexual abuse—for example, the archbishop of New Mexico, who subsequently resigned.[47] According to the sociologist Father Andrew Greeley (quoted in *Time* magazine), no less than one hundred thousand children have probably been sexually abused by priests in the United States alone, without any public exposure of the thousands of men involved by a Church that did not excommunicate them nor apparently even hand a single one over to civil authorities for prosecution.[48] Indeed, as heat from these scandals increased, the Church was forced to admit that these men were generally transferred to other parishes—where unsuspecting parents again trusted that their children were in safe and caring hands.[49]

In short, despite all its preaching about sexual morality, the Church seems to have colluded with pederasts and child molesters, protecting them rather than the children of their parishioners. Moreover, in a 1993 segment of the television program "60 Minutes," the Vatican spokesman sent to deal with these kinds of scandals still seemed more concerned with "damage control" to the Church's public image—that is, with protecting the Church hierarchy, and with this, its authority—than with protecting women and children from sexual predation by holding the sexual predators accountable.

Here again I want to emphasize that what we have been looking at are *not* problems exclusive to the Catholic hierarchy or other religious institutions. Rather, they are inherent in institutions—be they familial, political, economic, or religious—that are rigidly male dominated and authoritarian, which unfortunately is still the case with the Vatican as well as with the fundamentalist groups that are today worldwide the last unashamed bastions of dictatorial top-down rule.

In other words, as with sex, the problem is not one of religion but of *dominator* religion. But unfortunately this problem to varying degrees infects all the world's major religions since, in their institutionalized forms, they evolved in the context of dominator societies—societies in which, for much of our history, the heads of religious institutions have themselves ruled through force and fear, or worked hand in hand with despotic rulers (as in the alliance of the Church fathers with the emperor Constantine) lest, like Jesus, they be perceived as a threat to the established order.[50] Small wonder then that the high valuing of accountability, empathy, and love that (as in Jesus' teachings) lies at the core of many of the world's major religions has in practice so often been subsumed and distorted, even by the men who give it the most lip service. Moreover, further compounding the problem is that in the minds of men socialized to fit into dominator societies, the "soft" teachings of a caring morality are stereotypically associated with women and hence viewed as feminine and thus unmanly, while the harsh teachings of a coercive morality are, as

Paul Kivel notes, far more congruent with the masculine stereotype of stern paternal authority, be it temporal or divine.[51]

Yet it is out of a morality of caring rather than coercion—in other words, out of the partnership core of love, empathy, and accountability at the heart of most world religions—that some religious leaders are today trying to create a new sexual ethic. For instance, although at this writing there has not yet been any fundamental change in how mainstream religious congregations define what is sexually moral, in 1991 a special committee on human sexuality of the Presbyterian Church proposed that the Church expand its sexual borders to encompass premarital sex, bisexuality, and homosexuality—as long as the relations were governed by "justice-love." This was a major step toward leaving behind a sexual morality of insensitivity, coercion, and punishment and moving toward a sexual ethic of caring, empathy, and accountability. So also was the proposal in the same report (titled "Keeping Body and Soul Together: Sexuality, Spirituality, and Social Justice") stating that real sexual freedom can only exist in the context of "right-relatedness with self and others."[52]

That such proposals are being made within traditional religious institutions is a very important sign of forward movement. So also is the formation of organizations such as the Religious Coalition for Reproductive Choice (which has on its board eminent Christian and Jewish religious leaders) and the allied Clergy for Choice. Of particular interest is Catholics for a Free Choice, founded in 1973 to advocate noncoercive ways to achieve a decline in global birthrates as well as a fundamental change in official Catholic policy—which, as it points out, has in fact changed many times during the history of the Church (the teachings on slavery and usury being among the most salient cases).[53] But the changes in policy this grassroots ecumenical Catholic group envisions not only relate to altering the Vatican position banning artificial contraception; they constitute nothing less than a challenge to the Vatican's dictatorial authority, and with this, to its continued suppression of the right to dissent.[54]

Sexual Standards, Sexual Policies, and Sex Education

The directness of such groups' criticism of Church authority is particularly significant considering that only a few hundred years ago for far less than this people were condemned to painfully die for the sin of heresy. For example, in the July/August 1987 issue of the Catholics for a Free Choice publication *Conscience,* a woman dared to hold the pope accountable for his failures, writing that she would "like to ask him why he doesn't go from country to country telling men to stop raping," and why in her fifty-eight years as a Catholic she has not once heard a sermon about this, or the sinfulness of domestic violence, or the immorality of teaching women that their bodies, and particularly their sexuality, are somehow tainted with evil.[55]

Since then, first the Canadian and later the American bishops have issued pastoral statements addressing the question of domestic violence, and even though it is still not a major official Church priority, it is becoming so for some individual priests. In addition, not only among Christians but among Jews, Buddhists, Hindus, and Muslims more and more women and men both inside and outside religious denominations are today speaking out against the lack of empathy and accountability in many of our traditional religious teachings about sex and women—even though in some places it is still at the risk of their lives.

For example, in Bangladesh fundamentalist clerics offered a reward to anyone who kills the novelist Taslima Nasreen—and even threatened to launch a holy war if the government does not hang her (and does not also ban organizations working to spread literacy, health care, and family planning for women)—because of Nasreen's criticism of women's oppression, as she writes, "justified in the name of religion."[56] Similarly, the Pakistani poet Abida Khanum, who had to flee her homeland after being arrested and tortured for daring to question whether some of the repressive provisions of the Shari'a were really "the word of God," notes that the word *honor* in sexual relations has in Islam sometimes been a way of camouflaging the most barbaric and immoral acts.[57] The Iraqi writer Kanan Makiya (who wrote his book *Republic of Fear* under the pseudonym of Samir al-Khalil) also condemns the traditional Muslim teaching that men must have control over women's bodies, writing that "change for the better will only come in the Arab world when a new generation of young Arabs becomes incensed at the unacceptably cruel state of their world."[58] And in Algeria a group of eminent intellectuals, targeted by fundamentalists for assassination, wrote an open letter disseminated by the organization Women Living Under Muslim Laws accusing the authorities of collaborating in the murder of some of their colleagues "with the goal of instituting a social order based on the economy of the bazaar (à la Iran), and the locking up of women, as is the rule in all fascist regimes."[59]

In addition to this growing literature openly criticizing traditional religious sexual morality—and even pointing to the link between the sexual oppression of women and a generally oppressive or fascist society—there is today also a growing literature on new sexual standards to replace the old. Not surprisingly, a major contribution to this literature comes from feminist writings, where there is a heated controversy about what form this new sexual ethic should take.

Some writers, such as the anthropologist Gayle Rubin, have taken the position that a new sexual ethic should revolve primarily around whether sex is consensual. However, she qualifies this by adding that—rather than the traditional division between acceptable or good sex as heterosexual, married, monogamous, and reproductive, and bad sex as anything else— sexual acts should be judged "by the way partners treat one another, the level of mutual consideration, the presence or absence of coercion, and the quantity and quality of the pleasure they provide."[60]

Others have taken the position that a new sexual ethic would be animated by "feminine" values (which a few imply are connected with women's biology, although most see as culturally assigned). Thus, Haunani-Kay Trask in her book *Eros and Power: The Promise of Feminist Theory* focuses on what she calls a feminist Eros as the guiding principle in both homosexual and heterosexual relations. Like Cherrie Moraga, Audre Lorde, and Robin Morgan, Trask does not isolate sexuality from other intimate relations—particularly the relationship of child and mother—arguing that sexual love is first learned in the mother-infant bond, and more specifically through "intimate care of the body."[61]

This emphasis on sexual love is in turn criticized by other theorists, such as Carole Vance and Alice Echols, who worry that it "apotheosizes" the romanticism that has constricted women's sexual choices—and that from this it is but a small step to the "traditional values" that, in Echols's words, "discourage women from struggling toward sexual self-definition."[62] But still others, like Mariana Valverde in her book *Sex, Power and Pleasure*, vigorously critique the idea that the only ethical standard should be consent, arguing that what she calls "sexual libertarianism" overemphasizes individual autonomy in a society where power is still so unequally distributed.[63]

Though there is no agreement on many issues, this rich body of literature raises vital questions—notably what social changes are needed to support new sexual standards.[64] This is also an issue being raised by family therapists, lawyers, and physicians likewise aware that a new sexual ethic is not just a matter of changing individual relations but of changing social conditions—conditions relating not only to gender relations but to social class, ethnicity, age, sexual preference, and race.

Hence many of those who today write of new sexual standards also actively work to change national and international policies, a subject we will return to. Just one example are the efforts to change public policies that have prohibited sex education—for instance, Fran Hosken's efforts through her Women's International Network to disseminate her *Universal Childbirth Picture Book*[65] (which has already been translated into Spanish, French, and Arabic), and the efforts of organizations such as SIECUS (Sex Information and Education Council of the United States),[66] which has worked for many years for sex education in schools. But here too there is enormous opposition from the religious right, once again on the grounds that to educate young people about sex is immoral.

Actually, if we stop to think about it, what is immoral is *not* to educate young people about sex. Because for no other matter of importance in our lives—and sex is obviously of tremendous importance—would anyone think of advocating ignorance. Not only that, it is well known that all forms of repression have first and foremost relied on ignorance, which has throughout history served to maintain every kind of power imbalance.

Nonetheless, so successful has the religious pressure against sex education been that—although it has not stopped young people from experimenting with sex—even in a "modern" nation like the United States, the extent of sexual ignorance is staggering. For instance, a 1986 Lou Harris survey of American teenagers found that some teens believe a girl can get pregnant only if she is lying flat on her back during intercourse, that she has to have an orgasm to become pregnant, or that she cannot become pregnant the first time she has intercourse.[67] As for American adults, when in 1989 a large sample of Americans were given what the Kinsey Institute termed a sexual literacy test, as institute director June Reinisch put it, Americans flunked.[68]

Still, the opposition to sex education continues. And ironically, the fiercest opposition comes from the very people who most loudly condemn what they call the epidemic of teenage illegitimacy—even though there is no evidence that sex education leads young people to have sex, and strong indications that, on the contrary, it often helps them postpone having sex, or at the very least, to be more careful when they do.

But even more ironic is something else. This is that when in the name of "family values" such people urge instead the introduction into the school curriculum of Bible readings and other forms of religious instruction, they fail to note something that only gradually registered on my own consciousness as I wrote this book: that family relations are actually *not* valued in most of the central myths of our world's religions.

Tradition, Family, and Values

I want to start by reiterating that the problem we are dealing with is not religion per se but the dominator elements in our religious heritage and, just as important, that there are in most major religions significant partnership elements. For example, there are teachings and prayers in my own Jewish tradition that honor family relations and speak of love and sensitivity. There are many religious people of all faiths who truly value their families and express this in loving and sensitive ways. Nonetheless, it is truly stunning how antifamily some of the messages about families and family relations conveyed by many of our religious myths and dogmas really are.

For example, even though the Buddha is said to have returned to teach them his newfound spirituality, we are told that he left his wife and child to wander off in search of enlightenment. The Christian story of how Jesus was born and raised is even more problematic, since Jesus' divine father never had any kind of family relationship with Jesus' mother. Not only that, but we are even informed in the New Testament that Jesus disassociated himself from *his* family,[69] urging others to do the same.

Thus, in a passage in Matthew, Jesus is said to promise everlasting life to "every one that has forsaken houses, or brethren, or sisters, or father, or mother, or wife, or children" for his sake.[70] Again in Luke, he supposedly says that no man can be his disciple if he "hate not his father, and mother, and wife, and children, and brethren, and sisters."[71] According to these scriptures (although *not* according to the "heretic" Gnostic Gospels and to many legends that Mary Magdalene was Jesus' wife, and in yet another version of the sacred marriage bore his holy son),[72] Jesus never had sexual relations with a woman. Moreover, in official Christian writings, marriage is often described as the lesser of two evils, better than "sinful" sex out of wedlock but not as good as celibacy—as in the often-quoted New Testament statement attributed to Paul that it is "better to marry than to burn."[73]

Along with this distrust and devaluation of sexual intimacy, we find in many religious stories an equally pathological distrust and devaluation of women. The message is often that intimate relations with women are actually dangerous to men—as in the well-known tale of Samson and Delilah. And of course this is the implicit message of the most famous story in the Bible: the Genesis tale of how Eve's influence on Adam caused nothing less than humanity's fall.[74]

There are also religious stories where sex and women are not vilified, stories where women are presented as virtuous and the importance of family bonds is stressed. But the catch is that these stories almost invariably involve precisely the kinds of families that millions of women and men are today trying to leave behind: male-dominated, authoritarian families where women and children of both genders are rigidly subordinated to the male head of household, whose word is law.

This is certainly the message of Paul's commandments that women must be silent. It is the message of his statement that the relations of husband and wife are akin to those of the Lord Jesus and the Church. It is even the message found in religious mythologies where sexual love is not devalued—as in the famous Muslim story of Mohammed's sexual love for his favorite wife, Ayesha.[75] For here too it is clear that Mohammed is the undisputed ruler of his harem, again providing us the model of a dominator family—in this case, as in the Old Testament stories of Abraham and his wife and concubines, a polygamous one. In fact, even in the famous Hindu myth of Shiva's and Shakti's sexual love, which stresses that Shiva's power derives from Shakti, Shiva still has superior authority—as dramatically reflected in a religious iconography that often depicts him towering over her, sometimes twice her size.

But it is not only that family relations are authoritarian in these normative stories that children worldwide are taught as holy or sacred; they are also frequently violent. For example, many Hindu stories depict brutal family relations, with great violence between brother and brother. Also teaching that family relations are far from loving, and can in fact be extremely dangerous, is the pivotal Hindu story of how the great god Vishnu is saved from being killed by his own father through the sacrifice of a female baby—a teaching that female life is of little value, which, not coincidentally, is found in the prevailing religion of a society where the United Nations in 1990 reported that 25 percent of Indian girls do not live to the age of fifteen.[76]

The implicit message of the Christian myth of an "all-powerful and all-loving" Father who sacrifices his only son as a scapegoat for humanity's sins is also that family relations, particularly father-son relations, are dangerous. Family violence—that is, wife beating—is actually prescribed in some Muslim scriptures.[77] Then there are the barbaric biblical stories we looked at earlier—for example, the famous tale of Lot, where a father offers his daughters to a mob to be gang raped, as well as other Old Testament passages such as Exodus 21:15 and Deuteronomy 21:18–20 where we learn that a child's striking a parent, or just habitual rebelliousness, could be grounds for a death sentence.

If we really focus on all this—which, amazingly, the vast majority of religious scholars and writers do not—it is perhaps not so surprising that most of the men who head the world's major religions have failed to take a strong stand against family violence and abuse. Nor is it surprising that when these men preach to us of love, they do so in such abstract terms.

Love, the Body, and Pleasure

Indeed, if our most foundational intimate relations—the relations between parents and children and women and men—are essentially bonds of obedience by inferiors to superiors in which love by the superior is contingent on obedience by the inferior, how can these men be expected to see any human relations except in authoritarian terms? If these intimate human relations are of a lesser order than the so-called spiritual, how can they be expected to recognize that it is not disembodied love, but embodied love—the love celebrated by poets throughout the ages—that we humans most need and yearn for? Moreover, if the body is intrinsically base, how can they be expected to recognize that our intimate relations—that is, relations that involve our bodies—can be the most exalted expressions of our humanity, of all that is most fulfilling and ennobling?

If on top of this, these men themselves are expected to renounce all intimate relations as unworthy of truly spiritual men, how can we expect them to have real empathy for the joys and sorrows of love in the concrete rather than the abstract? How can they be expected to fully appreciate the importance of love expressed through our bodies, through the physical touching of a loved one, when they are supposed to never give or receive a tender caress, much less a passionate embrace?

Realistically then, such men can also not be expected to formulate what we so urgently need: an ethic for intimate (including sexual) relations. For at the core of an ethic for intimate relations is, by definition, the valuing of the human body (our own and that of others) as well as the equal valuing of the needs and desires of all humans. And this is precisely the opposite of the religious teaching that intimate relations are relations where orders are given and must be obeyed. Moreover, it is the opposite of the teaching that we must devalue our bodies (our own and those of others, particularly the bodies of women), and even beyond this, that bodily pleasure is somehow base and dangerous.

So the only thing we could expect from such men is what they have in fact given us: a morality of coercion rather than caring—as well as one that, to borrow Valverde's words, basically sees the bodily or "lower" desires as a "slippery slope": dark forces that unless strictly controlled by punishments or threatened punishments will inevitably propel us toward "an irreversible sinking into increasingly more perverse and more bizarre passions" along "a downward spiral descending to absolute perdition."[78]

This is by no means to say that all clerics hold such views. Nor is it to say that if we are successful in completing the shift to a world that orients more to partnership than domination, there will no longer be any need for what used to be called self-discipline, but psychologists now often call impulse self-regulation—a subject I will return to in chapter 19. For learning to not just follow momentary impulses is part of human maturation, of progressing from infancy to adulthood, and in the process learning to postpone, and if necessary forgo, gratification. Indeed, temporary sexual abnegation, and even a certain amount of tolerance for self-imposed pain in following one's goals or one's conscience, are choices that can give us great satisfaction.[79] But to recognize the value of self-regulation and of following one's conscience rather than one's momentary impulse is hardly the same as the blanket religious devaluation, even condemnation, of bodily pleasure as dangerous and profane.

All of which takes me back full circle, from still another perspective, to the basic issues of pain and pleasure that are the subtext for this book, and to how we have been taught to associate pleasure with such terms as *hedonism* and *narcissism,* with self-centeredness and selfishness, and even with the notion that one person's pleasure must somehow be at the expense of someone else's pain. In reality, fully experiencing pleasure entails being present, sentient, and aware. And being sentient and aware makes it possible to also feel empathy, and thus at least to a certain degree to feel what another is feeling. In other words, people who have learned to think they feel pleasure from tormenting others do so precisely because this human capacity for empathy has been blunted, in some cases extinguished. Because otherwise, for their own sake as well as that of others, they would try to spare them rather than give them pain.

This in turn takes us to something I touched on earlier: that this does not mean that in a society where developing (rather than blunting) this capacity is part of basic socialization, people would never hurt each other. It certainly does not mean that people would no longer make love passionately, that sex would never be a rough-and-tumble affair, or that, when in the heat of passion erotic sensations become ever more intense, the borders between pain and pleasure would not become blurred. Nor does it mean that no one would ever suffer, or cause others to suffer, the pain of being rejected in love. But what would be different is that people would find it more difficult to get pleasure from acts that deliberately hurt someone else, particularly someone with whom they have an intimate relationship.

Obviously such fundamental changes in socialization will require equally fundamental changes in all our institutions. But in the meantime we can begin to develop and disseminate a new partnership ethic for sexual relations in which, both inside and outside of marriage and in both homosexual and heterosexual relations, questions of fairness *are* relevant.

Such an ethic would teach boys and girls that while sex itself is not obscene, what *is* obscene is exploitive, degrading, and hurtful sex, and that sexual violence is not a mark of manliness but of meanness. It would help girls and boys see their own bodies with more reverence and respect, and thus also require it from others. It would make it possible for people to understand that conceiving a child is a matter for the most serious reflection and thoughtful choice, and that unless a baby is wanted by both partners, and can be adequately provided for, birth control is essential. And it would early on help people deal with love in the concrete rather than just the abstract.

This sexual ethic would teach that there is nothing wrong with sexual passion, that on the contrary, our human capacity for sustained intense sensation, for feeling deeply through all our senses—be it through beautiful music, art, poetry, dancing, or making love—is part of what makes us uniquely human. For the goal of this sexual ethic would be not to control or suppress this capacity, but to help us learn to align it with still another quality that is most highly developed in our species: our capacity for feeling and acting empathically.

Can we replace the old dominator morality with this new partnership sexual ethic as a step toward a new partnership sexual morality? And how can we help ensure it does not become yet another set of abstract principles, something to which people give lip service and nothing more? What is needed for a new empathic ethic of sexual and other intimate relations to become integrated into all our social institutions? These are some of the underlying questions in the next two chapters, as we briefly look at sex, economics, and politics.

CHAPTER 17

Sex, Power, and Choice: Redefining Politics and Economics

Politics is about power: about who has it, how it is defined, and how it is exercised. Since these are issues in all relationships—be they sexual or nonsexual, between parents and children, between women and men, or between different racial, religious, economic, and national groups— human relations are always political.

To be sure, this is not how politics has conventionally been defined. The reason is that power—which in dominator societies is equated with control of others—was something only those who rule were supposed to have. Accordingly, for most of recorded history, political struggles were primarily between members of ruling elites, with the mass of men only backups (usually instruments of violence) for ambitious individuals or interests trying to seize or maintain control. Moreover, for most of recorded history women were barred from power. So until recent times political struggles have primarily been between the men of the ruling classes, with women at best playing auxiliary behind-the-scenes roles to advance, or block, their goals.

During the last three centuries there have been major political changes. When in the sixteenth century Nicolo Machiavelli wrote his famous treatise *The Prince*, Western politics was still essentially a matter of struggles for power between nobles, kings, and princes, including the so-called princes of the Church. By the nineteenth century, when the British philosopher John Stuart Mill wrote his well-known book *On Liberty* and his less well-known essay *On the Subjection of Women,* political struggles already involved masses of men and women from all walks of life. In other words, there had been a shift from politics as just infighting between dominator elites to politics as attempts by masses of people through public discourse, the vote, and at times also violence, to fundamentally alter who has power, how it is defined, and how it is exercised.

One result has been a broadening of what we today call the political base: of those who get to vote and otherwise participate in political discourse. Another result has been a broadening of what is considered political—for example, the gradual recognition, as Kate Millett put it in her book of the same title, that there is such a thing as "sexual politics."[1] And as people increasingly challenged the use of pain or the threat of pain— and very specifically, pain to the body through violence—as a legitimate basis for power, still another result has been that the way power is defined and exercised is itself beginning to be seen as a key political issue.

At the same time, though more slowly, economics is also being reexamined and redefined. As Hazel Henderson notes in her pioneering work, conventional economic models still focus only on the narrow band of the formal economy[2]—where, as in traditional politics, relations have been primarily between men. But gradually the much wider bands of economic relations between men and women, women and women, men and men, and adults and children in what economists call the informal economy are beginning to be recognized.

In the process, more attention is also beginning to be given to the still generally unrecognized economic contributions of women in the so-called private sphere. As a consequence, the problems inherent in not only the exploitation of women's life-giving and sustaining services but also the exploitation of nature's life-giving and sustaining activities are beginning to be recognized. And so gradually is the interconnection between economics and politics, not only in the relations that until now have been the focus of both political and economic theory, but in our most intimate sexual and family relations.

These are some of the issues I plan to address in my next book.[3] Here I want to briefly deal with how economics and politics affect, and are in turn affected by, the social construction of sexuality and with how this interaction in turn impacts the construction of culture. I particularly want to focus on how—because, like sex, economics is at its most basic level about survival—we cannot ignore this fundamental aspect of our lives if we are to understand how sexual attitudes and behaviors are formed, maintained, and changed.

Genes, Politics, and Economics

It has become fashionable to look to sociobiological theories of female and male "sexual strategies" aimed at ensuring "reproductive success" to explain everything connected with both animal and human sexuality. But even for nonhuman species, as the biologist Niles Eldredge and the philosopher of science Marjorie Grene note in their critique of what they call ultra-Darwinism, trying to explain behavior primarily in terms of genes striving to reproduce themselves does not sufficiently emphasize the importance of behavior aimed at maintaining one's existence, rather than just passing on one's genes.[4] Moreover, whether or not some of the theories of sociobiologists help explain some species' sexual behaviors, we humans are very different from other species—if only because humans often choose to mate specifically intending *not* to have offspring.

Another genetically based explanation sometimes given for our sexual behaviors is that they are driven by hormones. There are certainly hormonal and other genetic factors in sex. But this is at best only a partial explanation. Obviously who we humans choose to have sex with, when we do it, and even how we do it is heavily influenced by our particular personal experiences and family backgrounds, as well as by social, economic, and cultural factors. And one of the most important of these factors is how a society's politics and economics allocate resources—and with this, power—to females and males.

A good entry point into this pivotal matter is for us to briefly revisit our closest primate relatives: the common chimpanzees and the pygmy chimpanzees. Because what we find here are major differences in both economics and politics. In one group, the common chimpanzees, male bonding—in political terms, the alliance of males—plays a key role in the group's power relations, and with this, in the economics of food control. In the other, the bonobos or pygmy chimpanzees, female bonding makes for a very different situation—one in which males do not displace females at feeding sites, females (particularly older females) seem to play an important role in determining access to food, and male coercion does not seem to enter into sexual relations.[5]

This is why the anthropologist Amy Parish, who has studied bonobos in a number of zoos, suggests that women today can learn a great deal from the contrast between the bonobos (where females form strong alliances) and the common chimps (where there is very little female bonding). For it verifies that the contemporary networking and organizing of women can be a key factor in changing entrenched patterns of male economic, political, and sexual control.[6]

One thing is certain. Contrary to what we have been told, women's economic and political power does not depend on how hard they work or how much they contribute to the general economic well-being.[7] For instance, in the traditional warlike and highly male-dominant Masai society, women contributed an enormous share of the economically productive work, including even the construction of houses, yet got to own only a few personal possessions.[8] What does matter—and to a very large extent determines women's sexual choices—is whether or not men have exclusive control of the society's institutional structure, and with this, its economic resources.[9]

For example, in times and places where men control all the economic resources, they can often divorce wives almost at will. This was the situation in much of the Middle East and Europe before Christianity, and is still the case in some traditional Muslim societies to our day.[10] Hence, in the Muslim world, divorce rates were higher before ideas of women's rights began to make inroads.[11]

On the other hand, in societies where women are not so economically dependent on men, women and not just men can generally divorce with ease. This is the case among the Navajo, a matrilineal society where men do not have one-sided economic control and women have a good deal of say in the distribution of resources.

Similarly, while some sociobiologists argue that plural marriages for men, but not for women, are natural because men, but not women, "incline" toward polygyny, most polygamous societies are societies where men, and not women, control economic resources. Indeed, if male promiscuity and female fidelity were simply a matter of "wired-in" sexual differences, there would be no need in these societies for laws forbidding women more than one husband—much less for practices such as the "honor killings" (sometimes through public stonings) of women who have sex outside of marriage.

Of course, it is not only between males and females that political factors—that is, questions of power—enter into economic and sexual relations. As we have seen, the control of productive economic resources, including people's productive labor, has for much of European history been in the hands of male elites—often "noblemen" who traced their lineage to warlords or warrior-kings who had amassed enormous wealth by the sword. And the laws these elites made to enforce their rule sometimes quite literally gave them the right to appropriate and exploit for their own use the bodies—and with this, both the sexual and nonsexual services—of their subjects.

Accordingly, in the slave societies of Western antiquity, as in the pre-abolitionist American South, the bodies of many men and women (as well as little girls and boys) could legally be sold and bought, like we today buy groceries, furniture, or other inanimate objects. Since they were property, slaves had no choice in what services (including sexual services) they were forced to render, little if any legal protection, and the prospect of terribly painful punishments and/or the pain of starvation if they tried to escape. Under feudalism, the bodily labor of both male and female serfs could still lawfully be appropriated by dominator elites. Moreover, the lord of the manor was sometimes still entitled to what historians call *le droit du seigneur,* or the right of the master to first "deflower" or sexually possess a serf's new bride. Later, under capitalism, women, men, and children were in many places forced to work long hours for little pay in unsafe and unsanitary conditions—once again with little choice or legal protection, under the threat of starvation if they failed to do so. And in different forms this control through the threat of pain continued in many places after communist revolutions. For in communist nations orienting to the dominator model, women's and men's labor—along with the nation's other economic resources—was made the property of a state in which, once again, a small elite of men ruled from the top, sharply circumscribing most men's and women's life choices through force and the fear of pain.

Today, at least in principle, the ownership of one person's body by another, the appropriation of a person's services, and the negation of a person's right to make fundamental life choices is almost universally condemned. But there is one area where, even in principle, all this has been particularly resistant to change. When it comes to women's bodies, women's services, and women's choices, the traditional notion that men should hold power, men should make choices, and men should control women's bodies is still ideologically, legally, and economically in place throughout much of our world today.

This is most obvious in societies where girls and women are sold into marriage or prostitution by their families. But even in societies where women themselves are not considered male property—that is, societies in which male economic and political control is less rigid—to the degree that women still have limited economic rights and choices, women's bodies are still essentially commodities.

There is here, however, a crucial difference. Rather than being bought and sold by others, in less rigid dominator societies it is women them-

SEX, POWER, AND CHOICE 335

selves who get to sell their sexual and nonsexual services, be it in exchange for long-range support in marriage or, as in prostitution, in exchange for a fee.

Obviously this does not mean that even in these kinds of societies all, or even most, women have consciously had sex for economic reasons. Indeed, even in the most rigid dominator societies women have sex because they are in love, because sex is a way of at least for a time being close to someone, or simply for sexual pleasure. But in societies where men have far more economic and political power than women, women will tend to use the one asset they have—their bodies—for economic survival and advancement. And the fewer economic opportunities a girl or woman has, the more she will be inclined to do this—regardless of whether sex will give her pleasure, and even regardless of whether it is bound to give her a great deal of pain.

The Economics of Prostitution

As I write this, although a growing percentage of sex workers are already infected with the AIDS virus, thousands of Asian girls and women—particularly from extremely poor regions such as the north of Thailand—are still selling themselves as prostitutes. The main reasons they do so are because it is a way of escaping dire poverty and hunger, because at least for a few years it offers them an opportunity to get paid far more than they could earn doing anything else, or because it offers them an opportunity to be helpful to their families by sending large portions of their earnings home—which many of these girls and women do.[12]

Indeed, large segments of the global economy are today dependent upon prostitution. This includes not only the girls and women who work in the sex tourist industry and the countless bars and sex emporiums where local men drink, gamble, and have sex with prostitutes, but the families who sell their daughters into prostitution or whom these women help support. It certainly includes those who derive even more profit from this work: the "madams" of brothels and the men who worldwide run the sex industry, be it as pimps or large-scale sex entrepreneurs. It also includes the police and other government officials who collect bribes to look the other way or are paid to regulate prostitution where it is legal.

As the feminist scholar Christine Overall succinctly put it, "Prostitution is a commercial enterprise."[13] Or in the words of the former sex worker Amber Hollibaugh: "The bottom line for any woman in the sex trades is economics. However a woman feels when she finally gets into the life, it always begins as survival—the rent, the kids, the drugs, pregnancy, financing an abortion, running away from home, being undocumented, having a 'bad' reputation, incest—it always starts as trying to get by."[14]

Because like other work, sex work is basically a means of surviving, of making a living, prostitutes have recently begun to organize like other workers, trying to improve their working conditions (particularly relating to health and safety), raise the status of their profession, and promote respect for the human rights of prostitutes.[15] Some women argue that intrinsically prostitution is no worse than other forms of paid labor, that while prostitution has often been a source of danger, disease, mistreatment, insecurity, indignity, psychological abuse, and physical and emotional pain for women, these are not essential elements, as sex work could still be done, and sometimes is, without them.[16] Moreover, as Overall points out, danger and injury "are not unique to sex work, for women can be and are subjected to disease, injury and psychological abuse inflicted by men in offices, factories, and even their own homes," and when clients are respectful and considerate it can be more pleasurable than other kinds of work women have often had to do.[17]

Certainly women organizing to protect the human rights and improve the working conditions of prostitutes is important, and may have some success. It may help dispel some of the prejudices against prostitutes, at the same time that it can help to lessen the health and safety risks to women who do sex work. In the short run, and in terms of the immediate lives of the women (and men) who are prostitutes, these are important efforts. But in the long term, the problem remains that, as Overall writes, prostitution as it has existed historically "is dependent both for its value and for its very existence upon the cultural construction of gender roles in terms of dominance and submission."[18]

As Overall writes, "In a culture where women's sexuality is used to sell, and women learn that sex is our primary asset, sex work is not and cannot be just a private business transaction, an exchange of benefits between equals, or an egalitarian trade."[19] In other words, it is hardly a "free-market" transaction, much less one taking place on what economists today like to call a level playing field.

Even beyond this, as Overall points out, what the prostitute ultimately offers for sale is the ritualization of "feminine" sexual submission. For be it in a man's relation with the "cheapest" streetwalker or the most expensive call girl (or in his relation with a male prostitute taking the subordinate role of the woman), the crux of the matter is that the man gets to do the choosing and the woman (or man taking the woman's traditional role) is there for the client's use, and all too often abuse. Thus, one prostitute describes the relationship between the male buyer and the female

seller as follows: "What they're buying in a way, is power. You're supposed to please them. They can tell you what to do, and you're supposed
to please them, follow orders."[20]

In short, prostitution is inevitably a transaction between *un*equals: one
where the buyers set the price, deciding what kinds of women (or little
girls or boys) are worth paying for, and the sellers have little if any power
to determine how their bodies will be used. This is why prostitution is not
amenable to reform—and why it is inevitable in a society where women's
bodies are still essentially commodities for sale to men, as is all too
vividly reflected in television ads for everything from cars to Coca-Cola,
where women's bodies are used as marketing come-ons.

However, the assumptions behind prostitution as an economic transaction through which men purchase women's bodies are actually not so
very different from the contractual assumptions behind "traditional"
marriage. For the traditional marriage contract (like the agreement between a man and a prostitute) is essentially also one of power imbalances:
one through which the less powerful woman unconditionally sells her
body to the more powerful man. Hence the failure even to our day in
some American states to recognize marital rape as a crime rather than a
"natural" aspect of a husband's entitlement to his wife's sexual services
in conformance to stereotypical masculine and feminine gender roles.

Women, Work, and Value

I want to again say that when I speak of stereotypical masculine and
feminine roles, I mean just that. I do not mean how women and men naturally behave in their relations with one another. Nor do I mean how they
actually behave. What I am referring to are the *cultural roles* women and
men have been pressured to play.

In reality, even those women and men who most closely conform to
dominator gender stereotypes on occasion depart from their prescribed
roles. Thus, even though prostitution is an institutionalization of male
power and female powerlessness, there are times when men go to prostitutes simply because they are in need of intimate contact, of touch, because they are lonely and have no one else to go to. Moreover, while
prostitutes may treat such men kindly, they may also try to use these relationships to turn the tables, exploiting men who become involved with
them, sometimes even ruining them—as the saying has it, "taking them
to the cleaners."

So while the dominator model of sex and economics has had very negative and painful consequences for women, it also causes men a good

deal of pain. As Friedrich Engels wrote more than a century ago, it makes it hard for men to know if they are loved for themselves or for their economic support—not to speak of how it inevitably links sex and money in both men's and women's minds.[21]

Still (and despite the continuing barrage of novels and films romanticizing women who "marry up"), women are often upbraided for being gold diggers out to marry men for their money. For a curious aspect of the dominator mythology with which men and women are bombarded to our day—for example, all the novels and films romanticizing women who would rather starve (along with their children) than consider something as crass as money—is that in a society where women have extremely limited economic choices (as women have had until very recently, and by and large still do) women must only marry or "give" themselves sexually for love, with never a thought about economic survival. But in fact—as it must be—survival is for women, as well as for men, a key consideration. So obviously, particularly when they were barred by custom from other means of making a living, women's expectation has had to be that they will be supported in exchange for fulfilling their traditional unpaid homemaker role. Or how else would they survive?

Consider, for example, that until recently among many middle-class couples it was deemed inappropriate for women to "work"—that is, to take a job for pay—lest it appear that their husbands were not good providers or feel threatened by their wives' independence. What this did was to still further perpetuate women's economic dependency on the sale of their sexual and nonsexual services to men, as not just the only honorable but potentially the most lucrative career for them. And what it also did was to further perpetuate the idea that the work women have traditionally performed in their homes is not really work, no matter how hard or how long a woman works—and therefore has no real economic value.

This devaluation of traditional "women's work"—indeed, in a very real sense its invisibilization—has been so effective that even women have learned to devalue what they do (as in the once-familiar phrase "I'm just a housewife").[22] In fact, it has been so effective that women have often felt that the highest possible feminine achievement was to turn themselves into symbols of their husbands' economic success by conspicuously not working—except as mannequins displaying expensive clothes, jewelry, and furs to advertise this success, and through hostessing and other activities designed to further advance their husbands' careers and self-worth that are also not generally considered work.

Today, dual-job couples have become commonplace in industrial nations such as the United States. But most women still earn far less than men when they work outside their homes. And child care is still seen primarily as the personal responsibility of individual women—rather than a responsibility to be shared by the children's father and the larger community, which the child will eventually enter as either a productive member or a nonproductive liability.

Moreover—and this is crucial—to our day economists still exclude from their calculations of economic productivity the socially essential labor of women in giving birth and caring for children. In the same way, they do not include in their statistical measures the equally essential labor performed by women worldwide in caring for the old, maintaining a clean home environment, nursing the sick, cooking (and in many areas of the world, also growing) food—and in myriad other ways toiling many hours every day to sustain and care for life.[23] And this exclusion of "women's work" continues, despite United Nations data gathered since 1975 (the beginning of the UN Decade for Women) indicating that women globally contribute two-thirds of the world's work hours, for which— given the imbalanced, unjust, and truly peculiar nature of the accounting characteristic of dominator economics—they globally earn only one-tenth of what men do and own a mere one-hundredth of the world's property.[24]

This is still one more aspect of the economics of domination—an economics that by making women's economic contributions invisible, or at best less valuable than whatever men do, constantly reinforces the notion that men deserve more money because they do more, work harder, and bring in more money. In fact, however, what gets paid more or less (or does not get paid at all) is determined by those who have the resources to pay. In other words—and this is again a critical point—determinations of what is valuable or productive are made by those who have control over the economic resources.

Whether someone's labor is paid well, or even paid at all, is not, as we are often told, purely an economic matter regulated by laws of demand and supply. As socialist economists have demonstrated in connection with the "working classes," and feminist economists have demonstrated in connection with "women's work," it is a matter of power relations— and thus as much a matter of politics as of economics.

Power, Productivity, and Reality

As we saw earlier, in the more egalitarian and peaceful societies of our prehistory—where the maternal principle was venerated and women's sexuality was associated with feminine power rather than powerlessness—the politics and economics of gender seem to have differed greatly from what we have learned to take for granted. Data indicate that here women played important roles in both the spiritual and day-to-day life of their communities, including the choice of how resources were utilized and distributed. Moreover, there are strong indications that maternity rather than paternity was here the chosen means of tracing children's descent.[25] Hence in these societies all children could be viewed as "legitimate." Most important, since they were all children of mothers, and each one a child of Mother Earth, their caretaking could be seen not only as a personal but also as a communal responsibility—as is still the case in some more partnership-oriented tribal societies today.

With the imposition of a dominator system, both women and children came to be seen as male property—with children whose paternity could not be established with certainty labeled "illegitimate." In the process, fatherhood became associated not so much with caretaking (as we still often find among more peaceful and egalitarian tribal societies) as with remote authority and punishment (as symbolized by Zeus, Jehovah, and other punitive father deities). But even though paternity and not maternity was now considered of primary social and economic importance, women were at the same time expected to devote their lives to caring for men and men's children—like slaves, merely in exchange for food, clothing, and shelter.

This notion that women's reproductive and productive services are male property—and with this, the notion that women should not be economically rewarded for their contributions—was undoubtedly first imposed by force and fear of force. But as we saw in Part I, with time it was also institutionalized; that is, it became embedded in the society's economic and political organization.

Since now men were to have exclusive control over the bodies of the women and children in their households—including control over the fruits of both their productive and reproductive labor—laws were passed abridging, and in some cases abrogating, women's property rights. At the same time, since men were now also to have exclusive control over their tribe's (and later their nation's) land and other productive economic resources, men took over the leading roles in all social institutions—from religion (and what was often closely connected, education) to government (which gave them control over the making of laws and other social rules). And gradually, through the workings of religion, law, economics, politics, education, and custom, this state of affairs came to be viewed as not only inevitable but desirable—either divinely or genetically ordained—even by women themselves.

In short, as long as women could be forced or persuaded to work either for free or for minimal economic rewards, and as long as men were by law in control of finances not only in the household but in the state, men and not women controlled money and other economic resources. And as long as religious and economic authorities asserted that only men should have the power to decide how money and other resources should be allocated (be it in the household or in society at large), women did not have the legitimate power to effectively alter the economic devaluation of whatever work they did—which came to be contemptuously labeled women's work. Most critically, as long as women continued to have little or no say in politics—as long as women were excluded from the legal, judicial, and administrative bodies that make laws and policies, including laws and policies that have until recently excluded women from entry into the better-paying professions and occupations—women did not have the power to change this imbalanced system.

Not only that, but as long as women continued to be systematically excluded from positions of religious and spiritual authority, they lacked the moral authority to change these power imbalances. Nor could they even question this state of affairs, as long as both women and men accepted the religious notion that it is women's duty, indeed the mark of their womanliness, that they remain silent and obediently accept men's authority as "heads of household" and heads of religious, political, and economic institutions—an authority said to derive from God the Father himself.

But what these religious dogmas, laws, and customs maintained was not only the sexual and economic subordination of women; they also maintained a generally unjust and uncaring system—one in which power was defined as the ability to dominate and exploit others, and the majority of people (both female and male) were dominated and exploited. And what they also maintained is a fundamental denial of reality: the failure to recognize that the most economically productive work *is* the work of caretaking—as without it human society would simply die out.

This dominator economics and politics that at its most basic level accords higher value to the kind of work that has caused, and continues to cause, so much pain—the work of developing, manufacturing, and "heroically" using weapons that cause pain to the human body rather than the caring and caretaking work that at every stage of our development can make our lives pleasurable and productive—lies at the heart of many of our most devastating global crises. For instance, can we really expect adequate funding for programs to clean up our environment and care for people's basic needs as long as the socially essential work of caretaking and cleaning is relegated to women for little or no pay? Can we really expect to leave behind the continuing exploitation by the North of the South—and the exploitation within the South by postcolonial native elites of their own people's labor—as long as we fail to address the fact that the half of humanity that contributes two-thirds of the world's work hours earns and owns so much less than the half that contributes one-third? As long as that basic model of economic relations remains in place, how can we expect people to grow up expecting equitable rather than inequitable economic relations? And as long as it is only natural and right for men to appropriate and exploit women's life-giving and sustaining services, why should it not be all right for men to also dominate and exploit nature's life-giving and sustaining services?

Rethinking Work, Welfare, and Economics

This devaluation of women's life-giving and sustaining economic contributions also lies at the heart of many of today's most painful personal crises. For instance, in an affluent nation like the United States women over the age of sixty (white women and women of color) are the single poorest segment of the population. A major reason these elderly women, most of them traditional homemakers, are condemned to painful poverty is that unlike men who have done military service, they receive no medical benefits or pensions for their services in rearing children. Similarly, millions of young American men today rot in prisons (at an average cost to taxpayers of more than thirty thousand dollars per prisoner per year) largely because funding could not be found for adequate child care, education (including education for nonviolent conflict resolution), and other programs that could have steered them away from crime.

Today in the United States enormous sums are spent on alcohol and drug abuse programs, prisons, and other remedial and/or punitive measures for adults—sums far greater than what it would have cost to provide economic and social support for adequate caretaking and education when these people were small, and thus to produce less damaged, psychologically healthier, and more productive adults. Similarly, all around us are millions of women with children who live in poverty because the children's fathers either cannot or do not choose to support them,[26] and because the work of mothers in raising children is not even in an affluent nation like the United States perceived as a community responsibility to be subsidized from community funds—even though subsidies for raising crops (not only for food to sustain life but for a crop like tobacco that destroys life) have long been handed out by the U.S. government.

Some affluent nations, particularly the more partnership-oriented Scandinavian "welfare states," do provide at least some support for the "women's work" of child care from community funds.[27] Here caretaking work is considered of economic value, as reflected in government subsidies to all parents and particularly to single mothers, as well as other programs that proceed from the premise that the health, education, and welfare of a nation's people is not just an individual but a communal responsibility.[28]

Significantly, because as a result of such policies these are nations with a highly educated population, this has *not* resulted in anything even remotely resembling a population explosion. On the contrary, because contraception and abortion are easily available, large families are now the Scandinavian exception rather than the norm. And just as significantly, even though in the United States programs to help those in need are often criticized on the grounds that they encourage people to be nonproductive and noncreative, the fact is that the Scandinavian nations, which pioneered such programs, have been highly creative and productive.

Many factors distinguish Scandinavian from American welfare programs. But perhaps the most important difference is that in Scandinavian nations welfare does not carry a social stigma, whereas in the United States mothers on welfare are treated with contempt—thus further robbing them of the self-respect and self-confidence people need to be successful at anything. In other words, the problem in the United States is not simply one of state subsidies, which are actually commonplace to U.S. businesses (be they subsidies to farmers or to military enterprises, which receive huge sums from the government to support their research and development activities). Neither is it simply one of abuses of government programs by dishonest people (which, as all the business and military scandals during the 1980s revealed, is also common among the well-to-do). Rather, it is that American welfare programs are basically bureaucratic versions of male-dominated families in which women are expected to do caretaking work for free (merely in exchange for food, shelter, and clothing for their children). Moreover, as in dominator families, women are in these programs subject to the control of others who treat them as incompetent inferiors, intrude into their sexual lives, suspect them of wrongdoing, and generally accord them little dignity, independence, or self-worth.

So when looked at from a dominator versus partnership (rather than capitalist versus socialist) perspective, it is hardly surprising that U.S.

top-down, nonparticipatory welfare programs, like Soviet programs of top-down, nonparticipatory socialism, have tended to discourage, rather than promote, personal responsibility and competency. Viewed from this perspective, it also becomes more understandable that during the late 1970s, the 1980s, and the early 1990s, when the United States was in the throes of a massive dominator regression, there was so much political propaganda against any governmental expenditures for caretaking, education, and other social services and that instead enormous sums were allocated to ever more efficient ways of maiming and killing people—including unprecedentedly huge governmental subsidies to business for the development of weapons systems. From this new perspective, it also makes sense that in the nations that have been in the forefront of the contemporary partnership movement—the Scandinavian nations—there has been the greatest progress toward gender equity, sexual freedom, availability of contraceptives, and the funding of "women's work," along with a generally much higher quality of life than in almost all other nations in this world.[29]

In this connection, it is sometimes said that the reason values such as caring and compassion can more readily guide social and economic policy in the Scandinavian world is that these are well-to-do nations with relatively small and homogeneous populations.[30] But other affluent nations with relatively small and homogeneous populations—for example, Saudi Arabia, which has far greater wealth—have social and economic policies guided by very different values. So there has to be something else. And if we compare Saudi Arabia and Scandinavia, we see that the most glaring difference is that one orients far more closely to the dominator model—and even more specifically, that in Saudi Arabia women's bodies, and the issue of these bodies, are still viewed as male property, whereas in Scandinavia women have far greater economic, sexual, and reproductive choices.

Clearly there is still not complete gender equity in Scandinavian societies. But Scandinavian policies regarding sex and gender—from laws permitting greater freedom of sexual expression to laws mandating paid parental leave for mothers or fathers—have been a model for progressive policies in the United States and other nations. Still, their more partnership-oriented economic policies are only a beginning—a small sample of what could happen if the shift from domination to partnership is successful.

For example, what would happen to the sharp class distinctions we still see in so much of our world—including the United States—if we devised social and economic inventions to give the "women's work" of caretaking financial value, instead of just a lot of rhetoric about family values? Since this work is needed in all families (even families where there are no children), would we continue to see such sharp class distinctions—and with this, such inequities in the distribution of resources?

What would happen to the form of power the French social theorist Pierre Bourdieu calls symbolic capital as the source of legitimate demands on the services of others,[31] as this caretaking work becomes truly valued? Would we not see a very different economic and political system—one more like that still found a few centuries ago among the isolated Basques, the last surviving indigenous non-Indo-European-language speaking people in Europe, where women could legitimately demand that their husbands do their utmost to preserve family property and men could not unilaterally dispose of (that is, control) economic resources?

As "women's work" becomes more highly valued, would we continue to see what the economist Amartya Sen calls patterns of sex bias in the allocation within households of resources for food, health care, and education that in parts of the world today condemns girl children to a lesser life, even to death?[32] And as this new economic system begins to emerge, would we not find that boys and men also have much greater incentive to do what we are already beginning to see today: to redefine fathering to include the caretaking activities formerly deemed appropriate only for mothers?

What would happen to sex and spirituality if caring behaviors were in reality, not just rhetoric, highly valued? Would we still see the erotization of violence and the sanctification of pain as such major themes in both myth and life? Or would we find very different myths—and realities—focusing more on love than on violence?

I will get back to some of these matters in the last chapter. But to close this chapter I want to say that only as we address these kinds of economic and political issues can we successfully deal with the overconsumption and overmaterialism that is increasingly recognized as both economically and ecologically unsustainable. For as long as human beings are forced to live in a system that at every turn impedes the fulfillment of their basic human needs—not only for love but for creative and spiritual expression—they will try to compensate for this in other ways, including the compulsive acquisition of ever more material goods.

I also want to say that as long as we still look at economics solely in terms of capitalism and communism, we ignore the fact that the dehumanization and objectification of human beings goes way back, not just to precapitalist and precommunist feudal and monarchic societies but long before then, to the slave societies of antiquity. So to deal with basic economic questions such as ownership—and specifically with the issue of ownership in relations of one-sided exploitation rather than two-sided mutuality—we need to start with the deconstruction of gender roles and sexual relations whereby the body of one person becomes the property of another and one individual becomes entitled to exploit another's productive and reproductive capacities. Perhaps most important, we need to re-examine the politics (or power relations) that have until now determined what kind of work is or is not economically rewarded—and with this, what is and is not "productive" work—an issue that, as we move from an industrial to a postindustrial information- and service-based economy in which the number of jobs in both farming and manufacturing is rapidly shrinking, is not only timely but extremely urgent.[33]

These are some of the questions—and choices—that will determine our future, as there can be no real cultural transformation unless we more clearly understand, and more effectively use, the material levers for social change. They also lead into the next chapter, where we will look at the strong contemporary movement toward a new integrated politics of partnership that no longer artificially severs the political and the personal.

CHAPTER 18

Toward a Politics of Partnership: Our Choices for the Future

Today it seems strange that three hundred years ago there were hardly any democratic governments. Perhaps three hundred years from now it will seem just as strange that matters so profoundly affecting our lives as sexual violence, child sexual abuse, reproductive freedom, freedom from sexual harassment, and freedom of sexual choice were not always considered of political importance. But just as three hundred years ago there were attempts to suppress public debate about representative governments as alternatives to monarchies, there are people today who argue that intimate relations—particularly sexual relations—are not fit subjects for public discourse, much less political debate.

This kind of suppression is an effective way of obscuring the fact that we have choices in how we structure human relations. It is also an effective way of preventing collective action aimed at broadening our life choices—which is what modern politics have basically been about.

To illustrate, a central theme in Western history texts is the modern struggle for freedom to choose how and whether to worship, rather than being forced to worship in a particular way.[1] Another major theme is the struggle for freedom to choose a representative government, rather than being forced to live under hereditary or militarily imposed rule. Still another theme in modern Western history has been the struggle for freedom to choose one's means of livelihood, rather than being forced into that prescribed by one's caste, class, or gender.

So the struggle for sexual freedom of choice (rather than being coerced to have sex through fear, force, or lack of access to other means of economic support), the struggle for freedom to choose heterosexual or homosexual relations (rather than compulsory heterosexuality), and the struggle for reproductive freedom of choice (rather than being forced to reproduce or coercively prevented from reproducing) follow earlier precedents. They are actually only the latest chapter in the still-unfolding story of how during the last few centuries masses of people all over the world have joined together to challenge the power imbalances inherent in dominator systems.

Historically, all renegotiations to achieve a greater balance of power—be they by nobles, merchants, workers, colonized peoples, or members of minority races or religions—have only begun to be successful when they shifted from individual action to group action. In other words, issues that were once considered nonpolitical—and thus not to be included in public discourse or debate—have to become political (in the sense of being collectively discussed and negotiated) if successful power renegotiations are to take place.

So what is different in our time is not that some of our most controversial political issues are matters that were formerly considered outside the sphere of political or organized group action. What is different is that for the first time in recorded history, many of these issues revolve around people's intimate relations: the relations that most directly involve our bodies. And what this signals is a shift into a second, integrated stage in the modern movement toward a partnership society.

Until now, most of the organized political action to create a more equitable and truly free society has focused primarily on the top of the dominator pyramid: on the so-called public sphere in which relations have been primarily between men, since women and children were traditionally excluded from participation. And far too little attention has been given to changing the foundations on which this pyramid rests: the day-to-day relations involving women, men, and children in the so-called private sphere.

As we have seen, there were changes in these relations, as there had to be for any social progress to be made. But even though these changes were a major factor in both the modern revolution in consciousness and the sexual revolution, they did not go deep enough. Moreover, large segments of the population have remained relatively unaffected by them. Hence there has not evolved a solid foundation for an integrated partnership social and ideological structure—in sharp contrast to the still-powerful dominator infrastructure, which is all of one cloth, with authoritarian families and dominator-dominated sexual and gender relations, bolstered by authoritarian religious dogmas, providing a solid base for an integrated dominator system.

As a result, even where there have been partnership gains, these have been extremely vulnerable to co-option. For instance, even democratically elected governments are still largely controlled by powerful economic interests such as weapons and gun lobbies, which spread propaganda blaming governments for all social ills. Similarly, now under the mantle of sexual freedom and freedom of speech, propaganda for hate and violence against institutionally disempowered groups continues unabated. Not only that, but in places where dominator family relations and gender stereotypes have been most resistant to change, partnership gains have all too often been wiped out. Here, particularly during periods of severe economic stress, the movement toward partnership has been reversed by dominator regressions that, be it under fascism, communism, nationalism, capitalism, or most recently religionism, have brought a return to less equity, more violence, and a more firmly entrenched male-superior female-inferior in-group versus out-group species model.[2]

These are some reasons we today sometimes hear of the death of liberalism and other progressive ideologies.[3] It is certainly true that unless we succeed in building the foundations for a fundamentally transformed system, the contemporary partnership thrust will continue to be co-opted and reversed. But just as Mark Twain once termed a false notice of his death "highly exaggerated," these obituaries too are premature.

In fact, there are important signs that despite the dominator backlash, we stand at the threshold of a new stage in politics that takes the struggle for freedom from coercive controls to its most basic level: to the choices that most directly impact our bodies. It is still very much a politics in the making, only just beginning to come together in stops and starts. But it has as its aim nothing less than a fundamental reconceptualization of power in all spheres of life, from our individual families to the family of nations. And in this it holds the promise that we may one day avoid further dominator regressions—and in the process create social institutions that can support, rather than impede, the more satisfying and pleasurable intimate relations we humans so need and want.[4]

The Emerging Politics of Intimate Choice

The most publicized aspect of the new politics focusing on the right to freedom of choice in matters that directly impact our bodies is the contemporary struggle by women for reproductive freedom. But before we go on to this struggle and to other aspects of the new politics of intimate choice, I want to pause a moment to say that contrary to what we are sometimes told, technologies of family planning are not just a modern phenomenon.

Condoms and pessaries (precursors of the modern diaphragm) go back long before modern history.[5] A precursor to a technology we consider supermodern, the intrauterine device or IUD, already seems to have been used in ancient Egypt.[6] There are even indications that in rudimentary form family planning may go all the way back to the Paleolithic, to the prehistoric association of menstruation and the moon.

As Beth Ann Conklin writes, medical research indicates that in the absence of artificial lighting moonlight tends to synchronize women's reproductive cycles—with ovulation associated with the full moon and the onset of menstruation associated with the new moon.[7] So given the fact that becoming pregnant just before, just after, or during menstruation is highly unlikely, Conklin proposes that the careful attention our Paleolithic ancestors paid to the movements of the moon may be connected with women's attempts to prevent or promote conception by attuning their sexual activities to lunar rhythms—and that this may be part of the story behind the Venus of Laussel's notched crescent moon.[8]

A way of preventing conception that undoubtedly goes back to very ancient times is sex where the man does not ejaculate inside the vagina. Herbal birth control technologies (which are still found in a number of non-Western cultures) undoubtedly also go back to ancient times, although it is hard to know how effective they were. As I noted earlier, contraceptive and abortive herbs were apparently also still dispensed by the "witches" or Wiccan wise women who in Europe served as healers and midwives until they were forcibly replaced by Church-trained male physicians.[9]

So contraception and abortion are hardly new. What is new is the organized political struggle of women, and men, for reproductive freedom of choice. And this struggle is not unrelated to the contemporary struggle of women to reenter medicine and science—as well as to reclaim positions of religious, political, and economic policymaking. For it is in all these places that determinations are made as to whether or not contraceptive and abortive technologies will be developed and marketed, and under what circumstances and by whom they may be used.

As we have seen, the control of women's bodies by men (both as individuals and as makers of religious edicts and/or secular laws) is a mainstay of dominator ideology and society.[10] Reproductive freedom of choice threatens this control, which is why the struggle to obtain it is so fundamental for women. Moreover, as a World Health Organization report put it, "without fertility regulation women's rights are mere words," since "a woman who has no control over her fertility cannot complete her education, cannot maintain gainful employment . . . and has very few real choices open to her."[11]

But men's and children's life choices are also radically limited by the unavailability of family planning—as we tragically see in regions where birthrates, and with this poverty rates, are highest. In fact, unless family planning technologies are available, the very future of our species is endangered, as every day there is further evidence that present population growth rates are ecologically disastrous.

Moreover, as with other issues in today's new politics of intimate choice, something else is at stake here that assumes even greater importance at a time when scientists are developing technologies such as in vitro fertilization, artificial insemination, and even technologies that may in the very near future replace birth with laboratory-created life. This is whether people's most intimate life choices should be in the hands of a small group of men (be they scientists or heads of religious, economic, and government institutions), or whether people should be able to make their own choices in matters that directly affect the human body in its most personal and basic functions and activities.

This question of who should control a person's most intimate life choices also underlies another matter that has only become a major political issue in recent years: sexual harassment. Like man-made policies about contraception and abortion, sexual harassment has been a socially condoned expression of the notion that women's bodies should be under male control. Or to borrow a term coined by the social psychologist David Loye, sexual harassment expresses a cultural construction of sex in which women's bodies are a form of symbolic property: property that men have a right to by virtue of being male.[12]

In the work place, sexual harassment asserts this "right" in relation to the very women who, sometimes at the cost of enormous effort, stress, and pain, have begun to see their bodies as their own by finding a means of surviving other than complete dependency on marital or other sexual relations with men. So whether it succeeds or not, sexual harassment has been a way of taking that hard-won sense of independence away by again forcing women to view their bodies through the eyes of others rather than their own. On a very practical and immediate level, sexual harassment has also been a means of excluding women from the male-dominated higher-paying trades by creating a work environment that is hostile, even dangerous, to women. It has often served to block women's professional career advancement, as noncompliance with unwanted sexual advances has been used by men to deprive women of promotions, and has even led to women being fired. But most fundamentally, sexual harassment is an infringement of the right to freedom of choice. For it is designed to coerce women to make their bodies available to men with whom they would otherwise not choose to have sex.

In this sense, women's struggle against the assertion of male entitlement to their bodies is not so different from the struggle for freedom that led to the establishment of the United States of America by what were once British colonies. For ultimately involved in both cases is not only the right to be seen by oneself and others as belonging to oneself rather than someone else, but the right to self-determination.

This same basic issue of self-determination also underlies the contemporary political battle over lesbian and gay rights. As with the right to freedom from sexual harassment, just a generation ago the idea of the right of heterosexual or homosexual freedom of choice as a political issue would have seemed beyond the pale. Yet just as the Clarence Thomas–Anita Hill hearings led to an unprecedented number of American women running for national, state, and local office in 1992, during the 1992 presidential campaign, gay men and lesbians came out of the political closet, forming fund-raising networks for sympathetic candidates.[13]

Again, just as with freedom of reproductive choice and freedom from sexual harassment, the struggle over freedom to choose homosexuality rather than, or in addition to, heterosexuality goes far deeper than at first meets the eye. For it too threatens the very foundations of a society in which men are supposed to control women and a small elite of men are supposed to control the mass of women and men.

To begin with, homophobia—the fear, hate, and all too often persecution of gay men and lesbians—is basically about the preservation of dominator masculine and feminine stereotypes and relations. The ridicule of "sissy" or "effeminate" gay men is still one more way of maintaining the tough, unempathic "macho" stereotype of masculinity appropriate for a dominator society. Not only that, but for an adult man to relate to another man by taking the stereotypically feminine role of wife or mistress challenges the whole notion that the only natural role for a man is to be the dominant party in intimate relations.[14]

Although in different ways, lesbian relations also threaten the traditional construction of gender roles. They offer women an alternative to the so-called traditional family: the male-dominated, procreation-oriented family that is the cornerstone of dominator society. Moreover, because they promote bonding between women, they can lead to what many lesbian groups in fact are today engaged in—social and political action for fundamental structural and ideological change.[15]

But homophobia is also inherent in dominator societies in still another way. It stems from the in-group versus out-group thinking characteristic of these societies, a kind of thinking that automatically equates difference with inferiority or superiority. So the persecution of gay men and lesbians has also served the same scapegoating function as sexism, racism, and anti-Semitism, of deflecting repressed fear and pain against disempowered out-groups.

Today in the United States the most rabid denunciations of homosexuality come from the rightist-fundamentalist alliance. Here we sometimes even find preachers quoting biblical passages prescribing death as the punishment for such "abominations." And tragically, as with other incitements of hate against socially disempowered groups, such pronouncements are not without effect—as shown by recent press reports of a young man who was beaten to death by a shipmate (while others just looked on) simply because he openly declared he was gay.

What can happen when this hate is incorporated in government policies has also recently been shown by press reports that the government of Iran "celebrated the new year" with the public beheading of three homosexual men and the even more prolonged and excruciatingly painful stoning to death of two women accused of being lesbians—executions which often last many hours, since according to Iranian law they have to be with stones "small enough so they don't kill the victim instantly."[16] Ironically, as the columnist Jack Anderson writes, this was the government headed by Hashemi Rafsanjani, whom "both George Bush and Ronald Reagan have called 'moderate.'"[17] But again, I want to emphasize that what we are here dealing with is not a matter of conventional political labels such as radical, moderate, or conservative, much less Republican or Democrat.

What we are here dealing with are fundamental issues of human rights. Even more specifically, what we are dealing with—as with the increasingly violent resistance to women's reproductive freedom—is one of the most entrenched, and basic, aspects of dominator politics: the view that one individual or group can legitimately coerce another individual or group through institutionally condoned threats or acts of violence.

The Old Politics of Violence

I have over the past several decades written and lectured extensively about human rights. I started in 1969, with a Friend of the Court brief to the Supreme Court of the United States urging it to interpret the Fourteenth Amendment to the U.S. Constitution so that women are included under the definition of persons in its equal protection clause.[18] Most recently, through a series of articles written from 1987 to 1993, I have proposed that governments and international organizations such as Amnesty International change their definition of human rights. My proposal is for what to my knowledge is the first truly integrated approach to human rights, one that no longer splits off the rights of the majority from human rights as merely "women's rights" and "children's rights" and recognizes that coercive violence is no less political in the place where we first learn about human relations—our homes.[19]

But it was only in the last year of writing this book that I began to probe the connection between this new integrated approach to human rights and issues relating directly to the human body. I asked myself what would happen if such issues became part of the discourse on constitutional law and human rights. An immediate answer was that protections regarding matters that directly affect the human body—such as protection from child beating, child sexual abuse, rape, compulsory childbearing, and other infringements of the basic human right of bodily integrity—would not only be constitutionally protected, but considered central to human rights theory. I also realized that if constitutional and human rights theory had been framed in a partnership rather than dominator context, these protections would have been there from the start. Because it is precisely the lack of bodily self-determination—be it for men as conscripted soldiers or for women as conscripted mothers—that is basic to dominator rather than partnership societies.

Even beyond this, I have come to see that constitutional and human rights theories need to be expanded to include in their conceptual frameworks the most basic of human rights: the right to live free of the fear of violence. Because as long as violence is not only accepted as appropriate but actually institutionalized—be it through warfare in international relations or wife and child beating in intimate relations—there is no realistic way we can build a society where the capacity to inflict pain on others is not the basis for power.

This is not to say that all violence would come under the purview of this right. For example, defensive violence or the violence of yanking a child back from running into traffic would not. But it would apply to the violence that is institutionalized to maintain rankings of domination.

As we have seen, in dominator societies this violence starts very early, with the confluence of caring and coercive touch in a child rearing where obedience to authority is a condition for parental love. It continues through the erotization of domination and violence that is characteristic of the social construction of sexuality in such societies. And until modern times in the West, and in many places still today, it has also been through the use of violence that despotic rulers have maintained control over their "subjects."

In the West, this control was often ritually dramatized—as it still is in some places today—through public exhibitions of the most brutal infliction of pain, not only to dissidents but to members of socially disempowered groups, like the women labeled witches publicly executed less than three hundred years ago in both Europe and some American colonies. These public exhibitions of the power to inflict pain served a number of social functions. They were warnings to those who might want to question the status quo. They taught people how powerless and vulnerable they were, as well as signaling who (like the "witches") could be scapegoated with impunity. And they served to desensitize people to suffering, and to even view it as entertainment, thus deadening empathy.

After the eighteenth-century Enlightenment, such public exhibitions of brutality gradually stopped in the West, at the same time that more democratic families along with more democratic governments began to emerge. Nonetheless, as part of the continuing struggle between partnership resurgence and dominator resistance, there continued to be violent backlashes in both the private and public spheres—for example, the rise in violence against women in the wake of both nineteenth- and twentieth-century feminism [20] and various other forms of scapegoating, from the neo-Nazi "skinhead" terrorism we see in parts of the West to the religious, tribal, and ethnic massacres we find in other regions of the world. And although in the West efforts to again institute public displays of brutality (for example, the bill introduced in the California legislature in 1994 that would have instituted public whippings for spray painting graffiti on walls and cars) have not been successful, a new way of achieving the same ends through modern technology continues unabated: the almost constant display on television and other mass media of the power to inflict pain on the body.

This electronic display of violence is certainly a vast improvement over the real-life executions through public drawings and quarterings, crucifixions, and other barbarities commonplace in the West in earlier times. Still, the amount of brutality dispensed to us through both television news and "entertainment" on our home screens is staggering. As David Barry writes, it is estimated that in the United States "the average child is likely to have watched 8,000 screen murders and more than 100,000 acts of violence by the end of elementary school"—a figure that will again double by the end of his or her teen years.[21] This is despite the fact that contrary to what we are sometimes told, violent programs do not get the highest ratings—in other words, that they are not, as their broad-casters claim, merely "what people want."[22]

Understandably, given the high U.S. crime rates (and particularly the increase in random violence among the young during the last genera-tion), most public discourse about this barrage of violence in the media is still focused on whether it leads to violent crimes by presenting violence as a way of dealing with life's conflicts, problems, and frustrations that is not only common, but exciting. There certainly is no lack of studies con-firming that the exponential rise in American violence during the decades after television was first introduced is not just coincidental. For example, the University of Washington epidemiologist Dr. Brandon Centerwall's ground-breaking studies of epidemics of violence show that in both the United States and Canada violent crimes increased almost 100 percent within a generation after television was introduced. By contrast, during some of those same years in South Africa violent crime rates actually dropped—only to also more than double after the introduction of televi-sion in 1975.[23] There are also hundreds of studies confirming the obvious: that television programming affects not just buying behaviors (the ex-plicit goal of the advertisers who fund it) but all kinds of behaviors, in-cluding children's level of aggression (which not surprisingly increases when children, particularly boys, since most violence modeled on televi-sion is by males, watch TV)[24] and even whether adults behave in hurtful or helpful ways (as shown by a research project directed by David Loye during the 1970s at the UCLA School of Medicine).[25]

So the growing public perception that television teaches children (and adults) not only violence but insensitivity as a way of life is extremely im-portant. But as George Gerbner (the former dean of the Annenberg School for Communication at the University of Pennsylvania and founder of the Cultural Environment Movement) notes, what is as yet not generally dis-cussed—and urgently needs to be—is how the way our world is por-trayed on television serves to maintain entrenched power imbalances.[26]

As Gerbner and others point out, there is in television "an overall pat-tern of programming to which total communities are regularly exposed over long periods of time" in which repetitive themes that cut across all kinds of programming are "inescapable for the regular (and especially heavy) viewers."[27] For example, the disproportionate ratio of male to fe-male characters on television (with two-thirds male and only one-third fe-male) all too graphically, though subliminally, communicates the message that men are more important than women. Similarly, the fact that the vic-tims of television violence are disproportionately women, minorities, and other socially disempowered groups communicates to the viewer who is, and is not, fair game for victimization. That members of such groups are generally restricted to a stereotypical range of roles and activities where they have, again in Gerbner's words, "less than their share of success and power" further helps to mold people's perceptions and expectations.[28]

Perhaps most important, as Gerbner, Gross, Morgan, and Signorielli write, is that in this symbolic world into which children are born, which they begin viewing before they can read or even talk, our world is presented as a "mean place"—one that requires "good violence" to combat the "bad violence" that would otherwise destroy us all. This, as Gerbner points out, inculcates in people a sense that "law and order" can only be maintained through brutal means. Not only that, it inculcates in people a simplistic in-group versus out-group mentality, which, as he also notes, serves to even further promote conservative values and gender stereotypes.[29] And of course, just as violent pornography desensitizes men to the real pain of rape victims, all our media violence (like the ritualized public executions of old) conditions people to be spectators to other people's pain without empathizing with them, much less taking action to stop it—and even (as in children's cartoons, where there are on the average no less than twenty-five violent incidents per hour)[30] to view the causing of pain to others as funny.

Yet despite all this pressure to deaden our human capacity for empathy—which is obviously successful with some—as part of the ongoing revolution in consciousness, the challenge to violence as a normal and legitimate means of attaining and maintaining power (be it in intimate or international relations) continues to mount. Indeed, although this too is still rarely noted in most contemporary political analyses, one of the most important developments in modern politics has been the unprecedented phenomenon of masses of people organizing, not just against those who violently oppress them, but against the oppression of others—and even against the use of violence itself.

The New Politics Against Violence

The condemnation of violence is age-old, as is nonviolent resistance to violence, as exemplified by the teaching of Jesus that we turn the other cheek. But collective political action to challenge the institutionalization of violence is a relatively recent phenomenon.

Although the Quakers (or Friends, as they prefer to be called) were already pacifists back in the seventeenth century, it was not until the nineteenth century that pacifism began to emerge as a social movement in the West. And not until the twentieth century—as exemplified by the numerous anti–Vietnam War protests—did rallies of many thousands of people protesting against the use of violence as a means of resolving international conflict become commonplace.

Similarly, while there have always been people who have condemned violence against religious, racial, and ethnic minorities, it was not until the twentieth century—as exemplified by the Nuremberg war crime trials of Nazis for genocide, the U.S. civil rights movement to stop racial violence, and the huge demonstrations in Germany during the 1990s against violence to foreigners—that large masses of people began organizing against the violence of ethnic, racial, and religious scapegoating. And even though many world governments continue to use force to maintain their power, increasingly—as evidenced by the United Nations' condemnation of the Chinese government's brutal suppression of nonviolent student protests in Tiananmen Square—we also see the rejection by people all over the world of this once generally accepted political violence as legitimate.

Not only that, but for the first time, violence in intimate relations is today becoming a major political issue. Again, there have always been people who opposed violence against children and women. But until recent times this violence has generally been considered a private or family matter that should not brook outside interference. And it has not, until now, been the focus of collective political action by large organized groups of people dedicated to exposing and ending what is sometimes accurately called terror in the home.

For instance, it is only because of this organized political action that today in the United States the reporting by physicians of child abuse is strongly supported by both privately and governmentally funded education programs. It is only because of the continuing efforts of many women's organizations that laws against assault and battery are at least in some places being applied to what was traditionally dismissed as mere "domestic violence." Similarly, it is only due to organized pressure that rape is today more frequently prosecuted—even though judges and juries still often expect rape victims to "fight back," something not expected of anybody else threatened by a knife, a gun, or just a large attacker.

Due to such organized efforts, shelters for battered women have also begun to be funded by both private and government agencies, particularly in North America and Europe. Again, at this writing there are still far too few such shelters—as evidenced by studies indicating that a large proportion of homeless women on our streets are fleeing violent homes.[31] And again, there is even here strong political opposition. One of the most jarring examples was the so-called Family Protection Act introduced by

Senator Paul Laxalt, which—highlighting what kind of family the senator was trying to protect—would have drastically cut funding for shelters for battered women.

Nonetheless, the organized political action to end the worldwide violence against women is having important results. For example, the World Health Organization, which a few decades ago still ignored the enormous health costs to women from the violence of genital mutilation, in 1992 announced that it would call for "tougher action" against what it once ignored as merely a "traditional practice." In India, laws against the traditional practice of bride burning are also beginning to be more frequently invoked, thanks to pressure from women's organizations. And because male violence against women is now beginning to be perceived as a social, rather than purely personal, problem, attention is also gradually being given to its astronomic economic costs—which in the United States alone are estimated at more than three billion dollars per year.[32] As a result, once again against strong resistance,[33] in 1994 the U.S. Congress as part of a larger crime bill adopted a milestone piece of legislation: the Violence Against Women Act.[34]

In addition to family violence against women and children, family violence against the elderly and disabled is also beginning to be systematically addressed, thanks in large part to the organized efforts of groups such as the Older Women's League. For example, in 1984 California began requiring agencies such as departments of social services and legal services to report incidents of elder abuse. The abuse of domestic workers by their employers is also increasingly addressed by national and international organizations. For instance, after the Gulf War, reports of abuse (including rape) of women imported to work in Kuwaiti households (long reported in the feminist press) began to attract international media attention. As already noted, violence against women and children in the international sex trade is also beginning to get more media coverage. In fact, what is beginning to come together in bits and pieces is something I and others have for many years called for: an international campaign against all forms of intimate violence through organized and coordinated education and political action.[35]

This campaign still needs far more political, moral, and financial support, particularly from the heads of the world's governments, religions, and international bodies such as the United Nations. But that all these hitherto ignored forms of intimate violence are today beginning to be challenged through organized political action is of pivotal, often life-and-death, importance for millions of children, women, and men worldwide. And it is also of critical importance in what it tells us about the emergence of a new kind of politics: a politics of empathy, based not on the in-group versus out-group thinking characteristic of a dominator worldview, but on the capacity to feel at one with others, particularly with members of traditionally disempowered groups.

Empathy, Gender, and the "Feminization" of Politics

Since empathy is one of our most important human attributes, there were undoubtedly even in the most rigid dominator societies people sensitive to the pain of others, as well as to the social injustices that make it possible for some people to cause other people so much pain. But the translation of this sensitivity into political action guided by the vision of a better society, as distinguished from individual rebellions and numerous earlier slave and peasant revolts, is relatively recent. And it too has gone through a number of stages.

In its first stage, the empathy animating progressive social movements was (except in the case of feminism) primarily by men for other men. This is not to say that there was no empathy for the suffering of women and children. But it was largely focused on their suffering due to class-based and race-based inequities.[36] For example, during the nineteenth century men of the more privileged classes (such as the socialist philosophers Karl Marx and Friedrich Engels) wrote with great feeling about the plight of the poor or "working-class man." Similarly, members of the primarily white and male "intelligentsia" wrote with great feeling about the suffering of men of the oppressed races, as exemplified by books such as Gunnar Myrdal's *An American Dilemma* and David Loye's *The Healing of a Nation*.[37]

But what distinguishes this second stage in the emergence of an organized politics of empathy is that it increasingly focuses on hitherto invisible groups such as children and women. This is a fundamental breakthrough. Indeed, in its focus on the prototypical out-group—women—it signals the gradual abandonment of the male-superior female-inferior, in-group versus out-group model of our species that is the basic model for racism, anti-Semitism, and all the other ways people unconsciously learn to think of "inferior" out-groups as not fully human. And it also takes the contemporary revolution in consciousness to a new level: one where the hidden subtext of gender we have been examining comes into plain sight.

As we have seen, the power through greater strength or force to dominate or control others, thereby restricting their life choices, has stereotypically been associated with masculinity. And the power to care for others, to nurture them through caring touch, thereby empowering them to develop and effectively broaden their life choices, has stereotypically been associated with femininity. Again, this does not mean that these gender differences are natural. Women can be very disempowering to others, and seemingly enjoy it. And men can derive great pleasure from nurturing and empowering behaviors—for example, the many men who are today caring for children.

But while men have traditionally been socialized to derive pleasure from power over others (as in Henry Kissinger's famous statement that power is the greatest aphrodisiac), women have generally been socialized to derive pleasure from a very different kind of power: the power to enable others, particularly their children and husbands, to actualize their potentials. In other words, the power stereotypically associated with femininity has been the power to care for others, while the power stereotypically associated with masculinity has been the power to control others. And even though all women and all men have by no means conformed to this socialization, these differences in gender socialization have for most of recorded or dominator history been reinforced by a social organization in which men have received rewards and encouragement when they equate power with control (the traditional definition of a leader being a man who has the power to give orders that will be obeyed) and women have been generally discouraged, and even punished, for trying to exercise this kind of power.

So a politics of empathy, or sensitivity to others, is basically a more stereotypically feminine politics—which helps explain why, in a world that still tends to devalue anything stereotypically associated with women, its emergence is still largely unremarked in mainstream progressive political discourse. Yet, ironically, it has begun to be discussed in precisely these terms by rightist-fundamentalist theorists who accurately perceive it as a threat to a system based on ranking rather than linking.

Thus, in an article called "The Ideology of Sensitivity" he wrote for the rightist-fundamentalist publication *Imprimis,* Charles Sykes ridicules the "absurdity" of feelings figuring in politics.[38] But actually, as his title highlights, what outrages him is the idea that "soft" or stereotypically feminine feelings such as sensitivity should figure in politics. For it is very clear from his article that Sykes has no trouble with stereotypically masculine feelings such as contempt and anger being part of politics. Quite the contrary, his prose drips with contempt as he excoriates those who assert that unequal opportunities rather than unequal capabilities account for discrimination. He is angrily disdainful of what he calls the "whining" of African Americans, other minorities, and women, all of whom he dismisses as "fabricating" victimization. He even more snidely dismisses the idea that hurtful and insensitive patterns of behavior that rob people of a sense of self-worth are effective means of denying out-groups equal opportunities.[39] And, along with his denial of the pain of others, so characteristic of those who believe it their God-given right to be superior, he scornfully denies that there is any connection between what he calls "private and public acts." But his angriest rhetoric is reserved for the idea that nurturance should have any place in politics through what he derisively calls a politics of sensitivity—lest, as he sarcastically puts it, "Big Nanny" replace "Big Brother."[40]

Sykes's view that sensitivity must at all costs be kept out of politics undoubtedly stems from his socialization for a masculinity that, as we have seen, requires the suppression in men of stereotypically feminine feelings such as empathy. And, albeit probably more on the unconscious than conscious level, it also stems from his unquestioning acceptance of the dominator dictum that women—and with this, anything associated with the feminine—have no place in politics. So it is not surprising that he is horrified that politics be contaminated by anything so "unmanly" as a more stereotypically feminine sensitive and empathic ethos.

Nonetheless—and once again, on a scale much larger than ever before—such a political ethos *is* beginning to gain momentum worldwide. Much of it is still rhetoric—as in former President George Bush's slogan of a "kinder and gentler" nation, which so sharply contrasted with his "hard," stereotypically masculine emphasis on weaponry and his continuation of the Reagan policies of slashing funds for health, education, and welfare. But some of it is beginning to affect both the substance and the style of political leadership in many world regions.

Certainly President Clinton's political style emphasizing health, education, and welfare as well as nonviolent conflict resolution, is far more stereotypically feminine than that of his predecessors—which undoubtedly accounts for some of the virulence of the attacks against him.[41] As Steven Stark writes in his analysis of political styles from a gendered perspective: "If other presidents tend to speak by lecturing us ('we have nothing to fear but fear itself' or 'ask not what your country can do for you'), Clinton often communicates by listening ('I feel your pain'). Whereas other presidents tended to address the country most effectively from above at a rostrum . . . the maternal hug and the 'all ears' attentive body language are the characteristics of this President."[42]

As Stark also notes, Clinton is not alone in this new style of leadership—or in his discomfort with military aggression and his relative ease with strong women such as his own partner, Hillary Rodham Clinton. Stark writes how "many baby boomers exhibit a more feminine style of leadership and rhetoric than previous generations." And of course, a key part of the movement toward a more stereotypically feminine or empathic political style is the ascendancy of women to high political office.

Not that all women who enter politics bring with them this new leadership style. Some, such as Margaret Thatcher, Indira Ghandi, and Benazir Bhutto, have tried to prove that they are not too "soft" or feminine through stereotypically masculine or "hard" leadership styles. However, as the sociologist Jessie Bernard, the psychologist Carol Gilligan, and the psychiatrist Jean Baker Miller note, because women are socialized to make relationships their primary priority, and because they are expected to internalize what Bernard calls a "female ethos of love/duty," they tend to be more sensitive to human needs.[43] Or as the president of the German Bundestag (Parliament), Professor Rita Süssmuth, said in a recent interview with a German newspaper, "we can expect from women different approaches and solutions to a number of problems connected with people living together" because "women tend to approach problems in a more pragmatic and action-oriented way which is more closely related to real life."[44]

Moreover, it is only as women rise in status that men can more comfortably themselves exhibit stereotypically feminine styles of behavior without feeling a loss in their own status. Thus, a number of well-known leaders who have strong women as partners in their personal lives, such as the Costa Rican ex-president Oscar Arias (winner of the Nobel Peace Prize) and the former Soviet president Mikhail Gorbachev, also have exhibited more empathic leadership styles. Not only that, men and women all over the world are increasingly recognizing, as Süssmuth succinctly put it, that what is needed is not to push "Mütterlichkeit" (a mothering, nurturing ethos) back into the confines of the household, but rather to fully incorporate it into politics, and thus social policy.

The Groundswell for Transformation

If we look only at what is conventionally considered political—governments and political parties, terrorism and armed revolutions, international agencies like the United Nations—the prospects for what Süssmuth proposes seem slim. Indeed, there are today signs of massive dominator systems' resistance and regression, be it the election of rightists and even fascists in the West, the mounting fundamentalist terrorism, the "ethnic cleansings" of Rwanda and the former Yugoslavia, the huge concentration of economic power in transnational corporate giants, or the loss of women's right to reproductive freedom in some of the former Eastern bloc nations. But if we also look at what is happening on the grass-roots level, despite press reports of growing alienation and apathy, we find that there are worldwide more people today involved in groups and organizations to create a more just and equitable society than ever before in recorded history.

In countries where there are electoral processes, these groups and organizations are essential to revitalize democracy, to support progressive political candidates, and to educate people to be politically active rather than to abandon politics to highly organized regressive interests—as happened in the 1994 U.S. elections when only one third of those eligible to do so voted.[45] But as essential as this is, when viewed from the perspective of *cultural transformation theory*, these grass-roots organizations— and their global networking through conferences on everything from the environment, economic justice, and peace to the empowerment of indigenous peoples, colonized peoples, women, and children, as well as through newsletters and/or electronic networks such as PEACE NET and ECONET—are also crucial for the foundational change we are here exploring. For increasingly their focus is not on just reforming existing social and cultural patterns, but rather on fundamental personal and social transformation.

To begin with, many of these groups are either explicitly or implicitly beginning to recognize the interconnection between the so-called private and public spheres. Hence many are beginning to integrate women's and children's rights, as well as sexual and spiritual issues, into their activities. Not only that, many are taking a much more holistic approach to politics, integrating activities to promote greater social justice, economic equity, and environmental consciousness with activities designed to empower people to right power imbalances in their day-to-day lives. And by so doing, they are beginning to provide the much needed nuclei for an emerging international partnership movement based on a new integrated politics of partnership: a politics aimed at nothing less than transforming our familial and sexual relations, our economic and work relations, our intranational and international relations, our relations with nature, and even our relations with our own bodies.

For example, the women in the Green Belt movement in Kenya and the Chipko movement in India have successfully organized nonviolent environmental actions, such as large groups of women hugging trees to save forests from being cut down.[46] But at the same time that these kinds of organized grass-roots actions are bringing many Kenyan and Indian women into environmental politics, they are also empowering these women to work toward bettering the lives of all Kenyan and Indian women. Another organization that combines an environmental focus with basic human concerns is the Ladakh Ecological Development Group, one of the most influential nongovernmental organizations in this remote Himalayan region. Its main focus is on protecting the people's indigenous lifestyle from both colonial exploitation and environmental degradation. But in the words of its founder Helena Norberg-Hodge, one of its aims is also that "equal voice should be given to female perspectives and values."[47]

Other grass-roots organizations focus primarily on the economic and social conditions that underlie wars and other forms of institutionalized violence. For instance, the Hawaii-based Center for Global Nonviolence, the Danish-based Center for Conflict Resolution, and the International Quaker American Friends Service Committee all address the economic injustices that have often led to the deflection of people's misery and frustration into civil and other wars. But they are also beginning to recognize that effectively dealing with poverty requires that stereotypically feminine activities such as feeding and caring for children receive adequate government support and, even beyond this, that if there is to be less violence both women and men need to learn nonviolent, rather than violent, conflict resolution.

Also helping to raise world consciousness about the human costs of a male socialization for violence—and particularly about how military training serves to brutalize men—are grass-roots groups such as the Mothers of the Plaza de Mayo in Argentina and Mothers of El Salvador, both composed of women who organized to protest against terrorist regimes that have "disappeared" their children. This too is an important focus of grass-roots men's groups such as the Oakland Men's Project, an organization that, as Paul Kivel (one of its founders) writes in *Men's Work,* was specifically formed to help men learn to leave behind patterns of thinking and behaving that lead not only to wife battering but to the acceptance of violent behaviors as legitimate in all kinds of relations.[48] Similarly, women's antinuclear groups such as those at Greenham Common in England, Comiso in Italy, and Pine Gap in Australia, Women for Meaningful Summits in the United States, and the Shibo Kusa women of Mount Fuji in Japan focus not only on international peace treaties and other traditional approaches but also on raising consciousness about what both women and men are taught about masculinity and femininity.[49]

Then there are organizations whose primary focus is on the shift from a dominator to a partnership sexuality. They too recognize that this will require fundamental changes in both women's and men's attitudes and national and international policies. For example, the *Coalition Against Trafficking in Women* headquartered at Pennsylvania State University works with women's organizations all over the world to raise public consciousness about the values and institutions that lie behind the sexual trade in women, and to lobby the United Nations and other international agencies to pressure governments to more vigorously enforce laws against it. Organizations of survivors of incest and other forms of childhood sexual abuse, as well as rape survivors, are also beginning to form worldwide, as are groups working against genital mutilation, child marriage, and other traditional customs in which sex is molded to fit the requirements of a dominator form of social organization. To give just one example, in Tanzania the Institute for Development and Training in 1993 introduced initiatives for the prevention of the genital and sexual mutilation of females.[50] Other organizations are working for government policies that promote rather than prevent reproductive freedom of choice, again not only in the United States but all over the world. And many organizations are working against the media erotization of violence, as well as the portrayal of women in degrading and dehumanizing ways; for example the California-based Media Watch founded by Ann Simonton (a former Miss California) for these ends.

A myriad of organizations focusing on the rights of children are also working to change both attitudes and government policies. Examples in the United States are the National Center for Children in Poverty at the Columbia University School of Public Health, which has focused both public and official attention on the shocking fact that during the last twenty years in the United States poverty rates have increased so steeply for children that by 1991 nearly one out of every four children under six lived in poverty, [51] and the Children's Defense Fund in Washington, DC, which works assiduously to bring the need for family policies that truly value children to public consciousness. Similarly, the Inter-American Children's Institute in Montevideo, Uruguay, and Defense for Children International are working to change both political and economic policies to improve the condition of children (and with this, society) worldwide. And some of these organizations specifically address issues of violence and abuse against children. For example, Healthy Families America, which is now operating out of more than fifty sites in sixteen states, provides help to overburdened young mothers and/or helps mothers who were themselves abused so they will not repeat this pattern with their own children.[52]

These kinds of organized efforts are of foundational importance to the emergence of an integrated partnership movement, since as we have seen, it is in our family relations that we first learn to respect human rights or to accept human rights violations as only natural and right. So also is the fact that in the wake of the first United Nations Decade for

Women (1975–1985), there are today thousands of groups worldwide specifically dedicated to the empowerment of women.

These groups are in many ways in the forefront of the much-needed integrated politics of partnership that no longer splits off issues of sex and gender from politics and economics. For instance, a whole host of women's organizations—from the Indian Self-Employed Women's Association (SEWA) and the Honduran Federation of Peasant Women to the Women and Development Unit (WAND) in the Caribbean and the African Association of Women for Research and Development (AAWORD) in West Africa—focus on the fact that worldwide poverty is to a disproportionate extent a "women's issue."[53] The Women's Rights Committee of the European Parliament recently called for studies to assess the economic and social value of women's unpaid work, particularly in respect to pensions.[54] In Hong Kong, five women's groups started a women's voter education program and are working on a women's platform.[55] From Prague, Czechoslovakia, comes an announcement of an ambitious new East-West Gender Studies Center.[56] The Maryam Babangida National Center for Women's Development is a self-sustaining and income-generating resource center for research, training, and mobilizing women toward self-emancipation. Women Living Under Muslim Laws (based in France), as well as the U.S.-based Sisterhood Is Global, the Center for Global Issues and Women's Leadership, Women's International Network (WIN) News, and the International Women's Rights Action Watch gather and publicize information about the human rights (and violations of these rights) of women worldwide.[57]

These and many other organizations worldwide have as their goal the implementation of the three interconnected goals of the first United Nations Decade for Women: equality, development, and peace.[58] And often these groups, particularly in the South, are supported by foundations from the North, including foundations specifically dedicated to funding women's groups, such as the Ms. Foundation, the Shaler-Adams Foundation, and the Global Fund for Women (which gives approximately two hundred grants per year to organizations dedicated to the empowerment of women worldwide).

There are also many organizations worldwide working to protect the rights of indigenous peoples, such as the International Indian Tribal Council and Women of All Red Nations (WARN). And there are thousands of organizations worldwide developing new approaches to economic development in which human development—and particularly the long-ignored needs, problems, and aspirations of women—is central. These range from more conventional politically oriented think tanks like the Washington DC–based Center for Policy Alternatives to alternative economics networks like the Other Economic Summit (TOES), and Development Alternatives With Women for a New Era (DAWN).[59] Along similar lines, and again integrating both the so-called private and public spheres in their activities, are groups like GOLUBKA and the Ecopolis Culture and Health Center in Moscow, dedicated to bringing into former Soviet-bloc countries an economic and social vision that goes beyond both communism and capitalism—one that includes equitable and fulfilling family and other personal relations.

A new economic and social vision guided by more stereotypically feminine values is also starting to infiltrate the world of business and finance. Organizations such as the World Business Academy, the Social Ventures Network, Business for Social Responsibility, and Students for Responsible Business are being formed to fundamentally transform the way business is done—in the words of the purpose statement of Students for Responsible Business, to foster a new generation of business leaders who "will achieve financial success while contributing to the creation of a more humane, just, and sustainable world."[60] There are also a growing number of foundations funded by these kinds of business leaders dedicated to empowering people on the grass-roots level—for example, the Katalysis and Earth Trust foundations' North/South Development Partnerships, which make village loans in Central America, particularly to entrepreneurial women.

Not only that, but in the last decade investment funds have appeared on the world stock markets, such as the Calvert Social Investment Fund, the Parnassus Fund, and the Women's Equity Mutual Fund, which include in their criteria for their investment portfolios the social and environmental impact of how business is conducted as well as how companies treat their employees, including their inclusiveness of women and minorities.[61] Moreover, these funds typically do not invest in companies that either make or sell weaponry, in other words, companies that—as is so dramatically reflected by the epidemic of violence in the United States associated with the proliferation of handgun and other weapons sales—do not make or sell products that have as their aim the causing of pain to others.

There is even an International Partnership Network now being organized, with a Partnership Research Group at the Chinese Academy of Social Sciences in Beijing exploring partnership roots in Asia and Centers for Partnership Education being formed in Germany in addition to those in the United States. And for these groups, catalyzed by the integrated partnership vision introduced in *The Chalice and the Blade* and *The Partnership Way*, as for a growing number of other empowerment-oriented organizations, the way relations between the female and male halves of humanity are structured in both the private and public spheres is central to any fundamental social and ideological transformation.

Spirituality, Justice, and the Body Politic

Another interesting feature of many of the organizations today springing up as potential nucleations for an international partnership movement—including even some of the new business organizations I mentioned earlier—is that they have a strong spiritual component. But it is not the old-style spirituality of either detachment from all that is of this world or of charitable endeavors that, while important, focus only on ameliorating the pain of poverty and illness. It is rather a spirituality that recognizes the responsibility of every one of us to do what we can to eradicate what the Norwegian sociologist Johan Galtung has called structural violence: not only the institutionalized use of physical violence, but also oppressive, exploitive, and discriminatory structures that deny people the food, shelter, health care, and education they need to maintain their bodies and develop their minds, or threaten to do so if they organize to change existing values and institutions.[62]

In short, it is a spirituality that puts into actual practice the partnership teachings that lie at the core of most world religions: the teachings of compassion, nonviolence, and caring. Even beyond this, it is a spirituality dedicated to empowering people so they can take action against oppression, exploitation, and discrimination, rather than passively accepting injustice in the hope of a better hereafter in which those who are unjust will be punished and those who patiently accept injustice will be rewarded.

Because it is a spirituality that does not consider what is of this world secondary, this new spirituality of empowerment also recognizes that politics can no longer ignore matters that directly impact the human body—that, as Michael Rossman writes, "the repression of bodily energies is a key element in the functioning of authoritarian social systems, and the freeing and rebalancing of our bodily vitality is essential to the struggle against them, as well as for the recreation of a freer order."[63] This also is the guiding philosophy of Capacitar, an organization whose name in Spanish means "to enable, encourage, or bring forth." Capacitar operates on many levels. For example, it collects funds and materials for groups of Latin American women and offers workshops on parenting, health care, and other skills that will enable them to make changes in their own lives and to work together for social change. But one of the main ways Capacitar helps women organize and form mutual support and social action networks is through spiritually oriented bodywork, including massage, guided imagery, and Tai Chi—methods involving direct, caring, pleasurable touch of the body.

Obviously this approach does not fit into the conventional model of activism as organizing for political confrontations, even though part of what Capacitar does is to empower people to stand up against injustice. But it fits well into a new partnership model of political organizing that recognizes the connection between politics and the body, as well as, to again borrow Rossman's words, the need to stop "making arbitrary boundaries between the practices of social therapy, personal psychological therapy, and bodily therapy."[64]

As Hillary Bendon writes in "Partnership: An Alternative to the Classic Bureaucratic Management Model," what Capacitar offers are "alternatives to suffering."[65] This phrase "alternatives to suffering" sums up an essential element of the new politics of partnership. For it takes the definition of political rights to its most basic level: to the right to be free from pain inflicted by the domination of others. And it also takes us back to *cultural transformation theory* and to what I have called the pain to pleasure shift—and to how this is integral to the shift from a dominator to a partnership social organization.[66]

Because what basically distinguishes the politics of domination and partnership are two very different ways of conceptualizing power: one that requires the institutionalization of pain and one that does not.[67] Of course, this does not mean that if the new grass-roots politics of empowerment ultimately attains its goal of social, economic, and cultural transformation there will no longer be any pain. But ultimately our choices for the future *are* between a social system that requires pain for its maintenance and one that does not.

These choices are today reflected in two very different kinds of politics that transcend the conventional differences between left and right, liberal and conservative, capitalist and communist, and even religious and secular. One, following the old rule through terror or alternately the terrorist–armed revolution pattern, is still the old politics of violence. The other is a new politics of transformation, not from the top down but from the ground up, through nonviolent and empathic means that can provide real alternatives to suffering.

But despite the fact that this new politics of partnership is today gathering momentum in all parts of our globe, it still does not get the attention of front-page headlines and lead stories on television that the old-style politics based on the power to inflict pain gets. Indeed, most of what is still reported as news in the world media is about suffering—be it the pain people suffer during natural disasters or the pain inflicted on them by other humans.

Accordingly, most of the leaders we still read about in our papers or see on television are the old-style "strong-man" types. Even the leaders of movements for social justice or political liberation that get mainstream media attention are generally those who still rely primarily on violence to effect change. And the far more interesting, and really new, news of the many thousands of organizations that have leaders who display a very different kind of strength—the strength of not only nonviolent resistance but of going against entrenched beliefs and institutions—are, except in small presses and alternative newsletters, still given only the most cursory coverage, if they are given any coverage at all.[68]

All of which takes us to the next, and final, chapter of this book, where we come full circle to what we began with: the myths and images that shape how we see ourselves and our world. For one of the great challenges we face today is to create and disseminate new myths and images that make it possible for us to see that we *do* have choices, that we are not doomed to eternal misery by "selfish genes" or "original sin"—and most important, that in the last analysis the choice of our future is up to us.

The New Eves and the New Adams: The Courage to Question, the Will to Choose, and the Power to Love

We all hunger for stories. Stories give form to our desires, feelings, and goals, molding how we view just about everything—from our own bodies to what is sacred or profane, good or bad, possible or impossible. Stories give us figures to emulate, imitate, admire, or abhor. And it is from the stories we are told that we in turn unconsciously fashion our own life scripts.

Most of us, like our parents before us, are not aware of all this. So we usually just tell our children the kinds of stories we were told or the stories easily available through popular books, magazines, films, and television. This is what my parents did with me, and I in turn did with my own children. So now they, like me and like most of us, face the task of reexamining and refashioning the stories and images that clutter our imagination: the task of becoming aware of the story lines we carry inside us, and of finding or creating stories and images that expand rather than limit our horizons.

This is why there is today so much interest in both very ancient and very new myths. This is not just, as we are sometimes told, a "New Age" fad. It stems from the recognition that many of our myths are not only inappropriate for our rapidly changing world but misleading about human possibilities. Most important, it stems from the growing consciousness that how we image our personal and social paths can profoundly affect both our own lives and those of others.

Again, this is not to say that all we have to do is change our stories and images. But even the most cursory glance at modern history shows that it is only because a small group of venturesome women and men dared to image different political, economic, and sexual relations—courageously challenging long-established institutions such as slavery and the divine right of kings to rule, and beliefs such as "if rape is inevitable relax and enjoy it" and "spare the rod and spoil the child"—that we have gradually been able to change many painful and inhuman realities.

As we have seen, this is basically what the modern revolution of consciousness is about: the gradual deconstruction and reconstruction of the stories and images that have for so long served to mold our minds, bodies, and souls to fit the requirements of a system driven by punishment, fear, and pain. As we have also seen, this revolution in consciousness is today moving into a second stage animated by the awakening consciousness that we do have choices, that we can make changes, and that these changes are essential in our high technology age of nuclear bombs and threatened ecological disasters.

There are no guarantees that we will succeed in freeing ourselves from the myths and structures that still bind us to dysfunctional, painful, and unjust ways of living and dying. But even attempting it is in itself an extraordinary adventure: a journey that is at the same time inward and outward, taking us toward ever deeper levels of consciousness and ever wider and more fulfilling life paths. Because, paradoxically, the more integrated we become as we strive to fashion our own life scripts, the more open we are to further changes in consciousness. And the more we dare to try out new paths, like all explorers of new territory, the more we open up further paths that make it possible for us to experience life in ways we never thought possible.

If I write of this with such conviction it is because as my own consciousness has radically changed over the last three decades, so also has my life. Certainly there has been pain, as there is for all of us who no longer try to numb ourselves through all the ways developed in dominator societies for people to go through life only half aware and awake, to deaden the pain we carry from our past or to blind us to the pain of others. There have even been times when it has been extremely painful, when I wondered if it was worth the struggle. But I can unequivocally say it was. For it has opened my mind, my heart, and in the sense of that which in all of us is most truly evolved, my soul. Above all, it has opened up for me the enormous possibilities of love, including a more loving acceptance of myself. And I am far from alone in this, as the search for new and different paths is today becoming a worldwide quest.

It is still by and large a quest by solitary travelers only slowly beginning to link with one another to discover that they are part of a new community in the making. It is certainly not yet a quest reflected in the mainstream stories of violence, depersonalized sex, alienation, brutality, and cynicism that, as George Gerbner and others have shown, maintain existing power imbalances. Yet if we persevere, some of the stories of those who today have the courage to question, the will to choose, and the determination to reclaim for ourselves and our children our unique human power to give and receive love will be the basis for new myths: myths about new Eves and new Adams who, against all obstacles, laid the groundwork for social structures that foster—rather than impede—the great capacity for pleasure from caring connections that, by the grace of evolution, has been given us to enjoy.

Our Creative Adventure

Since the emergence of our species, some of the most important changes on our planet have been human creations. To verify this, we need only look around us—not only at the cities and towns we live in, the cars and airplanes we travel in, the chairs we sit on, the tables we write on, the dishes we cook, and the plates we serve them on, but at our governments, our religions, our schools, our businesses, our laws, and of course our myths, symbols, and images. All these are human creations, and as such can be reinvented—as they have been all through human history in different places and times.

This is why we hear so much talk today of reinventing just about everything to meet the challenges of our time: our corporations, our government, our schools, and even our spirituality and sexuality. But if we are to reinvent our basic values and institutions, we also need to reinvent creativity.

The still-prevailing view of creativity is in itself an outgrowth of a dominator social and ideological organization. To begin with, it defines creativity as something apart from and above "ordinary" people and "ordinary" life, something that only a rare genius possesses and carries out in lofty isolation to create products that can only be viewed on special occasions in museums and other rarified spaces or used to revolutionize technologies of production or destruction. No distinction is made between inventiveness that expands people's life choices and enhances the quality of our lives, and inventiveness that restricts people's life choices and even (as with the Nazis' invention of mass extermination camps) more efficiently takes people's lives. Nor is any attention given to the social context of creativity (to what David Loye calls the nurturing "feminine" matrix of creativity in social systems) or to collaborative creativity—much less to the day-to-day creativity required in maintaining relationships or bringing up children (again stereotypically "women's work").

Such a limited, and limiting, definition of creativity makes sense for a society where men are ranked above women and an elite of men are ranked over everyone else. But it makes no sense for a more partnership-oriented society, which is why we are today seeing the gradual emergence of a very different view of creativity, not only among creativity researchers, artists, and executives who are instituting creativity training workshops in their corporations, but among thousands of "ordinary" women and men.[1]

This new way of looking at creativity recognizes that all humans are endowed with the capacity for creativity, and that while this capacity (like the ability to lift or run or any other human capability) varies from person to person, it can be developed—or hindered. It also recognizes, as Alfonso Montuori and Isabella Conti write, that creativity can be expressed in all realms, not just in the artist's loft or the rocket scientist's lab.[2] It therefore changes the classification of what is and is not a "creative product"—as much of contemporary art has also begun to do—recognizing that in fact it is "ordinary" creativity, the creativity we invest in our day-to-day lives, that is often most extraordinary since, as Elizabeth Dodson Gray writes, it can give far more meaning, and even sanctity, to our lives. It also no longer indiscriminately applies the term *creativity* to all inventiveness, including that designed to better dominate and kill. Rather it reserves the term *creativity* for those uses of inventiveness in line with the creative, rather than destructive, cycles of nature.[3]

But perhaps the most important thing about this new view of creativity is that it focuses extensively on the social context for creativity, on what supports or inhibits us in being creative, and even beyond this, on what is today called social creativity: the creation of social institutions, belief systems, and myths. In other words it recognizes, and thus opens up for both study and action, the fact that from the very beginning of our human adventure here on Earth we humans have been cocreators of our social evolution.

In terms of how we keep time (yet another human invention), it has only been approximately 250,000 years since this adventure began with the appearance of our human species. It has been 25,000 years since our

Paleolithic ancestors produced the first great Western works of art, works in which pairs of female and male animals and human sexuality were important themes. And it has now been approximately 2,500 years since religious myths of the sacred marriage of the Goddess and her divine lover and sacred images of female creative power faded from Western cultural consciousness.

Today our sacred images and myths tend to focus more on death, punishment, and pain than on sex, birth, and pleasure. We no longer celebrate the return of life every spring, nor do we have images of the vulva and phallus as sacred. Neither do we any longer have stories in our religious mythology in which nature's cyclic movements from dark to light, cold to warm, and especially fallowness to fruitfulness are linked with our own human cycles of life and death—stories in which the Earth from which life springs every year is imaged as a Great Mother to whose womb all life returns, like the cycles of vegetation, to be reborn.

But during the last twenty years, as I have become more aware of our most ancient Western images and myths, I have often been astonished by how much that is emerging in our time is reminiscent of our earlier, more partnership-oriented cultural roots. From this larger perspective, the "new spirituality" that no longer elevates man and spirituality over woman and nature does not seem all that new. And, as we have seen, the emerging consciousness of the link between human sexuality and spirituality has very ancient antecedents.

It is also striking how our ancestors' view of our Mother Earth as a living, pulsating, and miraculously interconnected whole is in our time beginning to reemerge, not only in mass consciousness but in scientific theories such as the "Gaia hypothesis"—Gaia being the Greek name for the Goddess-Creatrix.[4] Certainly bumper stickers proclaiming "Love Your Mother" and "Honor Our Mother Earth" acquire a far more powerful, and specific, meaning in the larger context of an earlier belief system where the world was seen as a divine Mother. There are even similarities between some of our environmental posters and ancient artistic images— for example, between the beautiful Minoan dolphin fresco in Knossos and the many images of dolphins we see today.

In short, be it in what we today would call our ancestors' ecological consciousness or in their more nature-and-body-centered spirituality, much in Western prehistory seems to prefigure the more partnership-oriented world view today struggling to emerge. But just as ancient images of woman's body as sacred did not emerge in a vacuum, the new beliefs, images, and stories more congruent with a partnership than dominator social organization that are in our time beginning to enter our consciousness are only surfacing because of the personal, cultural, social, and economic changes we have been examining.

The problem, however, is that even though at least in some world regions the last three centuries have brought fundamental changes in how people relate to one another in both the public and private spheres, the myths and images we find in our mainstream culture still to a very large extent reflect dominator rather than partnership relations. Part of this is a function of time lag, as it often takes a long time before new ideas and discoveries become incorporated into what is accepted as knowledge and truth. But a good part of it is because the old dominator stories and images have such a grip on our imagination, particularly on the imagination of our cultural gatekeepers: the academic, religious, economic, and educational establishments, and especially the publishers of books, magazines, and newspapers and the producers of television and radio news, entertainment programs, and films.

As a result, most of the stories and images in our mainstream culture still heavily focus on what keeps a dominator social organization going: pain or the threat of pain to the body. Unfortunately this is also true of much of our sacred imagery, which, as we have seen, came out of a time that was far more male dominated and authoritarian, a time when violence was sanctioned as divinely ordained.

Hence it is not surprising—although once we really look at them, it *is* shocking—how few of our religious images express love in intimate relations. We have no sacred images of sexual love or sexual pleasure since, as we saw earlier, only sex for procreation was condoned by the Church fathers, and even then only grudgingly. On the contrary, rather than focusing on pleasure, much of Christian religious imagery focuses on pain and cruelty, idealizing and actually sacralizing suffering (as in the endless images of martyred saints and Jesus' martyrdom on the cross). Even our religious imagery of parent-child and sibling relations focuses more on violence (as in the famous story of Cain and Abel) or rote obedience to an all-powerful paternal authority (as in Jesus' obedient sacrificial death and the often-painted image of Abraham's willingness to sacrifice his son Isaac to God). Not only that, but as I found when I again looked at the many icons and paintings of the Madonna and the baby Jesus from early medieval to modern times, even here a surprising number convey hardly any tenderness between mother and child.

So one of the great creative challenges of our time—critical, if we are to continue our human adventure in an age when the old ethos of domination and conquest is increasingly dysfunctional, even potentially suicidal—is to create for ourselves and our children images and stories of the sacred more congruent with a partnership than dominator social organization, images and stories in which giving and receiving pleasure and caring, rather than causing or submitting to pain, occupy center stage.

It is an enormous undertaking, against which there is tremendous resistance, not only from external forces but from inside all of us. Yet despite all of this, that is precisely what a courageous group of theologians, priests, nuns, rabbis, and, most important, "ordinary" women and men all over the world have already begun to do.

Remything the Sacred

Ours is not the first time in recorded history that religious myths that have served to maintain injustice and suffering have been challenged. For example, Elizabeth Cady Stanton's nineteenth-century *The Woman's Bible* provides a scathing commentary on the many biblical passages that present woman as villainous, subordinate, and/or inconsequential.[5] But although some of these earlier attempts to deal with religious myths that bind us to a dominator way of living call for alternatives that, as Stanton wrote in 1898, "teach more impressive and exalted lessons than the holy books of all the religions on earth,"[6] during the first phase of the modern revolution in consciousness the emphasis was primarily on critiques of existing myths—in other words, on deconstruction. It is only now, as we enter the second stage of this revolution in consciousness, that the emphasis is beginning to be more on reconstruction.

Some of those who are today, stone by stone, trying to lay the groundwork for a sacred mythology appropriate for partnership social and sexual relations are working within established traditions. They argue that we do not need to leave behind all our religious stories and images, that since there are so many different elements in our religions, we can select and strengthen what in them promotes more equitable, peaceful, and fulfilling ways of living. There are certainly in our Judeo-Christian religious heritage myths and stories that have strong partnership elements—for example, the many stories of Jesus' kindness and caring, as well as of his courageous defiance of the norms of his time when he freely associated with women (including some of the female disciples now being rediscovered).[7] Not only that, there are also myths and rites that still have strong traces of earlier partnership traditions under their dominator overlay.

For instance, in rethinking my own Jewish tradition, I realized that the beautiful Hebrew song "L'Cha Dodi," welcoming the beloved Kala or bride, most probably in some form harkens back to the ritual invocation of the Goddess and to myths of the sacred marriage. So also probably does the ceremony I loved watching my mother perform when I was a child: the Jewish rite where every Friday evening women light the Shabbat candles. Moreover, when I now myself repeat the same undulating hand movements my mother made over the candles, I see that when done slowly they are a form of ritual meditation.

There are also in Jewish tradition nature-celebrating holidays—for example, the festival of Succoth, when children dance under bowers made of leaves, fruits, and vegetables. This festival too probably in some form goes back to the agrarian Goddess-worshiping peoples who earlier lived in the Near East.

As I have already noted, there are also in the Old Testament many ethical precepts suitable for partnership relations. Examples are the requirement that orphans be cared for, as well as teachings such as those in Leviticus 19:18 that "thou shalt love thy neighbor as thyself." Then there are the Psalms, many of which present a gentle and comforting deity, and Jewish prayers that give thanks for our blessings and joys, including both the bounties and beauties of nature. There is even language such as that in 2 Isaiah 66:13 where, in sharp contrast to the many threats of punishment for those who fail to follow the commands of a divine Father or Lord, we find a feminine voice of God saying, "As one whom his mother comforteth, so will I comfort you."

In Christian tradition, we of course have Jesus' many teachings of stereotypically feminine values such as compassion and nonviolence. Here too we have clear traces of earlier holidays, such as Easter (so named after the ancient Spring Goddess of Northern Europe, Eostre, with her fertility symbols of eggs and rabbits)[8] celebrated to honor the return, or resurrection, of life every spring. The round wreath of Christmas, as Elizabeth Dodson Gray writes, probably also dates back to the Old Religion,[9] as does the mythological birth of a holy child as the representative of the new year—which used to be celebrated on the winter solstice but later was in modified form shifted to Christmas.

But while theologians such as Rosemary Radford Ruether, Helen Kenik, Thomas Berry, Rita Nakashima Brock, Walter Wink, Judith Plaskow, Matthew Fox, and others too numerous to list are attempting to strengthen the partnership elements in Jewish and Christian tradition— as Fox movingly writes, trying to refocus it on "original blessing" rather than "original sin"[10]—others are going outside this tradition in search of the myths, images, and rites we need for a more peaceful and equitable world. Some people are turning to Eastern teachings, such as those of the Dalai Lama, and to yoga and other forms of meditation, finding in such practices, as Justin O'Brien writes, "a transformative process that systematically awakes, coordinates, and realizes the latent resources in human nature for peaceful living and full self-awareness."[11] Others, as we have seen, are finding spirituality in both very old and very new myths about the ancient Goddess, and even, like the ritualists Starhawk and Luisah Teish, in recreating modern versions of Wicca (the name now given to the pre-Christian religion of some of the so-called witches) or earlier mother-centered African and Caribbean ceremonies.

As we have also seen, "ordinary" women and men are reinventing rituals to celebrate the act of birth giving, as well as ceremonies to honor a girl's first menses as an important rite of passage. Just as important, they are beginning to resacralize our day-to-day lives, reinvesting our daily acts of caring (from the preparation of food to caring for our environments, and above all, caring for one another and ourselves) with much greater fulfillment and meaning.

People are reinventing the sacrament of marriage by writing their own vows, even using their mutual pledges of love (instead of the words of a religious functionary) to proclaim their sacred bond. Most important, they are resacralizing the erotic—including both the most tender and the most passionate sex—bringing what in dominator religions is relegated to mysticism to where it rightfully belongs, into our everyday lives.

As the theologian Carter Heyward writes:

As we come to experience the erotic as sacred, we begin to know ourselves as holy and to imagine ourselves sharing in the creation of one another and of our common well-being. As we recognize the faces of the Holy in the faces of our lovers and friends, as well as in our own, we begin to feel at ease in our bodyselves— sensual, connected, and empowered. We become resources with one another of a wisdom and a pleasure in which heretofore we have not dared believe.

We begin to realize that God moves among us, transcending our particularities. She is born and embodied in our midst. She is ground and figure, power and person, this creative Spirit, root of our commonlife and of our most intensely personal longings. As the wind blows across the ocean, stirring up the seacreatures, causing them to tumble, rearranging them, the erotic crosses over among us, moving us to change the ways we are living in relation. Touched by this sacred power, we are never the same again.[12]

I believe that this reinvestment of our bodies and our intimate relations with the sacred is one of the most important building blocks for a new partnership spirituality that is both immanent and transcendent: one in which sacred pleasure rather than redemptive suffering is idealized. I also believe that the creation of a mythology that sacralizes the erotic and inspires us to transform ourselves and our societies will bring with it new myths, including myths of a sacred family appropriate for an equitable and democratic world. And once again, even though it goes against many of the norms that are our legacy from ancient dominator societies, this too is in bits and pieces already under way—for instance, in attempts by theologians, artists, and novelists to reinvest the Christian Mother of God with divinity.[13]

This reclamation of divinity for Mary is particularly important, since we obviously need to leave behind the idealization of a family in which only the father and the son, and not the mother, are divine. In fact, we also need to add to the pantheon of a holy family a divine daughter. For only then will we have a model for families in which all members are equally valued and respected.

But even though there are stories and images that are beginning to be modified in ways congruent with a partnership rather than dominator social organization, there are some myths that I think we will simply have to discard. These are myths such as the Hindu story of how the great god Vishnu was saved from death at his father's orders when a baby girl was sacrificed in his stead, the Judeo-Christian story of how Lot offered his young daughters to a mob to be raped to protect his angelic guests, as well as all the many versions of what the theologian Walter Wink calls the myth of redemptive violence—be it the story of God sending his son Jesus to die for humanity's sins, allegories of Christian soldiers marching to the fray, or our endless tales of killings by "heroic" knights, cowboys, cops, and most recently space cadets saving their countries, communities, or planets through their "superior" capacity to inflict pain.[14]

I realize that some will find the idea of abandoning such myths outrageous, even sacrilegious and immoral. But as we have seen, what is sacred and moral—just as what is normal and abnormal—is very different in a partnership and dominator context. I also realize that there will be those who will argue that it is impossible to transform our religious myths, that even though it is needed, it simply cannot be done. But as we have also seen, the transformation of religious myths has ample precedent. And there will undoubtedly be some who will argue that all our religious and secular myths of heroic violence merely symbolize the cosmic struggle between the forces of good and evil, God and Devil, Light and Darkness, or as Jungians like to put it, "man and his shadow"—that these myths just reflect human reality.

However, there is another way of looking at the reality of evil. On the cosmic level, as the Jewish mystic Baal Shem Tov said, it is more useful to view evil as the absence of good than as its opposite. I would add to this that on the human level a far more useful way of looking at evil is as the absence of those qualities that make us uniquely human: our enormous capacity for consciousness, choice, and most important, empathy and love.

This insight that love is the essence of both our humanity and what we call divine is actually the core teaching of great spiritual figures such as Jesus and Buddha. But despite the fact that Buddha and Jesus specifically preached, and often practiced, empathic and loving actions (as when Jesus healed the sick, comforted the grieving, multiplied loaves to feed the hungry, stopped the stoning of a woman accused of adultery, asked us to be nonviolent, and urged us to do unto others as we would have them do unto us), this teaching of love has in the context of a dominator society become distorted, rarified, and all too often perverted as a justification for the most barbaric and unloving acts.

This is why one of the most important creative challenges of our time is nothing less than to disentangle love from all the cruel meanings it has acquired over these last millennia of dominator history. And the exciting fact is that this too is already under way.

Relearning Love

We say we love our parents, our children, our mates, our friends, that we love Mozart, roses, sunsets, dancing, running, singing, cooking, gardening, and even that we love eating chocolate or reading a stimulating book. So *love* is our all-purpose word for everything that makes us feel good, especially everything that makes us feel connected both physically and spiritually with others of our kind.

Indeed, as we saw earlier, through chemicals such as endorphins and other neuropeptides which have only recently begun to be studied by scientists, in the course of evolution nature came to provide our species with an enormous capacity for pleasure from sex and from being cared for and being caring to others. This makes sense because we humans cannot survive without at least some measure of caring connection. In fact, as scientists are now also verifying, this is not only so when we are small but for our whole life.

To begin with, there is today a growing medical literature on the healing power of love. For example, in his book *Reversing Heart Disease,* Dr. Dean Ornish reports the results of a Yale University School of Medicine study showing that the "more people felt loved and supported, the less coronary arterial sclerosis they had."[15] Along similar lines, a 1988 review article in *Science* cited sixty-two studies, which "provide compelling evidence" that social support networks (variously defined as marital ties, friends and extended family, and group memberships) have a positive effect on surgical recovery time, as well as on both chronic and infectious diseases, while "lack of social support constitutes a major risk factor for mortality."[16]

There is also scientific evidence that engaging in caring behaviors is good for our health. For example, a 1988 study done by the University of Michigan Survey Research Center that followed twenty-seven hundred people in Tecumseh, Michigan, over a ten-year period found that regular volunteer work dramatically increased life expectancy. Significantly, this was especially so for men, who stereotypically do less caring work in their homes, with findings that men who did no volunteer work had a death rate during the ten-year study two and one-half times higher than those who volunteered at least once a week. Another survey of more than seventeen hundred women found that when engaged in helping behaviors to relatives, friends, and even total strangers they reported what Dr. Dean Edell calls a "helper's high," which, probably due to the triggering by altruistic behaviors of chemicals such as endorphins, the women linked to "decrease in stress-related disorders and headaches."[17]

All this verifies our own experiences: the fact that we feel better when we are kind and helpful to others. It also verifies the observation of the neurobiologist Humberto Maturana that we humans "depend on love and we get sick when it is denied us."[18] Even beyond this, it verifies something that many of us are beginning to understand: that to heal ourselves we also have to heal society.

For what we are beginning to wake up to today, as if from a long drugged sleep, is that we have for millennia structured our social institutions and our systems of values precisely in ways that serve to block, distort, and pervert our enormous human yearning for loving connections. We see this all too hideously in the carnage in our world, unrelenting and unremitting now for almost five thousand years. We see it, for the first time in history, on our movie and television screens in all its brutality and horror. We see it in still-lingering dominator economic institutions and practices that require the kinds of insensitive and hurtful behaviors that, as Jesus once allegorically said, would make it harder for a rich man to go to heaven than for a camel to go through the eye of needle. We see it in family relations that have all too often, ironically in the name of love, brutalized, numbed, and at best blunted our natural capacity for love. And we see it in the way love is portrayed in our mass media, and even in some of our most revered classics.

Thus, on our television screens, we find situation comedies such as "Married . . . With Children" presenting marital love in terms of "funny" abusiveness, insensitivity, and uncaring, while game shows such as "That's Amore" egg contestants on to insult and put down their "loved ones." In our classics, we find stories such as *Romeo and Juliet* idealizing a fourteen-year-old girl and a fifteen-year-old boy who hardly know each other dying for "love," and *Othello,* which has as its hero a man who kills for "love"—not exactly role models for healthy love. Then there are countless "bodice-ripper" romances marketed to women, hundreds of hopeless love stories (from *Dr. Zhivago* to the more recent *Bridges of Madison County*), and films such as *Tie Me Up! Tie Me Down!, The Piano,* and *Remains of the Day,* featuring women who fall in love with men who are either cruel and abusive, sexually predatory, or so emotionally stunted they are almost catatonic.

Yet despite all these portrayals of sexual love as more of a curse than a blessing, and despite all this modeling of unhealthy and violent behaviors in the name of love—or rather, precisely because of this—today many thousands of women and men are refusing to any longer buy into these old cultural norms. Again, critiques of romantic love as it has been culturally defined are hardly new. Neither, as we have seen, are attempts to restructure sexual and family relations. But it is only now, as we shift from the first to the second stage in both the contemporary revolution in consciousness and the sexual revolution, that the focus is shifting to the behavioral building blocks that are needed for either dominator or partnership intimate relations. For it is only now, on a scale never before seen in recorded history, that people are reevaluating, and trying to change, not only our social institutions but our day-to-day personal behaviors.

Once again, what is primarily reported in our mass media is the deconstructive (or destructive) part of what is happening—for example, the fact that along with rapid technological and social change there has been a rapidly rising divorce rate. Clearly this has not been without severe personal and social costs. But for many people the disintegration of old institutional forms has not been just a crisis but a creative opportunity—an opportunity for envisioning, and working to create, healthier and more satisfying personal and social alternatives. In fact, what the mass media still generally ignore, except for an occasional "human interest" feature story, is nothing less than what the sociologist Anthony Giddens calls the "transformation of intimacy"[19]—the unprecedented phenomenon of thousands of women and men who, stimulated by the sweeping social movements of our time, are consciously and deliberately trying to unlearn, and relearn, how to love.

Some are doing this through individual, family, and/or group therapies—therapies that have themselves shifted from the earlier aim of helping people "adjust" to helping people, in ever more empathic and caring ways, find healthier paths to living and loving. Others do so in self-help groups ranging from women's, men's, and couple's support groups to twelve-step groups that not only reject traditional feminine scripts of love as acceptance of pain and traditional masculine scripts that block men from "soft" or "feminine" emotions, but focus on helping people learn how to be more loving to their own "inner child." Still others do so through countless books focusing on self-esteem, self-healing, and healing our relationships, as well as through the thousands of workshops that today constitute a whole new industry focusing on helping people acquire the attitudes and skills—such as active listening, assertiveness, and above all, empathy—that make truly loving relations possible.

Not only that, but progressive educators are today, for the first time in the history of modern education, beginning to address education for love—or as it is sometimes called, education for emotional literacy—to help students learn ways of being and relating that equip them to fit into a partnership rather than dominator society.[20] This education, which can vastly accelerate what I have in this book called the pain to pleasure shift as a key factor in cultural transformation, is today still only slowly entering our school curriculum.[21] But as Daniel Goleman writes in *Connections: The Newsletter of Social and Emotional Learning* (published by the Yale Child Study Center), courses in the "core of emotional and social skills now being called 'emotional literacy'" are gradually emerging in both private and public schools.[22]

For example, at Jefferson High School in Portland, Oregon, Bill Bigelow and Linda Christiansen have for several years now taught their literature and history students empathy through what they call "interior monologues" in which students are encouraged to think from the perspective of different characters "in history, literature, or life."[23] The Self-Science curriculum developed by Karen Stone McCown of the Nueva Learning Center is designed to "raise the level of social and emotional competence in children as part of overall education."[24] Another program, now a requirement for grades six to ten and for the senior high school year at the Crossroads School in Santa Monica, California, is designed to "stimulate dimensions of intelligence often left out of traditional schooling: sensitivity to others, self-understanding, and intuition, imagination, and body wisdom."[25]

Despite enormous opposition, sex education—which helps children better understand both their own bodies and their intimate relations, as well as to identify and avoid sexually abusive behaviors—is also becoming more commonplace in schools.[26] Education for honoring diversity, for viewing those who are different from us with empathy and respect,[27] along with education for moral sensitivity, for a new morality of caring rather than coercion,[28] is also beginning to enter our classrooms. So also are classes to teach children the emotional and practical skills required in child care—which, as it turns out, are just as enthusiastically received by boys as by girls.

For example, in 1979 Education for Parenting was started at the initiative of Sally Scattergood, because she was "disturbed by the fact that childrearing, which is probably the most important task that most human beings will ever undertake, and one of vital importance for society, is ignored in our school curriculum."[29] Today it is taught in nine Philadelphia public schools in poor ghetto areas, all the way from kindergarten to high school, helping children learn not only the skills and the joys of parenthood but also its responsibilities. And these classes, as Myriam Miedzian writes, have also helped reduce teenage pregnancies and the replication, generation after generation, of physical and emotional child abuse.[30]

Miedzian notes that Education for Parenting recognizes that the assumption that good child rearing is something parents, particularly mothers, instinctively know is not only mistaken but dangerous—as even a glance at what scholars call the history of childhood shows.[31] As she points out, "Most parents have the capacity to love and nurture their children."[32] But whether that capacity is developed, or stunted and distorted, largely depends on what we are taught, and on how we ourselves experience parenting beginning when we are very small. And unfortunately, as we have seen, in "traditional" child rearing love has often not only been made conditional on unquestioning obedience to authority but has all too often been expressed through the confluence of caring with coercive touch.

Because this kind of child rearing in turn helps lay the groundwork for the erotization of domination and violence in later teenage and adult sexual relations, the teaching of parenting skills to both children and adults is an important component of an effective program of social education for healthy sex and love—and thus another sign of our entry into a second stage of the modern sexual revolution. It is also an important component of the much-needed new education for a more peaceful and equitable society. For, as we saw earlier, it is people's childhood experiences that have laid the groundwork for the replication, generation after generation, not only of a "love" in which pleasure is tinged with pain, but of habits of thinking and acting in which the cells, nerves, and tissues of our bodies become unwitting collaborators in the kinds of politics that—both in the public and private spheres—millions of people are today struggling to leave behind.

So the relearning of love in all of its forms, beginning with how we can be more loving parents to our children, is not, as conventional wisdom might have it, just a nice little frill to add to our educational curriculum if and when there is leftover funding from basic curriculum needs. If we are serious about creating a more democratic, less violent, truly civilized society, it *is* a basic curriculum need. It is certainly essential, after so many centuries of dominator socialization, to any realistic hope of freeing our body cells, nerves, and tissues to fully experience and express our powerful human yearning for connection. For, as the psychological research on love tells us, how we experience our relations with our caretakers profoundly affects all our later intimate relations.[33] Even beyond this, it affects how we relate to ourselves. So the new kind of education for partnership rather than dominator intimate relations that is today beginning to gain ground will also help us accept and love our own bodies— which, as Rita Freedman writes in her book *Bodylove,* is still another aspect of the new consciousness of what love is all about.[34]

The Challenge, the Creative Opportunity, and the Real Culture Wars

Will we succeed in this extraordinary chapter of our human adventure in forging new paths for ourselves and our children in which power is no longer equated with destruction and conquest—be it in war or the war of the sexes—but with creativity and caring, with those powers that are our species' unique evolutionary gifts?

To undertake nothing less than the creation of new cultural alternatives, to try to bring these into the mainstream, and to then try to ensure that they are institutionalized—that they are incorporated into our familial, political, economic, religious, and educational institutions so that the next generation does not again have to start from scratch—is a monumental task. It requires the will to go against not only the pull of millennia-old dominator myths and images but against the flood of new dominator myths and images that, like cancerous cells, today crowd out the new partnership myths and images struggling to emerge. It requires the will to go against established institutions that still reward antihuman behaviors, as in economic institutions that provide the lowest rewards for precisely those caring and caretaking behaviors that, as we are now learning, not only make us feel good but help us fight disease and prolong our lives. It even requires us to ask ourselves and others unheard-of questions, such as *whose* imagination, when we have fantasies that we know at the core of our being are products of a pathological social and ideological system. In short, it requires the will to choose not conformity but dissent—as did the small, and initially highly unpopular, minority that during the first phase of the modern revolution in consciousness defied authority to bring about the first important steps toward a partnership rather than dominator social and ideological organization.

It is precisely this great power of dissent—a power that scientific experiments show can be even stronger than the power of conformity—that we too have going for us in this second phase of the contemporary revolution in consciousness. Typically, given the dominator systems dynamics we have been examining, the experiments that have received the most attention are those by social scientists such as Solomon Asch demonstrating the power of conformity: how, for example, when six confederates of Asch said two lines were of equal length even though they were not, a majority of the subjects who followed them agreed—although it contradicted what their own eyes told them. What has not received even a fraction of the attention paid to that finding is what Asch's experiments demonstrated about dissent: that when just *one* of Asch's six confederates disagreed with the answers of the majority, the rate of conformity to majority opinion declined to a mere 5 percent![35]

Even beyond this, what we have going for us at this critical junction in our cultural evolution is that ours is a time of extreme systems disequilibrium, a time, as *cultural transformation theory* shows, when transformative change *can* happen—even in a relatively short time. This possibility of transformative change is further supported by the growing awareness—rapidly accelerating as we shift from the first to the second stage in the modern revolution of consciousness—that the mix of dominator myths and institutions with high technology is taking us to an evolutionary dead end.

So what we ultimately have going for us is the awakening consciousness of a species struggling to survive. And what we also have going for us is our enormous human creativity: the unique capacity of a species struggling to realize its highest potentials, especially our great human potentials for love, for creating ever new institutional and mythical forms.

As we have seen, changes in myths and realities go hand in hand. Changes in how people think and act lead to new stories and images. But these in turn facilitate the creation of new behavioral and institutional forms, which in turn make possible further changes in consciousness, and with this, new myths and images—which then in turn again stimulate our unique human capacity for creativity, inspiring us to make still further changes in all aspects of our lives.

So just as Theseus and some of the other Greek Argonauts were undoubtedly larger-than-life composites of some of the men who in our prehistory ushered in the shift to a world of violence and strong-man rule—a world where, as in Theseus's story, men's sexual relations were ideally devoid of love—some of the pieces for the archetypes and stories of tomorrow may one day also come from larger-than-life composites of real people who are in our time trying to usher in a very different world. These archetypes and stories will in turn inspire us to further change how we think, live, and love, which in turn will lead to new myths and images. And just as some of the myths we have inherited from ancient dominator societies were radical alterations of earlier themes—often, as in the Theseus legend's treatment of the ancient sacred marriage, parodies of what was once sacrosanct—we too can today use these same methods, as we work to clear the ground of the underbrush of dominator myths that keep getting in our way.

For example, many of our myths—all the way from ancient legends about the Trojan Wars to contemporary tales like *Star Wars*—deal with combat. A recurrent theme is the fashioning of ever more potent technologies for inflicting pain, from King Arthur's famed sword to science fiction arsenals bulging with body-disintegrating death rays and mind-destroying nerve gases. But suppose we now made up stories not about the kind of chemical warfare that makes people so sick they cannot fight, but about neuropeptide-like substances that make people feel so good they would rather not fight. Furthermore, rather than imagining a future of feuding galactic fiefdoms, as so many science fiction fantasies do, we could in these stories imagine a future in which empathy-and-caring-producing chemical "weapons" make it possible for people to use their energies, and financial resources, to care for others, including their "enemies," thereby saving a ton of money—as well as our planet.

Such transitional stories would still fit the beloved war epic format. But they would be far more novel and interesting—funny but also stimulating vehicles for changing peoples' consciousness about what is possible. They might even inspire some enterprising chemical company to explore such possibilities, or some military agency to fund scientists already doing neuropeptide research in a very different replay of the famous Manhattan Project that during the 1940s brought us the first atom bombs.

There is also room for playful innovativeness by reshuffling elements in some of our dominator classics, all the way from *The Taming of the Shrew* to *Rambo*, as was done in Danny Kaye's spoof of the Robin Hood legend in *The Court Jester*—which also managed to stand many masculine and feminine stereotypes on their heads. For example, we could try a redo of "Cinderella" in which, instead of passively accepting her oppression, she manages to enlist the help of one of her stepsisters in showing both the selfish and insensitive stepmother and the insensitive and neglectful father (who is so detached he does not even figure in the old story) how they can be decent parents—neither spoiling their children (as the stepmother did with her ill-fated daughters in the original tale) nor exploiting and abusing them (as was done with Cinderella). Of course, in this redo none of the three daughters would deign to even try on the famous slipper, sending the prince's agents packing with the message that no woman wants a man who is so shallow he thinks it is important that her body parts conform to set specifications.

A related area where there is much room for stories that are funny, at the same time that they change attitudes, is the sexual mythology found in both antiquated psychiatric theory and contemporary pornographic fantasy telling us that what men want and need to be sexually aroused is to humiliate, torture, beat, debase, and otherwise subordinate women. An example is the old saw of Freud's that men are only potent with women who are their inferiors—when in fact recent studies show that impotence is actually *less* frequent among dual-career couples, where women at least to some extent have a more equal position.[36] Not only that, these couples often report a richer and more exciting sex life.

So there is much material that can be used to help debunk the erotization of domination and violence, as well as other dysfunctional notions about sex. For instance, the idea that older people do not actively enjoy sex is today being shown by research as manifestly untrue. So also is the idea that men naturally are more interested in scoring than caring—when in fact one of the most dramatic developments during the second phase of the contemporary sexual revolution is that, at the same time that women have been moving toward a more stereotypically masculine sexual freedom, men have been moving toward a more stereotypically feminine linking of sex with meaningful relations. For instance, a survey published in 1994 by *Parade* magazine reported that 71 percent of men in a sample of more than one thousand people from all walks of life said they find it difficult to have sex without emotional involvement.[37] There are also books such as Robert Pasick's *Awakening From the Deep Sleep: A Practical Guide For Men in Transition*, designed to help men surrender to what Pasick calls sex as an "exquisitely pleasurable shared experience of affection,"[38] and *Transforming a Rape Culture*,[39] which not only exposes rape as the pathological act it is but shows that—far from being inevitable—much can be done (and is beginning to be done) to counteract its pervasiveness. As we saw earlier, there are films such as *Sex, Lies, and Videotape* where the Don Juan archetype is turned into a ridiculous figure, and the whole point is how crippling our sexual myths and stereotypes have been.

But there are other areas, where far less debunking is being done, which could also greatly profit from some gentle, but trenchant, irreverence. One of these is religion, as there is still a great deal of fear (not surprising, in light of so many warnings of dire, even eternal punishment) of poking fun at or in any way criticizing established religious leaders.

Of course, there would be loud cries of outrage from those who are today mounting an ever more frantic defense of dominator traditions in the name of God. But it can be pointed out that only a few centuries ago political satires of autocratic princes and kings were also beyond the pale; that in a democracy even religious leaders should no longer be exempt from criticism; and anyway, that playful irreverence is far less offensive than the invective and incitements to violence of a religious right that has today in the West launched what they aptly call a "culture war" in which—among other stealth tactics—they use religious myths that are the product of a time when the most brutal cruelties were perpetrated in the name of religion as a cover-up for their antidemocratic agenda.

As some social commentators have noted, a major factor behind the fundamentalist offensive of our time—be it Christian in the United States or Muslim and Hindu in other world regions—is the fear engendered by the difficulties of coping with a rapidly changing world.[40] This analysis makes sense, since the rigidities that have through pain or the threat of pain been built into the dominator psyche make it extremely difficult for people with this kind of personality structure to effectively deal with change, as shown by studies such as those of Frenkel-Brunswick in *The Authoritarian Personality*. From this larger perspective, it also makes sense that the attempts by fundamentalists to get things back "in control" should so heavily focus on reimposing strict controls on women—and even more specifically, controls on women's sexuality. For, as we have seen, this control is a linchpin of dominator social and ideological organization.

Given these underlying dynamics, it becomes more understandable that both Muslim fundamentalists and the Christian right are today focusing their attempts to regain control in a rapidly changing world on frantic efforts to maintain control over women, particularly over women's sexuality. Moreover, given their mythologies about "holy wars," it is also understandable that they should use "divinely approved" violence to do so—be it in the murders of thousands of women in Muslim nations, sometimes just for the "crime" of standing at a bus stop without covering their heads (as recently happened in Algeria),[41] or for the "crime" of performing legal abortions in the United States (as happened when members of the Christian right in the name of God murdered doctors who did so).

In fact, if from this perspective we look at today's fundamentalist Muslim violence—from Iran, Algeria, and Somalia to Pakistan, Bangladesh, and Kurdistan, all places where women are being hunted down and killed for any real or imagined "moral" infraction—what comes to mind are the European witch-hunts and inquisitions during the end of the Middle Ages and the onset of our modern era. For in both cases, we see how during an unsettled time fear and anger are deflected into violence against the traditionally disempowered half of humanity, as well as against disempowered religious and ethnic minorities and anyone who questions dominator religious myths. And in both cases, as the *Malleus Maleficarum* proclaimed some five hundred years ago, we see the blaming of women's "uncontrolled" sexuality for all of society's ills.

So what is happening today is in significant ways a replay of the same kinds of efforts that were used to oppose the Enlightenment in the West three hundred years ago. These efforts are more violent in those parts of the world where the revolution in consciousness and the sexual revolution that during the last three hundred years swept the West are still by and large in their first stages. But there is also increasing violence in the West, as the second phase of these revolutions is accurately perceived by those who still desperately cling to dominator mythologies as a threat to the very foundations of a system they believe to be divinely ordained.

There is thus no question that those who lead and finance the contemporary "culture wars" in the West are dangerous, not only in the short run but in the long run. Their goal is nothing less than a return to the "good old days," when all women and most men still knew their place in a system based on the ranking of man over woman, man over man, nation over nation, and man over nature—one in which, if they succeed, there will be neither freedom nor equality, as they will have absolute "divinely ordained" control.[42] So we need to defend ourselves much more vigorously and outspokenly against this kind of religious fascism, alert ourselves and others to its stealth tactics, and mobilize our legal, economic, and media resources to halt it. But the challenge for us is not to respond to the declaration of war of those who lead the flock of the religious right by also resorting to abusive and violent tactics. Rather, it is to deal with those who follow them with a compassion born from the understanding that they come from a place of great fear and pain—as well as by discrediting rightist fundamentalist leaders by exposing their real cultural agenda and the great damage they do, and by demonstrating it *is* possible to appropriately respond to rapidly changing environmental and social conditions in creative rather than destructive ways.

For in truth the "culture wars" of our time are not between religious versus "heathen" values, but between a dysfunctional and antihuman system that threatens to destroy us all and a new partnership system that is today struggling to emerge—thanks to the courageous efforts of thousands of people who no longer accept the myth that, like the Adam and Eve of Genesis, we humans are doomed to live in eternal fear, lovelessness, and pain. On one side are all those who still try to "adjust" to an inherently painful system because they think it is inevitable—be it through abusive and violent scapegoating and fantasies of a better hereafter, nihilism and cynicism, the excessive use of alcohol and drugs (including mood elevators and tranquilizers sold by the buckets in the United States), or the mind-numbing and empathy-deadening "entertaining" abuse and violence today mass marketed by our media. On the other side are those who have the courage to question the false myths of dominator inevitability, to face ourselves and our world, and most important, to try to change it.

Redefining Courage and Recreating Our Lives

This matter of courage takes us to another major change in consciousness—once again, one that is not reflected in most of the images and stories we still find in our mainstream culture, which are more like a rearview mirror reflecting our dominator past than an accurate reflection of much that is happening in our time. For more and more of us are today becoming aware that the old model of courage is of a courage born of anger, fear, and hate. Even more important, we are becoming aware that there is another kind of courage, a courage that at its most basic level is rooted in caring for others, be it for those we love or even total strangers: the courage to stand up to injustice. We are also becoming aware that it takes far more courage to challenge unjust authority without violence than it takes to kill all the dragons and monsters that populate all the stories still told to our children about what it means to be brave.

In my own life, my first lesson in the courage to challenge unjust authority from a position of love rather than hate came very early, when I was a little girl in Vienna. It was Crystal Night, so named because of all the windows of synagogues and homes smashed when the Nazis mounted their first mass roundup of Jews in Germany and Austria. When there came to our house that night five men headed by a Gestapo officer to "confiscate" what they wanted of our belongings and to drag my father away—which they did—my mother had the courage to stand up to them, to denounce them for their despicable actions, for daring to break in to loot and to so brutally treat a man who was kind and upright. And a remarkable thing happened. Whether it was because of her authoritative tone and demeanor (which the dominator personality is trained to respect) or partly out of greed (because the pack leader said that if she brought a certain sum of money to Gestapo headquarters he would see that my father was released), she saved not only my father's life but mine and hers as well. Because had he been sent to a concentration camp as so many men were that night, like many other Jewish women and children, we too would have stayed behind in hopes of his release—until we in turn were rounded up and killed.

For my mother to do what she did took enormous courage. But she not only had to muster the courage to risk her life unarmed with anything except her love; she also had to muster the courage to violate established norms, including the norms that to be "good" is the same as unquestioningly obeying those in positions of authority and that "good" women only speak softly and pleadingly, never demanding or asserting themselves.

I now think of this courage to challenge unjust authority from a position of love rather than hate as spiritual courage. I think of it as the courage to question our most hallowed and sanctified norms—as the young Jew named Jesus did almost two thousand years ago when he defied the religious and secular authorities of his day. And I think of it as the kind of courage today being displayed by countless women and men in all walks of life who are through their lives and actions defying still firmly entrenched millennia-old dominator traditions.

Some of them, as we already glimpsed, are teachers who will no longer teach what they call the "hidden curriculum" of obedience and uniformity[43] and instead help students recognize and resist all forms of oppression and work for a more equitable society, both through social action and by learning skills needed for living more productive and peaceful lives—as through new programs in nonviolent conflict resolution and peer mediation that are slowly entering our school curriculum.[44] Even though these programs are still rarely considered newsworthy, they are of enormous importance, as they make it possible for children to take responsibility for their own behaviors, rather than looking to authority figures—teachers, principals, and later clergy, cops, and/or "strong-man" leaders—to maintain law and order. In other words, this kind of early education provides children themselves with the tools to creatively deal with conflict, rather than to expect a "higher authority" to control their own and others' behavior. It also helps children acquire habits of impulse self-regulation, not out of fear but out of respect and concern for others—teaching them to link courage with sensitivity, consciousness of others, and an empathic sense of what is just and fair.

Another important area where courageous educators are challenging dominator norms is in trying to make education more gender holistic and multicultural, not only through women's studies or African-American studies, but through fundamental changes in the whole school curriculum—as well as in our informal education through the mass media. For example, in her article "Unlearning the Myths That Bind Us," Linda Christiansen writes of methods to help students reexamine stereotypes in children's stories, television programs, and films, and in their place develop for themselves new role models free from racism, sexism, and violence.[45] There are also curricula being developed in media literacy, such as those put out by the Los Angeles–based Center for Media Literacy, to help us detect the hidden messages in the media and gradually shift the focus of public discourse to the underlying issues that shape our lives and the lives of our children.

Dominator traditions are also today being challenged by other professionals—for example, by psychologists such as Arthur and Elaine Aron, whose work brings us new perspectives on love;[46] anthropologists such as Stuart Schlegel, whose fieldwork offers us insights into what a partnership tribal society is like;[47] sociologists such as Rob Koegel, who is editing a series of books on partnership education;[48] philosophers such as Min Jiayin, coordinator of the Chinese Partnership Research Group in Beijing; and economists such as Devaki Jain, Nirmala Banerjee, Hazel Henderson, Manfred Max-Neef, Amartya Sen, and countless others whose work particularly focuses on the unjust misdistribution of resources between North and South, Whites and Blacks, as well as men and women of all races.[49]

Many of those who today have the courage to challenge dominator traditions are artists. A notable example is Judy Chicago, one of the most important artists of modern times, whose monumental projects *The Dinner Party* and *The Birth Project* again honor woman's sexuality and her life-giving powers. There are countless others—from the Polish artist Krzyztof Wodicz, the American artists Bradley McCallum and Carrie Nordello, and the Vietnamese artist To Hoang, whose portrayals of suffering speak of caring and commitment to change rather than alienation and hopelessness, to the Australian-American artist Jane Evershed and the Rome-based artist BarBara Schaefer, whose images sing of the world as it can be, as well as thousands of others all over the world who are using art to "reenchant" both nature and life—including many whose paintings, sculptures, altars, and sacred spaces reclaim our ancient Goddess heritage while at the same time providing new images reflecting the emerging partnership consciousness of our time.[50]

Other courageous pioneers on the road to partnership are community organizers and social and environmental activists, again far too numerous to list, who also recognize the importance of new images and stories in bringing about personal and social transformation. Examples are Bernadette Cozart, founder of the Greening of Harlem Coalition, who is even planning a new Goddess Garden; George Singleton, of the Hope LA Horticulture Corps, who is working in the South Central Los Angeles area to raise consciousness about what he calls rape by consent;[51] the survivors of incest, rape, and other forms of intimate violence who organized the Clothesline Project, which uses art in the service of social activism;[52] and particularly close to my heart, the International Partnership Network: the women and men who through Centers for Partnership Education and other groups in the United States and elsewhere are using *The Partnership Way* (which I wrote with my partner, David Loye) as a tool for personal and social transformation.[53]

Others inspiring us to meet this creative challenge are storytellers such as Jean Houston and Brian Swimme; biographers such as Cathleen Rountree, whose *Coming Into Our Fullness: On Women Turning Forty* brings us new heroines for our time; autobiographers such as Arthur Melville, who *is* a new hero for our time; and musicians such as Mathew Callahan, whose lyrics express both outrage and hope.[54] Then there are writers, so many that I could not even begin to list and describe them here, spanning every conceivable subject, from biology, ecology, sexuality, and gender to the interconnection between environmental, social, and economic issues as well as between sexism, racism, and economic and social injustice.[55] Some of the pioneers on the road to partnership are young, such as Severn Cullis-Suzuki, founder of the Environmental Children's Organization. Others are old, such as Ashley Montagu, who in his nineties continues his indefatigable struggle to bring more sanity and caring into our intellectual discourse. Many focus specifically on remything the human body and human sexuality, and on bodily and spiritual healing.[56] Some are working on new creation myths—for example, Carolyn Marks, whose ritual story of a divine Mother and Father who together give birth to the world was performed in San Francisco at Grace Cathedral on New Year's Day 1987 (a partnership myth that I am proud to say was inspired by the work of Marija Gimbutas as well as my own). Still others are trying to help people create their own new myths, such as the women and men of the Irish-based Spectrum Productions Limited who are working on a television program that takes us from the Paleolithic to the present for use on interactive

CD-ROM disks.[57] Others use humor to both demythologize dominator stereotypes and inspire us to write our own life scripts instead—for example, Nicole Hollander, the creator of *Sylvia;* Garry Trudeau, the creator of *Doonesbury;* and the former television soap opera writer Linda Grover, who among other works creates provocative bumper stickers such as "Partnership Is Adam and Eve with a Happy Ending."

Some of the people who today have the spiritual courage to challenge dominator norms are well known.[58] But most are not, because—unlike the politicians, generals, rock stars, society people, sports figures, and other celebrities whose all-too-often trivial, and even destructive, activities receive so much media attention—their extraordinary personal and social creativity as yet receives little recognition. So still a further creative challenge for us is to find ways of bringing them to wider attention.

For it is these women and men of all races, nationalities, and faiths committed to creating not only new myths, institutions, and beliefs but new ways of living and relating in our day-to-day lives who today offer us the much-needed role models for our time of personal, cultural, social, and economic transition. Even beyond this, it is their struggles, trials, tribulations, and triumphs that will perhaps one day provide some of the raw materials for the stories still to be written of the new Adams and Eves who will be the progenitors of a new partnership culture on this Earth.

The Future of Sex, Love, and Pleasure

As I began to approach the end of this book and found myself again, as at its beginning, with far more boxes of notes and clippings than I could possibly put into just one chapter about all the people who individually and in groups are today trying to create a new partnership culture for our future, I kept thinking how fortunate I am that through my work I am in touch with so much that is positive and hopeful. I also thought of how there was a time in my own life when I had no idea that any of this transformative work was happening, just as I had no idea of how profoundly transformed my own life would be in the course of only three short decades. But the fact that I have myself experienced such profound transformation, and the fact that I know how many others are today committed to transforming themselves and our world, gives me a far surer sense that while it is by no means inevitable, we can succeed in forging new paths into a better future for ourselves and our children.

If we succeed, we will certainly look at many of our present myths, both scientific and religious, with astonishment. For example, we will wonder why, rather than emphasizing the incredible potentials that lie

latent in a human mind that scientists tell us is still only using a small
fraction of its enormous power, so many of our sociobiological myths
focus instead on earlier restrictions, on life forms whose potentials are
more limited than ours—communicating to us the message that because
our appearance on the evolutionary scene was preceded by more restricted life forms, we humans are more restricted than one would think.
We will certainly be amazed that our most famous story of human origins, the Genesis story of Adam and Eve, has absolutely nothing good to
say about sex, love, or pleasure, that it presents the human quest for
higher consciousness as a curse rather than a blessing, and that it does not
even touch on the awe and wonder we humans experience when we be-
hold or touch someone we love.

When I told David that I was in this last chapter planning to write of
this myth, he wrote a poem about it—one of many poems he has written
me since the day we first met eighteen years ago.[59] It is a poem called
"The New Adam and the New Eve," and it expresses in a few lines how
perhaps one day what is so vivid to us now may become the stuff of
which dreams, or nightmares, are made.

I had a terrible dream, she said.
You're safe, he murmured, cradling her.
No, it was terrible, she said, I cannot sleep.
I still see that glorious garden, the birds,
the fruits, the clear streams with pebbles of
agate and the trancelike wandering of green fish,
and you were there, and for a time it was good,
but then this terrifying old man came and told me
I must not think for myself. And soon a snake
came and said— He laughed. A talking snake!
Don't laugh, please don't laugh! She shuddered.
This was so real, more real than now, much more.
The snake offered me a brain and mind and when
I took them the old man came rushing in, his eyes
exploding, his mouth aghast, and cursing with
hurricane force he threw us from the garden.
And *you* blamed *me*, she cried, and in a world
of misery we fought for five thousand years.

The sun touched the window sill, touched
her hair: he touched the gold along her neck
and back and sighing she rolled over and for

a long time they held each other, then she rose.
Come see, she called, joyous beside the window.
In poured the full glory of the morning, the
copper-gold of sky, the far-off crowing, the
clear, muted laughter along the river, the
light, cool fragrance in from the fields.
It will be a good day, he said, smiling.
And night, she said. For years, they
both thought. For years and years.

I hope David's poem is prophetic, that we will really someday forget the myths and archetypes that have so long distorted how we view love, sex, our bodies, and just about everything in this world. That this is not impossible is demonstrated by how our earlier myths and images in which sex was sacred and woman's body was venerated rather than vilified were over time forgotten. It will not happen overnight. Perhaps even then we will never completely forget, because of the need to remember what happened so it will never happen again.

But one thing is certain. If we succeed in completing the shift from a dominator to a partnership world, both the realities and myths of our future will be very different from what they are now. For in this world we will be far more able to fully utilize all our senses and capacities—including senses and capacities we did not even know we had—to create the new institutional forms and myths that will make it possible for us to fully express the miracle, mystery, and joy of what mystics throughout the ages have called the sacred truth of our oneness in love.

In this world there will still be myths sacralizing suffering, as pain and death are part of the cycles of nature and of life. But there will be many more myths about the awe, wonder, and ecstasy that has been given us to feel, including the joy, awe, wonder, and ecstasy of physical love.

There will be stories about how we humans are conceived in delight and rapture, not in sin. There will be images spiritualizing the erotic, rather than eroticizing violence and domination. And rather than myths about our salvation through violence and pain, there will be myths about our salvation through caring and pleasure.

There may still in this world be divine creation stories, perhaps stories more as they once seem to have been—of a divine Mother who through sexual union with her divine lover brings forth all life. There may also be stories containing the insight buried in the epic of Gilgamesh that our sexuality is an important element of that which makes us human. There may even be stories about how there was once a time when, as Jakob Böhme wrote of the biblical story of Adam and Eve, woman and man were rent asunder. But in these myths that rift will be healed.

There will certainly be no myths about a deity who demands servility, suffering, and self-abasement. For if in this world the powers that govern the universe are imaged in human form, it will be as both a Mother and a Father who, far from begrudging us pleasure, bless our joys—like loving parents, deriving pleasure from our enjoyment. These divine parents will also encourage our quest for knowledge, rather than wanting to monopolize it. They will applaud our zest for life, rather than trying to stem it. And they will teach us to every day remember to live our lives to the fullest—and to help those around us to do so too.

Since there will in this world be no separation between the spiritual and the material, it will have an economic mythology in which not only our physical needs but our spiritual needs—our needs for meaning and justice, and the enormous pleasures we derive from caring—are taken into account. As children will be truly valued, there will be fewer, so that myths about families will be not only about biological mothers and fathers but about a whole host of loving caretakers. And these myths will be taught to children from babyhood on.

There will in this world be many rites to invest our daily lives with meaning, including rituals with flowers, candles, music, and wine. But these rituals will honor both our spiritual and physical bonds, as the two will be seen as intertwined. Some of these rituals may again be rites in which the union of female and male will be an ecstatic, and in the true sense of the word, magical act. But just as our ancestors' sexual rites must have developed out of people's experience of sex as an altered state of consciousness, as a means of connecting with what we call the divine, these rites too will come out of such authentic experiences—and not out of some mechanical use of Tantric yoga formulas or other technologies in which, as we read in some texts today, one person's body becomes no more than an instrument for another's spiritual use.

These rites will recognize that our most sacred touch is touch that gives pleasure. Hence some may be rites for when we touch our children, our friends, and our own bodies. All of them will have as their purpose not to frighten us with terrible punishments but to help us live in ways that, through the free flow of our natural capacities for empathy and caring, help us recognize what we call the divine in ourselves and others.

We still have a long way to go before we get to this world where spirituality can again be erotic and the erotic can again be spiritual, where sex can be a sacrament and our bodies shrines, where we will know in our everyday lives, and not just in moments of spiritual illumination, that it is through love that we expand ourselves to both literally and figuratively embrace others at the same time that we enfold ourselves into them and into that oneness mystics and lovers speak of as an experience of both exquisite passion and perfect peace.

But the path to that world is the path many women and men all over the world have chosen to take: the path of spiritual, sexual, and social healing. So even though most of us living now may never see this world, its promise sustains us on our journey into unknown realms, as we continue to create, and live, our unfolding human story.

THE DOMINATOR AND PARTNERSHIP MODELS:

Seven Basic, Interactive, and Mutually Supporting Differences

COMPONENT	DOMINATOR MODEL	PARTNERSHIP MODEL
1. Gender relations	The male is ranked over the female, and the traits and social values stereotypically associated with "masculinity" are valued more highly than those associated with "femininity."[1]	Females and males are equally valued in the governing ideology, and stereotypically "feminine" values such as nurturance and nonviolence can be given operational primacy.
2. Violence	A high degree of social violence and abuse is institutionalized, ranging from wife-and-child beating, rape, and warfare to psychological abuse by "superiors" in the family, the work place, and society at large.	Violence and abuse are not structural components of the system, so that both boys and girls can be taught nonviolent conflict resolution. Accordingly, there is a low degree of social violence.

1. Please note that the terms *"femininity"* and *"masculinity"* as used here correspond to the sexual stereotypes socially constructed for a dominator society (where masculinity is equated with dominance and conquest, and femininity with passivity and submissiveness) and *not* to any inherent female or male traits.

COMPONENT	DOMINATOR MODEL	PARTNERSHIP MODEL
3. Social structure	The social structure is predominantly hierarchic[2] and authoritarian, with the degree of authoritarianism and hierarchism roughly corresponding to the degree of male dominance.	The social structure is more generally egalitarian, with difference (be it based on gender, race, religion, sexual preference, or belief system) not automatically associated with superior or inferior social and/or economic status.
4. Sexuality	Coercion is a major element in mate selection, sexual intercourse, and procreation, with the erotization of dominance and/or the repression of erotic pleasure through fear. Primary functions of sex are male procreation and male sexual release.	Mutual respect and freedom of choice for both females and males are characteristic of mate selection, sexual intercourse, and procreation. Primary functions of sex are the bonding between female and male through the give and take of mutual pleasure, and the reproduction of species.
5. Spirituality	Man and spirituality are ranked over woman and nature, justifying their domination and exploitation. The powers that govern the universe are imaged as punitive entities, be it as a detached father whose orders must be obeyed on pain of terrible punishments, a cruel mother, or demons and monsters who delight in arbitrarily tormenting humans, and hence must be placated.	The spiritual dimension of both woman's and nature's life-giving and sustaining powers is recognized and highly valued, as are these powers in men. Spirituality is linked with empathy and equity, and the divine is imaged through myths and symbols of unconditional love.

2. As used here, the term *hierarchic* refers to what we may call a *domination* hierarchy, or the type of hierarchy inherent in a dominator model of social organization, based on fear and the threat of pain. Such hierarchies should be distinguished from a second type of hierarchy, which may be called an *actualization* hierarchy. An example from biology is the hierarchy of molecules, cells, and organs in the body: a progression toward a higher and more complex level of function. In social systems, hierarchies of actualization go along with the equation of power with the power to create and to elicit from oneself and others our highest potentials.

COMPONENT	DOMINATOR MODEL	PARTNERSHIP MODEL
6. Pleasure and pain	The infliction or threat of pain is integral to systems maintenance. The pleasures of touch in both sexual and parent-child relations are associated with domination and submission, and thus also with pain, be it in the so-called carnal love of sex or in submission to a "loving" deity. The infliction and/or suffering of pain are sacralized.	Human relations are held together more by pleasure bonds than by fear of pain. The pleasures of caring behaviors are socially supported, and pleasure is associated with empathy for others. Caretaking, love-making, and other activities that give pleasure are considered sacred.
7. Power and love	The highest power is the power to dominate and destroy, symbolized since remote antiquity by the lethal power of the blade. "Love" and "passion" are frequently used to justify violent and abusive actions by those who dominate, as in the killing of women by men when they suspect them of sexual independence, or in "holy wars" said to be waged out of love for a deity that demands obeisance from all.	The highest power is the power to give, nurture, and illuminate life, symbolized since remote antiquity by the holy chalice or grail. Love is recognized as the highest expression of the evolution of life on our planet, as well as the universal unifying power.

Use of Notes and Bibliography

My main concerns in deciding on the form for the references have been clarity, accessibility, and avoidance of unnecessary repetition.

As a general rule, the references for this book follow the format recommended by the Modern Language Association of splitting citations into Notes and Bibliography. In the case of books and periodicals, the Notes generally contain only the last name of the author and the date of publication, with the full citation listed in alphabetical order by the authors' last names in the Bibliography. In other words, most references in the Notes do not contain information such as the author's first name, the title of the book or article, and the publisher or periodical, which are listed in the Bibliography.

However, some references are cited only in the Notes. These are primarily references that cannot be listed by author. Examples are newspaper or magazine pieces that give no author, reports such as the *Human Development Report 1991*, entire issues of magazines (such as *WIN News*, Summer 1993), as well as listings of organizations and other miscellaneous items. There are exceptions, such as the Dartmouth Bible, which is listed by title in the Bibliography.

Many notes contain additional information or quotations that would have interrupted the flow but that may be of use to interested readers. Sometimes in addition to the author and date, I have also included the titles of books, articles, and periodicals because these offer important descriptive information to the reader (see, for example, note 11, Introduction).

In the Bibliography all entries are in alphabetical order by authors' last names. If there is more than one work by the same author, the earlier work is generally listed first. Where there is more than one publication by the same author in the same year, these publications are identified by letters after the date, in alphabetical order. For example:

Eisler, Riane. *The Chalice and the Blade: Our History, Our Future.* San Francisco: Harper & Row, 1987a.

———. "Woman, Man, and the Evolution of Social Structure." *World Futures: The Journal of General Evolution* 23 (April 1987b), 79–92.

———. "Human Rights: Toward an Integrated Theory for Action." *The Human Rights Quarterly* 9 (August 1987c), 287–308.

If there is more than one work in progress by the same author, the same format has been used. For example:

Loye, David. *The River and the Star: The Lost Story of the Great Scientific Explorers of Goodness.* Work in progress a.

———. *Moral Transformation.* Work in progress b.

I hope the reader will find the Notes and Bibliography helpful and easy to follow. I should add that the Bibliography only includes those works actually cited and is by no means a complete list of the works I drew upon in research for this book.

Notes

Please see "Use of Notes and Bibliography," on page 407.

OUR SEXUAL AND SOCIAL CHOICES: AN INTRODUCTION
(Pp. 1–12)

1. This was to be *Breaking Free*, followed by *Emergence*. Some materials for these books went into *The Partnership Way: New Tools for Living and Learning* (1990), which I wrote with my partner, the social psychologist and futurist David Loye. Some became part of this book.
2. For a more detailed discussion, see *The Chalice and the Blade*, (Eisler 1987a).
3. Islamic teachings differ from more extreme Christian views in that, as in Hebrew tradition, they do not look askance at marital sex—which the prophet Mohammed is said to have thoroughly enjoyed, particularly with his favorite wife. (See Mernissi 1987, 54–61.) But these teachings too tend to view the human body with suspicion and women—and particularly women's sexuality—as dangerous unless rigidly controlled by men.
4. For a discussion of this shift, see chapters 4, 6, 7, and 8 in *The Chalice and the Blade*.
5. Perry 1989.
6. In *The Chalice and the Blade* I make a distinction between hierarchies of actualization and hierarchies of domination and discuss how the former are more characteristic of the partnership model while the latter are characteristic of the dominator model. See also Eisler and Loye 1990, particularly charts on 179–190.
7. A new work on these issues is Henshaw 1994.
8. Gardner and Maier 1984, 77–78.
9. Much written about the Cathars focuses on the rejection by some of them of all that is of this world. While many Cathars exalted the spiritual over the worldly, this has to be understood in the context of a time when people's worldly actions—including those of the "princes" of the Church—were often extremely brutal. In fact, the Cathars were noted for their charity and compassion—in other words, for their efforts to improve people's lives in this world. Cathars gave high status to women, who are stereotypically supposed to embody the more "soft" or "feminine" values. As G. Rattray Taylor points out in *Sex in History*, they also sometimes conceptualized the deity in feminine form.
10. I have deliberately used Freud's term *man* because his work is so male-centered.
11. *Cultural transformation theory* is introduced in general terms in *The Chalice and the Blade*. Concise presentations also appear in articles I wrote for other scholarly books and periodicals; for example, in *World Futures* (1987b); in *The New Evolutionary Paradigm* (1991);

in *The Evolution of Cognitive Maps: New Paradigms for the Twenty-First Century* (1993a); in *Communication and Culture in War and Peace* (1993b); and in *Journal of Organizational Change Management* (1994).

To supplement the brief description of *cultural transformation theory* in this introduction, what follows are some passages from *The Chalice and the Blade*:

> One result of re-examining human society from a gender-holistic perspective has been a new theory of cultural evolution . . . which . . . proposes that underlying the great surface diversity of human culture are two basic models of society . . . the *dominator* . . . and the *partnership* model. . . . Cultural transformation theory . . . proposes that the original direction in the mainstream of our cultural evolution was toward partnership but that, following a period of chaos and almost total cultural disruption, there occurred a fundamental social shift. . . . At this pivotal branching, the cultural evolution of societies that worshiped the life-generating and nurturing powers of the universe . . . was interrupted. There now appeared on the prehistoric horizon invaders from the peripheral areas of our globe . . . who worshiped . . . the power to take rather than give life. (xvii)

> If we look at the whole span of our cultural evolution from the perspective of cultural transformation theory, we see that the roots of our present global crises go back to the fundamental shift in our prehistory that brought enormous changes not only in social structure but also in technology. This was the shift in emphasis from technologies that sustain and enhance life to the technologies symbolized by the Blade: technologies designed to destroy and dominate. (xx)

12. Michel Foucault points out that much of the modern discourse about sex has been co-opted by those in power to maintain that power (Foucault 1980). While Foucault's work is an important contribution, he tends to present a static, essentially unalterable view of society in which we are forever doomed to a dominator model. Foucault ignores the fact that there have in modern times been fundamental political and social changes, such as the shift from monarchies to republics, the abolition of slavery, and the gradual movement toward a more equitable family. Moreover, he ignores the fact that as psychology has amply documented, talking about once forbidden subjects is basic to healing. Only by articulating matters loaded with fears, false guilts, and distortions can we begin to see these matters from a different perspective. For a recent critique of Foucault's writings about sexuality from still another perspective, see Giddens 1992. Giddens points to a basic problem with Foucault's work: that in his discourse on sex he adopts a very conventional and (as we will explore, stereotypically "macho") stance on sex, which ignores both gender and intimacy—matters that, as Giddens points out, are basic to sex.

CHAPTER 1: FROM RITUAL TO ROMANCE
(Pp. 15–33)

1. As I will develop in Chapter 3, when I use the term *Goddess* I do not mean a female mirror image of what we today call God. We do not know if the word *Goddess* was used by our prehistoric ancestors. But in terms of the language available to us today, it expresses what so impressed our ancestors: the creative female power as symbolic of the life force that animates our universe.
2. Gimbutas 1989, 99.
3. Ibid., 260, and Gadon 1989, 43.
4. Gimbutas 1989, Plate 9.
5. Johnson 1988, 130, 131.
6. Gimbutas 1989, 102.
7. Gadon 1989, 18–19.
8. Marshack 1991, 293.

9. Gimbutas 1989, 231.
10. Ibid., 103.
11. Gadon 1989, 129. I will sometimes use the term *sacred marriage,* because it is a well-known description of sacral sex. But I prefer the term *sacred union.*
12. Accounts of how pornographic films are made bring out this lack of caring. Women tell how they are often in acute pain during filming, and how (as in the famous case of Linda Lovelace) they are sometimes terrorized by the men who profit from their services. See Barry 1979; Griffin 1981; Lovelace 1987; Steinem 1983.
13. *Hustler* also shows pictures of nude or scantily clad women in degrading positions, such as a woman having her face pushed into a toilet. A few years ago, this image was actually part of an ad to increase *Hustler* subscriptions (*Hustler,* July 1992). In a more recent issue of *Hustler* (January 1994), we find a woman with a leash around her neck on her hands and knees sniffing a puddle of urine while a man stands over her—together with a request urging readers to send in their own ideas for degrading photos of women.
14. *Penthouse,* December 1984; *Hustler,* June 1978.
15. Barry 1979, particularly chapter 4.
16. This was dramatically brought out when the American football hero O. J. Simpson was arrested on charges of brutally killing his ex-wife. She had repeatedly told police she was afraid he would kill her, begging them to do something about it instead of just talking to him and leaving. Even when Simpson was arrested on one occasion when he punched and kicked her so hard she was hospitalized, he only received two years probation—a sentence the city attorney who prosecuted the case called "a joke." In contrast, in San Diego, California, where the police formed a domestic violence task force, homicides decreased (Hastings 1994). For a recent article on the psychopathology of batterers, cautioning that short-term treatments may give the women living with them a false sense of security, see Vaselle-Horner and Ehrlich 1992.
17. Hoffman 1994; estimate of Child Sexual Abuse Treatment Program, reported in Stark 1984. Many books have been written about violence against women in the United States. For example, in *Intimate Violence: A Study of Injustice* (1989), Blackman discusses victim blaming, noting that this makes it possible not to identify with the victim, minimizing the observer's distress. Gordon's and Riger's *The Female Fear: The Social Cost of Rape* (1989) musters evidence in support of Brownmiller's (1975) contention that all men benefit from rape because it leads women to believe they must have a man to protect them from other men. Anthropologist Peggy Reeves Sanday's *Fraternity Gang Rape: Sex, Brotherhood, and Privilege on Campus* (1990), a study of gang rape (or "pulling train" as it is called by fraternity members), concludes that these exclusive male clubs reinforce male privilege by introducing adolescent boys to their future place in the male status hierarchy, conditioning men to interpret women's behavior as consensual and thus feel no guilt, and in fact be proud of their behavior.
18. *Women's International Network News* 16 (Summer 1990), 40. (*WIN News* is available from 187 Grant Street, Lexington, MA 02173.)
19. For the latest update of one of the first works in this area, see Hosken, *The Hosken Report: Genital and Sexual Mutilation of Females,* 4th ed. (1994). See also El Daree, *Sudan: National Study on the Epidemiology of Female Circumcision* (1980); Botti, "The Battle Against Excisions by Africans: A Survey of Actions in Three West African Countries" (1985); Salah Abu Bakr, *The Effect of Vulval Mutilation on the Nerve Supply: Anatomical Considerations,* Ministry of Health, Sudan (the monograph establishes these operations deprive women of the ability to enjoy genital sensation). There are numerous other materials, including the section on Genital and Sexual Mutilations of Females in every issue of *WIN News.* Alice Walker's 1992 novel *Possessing the Secret of Joy* deals with this issue from the perspective of an African-American woman. Clitorectomy is by no means exclusive to Africa, the Middle East, and Asia. In the West, the use of clitorectomies by physicians during the nineteenth century as a "cure for nymphomania" has been well documented (see Chapter 14).
20. A 1993 mailing from Women Living Under Muslim Laws prepared by Equality Now (Women's Action 5.1, November 1993) points out that even though girls have been taught to look forward to this mutilation as a rite of passage to womanhood, it leaves

even those who survive it with lifelong problems, including pain during intercourse and extreme complications during childbirth. The mailing includes a poem by Swido-Aidos, which won first prize in a poetry competition for female poets of Benadir, appealing to "all peace-loving people" to "protect, support, give a hand to innocent little girls." It appeals to recipients to write UNICEF urging it to fund the work of grassroots activists fighting to eradicate female genital mutilation.

21. See Chapters 5 and 6.
22. Brown 1965, 38–40.
23. Highwater 1990.
24. Foucault 1980. Ironically, despite his emphasis on politics and how sexuality has been used to maintain domination, Foucault takes the sexual domination of women so for granted that he ignores this most basic aspect of sexual politics. Some works dealing with how images of sex and the body are socially constructed that take this into account are Butler 1993; Giddens 1992; Laqueur 1990; and Nead 1992.
25. Pagels 1988.
26. St. Augustine, *City of God*, Book XIII, Chapter 14.
27. Kramer and Sprenger 1971.
28. Pagels 1988, 113.
29. Chapter 8 of *The Chalice and the Blade* details how early or so-called "primitive" Christianity—following the lead of Jesus—was an important partnership movement. But it also documents how the "orthodox" Church—with its rigid all-male priestly hierarchies, its authoritarianism, and its systematic violence through inquisitions, witch-hunts, and crusades—again became a dominator institution.
30. Harris and Levey 1975.
31. Highwater 1990, 95.
32. See Martin Luther, "Sermon of 1537," in Wehr 1990, 73. See also Wehr 1990, 32, quoting Luther on how "God chooses a Church for his Son to take for his own as a bride."
33. See, for example, Campbell 1974, 59. But see Atkinson for how, in the context of the male-dominated society of that time, the Christian idealization of motherhood that during the late Middle Ages accompanied the rise of devotion to the Virgin Mary became still another means for men to control women's sexuality, and with this, women's life choices.
34. Campbell 1974, 66.
35. Walker 1988, 9.
36. Song of Solomon 4:3, 5, King James Version. Scholars today question the accuracy of some King James Version lyrics. But because it is faithful to the basic themes of the Hebrew text (the pleasures of erotic love and the bounties of nature) and because its language is so well known, I have chosen it in preference to less familiar translations. A recent translation that more closely follows the original text is Falk 1990. Falk notes that, in her words, the Song of Songs "offers a thoroughly nonsexist view of heterosexual love" (Falk 1990, 134). As she writes, "Women in the Song speak as assertively as men, initiating action at least as often; so too, men are free to be as gentle, as vulnerable, even as coy" (ibid.). She also points out that many of the poetic fragments in the Song of Songs derive from what she calls "spring songs" celebrating the fruitfulness of nature (ibid., 154).
37. Song of Solomon 1:2, 13, King James Version.
38. Song of Solomon 2:12, King James Version.
39. Dartmouth Bible. See also 512–513 of the Dartmouth Bible for a summary of some interpretations of the meaning of the Song of Songs.
40. In line with the archaeological data we will examine indicating that prehistoric Goddess worship originated in societies that were more generally peaceful and egalitarian (the partnership model) is the passage in Jeremiah 44:17 where the men explain to him that they will not heed his orders to stop their wives from burning incense, offering libations, and baking cakes for the Queen of Heaven, because in the days when these practices prevailed there was peace and prosperity. They tell him: ". . . for then we had plenty of victuals, and were well, and saw no evil. But since we left off to burn incense to the Queen of

Heaven, and to pour out drink offerings unto her, we have wanted all things, and have been consumed by the sword and by the famine" (Jeremiah 44:17, Dartmouth Bible). For a discussion of the importance of the Goddess in Hebrew tradition, see Patai 1978.

41. In his book *The Sacred Marriage Rite* (1969) the Sumerologist Samuel Noah Kramer also makes the connection between the Song of Songs and the much earlier Inanna hymns. These older traditions can help explain why the Shulamite, as the representative of the Goddess, is black. This point is brought out by Birnbaum 1993. As Birnbaum notes, the lingering images of Black Madonnas (450 images are known still to exist throughout the world) harken back to a time when the Goddess was worshiped as the Earth Mother. According to her, the darkness of these images symbolizes the darkness of the earth.

42. Co-option, or the absorption and distortion of threatening elements and/or individuals into ruling structures, does not necessarily imply conscious intent. Although sometimes it is conscious, more often it is unconscious. In either event, it serves to neutralize threats to the established order—as when former leaders of opposition groups are absorbed into existing power structures.

43. Pagels 1988, 29.

44. See *The Chalice and the Blade,* Chapter 10.

45. The history of witch burning is pivotal to an understanding of Western history. See Christ 1987 and Appendix A, "The Burning Times," in Starhawk 1982. See also Atkinson 1991 for the suggestion that the large surplus of women over men, and thus the threat of large numbers of unmarried or "masterless" women, was a factor behind this large-scale torture and murder of women during the late Middle Ages. There is a great deal of controversy about how many women were killed. Some have placed estimates as high as several million. In her recent book, *Witchcraze: A New History of the European Witch Hunts* (1994), Anne Llewellyn Barstow places the figure closer to one hundred thousand—still an enormous number of women when one considers the size of the European population at that time. In this haunting book, Barstow amply supports her contention that "in much of Western Europe in the peak years of the craze, any woman might have felt like a hunted animal" (ibid., 148).

46. In Judeo-Christian tradition, this vilification of woman begins much earlier, as reflected in the Genesis story blaming Eve for humanity's ills. In addition, popular proverbs and tales derided women's intelligence, criticized them for speaking too much, for being vain and untrustworthy, and for the "uncleanliness" of their reproductive organs. But around 1300, accusations of witchcraft began. That this was *not* a spontaneous outbreak of mass hysteria and violence (as is sometimes claimed) but an officially blessed mass persecution of women is evidenced by the fact that in 1486 the Dominicans Heinrich Kramer and Jacob Sprenger published the *Malleus Maleficarum (Hammer of the Witches)*, with the approval of the pope. Sprenger and Kramer imagined women's sexual intercourse with Satan, and that so joined, women became the devil's followers. They prescribed procedures for dealing with these women, accused of everything from orgies on "Witches Sabbaths," cannibalism of newborns, gluttony, drunkenness, lewd dancing, intercourse with every variety of creature in every possible position, as well as making men impotent and women miscarry and driving horses mad (Anderson and Zinsser 1988, 164–166). They also believed that torture would free women from the devil's power. As a result, many confessions were obtained through torture.

As Anderson and Zinsser write: "Neighbors and relatives accused each other. Once accused, the victim could think of others. Almost always the village named women, often those outcast by choice or by poverty, women living outside the traditional patterns of their village's expectations." Usually, they continue, they "were the women ready to speak back, to quarrel, to curse those who angered or frightened them." It could be a diviner, a woman villagers believed could change the weather, a midwife. So "throughout Europe the wisewomen known for their cures and their curses were accused" (ibid., 168). By the end of the 1500s in some regions of Europe, no one could say anymore who was a witch and who was not. Starting as early as 1613 in the Netherlands, authorities began to refuse to hear new accusations. By the middle of the seventeenth century the horror of the witch-hunts began to end, closing what Anderson and

Zinsser rightly call "the most hideous example of misogyny in European history" (ibid., 172). Nonetheless, witch-hunts and executions sporadically continued during the eighteenth century in both Europe and the Americas.

47. See, for example, Faulkner 1985.

48. As Barstow writes, there is no question that this was a violent persecution of women, a deliberate attempt to terrorize women. To write about it in other terms is tantamount, as she puts it, to writing about the Nazi Holocaust, in which the majority of victims were Jewish, "without mentioning the fact that this was a violent persecution of Jews" (Barstow 1994, 4).

49. By then, the Church had completely desexed her, and male deities were the only depictions of the divine. But the Blessed Mother was still seen by the people as the divinity one prayed to, even though this was not the view of the religious authorities.

50. Some scholars such as Barbara Welter argue that when men idealize women it is still another device to maintain male dominance (Welter 1976, 21–41). Welter bases her argument on the Victorian idealization of female "virtue" I discuss in Chapter 14. But while there are certainly such crosscurrents in the troubadour literature, unlike the Victorian ideal woman, in these love songs female power rather than female powerlessness is emphasized.

51. Anderson and Zinsser 1988. As early as the eleventh century in the Rhone Valley of Provence, noblewomen were composing songs and poetic narratives. Of the 400 known singers and poets, or troubadours, 20 were women, called in the language of Provence "trobaritzes." Usually wives and daughters of landed noble families, they also sang of courtly love. But as Anderson and Zinsser point out, their verses ignored many of the formal trappings of the men's verses. In the free conversational tone of their poems, they idealized neither the lover nor love. Instead, they were direct, practical, sensual, and alternately expressed happiness, anger, sorrow, and passion (Anderson and Zinsser 1988, 307).

52. The trobaritz songs in particular stressed the character and behavior of the man, whether he was generous, upright, and wise, with intelligence and common sense. Or as one such song put it, whether he "be frank and humble, not pick fights with any man, be courteous with everyone . . . noble, loving and discrete . . . " (ibid., 307–308).

CHAPTER 2: ANIMAL RITES AND HUMAN CHOICES
(Pp. 34–52)

1. See, for example, Trivers 1985.

2. In recent sociobiological writings much is made of female choice. But generally in these discussions it is still males who present choices to females by actively soliciting sex, with females either accepting or rejecting them—even though females in a number of species (particularly among primates) frequently "present" to males, thus actively initiating sexual intercourse.

3. Fortunately, this is beginning to change. Examples of sociobiological works that either focus on females or present a more gender-balanced picture are Fisher 1992; Hrdy 1981; Kevles 1986; and Morbeck, Zihlman, and Galloway, in press. In fact, one of the debates of the last ten years has been whether the vast array of male reproductive traits has evolved (1) due to arbitrary female preferences for certain traits or (2) because choices of "attractive" characteristics are often correlated with functional qualities.

4. Some of these books have been highly publicized, for example, Ardrey's *The Territorial Imperative* (1966), which received enormous media coverage.

5. Even scientists such as E. O. Wilson sometimes make such inferences. For example, in his famous book *Sociobiology*, after citing selected animal and insect data to support his argument that male animals are fundamentally polygamous because the siring of more offspring by the "fittest" males gives an evolutionary advantage to the whole species (Wilson 1975, 327), Wilson contends that "reproductive advantages conferred by dominance" extend to our human species—supporting this with the sole example of the

Yanomama Indians of Brazil, a rigidly male-dominant, highly warlike tribe in which female infanticide is practiced and in which, according to one anecdotal anthropological account, the headman (who is polygamous) was said to be more intelligent than the other, nonpolygamous males (ibid., 288).

6. Books such as Kitcher's *Vaulting Ambition: Sociobiology and the Quest for Human Nature* (1985); Lewontin's, Rose's, and Kamin's *Not in Our Genes* (1984); Montagu's *Sociobiology Examined* (1980); and *Genes and Gender* edited by Tobach and Rosoff (1978) detail the fallacies of trying to "explain" human behaviors on this basis.

7. It is sometimes argued, particularly by primatologists, that because other primates in many ways foreshadow human capacities and behaviors, we are not all that unique. Certainly we share many traits with other primates. (See, for example, McGrew 1992, showing that the use of rudimentary tools is found among chimpanzees.) But if we look at human culture—not only human technology but the vast storehouse of ideas (including philosophy, science, poetry, etc.), images (including painting, sculpture, and film), as well as music and other unique human creations—the contrast with even our closest primate relatives, the chimpanzees, with whom we share 99 percent of our genetic heritage, is so vast that the term *unique* is appropriate. And while a 1 percent genetic difference between humans and chimpanzees may not seem that great, it is reflected in pivotal evolutionary changes, such as human genes that make it possible for our cranial bone structures to remain open after birth, thereby making possible further brain growth, and with this, the much greater mental capacities that distinguish our species.

8. De Waal 1989, 269. Other scholars, such as Jeanne Altmann, Tim Ransom, Thelma Rowell, Barbara Smuts, Nancy Tanner, and Adrienne Zihlman, have also emphasized the importance of affiliation and cooperation in primate social behaviors.

9. De Waal notes that even in adversarial situations, "the contested resource often is simply not worth putting a valuable relationship at risk, and if aggression does occur, both parties may hurry to repair the damage" (de Waal 1989, 270).

10. See Goldizen 1989.

11. Interestingly, this point was also made by E. O. Wilson, although the way he presents his ideas unfortunately sometimes contradicts this.

12. Csanyi 1989; Sahtouris 1989; Loye 1990, and work in progress b; Chaisson 1987; Capra 1982; Laszlo 1987. A number of these scholars are members of the General Evolution Research Group, of which Loye and I are two of the founding members.

13. Although there is some controversy about this, the generally accepted hypothesis is that this is why we find sexual reproduction in so many species. As Jerold M. Lowenstein writes, "So advantageous is sexual reproduction that it has evolved separately a number of times in a variety of different modes." This independent experimentation by nature in species as different as reptiles (where the sex of offspring is sometimes determined by the weather) and fish (where individuals sometimes alternate between being male and female) is humorously examined in Lowenstein 1992.

14. Because radiocarbon dating is only accurate to about fifty thousand years ago, there is a great deal of controversy regarding earlier evolutionary dates. I have chosen the figure of sixty-five million used in some recent works (see, for example, Howells 1993, 61).

15. Today most evolutionary biologists do not conceive of evolution by natural selection in this way. Their use of the phrase "survival of the fittest" does not equal "nature red in tooth and claw." It connotes that individuals with the inherent capacity to live and reproduce successfully in a given environment will become the more common variety. That is, in sociobiological terms, the "fittest" individuals are simply those who leave the most copies of their genes in subsequent generations. It is from this perspective that natural selection also seeks to explain the evolution of such things as maternal care, pair bonding, sheltering abilities, photosynthesis, whale song, and bat sonar.

16. Although there is some controversy about this, 250,000 years is the approximate date generally used for the appearance of *homo sapiens* (our own species). Earlier now extinct members of the *genera homo*, going back to *homo habilis,* are generally dated to approximately two million years ago.

17. Like most evolutionary changes, the evolution of human sexuality as a year-round, highly pleasurable, and primarily nonreproductive phenomenon is foreshadowed among other primates. As Frayser points out, primates engage in far more nonreproductive activity than most other mammals. Moreover, as among humans, among most primates, females appear to be just as interested in sex as males, partly because the clitoris is almost universal among primates (Frayser 1985, 41, 37). Like humans and some other mammals, primates sometimes also touch and stimulate their own genitals. So despite the sociobiological emphasis on reproduction (or as they put it, reproductive success), as Frayser writes, like humans, "primates may engage in sexual behavior beyond that necessary for reproduction because it is enjoyable in its own right" (ibid., 44). But although the evolution of nonreproductive year-round sexuality is foreshadowed among other primates, it takes a quantum leap first, as we will see, with the bonobos or pygmy chimpanzees, and then much farther with humans.

18. Although technically the term *hominid* includes our species, I will use it only to designate earlier, now extinct, members of the *genera homo* beginning with Australopithecus.

19. A reason the baboon was used as a model is that it lives in groups on savannahs, as was once believed our ancestors did. Recent discoveries cast doubt on this assumption.

20. See, for example, Rowell 1966 and Smuts 1985.

21. Fedigan 1982, 309.

22. See, for example, Ardrey 1961; Tiger and Fox 1971; and Washburn and Lancaster 1968. For some excellent critiques of these theories, see Fedigan 1982.

23. Recent observations of both common and so-called pygmy chimpanzees indicate they hunt. However, most of their food is not derived from hunting.

24. Zihlman and Tanner 1974; Tanner 1981.

25. Fedigan 1982, 319; McGrew 1992.

26. See Smuts 1985 about baboons. Based on her observations of savannah baboons, Smuts stresses that the female baboons she observed often mated not with the dominant males but with males with whom they had formed a friendship. In other words, rather than choosing the biggest and most aggressive male (presumably, as some sociobiologists tell us, because he has "superior" genes), they preferred males they did not have to fear. But as Smuts, de Waal, and others observe, sometimes a female primate stops having sex with a male because another male punishes her when she does.

27. Kano 1990, 62–70.

28. One reason is that adult bonobos are unlike adult common chimpanzees in important respects, including cranial and dental configuration (Zihlman 1989). Another may be that, as Suehisa Kuroda notes, like humans but unlike common chimps and other apes, bonobos tend to retain infant and juvenile body traits when they are mature—a characteristic called neoteny (Kuroda 1980, 195). This helps explain why pygmy chimpanzees were in the past often thought to be young chimpanzees rather than members of a separate species.

29. Kano 1980, 243. See also de Waal 1989, 178–179. Bonobos died quickly in captivity. Even now there are only approximately fifty bonobos in laboratories and zoos (compared to thousands of captive common chimpanzees). Observation of their social behaviors in zoos did not start for some time after they were classified as a separate species.

30. De Waal 1989, 175.

31. As Kano writes, the choice of position differs according to age, with face-to-face copulation more frequent in adolescents than in full adults, although data indicate that females tend to prefer the face-to-face position (Kano 1992, 141–142).

32. De Waal 1989, 199.

33. Kuroda 1980, 181.

34. Kano 1990, 64.

35. Ibid., 65.

36. As Kano writes, "Female bonobos are generally not afraid of males" (Kano 1990, 68). In fact, as the de Waal study of bonobo behavior in zoos brings out, smaller bonobos even tease larger and older ones (de Waal 1989, 195).

37. Kano writes about this at length in *The Last Ape: Pygmy Chimpanzee Behavior and Ecology* (1992).

38. Kano 1980, 243. Kuroda, who like Kano observed pygmy chimpanzees in the Wamba Preserve of Zaire, reports that "the affinitive interactions among the pygmy chimps seem to be the most frequent in the male/female combinations," leading him to conclude that "the pygmy chimp society may be said to be integrated by the male/female affinity, little differentiation by sex in the grouping and the affinitive relations, and by inter-individual tolerance and coherence" (Kuroda 1980, 195). White, who observed bonobos in Lomako rather than Wamba, found that when bonobos travel in smaller groups in which there is sometimes only one male (as contrasted to the typically larger multimale groups found in Wamba), female-female interactions are most important (White 1992). This was also the observation of Amy Parish, who has studied bonobos in captivity, again typically in small groups of five or six members where there is usually only one male (personal communication with Amy Parish, November 1993).

39. A book illustrating this is discussed in Chapter 5: Lila Abu-Lughod, *Veiled Sentiments* (1986). The segregation of women and rigid male dominance was also a major element in the ancient Greek and Hebrew societies we will examine in Chapter 6.

40. De Waal 1989, 195.

41. Kano 1980, 255–256.

42. Kano 1990, 67.

43. De Waal 1989, 199.

44. Ibid.

45. Smuts and Watanabe 1990.

46. The sexual interactions between bonobo females also seem to serve the function of cementing bonds, or alliances, between females, contributing to the fact that despite the male bonobos' somewhat larger size, theirs is not a male-dominated social organization.

47. Kano 1980, 253. As Kano also notes, "Estrous females with genital swelling (those clearly signalling sexual readiness and disposition to mate) were the majority of those involved." But anestrous females were not excluded. And on a few occasions, neither partner was in estrus. Kuroda and de Waal also confirm these sexual interactions.

48. For example, the *Random House Dictionary of the English Language* (2nd ed., 1987) defines *ritual* as "any practice or pattern of behavior regularly performed in a set manner."

49. Savage-Rumbaugh, who has worked extensively with bonobos in the laboratory, also reports frequent food sharing in association with sexual behavior (Savage-Rumbaugh and Wilkerson 1978). Parish's observations in the San Diego, Frankfurt, and Stuttgart zoos were that the majority of sex-for-food exchanges were among females and females. It is not clear whether this is the case in the wild (personal communications with Parish, October 1993).

50. Kano 1990, 70.

51. De Waal 1989, 261.

52. New field observations indicate that bonobos do more hunting than was previously thought. However, contrary to the "man the hunter" hypothesis, both males and females hunt. In most cases, the meat is shared with others (Hohmann and Fruth 1993).

53. Kuroda 1980, 195–196. Barbara Smuts also reports that among nonhuman primates, females and males can develop close bonds based on reciprocal sharing of social (versus material) benefits, as she observed among baboons. She proposes that hominids developed such bonds long before the evolution of a division of labor and that such bonds probably facilitated the development of food sharing among hominids and early humans (letter to author from Barbara Smuts, February 1, 1994; Smuts 1985).

54. Kano 1992, particularly Chapters 6, 7, and 8.

55. Kano 1990, 69.

56. Ibid. Such protection of young has also been observed in savannah baboons, among which adult males develop special bonds with the offspring of their close female associates (Smuts 1985).

57. Kano 1990, 62. As has happened with other species, such continuing violence may significantly alter bonobo behavior and social organization, pushing them toward more aggression and violence—until the bonobos as an intact species, or even as a species at all, cease to exist.

58. Zihlman, quoted in Schell 1991, 41.
59. For a recent article integrating what we are now learning about bonobos into an overview of primate and hominid evolution, see Zihlman 1989. Zihlman's theory that humans and chimpanzees diverged from a common ancestor resembling a small chimpanzee similar to the bonobo about five million years ago is based on both molecular and anatomical evidence. It also would support the view that in primate evolution a multilinear rather than a unilinear approach is more appropriate.
60. By this I do not mean to imply that animal and human behaviors can be evaluated by the same standards. For instance, among common chimpanzees, male control over females is individual and not institutionalized, as among some human societies.
61. Parish 1994; Smuts and Smuts 1993; Wrangham 1993. As Smuts and Smuts write, "Bonobo females, in contrast to chimpanzee females, routinely ally with one another against males" and thereby "gain protection from male aggression" (ibid., 34). And as both Smuts and Parish note, this has important implications for the contemporary attempts of women to organize. I will return to this subject in Part II. Here I want to address an issue raised in Parish's paper. Parish observed a group of captive bonobos in the Stuttgart Zoo in which the lone young male was on one occasion seriously injured in an attack by a female (as has also happened to the lone male in a number of other zoos). Parish believes that this may indicate that the use of force by females against males may also be common among bonobos in the wild, even though there have been no field reports of this. She may be correct, but I believe that drawing conclusions about patterns of aggression from studies of animals in captivity is problematic. Just as there is a high level of frustration, tension, and aggression among incarcerated humans, these factors must be considered in evaluating studies of the behavior of animals in captivity. Moreover, the composition of a group in the wild is not externally determined, as it is in a zoo. Nor are animals forced to stay with a particular group, as they are in captivity. Furthermore, there are indications that in bonobo social organization in the wild the young males in a group are sometimes the sons of the older and more powerful females—a situation very different from that of the lone males placed in all-female groups in captivity. So while there is undoubtedly some violence by older females against males in the wild, with the threat of this violence serving to deter male aggression against females, I would suggest that it is probably more extreme in captivity—a conclusion that seems congruent with evidence that although there is some violence among bonobos in the wild, it is not as severe or common as among common chimpanzees.
62. Kano 1990, 68. For example, Kano reports that Hata, a male in his prime, backed off rather than attacked after being threatened by Kiku, a female who was "smaller, weaker physically, young, and had been a group member for only a few years"—and whose "mobility was limited because of her clinging infant" (ibid.).
63. Wrangham 1993.
64. Kano 1990, 70.
65. Letter to author from Barbara Smuts, February 1, 1994. Smuts also notes that "female bonobos seem content to use their power primarily to thwart male aggression toward themselves (see Smuts and Smuts 1992 on this, pp. 34–35) and also, under some conditions, to gain priority of access to valuable resources (Parish)" (same letter from Smuts).
66. De Chardin 1959. After Darwin introduced his theories on evolution, documenting that life on this planet was not created in one fell swoop a few thousand years ago (as claimed by the biblical account) but evolved over billions of years, some nineteenth-century theorists tried to impute a divine purpose to this process. Contemporary systems thinking about evolution rejects this idea of an unfolding divine plan.
67. Eisler and Csanyi, unfinished manuscript; personal communications with Csanyi from 1988 to 1993.
68. Some primate females have very large clitorises (for example, the bonobos), so one could argue that they have very intense orgasms. However, the duration of the intercourse (not to speak of the orgasm) among monkeys and apes is extremely short. Also, there seems to be no aftermath (they usually just saunter off). Their facial expressions

are in some species indicative of indifference, if not boredom. Hence it is difficult to believe that theirs is the kind of experience that for humans can provide such ecstasy.

69. Sarah Blaffer Hrdy has proposed an alternate theory for the development of year-round sexuality and the capacity for multiple orgasms (Hrdy 1988).

70. Maturana and Varela 1987, 219–220.

71. Personal communications from Csanyi; Eisler and Csanyi, unfinished manuscript. Fisher (1992) makes a similar argument, though based on a different theory.

72. A documentary film of the Musuo (shown at the 1987 International Real-Life Film Festival in Paris) was made in 1986 by Tiensung Su, who with a Beijing film producer and camera team spent a half year in a canyon surrounded by primeval forest in the high mountains where Tibet, Yunan, and Sichun provinces overlap. The film was named "The Locale of Goddesses," apparently because, as Tiensung Su writes in his description of the film, "Goddess Gemu is the most beautiful and respectable Goddess among Musuo people." This description, based on the narration of the film, describes the Musuo as "a primitive matriarchy" in accordance with the terminology of the nineteenth-century anthropologist Lewis Henry Morgan, whose ideas it adopts. But it is a society where women and men play important roles (the women primarily in economic decision-making and the men in politics), and which in other respects can also more accurately be described as orienting primarily to the partnership model. The Musuo (or Moso, as it is sometimes spelled) are also described by Chuankang Shih in "The Yongning Moso," Ph.D. dissertation, Department of Anthropology, Stanford University, 1993, and by Naiqun Weng in "The Mother House," Ph.D. dissertation, Department of Anthropology, Rochester University, 1993. Some scholars believe that while the matrilinear structure is old, the custom of sexual partners only sleeping together at night but maintaining separate domiciles, is not (private communication with Steven Harrell, January 16, 1995). I want to express my appreciation to Professor Harrell for information about the ethnic customs and background of the people in this region, where there is an admixture of many cultural strains.

73. Most of the !Kung now live in a harsh environment, but there are indications that this is so because they were forced to migrate there. Even so, their environment is not so harsh as to require constant foraging.

74. However, there are indications that even in these harsh environments societies do not inevitably have to develop a dominator social organization.

75. It is interesting that Kano believes that the year-long sexual receptivity in hominids and humans developed in environments where food was abundant (Kano 1992, 217) and that the mother-centered type of family found among pygmy chimpanzees (with strong bonds between mothers and sons) may have been the basis for a human family of shared bonds between females and males and mutual care of offspring (ibid.).

76. This is discussed in detail in Part II.

CHAPTER 3: SEX AS SACRAMENT
(Pp. 53–71)

1. For a book documenting how Western science has basically been a male club, see David Noble, *A World Without Women: The Christian Clerical Culture of Western Science* (1992).

2. See, for example, Eisler 1987a; Gimbutas 1991; Marshack 1991.

3. Marshack 1991, 297.

4. Gadon 1989, 16–17; Gimbutas 1989, 105, Figure 173.

5. Marshack 1991, 171.

6. Ibid., 173 (emphasis in original).

7. Ibid.

8. Leroi-Gourhan 1971, 120.

9. These kinds of traditions were also found not so long ago in a number of Native American cultures and other tribal societies. For example, the Creek Indians celebrated a Green Corn Festival that used to include a night of "free love."

10. In this sense, I believe that the earliest religion was probably closer to what we call monotheistic. But it was monotheistic in a nonexclusionary way, as many of the same attributes and functions of different aspects of the deity were found in different cultures.
11. Marshack 1991, 318.
12. Turnbull 1961.
13. I will return to this subject in a more contemporary context in Chapter 15.
14. As noted in Chapter 1, B.C.E. (before the Common Era) is preferred by contemporary scholars to B.C. (before Christ) because it is a more ecumenical, more culturally inclusive term. It has recently been adopted by the American Academy of Religion.
15. Gadon 1989, 10.
16. This is not to say that they understood, as we do now, how the female ova and the male semen combine to produce life, much less that each parent contributes an equal number of chromosomes to their offspring. Indeed, these facts were not known until very recently, as even nineteenth-century scientific authorities like Herbert Spencer still insisted that woman's womb is no more than the soil in which the male seed grows—in other words, that only men are the life-givers. But contrary to what we still read in many books about the Paleolithic and the Neolithic, there are in both Paleolithic and Neolithic art strong indications that these people were fully aware of the relationship between sexual union and procreation.
17. The archaeologist Marija Gimbutas believes that the bucrania of Çatal Hüyük are the female uterus and fallopian tubes. I do not agree, although it is possible that they had more than one meaning, as symbols often do.
18. Mellaart 1967, 148.
19. Not surprisingly, if only because they bred domestic animals.
20. Gimbutas 1982, 228–230.
21. Ibid., 188.
22. Goodison 1989.
23. Ibid., 45.
24. Gimbutas writes that in prehistory, "the worship of the sun (definitely as Goddess of Regeneration herself) is well known in such famous monuments as New Grange in Ireland or Gavrinis in Brittany." She also notes that "this was the worship of the Winter sun and the monuments are aligned with the rising of the Winter sun." So, as she writes, there was in northern European tradition not only the Indo-European sun god (the god of the shining sun associated with the seasons of the year), but the association of the sun with the Goddess of Old Europe (letter to author from Gimbutas, November 14, 1992).
25. Leviticus 12:6–7, King James Version.
26. Patai 1978.
27. For a new scholarly work analyzing some of these narratives, as well as other Mesopotamian texts showing the important role of both female deities and priestesses and other temple officials, see Henshaw 1994.
28. Wolkstein and Kramer 1983, 125.
29. Ibid., xiii, 124.
30. Ibid., 116. Similarly, in *Myths of Enki, The Crafty God,* which he wrote with John Maier, Kramer again writes of this shift, this time using the conceptual framework introduced in *cultural transformation theory.* He writes that power shifted from the *ensi* (the earlier title for the chief political authority) to the *lugal* and that "within this change may be glimpsed what Riane Eisler calls a 'cultural transformation' . . . from a 'partnership' society, in which diversity of role is not equated with inferiority and superiority, to a 'dominator' society, in which roles—especially sex roles—are ranked on the basis of superior and inferior" (Kramer and Maier 1989, 19).
31. Wolkstein and Kramer 1983, 33.
32. Ibid., 37.
33. Ibid.
34. Ibid., 37–38.
35. Ibid., 39.
36. Ibid., 42.
37. Ibid., 43.

38. Ibid., 39, 41.
39. Ibid., 47.
40. Gadon 1989, 129.

CHAPTER 4: SEX AND CIVILIZATION
(Pp. 72–83)

1. See, for example, Eisler 1987a; Gimbutas 1982, 1989, 1991; Mellaart 1967; Platon 1966.
2. Gylany is a composite of gy (from the Greek gyne or woman) and an (from andros or man). The l between them is the first letter of the Greek verb lyos, which has the double meaning of set free (as in catalysis) and resolve (as in analysis). In English the l stands for linking.
3. See Chapter 7, as well as The Chalice and the Blade, for a discussion of how Cain (the farmer) is accused of being the aggressor in this story that, like so much of Western mythology, is written from the perspective of the victors (the pastoralist invaders we will get to in the chapter that follows).
4. Hesiod, Works and Days. Quoted in Robinson 1968, 12–13.
5. As noted before, I distinguish between hierarchies of domination and actualization.
6. See Chapter 7 for a discussion of this. For example, that the hybrid, fantastic figures of this earlier art are not yet dualistic is borne out by Lambert 1987, 37–52. Lambert shows that the representation of the Gorgon Medussa derives from earlier Humbaba figures, which were even before that representations of the lahama—creatures of the sea, usually thought to be quite benevolent. See also Kramer and Maier 1989, 45, where the lahama "speak tenderly to Enki."
7. For these concepts see Sheldrake 1988 and Laszlo 1993.
8. Gimbutas 1991, 324.
9. See ibid., 324, and Gimbutas 1989, p. xx. Gimbutas writes: "The difficulty with the term matriarchy in twentieth century anthropological scholarship is that it is assumed to represent a complete mirror image of patriarchy or androcracy—that is to say, a hierarchical structure with women ruling by force in place of men. This is far from the reality of Old Europe. Indeed, we do not find in Old Europe, nor in all of the Old World, a system of autocratic rule by women with an equivalent suppression of men. Rather, we find a structure in which the sexes are more or less on equal footing, a society that could be termed a gylany. This is a term coined by Riane Eisler . . . I use the term matristic simply to avoid the term matriarchy, with the understanding that it incorporates matriliny" (Gimbutas 1991, 324).
10. As Frank et al. (1990) note, the Basque (who still survive in the Pyrenees in southwestern France and northern Spain, but occupied a much larger area in Roman times) were characterized by an indigenous religious belief system in which the worship of a Mother Goddess figure known as Andrea Mari played a prominent role. In the family, the wife was known as "Mistress of the House." Upon marriage, the male moved into his wife's home and assumed her name. Though inheritance laws did not discriminate against male children, upon marriage the husband could not sell or otherwise alienate any of the marital property, even though he was charged with the task of increasing the wealth of the house through proper management and hard work. To ensure the protection of the family's assets, only women could do this. Women also served as religious representatives or spokespersons of the family unit, as well as representatives to political assemblies, and apparently this continued as late as the sixteenth century. After the institution of the Napoleonic Codes, Basque women lost most of their traditional rights (against which they protested vigorously, but with no success). Even now, though the position of Basque women is nothing like what it once was, there are traces of a different earlier social organization. It is noteworthy that the world famous Mondragon cooperative is a Basque institution (Frank et al. 1990, 133–157).
11. It may well be that in the less violent prehistoric societies we have been examining, men took a far greater role in child care than men characteristically do in highly warlike and

male-dominated societies, as these were societies in which *both* women and "feminine" behaviors could be more highly valued. For a recent study on the relation between greater male participation in child care, greater gender equity, and less aggressive behaviors in males, see Coltrane 1992. See also Chapter 12.

12. Gimbutas 1991, 324.
13. Mara Keller has recently proposed the phrase "Chthonic Crete" to describe the Goddess-worshiping civilization of Crete. "Chthonia" was a term the ancients used to refer to Crete (Keller 1992).
14. Willetts 1977, 112–113.
15. Platon 1966.
16. See Eisler 1987a, 105–106; Eisler and Loye 1990.
17. Gimbutas sometimes uses the term *temple-palace* as a compromise (letter to author from Marija Gimbutas, November 14, 1992).
18. This is how a Mexican bull-vaulting film was made, as I was informed in Heraklion, Crete, September 1992. I was also informed that there was a group in Crete trying to recreate this process by raising bulls and practicing bull-vaulting with them beginning when they were still very small.
19. As Willetts notes, "Although scenes of ceremony are common in Minoan art, no kingly figure takes part in or presides over any of them." Willetts also points out that "there is massive pictorial evidence, from the Miniature Frescoes onwards, for the predominant position of women in such scenes and in Minoan culture as a whole" (Willetts 1977, 112).
20. Ibid., 111.
21. Gimbutas points out that these themes are also often found in the island of Santori or Thera (letter to author from Marija Gimbutas, November 14, 1992).
22. Willetts 1977, 113.
23. Hawkes 1968, 131.
24. Ibid.
25. Ibid., 134.
26. Letter to author from Kjell Aartun, February 7, 1991. If Aartun is right, we may have still another confirmation that the sacred marriage was an important rite in Minoan Crete. This information could provide another link in the chain of evidence that for thousands of years—from the Paleolithic twenty-five thousand years ago to the Bronze Age civilization of Minoan Crete only thirty-five hundred years ago—sex was a religious rite and sexuality and spirituality were inextricably intertwined.
27. Hawkes 1968, 113.
28. Ibid., 110.
29. Ibid., 113.
30. Hawkes notes that "at least from the time of the later palaces the men usually kept their hair long, allowing it to fall down their backs, and often, like the women, bringing locks forward to hang in front of the ears" (Hawkes 1968, 113). She further notes that although sexual differences are accentuated, in many ways the bodies of women and men are in their litheness, general size, and emphasis on a small waist rather similar.
31. As noted earlier, the various Minoan city-states, and even their shorelines, were generally unfortified. For more details on the partnership elements in Minoan civilization, see Eisler 1987a.
32. For a discussion of these terms in the context of *cultural transformation theory,* see *The Chalice and the Blade,* especially xvii–xxiii, 135–137, 173–203.

CHAPTER 5: FROM EROS TO CHAOS
(Pp. 84–102)

1. Hesiod, *Theog,* 116. Quoted in Harrison 1962, 626.
2. Harrison 1962, 630.
3. Ibid., 647.

4. As Harrison points out, this is clear not only from philosophical and poetic writings but also from classical artistic depictions (Ibid., 647). For a book illustrating the further transformation of Eros, first during Roman times to a small child, and then during Christian times to images of angels, see Kunstmann 1964.

5. Harris and Levey 1975, 888.

6. Ibid.

7. Engels 1972.

8. De Beauvoir 1968, Chapter 5.

9. Ibid., 75.

10. Childe 1958, 109, 119, 123.

11. Mallory 1989, 259–260.

12. Ibid., 266.

13. Ibid., 270. To this day, Childe's legacy of the idealization of the Indo-Europeans as the "promoters of true progress" lingers on. One of its latest revivals has come from the British archaeologist Colin Renfrew, who recently argued that rather than heralding the destruction of earlier European farming societies, the Indo-Europeans were themselves the farmers (Renfrew 1988). But, as Mallory points out, Renfrew's claim that it was actually due to the Indo-Europeans that farming was developed and spread from Anatolia into the European continent is contrary to the evidence, as there is no question that the Indo-European incursions into Europe that began in the late fifth and early fourth millennia B.C.E. were by pastoralists. As Mallory also notes, Renfrew's thesis contradicts the archaeological evidence indicating farming was introduced in both Anatolia and in Europe long before the Indo-European incursions. Mallory also curtly dismisses Renfrew's claim that Indo-European languages spread not by conquest but along with "the peaceful diffusion of agriculture" by Neolithic Indo-Europeans from Anatolia. He writes: "Any attempt to tie the initial Neolithic (farming) colonization of Europe to the spread of the earliest Indo-Europeans is really not congruent with either the linguistic or archaeological evidence and, indeed, does not even provide the economy of explanation which should have been one of its major attractions. Anatolia is the wrong place at the wrong time, and migrations from it give the wrong results" (Mallory 1989, 181).

14. The evidence indicates that initially through force and fear, and then also through fundamental institutional and ideological changes, this new population group gradually came to control more and more of the economic, religious, artistic, and even mythical (not to speak of military) contexts of the surviving Europeans' lives. So what at first may have continued as bilingual societies (with, as in India, the native populations subordinated as slaves or lower castes) eventually became Indo-European-speaking societies.

15. Mallory 1989, 238.

16. Gimbutas 1991, 399. Gimbutas died in February 1994.

17. Gimbutas 1991, 399.

18. This Indo-European view of what happens after death is reflected in later Greek mythology, where Hades (the realm of the dead) is still described as a dank and dark world where lonely "shades" (or spirits) wander around forlornly. Confusingly, the Greek word *Hades* also describes the god of the underground in Greek mythology.

19. Gimbutas 1991, 400.

20. Gimbutas describes these sacrificial graves as "suttee" burials, a term borrowed from the Indian name for throwing widows (often mere children in his harem) into a man's funeral pyre, which has continued in India to our day—and was also there introduced by the Indo-European or Aryan invaders who conquered the indigenous Goddess-worshiping population. It is sobering to reflect that the Aryan or Vedic-Hindu practice of suttee was promulgated in Hindu scriptures as a sacred, loving "choice" for widows.

21. There is some controversy about whether human sacrifice was practiced in the earlier Goddess-worshiping societies. This is discussed in Chapter 7.

22. See, for example, Numbers 31:9, 17, 18, King James Version.

23. For a more detailed description of this fundamental cultural shift, and how the process was not only one of armed conquest, see *The Chalice and the Blade,* Chapters 4, 6, and 7.

24. Mallory 1989, 222; map on 144.

25. For a discussion of why the Nazis drew so much from Indo-European mythology, as well as some of the similarities between them and the Kurgans, see Eisler 1987a, Chapter 12.
26. Taylor 1954.
27. DeMeo 1986, maps on 425.
28. DeMeo 1991.
29. Ibid., 249.
30. DeMeo was heavily influenced by the work of Wilhelm Reich, one of the pioneers in the social psychology of sex (see, for example, Reich 1970b and 1971). During the 1940s Reich was sent to prison for defying a court order banning interstate shipment of his "orgone box" and authorizing the banning of all existing copies of his books containing the word *orgone*. Contrary to some accounts, he was never convicted of fraud. In fact, he did not even appear in person to defend what he considered an unethical and malicious persecution. Later he was charged with contempt for technical violations of the original injunction, and at the contempt proceedings he was denied the right to present any evidence. When his appeal was denied, he was thrown in jail, dying shortly afterward (letter to author from James DeMeo, December 6, 1992). During the 1940s and 1950s Reich's work was attacked in some medical journals and scientific books. While Reich's work is still controversial, it is today recognized by many researchers and therapists as an important foundation for body- as well as mind-based therapies.
31. As DeMeo points out, the problem is to some extent semantic, as Reich asserted that sexual repression profoundly affects the "macho," Don Juan character, whom he viewed as "biophysically a very damaged individual" (letter to author from DeMeo, December 6, 1992).
32. Sanday 1981, 158. Sanday's book is a pioneering study presenting an environmentally oriented theory of gender relations, selection of male or female deities, and the incidence of rape, connecting these with whether an environment is hostile or nurturing.
33. The circumcision of boys remains controversial. Some, including DeMeo, believe it is a sadistic and damaging practice. Others staunchly defend it, pointing to studies indicating that it offers a high degree of protection against urinary tract and kidney infections, as well as against cancer of the penis.
34. In Africa, pastoralist villages have recently been encouraged to return to hunting, because it is so much less ecologically damaging to the land and also does not so drastically encroach on other (increasingly scarce) species' habitats.
35. Moore and Gillette 1991, 89.
36. Abu-Lughod 1986, 131–132.
37. Ibid., 149, 150.
38. Ibid., 148.
39. Ibid., 152, 154.
40. Ibid., 153.
41. Ibid., 152.
42. Ibid., 154.
43. Ibid., 155.
44. Ibid., 157, 158.
45. Another social scientist who brings out some of these connections is the sociologist Fatima Mernissi. She writes that in Muslim North African society a man's prestige is linked "in an almost fatal way to the sexual behaviour of the women under his charge, be they his wives, sisters, or unmarried female relatives" (Mernissi 1987, 161). So extreme is this that even a man who has a wife or sister working in an office or going to school "runs a very serious chance of seeing 'his honour soiled'" (ibid.). Mernissi also notes that the differential socialization of boys and girls about sexuality is the source of great tension for both. Whereas men "are encouraged to expect full satisfaction of their sexual desires, and to perceive their masculine identity as closely linked to that satisfaction," women are from an early age "taught to curb their sexual drives" and even told about "the penis's 'destructive' effects . . . " (ibid.). In sharp contrast, Mernissi writes that a boy's penis is "the object of a veritable cult on the part of the women rearing him" and how, "as a boy matures, the fact that men have privileges such as polygamy and repudiation,

which allow them not only to have multiple sexual partners but also to change partners at will, gives him the impression that society is organized to satisfy his sexual wishes" (ibid., 162). But as he meets all the prohibitions that are imposed on having sex (finding out that "if he wants to satisfy his sexual needs, he must break the law and have illicit intercourse") his anger often "turns toward the family and women" (ibid., 162–163). Like DeMeo, Mernissi also draws on the sexual-social theories of Wilhelm Reich. She discusses these in Chapter 9 of her book, which sharply critiques fundamentalist Muslim codes. She observes that "the traditional order, empowered by the codification of the *shari'a* in the modern family code, views men and women as antagonists and dooms the conjugal unit to conflict" (ibid., 163).

46. Abu-Lughod 1986, 158.
47. Ibid., 159. Not all Islamic scholars would agree. Neither would all Islamic women, who sometimes see in their veiling and seclusion a protection from contact with a male world that poses great dangers to them. This is an extreme variation of the dominator tenet that all women need a man to protect them—from other men—and hence that female dependency and subservience is only natural. Ironically, as part of the Islamic nationalist independence movements, some women have even readopted the veil as a rejection of Western values, and thus a symbol of "liberation." See, for example, Reeves 1989.
48 Abu-Lughod 1986, 138.
49. Ibid., 183–185, 264.
50. Gies and Gies 1987, 198–199. See also *Journal of Psychohistory* 15 (Summer 1987), special issue on the history of childhood. See also Chapter 10.
51. DeMeo 1986, 2.
52. Reich 1971b.

CHAPTER 6: THE REIGN OF THE PHALLUS
(Pp. 103–125)

1. Homer, *Iliad,* Fitzgerald translation 1975, 17 & 20.
2. Ibid., 30–31.
3. James 1959, 89.
4. The *Oresteia* and what it tells us of how dramatically sexual and social relations had been altered by the shift from a partnership to a dominator model are explored in *The Chalice and the Blade,* Chapter 8.
5. Rockwell 1974, 162.
6. Peradotto and Sullivan 1984, 33.
7. Keuls 1985, 5.
8. Ibid., 6.
9. There are important exceptions, such as Coontz and Henderson 1986; Peradotto and Sullivan 1984; Pomeroy 1975.
10. Keuls 1985, 13.
11. Ibid., 209.
12. Ibid., 7.
13. Ibid.
14. Ibid., 206.
15. Ibid., 7.
16 Aristotle, *Politics* 51.2, cited in Keuls 1985, 208.
17. Keuls 1985, 208–209.
18. Dover 1984, 149, 151.
19. Keuls 1985, 47.
20. Kaempf-Dimitriadou, cited in Keuls 1985, 52.
21. Ibid., 176.
22. Ibid., 160.

23. This would further limit and suppress women's capacity for sexual enjoyment, as well as reinforcing their and their husbands' perception that for women sex with men is not to be an act of love, but rather of submission and domination.

24. Keuls 1985, 7.

25. Ibid., 187, 200.

26. *Against Neaera* 59, 122 (commonly attributed to Demosthenes, though probably not written by him), quoted in Keuls 1985, 99.

27. Keuls 1985, 146.

28. Ibid., 86–87.

29. Ibid., 90. See also Xenophon, *Conversations of Socrates* "The Estate Manager," where Ischomachus' wife is the central figure in his account of their dialogues (actually mostly his condescending monologues) on how to manage his house, but she is never addressed or mentioned except as "my wife" (Xenophon 1990, 289–359).

30. Xenophon, quoted in Keuls 1985, 102.

31. Keuls 1989.

32. Bonfante-Warren 1984, 229.

33. Not surprisingly, many earlier attitudes about sex, women, and pleasure are reflected in some of the surviving Etruscan art. Like the art of Minoan Crete, where women were also not subordinate, it is an art of vivid natural colors and fluidity.

34. Warren 1984, 236.

35. For an account of Aspasia's life (including persuasive evidence that she was *not,* as still commonly believed, a hetaera) and her relationship to Pericles (including her trial in 432 B.C.E. in which Pericles defended her), see Montuori 1988, 201–226.

36. Dover 1984, 155.

37. Aristophanes ridicules this to some extent, but that he writes of it at all indicates that it not only existed but excited popular interest.

38. This evidence is convincingly detailed in Chapter 16 of *The Reign of the Phallus,* where Keuls shows that women had both the motive and opportunity, and unlike free males had no other way of publicly protesting (Keuls 1985, 392).

39. Kramer 1963, 322.

40. Kramer 1981, 179.

41. Bury, Cook, and Adcock 1971, 154–157.

42. This institutionalization of violence is strikingly evident in the routine brutality of punishments in the laws of the Fertile Crescent, such as the cutting off of noses, ears, and hands for all kinds of offenses, particularly in Assyrian law, as Gerda Lerner points out in Chapters 4 and 5 of *The Creation of Patriarchy* (1986). Although I do not agree with Lerner's structuralist neo-Marxist approach, which attributes the shift to male dominance to greater social complexity and tends to minimize the importance of prehistoric data, she makes an important contribution to our knowledge that rather than being inevitable, male dominance is a social construct.

43. Rohrlich-Leavitt 1977, 43.

44. Ibid., 57. As Rohrlich-Leavitt writes, "With no voice in the laws that were passed primarily to protect the wealth and power of the elite groups, [women] were deprived of education and ousted from lucrative and prestigious professions. Segregated from the kinship group, they were made totally dependent on the male heads of the patrilineal family." Moreover, "women could be divorced on the slightest pretext, in which case they had few alternatives to prostitution, or they could be sold into slavery. Finally, they could suffer the death penalty not only for the new crime of adultery, but for minor acts of independence" (57).

45. Ibid., 55. As John Maier notes, even the legend of Gilgamesh (which dwells on the humiliation and defeat of the goddess Ishtar by Gilgamesh and his companion Enkidu) contains clues to this. He writes that when he and John Gardner translated *Gilgamesh* (1985), they were struck by the prominent role played in the story by a woman called both a *shamhatu* and a *harimtu* (both terms having to do with women, in the service of Ishtar, offering "sacred pleasure"). As I noted in the Introduction, it is she who in this

tale is "the means of transforming the beast Enkidu into a human being" (letter to author from John Maier, September 6, 1993). Accompanying the transition of these women from independent and powerful representatives of the Goddess to servants (indeed, property) of male masters (both divine and temporal) came many new myths in which the Goddess herself was either killed or raped. Thus, we first meet the powerful Sumerian god Enlil when we read of his rape of the goddess Ninlil. But in Palestine, even though archaeological evidence shows that the people's worship of the Goddess lasted throughout the monarchies and as late as the exile itself, the Goddess was completely written out of religious scripture.

46. See, for example, Teubal 1984. It is interesting in this connection that in 1 Samuel 28:4–25 we read that Saul turns to the woman sometimes referred to as the witch of Endor to bring up the spirit of Samuel. This would indicate that the belief in the magical power of women as priestesses to effect the return of the dead still lingered during biblical times. It is also interesting that what Saul asks seems to stem from an earlier faith in what we today might call the rebirth of the soul—suggesting that perhaps in Neolithic times the aim of funerary rites was not literal but spiritual rebirth.

47. Plaskow 1990, 38–39.

48. See, for example, Deuteronomy 22:13–21.

49. Deuteronomy 22:13–21 provides the rules for the situation where a man suspects that his bride is not a virgin.

50. Two books that document the real basis of traditional adultery prohibitions—and that adultery was a crime against male property rights in women—are Countryman 1988, particularly 157–159, and Daly 1973. See also Chapter 7 of *The Chalice and the Blade*.

51. The playwright-actress Carol Lynn Pearson has included a powerful dramatization of this story from the perspective of the Levite's host's daughter in her one-woman play *Mother Wove the Morning*.

52. It is becoming increasingly apparent that these continuing stonings of women are often politically motivated. Women who have shown any sign of independence, or who are felt to have undue power, are today at risk of being called prostitutes by fundamentalists, the brutal violence against them serving as an example to other women not to try to take roles monopolized by men. For example, at the beginning of January 1993, four women accused of prostitution were publicly stoned to death in a northern town of Somalia, an act that Hibaaq I. Osman in her story for *Ms.* magazine suggests was part of "a ferocious backlash against the accomplishments of women" who during the civil war began to take more leading roles in the country's economic life (Osman 1993, 12).

53. Feminist theologians are trying to use these elements as the basis for a more partnership-oriented religious ethic. See, for example, Mollencott 1977 and 1987; Plaskow 1990.

54. Many of the early laws of Rome are attributed to Romulus, its legendary founder. To buttress male sexual control over females, Romulus fashioned laws that made adultery by a woman punishable by death. Romulus also compelled the citizens of Rome to "rear every male child and the first born of the females" (Lefkowitz and Fant 1982, 173).

55. Ibid., 202. Later "reforms" that made marriage without *manus* a legal alternative were for women a mixed blessing. They generally also deprived women of claims to their husbands' estates (Hallett 1984, 244).

56. Lefkowitz and Fant 1982, 176. Another Roman law provided that "if a daughter-in-law strikes her father-in-law she shall be dedicated as a sacrifice to his ancestral deities"—in plain language, killed (ibid., 174). Further enforcing male control over women were laws practically permitting husbands to divorce their wives at will. Thus we read in Valerius Maximus's *Memorable Deeds and Sayings* that Gaius Sulpicius Gallus "divorced his wife because he had caught her outdoors with her head uncovered," and that another man, Quintus Antistius Vetus, "divorced his wife because he had seen her in public having a private conversation with a common freedwoman" (ibid., 176).

57. Ibid., 239.

58. Hallett 1984, 248.

59. Ibid., 253, 246.

60. Ibid.
61. For a discussion of Jesus and partnership, see Chapter 9 of *The Chalice and the Blade.*
62. Peradotto and Sullivan 1984, 3.
63. *The Golden Ass of Apuleius,* translated by Graves 1954.
64. Suetonius 1896.
65. Ibid.

CHAPTER 7: THE SACRED MARRIAGE IN A DOMINATOR WORLD (Pp. 126–142)

1. This is discussed in depth in Part II.
2. A theory advanced by Mara Keller is that by Mycenaean times the ruler of Knossos was in fact a tyrannical overlord who exacted from the Athenians tribute in the form of maidens and youths to be sacrificed—according to another legend, because the Athenians had killed Minos's son. In either case, the Theseus legend reflects the shift from the earlier Goddess-centered mythology, in which Ariadne, as the representative of the Goddess, would never have been merely an instrument for Theseus's temporary use. It certainly reflects the ascendancy of Athenian rather than Mycenaean power (Keller, in progress).
3. "The Descent of Inanna," Wolkstein and Kramer 1983, 51–90; 156–157.
4. Zeus himself was a noted rapist and abductor of both mortal and divine women, reflecting (and reinforcing) the shift from partnership to dominator male-female relations.
5. Marshack 1991, 320, Figure 189.
6. Letter to author from John Maier, September 6, 1993.
7. For example, a *pithoi* or large jar containing the excarnated bones of two children, which the archaeologist Lucy Goodison believes was probably from early Mycenaean times, seems to have been not a sacrifice but a secondary burial, as the use of large jars for this purpose was a common Aegean custom that undoubtedly lasted well into Mycenaean times. Another archaeological find highly publicized as evidence of a Minoan custom of sacrifice was written up in *National Geographic* (February 1981, 220–224). But according to Platon and other Greek archaeologists, what was described there as an "interrupted sacrifice" to try to avert an earthquake was actually nothing of the kind. They note that what one archaeologist termed an altar was actually a wall that fell during the earthquake. And rather than a "priest" and an "intended victim," the two men found crushed at the site were simply killed when the building collapsed (meeting of the author with Nicolas Platon and Anastasia Platon in Athens in 1989).
8. Mellaart 1967, 77.
9. Gimbutas 1991, 296.
10. Ibid., 292. These secondary burials seem to have entailed elaborate ceremonies. "Special days for the return of the bones to the ancestors were joyously celebrated," writes Gimbutas about some of the famous tomb sanctuaries in the Orkney Islands. "Remains of feasting are abundant: bones of sheep, goats, cattle, pigs were found within the chamber." These massive megalithic tombs were also sites of music and dance on these ritual occasions. As Gimbutas writes, "We know that dance was associated with funeral rites of the Sardinian Hypogea and other monuments" (ibid, 294).
11. Goodison 1989, 113; 114–115.
12. Also supporting the contention that predominator agrarian peoples of the Neolithic preferred to make offerings of fruits from the earth rather than blood sacrifices is the biblical account of how the prophet Jeremiah rails against the people for backsliding to the worship of the Goddess and is told by the men that when their wives baked cakes for the Queen of Heaven they had prosperity and peace (Jeremiah 44:17).
13. For a discussion of this archaeological evidence, see Stager and Wolff 1984. Stager and Wolff describe a large complex of sandstone and limestone burial monuments dating from approximately 750 B.C.E. to 250 B.C.E. (in other words, beginning several thousand

years after the Neolithic and approximately seven hundred years after the fall of Minoan Crete) where many thousands of urns containing the burned remains of the bones of both young animals and human babies and infants were deposited. The urns from the earliest level (from about 750 B.C.E. to 600 B.C.E.) contain primarily sacrifices of young animals (like the calf and roe sacrifices we read about in the Bible), although there are also some human remains, which the authors describe as either stillborn or newborn babies. The second level (from about 600 B.C.E. to the third century B.C.E.) is where the finds of bones of babies and even infants escalate. But at this point, this is still primarily confined to the tombs of the ruling classes—only gradually spreading to the general population during the third and final period. This would indicate that the sacrifice of babies and infants was introduced by people who took over as overlords, rather than being indigenous to the earlier culture that was in many of the later prehistoric civilizations still largely composed of conquered people (as dramatically evidenced in India, where they were confined to the lower castes). However, some of the sacrifices in Carthage are to the goddess Tanit who, like Ishtar and Astarte in Canaan and Athena in Greece, was by now also a war goddess—in other words, a co-option of an earlier deity to fit dominator requirements. This has led scholars to conclude that the Carthaginian practice of human sacrifice may also have been present in earlier Goddess-worshiping prehistoric societies. I should add that there are those who are skeptical about Carthaginian child sacrifice, including Claude Schaeffer, who excavated Ugarit. (Some of this is discussed in the Stager and Wolff article, on p. 38, although their conclusions are to the contrary.) I should add that there are scholars such as Moshe Weinfeld and Helene Benichou-Safar who discount the biblical accusations of "Molech worship" and child sacrifice as "prophetic-poetic hyperbole" (ibid.).

14. For example, Dalley's *Myths from Mesopotamia* (1989), a translation of key Mesopotamian texts, does not mention ritual killing of the king during the festival (letter to author from John Maier, September 6, 1993).

15. Frazer 1922, 1969, 6. Frazer argued that stories such as that of a "king of the wood" who had to pluck the branch of a certain tree associated with the goddess Diana and then slay his predecessor in a grove near a temple in Nemi "must have been handed down from a time beyond the memory of man, when Italy was still in a far ruder state." He buttressed his argument with analogies from nineteenth-century anthropological accounts of "primitive tribes," which in fact had very little in common with the Neolithic societies we have been examining, as they were characteristically male-dominant, authoritarian, and violent, with the periodic replacement of one chieftain by a younger and stronger one as a means of ensuring "strong-man" rule. Frazer's theories have long since been rejected by most scholars. As Walter Burkert writes in his book *Structure and History in Greek Mythology and Ritual,* "Frazer's 'god of vegetation' is post-classic allegory transformed into a genetic theory of religion; we may leave it to rhetoric and poetry from whence it sprang" (quoted in Goodison 1989, 45).

16. Wink 1992.

17. It is generally believed that *Enuma Elish* is quite a late text, from the reign of Nebuchadnnezzar I (1125–1104 B.C.E.) (letter to author from John Maier, September 6, 1993).

18. Sandars's translation of *Gilgamesh* 1960, 88.

19. Letter to author from John Maier, September 6, 1993.

20. This episode is more extensively dealt with by John Gardner and John Maier in their translation of *Gilgamesh* (1985), which unlike most earlier translations includes comments specifically relating to the main themes of this book: how sexuality was once associated with the sacred. See, for example, 23–25; 77–80.

21. She also notes that although "by a most unhappy chance our main evidence as to the Sacred Marriage of the mysteries comes to us from the Christian fathers," who "see in its beautiful symbolism only the record of unbridled license" (Harrison 1962, 534), even "they confess that the pagan mysteries of marriage were believed by the celebrants to be spiritual" (ibid., 538).

22. Keuls 1985, 351.

23. Keller 1988, 31.
24. There are various versions of the Demeter-Persephone myth, involving a number of sacred sexual unions. One of these is between the Goddess Demeter and her lover Iason. Homer tells us of this union in the *Odyssey*. "So too fair-haired Demeter once in the Spring did yield to love," he writes, "and with Iason lay in a new plowed field" (Homer, *Odyssey* 5.125). But a later myth tells of Demeter's "forceful violation" by Iason.
25. Keuls 1985, 351; Keller 1988, 49.
26. According to Keller, "There are several sources indicating a time when the rites of Demeter, like the Mystery religion of Pythagoras, did not include the sacrifice of meat but instead shared the 'gentler foods' of fruits and grains" (ibid., 51).
27. It is interesting, as Keuls notes, that in the classical Greek language the word for pig, *choiros*, also denotes the female sex organs, particularly the vagina, a circumstance that was "especially dear to the comic playwrights." The Greek word for wild sow, *capraina*, also denoted a "lustful" woman, which, as Keuls writes, to the Athenian mind was the equivalent of "lewd" woman. The ancient association of the pig or sow with female sexuality and fertility seems to have given the pig a double meaning in these rites.
28. Keuls 1985, 352. Not surprisingly in view of their lives of extreme personal and sexual repression, this was through a socially sanctioned wildness. For the Thesmophoria served as an institutionalized pressure release valve. These secret rites—of which we know little except from vase decorations and classical Greek comic plays satirizing them (written by men, who were not admitted to these festivals)—apparently gave women permission to use ribald joking and act out other gender role reversals. At the same time, they seem to have preserved ancient customs, such as orgiastic dancing and the offering of seeds of grain to the Goddess. And they made it possible for women to express some of their pent-up angers and frustrations (Keller, in progress).
29. In one legend, because the women of Thrace were offended by his inattention to their sexual advances (presumably, as Ovid intimates, because he became a homosexual), they tore him to pieces. According to another legend, it was actually Dionysus who caused the wives of the Thracian men to murder their husbands and tear Orpheus to pieces, because Dionysus was enraged that Orpheus taught the Thracian men to worship the sun god (Apollo) instead. In either case, in these stories it is women who do Orpheus in.
30. Keuls 1985, 353. According to legend the Orphic Mysteries reformed the Dionysian rites, involving an initiation process in which initiates purified themselves through abstinence from meat, and as in the Eleusinian Mysteries, could have no blood guilt on their hands.
31. While the Greek Dionysian rites and the later Roman Bacchae dramatized violence and sexual antagonism as well as the cult of the phallus (as during the Greater Dionysian public processions when giant phalluses were carried by men through the streets), they also had another side. As we see on vase paintings from the fifth century B.C.E., the Athenians also sometimes showed Dionysus in scenes of harmonious family life, with his wife Ariadne at his side and his son Oenopion on his lap (Keuls 1985, 373).
32. The first European opera was *Orpheus and Euridice* by Peri in 1600. At least twenty-six operas were composed about Orpheus in the 1600s and twenty-four in the 1700s (Abraham 1994).
33. Conversations with David Loye, 1993.
34. For a discussion of Eros and Thanatos that counters Freud's thesis in *Civilization and Its Discontents*, see Marcuse 1955.

CHAPTER 8: THE LAST TRACES OF THE SACRED MARRIAGE (Pp. 143–157)

1. For a recent work on mind-altering plants, see McKenna 1992.
2. *Encyclopedia of Religion*, vol. 14, 247.
3. Walker 1988, 349.

4. Weisman 1990, reporting details of the Shinto ceremony performed by the new emperor..
5. Feuerstein 1989, 253.
6. Ibid.
7. Ibid., 252, 255.
8. According to the theologian Elizabeth Dodson Gray, the Christmas wreath, which is now standard on doors of American houses and apartments during the Christmas season, is the circle symbol that the Hindus called the yoni, signifying the circle of the woman's vagina, which stretches to give birth (Gray 1988, 50).
9. Feuerstein 1989, 275.
10. Feuerstein (1989) refers to the dormant kundalini-shakti energy as the "sleeping princess" (266) and the "sleeping goddess kundalini" (267). He also translates the term *kundalini* as "she who is coiled," in accordance with some descriptions of kundalini as a sleeping serpent coiled three and a half times around a phallus (265).
11. Many scholars are today using the term *Hebrew Bible* instead of *Old Testament* because the latter imposes a Christian name on what was once simply the bible for Hebrews. I have here chosen to continue the older usage since Hebrew Bible is still not generally used, and many readers would not know what it refers to.
12. Keller 1988, 30.
13. Regardie 1970, 42.
14. Thus in Hosea we read that Yahweh speaks as follows: "And I will betroth thee unto me for ever; yea, I will betroth thee unto me in righteousness, and in judgment, and in lovingkindness, and in mercies. I will even betroth thee unto me in faithfulness: and thou shalt know the Lord" (Hosea 2:19, 20, King James Version).
15. Wehr 1990, 73.
16. Martin Luther sermon, 14 October 1537, quoted in Wehr 1990, 73.
17. Wehr 1990, 71.
18. A thought-provoking book on the connection between the worship of Black Madonnas (images of which are found all over the world) and revolts against oppression, not only by women but also by men, is Birnbaum 1993. For an earlier essay highlighting the importance of the Black Madonna in European folk tradition, see Perry 1990.
19. Wehr 1990, 72.
20. Maitland 1987, 127.
21. Ibid.
22. Ibid., 130.
23. The equation of men with spirituality and women with the bodily or carnal is characteristic of many dominator religions. Nonetheless, the feminine ideal in popular discourse, for example in the Victorian era, is sometimes the opposite, with women entrusted with "civilizing" men through their more spiritual bent. We will deal with some of these contradictions, and how in the end they serve to buttress male control, in Chapter 11.
24. Maitland 1987, 130–131. As Maitland writes, in continuing to encourage in women a sadomasochistic relationship with "an invisible omnipresent and all-male God," the Church "also gives a subliminal justification to every wife-batterer, every rapist, every pornographer, and every man who wishes to claim 'rights,' the rights to abuse, over women" (ibid., 128). She also notes that this is still in modern times a relationship celebrated by the Church, for example in its canonization in 1950 of Mariana de Flores, a seventeenth-century woman described in the *Penguin Dictionary of Saints* as engaging in penitential practices that "savour of morbid fanaticism"—a woman who, as Maitland writes, completely bought into the androcratic tenet that for women accepting, and even seeking, masochistic suffering is the mark of true "femininity" (ibid., 127, 128, 135).
25. Fox 1986, 350, 361.
26. Though the emphasis on suffering and death in the medieval Church is very strong, there is also, albeit less visibly, a more life-affirming strain. See, for example, Fox 1983.
27. It is true that the mechanistic scientific paradigm, and particularly the view of the human body as a machine, needs to be left behind. But to lay all our problems at the feet of Newtonian science and Cartesian rationalism flies in the face of thousands of years of

dominator history—not to speak of the fact that the mind/body split antedates these developments by a very long time and is by no means exclusive to modern Western scientific thinking. This is discussed in Part II. See also the chart "The Dominator and Partnership Models" on pp. 403–405.

28. Taylor 1954, 126.
29. The Albigenses Crusade led not only to the genocide of the Cathars but to the wholesale massacre of thousands of other women, men, and children, the devastation of whole regions of France, and the destruction of the high medieval Provençal culture that gave birth to the troubadour and trobaritz tradition of courtly love. See Briffault 1965.
30. This focus on an afterlife is generally not found in Hebrew tradition, but as we saw does have early Indo-European roots. Thus, among the Indo-European Greeks and the later Romans some philosophers wrote of rewards and punishments in an afterlife, as Robin Lane Fox notes in his book *Pagans and Christians.* He writes that "Plato and Pythagoras had bequeathed to their followers a clear image of rewards and punishments in the next life" and that later Platonists such as Plutarch warned about the fate of the soul after death (Fox 1986, 95). He also points out that "it is hard to judge how far these concerns extended to a wider public" (ibid., 96). But certainly these pagan philosophers did not, as do Christian writers, teach that life after death is more important than life in this "earthly vale of tears."
31. De Rougemont 1956, 131–132.
32. De Rougemont 1956.
33. Through the fusion of the "female" mercury (or moon) and the "male" sulphur (sun).
34. Wehr 1990, 91–95.
35. Ibid., 56.
36. Wehr 1990. Wehr writes that, a century after the Reformation, this famous mystic reported how, in mystical union with the divine, his spirit "broke through the gates of Hell" when he was "encompassed by love, as a beloved bride is embraced by her bridegroom" (ibid., 77). Böhme even wrote of the need "to tincture Venus and Mars," by which, as Charles Muses points out, he meant that only through the reconnection of woman and man will there be human regeneration and harmony (Muses 1951, 150).
37. Böhme even contended that a return of humanity to an earlier androgynous state was Christ's mission on this Earth (Muses 1951, 150). But Böhme also believed that this much-desired "androgynous male-female wholeness he wrote about could not come to pass without Christ's suffering and death" (Wehr 1990, 72). "When Christ on the Cross once more redeemed man's virgin male-female image, and colored it with heavenly blood in divine love," Böhme wrote of his beatific vision, "Christ changed the sleeping Adam from being man and woman, back to his original angelic image"—an image that to Böhme healed the split between Adam and Eve after the Fall (Muses 1951, 81).

CHAPTER 9: FROM ANCIENT TO MODERN TIMES (Pp. 161–178)

1. As is developed in *The Chalice and the Blade,* this struggle is not new. For instance, Chapter 8 documents the gylanic or partnership nature of early Christianity, including the fact that women had important leadership positions in this movement, that it was perceived by the Roman and Jewish authorities of the time as a threat to their domination, and that Jesus' teaching of caring, compassion, and nonviolence frontally challenged basic premises of a dominator society. For a recent work on women's leading roles in early Christianity, see Torjesen 1993.
2. Homosexuality is today being more adequately treated in many excellent books. The way non-Western cultures, as well as subcultures within Western culture, construct sexuality is also being examined by scholars, some of whom will be cited in later chapters.
3. Millett 1970; Rich 1976; Heyward 1984; Cooey, Farmer, and Ross 1987.

4. Lynda Nead's *The Female Nude* (1992), which examines how the "male gaze" has defined representations of the female body in most Western art until recent times, is one of a number of feminist books addressing this fundamental issue.
5. Nead 1992, 17.
6. Johnson 1994, 59.
7. Ibid., see particularly Chapter 3.
8. Ibid., 58.
9. Freud 1962, 62.
10. Christ 1987a; Fox 1983, 1988; Gray 1988, 1994; Heyward 1984. See also Chapters 13 and 14.
11. Olds 1956.
12. In his study of what he calls the psychobiology of sexual experience, Davidson notes that "it qualifies by the simplest definition as a qualitative departure from usual experience" (Davidson 1980, 292).
13. Ibid., 292, 295. Another researcher, Charles Tart, describes altered states of consciousness in terms of two sets of forces. The first tends to produce disruption or destabilization of the existing state of consciousness, such as drugs or intense physical experiences like extreme exhaustion or excitation. The second involves processes of relaxation, as in sleep, meditation, and hypnosis. Orgasmic states seem to involve *both* these conditions. There is characteristically intense physical stimulation, which tends "to disrupt the normal state of consciousness." And there is also intense relaxation, a "letting go" that is also characteristic of mystical and other spiritual trances (ibid., 292–293).
14. Margulis 1987, 109.
15. Other animals also have systems of communication, from the warning calls of many mammals to the mating calls of many birds and primates. But with the possible exception of whales, none has as complex a system of communication.
16. Maturana and Varela 1987, 222.
17. Tanner 1981. This conclusion is also supported by the Vietnamese linguistic scholar Huynh Sanh Thong, who cites evidence that "it was from a small number of seed-mono-syllables, each of which signified 'mother,' that sprouted forth new words eventually giving rise to the forest of languages in the world today." As he vividly puts it, "in the beginning was the Word and the word was *ma*" (Huynh Sanh Thong 1990, 33).
18. Maturana and Varela 1987, 219–223. They write that "food sharing and male participation in the care of the young" were important factors in the early human groupings that first developed language, pointing out that food sharing between adults would have been more likely to develop in a species where year-round sexual intercourse is found (ibid., 222). This is already foreshadowed by the bonobos, as we saw in Chapter 2. I want to add that, as pointed out in Chapter 2, this male participation in the care of the young can occur in different familial and social contexts, including societies where the care of the young is not only a parental but also a communal responsibility.
19. Maturana 1990, xiv.
20. Maturana and Varela 1987, 234. "Language," they note, "is a condition *sine qua non* for the experience of what we call mind" (ibid., 231). They also note that consciousness, along with mind, "belong to the realm of sexual coupling"—a realm where, as they repeatedly stress, human sexuality played a germinal evolutionary role (ibid., 234).
21. Ibid., 246.
22. Montagu 1986.
23. Ibid.
24. Maturana 1990, xv. Other species also display signs of what we call loving feelings. This is particularly striking in the more complex, long-lived, and intelligent species such as dolphins, elephants, whales, and some of our fellow primates.
25. It is likely that pain and pleasure were also useful signals in relation to feeding, with bitter or unpleasant sensations elicited from poisonous food, at the same time that pleasurable sensations signaled that a food was fit to eat.
26. I want to express my appreciation to Dean Di Sandro, whose provocative essay "Endorphin, a Substitute for Attachment: When Love Is an Everyday Endogenous Opiate"

(unpublished paper), followed by conversations and written communications, first suggested this line of thinking to me.

27. Liebowitz 1983; Walsh 1991, 99; Fisher 1992. For how scientists are exploring the use of these types of chemicals with patients suffering from chronic depression, see Sabelli and Javaid (undated). That people with low levels of these types of chemicals suffer from chronic depression opens the door to speculations that since chronic depression is often related to lack of early love and even abusive and/or violent childhoods, this kind of chemical malfunction may, at least in part, result from such early life experiences—again highlighting the importance of love in healthy human development.

28. As I noted earlier, I am here using the term *evolved* not as a verb, which is how biologists use it, but as an adjective to connote a value judgment, which is how it is used by philosophers as well as in popular parlance.

29. Richards 1987, 207.

30. Ibid., 208. See also the slightly different Darwinian pattern for moral development discussed in Loye 1994.

31. Huxley 1953.

32. Maslow 1968.

33. Loye 1990. See also Loye 1994 and work in progress b.

34. Teilhard de Chardin 1959.

35. Chaisson 1987, 227.

36. For a discussion of attractors in the context of *cultural transformation theory,* see *The Chalice and the Blade,* particularly Chapter 10. For a discussion of nonlinear dynamics and attractors from a mathematical perspective, see Abraham and Shaw 1984.

CHAPTER 10: WAKING FROM THE DOMINATOR TRANCE (Pp. 179–200)

1. See Chapters 10 and 11, *The Chalice and the Blade.*

2. *The Chalice and the Blade* describes this point-counterpoint.

3. Although this idea is usually said to have originated with Western philosophers such as Locke, its manifestation in Native American tribal societies such as the Iroquois antedates this. For an early work on this, see Collier 1947. Although Collier tends to overidealize indigenous societies, his work is important. An essay relating to this subject, focusing on the eighteenth-century Shawnee Nation leader Queen Coitcheleh, is Schaaf 1990. Schaaf brings out that to the extent that some of the Native American tribal societies were more democratic, women in these societies also had higher status.

4. Our school curriculum prominently features men such as John Locke, Adam Smith, and even in our anti-communist U.S. political climate, Karl Marx and Friedrich Engels. But if we want such in-depth treatment of Frederick Douglass, Sojourner Truth, and other Afro-American leaders, we have to go to the intellectual ghetto of black studies. Similarly, to find out about the major contributions of the feminist thinkers and theorists who led the struggle for women's human rights, one has to go to the intellectual ghetto of women's studies.

5. This began at the end of the Middle Ages (Gies and Gies 1987).

6. For example, in Proverbs 23:13–14 (King James Version) we read: "Withhold not correction from a child: for if thou strike him with the rod, he shall not die. Thou shalt beat him with the rod, and shalt deliver his soul from hell." It is then not surprising that until recent times, and in some places still today, corporeal punishment was routinely used in church-run schools.

7. Gies and Gies 1987. For instance, as Stuart Schlegel (1970) writes, the family structure of the Tiruray people is basically egalitarian.

8. A now-classic book on this subject by the Swiss psychoanalyst Alice Miller is *For Your Own Good: Hidden Cruelty in Child-Rearing and the Roots of Violence* (1983).

9. Quoted in deMause 1987, 426.

10. Ibid., 427. Although deMause still subscribes to the nineteenth-century evolutionary theory of a linear rise from apes to savages to "civilized man" and claims that all human societies until now have been characterized by physically (and sexually) abusive child rearing—which I cannot agree with—and although he often interprets materials from both history and prehistory in ways with which I strongly disagree, he has been a pioneer in bringing to light institutionalized patterns of cruelty and abuse in child rearing.
11. Ibid.
12. Scheck 1987.
13. Taylor 1987, 443, 444.
14. Ariès 1962; deMause 1974; Shorter 1975. Ariès argues that until the seventeenth century even the concept of childhood may have been unknown—or at least very different from what later emerged. He points to how until the end of the medieval period children were regarded as not different from adults, just smaller. He shows that in medieval art (and in much of earlier classical art) children, even babies, often have adult faces—for instance, the baby Jesus and the little cherubs or angels in most medieval icons.
15. John Boswell's *The Kindness of Strangers* reports some of these data, including fifteenth-century records from La Scala, Italy, showing that only 13 percent of children in foundling homes survived to the age of six as compared to 83 percent of children sent away from home to nurse with wet nurses (Boswell 1988, 421).
16. Gies and Gies 1987.
17. Taylor 1985.
18. Eisler 1993c; 1993d.
19. Berghold 1991.
20. Ibid., 238.
21. Harman 1988.
22. Adorno, Frenkel-Brunswick, et al. 1964.
23. Miller 1983.
24. Blake 1994.
25. Ibid., 682.
26. Ibid.
27. As Degler writes, it was not accidental that "the decline of physical punishment coincided with the rise in the importance of women within the family and their increasing concentration upon child-rearing and home," for "as the gentler sex, traditionally, it was only to be expected that under their aegis a more gentle approach would be taken toward children" (Degler 1980, 89).
28. Bradshaw 1988; Schaef 1987.
29. Almost every week there are news stories about men who shoot, stab, set fire to, and otherwise turn their rage at being left by their wives against their "loved ones"—including their own children. For instance, the Associated Press reported on July 12, 1993, that a California man fatally shot his son and daughter and then turned the gun on himself after holding the children hostage at his estranged wife's home for nine hours. The high statistics on rape and other forms of intimate violence also reflect a huge jump in reports of these crimes, which were formerly often not prosecuted. It also reflects population growth. But there is certainly a backlash factor in this as well.
30. See, for example, Mills 1994, "Survey Dispels Common Myths About Families: Parental Behavior More Important Than Parental Number," reporting findings from a study of American families conducted by the psychologist Nicholas Zill and the demographer Christine Winquist Nord using new national survey data and state and local statistics, released by Childtrends, Inc., a nonprofit, nonpartisan research organization.
31. See, for example, Marcuse 1955; Reich 1970a, 1970b, 1971.
32. See, for example, MacKinnon 1982; Millett 1970.
33. Among the milestone writings of that period were Gloria Steinem's exposé of the unglamorous and exploited lives of the Playboy bunnies, which first appeared in 1963 and is included in her *Outrageous Acts and Everyday Rebellions* (1983); Laura Lederer's anthology *Take Back the Night* (1980), with important contributions by writers including Tracey Gardner, Kathleen Barry, Diana Russell, Luisah Teish, Adrienne Rich, and Robin

Morgan; Susan Griffin's *Rape: The Politics of Consciousness* (1986); and Susan Brown-miller's *Against Our Will: Men, Women, and Rape* (1975). Works by many of these authors are in the Bibliography.

34. Foucault 1980. See also Giddens 1992, Chapter 2.
35. For example, some of these preachers assert that when Armageddon comes (which they contend is imminent), only "chosen" fundamentalist Christians will be saved. They paint vivid pictures of freeway crashes and other catastrophes during Armageddon, promising the ascension from their cars into heaven of only the bodies of those who have seen the "truth."
36. In his classic cross-cultural work on ideology and values, the social psychologist Milton Rokeach found that fascism is the one modern ideology that still openly devalues both freedom and equality, thus justifying the suppression of both (Rokeach 1973, particularly 172–173). In other words, even though the suppression of freedom and equality is characteristically justified in "pure" dominator ideologies, for example in the monarchism that to varying degrees held sway in the West until the Enlightenment, fascism is the only contemporary ideology that still justifies their suppression. Yet while fascism has been massively discredited in this century, the subordination of both freedom and equality to "higher" goals still remains entrenched in the authoritarian factions of some of the world's religions. (This is analyzed in Loye, *The River and the Star,* work in progress a. See also Chapter 11 of *The Chalice and the Blade* for a discussion of modern fascist regimes as a regression to a "pure" dominator society, using modern technologies for more effective domination and destruction.)
37. Anthony Giddens notes how the recent spate of self-help books both reflect and contribute to this movement, and hence to a more democratic society (Giddens 1992).

CHAPTER 11: BONDAGE OR BONDING
(Pp. 201–221)

1. See "'Remember the Ladies': Abigail Adams vs. John Adams," in Rossi 1973, 7–15.
2. In fairness to Jefferson, some of his letters indicate that he wanted to get a grievance about slavery into the Declaration of Independence. See Becker 1972.
3. Okin 1979, 200.
4. Ibid., 163–164.
5. Kerber 1980, 25.
6. The term *erotization* is a derivative of erotism, an alternative to eroticism. Since I have used eroticism, I might be expected to use the term *eroticization.* But this is an extremely awkward word on which not only the tongue but the mind stumbles. By contrast, erotization is direct and forceful, and its meaning is clear. This is why I have chosen it.
7. Kerber 1980, 20. This insight, that what we conventionally define as political is inextricably interrelated with what is still conventionally seen as personal, is a major theme in feminist literature.
8. It is said that Pope Julius II founded such a house in Rome (Lewinsohn 1958, 135).
9. I use the term *medieval Christian Church* to describe the religious hierarchy that allied itself with the Roman emperor to control what became the official or state religion of Western Europe. The term *medieval* is generally used to describe the period between the fourth or fifth centuries and the fifteenth century. Since the split between Catholicism and Protestantism did not occur until the sixteenth century, the term *Christian Church* rather than *Catholic Church* is appropriate. Indeed, some Reformation leaders were just as antisexual as their Catholic counterparts, and in some cases more so. I do not mean to imply that all Christian leaders took this position. Many Christians today reject this and other repressive aspects of earlier Catholic and Protestant teachings.
10. Ranke-Heinemann 1990. See particularly pages 4–5 on Siricius. Even though Jesus is presented as celibate in the Scriptures included by the Church fathers in the New Testament, in the "heretic" Gnostic Gospels there are allusions to his love for Magdalene, who according to some was not only his "favorite disciple" but his wife. And although

Jesus did not explicitly preach against polygamy, as Ranke-Heinemann notes, by rejecting the double standard for adultery, in which "the wife belonged to her husband but
the husband did not belong to his wife," he did so implicitly (ibid., 1990, 34–35).

11. Ibid., 5. Siricius was hardly alone in his disgust for sex. James A. Brundage quotes
Arnobius, a Christian writer of circa 327, who wrote that it was blasphemy even to
imagine that Jesus could have been "born of filthy coupling and that He came into the
light as the result of obscene gropings and the spewing forth of senseless semen." He
notes that St. Jerome declared that "all sexual relations, even in marriage, were intrinsically evil and unclean." And he stresses that "the horror of sex was not the peculiar
aberration of a few eccentrics among the Church Fathers; rather it was squarely in the
mainstream of patristic teaching" (Brundage 1990, 196). Another work that forcefully
brings this out is Karen Jo Torjesen, *When Women Were Priests* (1993).

12. Ranke-Heinemann 1990, 6.

13. Fox 1986, 361. Even Epicurus distinguished between sexual enjoyment and other types
of pleasure, declaring in one of his writings that "sexual intercourse has never done a
man good and he is lucky if it has not harmed him" (Brundage 1990, 214).

14. Ranke-Heinemann 1990, 90, 122, 123. L. William Countryman points out in his book
Dirt, Greed, and Sex (1988) that this Christian notion of women's dangerous impurity
and the need to protect men from it is antedated by Old Testament passages—for instance, the prohibition of intercourse with a menstruating woman (Leviticus 18:19;
20:18) and the requirement that women be purified after childbirth, with the mother's
purification twice as long after the birth of a daughter as after bearing a son (Leviticus
12). As Countryman notes, though the prohibition is of sexual intercourse, clearly "the
text speaks as if the danger lay in the women" (Countryman 1988, 29). Countryman argues that these physical purity concerns were rejected by most early Christian writers
(ibid., 138). Nonetheless, as he writes, "the Jesus who regularly preferred the company
of the impure to that of the religious authorities of his day or who predicted that tax col-
lectors and prostitutes would more readily gain entrance into the reign of God than the
devout would not have been a popular figure in the Church itself in most of the suc-
ceeding Christian centuries" (ibid., 143).

15. For a recent work on the witch-hunts see Barstow 1994.

16. See, for example, Ranke-Heinemann 1990, 96–97.

17. Ibid., 163.

18. Ibid., 145.

19. An example is the Anglo-Saxon penitential put together between 690 and 710 by the
Greek monk Theodore, who, as the archbishop of Canterbury, was to organize the English Church (ibid., 149).

20. Ibid., 149, 150.

21. Ibid., 150.

22. Ibid., 146–147.

23. Ibid., 155.

24. Ibid., 154.

25. Ibid.

26. Anderson and Zinsser 1988, 256.

27. Ranke-Heinemann 1990, 154–155.

28. Lewinsohn 1958, 133–134. Lewinsohn does comment on the barbarity of this practice.

29. This practice lingered into historic times, as reflected in the famous quarrel between the
Church and Henry VIII, who broke with Rome over the Church's ban on divorce, and
then, instead of divorcing his wives, got rid of a number of them by killing them.

30. Gies and Gies 1987.

31. Despite the cruelty of many of its edicts concerning sexual and family relations, the
Church also helped to soften—though not eradicate—some brutalities of dominator
family relations. Notably, it condemned infanticide, which was still widely practiced in
Europe all through the early Middle Ages, particularly the selective infanticide of girl
babies that was often the result of the Germanic practice of placing the infant before the
father immediately after birth and killing it unless he accepted it and gave it a name
(Gies and Gies 1987, 34–35).

32. Eisler 1987c.
33. Blackstone 1765; Eisler 1977.
34. Ibid.
35. Ibid.
36. For a comprehensive report on the sexual slavery of women, see Kathleen Barry, *Female Sexual Slavery* (1979), particularly Chapter 4, "The Traffic in Sexual Slaves."
37. *The Women's Watch* 5 (January 1992), 5.
38. *San Francisco Examiner,* December 8, 1991, quoted in *Women's Watch* 5 (January 1992), 5.
39. This failure to protect girls and women is sometimes rationalized on the basis that some of them "consented" to their sexual enslavement because they were already prostitutes—as if that meant consent to being locked up and forced to sexually service dozens of men a day, often in the bargain being beaten up and tortured by the very pimps who lured them into prostitution.
40. See "Saudi Arabia: Update on Women at the Wheel," *Ms.*, November/December 1991, 17. See also Mackey 1990, which describes the rigid male dominance in this society and how it circumscribes not only women's sexual options but all aspects of their lives.
41. CNN World Report shown during the Gulf War.
42. Stalin abolished legal abortion in 1936, and it was only in 1955, as efforts began to be made to eradicate the cult of Stalinism, that abortion was again legalized in the Soviet Union (Robotham 1974, 160, 163).
43. Reich 1970a, xxiii. Foreshadowing what modern archaeology is now documenting, Reich also wrote that authoritarianism "reflects a patriarchal authoritarian civilization of thousands of years standing" which appeared at a "relatively late stage of culture" (ibid., 24).
44. Ibid.
45. See Millett 1970 for a feminist classic on this issue.
46. Koonz 1977, 469.
47. Ihara Saikaku's *The Great Mirror of Male Love* (1990) highlights this.
48. Especially in large towns, women were forced to live together in homes under the control of a guardian who was authorized to perform these temporary marriages. Frequently these homes were established at government initiative, especially when the women were young war widows or orphans (*Women Living Under Muslim Laws,* No. 62.2).
49. Wendy Chapkis, quoted in Simonton 1991, 5.
50. It is shocking that even the American Civil Liberties Union (ACLU), which in other respects makes a major contribution to the protection of human rights, has failed to budge from its stance of defending pornographic woman-hating-and-torturing images under the First Amendment. According to Ann Simonton, groups campaigning against antipornography activists are heavily supported by pornography enterprises, including even Feminists for Free Expression, an organization whose treasurer works for *Penthouse* and whose board member Marsha Pally is *Penthouse*'s film critic and receives grants from *Penthouse* and *Playboy* (Simonton 1994, 1). Simonton also reports that the National Coalition Against Censorship is partly funded by *Playboy* and *Penthouse*, which Simonton links with the fact that its executive director writes op-ed pieces "to fuel hostile attacks on the work and lives of Dworkin and MacKinnon"—the two most visible U.S. antipornography activists (ibid.).
51. Scott 1983. As Scott writes, some women find in this sexual role reversal a way of acting out their otherwise forbidden anger "at men for oppressing women" through "the combination of erotic stimulation and the symbolic punishment and penance."
52. Rousseau 1945, 13–16.
53. One of the most astounding passages in Rousseau's autobiography concerns these acts—made even more heartless by the fact that a very large number of children put in foundling homes during this period died. Rousseau wrote passionately of justice, sensitivity to others, and in his words, "the true, the beautiful, and the just." But he saw nothing false, unjust, or ugly in bringing children into this world only to abandon them. The barbarity of Rousseau's double standard for behaviors in the public and private spheres

is perhaps most jarringly reflected in the following passage, in which Rousseau writes of his deliberations before deciding that Thérèse's third child by him should, like the first two, be abandoned:

> While philosophizing upon the duties of man, an event occurred which made me reflect more seriously upon my own. Thérèse became pregnant for the third time. Too honest towards myself, too proud in my heart to desire to belie my principles by my actions, I began to consider the destination of my children and my connection with their mother, in the light of the laws of nature, justice, and reason. . . .
>
> If I was wrong in my conclusions, nothing can be more remarkable than the calmness with which I abandoned myself to them. If I had been out of those low-born men, who are deaf to the gentle voice of Nature, in whose heart no real sentiment of justice or humanity ever springs up, this hardening of my heart would have been quite easy to understand. But is it possible that my warm-heartedness, lively sensibility, readiness to form attachments, the powerful hold which they exercise over me, the cruel heartbreakings I experience when forced to break them off, my natural goodwill towards all my fellow-creatures, my ardent love of the great, the true, the beautiful, and the just; my horror of evil of every kind, my utter inability to hate or injure, or even to think of it; the sweet and lively emotion which I feel at the sight of all that is virtuous, generous, and amiable; is it possible, I ask, that all these can ever agree in the same heart with the depravity which, without the least scruple, tramples underfoot the sweetest of obligations? No! I feel and loudly assert—it is impossible. Never, for a single moment in his life, could Jean Jacques have been a man without feeling, without compassion, or an unnatural father. . . . If I had left them with Madame d'Epinay or Madame de Luxembourg, who, from friendship, generosity, or some other motive, expressed themselves willing to take charge of them, would they have been happier, would they have been brought up at least as honest men? I do not know; but I do know that they would have been brought up to hate, perhaps to betray, their parents; it is a hundred times better that they have never known them.
>
> My third child was accordingly taken to the Foundling Hospital, like the other two. The two next were disposed of in the same manner, for I had five altogether. This arrangement appeared to me so admirable, so rational, and so legitimate, that, if I did not openly boast of it, this was solely out of regard for the mother. (Rousseau 1945, 366–368)

54. This fundamental matter has been strangely ignored in most political writings. A notable exception is Scarry 1985.

55. Hegel's parable of the master and the slave is explicit, while in most of Freud's work this assumption is more implicit (except in his parable of social origins, where he too makes it explicit). Jean-Paul Sartre (whose long-term lover Simone de Beauvoir wrote a piece eulogizing the Marquis de Sade as a great philosopher) was in his own life apparently very aware of the miseries of this arrangement, although in his play *No Exit* (believed to be largely autobiographical), he too presents it as basically inevitable.

CHAPTER 12: MAKING LOVE OR MAKING WAR (Pp. 222–243)

1. For an analysis of how this relates to images of pregnancy (or more accurately, the absence of such images in our culture), see Wilshire 1988. For a work that goes to the heart of the erotization of domination and violence, see Morgan 1989.

2. Colin Wilson, quoted in Brownmiller 1975, 326–327.

3. Stoller 1979, 6, 23, 26.
4. Ibid., 151.
5. Freud 1963, 92.
6. An example is Camille Paglia, who contemptuously accuses women who complain of rape as "whining." In her view, male sexual aggression is even the motor for creativity—and a reason that, according to her, women are not as creative as men. Paglia, who does not seem to notice that this also dismisses her own work as less creative, is even quoted on her own sex life as being "a disaster, an absolute disaster" because she does not want to "submit." (*San Francisco Examiner*, July 7, 1991, Image section, p. 11).
7. See, for example, McConahay and McConahay 1977, and Coltrane 1988.
8. See, for example, Bleier 1984 and Fausto-Sterling 1984.
9. Schachter and Singer 1962. See also Aron and Aron 1989, 35–38. The design of the experiment was actually more complicated. There were several other subgroups. One group, having been told to expect adrenaline side effects, showed little emotion of any kind and just watched the confederates going through their antics. But those who were aroused and had no explanation or were given the wrong explanation showed the kind of emotion congruent either with the "anger condition" or the "euphoria condition."
10. For some comments from girls asked about this, see Minton 1992.
11. *Macho* is a Spanish word that means male. But in English it is commonly used to connote the equation of masculinity with domination and violence, because in some Spanish-speaking regions "machismo" is equated with what scholars today term hypermasculinity (proving manliness through acts of violent domination, be it of one's own feelings or of other human beings or animals). But there is here also an element of projection onto Latin men of racial and ethnic prejudices.
12. Tomkins stresses that cultural scripts (and the roles and scenes they contain) are effective because they are heavily laden with emotions or affect—which is why cultural scripts related to sex are particularly effective in both masculine and feminine socialization.
13. Tomkins 1984, 23. Tomkins stresses that the macho script originated "from a society which accepted slavery as well as living by the sword" (ibid., 24).
14. Tomkins 1984, 25. As he and Donald Mosher write, "The cultural descendent of the nomadic warrior is the macho man" (Mosher and Tomkins 1988, 64).
15. Tomkins's and Mosher's use of *macho* in this sense deviates from the Latin stereotype. While men are in most Spanish-speaking cultures seen as superior to women, and male dominance is by and large a given, the Latin definition of real masculinity permits a man certain "soft" emotions—albeit only in certain contexts, as with his children, in wooing women, or in being rejected by them, when he is socially permitted to cry.
16. Mosher and Tomkins 1988, 67.
17. As Barbara Kanner points out, this same ideology lay behind the socialization of boys through the exclusive English public schools where parents sent their sons to "stop them from being milksops and where they would be out of reach of the molly coddling influence of women." Here, as Kanner writes, "The institutional techniques of starvation, cold, flogging and fistcuffs were among the chief mechanisms for turning boys into brave, self-reliant, self-governing gentlemen committed to masculine ideals." Kanner also notes how training boys for "conforming to absolute obedience and achieving self-mastery," and for "appraising achievement through athleticism and proof of patriotism" relates to military training (Kanner 1990, xviii–xix).
18. Mosher and Tomkins 1988, 71.
19. This view of rape as a "prank" recently made international news when the headmistress of a school in Kenya spoke of the killing of nineteen girls by the boys in the school when they resisted being raped. Her astonishing comment, reported in the Kenyan press and then in the *New York Times* (August 4, 1991), was: "The boys never meant any harm against the girls. They just wanted to rape" (Hosken 1991, 37).
20. Thus, among the Masai of Africa, boys were segregated from the tribe to "play" at war until the time came to do it in real life. Even today, not only in military training camps all over the world but in all-male gangs and all-male football or soccer teams, the same ideals of aggressive masculinity are promulgated.

21. Mosher and Tomkins 1988, 72–73.

22. For example, during the 1950s it was common in basic training or boot camp to call men who were perceived as not tough or macho enough "pussies." Men who did not dominate women but were submitting to any form of female leadership were called "pussy-whipped." This derisive term is still used to shame men for lack of "masculinity" or dominance over women today.

23. Arken and Dobrofsky 1978, 161.

24. Ibid., 160.

25. See, for example, Schmitt 1994.

26. As Barbara Ehrenreich writes in her foreword to Theweleit's book, these were men like Rudolf Höss, who later was to become the commandant of the death camp at Auschwitz, men who during the years before the Nazi takeover "fought Polish communists and nationalists, the Russian Red Army and Latvian and Estonian nationalists in the Baltic region, and the German working class throughout Germany" (Theweleit 1987, ix).

27. Theweleit 1987, 186–187.

28. Ibid., 194–195.

29. Ibid., 196.

30. Introduction to the *Gambler's Songbook*, USAF 77th Tactical Fighter Squadron, Upper Heyford, Oxon; compiled by Capt. George "Kelmaniac" Kelman, Capt. Thomas "Tunes" Theobald, Capt. Mike "Boomer" Clowers, Capt. Tom "Grunt" Carmichael, and SRA John "The Kid" Galleta (so named for the pilots' squadron nicknames), quoted in Smith 1989, 122–123.

31. Ibid.

32. Ibid.

33. Ibid.

34. *American Psycho*, quoted in *Los Angeles Times*, December 18, 1990.

35. Lafferty and Brice 1992.

36. *Media Watch Action Agenda*, Spring 1994, 14.

37. See, for example, "Really Socking It to Women," *Time*, February 7, 1977, 58–60.

38. In texts where these kinds of works are described as great works of literature there is hardly ever any mention of these matters, with the focus of literary critics on the beauty of the style rather than on the horrible normative messages these writings convey. Many feminist works deal with this issue—for example, Dworkin 1987; Millett 1970; Morgan 1989; Smith 1989.

39. This is largely due to the untiring efforts of feminists in the last few decades, particularly through the first United Nations Decade for Women from 1975 to 1985.

40. Senate Judiciary Committee, fact sheet in support of Senate Bill 15, "Violence Against Women Act," introduced by Senator Joseph Biden, August 29, 1990.

41. Ibid.

42. Eisler 1987b.

43. Sen 1990a; "The Lesser Child: The Girl in India," a report prepared by the Indian government to mark South Asia's Year of the Girl Child in 1980, quoted in Crossette 1990.

44. As the historian Barbara Kanner writes, "Brutality toward a good proportion of poor and working-class wives has long been documented by social observers, reporters, philanthropists, and police courts," for example Frances Power Cobbe's article, "Wife Torture in England," which assisted the campaign for the Matrimonial Causes Act of 1878 (Kanner 1990, xxxi).

45. For example, only a few years ago in Kenya legislators openly defended wife beating as traditional. Latin America men who kill their wives for the slightest "disobedience" (like going to school against their orders or not making them tea) are to this day all too often let off scot-free by courts who likewise view male control over women as a traditional prerogative, as was recently publicized in a segment of the TV show "60 Minutes."

46. See *New York Times*, May 26, 1987, section 1, p. 21; *New York Times*, May 31, 1987, section 1, p. 18; *New York Times*, November 1, 1987, section 1, p. 65, for some reports of what happened when Lawrence Singleton, the man who committed this horrible crime, was paroled after serving only eight years in prison; how he was equipped with a bulletproof

vest and a police guard, and ultimately installed in a trailer under twenty-four-hour police protection at a cost to the State of California of $1,300 per day. This, when there was
no compensation for the fifteen-year-old girl whose arms he chopped off with an axe for
her permanent mutilation and traumatization, and when there is somehow no money to
guard women who plead with the police to protect them from men who all too often end
up by killing them. More recently, the so-called College Terrace Rapist, convicted in 1982
of twenty-three crimes after he confessed to some one hundred rapes, mostly of college-
age women in a number of northern California cities and towns, was paroled after
serving only half of his twenty-five-year sentence. Again at taxpayer cost, during his
three-year parole (during which he will reside in a two-bedroom, one-bath bungalow at
a minimum security conservation camp, where he spends most of his time reading and
watching television, according to a camp spokesman), this man too will be under
twenty-four-hour surveillance ("Freed Rapist Under Total Surveillance," Associated
Press, March 25, 1994; "State to Keep Rapist in Modoc County," Associated Press, March
26, 1994).

47. For one perspective, see Bart and O'Brien 1985; Brownmiller 1975; Lederer 1980;
MacKinnon 1982, 1993; and Russell 1988, 1993. For a different perspective, see some of
the publications of the American Civil Liberties Union, for example, their brief in the
1984 case *American Booksellers v. Hudnut.*

48. Raine, Brennan, and Mednick 1994.

49. See, for example, Donnerstein 1980, Feschbach and Malamuth 1978.

50. Linz, Donnerstein, and Penrod 1984, 130. This article contains a survey of some of the
research in this area.

51. For a short account of Pavlov's experiments, see Miller 1962, 181–182.

52. Linz, Donnerstein, and Penrod 1984, 144.

53. Berkowitz 1974, 165–176.

54. Bandura and Menlove 1968.

55. Suetonius 1896.

56. Miles 1989, 56–57.

57. Ibid., 156.

58. Ibid., 147.

59. In these paintings, as in Rembrandt's later *Susanna and the Elders* and in Manet's famous
picnic scene, only the women are naked while the men are wearing clothes.

60. Nasreen 1993.

CHAPTER 13: SEX, GENDER, AND TRANSFORMATION
(Pp. 244–264)

1. Though it is hard to tell to what extent young women who today talk of male bodies in
the same graphic sexual language once reserved for men are doing what women have
always wanted to do, and to what extent it is a matter of imitating behaviors associated
with male power and male prerogatives, clearly for women sex purely for pleasure can
be just as exciting and enjoyable as for men.

2. William Jankoviak and Edward Fisher study quoted in Livermore 1993, 33. Jankoviak
and Fisher even speculate that in those few cultures where they did not find such evidence, it was mainly because the anthropologists did not broach the subject.

3. 1988 study by Beverly Fehr, quoted in Livermore 1993, 34.

4. Prigogine and Stengers 1984. This is the same approach that informs the work of scientists such as Ralph Abraham, Fritjof Capra, Vilmos Csanyi, David Loye, and Humberto
Maturana. See, for example, Abraham and Shaw 1984; Capra 1982; Csanyi 1989; Loye
1995; and Maturana and Varela 1980.

5. See Introduction and Chapter 10, *The Chalice and the Blade.* See also Loye and Eisler 1987.

6. Loye 1995.

7. Marx and Engels 1960, 115.

8. Eisler 1987a, 1987b, 1991, 1993a, 1993b.

9. Csanyi 1989.

10. For details, see Winter 1973 and *The Chalice and the Blade,* Chapter 10.

11. Winter calls these stories Don Juan stories after the legendary hero of folk tales, celebrated literary works such as Goethe's *Faust,* and even one of the world's most beloved operas, Mozart's *Don Giovanni.* Don Juan is a man who compulsively seduces (or, as in Don Giovanni's case, rapes) women. In some versions he is punished; in *Faust,* by the loss of his immortal soul. But by and large the tenor of Don Juan stories is one of admiration for his manly exploits.

12. Giddens 1984, xxi. Giddens's theory of structuration focuses on the interactive processes through which this happens.

13. This is explored in *The Chalice and the Blade.*

14. Kimmel 1987, 127.

15. Ibid., 126–127.

16. Ibid., 128–133. As in the 1691 pamphlet "Restored Maidenhead," to counter any real female sexual independence, some men (like some men today) argued that it is well known that women want to be raped (ibid., 133).

17. Ibid., 135–136.

18. Roszak 1969, 96.

19. Kerber and Mathews 1982, 222–225. This high toll in lives was due to the fact that the women were locked in so they could not go outside, even to go to the bathroom, except at designated times. Unfortunately such practices are still found in some regions of the world today—for example, in some of the "maquilladora" sweatshops in Mexico, the Philippines, and other regions where cheap female labor is exploited. It also sometimes still leads to tragedies, like the fire at the Kader Industrial Company plant outside Bangkok, reported in the international press where many women's lives were again lost. (See *Ms.,* July/August 1993, 15, for a report of how more than two hundred workers, almost all women, were crushed behind locked doors and under collapsed stairwells at this plant where doors were always kept locked from the outside.)

20. Unfortunately, as often happens in dominator politics, in the struggle for the vote, two traditionally disempowered groups—black men and white women—were pitted against each other. Some suffragist leaders wrote resentfully of the unfairness of giving uneducated black men the vote while denying it to educated women. Their invocation of racial stereotypes in turn led to resentment, leading to a still-lingering rift. For an account of this, see Davis 1983.

21. See, for example, *Human Development Report 1991* (New York: Oxford University Press, 1991), 179.

22. Brod 1987, 40. As Brod writes, "The overgeneralization from male to generic human experience not only distorts our understanding of what, if anything, is truly generic to humanity but also precludes the study of masculinity as a *specific male* experience, rather than a universal paradigm for *human* experience" (ibid.). This is one reason Brod argues that although de facto most of what we are taught about the human condition has been "men's studies"—that is, written by men about men—there is a need for a discipline that "raises new questions and demonstrates the inadequacy of established frameworks in answering old ones" (ibid., 41).

23. Koegel 1994. Reprints of "Healing the Wounds of Masculinity" can be obtained from the Center for Partnership Studies, P.O. Box 51936, Pacific Grove, CA 93950.

24. Callahan 1993.

25. Castelot 1971, 377.

26. Beneke, 1993.

27. See Chapter 12, *The Chalice and the Blade.*

28. Stephenson 1991; see also Miedzian 1991.

29. See, for example, Kimmel and Mosmiller 1992.

30. Brod 1987, 1.

31. Brod 1987.

32. Clatterbaugh 1993, 6.

33. Brod 1987, 209.
34. Coltrane 1988, 1073.
35. Even the legendary Dr. Benjamin Spock, who for many decades wrote books on parenting in which fathers barely figured, finally changed his position. In the 1976 edition of his classic *Baby and Child Care*, he wrote that a father needs to more equally participate in child care because by so doing he "will do best by his children, his wife *and himself*" (quoted in Gerzon 1982, 196).
36. Quoted in Gerzon 1982, 207.
37. Brod 1987, 121.
38. Dittes writes that "a lot of the crippling that has come to light is the crippling done by men" who "are taught and induced to do it so compellingly that it often becomes automatic and unthinking" (Dittes 1985, 113).
39. McGill 1985, xvii, 255.
40. Barbeau 1982, 121.
41. Monet 1948. Casanova wrote of the period in France during the reigns of Louis XV and Louis XVI, but his autobiography did not appear until the early nineteenth century.
42. For example, as Karen Wright writes, "Paralysis victims bereft of feeling below the waist often get erections and ejaculate without having a climax and prepubescent boys can achieve orgasm, even multiple ones, without ejaculating" (Wright 1992, 56).
43. Adorno, Frenkel-Brunswick, et al. 1964.
44. A study of 336 students in 1971 at Heidelberg University (then a center of radical activity) by Ronald Grosarth-Maticek, originally reported in the German journal *Sexualmedizin*, described in "Revolution Yes, Orgasm No" in *Cambio 16* of Madrid, October 22, 1978, and in *Atlas World Press Review*, February 1979, 12.
45. Ibid.
46. Sabo 1989, 38.
47. Ibid., 39.
48. Ibid.
49. "The specific callous sexual act that is to count as manly varies," they write. It can be "'You're not a real man until you catch the clap,' or 'You're not a real man until you've scored ten times,' or 'You're not a real man unless you take what you need'" (Mosher and Tomkins 1988, 72). But the sex is not for the man himself but for his peers. As they put it, "Sol Gordon's joke has it that neither party enjoys their initial experience with sexual intercourse, the boy gets his orgasm the next day when he tells his friends" (ibid.).
50. Sabo 1989, 39.
51. Faludi 1991.
52. For an analysis of these various perspectives, see Clatterbaugh 1989; Kimmel 1987.
53. Quoted in Faludi 1991, 308–312.
54. Bly 1991, 38–42. The third and fourth issues of *Masculinities* was devoted to the subject of profeminist men responding to the men's movement, and featured a number of incisive critiques of Bly and others in the so-called mythopoetic men's movement. There have also been important critiques by women of Bly. One of the most interesting and funny ones is "Pumping Iron John" by Jane Caputi and Gordene O. MacKenzie, in *Women Respond to the Men's Movement* (1992).
55. Roszak 1969, 92–93.
56. A number of studies show that the cultural movement to a masculinity of male supremacy presages violence and repression. Thus, Roszak writes of the dominator backlash that eventually led to World War I, "Compulsive masculinity is written all over the political style of the period." Just as violence, and particularly sexual violence, is often the outcome of all-male drinking sessions, Roszak writes of those years as "one long drunken stag party where boys from every walk of life and every ideological persuasion goad one another on to ever more bizarre professions of toughness, daring, and counterphobic mania—until at last the boasting turns suicidal and these would-be supermen plunge the whole of Western society into the bloodbath of world war" (Roszak 1969, 92). See also David McClelland's study of times when the emphasis in popular culture is to downgrade "affiliation" (more "feminine" peaceful and compassionate values) and reidealize "power" (more "masculine" or "hard" values) and David Winter's study of

times when Don Juan "lady-killer" type fiction proliferates (McClelland 1980, Winter 1973).

57. Pleck in Brod 1992. See also Hagen, *Women Respond to the Men's Movement* (1992).
58. Knoll Evans, personal communication and work in process.
59. Roszak 1969, 101.
60. Winter 1973; personal communication with Knoll Evans; personal communication with a psychiatrist who lived in and worked with women in Saudi Arabia.
61. For some alternative scripts of masculinity and femininity, see Eisler and Loye 1990, especially the section on dominator and partnership heroes and heroines.
62. Ibid. See also Callahan 1993, which contains conversations with Loye and Eisler.
63. Stoltenberg 1990, 129. See also Stoltenberg 1993.
64. Stoltenberg 1990, 110, 129, 130.
65. This was the 18th National Conference on Men and Masculinity, held in 1991 and sponsored by the National Organization of Men Against Sexism, 54 Mint Street, Suite 300, San Francisco, CA 94103.
66. This 1993 conference, which I helped organize, was held in Coeur d'Alene, Idaho, and used the new integrated model for human rights proposed in Eisler 1987c; 1993c; 1993d.

CHAPTER 14: GETTING OUT OF PRINCE CHARMING'S SLIPPER (Pp. 265–286)

1. Publications and videos on this are available from the American Association of University Women Educational Foundation in Annapolis Junction, MD, based on findings that the U.S. school system shortchanges girls. One of the major factors is that teachers pay far more attention to boys than to girls, often rewarding boys for calling attention to themselves, while rewarding girls for being quiet and docile. See also Sadker and Sadker 1994; Orenstein 1994.
2. A recent book by an Episcopal bishop on how the Christian story of Mary has been a "subtle, unconscious source for the continued oppression of women" is John Shelby Spong's *Born of a Woman* (1992).
3. Even Judith, a heroic biblical figure, is presented as using her sexual powers against a man, in this case the tyrannical Holofernes, whom she decapitates.
4. Walker 1994, 22–25.
5. Alan Dundes, quoted in Wilstein 1989, A5. Charles Perrault wrote this version of "Little Red Riding Hood" in 1697.
6. There are still some fairy tales, such as "Snow White and the Seven Dwarfs," where the female protagonist displays a certain measure of spunk.
7. See Sinclair 1993, an in-depth analysis from the perspective of a mother of two daughters with eating disorders whom she helped through a technique she calls cohealing. See also Orbach 1978.
8. Feminist psychologists have shed important light on bulimia and anorexia by placing these eating disorders in their social context. For example, feminist analyses point out that trying to control one's bodily proportions often seems more doable to women than exercising real control over their lives in a society where women's life options, and thus power, are still very limited—so much so that even in their relations with men, women are expected to passively wait for men to call them or propose marriage rather than doing anything to change their situation, as this is still considered overly aggressive.
9. Personal conversation with an editor from a mainstream women's magazine.
10. See Steinem, "Sex, Lies, and Advertising" (1990) for a detailed exposé of how the women's magazines are censored.
11. In some recent versions, this part has been expurgated, but it is still in the "classic" story.
12. One of the most horrendous examples is the Chinese parable of the virtuous daughter-in-law who during a time of famine cuts off pieces of her own flesh in order to serve them to her husband and his venerable parents.

13. Like other effective pieces of dominator propaganda, the Sheherezade story has also been popularized through music, as in Rimsky-Korsakov's famous Sheherezade Suite, and (as with "Cinderella") an opera. Disney's *Sleeping Beauty* has vividly brought this same message of female helplessness to many millions more children.

14. In contrast to most female characters in Western literature, Roxana is, in Bram Dijkstra's words, a "levelheaded, intelligent, and extraordinarily tenacious" businesswoman, perfectly capable of "surviving and thriving" even in the predatory business world that already in the eighteenth century was beginning to provide men yet another battlefield on which to prove their "masculinity" (Dijkstra 1986, 6). Nonetheless, even this story has an obligatory "moral" ending—though it is without much impact, since it does not happen until the very last paragraph, when abruptly "the blast of Heaven" falls, and after years of flourishing, the heroine is suddenly plunged into misery.

15. Dijkstra 1986, vii.

16. For a book documenting some of the harsh realities, which sharply contrast with the myths, of the nineteenth century, see Vicinus 1973.

17. The French novelist Émile Zola wrote of the prostitute heroine of his *Nana* as a "lewd creature of the jungle" (Dijkstra 1986, 240). The poet Baudelaire referred to women as "flowers of evil" (ibid., 245). Artists painted nude women tempting spiritual men with their bodies or cavorting with goat-footed satyrs (ibid., 255). And in canvas after canvas these dangerous creatures consorted with serpents—as Dijkstra points out, a direct slam at nineteenth-century feminists, for whom the snake-headed Medusa was a symbol, as well as "a nightmare visualization of woman as predatory sexual being" (ibid., 238).

18. Ibid., 238. As Walter Pater wrote in *Marius the Epicurean* (1885), this version of Diana was "a Deity of Slaughter—the Taurian goddess, who requires the sacrifice of shipwrecked sailors, thrown on her coasts" (ibid., 239).

19. Ibid., 351.

20. Ibid., 346.

21. Byron and a host of other famous poets also eulogized dead women.

22. Kanner 1990, xxxiv–xxxv. For two powerful stories about women who could not conform to these myths, see Kate Chopin's, *The Awakening*, which was originally published in 1899 and reissued in 1972, and Charlotte Perkins Gilman's "The Yellow Wallpaper," originally published in 1892 and included in the *Charlotte Perkins Gilman Reader* (1980).

23. Dijkstra 1986, 328.

24. For a study of how race, gender, and class are interlocking systems of domination, see Glenn 1992.

25. Some recent writings by Black feminists on the divisions—as well as unities—between women of different races are Collins 1991, and James and Busia 1993.

26. Quoted in Spender 1983, xi.

27. Some works by Black feminists on this subject are Bannerji et al. 1991; Davis 1983; hooks (who chooses to not capitalize her name) 1984.

28. For example, as the poet Abida Khanum writes in her book *Forgotten Hostages: The Women of Islam* (work in progress), in Pakistan when a boy is born, there is celebration, whereas women sing laments upon the birth of a girl. For a documentary on the devaluation of girl babies in India, see the CBS program "60 Minutes," January 24, 1993. Traveling vans now provide ultrasound equipment to check the sex of the fetus, with the result that abortions of baby girls are soaring. Thus, in one district of India in 1991, out of 931 abortions 929 were of female fetuses.

29. See, for example, Sen 1990a.

30. If the men they live with continue to be abusive, their self-worth plummets even further, leading to the vicious cycle described by Forward 1986 and Norwood 1986.

31. This is a point brought out by French 1985. See also Caplan 1985.

32. See, for example, Rich 1976; Caplan 1989; and Chesler 1991.

33. For example, a psychoanalyst who accepted a contract to work in Saudi Arabia (being a woman, this meant working only with women) told me how shocked she was by all the unconscious ways in which women in that society expressed this resentment toward ·

men. She reported acts such as sexual abuse of male babies (for instance, grandmothers sucking baby boys' penises) and women egging their sons on to ever greater recklessness (reflected in the many abandoned Cadillacs and other expensive foreign cars found on Saudi Arabian roads after crashes due to driving at incredibly high speeds) (personal communication with a psychoanalyst who did not wish to have her name revealed).

34. Spender 1983, 2–3. For an excellent earlier book on this subject, see Kraditor 1968.
35. Spender 1983, 2–3.
36. As anyone who looks at the pictures of some of the women who have identified them-selves as feminists knows, most of them are actually quite good looking. In fact, some of the more outspoken (whose pictures occasionally get into newspapers) are extremely good looking, women such as Gloria Steinem, Patricia Schroeder, Kate Michelman, Alice Walker, Jill Eikenberry, and Jane Fonda, to name but a few. But one of the characteristics of "feminine" superscripts is that, like other forms of bias, even when they contradict what one sees, experiences, and feels—as illustrated in the story of the naked emperor whose nudity was perceived only by one untutored child—they are so powerful that they supersede the evidence from one's own eyes.
37. Proving that women, and not just men, have been effectively brainwashed, the maker of *Boxing Helena* was a woman, Jennifer Chambers Lynch.
38. Many books deal with this hidden history—for example, Flexner 1959; Newcomer 1959; Kerber and Mathews 1982; Lerner 1979; Millett 1970; and for a more international and multicultural perspective, books such as Collins 1990; James and Busia 1993; and Morgan 1984; as well as documents such as *The State of the World's Women 1985,* available from the United Nations. There are also anthologies of important feminist writings—for example, *Modern Feminisms* (1992), edited by Heilbrun and Miller; *The Feminist Papers* (1973), edited by Rossi; and *Feminism: The Essential Historical Writings* (1972) and *Feminism in Our Time* (1994), edited by Schneir.
39. Quoted in Caplan 1985, 164.
40. Cassell 1984.
41. Friday 1991. As Ti-Grace Atkinson writes, when women assert themselves more, they tend to have different kinds of sexual fantasies in which they are no longer "the passive recipient or helpless victim of the man's sex drive" (quoted in Caplan 1985, 166).
42. As Ehrenreich, Hess, and Jacobs (1987) note, even though there is here also a strong ten-dency toward sadomasochistic sex, it is a measure of the influence of the women's movement that even in these circles sexual pleasure for women is a fit subject at all.
43. Leo 1984.
44. Ehrenreich, Hess, and Jacobs 1987.
45. Gould 1987, 18.
46. Christ 1987a; Gray 1988; Plaskow and Christ 1989; Lorde 1984; Sjöö and Mor 1987; Chicago 1979, 1985; Gadon 1989; Orenstein 1990; Noble 1990; Starhawk 1982; Teish 1985; Wilshire 1994.
47. Heyward 1989.
48. Lorde 1984, 53, 56, 58.
49. Noble 1990, 198.
50. Gadon 1989, 305; Heyward 1989, 3, 101.

CHAPTER 15: SEX, LIES, AND STEREOTYPES (Pp. 287–307)

1. Martin 1991.
2. Ibid., 485–486.
3. Alberts 1983, 795.
4. Martin 1991, 488–489.

5. Ibid., 486–487.
6. Ibid., 489. Scientists even attribute to the sperm stereotypically masculine choices—for example, in an article in the journal *Cell* we are informed that the sperm makes an "existential decision" to penetrate the egg (Shapiro 1987, 293). By contrast, in an article they wrote for *Medical World News*, Gerald and Helen Schatten likened the egg's role to that of Sleeping Beauty: "a dormant bride awaiting her mate's magic kiss, which instills the spirit that brings her to life" (Schatten and Schatten 1984, 51).
7. Martin 1991, 493. Interestingly, in contrast to most biology texts, Woody Allen's film *Everything You Always Wanted to Know About Sex But Were Afraid to Ask* more accurately portrays this process in a sequence where he plays a recalcitrant sperm, engaged in shy avoidance rather than forceful pursuit.
8. Baltz, Katz, and Cone 1988, 643, 650.
9. As one researcher told Martin, the sperm tries to escape all the time "like Br'er Rabbit getting more and more stuck to Tar Baby the more he wriggles" (Martin 1991, 493).
10. Schatten and Schatten 1984, 51.
11. Martin 1991, 494.
12. Ibid.
13. Ibid., 491.
14. Wassarman 1988, 78–84.
15. As Martin comments, "At the very least, the imagery keeps alive some of the hoariest old stereotypes about weak damsels in distress and their strong male rescuers" (Martin 1991, 500).
16. Ibid., 486.
17. Douglas 1975, 62.
18. I want to add that in many cultures, coming-of-age ceremonies for boys, as well as girls, involve isolation, and that isolation can be a spiritual time of turning inward to prepare for adult life. In some societies, the girl's isolation may still have this element. But there is in rigidly male-dominant societies typically not just a sense of awe but a sense of danger and disgust associated with menstruation.
19. Turnbull 1961, 185–186.
20. Ibid., 154, 187.
21. Ibid. The *elima* can at times be a rough-and-tumble affair, with a lot of physical interaction, including even battles between the girls and the boys with strong sexual overtones. I should here say, as I have stressed all along, that because a society orients more to partnership than domination does not mean it will be violence-free. But, and this is the case among the BaMbuti and other more partnership-oriented tribal societies, this violence is not institutionalized in rigid dominator-dominated patterns or positively valued, as it is in the societies where women are rigidly controlled by men. So, in sharp contrast to the situation among the more androcratic neighboring villages, BaMbuti girls can be not only sexually but physically aggressive. Moreover, among the BaMbuti there is no stigma of inferiority attached to being a woman—all of which is reflected in the way a girl's first "blessing by the moon" is greeted.
22. Benedict 1959, 112. Another tribal society that orients more to partnership is the Tiruray, studied by the anthropologist Stuart Schlegel when he did his fieldwork in the Philippines (Schlegel 1970, and work in process). Schlegel points out that among the Tiruray menstruation is referred to as *adat libun* (women's custom), and that *adat* or *custom* is for the Tiruray a very positive word (personal communication with Stuart Schlegel, professor emeritus of anthropology, University of California at Santa Cruz, October 1993).
23. A work dealing with this and other subjects related to menstruation is Schuttle and Redgrove 1990.
24. See Noble 1990. See also discussion on sacrifice in Chapter 7.
25. Noble 1990 and Gray 1988.
26. Men also have biological cycles. Recent studies indicate that men have both daily and seasonal cycles of testosterone elevation. Their testosterone levels appear to be lower in the spring and higher in the fall. And from day to day, they seem to be lowest around

8 P.M. and peak around 4 A.M.—a discovery that led sex researcher June Reinisch to quip: "When people say women can't be trusted because they cycle every month, my response is that men cycle every day, so they should only be allowed to negotiate peace treaties in the evening" (quoted in Gorman 1992, 51).

27. For a book stressing this factor, see Berman 1984.

28. Genesis 1:28. There are also passages that speak of man as a steward in this respect, which are today being used by those who find a biblical authority for environmentalism. See, for example, Countryman 1988.

29. I have written about the need to develop a new system for classifying different kinds of technologies in accordance with their uses, rather than just throwing everything from can openers to nuclear bombs into the same classification (Eisler 1988).

30. Increasingly, problems with damming and other measures instituted without attention to long-range consequences are coming to the fore, as in the 1993 floods in the American Midwest, as well as the great floods that inundated parts of Germany at the end of that same year. See, for example, Calfield 1984.

31. Adams 1994; Diamond and Orenstein 1990; Shiva 1988; Anderson 1991.

32. Gray 1988, 1.

33. Leviticus 12.

34. There is movement in this direction in some mainstream congregations. For example, in the Episcopal Church, the 1979 revision of the official Book of Common Prayer (BCP) changed the previous Churching of Women Service, which focused on the mother's survival through the "ordeal" of birth, to a service called Thanksgiving for the Birth or Adoption of a Child, which emphasizes the miracle of birth.

35. Horton 1994. The struggle of women to reclaim their ancient role as birth attendants is not easy. For example, insurance companies still generally refuse to provide malpractice insurance for licensed midwives. For an overview of the struggle in the early eighteenth century between midwives and the Church-trained physicians who were already beginning to take over the delivery of babies, see Tatlock 1992.

36. Quoted in Gray 1988, 53.

37. This legislation was first introduced in Minneapolis. But to date, this type of legislation has been held unconstitutional in the United States. In 1992 the Canadian Supreme Court used the MacKinnon/Dworkin balancing-of-rights approach to redefine obscenity in a case that held that the right of people to life and to freedom from sadistic violence must take precedence over freedom of speech (Associated Press, March 5, 1992; see also Landsberg 1992). Charges that this ruling has been discriminatorily used against gay and lesbian pornography have been made. This may be true, but the fact is that, as Ann Simonton writes in *Media Watch,* this kind of discriminatory enforcement of laws against pornography and obscenity also was found in Canada before this ruling. An important recent book on pornography and free speech is Catharine A. MacKinnon, *Only Words* (1993). See also MacKinnon 1982.

38. Kaplan 1974, 147.

39. Brecher 1979, 184; Kaplan 1974, 388–389; Reinisch with Beasley 1990, 96.

40. Reinisch with Beasley 1990, 77.

41. Genesis 38:10, King James Version; Hair 1962; MacDonald 1967.

42. Quoted in Hall 1992, 367.

43. *Beautiful Dreamers* (1991, directed by John Kent Harrison) was based on the true story of a British physician who sought to end such barbaric practices in mental institutions.

44. Groneman 1994, 341.

45. Laqueur 1990. Women were long considered to be highly sexual. However, during the eighteenth century the idea that women have far less sex drive than men began to be promulgated by the medical establishment.

46. Groneman 1994, 349.

47. As Groneman writes, those who performed these operations (gynecologists) "were generally more enthusiastic about the operation than were neurologists, psychiatrists, and other physicians" (ibid., 350). As Groneman also notes, castration (which produces the

same effect in men as the removal of ovaries produces in women) was never considered an appropriate treatment for satyriasis (the medical term for what was considered the male counterpart of nymphomania); neither was cutting off the penis (ibid., 352).

48. Ibid., 349.
49. Quoted in Groneman 1994, 357.
50. Ibid., 359.
51. Reinisch with Beasley 1990, 203.
52. Conner 1993, Introduction. Among the reindeer-herding peoples of Siberia, believed by many to be ancestors of Native Americans, homosexual men can marry other men and live with them in much the same way they would if one of them were a woman (Walter L. Williams 1986). Among Polynesians, homosexual individuals (*mahus*) were often attached to the chief's household and held prestigious positions (ibid.).
53. Conner 1993. Some scholars believe that male homosexual priesthoods first appeared with the shift to a male-dominated social organization, arguing that men usurped the roles traditionally assigned to priestesses. Others believe that these men, like priestesses, served the Goddess from earliest times—a position for which Conner makes an interesting case. Actually, there may be truth in both arguments: perhaps originally both priestesses and priests served the Goddess, but with the shift to a dominator system priests began to displace priestesses even in religions where a female deity was still venerated.
54. Contrary to prevailing beliefs, as Reinisch and Beasley write, it is "not true that people become homosexuals because they were seduced by an older person of the same sex in their youth" (Reinisch with Beasley 1990, 36). On the contrary, some women who choose a lesbian lifestyle were influenced in this choice by negative, debasing, and often traumatic heterosexual experiences—for example, sexual abuse by their fathers or rape.
55. As Elaine Showalter reports in *Sexual Anarchy*, there has been a critique of those gay men who, as Susan Sontag harshly put it, "reconstituted themselves as something like an ethnic group, one whose distinctive folkloric custom was sexual voracity, and the institutions of urban homosexual life became a sexual delivery system of unprecedented speed, efficiency, and volume," as typifying everything that was most brutal and exploitive in male sexuality. However, since the advent of AIDS, this type of behavior and the macho values animating it seem to have substantially changed, with one recent study showing that between 1984 and 1987 the percentage of gay urban men in monogamous relationships doubled (Showalter 1990, 186).
56. As Kathleen Canning writes, the term *postmodernist*, like the term *linguistic turn*, has become a catch-all phrase for what are sometimes widely different critiques of established historical paradigms, narratives, and chronologies. Postmodernism "encompasses not only poststructuralist literary criticism, linguistic theory, and philosophy, but also cultural and symbolic anthropology, new historicism, and gender history" (Canning 1994, 369). It also builds on Marxist and feminist analyses of how mainstream historical, literary, and social scientific accounts have often served to maintain the interests of those who hold power. For a discussion of some of the foundational works of postmodern inquiry, see Skinner 1985. For a recent critique of postmodernism, see Spretnak 1991.
57. Gadamer 1976; Habermas 1971; Kuhn 1970; Derrida 1981; Foucault 1979; Kristeva 1978; Laqueur 1990; Lyotard 1984; Rorty 1979; Scott 1988.
58. Gergen 1991.
59. See, for example, Derrida 1981.
60. Gadamer 1976.
61. Canning 1994, 368. Two collections of essays with very different positions on postmodernism are Butler and Scott 1992 and Nicholson 1990.
62. See, for example, Riley 1988. For two strong critiques of the postmodern deconstruction of feminist theory see Bordo 1990 and Hartsock 1990.
63. Hartsock 1990, 163.
64. Baudrillard 1983, 38.

65. Kearney 1995.
66. Gablik 1991.
67. Montuori and Conti 1992.

CHAPTER 16: MORALITY, ETHICS, AND PLEASURE
(Pp. 308–329)

1. David was upbraided by Nathan, as we learn in 2 Samuel 12:7–24, where Nathan gives him a severe dressing down and prophesies that the child that is born to him will die. But then we learn that Bathsheba bears David another child, Solomon, "and the Lord loved him." In any event, David did not get stoned to death.
2. In *The River and the Star: The Lost Story of the Great Scientific Explorers of Goodness,* David Loye makes a distinction between a morality of coercion and a morality of caring, showing how the former grew out of a dominator social organization (Loye, work in progress a).
3. "Epidemic of STD's Forecast," *Associated Press,* January 4, 1991. See also Jacobson 1992.
4. Altman 1992. The Harvard findings are reported in a book edited by Dr. Jonathan Mann, Dr. Daniel Tarantola, and Thomas W. Netter, *AIDS in the World 1992* (1992).
5. Ibid.
6. In 1993, the Federal Drug Administration approved sale of a female condom in the United States, protection for women who have sex with men who will not use condoms.
7. Waken 1993.
8. Reported in "AIDS Is Spreading Rapidly and Ominously Throughout Africa," *New York Times,* September 16, 1990, 14.
9. Reported in "Does AIDS Mean Humiliation?" From *WomenIssue* in a February 1992 newspaper clipped by Barbara Good (a coordinator of the Coalition Against Trafficking in Women) on her 1992 tour of meetings with women leaders in Asia. The story also reported that the man responsible for this young woman's death continues to live "a respected life" as "he is protected by some influential people."
10. At the same time, heterosexual men who have contracted AIDS, such as the sports figure Magic Johnson—who essentially admitted that he had probably infected many women (he claimed he has slept with more than two thousand women)—have generally been viewed with sympathy, in yet another variation of the dominator double standards for those who hold power and those who do not.
11. Given the nature of prostitution as a transaction where the prostitute (female or male) often has little control over the use of condoms, the rapid spread of AIDS in places such as Thailand and India can hardly be blamed on prostitutes.
12. There is a strong grass-roots religious movement for social change, as exemplified by Catholic liberation theology. But even though a number of papal encyclicals speak of a just society and the plight of the poor, and Catholic bishops have, particularly in Latin America, sometimes supported liberation theology, there is still a tendency for the Church to laud those who do charity work for the poor but to condemn those who work for fundamental social and economic change. Moreover, even the Catholic liberation theology movement has, with only a few exceptions, ignored the fact that worldwide, women are the bulk of the poor and the poorest of the poor.
13. Contaminated blood transfusions account for only a small percentage of cases.
14. "AIDS Is Spreading . . . ," *New York Times,* September 16, 1990, 14.
15. The anonymity of the sex was sometimes absolute, in that in some of the places where it took place there was a wall between the participants, with a hole where one man placed his anal opening or mouth and another man entered it from the other side.
16. See, for example, Rhodes 1991. See also Powers 1992.
17. "AIDS Is Spreading . . . ," *New York Times,* September 16, 1990, 15.
18. Ibid.

19. Ibid.
20. Personal communication with Fran Hosken, 1992.
21. Hosken 1986.
22. *1994 World Population Data Sheet,* cited in *World Population News Service POPLINE,* May–June 1994, 1.
23. See, for example, Eisler 1986.
24. See, for example, Nullis 1992.
25. *World Population News Service POPLINE,* November–December 1992, 1. Another source of information in this area is Population Action International in Washington, DC.
26. Hume 1991, 17.
27. Quoted in Beck 1992–93, 78.
28. It is encouraging that the Catholic Church has during the twentieth century moved toward an official endorsement of social and economic justice in accordance with the original teachings of Jesus. There are certainly many Catholic priests and nuns who vigorously work for these ends in many parts of the world. But unfortunately, as many of their accounts attest, they are all too often *not* supported by Church officials. *With Eyes to See: A Journey From Religion to Spirituality* (1992) by Arthur Melville, a former Catholic priest who joined the peoples' struggle for economic justice in Guatemala, gives a moving account of this problem through the eyes of a sensitive man who gradually began to free himself from his religious and cultural programming and defied the Church hierarchy.
29. The old argument was that economic development is the key to lower population—despite the fact that some Arab states that are among the richest in the world have very high birthrates because of the low status and lack of independence of women. By contrast, poorer nations such as Indonesia, Thailand, and Mexico have begun to pursue policies designed to increase access to child health and family planning services, to support literacy and education (particularly among women), and to generally raise the status of women. While they still have a long way to go in implementing these measures, these nations have already had dramatic decreases in their population growth rates. For example, Indonesia's female literacy rate is 62 percent, while the country's population (the fourth largest in the world) is growing annually by only 1.8 percent (Jyoti Shankar Singh, director of the Technical and Evaluation Division of the UNFPA, quoted in Hertsgaard 1993, 72).
30. The extent of this is dramatically highlighted by how, during the United Nations preparatory planning sessions for the 1994 International Conference on Population and Development in Cairo, the Holy See made no less than 147 objections to the Proposed Program of Action (which included strong language on the empowerment of women), even objecting to such phrases as "family planning," "reproductive rights," "reproductive health," and, amazingly, "safe motherhood" (*World Population News Service POPLINE,* May–June 1994, 3).
31. This "nonfallible" declaration by Pope John Paul II, telling Catholics that the issue of women becoming priests is not open to debate and that his views must be "definitively held by all the church's faithful," came three days after the Vatican unveiled the English translation of its new universal catechism—originally submitted with gender-neutral language but altered to refer to *man,* for example, instead of *humanity* (Cowell 1994).
32. *World Population News Service POPLINE,* November–December, 1992, 1. This shift in policy was first announced at the 1984 Conference on Population in Mexico City, where (astonishingly, considering that overpopulation is such a visible problem in Mexico City), the Reagan administration announced that there is no population problem. An exposé of how President Reagan agreed to alter U.S. foreign aid programs to comply with the Vatican appeared in *Time* magazine on February 24, 1992. For a more detailed analysis, see Steven D. Mumford's 1992 article "Papal Power: U.S. Security Population Directive Undermined by Vatican With 'Ecumenism' a Tool," in *The Human Quest,* a publication of Churchman Associates, 1074 23rd Ave. North, St. Petersburg, FL 33704. After President Clinton took office, U.S. support for international family planning aid was reinstated

(see Burdett 1993). See also "Clinton Overturns Mexico City Policy With Stroke of Pen" (*World Population News Service POPLINE,* January–February 1993), reporting that President Clinton signed an executive memorandum on his third day in office terming the conditions set forth in the Mexico City policy "excessively broad" and "unwarranted."

33. Ibid.

34. Prescott 1986.

35. By failing to vigorously address the cultural, social, and economic factors behind abortion—including poverty, and since a large number of abortions are sought by unmarried women, lack of adequate social supports for single-parent families—they fail to address the conditions that often lead women to view abortion as their only realistic choice.

36. Ruether 1993, 10.

37. Ibid.

38. Portugal and Claro 1993, 30.

39. The alliance between the Vatican and the Saudi-controlled World Muslim League goes back to at least 1982, when a conference was held in Italy to push the argument that "consumption and better distribution of wealth," not overpopulation, should be the world's top environmental priority—an ironic plank, given the fact that the Vatican and the oil emirates together control, and have failed to redistribute, such an enormous share of the world's wealth. I should here add that the position of Muslim leaders is by no means unanimously pronatalist, with some very concerned about rapid population growth (Beck 1992–93, 78).

40. Nonetheless, in the end this alliance fizzled, and most Islamic states endorsed the Conference's Program for Action, including strong planks on family planning and gender equity, despite the Vatican's assertions that it violated morality. Still, as Ruether writes, there is a real danger of further alliances between the Vatican and fundamentalist Muslims around shared views on "family values" (Ruether 1994/95). For how feminist lobbying played an important part in the conference's final declaration of policy, see Correa and Petchesky, 1994; Cowell 1994.

41. September 1994 emergency mailing from Population Communication International in New York City. A recent cross-cultural study of eighty-nine nations verifies the connection between gender equity or inquity and a generally higher or lower quality of life. It also shows a highly significant correlation between prevalence of contraception as an indicator of gender equity and a generally higher quality of life (Eisler, Loye, and Norgaard 1995). This monograph, *Gender Equity and the Quality of Life,* can be ordered for $20 from the Center for Partnership Studies, P.O. Box 51936, Pacific Grove, CA 93950.

42. It is instructive that pronatalism has been a hallmark of dominator regressions throughout modern history—be they under Hitler, under Stalin, or under Khomeini.

43. This is analyzed in Hume 1991.

44. Loye works in progress a, b, and c. See also Loye 1990 and 1992.

45. Examples are the gunning down of demonstrators against the czars in Russia and the use of force against American labor organizers in the early twentieth century.

46. Hewitt et al. 1993.

47. See "Archbishop Resigns," *Associated Press,* April 7, 1993, reporting the resignation of Archbishop Robert F. Sanchez, 59, after allegations surfaced that he had had sex over a period of many years with several women, some of them teenagers.

48. Quoted in Ostling 1993, 44.

49. These sex scandals were for years written about in the feminist press. After the mainstream press at last began to write about this "delicate" subject, men as well as women began to come forward to tell that they were sexually abused by their trusted priests.

50. This is still a problem for more partnership-oriented religious groups today and has in some places resulted in the persecution and killing of members of such groups. For example, in Iran members of the Baha'i faith (which gives high value to the education of women and, except for the highest positions, does not exclude women from leadership) have been violently persecuted since Khomeini's so-called Islamic revolution.

51. This problem is forcefully brought out by Kivel 1992, 140.

52. Briggs 1991. Some congregations, such as the Unitarians and the Quakers, have already incorporated such principles into their religious canons.

53. For the history of Catholic doctrine on contraception, as well as what is today being done to once again achieve changes, see Maggie Hume, *Contraception in Catholic Doctrine: The Evolution of an Earthly Code,* published in 1991 by Catholics for a Free Choice in Washington, DC.

54. There are many other organizations working independently for reform, for example, the Association for the Rights of Catholics in the Church in Delrand, New Jersey. There are also publications, such as *Bread Rising* in Minneapolis and *Church Watch* in Chicago, the French *Golias,* the Brazilian *Rumos,* and the Canadian Catholic *New Times,* as well as more mainstream publications such as *The National Catholic Reporter* and the British *The Tablet.*

55. Letter by Joan D. Uebelhoer, reprinted under the heading of "Let the Pope Visit My Clinic," in the Spring/Summer 1993 issue of *Conscience.*

56. Nasreen 1993; Hazarika 1994; "Thousands of Protestors Demand Author's Death," *Associated Press, English News International,* June 12, 1994 (reprinted in a mailing by Women Living Under Muslim Laws, June 1994).

57. Abida Khanum, *Forgotten Hostages: The Women of Islam,* work in progress.

58. Excerpt from Makiya's *Republic of Fear* (1993) reprinted under the title of "Rape in the Service of the State" in *The Nation,* May 10, 1993. It is significant that Makiya writes that "women's bodies are deemed simultaneously the font from which all honor derives and a source of *fitna,* or public sedition" (*The Nation,* 630). If one substitutes the word *domination* for *honor,* it summarizes the hidden underpinnings of this kind of sexual morality, be it Eastern or Western, Northern or Southern.

59. Circular letter distributed by Women Living Under Muslim Laws, an international network headquartered in France, Boite Postale 23-34790 Grabels, Montpellier, France, dated July 15, 1993.

60. Rubin 1984, 283.

61. Trask 1983, 135.

62. Echols 1984, 65.

63. Valverde 1987.

64. Most feminist writings in one way or another deal with sexuality. And because in dominator societies gender, sex, class, race, and ethnicity form interlocking systems of domination, there have in recent years been important books by Black feminists dealing with these issues—for example, Patricia Hill Collins, *Black Feminist Thought* (1991); Angela Davis, *Women, Race, and Class* (1983); bell hooks, *Feminist Theory: From Margin to Center* (1984).

65. Hosken 1981. The *Universal Childbirth Book: A Picture Story of Reproduction From a Woman's View,* with illustrations by Marcia L. Williams, can be obtained by writing to WIN News, 187 Grant St., Lexington, MA 02173.

66. SIECUS, 130 West 42nd St., Suite 2500, New York, NY 10036.

67. "American Teens Speak: Sex, Myths, TV, and Birth Control," a poll conducted for the Planned Parenthood Federation of America by Louis Harris and Associates, 1986.

68. Reinisch with Beasley 1990, 1. The majority of those surveyed correctly answered only half or less of the questions, and therefore, in accordance with conventional grading standards, received an F. Only 4 percent got B's; and less than half of 1 percent got A's (ibid.). However, one of the more hopeful findings was that women eighteen to forty-four years and men thirty to forty-four scored higher than other age groups—with 55 percent of women as against 52 percent of men in these groups passing. As Reinisch and Beasley comment, "These Americans came of age sexually during an era characterized by the women's movement, the Pill, and books about female sexuality," a time when (partly explaining why women scored somewhat higher) "women were beginning to believe that they had a *right* to sex information, and there was greater access to higher education for both sexes" (ibid., 20, emphasis in original).

69. For instance, in John 2:5, he is quoted harshly telling his mother, "Woman, what have I to do with thee?" and in Matthew 12:48, when he is told his mother and brothers are standing nearby waiting to speak to him, he supposedly curtly asks, "Who is my mother? And who is my brethren?" (King James Version).

70. Matthew 19:29. The theologian Walter Wink argues that if Jesus made such statements, it was because he was against the authoritarian, male-dominated family of his time as the chief purveyor of dominator values, and not because he was against families (Wink 1992, 118–120). He writes that Jesus "created a counter-family, based not on the blood-line but on voluntary profession of partnership values (Mark 3:31–35)" (letter to author from Wink, September 15, 1994). However, this is not explicitly apparent from these biblical passages.

71. Luke 14:26. See also Matthew 10:34–37, where it is made to seem that Jesus again urges family discord, at the same time minimizing the importance of family love.

72. For a recent work probing this legend, see Starbird 1993.

73. Corinthians 7:9.

74. Genesis includes two human creation stories, and in one women and men are equal. But the story of Eve's creation from Adam's rib and the story blaming Eve for the Fall have been emphasized.

75. After the death of Mohammed's first wife, Khadija, a rich widow who was substantially older than he, Mohammed decided to marry a six-year-old girl, Ayesha, daughter of one of his friends. It was for this Ayesha, who as Richard Lewinsohn writes "brought her toys with her when she entered the house of a man who was old enough to have been not merely her father, but her grandfather," that Mohammed developed the sexual passion he retained to the end of his days. Nonetheless, in contrast to his marriage to Khadija, which had been monogamous and apparently faithful on both sides, this marriage was the beginning for Mohammed of a large harem that, as Lewinsohn writes, "grew even faster than his empire" (Lewinsohn 1958, 102–103). So it would seem that Mohammed's family life is actually a model for child molestation of a kind men are today prosecuted for in courts of law, as well as of polygamy.

76. "The Lesser Child: The Girl in India," prepared by the Indian government for South Asia's Year of the Girl Child in 1980, reports these UNICEF findings (Crossette 1990).

77. For example, the Koran attributes the following words to Mohammed himself: "Men have authority over women because God has made the one superior to the other, and because they spend their wealth to maintain them. Good women are obedient. They guard their unseen parts because God has guarded them. As for those from whom you fear disobedience, admonish them and send them to beds apart and beat them." See Pickthall's 1953 translation of the Koran, 83.

78. Valverde 1987, 150–151.

79. Even lifelong sexual abnegation has for some people been a choice preferable to the available alternatives. For example, nuns have often chosen it in lieu of becoming a subordinate and "silent" wife. And since for much of Western history men of the upper classes had only the choice of the military or the clergy, sensitive men often chose the latter—and with it (as required by the Church) a vow of lifelong celibacy.

CHAPTER 17: SEX, POWER, AND CHOICE
(Pp. 330–346)

1. Millett 1970.

2. Henderson 1981 and 1991.

3. I am hesitant to talk about a new book, since, as I explained in the beginning of this book, my plans for works that I had announced earlier changed. I hope that this time I will produce the book on Partnership Economics I plan to write next.

4. Eldredge and Grene 1992.

5. Perhaps in part because bonobo males balance this through their somewhat larger size, even though female groups sometimes displace males at feeding sites, in many other respects, including one-to-one relations, females do not here dominate males.

6. Personal communications with Amy Parish, 1992–93. For an important article highlighting how what she calls women's "networks of love and support" were a key factor in early twentieth-century political activism, see Cook 1982.

7. This position is still sometimes advanced by some Marxists.

8. *Masai Women*, Granada Television International, 1974, Melissa Llewelyn-Davies, producer.

9. In other words, the crux of the matter is not, as some Marxists have contended, the degree to which women contribute to the society's economy. The crux is whether a society orients primarily to a partnership or a dominator organization—and this is so whether societies are technologically primitive or advanced.

10. For an analysis of family laws and practices in Muslim societies, see Mernissi 1987.

11. Fisher 1992, 108.

12. In parts of Thailand, at least before the spread of AIDS, a woman could return to her village after a few years of doing sex work to marry and otherwise be accepted into the community. This is not the case in other regions of Asia, or for that matter in most places in the world, where prostitution carries a terrible social stigma.

13. Overall 1992, 709.

14. Hollibaugh 1988.

15. For example, CORP (Canadian Organization for the Rights of Prostitutes) and COYOTE (Call Off Your Old Tired Ethics). See also Pheterson 1989.

16. Overall 1992, 711.

17. Ibid.

18. Ibid., 719.

19. Ibid., 721.

20. Ibid., 722.

21. Engels 1972.

22. For a classic work on how women internalize their own devaluation, see Miller 1976. It offers positive alternatives, as well as an excellent psychosocial analysis.

23. See, for example, Waring 1988.

24. Reported in *The State of the World's Women 1985* (New York: United Nations, 1985).

25. For an article tracing the shift to male control in matrilineal tribes such as the Kaguru of Africa, where there are still, however, traces of an earlier power balance between women and men, see McCall 1982.

26. In recent years there have been more government efforts to collect court-awarded child support. Even now these efforts are halfhearted and less effective than they could be, as illustrated by the fact that a 1989 study by the inspector general of the Department of Health and Human Services found that military personnel were in arrears on child support payments totaling more than $176 million dollars—a ridiculous situation since the military has records of where its personnel are stationed, which could electronically be made available to state agencies seeking to collect child support (Dixon, 1993).

27. President Bush's 1991 Commission for Children and the Family suggested child-care allowances, but he ignored this. Such allowances would have changed the status of welfare mothers to one of far greater dignity and self-worth, thus undermining the notion that all women must be under male control in father-headed families.

28. For example, the Scandinavians were pioneers in areas such as family leave legislation, which then served as a model for other industrialized nations such as Germany. In the United States, it was not until President Clinton took office that the Family Leave Act was successfully introduced and passed by Congress. Even then, unlike policy in the Scandinavian nations and Germany, it provides for only unpaid parental leave.

29. United Nations Development Reports have been published annually since 1990 by the Oxford University Press. Based on quantified measures of a nation's quality of life (ranging from average life expectancy to hazardous waste generation), they consistently give top ranking to the Scandinavian nations and support the conclusion that, as the 1991 report puts it, lack of political commitment, not financial resources, is often the real cause of human neglect. For a new quantified study showing a significant correlation between a higher or lower general quality of life and gender equity or inequity, see Eisler, Loye, and Norgaard 1955 (available from the Center for Partnership Studies, P.O. Box 51936, Pacific Grove, California 93950).

30. It is certainly true that during times of economic trouble, as in Sweden during recent years, there are cutbacks in these programs as the tax base shrinks. But the underlying issue is the choice of funding allocations.

31. Bourdieu 1989; Brubaker 1985.
32. Sen 1990b.
33. Several decades ago, the liberal economist Robert Theobald proposed a guaranteed income as an economic floor (Theobald 1967). More recently, the conservative economist Milton Friedman has proposed a negative income tax as a necessary measure for social stability in an age of shrinking employment. In the new partnership approach to economics that I am developing, I am proposing that such measures be linked to rewarding caretaking work, both on the family and social level. There are many reasons for this, including the need to give value to this kind of work. But equally important is that people need a sense that their lives have meaning, that what they do is important—which is one of the reasons that top-down welfare programs that are handouts from bureaucratic structures that do not recognize the value of what the recipient does have not achieved their ends (Eisler, *Partnership Economics*, work in progress).

CHAPTER 18: TOWARD A POLITICS OF PARTNERSHIP (Pp. 347–371)

1. The imposition of a belief system can take different forms. Thus, in Soviet-style communism, where traditional religion was forbidden, Lenin became a cult object, with communism almost like a state religion. See Chapter 11 of *The Chalice and the Blade*.
2. See chapters 11 and 12 of *The Chalice and the Blade* for a more detailed discussion of these regressive dynamics. See also Loye 1977; Eisler and Loye 1983.
3. See Loye 1977; Eisler and Loye 1983.
4. The picture sketched in these pages of the three-hundred-year modern movement toward a politics of partnership is explored in depth by David Loye from the moral perspective developed in *The River and the Star* (work in progress a) and in terms of psychological dynamics in *The Leadership Passion* (Loye 1977).
5. McLaren 1990.
6. Hieroglyphics indicate the practice of inserting a small pebble through the cervix into the uterus, which is the same principle as the IUD.
7. Conklin 1980.
8. Ibid. As Conklin writes, "Traditional beliefs in every continent associate female reproductive cycles with the moon." She notes that the full moon is often seen as the best time for conception (as in the orgiastic spring festivals of the lower castes of the Kol in India and the preference for marriages at or before the full moon among the Kikuyu of East Africa) (ibid., 30). Conversely, ethnographic data (for example, from the Trobriand Islands) suggests a connection between high sexual activity during dark moonless or new moon nights and a low incidence of premarital pregnancy (ibid., 40–48).
9. Faulkner 1985.
10. It is noteworthy that courageous Catholic nuns have publicly called the Church's position prohibiting family planning immoral.
11. Nullis 1992.
12. Conversations with David Loye, June 1994.
13. See, for example, Boxall 1992.
14. This is why in warrior societies of the ancient Greek and Samurai type, where male homosexuality was idealized rather than condemned, this was only so for relations between men and boys—that is, between individuals of unequal power.
15. For an article on contemporary lesbian relations, see Peplau, Cochran, Rook, and Pedesky, "Loving Women: Attachment and Autonomy in Lesbian Relationships" (1978). There is a growing literature by scholars, poets, novelists, and other writers about this subject. For example, *Signs* devoted its Summer 1993 issue to "theorizing lesbian experience," with contributions by many scholars (*Signs*, Vol. 18, No. 4, Summer 1993).
16. Anderson 1990. Anderson reports that "Iranian officials have also admitted to at least 26 executions by stoning last year. Fourteen were women 'convicted of adultery or prostitution.' In one case, twelve women and three men were stoned to death on a soccer field by spectators who had come for the soccer game." He goes on to note that "Iran's law spells

out the rules for stoning—the rocks must be small enough so they don't kill the victim instantly, but large enough so they can be called stones" (ibid.). These executions continue. For example, according to a February 1, 1994, Reuters report, a married Iranian woman, Mina Kolvat, was stoned to death in Tehran's Evin prison for adultery (mailing from Women Living Under Muslim Laws, April 6, 1994). That same mailing reports that a prominent Iranian academic set herself on fire in public and later died protesting the treatment of women by the Islamic Republic of Iran. A professor of psychoanalysis at the university, she had been dismissed from her academic position for failing to observe strictly the prescribed rules of the *Hijab*, i.e., covering herself according to the government's regulations. The mailing also reports that "a widespread campaign continues to enforce Islamic dress, which sometimes leads to physical violence on the street" (ibid.).

17. Ibid.

18. This brief and the Reed case, which in 1971 finally held that in some cases, gender-based discrimination violates the Fourteenth Amendment, is discussed in Eisler 1978.

19. Eisler 1987c, 1993c, 1993d.

20. Roszak 1969.

21. Barry 1993, 8.

22. For example, according to a University of Pennsylvania study presented at the annual convention of the National Television Program Executives in Miami Beach, Florida, on January 27, 1994, the average Nielsen ratings during the past five seasons were higher for nonviolent programs than for violent ones, and the audience share for such programs was also higher. George Gerbner announced these findings in his January 27, 1994, press release for the Cultural Environment Movement (P.O. Box 31847, Philadelphia, PA 19104), which promotes networking to change the media.

23. Centerwall 1992. See also "A Tale of Three Countries: Homicide Rates Rise After Television's Arrival," *Media and Values,* Summer 1993, 12–13.

24. Tannis Macbeth Williams 1986. Particularly noteworthy is that parents who grew up watching television tend to use more violence in child rearing—helping to explain some of the rise in family violence we read about in our press (Eron and Huesmann 1984).

25. Loye, Gorney, and Steele 1977.

26. Gerbner 1994; Gerbner, Gross, Morgan, and Signorielli 1994.

27. Gerbner, Gross, Morgan, and Signorielli 1994, 20, 25.

28. Gerbner 1994, 139.

29. Gerbner 1994; Gerbner, Gross, Morgan, and Signorielli 1994. For example, Gerbner, Gross, Morgan, and Signorielli report that most groups of heavy viewers consistently scored higher on a sexism scale, and third and fourth graders who watched more television were more likely to stereotype activities such as cooking and playing sports and qualities such as warmth and independence along traditional gender-role lines (ibid., 31). They note that heavy viewers are more likely to label themselves moderates—even though when their positions on political issues are examined, their views are much closer to those of conservatives. So what these researchers call mainstreaming tends to bend people to the right, at the same time that it sets up unmeetable expectations, such as more social services but lower taxes (ibid., 31–32).

30. Barry 1993, 10.

31. For example, a recent survey of homelessness in London revealed that 40 percent of homeless women were fleeing violent homes (Henry 1994, 11).

32. These were some of the hitherto hidden statistics publicized during the 1990 and 1991 U.S. Senate hearings on violence against women. The three billion dollar sum, based on the cost of medical and psychological bills, absenteeism, lost wages, insurance, and police, court, and prison costs, does not include the economic costs of women's wasted human potential from chronic injuries, anxiety, feelings of lack of self-worth, and desperation, or the physical and psychological costs to the children of these women.

33. For example, the lead editorial of the *Monterey County Herald* of July 13, 1993, fretted that men of wealth might be "a tempting target" under the act's civil rights remedies.

34. This crime bill, passed in large part because of the persistence of President Clinton against the massive lobbying of the weapons manufacturers and the National Rifle As-

sociation, increases penalties for repeat sexual assault offenders and, for the first time, also includes a civil rights remedy for violent crimes motivated by gender (*The Woman Activist Extra,* August 26, 1994. *The Woman Activist* is published monthly by The Woman Activist, 2310 Barbaur Rd., Falls Church, VA 22043).

35. Eisler 1993c and 1993d.
36. This is dramatically shown by the history of Marxist revolutions, where women's rights, if considered at all, were viewed as peripheral to the "real" struggle.
37. Myrdal 1962, Loye 1971. Loye is currently rewriting and updating this book which, along with Myrdal's, won the Anisfield-Wolfe award for the best scholarly book on race relations.
38. Sykes 1992.
39. Cornel West, a professor at Princeton University, points out that this kind of thinking has greatly distorted the realities of Black Americans, who are now told (sometimes by conservative Blacks themselves) that they should "see themselves as agents, not victims." He writes that what "is particularly naive and peculiarly vicious about the conservative behavioral outlook is that it tends to deny the lingering effect of Black history—a history inseparable from, though not reducible to victimization.... This ahistorical perspective contributes to the nihilistic threat within Black America in that it can be used to justify right-wing cutbacks for poor people struggling for decent housing, childcare, healthcare, and education" (West 1993, 14).
40. Sykes 1992, 1, 3.
41. Many of the same criticisms that are leveled against President Clinton were also leveled against Lincoln, who was ridiculed for his propensity to try to make compromises (which was seen as indecisiveness) and for cowardice (because he wanted to avoid the bloodshed of the Civil War), yet whose empathy for others (particularly for Black slaves) is what he is most remembered for in American history.
42. Stark 1993. Stark notes that "the Clinton style is a textbook example of a leader who communicates in ways often more characteristic of women than men." Moreover, "if traditional gender roles dictate that women care for the home while men police the perimeter, Clinton is the first president in more than fifty years to make domestic affairs his preoccupation" (ibid.).
43. Bernard 1981; Gilligan 1982; Miller 1976.
44. Quoted in the *Kölner Staadt-Anzeiger,* weekend edition, October 2–3, 1993, 4.
45. Larsen 1994.
46. A book on environmental activism is Wallace 1993. It has a chapter on Wangari Maathai of Kenya, founder of the Green Belt movement. See also Lappe and DuBois 1994.
47. Quoted in "Survival Economics," *Earth Island Journal,* Spring 1992, 28.
48. Kivel 1992.
49. Peterson and Runyan 1993, 126–127.
50. Ibid., 44.
51. "Five Million Children: 1993 Update," National Center for Children in Poverty at Columbia University in New York City.
52. Healthy Families America was featured in an "All Things Considered" program on National Public Radio on April 19, 1994, with Michelle Trudeau reporting.
53. Peterson and Runyan 1993, 141–142.
54. Ibid., 64. This book looks at politics from a gender-sensitive perspective.
55. *Women's Watch* 5 (January 1992), 9. *Women's Watch* is published by the Humphrey Institute of Public Affairs, University of Minnesota, 301 19th Ave. South, Minneapolis, MN 55455.
56. Ibid.
57. The Sisterhood Is Global Institute is located at 4343 Montgomery Ave., Suite 201, Bethesda, MD 20814; the Center for Global Issues and Women's Leadership is located at Rutgers University, P.O. Box 270, New Brunswick, NJ 08903; Women's International Network News is located at 187 Grant St., Lexington, MA 02173; International Women's Rights Action Watch is located at the Humphrey Institute of Public Affairs, University of Minnesota, 301 19th Ave. S, Minneapolis, MN 55455.

58. The first UN Decade for Women also resulted in the establishment of a number of UN bodies such as the United Nations International Research and Training Institute for the Advancement of Women (INSTRAW), the United Nations Development Fund for Women (UNIFEM), and the Division for the Advancement of Women (DAW)—bodies that, though still poorly funded and forced to struggle every inch of the way to mainstream their work, have in a very short time made significant contributions. For example, INSTRAW publishes a quarterly, *INSTRAW News*, that reports important research, disseminates materials that other organizations and individuals can use, and promotes networking around development issues by women worldwide. Inquiries can be addressed to INSTRAW, DCI-1106, United Nations, New York, NY 10017, fax (212) 963–2978. See also Pietila and Vickers 1994 for an excellent book on the UN Decade for Women.

59. DAWN, Institute of Social Studies Trust (ISST), SMM Theatre Crafts Building, 5 Deen Deyal Upadhyay Marg., New Delhi 110 002, India.

60. World Business Academy, 433 Airport Blvd., Suite 416, Burlingame, CA 94010; Bay Area Business for Social Responsibility, 3220 Sacramento St., San Francisco, CA 94115; Students for Responsible Business, 1388 Sutter St., Suite 1010, San Francisco, CA 94109.

61. There also are businesses such as the San Francisco–based Working Assets, (which competes with AT&T, MCI, and Sprint for long-distance subscribers and gives a percentage of its revenues to groups working for peace, human rights, economic justice, and a clean, safe environment) and organizations such as Coop America in Washington, DC (which publishes lists of socially and environmentally conscious businesses).

62. Galtung 1980.

63. Rossman 1979, 93. Rossman, who in the 1960s was still enmeshed in the old-style politics of groups such as Students for a Democratic Society (SDS) (which was said to advocate violence as a means to a more just society) writes that like many other "veterans of the New Left," he at first turned to disciplines of the body-mind-spirit to retreat from or transcend politics, but that for him bodywork "turned out to be an intense form of meditation" that eventually led him to understand that "our social condition is reflected in our bodies, and can be approached through them as well" (ibid., 95).

64. Ibid., 101.

65. Bendon 1994, 29.

66. As I have developed in earlier chapters and in other writings (Eisler 1987a, 1987b, 1991, 1993a), *cultural transformation theory* predicts that during periods of social, economic, technological, and cultural disequilibrium there can be a strong movement for transformative change. It also posits that at a certain point small scattered nodules of people organizing for change at the periphery of the system can link to form the critical mass of a new "attractor" that can pull the institutional infrastructure and belief system in a partnership direction. However, *cultural transformation theory* also underlines that there is another possible outcome. As has happened repeatedly in our history, through the dynamics of dominator backlash and co-option, the new attractor may become one that only gives a new partnership "face" to domination. That is, rather than leading to a new partnership organization where the mutual giving and receiving of benefits or pleasure primarily holds relations together, the result can be merely a new version of a dominator system. Masquerading as a doctrine of love and "brotherhood" can be the same old secular or religious fascism still based on the idealization, and even erotization, of domination and submission. Or behind proclamations of world peace, the same forces can, either directly through brute force or indirectly through economic pressures, continue to use the power to inflict pain in order to maintain the old hierarchies of domination. Loye (work in progress a) explores these dynamics in terms of his concept of a hybrid dominator-partnership morality.

67. This is most apparent in rigid dominator societies—with their strong-man rule in both the family and the state and their high level of institutionalized violence (from child and wife beating to "heroic" or "holy" warfare). Here the only alternative to suffering is making others suffer instead by taking the role of dominator rather than dominated. Or if that is not possible, it is to deny one's pain by identifying with those who cause it and to deflect

one's frustration and anger against socially disempowered groups—or if one is a member of such a group, against oneself, as women and minorities have been taught to do.

68. There are alternative publications that do give coverage to such leaders, such as *In These Times* (a not-for-profit biweekly newsmagazine), *Ms., Woman of Power, WIN News, Common Ground,* as well as countless newsletters of groups ranging from the U.S.-based Friends (Quakers), the American Association of University Women, Women for Economic Justice, the Older Woman's Leauge, the Elmwood Institute, Population Action International, and the Population Institute to the French-based Women Living Under Muslim Laws, the British-based Right Livelihood Award Foundation, and the Geneva-based Green Cross.

CHAPTER 19: THE NEW EVES AND THE NEW ADAMS (Pp. 372–401)

1. For a more detailed discussion, see Montuori and Conti 1993; Eisler and Montuori 1995.
2. Montuori and Conti 1993.
3. Eisler and Montuori 1995, Eisler 1988.
4. Lovelock 1979.
5. Stanton 1885.
6. Ibid., 9.
7. For a recent book thoroughly documenting this, see Torjesen 1993. For other works on this subject, see Fiorenza 1983; Gray 1994; and Chapter 7 of *The Chalice and the Blade.*
8. Bowman 1994, 17. The Saxon goddess Eostre, or Ostara, may actually be of Babylonian origin and is the northern form of Astarte. Meg Bowman's *Goddesses, Witches, and the Paradigm Shift* is available from the Women and Religion Task Force at P.O. Box 21506, San Jose, CA 95151.
9. Gray 1988.
10. Fox 1981 and 1983.
11. O'Brien 1981, 370.
12. Heyward 1989, 102.
13. See, for example, Bradley 1983.
14. Wink 1992. Like Wink and other theologians and historians, such as Elizabeth Dodson Gray, Mary Daly, Joanne Carlson Brown, Carol R. Bohn, Rita Nakashima Brock, and Philip Greven, I believe that, as Gray puts it, we also need to deal with the myth of an abusive God the father who demands and carries out the suffering and death of his own son as part of that tradition of redemptive violence (Gray 1994, 48).
15. Ornish 1990, 90.
16. House, Landis, and Umberson 1988.
17. Edell 1991, 2.
18. Maturana 1990, xv.
19. Giddens 1992.
20. Efforts to teach children ways of being and relating are not new. Indeed, much of traditional schooling is designed to teach students ways of being and relating that socialize them to fit into and perpetuate a dominator society.
21. I want to especially thank Rob Koegel for his invaluable help in educating me about teachers' efforts to introduce partnership education into our schools.
22. Goleman 1994a, 2.
23. Bigelow and Christiansen 1993, 18.
24. Goleman 1994b, 10. The Child Development Program, which has as its aim making schools into "caring communities where children feel valued," encourages schools to "invent new traditions and reshape existing ones as they reweave the fabric of school life to emphasize values of kindness, fairness, and personal responsibility" ("The Child Development Project," *Connections* 1, June 1994, 8).

25. Shelley Kessler, one of the originators of the program, quoted in "The Mysteries Program," *Connections* 1 (June 1994), 4.

26. See, for example, Sears 1992, and Stein and Sjostrom 1994. The Stein and Sjostrom book, *Flirting or Hurting?*, is available by calling 617-283-2510.

27. See, for example, Tenorio 1994 and "Rethinking Our Classrooms: Teaching for Equity and Justice," a special issue of *Rethinking Schools*, published in 1994 by Rethinking Schools, 1001 East Keefe Ave., Milwaukee, WI 53212.

28. See Noddings 1994 and Loye work in progress c.

29. Quoted in Miedzian 1991, 118.

30. Miedzian 1991, 118–131.

31. Ibid., 118.

32. Ibid., 119.

33. One of the pioneering works in this area was Bowlby 1969. For a summary of the theories of Bowlby and others, see Shaver, Hazan, and Bradshaw 1988.

34. Freedman 1989.

35. Asch 1952.

36. These were the findings of the psychologist Constance Avery-Clark based on studies at the Masters and Johnson Institute indicating that more than twice as many husbands with nonworking wives complained of impotence and lack of sexual desire as did those in two-career marriages. Avery-Clark also found that "professional women have less difficulty being orgasmic than other women, because they do a better job of letting their partner know what they need" (quoted in Rubenstein 1985, 155).

37. Clements 1994.

38. Pasick 1992.

39. Buchwald, Fletcher, and Roth 1993.

40. Mernissi 1987.

41. *Women Envision*, June 1994, reports that on March 30, 1994, two unveiled young women, aged nineteen and twenty, were killed by gunmen while waiting at a bus stop (*Women Envision* is published by Isis International, P.O. Box 1837, Quezon City Main, Quezon City 1100, Philippines). The July 27, 1994, *Alert for Action* of Women Living Under Muslim Laws reports that more than 550 women have been murdered in Kurdistan, with the government remaining silent or even encouraging the situation through various laws directed against women, as is the case in other nations where religious fundamentalists have taken control.

42. Just how dangerous these leaders are is all too evident from their own words. For example, Randall Terry of Operation Rescue recently had this to say to his followers: "I want you to just let a wave of intolerance wash over you. I want you to let a wave of hatred wash over you. Yes, hate is good" (quoted in *Christian Century*, August 10–17, 1994, 742). A button for sale at the recent Republican state convention in Virginia read "Where Is Lee Harvey Oswald When America Really Needs Him?" (quoted in the July 18, 1994, *New Yorker*, and in *Christian Century*, August 10–17, 1994, 742).

43. Fullan 1994, 18. *Cooperative Learning* (available by calling 408-426-7926), as well as *Rethinking Schools* and *Connections*, are good sources of information on educators who are trying to teach students the causes of, and alternatives to, social injustice.

44. For instance, as David W. Johnson, Roger T. Johnson, Bruce Dudley, and Robert Burnett write in "Teaching Students to be Peer Mediators," students are today being taught skills of self-regulation, negotiation, conflict mediation, and peace making through programs such as the Resolving Conflict Creatively Program (RCCP), which is now serving 4,000 teachers and 120,000 students in New York City, with school districts in Anchorage, New Orleans, southern California, and New Jersey in various stages of replication (Johnson, Johnson, Dudley, and Burnett 1992).

45. Christiansen 1994.

46. Aron and Aron 1986.

47. Schlegel 1970.

48. Koegel is planning a series of books on education, including multicultural education, based on the conceptual framework of the partnership and dominator models. People

interested in forming a network of partnership educators can contact Rob Koegel at the Sociology Department, College of Technology, SUNY Farmingdale, Farmingdale, NY 11735.

49. See for example Jain and Banerjee 1985; Sen 1990a and 1990b. There are countless other professionals today also challenging dominator traditions, from physicians such as Dr. Fleur Sack, who documents the disastrous results of the male-as-norm approach to medical research, including research on AIDS (Sack with Streeter 1992), and Warren Bennis and Peter Block, who write of new empowering leadership styles (Bennis 1986 and Block 1990) to Arvonne Fraser, Peter Juviler, and Charlotte Bunch in the human rights field, and people trying to imbue large corporations such as DuPont and Volkswagen with more partnership-oriented values, such as Daniel Goudevert (former chairman of Volkswagen) and Peter Meyer-Dohm (director of Volkswagen's International Partnership Initiative), as well as new-style entrepreneurs, such as Anita Roddick, founder of the Body Shop, who sees business as an opportunity to market images and stories that raise consciousness about human rights and environmental issues.

50. See Chicago 1979 and 1985. Another example is the Swedish artist Monica Sjöö, whose painting of a female God giving birth caused an international uproar. For some images of Sjöö's work, see Sjöö and Mor 1987. A recent book of images and poems by Jane Evershed is *More Than a Tea Party* (1994). Some recent books about other artists are Gadon 1989 and Orenstein 1990. Gablik 1991 introduces the concept of the reconstruction, rather than deconstruction, of art—a very useful term. Another important source for new images as well as articles by some of these artists is *Woman of Power* (P.O. Box 2785, Orleans, MA 02653)—for example, the Winter 1994 issue, which has the theme of "Sacred Spaces." In addition, there are new publications such as *New Moon* with art, stories, and new rites for young girls (*New Moon*, P.O. Box 3587, Duluth, MN 55803).

51. Private communication from George Singleton, director, Hope LA Horticulture Corps.

52. *Woman of Power*, Winter 1994, 33.

53. Eisler and Loye 1990. For information on the partnership network, write Center for Partnership Studies, P.O. Box 51936, Pacific Grove, CA 93950.

54. Houston 1987; Swimme 1985; Rountree 1991; Melville 1992. Mathew Callahan is also the author of *Sex, Death, and the Angry Young Man: Conversations with Riane Eisler and David Loye* (1993).

55. See, for example, Capra 1982; hooks 1993; Hubbard 1990; Laqueur 1990; Merchant 1992; Steinem 1983; West 1993.

56. For example, Byllye Y. Avery, founder of the National Black Women's Health Project; Marsha Saxton, director of the Project on Women and Disability; Kathleen Barry, founder of the Coalition Against Trafficking in Women.

57. Spectrum Productions Ltd. can be reached by writing to Room 8, c/o Annex 8, RTE, Donnybrook, Dublin 4, Ireland.

58. Examples include Daw Aung San Suu of Myanmar (formerly Burma), who gained international press attention when she won the Nobel Peace Prize; Gloria Steinem, who for more than three decades has inspired us with her vision, humor, and courage; Amos Wako, attorney general of Kenya who recently suggested laws be reformed to allow the prosecution of men who have sex with their wives without prior consent; Mary Robinson, the president of Ireland, who has been an outspoken advocate of women's rights; Vice President Al Gore of the United States, who has been a leader in raising environmental consciousness; his wife, Tipper Gore, who has been in the forefront of raising consciousness about the need for images that no longer demean women and women's sexuality; as well as filmmakers such as Barbra Streisand and Robert Redford, who use their talents to bring us stories that both entertain and inspire.

59. We are in the process of putting these poems together into two collections for future publication: *100 Days of Love* and *1,000 Days of Love*.

Bibliography

Please see "Use of Notes and Bibliography," on page 407.

Abraham, Ralph. *Chaos, Gaia, Eros.* San Francisco: HarperSanFrancisco, 1994.

Abraham, Ralph, and Christopher Shaw. *Dynamics: The Geometry of Behavior.* Santa Cruz, CA: Aerial Press, 1984.

Abu-Lughod, Lila. *Veiled Sentiments.* Berkeley: University of California Press, 1986.

Adams, Carol, ed. *Ecofeminism and the Sacred.* New York: Continuum, 1994.

Adorno, T. W., Else Frenkel-Brunswick, Daniel Levinson, and R. Nevitt Stanford. *The Authoritarian Personality.* New York: Wiley, 1964.

Alberts, Bruce, et al. *Molecular Biology of the Cell.* New York: Garland, 1983.

Altman, Warren K. "Researchers Report Much Grimmer AIDS Outlook." *New York Times,* June 4, 1992, A1.

Anderson, Bonnie S., and Judith P. Zinsser. *A History of Their Own: Women in Europe.* Vol. 1. New York: Harper & Row, 1988.

Anderson, Jack. "Iran Homosexuals Fear for Lives." *Monterey Herald,* January 22, 1990.

Anderson, Lorraine, ed. *Sisters of the Earth.* New York: Vintage Books, 1991.

Ardrey, Robert. *African Genesis.* New York: Dell, 1961.

———. *The Territorial Imperative.* New York: Atheneum, 1966.

Ariès, Philippe. *Centuries of Childhood.* London: Cape, 1962.

Arken, William, and Lynne Dobrofsky. "Military Socialization and Masculinity." *Journal of Social Issues* 34 (Winter 1978), 151–168.

Aron, Arthur, and Elaine M. Aron. *Love and the Expansion of Self.* New York: Hemisphere, 1986.

———. *The Heart of Social Psychology.* Lexington, MA: Lexington Books, 1989.

Asch, Solomon E. *Social Psychology.* Englewood Cliffs, NJ: Prentice-Hall, 1952.

Atkinson, Clarissa. *The Oldest Vocation: Christian Motherhood in the Middle Ages.* Ithaca, NY: Cornell University Press, 1991.

Baltz, J. M., David F. Katz, and Richard A. Cone. "The Mechanics of the Sperm-Egg Interaction in the Zona Pellucida." *Biophysical Journal* 54 (October 1988).

Bandura, Albert, and Frances L. Menlove. "Factors Determining Vicarious Extinction of Avoidance Behavior Through Symbolic Modeling." *Journal of Personality and Social Psychology* 8 (1968), 99–108.

Banerji, Himani, Linda Carty, Kari Dehli, Susan Heald, and Kate McKenna. *Unsettling Relations: The University as a Site of Feminist Struggles.* Boston: South End Press, 1991.

Barbeau, Clayton. *Delivering the Male.* San Francisco: Harper & Row, 1982.

Barry, David S. "Growing Up Violent." *Media and Values,* Summer 1993, 8–11.

Barry, Kathleen. *Female Sexual Slavery.* New York: Avon Books, 1979.

Barstow, Anne Llewellyn. *Witchcraze: A New History of the European Witch Hunts.* London and San Francisco: Pandora, 1994.

Bart, Pauline B., and P. H. O'Brien. *Stopping Rape.* New York: Pergamon, 1985.

Baudrillard, Jean. *Simulations.* New York: Columbia University, Semiotext, 1983.

Beck, Roy. "Religions and the Environment: Commitment High Until U.S. Population Issues Raised." *The Social Contract* 3 (Winter 1992–93), 76–89.

Becker, Carl. *Declaration of Independence.* New York: Knopf, 1972.

Bendon, Hillary. "Partnership: An Alternative to the Classic Bureaucratic Management Model." Master's research project, Monterey Institute of International Studies, May 1994.

Benedict, Ruth. *Patterns of Culture.* New York: Mentor Books, 1959.

Beneke, Tim. "Deep Masculinity as Social Control: Foucault, Bly and Masculinity." *Masculinities* 1 (Summer 1993), 13–19.

Bennis, Warren. *Leaders.* New York: Harper & Row, 1986.

Berghold, Joe. "The Social Trance." *Journal of Psychohistory* 19 (Fall 1991), 221–247.

Berkowitz, Leonard. "Some Determinants of Impulsive Aggression." *Psychological Review* 81 (1974), 165–176.

Berman, Morris. *The Reenchantment of the World.* New York: Bantam Books, 1984.

Bernard, Jessie. *The Female World.* New York: Free Press, 1981.

Bigelow, Bill, and Linda Christiansen. "Promoting Social Imagination Through Interior Monologues." *Rethinking Schools* 8 (Winter 1993), 18.

Birnbaum, Lucia. *Black Madonnas.* Boston: Northeastern University Press, 1993.

Blackman, Julie. *Intimate Violence.* New York: Columbia University Press, 1989.

Blackstone. *Commentaries on the Laws of England.* Oxford: Clarendon Press, 1765.

Blake, C. Fred. "Foot-Binding in Neo-Confucian China and the Appropriation of Female Labor." *Signs* 19 (Spring 1994), 676–712.

Bleier, Ruth. *Science and Gender.* New York: Pergamon Press, 1984.

Block, Peter. *The Empowered Manager.* San Francisco: Jossey-Bass, 1990.

Bly, Robert. "The Need for Male Initiation." In *To Be a Man,* edited by Keith Thompson, 38–42. Los Angeles: Tarcher, 1991.

Bonfante-Warren, Larissa. "The Women of Etruria." In *Women in the Ancient World,* edited by John Peradotto and J. P. Sullivan. Albany, NY: State University of New York Press, 1984.

Bordo, Susan. "Feminism, Postmodernism, and Gender Skepticism." In *Feminism/Postmodernism,* edited by Linda J. Nicholson, 133–156. New York: Routledge, 1990.

Boswell, John. *The Kindness of Strangers.* New York: Pantheon, 1988.

Botti, Odile. "The Battle Against Excisions by Africans: A Survey of Actions in Three West African Countries." *Marie Claire* (November 1985).

Bourdieu, Pierre. "Social Space and Symbolic Power." *Sociological Theory* 7, 1989, 14–25.

Bowlby, John. *Attachment and Loss.* Vol. 1. New York: Basic Books, 1969.

Bowman, Meg, ed. *Goddesses, Witches, and the Paradigm Shift.* Vol. 2. San Jose, CA: Women and Religion Task Force, Unitarian Universalist Association, 1994.

Boxall, Bettina. "Gays Alter Dynamics of Politics." *Los Angeles Times,* September 15, 1992, A24.

Bradley, Marion Zimmer. *The Mists of Avalon.* New York: Knopf, 1983.

Bradshaw, John. *Bradshaw on the Family.* Pompano Beach, FL: Health Communications, 1988.

Brecher, Edward M. *The Sex Researchers.* Expanded ed. San Francisco: Pacific Press, 1979.

Briffault, Robert. *The Troubadours.* Bloomington, IN: Indiana University Press, 1965.

Briggs, David. "Report on Sexuality Stirs Up Presbyterians." *Associated Press,* June 1, 1991.

Brod, Harry. *The Making of Masculinities: The New Men's Studies.* Boston: Allen & Unwin, 1987.

Brown, Roger. *Social Psychology.* New York: Free Press, 1965.

Brownmiller, Susan. *Against Our Will.* New York: Simon & Schuster, 1975.

Brubaker, Rogers. "Rethinking Classical Theory: The Sociological Vision of Pierre Bourdieu." *Theory and Society* 14 (November 1985), 745–775.

Brundage, James A. "Better to Marry Than to Burn?" In *Views of Women's Lives in Western Tradition,* edited by Frances Richardson Keller, 195–216. Lewiston, NY: Edwin Mellen Press, 1990.

Buchwald, Emilie, Pamela R. Fletcher, and Martha Roth, eds. *Transforming a Rape Culture.* Minneapolis, MN: Milkweed Publications, 1993.

Burdett, Hal. "US Will Support Reproductive Choice, Including Abortion." *World Population News Service POPLINE,* May/June 1993, 1.

Burkert, Walter. *Structure and History in Greek Mythology and Ritual.* Berkeley: University of California Press, 1979.

Bury, J. B., S. A. Cook, and F. E. Adcock. "The Law of Ancient Babylonia." In *Man in Adaptation,* edited by Y. A. Cohen, 154–157. Chicago: Aldine, 1971.

Butler, Judith, and Joan W. Scott, eds. *Feminists Theorize the Political.* New York and London: Routledge, 1992.

Callahan, Mathew. *Sex, Death, and the Angry Young Man: Conversations with Riane Eisler and David Loye.* Ojai, CA: Times Change Press, 1993.

Campbell, Joseph. *The Mythic Image.* Princeton, NJ: Princeton University Press, 1974.

Canning, Kathleen. "Feminist History After the Linguistic Turn." *Signs* 19 (Winter 1994), 368–404.

Caplan, Paula J. *The Myth of Woman's Masochism.* New York: Dutton, 1985.

———. *Don't Blame Mother.* New York: Harper & Row, 1989.

Capra, Fritjof. *The Turning Point.* New York: Bantam Books, 1982.

Caputi, Jane, and Gordene O. MacKenzie. "Pumping Iron John." In *Women Respond to the Men's Movement,* edited by Kay Leigh Hagen. San Francisco: HarperSanFrancisco, 1992.

Cassell, Carol. *Swept Away.* New York: Simon and Schuster, 1984.

Castelot, André. *Napoleon.* New York: Harper & Row, 1971.

Caufield, Catherine. *In the Rainforest.* New York: Knopf, 1984.

Centerwall, Brandon, MD. "Television and Violence." *Journal of the American Medical Association* 267 (June 1992), 3059–3063.

Chaisson, Eric. *The Life Era.* New York: Atlantic Monthly Press, 1987.

Chesler, Phyllis. *Mothers on Trial.* San Diego: Harcourt Brace Jovanovich, 1991.

Chicago, Judy. *The Dinner Party.* New York: Anchor Press/Doubleday, 1979.

———. *The Birth Project.* New York: Doubleday, 1985.

Childe, V. Gordon. *The Dawn of European Civilization.* New York: Knopf, 1958.

Christ, Carol P., ed. *Laughter of Aphrodite.* San Francisco: Harper & Row, 1987.

Christiansen, Linda. "Unlearning the Myths That Bind Us." *Rethinking Schools* 8, Summer 1994 (Special Issue on Teaching for Equity and Justice), 8–12.

Clatterbaugh, Kenneth. "Masculinist Perspectives." *Changing Men* 20 (Winter/Spring 1989), 4–6.

———. "The Mythopoetic Foundations of New-Age Patriarchy." *Masculinities* 1 (Summer 1993), 2–12.

Clements, Mark. "Sex in America Today." *Parade,* August 7, 1994, 4–6.

Collier, John. *Indians of the Americas.* New York: Mentor, 1947.

Collins, Patricia Hill. *Black Feminist Thought.* New York: Routledge, 1991.

Coltrane, Scott. "Father-Child Relationships and the Status of Women." *American Journal of Sociology* 93 (March 1988), 1060–1095.

———. "The Micropolitics of Gender in Nonindustrial Societies." *Gender and Society* 6 (March 1992), 86–107.

Conklin, Beth Ann. "Lunar Cycles and Reproductive Rhythms." Thesis for master's in anthropology, University of Iowa, May 1980.

Conner, Randy P. *Blossom of Bone.* San Francisco: HarperSanFrancisco, 1993.

Cooey, Paula M., Sharon A. Farmer, and Mary Ellen Ross, eds. *Embodied Love.* San Francisco: Harper & Row, 1987.

Cook, Blanche Wiesen. "Female Support Networks and Political Activism: Lillian Wald, Crystal Eastman, Emma Goldman." In *Women's America,* edited by Linda K. Kerber and Jane De Hart Mathews. New York: Oxford University Press, 1982.

Coontz, Stephanie, and Peter Henderson, eds. *Women's Work, Men's Property.* London: Verso, 1986.

Correa, Sonia, and Rosalind Petchesky. "Exposing the Numbers Game." *Ms.,* September/October 1994, 10–17.

Countryman, L. William. *Dirt, Greed, and Sex.* Philadelphia: Fortress Press, 1988.

Cowell, Alan. "Pope Affirms Women Can't Be Priests." *New York Times,* May 31, 1994.

Crossette, B. "Twenty-five Percent of Girls in India Die by Age Fifteen, UNICEF Says." *New York Times,* October 5, 1990.

Csanyi, Vilmos. *Evolutionary Systems and Society: A General Theory.* Durham, NC: Duke University Press, 1989.

Dalley, Stephanie. *Myths From Mesopotamia.* Oxford, England: UP, 1989.

Daly, Mary. *Beyond God the Father.* Boston: Beacon Press, 1973.

Dartmouth Bible. Boston: Houghton Mifflin, 1950.

Davidson, Julian N. "The Psychobiology of Sexual Experience." In *The Psychobiology of Consciousness,* edited by Julian N. Davidson and Richard J. Davidson. New York: Plenum Press, 1980.

Davis, Angela. *Women, Race, and Class.* New York: Vintage Books, 1983.

de Beauvoir, Simone. *The Second Sex.* New York: Modern Library, 1968. (Original work published in French in 1949.)

Degler, Carl N. *At Odds: Women and the Family in America From the Revolution to the Present.* New York: Oxford University Press, 1980.

deMause, Lloyd. "Schreber and the History of Childhood." *Journal of Psychohistory* 15 (Summer 1987), 423–430.

———, ed. *The History of Childhood.* New York: Psychohistory Press, 1974.

DeMeo, James. *On the Origin and Diffusion of Patrism.* Doctoral dissertation, Geography Department, University of Kansas, 1986.

———. "The Origins and Diffusion of Patrism in Saharasia, c. 4000 B.C.E." *World Futures* 30 (March–May 1991), 247–271.

de Rougemont, Denis. *Love in the Western World.* New York: Schocken Books, 1956.

Derrida, Jacques. *Dissemination.* Chicago: University of Chicago Press, 1981.

de Waal, Frans. *Peacemaking Among Primates.* Cambridge, MA: Oxford University Press, 1989.

Diamond, Irene, and Gloria Feman Orenstein, eds. *Reweaving the World: The Emergence of Ecofeminism.* San Francisco: Sierra Club Books, 1990.

Dijkstra, Bram. *Idols of Perversity.* Oxford, England: Oxford University Press, 1986.

Dittes, James E. *The Male Predicament.* San Francisco: Harper & Row, 1985.

Dixon, Jennifer. "Support Often Uncollected From Parents in Military." *Associated Press,* June 13, 1993.

Donnerstein, Edward. "Aggressive Erotica and Violence Against Women." *Journal of Personality and Social Psychology* 39 (1980), 269–277.

Douglas, Mary Tew. *Implicit Meanings.* Boston: Routledge & Kegan Paul, 1975.

Dover, K. J. "Classical Greek Attitudes to Sexual Behaviour." In *Women in the Ancient World,* edited by John Peradotto and J. P. Sullivan. Albany, NY: State University of New York Press, 1984.

Dworkin, Andrea. *Intercourse.* New York: Free Press, 1987.

Echols, Alice. "The Taming of the Id." In *Pleasure and Danger,* edited by Carole S. Vance. London: Routledge & Kegan Paul, 1984.

Edell, Dean, MD. "To Your Health." *Edell Health Letter,* April 1991, 2.

Ehrenreich, Barbara, Elizabeth Hess, and Gloria Jacobs. *Re-making Love: The Feminization of Sex.* Garden City, NY: Anchor Press/Doubleday, 1987.

Eisler, Riane. *Dissolution.* New York: McGraw-Hill, 1977.

———. *The Equal Rights Handbook.* New York: Avon Books, 1978.

———. "Population Pressure, Women's Roles, and Peace." In *World Encyclopedia of Peace,* 292–294. New York: Pergamon Press, 1986.

———. *The Chalice and the Blade: Our History, Our Future.* San Francisco: Harper & Row, 1987a.

———. "Woman, Man, and the Evolution of Social Structure." *World Futures: The Journal of General Evolution* 23 (April 1987b), 79–92.

———. "Human Rights: Toward an Integrated Theory for Action." *The Human Rights Quarterly* 9 (August 1987c), 287–308.

———. "Technology at the Turning Point." *Woman of Power,* Fall 1988, 6–12.

———. "Cultural Evolution: Social Shifts and Phase Changes." In *The New Evolutionary Paradigm,* edited by Ervin Laszlo, 179–200. New York: Gordon & Breach, 1991.

———. "Technology, Gender, and History: Toward a Nonlinear Model of Social Evolution." In *The Evolution of Cognitive Maps: New Paradigms for the Twenty-*

first Century, edited by Ervin Laszlo, Ignazio Masulli, Robert Artigiani, and Vilmos Csanyi, 181–203. New York: Gordon & Breach, 1993a.

———. "From Domination to Partnership: The Foundations for Global Peace." In *Communication and Culture in War and Peace,* edited by Colleen Roach, 145–174. Newbury Park, CA: Sage Publications, 1993b.

———. "The Challenge of Human Rights for All: What We Can Do." In *Creating the 21st Century: Rights, Responsibilities, and Remedies,* edited by Howard F. Didsbury, Jr., 99–117. Washington, DC: World Futures Society, 1993c.

———. "The Rights of Women, Children, and Men." In *Human Rights for the 21st Century,* edited by Bertram Gross and Peter Juviler. Armonk, NY: M.E. Sharpe, 1993d.

———. "From Domination to Partnership: The Hidden Subtext for Sustainable Change." *Journal of Organizational Change Management* 7 (1994): 35–49.

———. *Partnership Economics.* Work in progress.

Eisler, Riane, and Vilmos Csanyi. "Human Dimorphism and Social Structure." Unfinished manuscript.

Eisler, Riane, and David Loye. "The Failure of Liberalism: A Reassessment of Ideology From a New Feminine-Masculine Perspective." *Political Psychology* 4 (1983), 375–391.

———. *The Partnership Way.* San Francisco: HarperSanFrancisco, 1990.

Eisler, Riane, David Loye, and Kari Norgaard. *Gender Equity and the Quality of Life: A Global Survey and Analysis.* Pacific Grove, CA: Center for Partnership Studies, 1995.

Eisler, Riane, and Alfonso Montuori. "Creativity, Gender, and Society." In *Social Creativity,* Vol. 3, edited by Alfonso Montuori and Ronald Purser. Creskill, NJ: Hampton Press, 1995.

El Daree, Dr. Asma. *Sudan: National Study on the Epidemiology of Female Circumcision.* Khartoum: University of Khartoum, Department of Community Medicine, 1980.

Eldredge, Niles, and Marjorie Grene. *Interactions: The Biological Context of Social Systems.* New York: Columbia University Press, 1992.

Encyclopedia of Religion. New York: Macmillan, 1987.

Engels, Friedrich. *The Origin of the Family, Private Property, and the State.* New York: International Publishers, 1972. (Original work published in German in 1884.)

Eron, Leonard D., and L. Rowell Huesmann. *Advances in the Study of Aggression.* Orlando, FL: Academic Press, 1984.

Evershed, Jane. *More Than a Tea Party.* San Francisco: HarperSanFrancisco, 1994.

Falk, Marcia. *The Song of Songs.* San Francisco: HarperSanFrancisco, 1990.

Faludi, Susan. *Backlash: The Undeclared War Against American Women.* New York: Crown, 1991.

Faulkner, Wendy. "Medical Technology and the Right to Heal." In *Smothered by Invention: Technology in Women's Lives,* edited by Wendy Faulkner and Erik Arnold. London: Pluto Press, 1985.

Fausto-Sterling, Anne. *Myths of Gender.* New York: Pergamon Press, 1984.

Fedigan, Linda Marie. *Primate Paradigms.* Montreal: Eden Press, 1982.

Feschbach, Seymour, and Bernard Malamuth. "Sex and Aggression." *Psychology Today,* November 1978, 111, 116.

Feuerstein, Georg. *Yoga: The Technology of Ecstasy.* Los Angeles: Tarcher, 1989.

Fiorenza, Elizabeth Schüsler. *In Memory of Her*. New York: Crossroads, 1983.

Fisher, Helen E. *Anatomy of Love*. New York: Norton, 1992.

Flexner, Eleanor. *Century of Struggle*. Cambridge: Harvard University Press, 1959.

Forward, Susan. *Men Who Hate Women and the Women Who Love Them*. New York: Bantam Books, 1986.

Foucault, Michel. *Discipline and Punish*. New York: Vintage Books, 1979.

———. *The History of Sexuality, Vol. 1*. New York: Vintage Books, 1980.

Fox, Matthew, ed. *Western Spirituality: Historical Roots, Ecumenical Routes*. Santa Fe, NM: Bear & Company, 1981.

———. *Original Blessing*. Santa Fe, NM: Bear & Company, 1983.

Fox, Robin Lane. *Pagans and Christians*. San Francisco: Harper & Row, 1986.

Frank, Roslyn M., with Susan Ayers, Monique Laxalt, Shelly Lowenberg, and Nancy Vosburg. "Etxeko-Andrea: The Missing Link? Women in Basque Culture." *Views of Women's Lives in Western Tradition*, edited by Frances Richardson Keller, 133–157. Lewiston, NY: Edwin Mellen Press, 1990.

Frayser, Suzanne G. *Varieties of Sexual Experience*. New Haven, CT: HRAF Press, 1985.

Frazer, James G. *The Golden Bough*. New York: Macmillan, 1922, 1969.

Freedman, Rita. *Bodylove*. New York: Harper & Row, 1989.

French, Marilyn. *Beyond Power*. New York: Ballantine, 1985.

Freud, Sigmund. *Three Contributions to the Theory of Sex*. New York: Dutton, 1962.

———. *General Psychological Theory*. New York: Collier Books, 1963.

Friday, Nancy. *Women on Top*. New York: Simon & Schuster, 1991.

Fullan, Michael. "Masks of the Teacher." *Edges* 6 (Spring 1994), 14–18.

Gablik, Suzi. *The Reenchantment of Art*. New York: Thames & Hudson, 1991.

Gadamer, Hans-Georg. *Philosophical Hermeneutics*. Berkeley: University of California Press, 1976.

Gadon, Elinor. *The Once and Future Goddess*. San Francisco: Harper & Row, 1989.

Galtung, Johan. *The True Worlds*. New York: Free Press, 1980.

Gardner, John, and John Maier, trans. and eds. *Gilgamesh*. (Translated from the Sin-Leqi-Unninni version.) New York: Vintage, 1985.

Gerbner, George. "The Politics of Media Violence: Some Reflections." In *Mass Communication Research*, edited by Cees J. Hamelink and Olga Linne, 133–145. Norwood, NJ: Ablex, 1994.

Gerbner, George, Larry Gross, Michael Morgan, and Nancy Signorielli. "Growing Up With Television." In *Media Effects*, edited by Jennings Bryant and Dolf Zillmann, 17–41. Hillsdale, NJ: Erlbaum, 1994.

Gergen, Kenneth J. *The Saturated Self*. New York: Basic Books, 1991.

Gerzon, Mark. *A Choice of Heroes*. Boston: Houghton Mifflin, 1982.

Giddens, Anthony. *The Constitution of Society*. Berkeley: University of California Press, 1984.

———. *The Transformation of Intimacy*. Stanford, CA: Stanford University Press, 1992.

Gies, Frances, and Joseph Gies. *Marriage and the Family in the Middle Ages*. New York: Harper & Row, 1987.

Gilligan, Carol. *In a Different Voice*. Cambridge, MA: Harvard University Press, 1982.

Gimbutas, Marija. *The Goddesses and Gods of Old Europe.* Berkeley: University of California Press, 1982.

———. *The Language of the Goddess.* San Francisco: Harper & Row, 1989.

———. *The Civilization of the Goddess.* San Francisco: HarperSanFrancisco, 1991.

Glenn, Evelyn Nakano. "From Servitude to Service Work." *Signs* 18 (Autumn 1992), 1–43.

Goldizen, Anne Wilson. "Social Relationships in a Cooperatively Polyandrous Group of Tamarins." *Behavioral Ecology and Sociobiology* 24 (1989): 79–89.

Goleman, Daniel. "A Great Idea in Education." *Connections* 1 (June 1994a), 2.

———. "Emotions 101." *Connections* 1 (June 1994b), 10.

Goodison, Lucy. *Death, Women, and the Sun.* London: University of London, 1989.

Gordon, Margaret, and Stephanie Riger. *The Female Fear: The Social Cost of Rape.* New York: Free Press, 1989.

Gorman, Christine. "Sizing Up the Sexes." *Time,* January 20, 1992.

Gould, Stephen Jay. "Freudian Slip." *Natural History,* February 1987, 14–21.

Graves, Robert, trans. *The Golden Ass of Apuleius.* New York: Pocket Library, 1954.

Gray, Elizabeth Dodson, ed. *Sacred Dimensions of Women's Experience.* Wellesley, MA: Roundtable Press, 1988.

———. *Sunday School Manifesto.* Wellesley, MA: Roundtable Press, 1994.

Griffin, Susan. *Pornography and Silence.* New York: Harper & Row, 1981.

———. *Rape: The Politics of Consciousness.* San Francisco: Harper & Row, 1986.

Groneman, Carol. "Nymphomania." *Signs* 19 (Winter 1994), 337–367.

Habermas, Jürgen. *Knowledge and Human Interests.* Translated by Jeremy J. Shapiro. Boston: Beacon Press, 1971.

Hagen, Kay Leigh, ed. *Women Respond to the Men's Movement.* San Francisco: HarperSanFrancisco, 1992.

Hair, E. H. "Masturbatory Insanity." *Journal of Mental Science* 108 (1962), 1–25.

Hall, Lesley A. "Forbidden by God, Despised by Men." *Journal of the History of Sexuality* 2 (January 1992), 365–387.

Hallett, Judith P. "The Role of Women in Roman Elegy: Counter-Cultural Feminism." In *Women in the Ancient World,* edited by John Peradotto and J. P. Sullivan. Albany, NY: State University of New York Press, 1984.

Harman, Willis. *Global Mind Change.* Indianapolis, IN: Knowledge Systems, 1988.

Harris, William H., and Judith S. Levey, eds. *The New Columbia Encyclopedia.* New York: Columbia University Press, 1975.

Harrison, Jane Ellen. *Prolegomena to the Study of Greek Religion.* London: Merlin Press, 1962. (Original work published in 1903.)

Hartsock, Nancy. "Foucault on Power: A Theory for Women." In *Feminism/Postmodernism,* edited by Linda J. Nicholson, 157–175. New York: Routledge, 1990.

Hastings, Deborah. "Simpson Arrest Focuses Attention on U.S. Spousal Abuse Problem." *Associated Press,* June 22, 1994.

Hawkes, Jacquetta. *Dawn of the Gods.* New York: Random House, 1968.

Hazarika, Sanjoy. "Bangladesh Seeks Writer, Charging She Insults Islam." *New York Times,* June 8, 1994.

Heilbrun, Carolyn, and Nancy Miller, eds. *Modern Feminisms.* New York: Columbia University Press, 1992.

Henderson, Hazel. *The Politics of the Solar Age.* New York: Anchor Books, 1981.

———. *Paradigms in Progress.* Indianapolis, IN: Knowledge Systems, 1991.

Henry, Margaret. "Domestic Violence." *Toward Freedom,* March 1994.

Henshaw, Richard A. *Female and Male: The Cultic Personnel, the Bible, and the Rest of the Ancient Near East.* Alison Park, PA: Pickwick Press, 1994.

Hertsgaard, Mark. "Still Ticking . . . " *Mother Jones,* March/April 1993, 72.

Hewitt, Bill, Lyndon Stambler, Julie Klein, and Doris Bacon. "The Body Counters." *People,* April 12, 1993, 35–37.

Heyward, Carter. *Touching Our Strength.* San Francisco: Harper & Row, 1989.

Highwater, Jamake. *Myth and Sexuality.* New York: Penguin, 1990.

Hoffman, Lisa. "Rape Study Says 51% of Victims Under 18." *Scripps Howard News Service,* June 23, 1994.

Hohmann, Gottfried, and Barbara Fruth. "Field Observations on Meat Sharing Among Bonobos." Paper presented at the Max Planck Society and Zoology Institute of the University of Munich, Germany, 1993.

Hollibaugh, Amber. "On the Street Where We Live." *Women's Review of Books,* January 1988, 1.

Homer. *Iliad.* Translated by Robert Fitzgerald. New York: Anchor Books, 1975.

hooks, bell. *Feminist Theory.* Boston: South End Press, 1984.

———. *Sisters of the Yam: Black Women and Self-Discovery.* Boston: South End Press, 1993.

Horton, Richard. "Unnecessary Caesarian Sections in U.S.A." *Lancet,* May 28, 1994, 1351.

Hosken, Fran. Pictures by Marcia L. Williams. *The Universal Childbirth Picture Book.* Lexington, MA: Women's International Network News, 1981.

———. "Why AIDS Pattern Is Different in Africa." *New York Times,* December 15, 1986, Letters section.

———. "Rape and Murder at Kenyan Catholic Boarding School in Meru." *Women's International Network (WIN) News* 17 (Autumn 1991), 37.

———. *The Hosken Report: Genital and Sexual Mutilation of Females.* 4th ed. Lexington, MA: Women's International Network News, 1994.

House, J. S., K. R. Landis, and D. Umberson. "Social Relationships and Health." *Science* 29 (July 1988), 540–550.

Houston, Jean. *The Search for the Beloved.* Los Angeles: Tarcher, 1987.

Howells, William W. *Getting Here.* Washington, DC: Compass Press, 1993.

Hrdy, Sarah Blaffer. *The Woman That Never Evolved.* Cambridge, MA: Harvard University Press, 1981.

———. "The Primate Origins of Human Sexuality." In *The Evolution of Sex,* edited by Robert Bellig and George Stevens, 101–136. San Francisco: Harper & Row, 1988.

Hubbard, Ruth. *The Politics of Women's Biology,* New York: Rutgers University Press, 1990.

Hume, Maggie. *Contraception in Catholic Doctrine.* Washington, DC: Catholics for a Free Choice, 1991.

Huxley, Julian. *Evolution in Action.* New York: Harper & Row, 1953.

Huynh Sanh Thong. "Mother's Tongue and Slang." *Journal of Unconventional History* 2 (Fall 1990), 31–61.

Jacobson, Jodi. "The Other Epidemic." *World Watch,* May/June 1992, 10–17.

Jain, Devaki, and Nirmala Banerjee, eds. *Tyranny of the Household: Women in Poverty.* New Delhi: Shakti Books, a division of Vikas Publishing, 1985.

James, Edwin Oliver. *The Cult of the Mother Goddess.* London: Thames & Hudson, 1959.

James, Stanlie M., and Abena P. A. Busia, eds. *Theorizing Black Feminism.* London: Routledge, 1993.

Johnson, Buffie. *Lady of the Beasts.* San Francisco: Harper & Row, 1988.

Johnson, David W., Roger T. Johnson, Bruce Dudley, and Robert Burnett. "Teaching Students to Be Peer Mediators." *Educational Leadership,* September 1992, 10–13.

Johnson, Don Hanlon. *Body, Spirit and Democracy.* Berkeley, CA: North Atlantic Books, 1994.

Kanner, Barbara. *Women in English Social History 1800–1914.* New York: Garland Publishing, 1990.

Kano, Takayoshi. "Social Behavior of Wild Pygmy Chimpanzees (*Pan paniscus*) of Wamba." *Journal of Human Evolution* 9 (1980), 243–260.

———. "The Bonobos' Peaceable Kingdom." *Natural History,* November 1990, 62–70.

———. *The Last Ape.* Stanford, CA: Stanford University Press, 1992.

Kaplan, Helen. *The New Sex Therapy.* New York: New York Times Book Co., 1974.

Kearney, Richard. "The Narrative Imagination." In *Social Creativity, Vol. 1,* edited by Alfonso Montuori and Ronald Purser. Creskill, NJ: Hampton Press, 1995.

Keller, Mara Lynn. "The Eleusinian Mysteries of Demeter and Persephone." *Journal of Feminist Studies in Religion* 4 (Spring 1988), 27–54.

———. "Chthonian Crete of the Earth Mother Goddess." Paper presented at the First International Minoan Celebration of Partnership, Crete, Greece, October 8, 1992.

———. *The Greater Mysteries of Demeter and Persephone.* Work in progress.

Kerber, Linda. *Women of the Republic.* Chapel Hill, NC: University of North Carolina Press, 1980.

Kerber, Linda, and Jane DeHart Mathews, eds. *Women's America.* New York: Oxford University Press, 1982.

Keuls, Eva. *The Reign of the Phallus: Sexual Politics in Ancient Athens.* Berkeley: University of California Press, 1993.

———. "The Partnership-Dominator Models of Social Organization." Paper given at the Western Association of Women Historians Conference, June 10, 1989, Asilomar, Pacific Grove, CA.

Kevles, Bettyann. *Females of the Species.* Cambridge, MA: Harvard University Press, 1986.

Khanum, Abida. *Forgotten Hostages: The Women of Islam.* Work in progress.

Kimmel, Michael S. "The Contemporary 'Crisis' of Masculinity in Historical Perspective." In *The Making of Masculinities,* edited by Harry Brod. Boston: Allen & Unwin, 1987.

Kimmel, Michael S., and Thomas E. Mosmiller, eds. *Against the Tide: Pro-Feminist Men in the United States 1776–1990.* Boston: Beacon Press, 1992.

Kitcher, Philip. *Vaulting Ambition: Sociobiology and the Quest for Human Nature.* Cambridge, MA: MIT Press, 1985.

Kivel, Paul. *Men's Work.* New York: Ballantine Books, 1992.

Koegel, Rob. "Healing the Wounds of Masculinity: A Crucial Role for Educators." *Holistic Education Review* 7 (March 1994).

Koonz, Claudia. "Mothers in the Fatherland." In *Becoming Visible: Women in European History,* edited by Renate Bridenthal and Claudia Koonz, 445–473. Boston: Houghton Mifflin, 1977.

Kraditor, Aileen S., ed. *Up From the Pedestal: Selected Writings in the History of American Feminism.* Chicago: Quadrangle Books, 1968.

Kramer, Heinrich, and James (Jacob) Sprenger. *Malleus Maleficarum.* New York: Dover, 1971. (Original work published in 1486.)

Kramer, Samuel Noah. *The Sumerians.* Chicago: University of Chicago Press, 1963.

———. *The Sacred Marriage Rite.* Bloomington, IN: Indiana University Press, 1969.

———. *History Begins at Sumer.* 3rd rev. ed. Philadelphia: University of Pennsylvania Press, 1981.

Kramer, Samuel Noah, and John Maier. *Myths of Enki, The Crafty God.* New York: Oxford University Press, 1989.

Kristeva, Julia. *Semiotikè.* Madrid: Fundamentos, 1978.

Kuhn, Thomas. *The Structure of Scientific Revolutions.* 2nd rev. ed. Chicago: University of Chicago Press, 1970.

Kunstmann, Josef. *The Transformation of Eros.* London: Oliver & Boyd, 1964.

Kuroda, Suehisa. "Social Behavior of the Pygmy Chimpanzees." *Primates* 21 (April 1980), 181–197.

Lafferty, Elaine, and Tammy Brice. "Suddenly They Hear the Words." *Los Angeles Times,* July 6, 1992, B9.

Lambert, W. G. "Gilgamesh in Literature and Art." In *Monsters and Demons in the Ancient and Medieval Worlds,* edited by Ann E. Farkas, Prudence O. Harper, and Evelyn B. Harrison, 37–52. Mainz on Rhine: Von Zabern, 1987.

Landsberg, Michelle. "Antipornography Breakthrough in the Law." *Ms.,* May/June 1992, 14–15.

Lappe, Francis Moore, and Paul DuBois. *The Quickening of America.* San Francisco: Jossey-Bass, 1994.

Laqueur, Thomas. *Making Sex: Body and Gender From the Greeks to Freud.* Cambridge, MA: Harvard University Press, 1990.

Larsen, Leonard. "American Democracy's Shame." *Scripps Howard News Service,* November 16, 1994.

Laszlo, Ervin. *Evolution.* Boston: Shambhala, 1987.

———. *The Creative Cosmos.* Edinburgh: Floris Books, 1993.

Lederer, Laura, ed. *Take Back the Night.* New York: William Morrow, 1980.

Lefkowitz, Mary R., and Maureen B. Fant, eds. *Women's Life in Greece and Rome.* Baltimore, MD: Johns Hopkins University Press, 1982.

Leo, John. "Sex in the '80s: The Revolution Is Over." *Time,* April 9, 1984.

Lerner, Gerda. *The Majority Finds Its Past.* New York: Oxford University Press, 1979.

———. *The Creation of Patriarchy.* New York: Oxford University Press, 1986.

Leroi-Gourhan, André. *Prehistoire de l'Art Occidental.* Paris: Edition D'Art Lucien Mazenod, 1971.

Lewinsohn, Richard. *A History of Sexual Customs.* New York: Fawcett Publications, 1958.

Lewontin, R. C., Steven Rose, and Leon J. Kamin. *Not in Our Genes.* New York: Pantheon, 1984.

Liebowitz, Michael. *The Chemistry of Love.* New York: Berkeley Press, 1983.

Linz, Daniel, Edward Donnerstein, and Steven Penrod. "The Effects of Multiple Exposures to Filmed Violence Against Women." *Journal of Communication* 34 (Summer 1984), 130–147.

Livermore, Beth. "The Lessons of Love." *Psychology Today,* March/April 1993.

Lorde, Audre. "Uses of the Erotic: The Erotic as Power." In *Sister Outsider, Essays and Speeches by Audre Lorde.* Freedom, CA: Crossing Press, 1984.

Lovelace, Linda. *Ordeal.* New York: Berkley Publishers, 1987.

Lovelock, James. *Gaia: A New Look at Life on Earth.* London: Oxford University Press, 1979.

Lowenstein, Jerold M. "Nine Ways to Have Sex." *Pacific Discovery,* Fall 1992, 40–41.

Loye, David. *The Healing of a Nation.* New York: Norton, 1971.

———. *The Leadership Passion: A Psychology of Ideology.* San Francisco: Jossey-Bass, 1977.

———. "Moral Sensitivity and the Evolution of Higher Mind." *World Futures: The Journal of General Evolution* 30 (1990), 41–51.

———. "Cooperation and Moral Sensitivity." In *Cooperation: Beyond the Age of Competition,* edited by Allan Combs, 24–35. New York: Gordon & Breach, 1992.

———. "Charles Darwin, Paul MacLean, and the Lost Origins of 'The Moral Sense': Some Implications for General Evolution Theory." *World Futures: The Journal of General Evolution* 40 (1994), 187–196.

———. "The Psychology of Prediction in Chaotic States." In *The Proceedings of the Society of Chaos Theory in Psychology,* edited by Robin Robertson and Allan Combs. Hillsdale, NJ: Erlbaum, 1995.

———. *The River and the Star: The Lost Story of the Great Scientific Explorers of Goodness.* Work in progress a.

———. *Moral Transformation.* Work in progress b.

———. *Moral Sensitizing.* Work in progress c.

Loye, David, and Riane Eisler. "Chaos and Transformation: Implications of Nonequilibrium Theory for Social Science and Society." *Behavioral Science* 32 (1987), 53–65.

Loye, David, Roderick Gorney, and Gary Steele. "Effects of Television." *Journal of Communications* 27 (1977), 206–216.

Lyotard, Jean Francois. *The Postmodern Condition.* Minneapolis: University of Minnesota Press, 1984.

MacDonald, Robert H. "The Frightful Consequences of Onanism." *Journal of the History of Ideas* 28 (1967), 423–431.

Mackey, Sandra. *The Saudis.* New York: Signet, 1990.

MacKinnon, Catharine. "Feminism, Marxism, Method and the State." *Signs* 7 (Spring 1982), 515–544.

———. *Only Words.* Cambridge, MA: Harvard University Press, 1993.

Maitland, Sara. "Passionate Prayer: Masochistic Images in Women's Experience." In *Sex and God: Some Varieties of Women's Religious Experience,* edited by Linda Hurcombe, 125–140. New York: Routledge & Kegan Paul, 1987.

Makiya, Kanan. *Republic of Fear.* New York: Norton, 1993.

Mallory, J. P. *In Search of the Indo-Europeans: Language, Archaeology, and Myth.* London: Thames & Hudson, 1989.

Mann, Dr. Jonathan, Dr. Daniel Tarantola, and Thomas W. Netter, eds. *AIDS in the World 1992.* Cambridge, MA: Harvard University Press, 1992.

Marcuse, Herbert. *Eros and Civilization*. New York: Vintage Books, 1955.

Margulis, Lynn. "Early Life." In *Gaia,* edited by William Irwin Thompson, 98–109. Hudson, NY: Lindisfarne Press, 1987.

Marshack, Alexander. *The Roots of Civilization*. Mount Kisco, NY: Moyer Bell Ltd., 1991.

Martin, Emily. "The Egg and the Sperm: How Science Has Constructed a Romance Based on Stereotypical Male-Female Roles." *Signs* 16 (Spring 1991), 485–501.

Marx, Karl, and Friedrich Engels. *Werke,* Vol. 8. Berlin: Dietz Verlag, 1960. (Written in the nineteenth century.)

Maslow, Abraham. *Toward a Psychology of Being*. New York: Van Nostrand-Reinhold, 1968.

Maturana, Humberto. Preface to *El Caliz y La Espada* (Spanish edition of *The Chalice and the Blade*) by Riane Eisler. Santiago, Chile: Editorial Cuatro Vientos, 1990.

Maturana, Humberto, and Francisco Varela. *Autopoeisis and Cognition*. Boston: Reidel, 1980.

———. *The Tree of Knowledge*. Boston: Shambhala, 1987.

McCall, Daniel. "Mother Earth: The Great Goddess of West Africa." In *Mother Worship: Theme and Variations,* edited by James J. Preston. Chapel Hill, NC: University of North Carolina Press, 1982.

McClelland, David. *Power*. New York: Irvington, 1980.

McConahay, Shirley, and John McConahay. "Sexual Permissiveness, Sex Role Rigidity, and Violence Across Cultures." *Journal of Social Issues* 33 (1977), 134–143.

McGill, Michael E. *The McGill Report on Male Intimacy*. New York: Harper & Row, 1985.

McGrew, W. C. *Chimpanzee Material Culture*. Cambridge, England: Cambridge University Press, 1992.

McKenna, Terence. *Food of the Gods*. New York: Bantam Books, 1992.

McLaren, Angus. *A History of Contraception*. Oxford & Cambridge, England: Blackwell, 1990.

Mellaart, James. *Çatal Hüyük*. New York: McGraw–Hill, 1967.

———. *The Neolithic of the Near East*. New York: Scribner's, 1975.

Melville, Arthur. *With Eyes to See: A Journey From Religion to Spirituality*. Walpole, NH: Stillpoint Publishing, 1992.

Merchant, Carolyn. *Radical Ecology*. New York: Routledge, 1992.

Mernissi, Fatima. *Beyond the Veil*. Bloomington, IN: Indiana University Press, 1987.

Miedzian, Myriam. *Boys Will Be Boys*. New York: Anchor Books, 1991.

Miles, Margaret R. *Carnal Knowing*. Boston: Beacon Press, 1989.

Miller, Alice. *For Your Own Good*. New York: Farrar, Straus & Giroux, 1983.

Miller, George A. *Psychology*. New York: Harper & Row, 1962.

Miller, Jean Baker. *Toward a New Psychology of Women*. Boston: Beacon Press, 1976.

Millett, Kate. *Sexual Politics*. New York: Doubleday, 1970.

Mills, Kim I. "Survey Dispels Common Myths About Families." *Associated Press,* September 5, 1994.

Minton, Lynn. "Do Girls Prefer Boys Who Treat Them Badly?" *Parade,* February 2, 1992, 13.

Mollencott, Virginia Ramey. *Women, Men, and the Bible.* Nashville, TN: Abingdon, 1977.

————, ed. *Women of Faith in Dialogue.* New York: Crossroads, 1987.

Monet, Joseph, ed. *Casanova's Memoirs,* by Giovanni Casanova. Abridged ed. New York: Hillman Periodicals, 1948.

Montagu, Ashley. *The Direction of Human Development.* New York: Hawthorn Books, 1955, 1970.

————. *Sociobiology Examined.* New York: Oxford University Press, 1980.

————. *Touching.* 3d ed. New York: Harper & Row, 1986.

Montuori, Alfonso, and Isabella Conti. *From Power to Partnership.* San Francisco: HarperSanFrancisco, 1993.

Montuori, Mario. *Socrates: An Approach.* Amsterdam, Holland: J. C. Gieben Publishers, 1988.

Moore, Robert, and Douglas Gillette. *King, Warrior, Magician, Lover.* HarperSanFrancisco, 1991.

Morbeck, Mary Ellen, Adrienne L. Zihlman, and Alison Galloway, eds. *Life History, Females, and Evolution.* Princeton, NJ: Princeton University Press, in press.

Morgan, Robin. *The Demon Lover: On the Sexuality of Terrorism.* New York: Norton, 1989.

————, ed. *Sisterhood Is Global.* New York: Anchor, 1984.

Mosher, Donald L., and Silvan S. Tomkins. "Scripting the Macho Man." *Journal of Sex Research* 25 (February 1988), 60–84.

Mumford, Steven D. "Papal Power: U.S. Security Population Directive Undermined by Vatican With 'Ecumenism' a Tool." *The Human Quest,* May/June 1992, 15–18.

Muses, Charles A. *Illumination on Jakob Böehme.* 2nd ed. New York: Kings Crown Press, Columbia University, 1951.

Myrdal, Gunnar. *An American Dilemma.* New York: Harper & Row, 1962.

Nasreen, Taslima. "Sentenced to Death." *New York Times,* November 30, 1993.

Nead, Lynda. *The Female Nude.* London: Routledge, 1992.

Newcomer, Mabel. *A Century of Higher Education for American Women.* New York: Harper, 1959.

Nicholson, Linda J., ed. *Feminism/Postmodernism.* New York: Routledge, 1990.

Noble, David F. *A World Without Women: The Christian Clerical Culture of Western Science.* New York: Knopf, 1992.

Noble, Vicki. *Shakti Woman.* San Francisco: HarperSanFrancisco, 1990.

Noddings, Nel. "Learning to Engage in Moral Dialogue." *Holistic Education Review* 7 (Summer 1994).

Norwood, Robin. *Women Who Love Too Much.* New York: Pocket Books, 1986.

Nullis, Clare. "WHO Says Women Helped by Contraception." *Associated Press,* June 25, 1992.

O'Brien, Justin. "Yoga and the Western Consciousness." In *Western Spirituality,* edited by Matthew Fox, 370. Santa Fe, NM: Bear & Company, 1981.

Okin, Susan Moller. *Women in Western Political Thought.* Princeton, NJ: Princeton University Press, 1979.

Olds, James. "Pleasure Centers in the Brain." In *Frontiers of Psychological Research: Readings From Scientific American,* edited by Stanley Coopersmith, 54–59. San Francisco: W. H. Freeman, 1956.

Orbach, Susie. *Fat Is a Feminist Issue.* New York: Berkeley Books, 1978.

Orenstein, Gloria. *The Reflowering of the Goddess.* New York: Pergamon Press, 1990.

Orenstein, Peggy. *Schoolgirls: Young Women, Self-Esteem, and the Confidence Gap.* New York: Doubleday, 1994.

Ornish, Dean, MD. *Reversing Heart Disease.* New York: Ballantine, 1990.

Osman, Hibaaq I. "Somalia: Will Reconstruction Threaten Women's Progress?" *Ms.*, March/April 1993, 12.

Ostling, Richard. "The Secrets of St. Lawrence." *Time,* June 7, 1993, 44.

Overall, Christine. "What's Wrong with Prostitution?" *Signs* 17 (Summer 1992), 705–724.

Pagels, Elaine. *Adam, Eve, and the Serpent.* New York: Random House, 1988.

Parish, Amy Randall. "Sex and Food Control in the 'Uncommon Chimpanzee.'" *Ethology and Sociobiology* 15 (1994), 157–179.

Pasick, Robert. *Awakening From the Deep Sleep.* San Francisco: HarperSanFrancisco, 1992.

Patai, Raphael. *The Hebrew Goddess.* New York: Avon, 1978.

Peplau, Letitia Anne, Susan Cochran, Karen Rook, and Christine Pedesky. "Loving Women." *Journal of Social Issues* 34, (1978), 7–27.

Peradotto, John, and J. P. Sullivan, eds. *Women in the Ancient World.* Albany, NY: State University of New York Press, 1984.

Perry, Mary Elizabeth. "Deviant Women and Cultural Transformation." Paper presented in the panel "Dominator and Partnership Models as Analytical Tools," 20th Anniversary Conference of the Western Association of Women Historians, Asilomar, Pacific Grove, CA, 1989.

———. "The Black Madonna of Montserrat." In *Views of Women's Lives in Western Tradition,* edited by Frances Richardson Keller, 110–128. Lewiston, NY: Edwin Mellen Press, 1990.

Peterson, V. Spike, and Anne Sisson Runyan. *Global Gender Issues.* Boulder, CO: Westview Press, 1993.

Pheterson, Gail, ed. *A Vindication of the Rights of Whores.* Seattle: Seal Press, 1989.

Pickthall, Mohammed Marmaduke. *The Meaning of the Glorious Koran.* New York: New American Library, 1953.

Pietilä, Hilkka, and Jeanne Vickers. *Making Women Matter: The Role of the United Nations.* London: Zed Books, 1994.

Plaskow, Judith. *Standing Again at Sinai: Judaism from a Feminine Perspective.* New York: Harper & Row, 1990.

Plaskow, Judith, and Carol P. Christ. *Weaving the Visions.* San Francisco: Harper & Row, 1989.

Platon, Nicolas. *Crete.* Geneva: Nagel Publishers, 1966.

Pomeroy, Sarah. *Goddesses, Whores, Wives and Slaves.* New York: Schocken Books, 1975.

Portugal, Ana Maria, and Amparo Claro. "Virgin and Martyr." *Conscience,* Spring/Summer 1993, 30.

Powers, John. "An Unreliable Memoir: The Film Maker and the Prostitute." *LA Weekly,* March 6–12, 1992, 18.

Prescott, James W. "The Abortion of *The Silent Scream.*" *The Humanist,* September/October 1986, 10–17.

Prigogine, Ilya, and Isabel Stengers. *Order Out of Chaos.* New York: Bantam, 1984.

Raine, Adrian, Patricia Brennan, and Sarnoff A. Mednick. "Birth Complications Combined with Early Maternal Rejection at Age 1 Year Predispose to

Violent Crime at Age 18 Years." *Archives of General Psychiatry* 51 (December 1994), 984–988.

Ranke-Heinemann, Uta. *Eunuchs for the Kingdom of Heaven.* New York: Doubleday, 1990.

Reeves, Minou. *Female Warriors of Allah.* New York: Dutton, 1989.

Regardie, Israel. *Garden of Pomegranates.* St. Paul, MN: Llewellyn, 1970.

Reich, Wilhelm. *The Mass Psychology of Fascism.* Salinas, CA: Masters of Perception Press, 1970a.

———. *Function of the Orgasm.* New York: Farrar, Straus & Giroux, 1970b.

———. *The Sexual Revolution.* New York: Octagon Books, 1971.

Reinisch, June M., with Ruth Beasley. *The Kinsey Institute New Report on Sex.* New York: St. Martin's, 1990.

Renfrew, Colin. *Archaeology and Language.* Cambridge, England: Cambridge University Press, 1988.

Rhodes, Richard. "Death in the Candy Store." *Rolling Stone,* November 28, 1991, 64.

Rich, Adrienne. *Of Woman Born.* New York: Norton, 1976.

Richards, Robert J. *Darwin and the Emergence of Evolutionary Theories of Mind and Behavior.* Chicago: University of Chicago Press, 1987.

Riley, Denise. *Am I That Name? Feminism and the Category of "Women" in History.* Minneapolis: University of Minnesota Press, 1988.

Robinson, John Mansley. *An Introduction to Early Greek Philosophy.* Boston: Houghton Mifflin, 1968.

Robotham, Sheila. *Women, Resistance, and Revolution.* New York: Vintage, 1974.

Rockwell, Joan. *Fact in Fiction.* London: Routledge & Kegan Paul, 1974.

Rohrlich-Leavitt, Ruby. "Women in Transition." In *Becoming Visible,* edited by Renate Bridenthal and Claudia Koonz. Boston: Houghton Mifflin, 1977.

Rokeach, Milton. *The Nature of Human Values.* New York: Free Press, 1973.

Rorty, Richard. *Philosophy and the Mirror of Nature.* Princeton: Princeton University Press, 1979.

Rossi, Alice, ed. *The Feminist Papers.* New York: Bantam, 1973.

Rossman, Michael. "Notes on the Tao of the Body Politic." In *New Age Blues.* New York: Dutton, 1979.

Roszak, Theodore. "The Hard and the Soft." In *Masculine/Feminine,* edited by Betty Roszak and Theodore Roszak, 92–93. New York: Harper Colophon Books, 1969.

Rountree, Cathleen. *Coming Into Our Fullness: On Women Turning Forty.* Freedom, CA: Crossing Press, 1991.

Rousseau, Jean Jacques. *The Confessions of Jean-Jacques Rousseau, 1712–1778,* Book 1. New York: Modern Library, 1945.

Rowell, Thelma E. "Forest Living Baboons in Uganda." *Journal of Zoology* 149 (July 1966), 344–364.

Rubenstein, Carin. "Making Time for Love." *Working Woman,* October 1987, 155–169.

Rubin, Gayle. "Thinking Sex." In *Pleasure and Danger,* edited by Carole S. Vance. London: Routledge & Kegan Paul, 1984.

Ruether, Rosemary Radford. "Women, Sexuality, Ecology, and the Church." *Conscience,* Spring/Summer 1993, 6–11.

———. "The Alliance That Fizzled." *Conscience,* Winter 1994/95, 20–21.

Russell, Diana. *The Secret Trauma.* New York: Basic Books, 1986.

————. "Pornography and Rape." *Political Psychology* 9 (1988), 41–73.

————. *Against Pornography: The Evidence of Harm.* Berkeley, CA: Russell Publications, 1993.

Sabelli, Hector C., and Javaid I. Javaid. "Phenylethylamine Modulation of the Libido." Undated. Obtain by writing Hector C. Sabelli, Department of Psychiatry, Rush Medical Center, Chicago, IL.

Sabo, Don. "The Myth of the Sexual Athlete." *Changing Men* 20 (Winter/Spring, 1989), 38–39.

Sack, Fleur, MD, with Ann Streeter. *Romance to Die For.* Deerfield Beach, FL: Health Communications, 1992.

Sadker, Myra, and David Sadker. *Failing at Fairness.* New York: Scribner's, 1994.

Sahtouris, Elisabet. *Gaia.* New York: Pocket Books, 1989.

Saikaku, Ihara. *The Great Mirror of Male Love.* Stanford, CA: Stanford University Press, 1990.

Sandars, N. K., trans. and ed. *The Epic of Gilgamesh.* New York: Penguin Books, 1960.

Sanday, Peggy Reeves. *Female Power and Male Dominance.* Cambridge, England: Cambridge University Press, 1981.

————. *Fraternity Gang Rape.* New York: New York University Press, 1990.

Savage-Rumbaugh, E. Sue, and Beverly J. Wilkerson. "Socio-Sexual Behavior in *Pan paniscus* and *Pan troglodytes.*" *Journal of Human Evolution* 7 (1978), 327–344.

Scarry, Elaine. *The Body in Pain.* New York: Oxford University Press, 1985.

Schaaf, Gregory L. "Queen Coitcheleh and the Women of the Lost Shawnee Nation." In *Views of Women's Lives in Western Tradition,* edited by Frances Richardson Keller, 158–167. Lewiston, NY: 1990.

Schachter, Stanley, and Jerry Singer. "Cognitive, Social, and Physiological Determinants of Emotional State." *Psychological Review* 69 (1962), 379–399.

Schaef, Anne Wilson. *When Society Becomes an Addict.* San Francisco: Harper & Row, 1987.

Schatten, Gerald, and Helen Schatten. "The Energetic Egg." *Medical World News,* January 23, 1984, 51–53.

Scheck, Raffael. "Childhood in German Autobiographical Writings, 1740–1820." *Journal of Psychohistory* 15 (Summer 1987), 391–422.

Schell, Ellen Ruppel. "Flesh and Bone." *Discover,* December 1991, 37–42.

Schlegel, Stuart. *Tiruray Justice.* Berkeley: University of California Press, 1970.

————. *Don't Give Anyone a Bad Gall Bladder.* Work in progress.

Schmitt, Eric. "Military Struggling to Stem an Increase in Family Violence." *New York Times,* May 23, 1994, A1.

Schneir, Miriam, ed. *Feminism.* New York: Vintage Books, 1972.

————. *Feminism in Our Time.* New York: Vintage Books, 1994.

Schultz, Ken. "Abuse of Elderly Wears Many Faces." *The Monterey Herald,* May 24, 1992, 1.

Schuttle, Penelope, and Peter Redgrove. *The Wise Wound.* New York: Bantam, 1990.

Scott, Gini Graham. *Erotic Power.* New York: Citadel Press, 1983.

Scott, Joan W. *Gender and the Politics of History.* New York: Columbia University Press, 1988.

Sears, James. *Sexuality and the Curriculum.* New York: Teachers College Press, 1992.

Sen, Amartya. "More Than 100 Million Women Are Missing." *The New York Review,* December 20, 1990a, 61–66.

———. "Gender and Cooperative Conflicts." In *Persistent Inequalities: Women and World Development,* edited by Irene Tinker, 123–149. New York: Oxford University Press, 1990b.

Shapiro, Bennet M. "The Existential Decision of a Sperm." *Cell* 49 (May 1987), 293–294.

Shaver, Phillip, Cindy Hazan, and Donna Bradshaw. "Love as Attachment." In *The Psychology of Love,* edited by Robert J. Sternberg and Michael L. Barnes. New Haven, CT: Yale University Press, 1988.

Sheldrake, Rupert. *The Presence of the Past.* London: Collins, 1988.

Shiva, Vandana. *Staying Alive.* London: Zed Books, 1988.

Shorter, Edward. *The Making of the Modern Family.* New York: Basic Books, 1975.

Showalter, Elaine. *Sexual Anarchy.* New York: Viking, 1990.

Simonton, Ann J. "The Torture Circus Comes to Town." *Media Watch* 5 (Summer 1991), 5.

———. "Slandering Anti-Pornography Feminists." *Media Watch Action Agenda,* Spring 1994, 1.

Sinclair, Hope. *Cohealing.* Berkeley, CA: Regent Press, 1993.

Sjöö, Monica, and Barbara Mor. *The Great Cosmic Mother.* San Francisco: Harper & Row, 1987.

Skinner, Quentin, ed. *The Return of Grand Theory in the Human Sciences.* Cambridge, MA: Cambridge University Press, 1985.

Smith, Joan. *Misogynies.* New York: Fawcett Columbine, 1989.

Smuts, Barbara. *Sex and Friendship in Baboons.* New York: Aldine, 1985.

Smuts, Barbara, and Robert W. Smuts. "Male Aggression and Sexual Coercion of Females in Nonhuman Primates and Other Mammals." *Advances in the Study of Behavior* 22 (1993), 1–63.

Smuts, Barbara, and John Watanabe. "Social Relationships and Ritualized Greetings in Adult Male Baboons." *International Journal of Primatology* 11 (1990), 147–170.

Spender, Dale, ed. *Feminist Theorists.* New York: Pantheon, 1983.

Spong, John Shelby. *Born of a Woman.* San Francisco: HarperSanFrancisco, 1992.

Spretnak, Charlene. *States of Grace.* San Francisco: HarperSanFrancisco, 1991.

Stager, Lawrence E. and Samuel R. Wolff. "Child Sacrifice at Carthage—Religious Rite or Population Control?" *Biblical Archaeology Review,* January/February 1984, 31–51.

Stanton, Elizabeth Cady. *The Woman's Bible.* New York: European Publishing Company, 1885. Reprinted as *The Original Feminist Attack on the Bible,* by Elizabeth Cady Stanton with a modern introduction by Barbara Welter. New York: Arno Press, 1974.

Starbird, Margaret. *The Woman With the Alabaster Jar: Mary Magdalene and the Holy Grail.* Santa Fe, NM: Bear & Company, 1993.

Starhawk. *Dreaming the Dark.* Boston: Beacon Press, 1982.

———. *Truth or Dare.* San Francisco: Harper & Row, 1988.

Stark, Elizabeth. "The Unspeakable Family Secret." *Psychology Today,* May 1984, 40–46.

Stark, Steven. "Practicing Inclusion, Consensus: Clinton's Feminization of Politics." *Los Angeles Times,* March 14, 1993.

Stein, Man, and Lisa Sjostrom. *Flirting or Hurting? A Teacher's Guide on Sexual Harassment in Schools for 6th–12th Graders.* Washington, DC: National Education Association, 1994.

Steinem, Gloria. *Outrageous Acts and Everyday Rebellions.* New York: Holt, Rinehart & Winston, 1983.

———. "Sex, Lies, and Advertising." *Ms.* premier issue, July/August 1990, 18–28.

Stephenson, June. *Men Are Not Cost-Effective.* Napa, CA: Diemer, Smith, 1991.

Stoller, Robert. *Sexual Excitement.* New York: Pantheon, 1979.

Stoltenberg, John. *Refusing to Be a Man.* New York: Penguin Books, 1990.

———. *The End of Manhood.* New York: Penguin Books, 1993.

Suetonius, Tranquillus. *The Lives of the Twelve Caesars.* London: George Bell & Sons, 1896. (Originally written in classical Roman times.)

Swimme, Brian. *The Universe Is a Green Dragon.* Santa Fe, NM: Bear & Company, 1985.

Sykes, Charles. "The Ideology of Sensitivity." *Imprimis* 21 (July 1992), 1–6.

Tanner, Nancy N. *On Becoming Human.* Cambridge, England: Cambridge University Press, 1981.

Tatlock, Lynne. "Speculum Feminarum." *Signs* 17 (Summer 1992), 725–760.

Taylor, G. Rattray. *Sex in History.* New York: Ballantine Books, 1954.

Taylor, Karen. "Venereal Disease in Nineteenth-Century Children." *Journal of Psychohistory* 12 (1985), 431–464.

———. "Blessing the House." *Journal of Psychohistory* 15 (Summer 1987), 431–454.

Teilhard de Chardin, Pierre. *The Phenomenon of Man.* New York: Harper & Brothers, 1959.

Teish, Luisah. *Jambalaya.* San Francisco: Harper & Row, 1985.

Tenorio, Rita. "Race and Respect Among Young Children." *Rethinking Schools* 8 (Summer 1994).

Teubal, Savina J. *Sarah the Priestess.* Athens, OH: Swallow Press, 1984.

Theobald, Robert, ed. *The Guaranteed Income.* New York: Doubleday, 1967.

Theweleit, Klaus. *Male Fantasies.* Minneapolis, MN: University of Minnesota Press, 1987.

Tiger, Lionel, and Robin Fox. *The Imperial Animal.* New York: Dell, 1971.

Tobach, Ethel, and Betty Rosoff, eds. *Genes and Gender.* New York: Gordian Press, 1978.

Tomkins, Silvan S. "Script Theory." Working paper for meeting of the Society for Personology, Asilomar, Pacific Grove, CA, June 1984.

Torjesen, Karen Jo. *When Women Were Priests.* San Francisco: HarperSanFrancisco, 1993.

Trask, Haunani-Kay. *Eros and Power.* Philadelphia, PA: University of Pennsylvania Press, 1983.

Trivers, Robert. *Social Evolution.* Menlo Park, CA: Benjamin/Cummings, 1985.

Turnbull, Colin M. *The Forest People.* New York: Simon & Schuster, 1961.

Valverde, Mariana. *Sex, Power and Pleasure.* Philadelphia, PA: New Society Publishers, 1987.

Vaselle-Horner, Renata, and Annette Ehrlich. "Male Batterers." In *Intimate Violence,* edited by Emilio Viano, 139–151. Washington, DC: Hemisphere, 1992.

Vicinus, Martha. *Suffer and Be Still.* Bloomington, IN: Indiana University Press, 1973.

Waken, Daniel J. "Pope Urges Chastity to Halt AIDS," *Associated Press,* February 2, 1993.

Walker, Alice. *Possessing the Secret of Joy.* New York: Harcourt Brace Jovanovich, 1992.

———. "Giving the Party." *Ms.*, May/June 1994, 22–25.

Walker, Barbara. *The Woman's Dictionary of Symbols and Sacred Objects.* San Francisco: Harper & Row, 1988.

Wallace, Aubrey. *Eco-Heroes.* San Francisco: Mercury House, 1993.

Walsh, Anthony. *The Science of Love.* Buffalo, NY: Prometheus Books, 1991.

Waring, Marilyn. *If Women Counted.* San Francisco: Harper & Row, 1988.

Washburn, Sherbourne, and Chet S. Lancaster. "The Evolution of Hunting." In *Man the Hunter,* edited by Richard B. Lee and Irven DeVore, 293–303. Chicago: Aldine, 1968.

Wassarman, Paul M. "Fertilization in Mammals." *Scientific American,* December 1988, 78–84.

Wehr, Gerhard. *The Mystical Marriage.* Wellingborough, England: Aquarian Press, 1990.

Weisman, Steven R. "Akihito Performs His Solitary Rite." *New York Times,* November 23, 1990.

Welter, Barbara. "The Cult of True Womanhood." In *Dimity Convictions,* edited by Barbara Welter, 21–41. Athens, OH: Ohio University Press, 1976.

West, Cornel. *Race Matters.* Boston: Beacon Press, 1993.

White, Frances J. "Pygmy Chimpanzee Social Organization." *American Journal of Primatology* 26 (1992), 203–214.

Willetts, R. F. *The Civilization of Ancient Crete.* Berkeley: University of California Press, 1977.

Williams, Tannis Macbeth. *The Impact of Television.* Orlando, FL: Academic Press, 1986.

Williams, Walter L. *The Spirit and the Flesh.* Boston: Beacon Press, 1986.

Wilshire, Bruce. "Introduction. Book Review Symposium." *World Futures* 25 (1988), 283–286.

Wilshire, Donna. *Virgin, Mother, Crone.* Rochester, VT: Inner Traditions, 1994.

Wilson, E. O. *Sociobiology.* Cambridge, MA: Harvard University Press, 1975.

Wilstein, Steve. "Cal Anthropologist Stakes Claim *Little Red Riding Hood* Is a Fake." *Monterey Herald,* September 10, 1989, A5.

Wink, Walter. *Engaging the Powers.* Minneapolis, MN: Fortress Press, 1992.

Winter, David. *The Power Motive.* New York: Free Press, 1973.

Wolkstein, Diane, and Samuel Noah Kramer. *Inanna.* New York: Harper & Row, 1983.

Wrangham, Richard W. "The Evolution of Sexuality in Chimpanzees and Bonobos." *Human Nature* 4 (1993), 47–79.

Wright, Karen. "Evolution of the Big O." *Discovery,* June 1992.

Zihlman, Adrienne. "Common Ancestors and Uncommon Apes." In *Human Origins,* edited by John R. Durant, 81–105. Oxford, England: Clarendon Press, 1989.

Zihlman, Adrienne L., and Nancy N. Tanner. "Becoming Human: Putting Women in Evolution." Paper presented at the annual meeting of the American Anthropological Society, Mexico City, 1974.

Acknowledgments

This book is dedicated to my partner and husband, David Loye. The reason, besides my love for him, is simple: I could not, and would not, have written *Sacred Pleasure* were it not for him. So I want to begin my acknowledgments by saying thank you, David, for all your loving support, intellectual stimulation, editorial advice, caretaking, knowledge, time, effort—and, above all, for being you.

There are two others whose help has also been indispensable: Constance Fishman and Hannah Liebmann. Without Connie's dedicated, and amazingly accurate, efficient, and intelligent work at the computer and other organizational skills, and without Hannah's multifaceted abilities, from editing to sorting to holding my hand through times of paper overwhelm and inspiring me through our longtime nurturant friendship to somehow solve the problems that beset one in writing a book such as this, I could not have kept working so long and so hard—nor would the process have been half as enjoyable. I particularly want to express my admiration for Connie's heroism during the last rush to meet our deadline, when she persisted at the computer wrapped in a blanket to stave off the chills preceding a temperature that rose, once she got home, to 104 degrees.

I also owe a great debt of gratitude to the women and men who so generously gave of their time and counsel to read and comment on all or most of this book in manuscript. They include, in alphabetical order, Carole Anderson, Art Aron, Mathew Callahan, Annette Ehrlich, Natasha Josefowitz, Frances Richardson Keller, Mara Lynn Keller, Rob Koegel, John Maier, Monty (Alfonso) Montuori, Kari Norgaard, and Stuart Schlegel. In addition, I want to acknowledge my great debt to Ashley Montagu both for his inspiration and his encouragement of my work.

I also want to thank those who reviewed parts of this book in manuscript for their important insights and information. These include, in alphabetical order, Robin Balliger, Harry Brod, Scott Carroll, my daughters, Andrea Eisler and Loren Eisler, Ira Fishman, Fred Jealous, Eva Keuls, Emily Martin, Arthur Melville, Jim DeMeo, Uta and Peter Meyer-Dohm, Amy Parish, Hector Sabelli, Bonia Shur, Linda Silverman, Barbara Smuts, Marsha Utain, Walter Wink, Adrienne Zihlman, and the late Marija Gimbutas.

I also want to express my gratitude to my agent, the Ellen Levine Agency in New York, particularly to Ellen Levine as well as Diana Finch, and to my publishers, HarperSanFrancisco, especially to my editor Barbara Moulton, but also to Lorraine Anderson, Lisa Bach, Judy Beck, Martha Blegen, Ani Chamichian, Nancy Fish, Terri Goff, Tom Grady, Shelly Meadows, Mary Peelen, Jaime Robles, Robin Seaman, Hilary Vartanian, Michele Wetherbee, and to all those who in one way or another took part in the birthing of this book.

I especially want to thank Bernardine Abbott of the Monterey Peninsula College Library, as well as Mary Anne Teed, Julia Batchev, Kirk Hall, Deborah Ruis, and Judy White of the MPC Library, and Topsy Smalley of the Cabrillo College Library; Janet Bombard, Lani Fremier, Tamara Hennessy, Arlene Hess, and Halina Szczesiak of the Harrison Memorial Library in Carmel; and Victor Bausch, Joe Johnson, Pamela Jungerberg, and Janis Rodman of the Monterey Library.

There are many others who, in one way or another, have been supportive to me during the seven years of research, thinking, rethinking, writing, and rewriting of this book, such as Gwen Withers, who helped me with the final preparation of the notes, and John Mason, who helped me with the cover. In fact, there are far too many to list here.

I particularly want to express my gratitude to the women and men who have formed partnership discussion groups, Centers for Partnership Education and the International Partnership Network. I also want to thank the women and men from all over the world who, since the publication of *The Chalice and the Blade*, have written me or come up to me at lectures to share their experiences and their work of personal and cultural transformation. Your communications have meant a great deal to me and have helped sustain my energies over the many years of intensive work on this book.

Riane Eisler
January 1995

Index

Aartun, Kjell, 81
Abortion, 214, 315–17. *See also* Family
    planning
Abu-Lughod, Lila, 97–99
Abuse. *See* Sexual abuse
Accountability, in morality of coercion or
    caring, 318–21
Adam and Eve, 23, the new, 398–99
Adams, Abigail, 201
Adams, Carol, 295
Advertising, 234, 268–70
African Association of Women for Research
    and Development (AAWORD), 367
AIDS, 309–14
Alcott, Louisa May, 271
Altered states of consciousness (ASCs), 145,
    170, 433n.13
Altmann, Jeanne, 38
Anderson, Bonnie, 32
Anderson, Lorraine, 295
Androcratic societies. *See* Dominator soci-
    eties
Animals, study of, 34–36
Antinuclear groups, 365
Archetypes, feminine, 265–67, 272–75, 284
Ardrey, Robert, 38
Arias, Oscar, 363
Ariès, Philippe, 184, 185
Aristotle, 107
Arken, William, 229–30
Aron, Arthur, 395
Aron, Elaine, 395
Art: challenging dominator culture, 395;
    Christian, 240–41; prehistoric, 16–18,
    53–66, 75–77
Aryans. *See* Indo-Europeans
Asch, Solomon, 388
Athens: male domination in, 110–12; part-
    nership elements in, 112–14; sexual rela-
    tions in, 107–10; women in, 104–7
Augustine, Saint, 22–24

Bachofen, J. J., 87
Bandura, Albert, 239
Banerjee, Nirmala, 395
Barbeau, Clayton, 255
Bardot, Brigitte, 266
Barry, David, 355
Barry, Kathleen, 212
Baudrillard, Jean, 305
Bedouins, 97–99

Behn, Aphra, 249, 279
Bendon, Hillary, 370
Benedict, Ruth, 292
Beneke, Tim, 253
Bennett, Emmett L., 80
Berghold, Joe, 186–87
Berkowitz, Leonard, 239
Bernard, Jessie, 363
Berry, Thomas, 379
Bhutto, Benazir, 363
Bigelow, Bill, 385
Birth: in Neolithic art, 63–64, 65–66, 78;
    resacralizing, 296–98
Black Madonna, 151, 267
Blade, 75, 166
Blake, C. Fred, 188
Bly, Robert, 258–59, 260
Body, 1, 3, 4, 9, 11, 12, 14, 15, 16; in art of
    prehistory, 54; as commodity, 335–37; as
    corrupting to spirit, 22–25; dehumaniza-
    tion of female body, 18–19, 235; and eco-
    momics and politics, 333–35; erotization
    of inflicting pain to, 226–35; loving
    touch to, 168; myths about woman's
    body, 265–70, 273–75; politics of, 163–66,
    188–89, 205, 211, 213–21, 222–26; as
    property, 344, 346; resacrilization of
    woman's body, 284–86; sacrilization of
    pain to, 167; valuing of, 327–29; woman's
    body as magical vessel, 25–27
Bogart, Humphrey, 233
Böhme, Jakob, 156, 400
Boland, Raymond, 315
Bondage, 218
Bonding: in chimpanzees, 41–42, 332–33;
    sexual pleasure, 4, 7, 50–51, 156–57
Bonfante-Warren, Larissa, 112–13
Bonobos, 40–43, 416nn.28–29, 417n.38;
    bonding among, 41–42, 332–33; social
    organization of, 41, 46–48
Bourdieu, Pierre, 345
Bradshaw, John, 193
Brain: and language and consciousness,
    172–73; and sexuality and love, 169–70
Brando, Marlon, 233
Breuil, Abbé, 54, 59
Brock, Rita Nakashima, 379
Brod, Harry, 196, 254
Brownmiller, Susan, 196
Brutality, 224–26. *See also* Violence
Buddhism, mythology of, 25

Bull God, 8–9, 62, 130
Bullough, Vern, 282
Bush, George, 362
Business for Social Responsibility, 368

Callahan, Mathew, 253, 396
Calvert Social Investment Fund, 368
Cannibal Corpse, 234
Canning, Kathleen, 305
Capacitar, 369–70
Caplan, Paula, 278
Capra, Fritjof, 36
Caring, 164, 174, 199–200, 244–45, 263, 339;
    among bonobos, 45; health benefits of,
    382–83; work involving, 342–45. *See also*
    Love: Sexual ethic
Carson, Rachel, 295
Casanova, 255, 256
Cassell, Carol, 281
Çatal Hüyük, 62–64, 132
Cathars, 8, 409n.9
Cather, Willa, 272
Catholic Church, 318; on family planning,
    315, 316, 317; movement for change in,
    321, 451n.12, 454n.54; Muslim alliance
    with, 317, 453n.39; sex scandals in,
    319–20. *See also* Christian Church; Reli-
    gion
Center for Conflict Resolution, 365
Center for Global Issues and Women's
    Leadership, 367
Center for Global Nonviolence, 365
Center for Partnership Studies, 456n.29
Centerwall, Brandon, 356
Chaisson, Eric, 36, 176
Chalice, 75
The Chalice and the Blade (Eisler), 11, 73, 85,
    105, 409n.11
Chamberlain, Wilt, 244–45
Change, 194–97, 460n.66. *See also* Transfor-
    mation
Chesler, Phyllis, 278
Chicago, Judy, 272, 284, 395
Childbirth. *See* Birth
Childe, V. Gordon, 88
Child rearing: changes in, 190–92; domina-
    tor trance and abusive, 186–89; educa-
    tion for, 386; violent traditions in,
    183–84. *See also* Fatherhood; Mother-
    hood
Children: organizations for rights of, 366;
    sexual abuse of, 184–85, 280–81; social-
    ization of female, 226–29, 270–72
Children's Defense Fund, 366
Chimpanzees: common, 40, 46–47. *See also*
    Bonobos
China: foot binding in, 188–89; infanticide
    in, 236; mysticism in, 145

Chipko movement, 364
Choice: conscious, 52; creativity and,
    374–75; in intimate relations, 349–53; of
    partnership or dominator politics,
    347–52, 370–71
Christ, Carol, 169, 284
Christian Church: on body as corrupt,
    22–24; double standard of, 208–9;
    medieval, 154–57; and pagan deities,
    148–49; sacred marriage in, 150–51;
    sexuality teachings of, 202–5; sexual
    obsession of, 205–8; vilification of sexual
    pleasure by, 29–32; witch-hunts by, 31,
    204, 413nn.45–46; and women's sexual
    slavery, 209–10. *See also* Catholic Church;
    Religion
Christiansen, Linda, 385, 395
Cinderella, 267–68, 270–72
Clafflin, Tennessee, 195
Clatterbaugh, Ken, 254
Clinton, Bill, 362
Clinton, Hillary Rodham, 362
Coalition Against Trafficking in Women,
    365–66
Coltrane, Scott, 254
Conditioning, linking sex with violence,
    238–39
Conklin, Beth Ann, 350
Connection, yearning for, 169–71, 181–82
Consciousness, 173; about femininity,
    276–80; altered states of, 145, 170,
    433n.13; changes in, 179–80, 190, 201–02,
    373–74; revolution in, 182, 192–93, 273,
    388, 397–401; and social systems, 247
Contraception, 207, 214, 314–17, 350–51
Cooey, Paula, 163
Co-option, 29, 413n.42; of Goddess worship,
    29; of pagan deities by Christian Church,
    148–49; of sexual revolution, 197–200
Copland, James, 300
Courage, spiritual, 393–97
Cozart, Bernardette, 396
Creativity, reinventing, 374–78
Crete. *See* Minoan society
Csanyi, Vilmos, 36, 49, 50, 247
Cullis-Suzuki, Severn, 396
Cultural transformation theory, 40, 176, 180,
    245, 248, 364, 370; on change, 177, 194,
    388, 460n.66; as framework, 11, 409n.11;
    on social systems, 245–48
Culture, creating new, 387–93; Western, 126.
    See also Partnership culture
"Culture wars," 392–93

Danuwar, Geeta, 311
Darwin, Charles, 175–76
Davidson, Julian, 170
Death: Indo-European preoccupation with,

90; and medieval Christianity, 154–57; Neolithic view of, 64–65; and sacred marriage, 151–54. *See also* Thanatos
de Beauvoir, Simone, 87–88
de Clairvaux, Christian, 151
Deconstruction: co-option of, 198; of femininity, 276, 278–80; of love, 384; of masculinity, 254
Defense for Children International, 366
Defoe, Daniel, 271
Degler, Carl, 190
deMause, Lloyd, 183, 184, 185
DeMeo, James, 92–94, 101–2
Demonization, of mythical figures, 130–31, 135–36
Denial: coming out of, 178, 191–92; in dominator societies, 187; of violence in child rearing, 186, 187, 189
de Rougemont, Denis, 155
Derrida, Jacques, 303
Deutsch, Helene, 224–25
Development Alternatives with Women for a New Era (DAWN), 368
de Waal, Frans, 35, 41, 42, 43, 44, 46
Diamond, Irene, 296
Dijkstra, Bram, 272–74
Dionysian Mysteries, 138–39
"Discovery of paternity" theory, 86
Dittes, James, 255
Dobrofsky, Lynn, 229–30
Dohm, Hedwig, 181, 279
Domination: assumption of, 181–82; in Athens, 110–12; in church's sexuality teachings, 204–5; economics of, 117–20, 333–35, 340–42; erotization of, 202, 206, 436n.6; theories on origins of, 85–88
Dominator configuration, 4–7, 20–22, 47, 68, 86, 88–93, 95, 100–02, 164–66, 222–23, 238–41, 247–48, 294, 340–42, 370–71; charts, 403–05
Dominator model, 4–6; in chimpanzee social organization, 46–48; courage to challenge, 393–97; cultures with, 20; of family, 189–94; versus partnership model, 403–5
Dominator morality, 116–20, 318–21. *See also* Sexual morality
Dominator societies: economic and political power in, 333–35; laws of, 114–17; origins of, 91–93; reconceptualization of female body in, 164–66; Rome as, 121–24; valued work in, 341–42. *See also* Athens
Dominator trance: awakening from, 191; and families, 186–89
Donnerstein, Edward, 237, 239

Double standard: of Christian Church, 208–9; for freedom and equality, 201–2; for morality, 308–9; for slavery, 212; for violence, 237–38
Douglas, Mary, 291
Douglass, Frederick, 181, 251
Dover, K. J., 108
Dundes, Alan, 267
Dworkin, Andrea, 299

Eastern religion: sacred marriage elements in, 145–46; sex and spirituality in, 8
East-West Gender Studies Center, 367
Eastwood, Clint, 233
Eating disorders, 268, 445n.8
Echols, Alice, 323
ECONET, 364
Economics, 331; of domination, 117–20, 333–35, 339–42; marriage as survival, 338; of partnership, 339–40, 343, 344–46; and productivity, 339, 341; of prostitution, 335–37; in Scandinavia, 343–44; and sex, 332–37; of work, 337–39, 342–45
Ecopolis Culture and Health Center, 368
Edell, Dean, 383
Education: for emotional literacy, 385; for love, 385–86; for parenting, 386
Ehrenreich, Barbara, 281, 282
Eldredge, Niles, 332
Eleusinian Mysteries, 137–38
Ellis, Bret Easton, 233
Emotional literacy, 385
Empathy, 96, 121, 227, 230, 245, 263, 312, 320, 321, 322, 328, 329
Empathy, politics of, 360–63
Engels, Friedrich, 87, 181, 338, 360
Environment: control of, 293–96; organizations working to protect, 364–65; pastoralism's effect on, 95–96
Eros: change in image of, 84; in myths, 140–42. *See also* Love
Erotic love, 15, 18, 28, 32, 69–71, 284–86, 399–401; as armed male deity, 84, 85, 99
Erotization: of domination, 202, 206, 436n.6; of violence, 206, 223, 233–35, 241–42
Etruscans, 112–13
Evans, Knoll, 260
Evans, Sir Arthur, 78
Eve, 266; Adam and, 23, 398–99
Evershed, Jane, 395
Evil, 134–36, 381–82
Evolution, 36–37; cultural, 85–91, 175–77; human, 37–40; of love, 172–73, 175; multilinear theory of, 40, 46–52, 100; of sexuality, 48–50; of sexuality to reduce violent conflict, 43–44

Fairy tales, 267–71. *See also* Myths
Faludi, Susan, 258
Family: and dominator religion, 325–26; and dominator trance, 185–89; history of, 182–85, 189–94; partnership versus dominator model of, 189–94; with sexual pleasure bonding, 50–51
Family planning, 207, 214, 314–17, 350–51
Family Protection Act, 358–59
Family values, 121, 193–94, 324–26
Fantasies: men's, 233–35; women's, 280–81
Farmer, Sharon, 163
Fascism, religious, 199, 322, 392
Fatherhood, 254–55. *See also* Child rearing
Federation of Peasant Women (Honduras), 367
Fedigan, Linda Marie, 38
Female sexual slavery, 106–07, 111, 209–13; relation to political repression, 213–21
Femininity, 403; in advertising, 268–70; archetypes of, 265–67, 272–75; deconstruction and reconstruction of, 276, 278–80; in fairy tales, 267–68, 270–71; in literature, 271–74. *See also* Gender
Feminism, 163, 179, 181, 190, 195–96, 212, 217, 236, 250, 252, 259, 262, 269, 276, 278–80, 291, 301, 304, 305, 335
Feminization, of politics, 360–63
Feuerstein, Georg, 146–47, 284
Fisher, Edward, 244
Flexner, James Thomas, 183, 185
Foucault, Michel, 22, 197, 303, 410n.12
Fox, Matthew, 169, 379
Fox, Robin, 38
Franklin, Miles, 272
Freedman, Rita, 387
Frenkel-Brunswick, Else, 187, 256–57, 391
Freud, Sigmund, 9, 195, 220, 224–25, 280; Oedipus complex of, 140, 260, 278
Friday, Nancy, 281
Fuller, Margaret, 279
Fundamentalism, religious, 198–99, 391–93

Gablik, Suzi, 305–6
Gadamer, Hans-Georg, 303, 304
Gadon, Elinor, 61, 284, 285
Gage, Matilda Joslyn, 181, 279
Galtung, Johan, 369
Gender: challenge to stereotypes, 249–55, 261–64; changes in roles and relations, 163–66, 190–200; in partnership and dominator models, 403; stereotypes, 244–45, 247–49; charts, 403. *See also* Femininity, Masculinity
Genetics, and sexual behavior, 332
Genet, Jean, 221

Genital mutilation: and dominator societies, 94–95; female, 20, 411nn.19–20; and political repression, 214
Gentleman, 32
Gerbner, George, 356–57, 374
Gergen, Kenneth, 304
Ghandi, Indira, 363
Giddens, Anthony, 199, 248, 384
Gies, Frances, 182, 184, 185
Gies, Joseph, 182, 184, 185
Gilgamesh, 136–37
Gilligan, Carol, 363
Gilman, Charlotte Perkins, 276
Gimbutas, Marija, 17, 63, 65, 73, 132, 396; on Kurgans, 89–90, 91, 92; on matristic societies, 77–78
Global Fund for Women, 367
Goddess, 16, 57–58, 410n.1; archetype of, 265, 266, 267, 284; in prehistoric art, 16–18, 59, 60–61; reclamation of, 267, 284–86; sacred marriage of, 127. *See also* Inanna hymns
Goddess worship, 29, 78, 80, 81, 412n.40
Goldman, Emma, 195, 272, 279
Goleman, Daniel, 385
GOLUBKA, 368
Goodison, Lucy, 64–65, 133
Gorbachev, Mikhail, 363
Gould, Stephen Jay, 283
Gray, Elizabeth Dodson, 169, 284, 296, 375, 379
Greeley, Father Andrew, 319–20
Green Belt movement, 364
Grene, Marjorie, 332
Griffin, Susan, 29, 196
Grimm, Jacob, 267
Grimm, Wilhelm, 267
Groneman, Carol, 301
Grover, Linda, 397
Gylany, 74, 77, 83, 135, 156–57, 421n.2

Habermas, Jürgen, 303
Hallett, Judith P., 22
Harlow, Harry, 22
Harlow, Margaret, 22
Harman, Willis, 186
Harrison, Jane Ellen, 84, 137
Haskall, Molly, 281
Hawkes, Jacquetta, 80, 81–82
Hayworth, Rita, 266
Healthy Families America, 366
Hegel, Georg Wilhelm Friedrich, 220
Henderson, Hazel, 331, 395
Hermes, mutilation of statues of, 114
Hess, Elizabeth, 281, 282
Heyward, Carter, 163, 169, 284, 380

Hierarchy: actualization, 79, 404n.2; domination, 79, 87, 404n.2

Hieros gamos, 7–8, 62, 101. *See also* Sacred marriage

Highwater, Jamake, 22, 23, 24

Hinduism, mythology of, 24–25

Hira, Subhash K., 313

Hitchcock, Alfred, 233

Hite, Shere, 281, 283

Hollander, Nicole, 397

Hollibaugh, Amber, 335

Hominids, 37–40, 416n.18

Homophobia, 352–53

Homosexuality, 250, 302–3; in Athens, 107–8; in Christian mysticism, 151; freedom to choose, 352–53; pornography with, 262; in primates, 43, 417n.46; and sadomasochism, 221

"Honor killings," 20, 98, 214, 333

hooks, bell, 196

Hosken, Fran, 313, 323–24

Houston, Jean, 396

Human rights: and the family, 185–86; integrated theory, 353—54; organized efforts of, 366; and sexual relations, 303; standards for, 303–07; and violence, 353–54

Human sacrifice, 90, 100, 102, 128, 130–35, 140, 428n.13

Huxley, Julian, 176

Hypermasculinity: sex with, 256–58; socialization for, 226–29

Iliad, 103–4

Impulse: self-regulation, 328, 394

Inanna hymns, 67–71, 132–33, 134

Indian culture, art of, 17

Indo-Europeans, 88–91

Infanticide, 110–11, 236, 437n.31

Institute for Development and Training (Tanzania), 366

Inter-American Children's Institute, 366

International Indian Tribal Council, 367

International Partnership Network, 368–69

International Quaker American Friends Service Committee, 365

International Women's Rights Action Watch, 367

Intimacy: dominator religion on, 325; need for, 169,171; sex without, 256, 257–58

Intimate relations: choice in, 349–53; history of, 163–66, 182–85, 189–200; importance of, 255; and politics, 347–49; violence in, 358–60. *See also* Caring; Love; Sexual ethic

Islam. *See* Muslims

Jacobs, Gloria, 281, 282

Jain, Devaki, 395

James, E. O., 104

Jankoviak, William, 244

Japan, mysticism in, 145–46

Jefferson, Thomas, 201

Jeffers, Robinson, 234

Jesus, 141–42, 325, 379

Jiayin, Min, 395

John Paul II, Pope, 310, 314

Johnson, Don Hanlon, 166

Johnson, Virginia, 50, 196, 282

Jovian, 203

Kanner, Barbara, 274

Kano, Takayoshi, 41, 42, 43, 44–45, 47

Kaplan, Helen Singer, 300

Katalysis Foundation, North/South Development Partnerships, 368

Kaye, Danny, 389

Kearney, Richard, 305

Keller, Mara, 137, 138

Kenik, Helen, 379

Kerber, Linda, 202

Keuls, Eva, 105–6, 108, 109, 110, 111, 112, 114, 138, 139

Khanum, Abida, 322

Kimmel, Michael, 249, 250

Kinsey, Alfred, 195

Kissinger, Henry, 361

Kivel, Paul, 321, 365

Koegel, Rob, 252, 395

Kolontai, Alexandra, 195

Kramer, Samuel Noah, 67, 68, 114

Kristeva, Julia, 303

Kuhn, Thomas, 72, 303

Kurgans, 89–91

Kuroda, Suehisa, 41, 44

Ladakh Ecological Development Group, 364–65

Lafitau, Joseph Francois, 302

Langton, Stephen, 208

Language, 172–73; for reproductive biology, 288–91; slang, 222–23

Laqueur, Thomas, 301, 303

Laszlo, Ervin, 36, 76

Lawrence, D. H., 234

Laxalt, Paul, 359

Lederer, Laura, 196

Lennon, John, 254–55

Leroi-Gourhan, André, 55, 56

Lesbians, 221, 302, 352

Liebowitz, Michael, 174

Linz, Daniel, 237, 239

Locke, John, 181, 201

Lorde, Audre, 284, 285, 323

Love: biology and chemistry of, 173–75; in

dominator and partnership models, 405; education for, 385–86; embodied or disembodied, 168–69, 327, 399–401; evolution of, 172–73, 175; free, in Athens, 109–10; health benefits of, 382–83; in media, 383–84; romantic, 244; in Rome, 121–22; as yearning for connection, 170–71; charts, 405. *See also* Eros
Love elegies, Roman, 121–22
Loye, David, 36, 141, 176, 246, 261, 318, 351, 356, 360, 375, 396, 398–99
Luther, Martin, 150, 208
Lyotard, Jean Francois, 303

McCallum, Bradley, 395
McCown, Karen Stone, 385
McGill, Michael, 255
Machiavelli, Nicolo, 330
Macho, 440n.11, 440n.15; in men's movement, 259; socialization for, 226–29
MacKinnon, Catharine, 299
Maier, John, 131, 137
Mailer, Norman, 234–35
Maitland, Sara, 152, 153
Makiya, Kanan, 322
Male bride, in Christian sacred marriage, 150–51
Male preference, 276–77
Malleus Maleficarum, 23, 31
Mallory, J. P., 89, 90, 91
"Man the hunter" theory, 38–39
Mann, Jonathan, 309
Marcus Aurelius, 204
Marcuse, Herbert, 195
Margulis, Lynn, 171
Markham, Beryl, 272
Marks, Carolyn, 396
Marriage: assumptions behind, 337; for economic survival, 338; Engels on, 87; reinventing sacrament of, 380; women as property in, 210–11. *See also* Sacred marriage
Marshack, Alexander, 17, 54–55, 56, 59
Martin, Emily, 288, 289–91
Marx, Karl, 181, 198, 246, 360
Mary, 8, 151, 203, 266, 381
Maryam Babangida National Center for Women's Development, 367
Masculinity, 403; changing view of, 252–55. *See also* Gender; Hypermasculinity
Masculinization, of sacred marriage, 148–51
Maslow, Abraham, 176
Mass media. *See* Media
Masters, William, 50, 196, 282
Masturbation, 300–301
Matriarchy, 421n.9
Matrifocal societies, 77–78

Matristic societies, 77–78
Maturana, Humberto, 10, 49, 172–73, 174, 383
Maximus, Valerius, 121
Max-Neef, Manfred, 395
May Day celebrations, 8, 56
Mayhew, Henry, 183
Media: love in, 383–84; partnership movement in, 371, 461n.68; violence in, 233–35, 355–57
Media Watch, 366
Mellaart, James, 62, 73, 91, 132
Melville, Arthur, 396
Men: dehumanization of, 121; fantasies of, 233–35; as scholarship focus, 53, 180; socialization of, 226–33, 245, 253–54. *See also* Domination; Masculinity
Men's movement, 248–49, 252–62
Menstruation, 291–93, 296–97
Merchant, Carolyn, 296
Messner, Michael, 254
Miedzian, Myriam, 386
Miles, Margaret, 240
Military: language in, 223; socialization in, 229–33
Miller, Alice, 187
Miller, Henry, 234
Miller, Jean Baker, 363
Millett, Kate, 163, 331
Mill, John Stuart, 251, 330–31
Minoan society, 116, 133; myth of Theseus, Ariadne, and Minotaur from, 128–30, 134; as partnership-oriented, 78–83
Monroe, Marilyn, 266, 306
Montagu, Ashley, 38, 173, 219–20, 396
Montgaudier baton, 54, 55, 56
Montuori, Alfonso, 375
Moraga, Cherrie, 323
Morality: of caring or coercion, 299, 321, 327. *See also* Dominator morality; Sexual morality
Moral sensitivity, 261
Mor, Barbara, 284
Morgan, Louis H., 87
Morgan, Robin, 196, 323
Morris, Sydney Amara, 298
Mosher, Donald, 227–29, 256, 257, 258
Motherhood, 277–78. *See also* Child rearing
Mothers of the Plaza de Mayo, 365
Mountcastle, Vernon, 288
Movies, 233
Ms. Foundation, 367
Muslims: Catholic alliance with, 317, 453n.39; divorce by, 333; genital mutilation by, 20, 411n.20; honor killings by, 20, 98, 214, 333; questioning teachings of, 322; repression of women by, 213–14; sexuality for, 97–99, 424n.45; on sex and

women, 5, 409n.3; veiling of women by, 98–99, 425n.47

Myrdal, Gunnar, 360

Mysticism, 144; and partnership-oriented societies, 156–57; and sex, 144–48; and suffering, 151–54

Myths, 22, 135–37; and changing consciousness, 372–73; defeminization of, 138–39, 148–51; of Greek Mysteries, 137–40; of Orpheus, 140–42; with partnership culture, 398–400; reinventing sacred, 378–82; revising traditional, 388–91; and sexuality, 22–25; shift from Eros to Thanatos in, 140–42; of Theseus, Ariadne, and Minotaur, 128–30, 134; transformation of, 372–82, 397–401; Western, 74, 127. See also Fairy tales

Nakajima, Hiroshi, 309

Nasreen, Taslima, 322

National Center for Children in Poverty, 366

Nature, control of, 95, 293–96

Neolithic era, 16; archaeological evidence from, 73–75; art of, 16–18, 62–66; death rites in, 64–65

Nicholson, Jack, 233

Noble, Vicki, 132, 284, 285

Norberg-Hodge, Helena, 365

Nordello, Carrie, 395

Normalization, of horror, 241–42

Nu-man, Fareed, 315

NWA, 234

Nymphomania, 280, 301

Oakland Men's Project, 365

O'Brien, Justin, 379–80

Obscenity, 298–300

Orenstein, Gloria, 284, 296

Orgasm, 49, 170, 282–83, 433n.13

Ornish, Dean, 382

Orpheus and Euridice, 140–41

Orphic Mysteries, 139–40

The Other Economic Summit (TOES), 368

Overall, Christine, 335, 336

Pagels, Elaine, 23, 24

Pain: in dominator and partnership models, 405; and institutionalization of trauma, 99–102; as pleasure, 219–20; public exhibition for social control, 106, 118, 211, 218, 240, 355–57; shift to pleasure, 3, 175, 177; socialization to endure, 188–89; as valuable, 153–54, 178; women and men choosing, 277; charts, 405

Paleolithic era, art of, 16, 53–62

Pankhurst, Emmeline, 181

Parish, Amy, 41, 47, 332

Parnassus Fund, 368

Partnership, 74

Partnership culture: archaeological evidence of, 73–75; in Athens, 112–14; of future, 397–401; Minoan society as, 78–83; mysticism as link to, 156–57; Orpheus and Euridice myth as, 140–41; in Rome, 121–22

Partnership configuration, 4–7, 20–22, 47–48, 73–75, 78, 80–83, 114, 286, 292–93, 328–29, 339–40, 343–44, 354, 370–71, 379–81, 385–87, 399–401; charts, 403–05

Partnership model, 6–7; in chimpanzee social organization, 46–48; of family, 189–94; societies moving toward, 21; versus dominator model, 403–5

Partnership movement, 262–64; in media, 371; organizations promoting, 363–69; pioneers, 394–97; spirituality in, 369–70

Pasick, Robert, 390

Partnership and dominator origins: summary, 100–102

Pastoralism, 94–96; of Bedouins, 97–99; and patriarchy, 88, 89, 93; psychological armoring with, 96–97

Patai, Raphael, 67

Patrist societies, origins of, 92–93

Pavlov, Ivan, 238

PEACE NET, 364

Peckinpah, Sam, 233

Penrod, Steven, 237, 239

Peradotto, John, 123

Perrault, Charles, 267

Perry, Mary Elizabeth, 6

Phaistos Disc, 81

Phallicism, 105, 108

Plaskow, Judith, 284, 379

Platon, Nicolas, 132

Pleasure, 2, 3, 11, 167–68, 328, 399–400; to avoid tension and violence, 46; celebration in prehistory, 58–59; in dominator and partnership models, 405; evolution of, 174–75; pain as, 219–20; sacred, 167–69; sexual, 29–32, 50–51, 58–61; of sexual love, 70–71, 97–99; shift to, 3; charts, 405

Pleck, Joseph, 254

Pliny the Younger, 121–22

Politics, 330–33; against violence, 357–60; and choice, 347–52, 370–71; of culture wars, 391–93; dominator, 117–20, 333–35; of empathy, 360–63; and intimate relations, 347–53; organizations for transforming, 363–69; of partnership, 348–49, 363–71; repression in, 213–16; and spirituality, 369–70; of violence, 353–57

Population growth, 314–17

Pornography, 6, 18, 124, 438n.50; desensitization with, 237–38; as institutionalizing male supremacy, 262; legislation on, 298–300; religious, 240-41; sexual images in, 18–19

Postmodernism, 303–7, 450n.56

Power, 163, 330–31; dissent, 387–88; in dominator and partnership models, 285, 405; and economics, 341–43; female sexual, 60–62, 78; imbalances, 337; in prostitution, 336–37; charts, 405

Powerlessness, in fairy tales, 267–68, 270–71

Prigogine, Ilya, 245

Prostitution: and AIDS, 311–12; economics of, 335–37; temple, 8

Psychological armoring, 94–97

Psychosexual armoring, 124

Rajneesh, Sri, 245

Ranke-Heinemann, Uta, 203, 204, 208

Rape, 19, 20, 118–19, 235, 280, 314, 326, 366; in Athens, 108; fantasies of, 281; as prank, 228, 440n.19

Rebirth: in Neolithic cultures, 64, 65; in Paleolithic art, 55–62

Reconstruction: of femininity, 278–80; of masculinity, 254; uncertainty over, 199–200

Redgrove, Peter, 284

Regardie, Israel, 149

Reich, Wilhelm, 94, 195, 215, 256, 424n.30

Reinisch, June, 324

Religion: dominator elements in, 324–26; Eastern, 8, 145–46; fundamentalist, 198–99, 391–92; partnership elements, 119, 166, 202, 314, 320–21, 325, 369; partnership myths in, 25–29, 378–80; sex/spirituality link in, 25–29; Western, 4–5, 7–8. See also Catholic Church; Christian Church; Muslims

Repression: by Muslims, 213–14; sexual and political, 213–16

Reproductive biology: Paleolithic knowledge of, 61–62; sexual stereotypes in, 288–91

Reproductive choice, 195–96, 211, 214, 279, 314–18, 349–51, 363, 366. See also Abortion; Family planning; Sex education

Reusch, Helga, 80

Rich, Adrienne, 163, 196, 278

Richards, Robert J., 175

Rites of spring, in prehistoric art, 55–56

Rites of alignment, 76, 132

Rituals, 296–97; animal behavior, 43–44; with partnership culture, 400

Rockwell, Joan, 104

Rohrlich-Leavitt, Ruby, 80, 116–17

Rome, 17, 121–24

Rorty, Richard, 303

Rossman, Michael, 369, 370

Ross, Mary Ellen, 163

Roszak, Theodore, 250, 259, 260

Rountree, Cathleen, 396

Rousseau, Jean-Jacques, 202, 220, 438n.53

Rowell, Thelma, 38

Rubin, Gayle, 323

Ruether, Rosemary Radford, 316, 379

Russell, Dianna, 280

Sabo, Don, 196, 257–58

Sacred: definition of, 76; pleasure, 3, 58–60, 70–71, 167–69; remything of, 378–82; renaming of, 296–98; sex as, 76–77

Sacred marriage, 62, 63; in Goddess myths, 127, 134; in Greek Mysteries, 137–40; of Inanna, 67, 68–71; masculinization of, 148–51; and mysticism, 143–48; mythical views of, 134–37, 140–42; in myth of Theseus, Ariadne, and Minotaur, 129–30, 134

Sacred union, 7–8, 18, 101, 411n.11. See also Sacred marriage

Sadomasochism (S/M), 151–54, 212, 217–19, 220, 257; homosexual, 221

Sahtouris, Elisabet, 36

Sanday, Peggy Reeves, 94

Sanger, Margaret, 195

Sartre, Jean-Paul, 220

Scandinavia, 343–44

Scattergood, Sally, 386

Schaef, Anne Wilson, 193

Schaefer, BarBara, 395

Schatten, Gerald, 290

Schatten, Helen, 290

Scheck, Raffael, 183, 185

Schlegel, Stuart, 395

Schwarzenegger, Arnold, 233

Science and technology, in partnership or dominator context, 293–96

Scientific paradigm, new, 245–46

Scott, Gini Graham, 218

Scott, Joan W., 303

Self-Employed Women's Association (SEWA) (Indian), 367

Sen, Amartya, 345, 395

Sex: association with pain in dominator societies, 94, 102; brutality in, 224–25; Church's obsession with, 205–08; in Minoan society, 81–83; and mysticism, 144–48; nonreproductive, 4, 42, 44–45; as sacred, 65–71, 76–77, 78–83; social construction of, 22; and spirituality, 7–9, 200, 284–86; and violence, 239–41; charts, 404

Sex education, 323–24, 385
Sex killings, 224. *See also* "Honor killings"
Sex, Lies, and Videotape, 287, 390–91
Sexual abuse, of children, 184–85, 280–81
Sexual athlete, 257–58
Sexual compulsivity, 123–24, 255–56
Sexual ethic, 309; new, 321–23, 327, 328–29. *See also* Sexual morality
Sexual harassment, 351–52
Sexual imagery: in ancient cultures, 16–18; in modern world religions, 26–29; in Neolithic art, 16–18, 62–66; in Paleolithic art, 16–18, 53–62
Sexuality: animal, 34–36; in Athens, 107–10; Christian Church's teachings on, 202–5; in dominator and partnership models, 4–7, 404; in dominator societies, 93, 94; evolution of human, 48–50; and myths, 22–25; women's, 273–75, 280–84; as yearning for connection, 169–71; charts, 404
Sexual morality, 309; AIDS and traditional, 309–14; double standard for, 308–19; questioning of religious, 321–23; in sex scandals, 319–20. *See also* Dominator morality; Sexual ethic
Sexual perversion, 300–03
Sexual pleasure: bonding for, 50–51; Christian Church's vilification of, 29–32; in prehistoric art, 58–61. *See also* Pleasure
Sexual revolution, 179, 195–97, 282–83; co-option of, 198–200; second phase of, 12, 199–200, 283–86, 384, 386, 390, 392
Seyfarth, Robert, 38
Shakespeare, William, 223, 271
Shaler-Adams Foundation, 367
Sheldrake, Rupert, 76
Shiva, Vandana, 296
Shorter, Edward, 184, 185
Simonton, Ann, 366
Sinatra, Frank, 234
Singleton, George, 396
Singleton, Lawrence, 441n.46
Siricius, Pope, 203
Sisterhood Is Global, 367
Sjöö, Monica, 284
Slavery, 334; in Athens, 106–7; Indo-European, 90–91; and pastoralism, 96–97; women's sexual, 90, 106–107, 111, 209–16
Smith, Adam, 181, 198
Smith, Joan, 232
Smuts, Barbara, 38, 43, 47
Social context: for creativity, 375; for male violence, 225–26
Socialization: to mold body to wishes of others, 188–89; of females, 270–72; of

males, 226–33, 245, 253–54; with new sexual ethic, 328–29; organizations raising consciousness about, 365
Social organization: of bonobos, 41, 46–48; sexuality as basis of human, 49–51
Social structure, in dominator and partnership models: charts, 404
Social systems, cultural transformation theory on, 245–48
Social Ventures Network, 368
Societies: matrifocal or matristic, 77–78; patrist, 92–93. *See also* Dominator societies; Minoan society
Soderbergh, Steven, 287
Song of Solomon. *See* Song of Songs
Song of Songs, 28–29
Spencer, Herbert, 176
Spender, Dale, 278–79
Spirituality: and Church's sexual obsession, 206; in dominator and partnership models, 404; and economics, 345; future of, 378–82; immanent and transcendent, 168–69; nature-based, 62–65, 76; partnership, 169; in partnership movement, 369–70; personal journey, 168; and politics, 369–70; and sex, 7–9, 284–86; charts, 404
Stanton, Elizabeth Cady, 181, 378
Starhawk, 284, 380
Stark, Steven, 362–63
Steinem, Gloria, 196
Stereotypes, in reproductive biology, 288–91. *See also* Gender
Stoller, Robert, 224
Stoltenberg, John, 196, 261–62
Stone, Lucy, 279
Stories. *See* Fairy tales; Myths
Strum, Shirley, 38
Students for Responsible Business, 368
Suffering, and Christian mystical marriage, 151–54
Sullivan, J. P., 123
Sumeria: hymns of Inanna in, 67–71; laws of, 114–17
Sun, as female, 65, 420n.24
Süssmuth, Rita, 363
Swimme, Brian, 396
Sykes, Charles, 361

Tanner, Nancy, 38–39, 172
Tantric yoga, 8, 17, 27–28, 146–48
Taylor, G. Rattray, 30, 92, 154
Taylor, Karen, 183, 184–85
Teilhard de Chardin, 49, 176
Teish, Luisah, 284, 380
Television, 356–57; love on, 383–84; violence on, 233

Thanatos, in myths, 140–42. *See also* Death
Thatcher, Margaret, 363
Theweleit, Klaus, 231–32
Thompson, William Irwin, 284
Tiger, Lionel, 38
Tolstoy, Leo, 234
Tomkins, Silvan, 226–29, 256, 257, 258
Touch, 22, 173; confluence of care and hurt in dominator intimate relations, 189–90. *See also* Body; Connection, yearning for; Pain; Pleasure
Tov, Baal Shem, 381
Transformation, 177–78; of politics, 363–69. *See also* Change
Transformative knowledge, 2
Trask, Haunani-Kay, 323
Trauma, institutionalization of, 93–94, 99–102
Trobaritzes, 8, 32–33, 414n.51
Troubadours, 8, 32–33
Trudeau, Garry, 397
Truth: changing, 72–73; and myths, 22
Truth, Sojourner, 181, 272
Turnbull, Colin M., 291–92
2 Live Crew, 234

Valverde, Mariana, 323, 327
Vance, Carole, 323
Van Effenterre, Henri, 80
Varela, Francisco, 50, 172–73
Vedder, Elihu, 274
Veiling, of Muslim women, 98–99, 425n.47
Venus of Laussel, 60–61
Violence: against women, 19–20, 235–37; in child rearing, 183–84; in Christian art, 240–41; domestic, 235, in dominator and partnership models, 403; erotization of, 206, 223, 233–35, 241–42; linked to sex, 224–25, 237–41; male, in crime, 253; in male socialization, 226–29; in military training, 229–33; and politics, 353–60; social context for male, 225–26; charts, 403
Violence Against Women Act, 359

Walker, Alice, 267
Walker, Barbara, 132
Warhol, Andy, 306
"War of the sexes," 181, 222, 223, 235
Washburn, Sherwood, 38

Wassarman, Paul, 290
Watanabe, John, 43
Waterhouse, Helen, 80
Welfare, 343–44
Western religion: sex and spirituality in, 7–8; view of sex and women in, 4–5. *See also* Catholic Church; Christian Church
White, Frances, 41
Willetts, R. F., 79, 80
Wilshire, Donna, 284
Wilson, Colin, 224
Wilson, Robert Anton, 284
Wink, Walter, 134, 379
Winter, David, 248
Witch-hunts, by Christian Church, 31, 204, 207, 294, 413n.45-46
Wodicz, Krzyztof, 395
Wolkstein, Diane, 67
Women: in Athens, 104–7; changes in consciousness, 276–80; domestication of, 120–21; fantasies of, 280–81; male-dominant religious view of, 5; organizations for rights of, 366–68; not passive victims, 275–76; pornographic images of, 18–19; reclaiming sexuality, 280–84; reconceptualization of body of, 164–65; resacrilizing the erotic, 284–86; resistance to domination, 114–15, 279; socialization of, 270–72; violence against, 19–20, 235–37
Women of All Red Nations (WARN), 367
Women and Development Unit (WAND), 367
Women Living Under Muslim Laws, 367
Women's Equity Mutual Fund, 368
Women's International Network (WIN) News, 367
Women's movement, 248–49, 251, 262
Women's Rights Committee of European Parliament, 367
Women's work, 338–39, 343
Woodhull, Virginia, 195
Work: caretaking, 342–45; valued, 341–42; by women, 338–39, 343
World Business Academy, 368
Wrangham, Richard, 47

Zihlman, Adrienne, 38–39, 46, 172
Zinsser, Judith, 32
Zoroaster, 24

PERMISSIONS